ISBN 978-1-332-94819-2
PIBN 10441721

1 MONTH OF
FREE
READING

at

www.ForgottenBooks.com

By purchasing this book you are eligible for one month membership to ForgottenBooks.com, giving you unlimited access to our entire collection of over 1,000,000 titles via our web site and mobile apps.

To claim your free month visit:

www.forgottenbooks.com/free441721

English
Français
Deutsche
Italiano
Español
Português

www.forgottenbooks.com

Mythology Photography **Fiction**
Fishing Christianity **Art** Cooking
Essays Buddhism Freemasonry
Medicine **Biology** Music **Ancient
Egypt** Evolution Carpentry Physics
Dance Geology **Mathematics** Fitness
Shakespeare **Folklore** Yoga Marketing
Confidence Immortality Biographies
Poetry **Psychology** Witchcraft
Electronics Chemistry History **Law**
Accounting **Philosophy** Anthropology
Alchemy Drama Quantum Mechanics
Atheism Sexual Health **Ancient History**
Entrepreneurship Languages Sport
Paleontology Needlework Islam
Metaphysics Investment Archaeology
Parenting Statistics Criminology
Motivational

THE SERMONS AND CONFERENCES

—— OF ——

JOHN TAULER

OF THE ORDER OF PREACHERS

Surnamed "THE ILLUMINATED DOCTOR"

—— BEING ——

HIS SPIRITUAL DOCTRINE

First Complete English Translation with Introduction and Index

—— BY ——

VERY REV. WALTER ELLIOTT
Of the Paulist Fathers

1910
APOSTOLIC MISSION HOUSE
BROOKLAND STATION
WASHINGTON, D. C

APR 25 1952

DEDICATION

This translation is affectionately dedicated to Father A. P. Doyle, C. S. P., without whose zealous and skillful co-operation it could not have been published.

W. E.

This Volume is

No._____
of Five Hundred Copies.

Patrons

1   His Eminence James Cardinal Gibbons, Archbishop of Baltimore.

1   His Excellency Diomede Falconio, Apostolic Delegate.

Patrons among the Archbishops

2   Most Rev. Jas. H. Blenk, D.D., Archbishop of New Orleans, La.

3
4   Most Rev. J. L. Spalding, D.D., Peoria Ill.
5

6
7   Most Rev. J. M. Farley, D.D., Archbishop of New York
8

9
10   Most Rev. John Ireland, D.D., Archbishop of St. Paul

11
12
13
14
15
16   Most Rev. P. J. Ryan D.D., Archbishop of Philadelphia, Pa.
17
18
19
20

21
22   Most Rev. J. E. Quigley, D.D., Archbishop of Chicago

23
24   Most Rev. J. J. Keane, D.D., Archbishop of Dubuque, Iowa

25   Most Rev. P. W. Riordan, D.D., Archbishop of San Francisco

Patrons among the Bishops

26   Alerding, Rt. Rev. H. J., Bishop of Fort Wayne, Ind.

27   Allen, Rt. Rev. Edward, Bishop of Mobile, Ala.

28 }
29 }   Bonacum, Rt. Rev. Thos., Bishop of Lincoln, **Neb.**

30   Burke, Rt. Rev. Maurice F., Bishop of St. Joseph, Mo.

31 }
32 }   Canevin, Rt. Rev. Regis, Bishop of Pittsburg, Pa.

33   Carroll, Rt. Rev. John P., Bishop of Helena, Mont.

34 }
35 }   Colton, Rt. Rev. Chas., Bishop of Buffalo

36 }
37 }   Conaty, Rt. Rev. Thos. J., Bishop of Los Angeles, **Cal.**
38 }

39 }
40 }   Corrigan, Rt. Rev. Owen B., Auxiliary Bishop of Baltimore.

41 }
42 }   Cusack, Rt. Rev. Thos. F., Auxiliary Bishop of New York
43 }

44 }
45 }   Dunne, Rt. Rev. Edw. J., Bishop of Dallas, Texas

46   Fox, Rt. Rev., Joseph J., Bishop of Green Bay, Wis.

47   Garrigan, Rt. Rev. P. J., Bishop of Sioux City, Iowa

48   Garvey, Rt. Rev. E. A., Bishop of Altoona, Pa.

49 }
50 }   Grace, Rt. Rev. Thos., Bishop of Sacramento, **Cal.**

51
52
53
54
55
56
57
58   Harkins, Rt. Rev. Matthew, Bishop of Providence, **R.** I.
59
60
61
62
63
64
65

66	Haid Rt. Rev. Leo, O.S.B., Bishop of North Carolina
67 68	Hennessey, Rt. Rev. John, Bishop of Wichita, Kan.
69	Heslin, Rt. Rev. Thos., Bishop of Natchez, Miss.
70 70a 70b	Hoban, Rt. Rev. M. J., Bishop of Scranton, Pa.
71	Janssens, Rt. Rev. John, Bishop of Belleville, Ill.
72	Koudelka, Rt. Rev. Joseph M., Auxiliary Bishop of Cleveland
73 74	Keane, Rt. Rev. J. J., Bishop of Cheyenne, Wyo.
75	Maes, Rt. Rev. Camillus P., Bishop of Covington, Ky.
76	Monaghan, Rt. Rev. J. J., Bishop of Wilmington, Del.
77 78	Muldoon, Rt. Rev. P. J., Bishop of Rockford, Ill.
79 80	McGolrick, Rt. Rev. Jas., Bishop of Duluth, Minn.
81	Northrop, Rt. Rev. H. P., Bishop of Charleston, S. C.
82	O'Connell, Rt. Rev. D. J., Auxiliary Bishop of San Francisco
83 84	Prendergast, Rt. Rev. E. F., Auxiliary Bishop of Philadelphia, Pa.
85	Schinner, Rt. Rev. A. F., Bishop of Superior, Wis.
86 87	Trobec, Rt. Rev. James, Bishop of St. Cloud, Minn.
88 89 90	Van de Vyver, Rt. Rev. A., Bishop of Richmond.
91	Lenihan, Rt. Rev. M. C., Great Falls, Mont

𝕻atrons among the 𝕻relates

101	Connolly, Rt. Rev. Mgr. J. N., New York
102 103	Duffy, Rt. Rev. Mgr. J. S., Brooklyn, N. Y.
104 105 106	Edwards, Rt. Rev. Mgr. John, New York

107	
108	
109	Lavelle, Rt. Rev. Mgr. Michael V. G., New York
110	
111	
112	McNamara, Rt. Rev. Mgr. P. J., Brooklyn, N. Y.
113	McCready, Rt. Rev. Mgr. Charles, New York.
114	
115	McGean, Rt. Rev. Mgr. James, New York.
116	McCarty, Rt. Rev. Mgr. Edw., Brooklyn
117	O'Brien, Rt. Rev. Mgr. John, East Cambridge, Mass.
118	Tihen, Rt. Rev. Mgr. J. H. Wichita, Kans.
119	Wall, Rt. Rev. Mgr. F. A., New York
120	Engel, Rt. Rev. Peter, O.S.B., Collegeville, Minn.

Patrons among the Priests

124	Buckley, Rev. John, Delavan, Wis.
125	Bresnahan, Rev. Patrick J., Tallahassee, Fla.
126	Brosnahan, Rev. Timothy, Waltham, Mass.
127	Brancheau, Rev. L. D., Lansing, Mich.
128	Corrigan, Rev. M. F., Dunmore, Pa.
129	Carroll, Rev. John H., Wallingford, Conn.
130	Cavanaugh, Very Rev. John, C.S.C., Notre Dame University
131	Corrigan, Rev. George W., Newark, N. J.
132	Chidwick, Very Rev. John, St. Joseph's Seminary, Dunwoodie.
133	Coyle, Rev. Richard, LL.D., Jamestown, N. Y.
134	Coopman, Rev. A. R., Anaconda, Mont.
135	Crowe, Very Rev. John W., Routt College, Jacksonville, Ill.
136	
137	Connolly, Rev. M. D., San Francisco, Cal.
138	
139	Cleary, Rev. J. M., Minneapolis, Minn.
140	Carrigan, Rev. J. P., Denver, Col.
141	Cunnion, Rev. Malick, New York
142	Coyle, Rev. James E., Birmingham, Ala.
142a	Dobbin, Rev. W. A., Darwin, Minn.
143	Driscoll, Rev. J. J., Jerseyville, Ill.
144	Dixon, Rev. G. J., Blossburg, Pa.
145	Dougherty, Rev. James, Canandaigua, N. Y.

146	Devlin, Rev. Thos., Pittsburg, Pa.
147	Duggan, Rev. Thos. S., Hartford, Conn.
148	Dougherty, Rev. W. F., Bronx, New York City
149	Donnellon, Rev. John J., Erie, Pa.
150	Dillon, Rev. John J., Albany, N. Y.
151	Eisler, Rev. Geo. J., Caledonia, N. Y.
152	Early, Rev. J. L., Hopkinton, Mass.
153	Ellis, Rev. John H., Sacramento, Cal.
154	Foley, Rev. Maurice P., St. Augustine, Fla.
155	Finn, Rev. Thos., Rockford, Ill.
156	Gallagher, Rev. Michael, Washington, D. C.
157 158	Huntman, Rev. Gerard, 405 W. 125th Streeet, New York
159	Hamel, Rev. J. J., Olean, N. Y.
160 161	Hanna, Rev Edward, D.D., Rochester, N. Y.
162	Hogan, Rev. Thaddeus, Trenton, N. J.
163	Hackett, Rev. Edw. J., Mobile, Ala.
164	Hally, Rev. Jas. A., Wyandotte, Mich.
165	Howlett, Rev. M. J., Loveland, Col.
166 167	Jennings, Rev. Gilbert, Cleveland, Ohio
168	Kress, Rev. William, Stephens, Cleveland, Ohio
169 170	Kirwin, Rev. James, Galveston, Texas.
171 172	Keane, Rev. Francis, Pittsburg, Pa.
173	Kehoe, Rev. Francis B., Alton, Ill.
174 175 176 177 178 179 180 181 182 183	Lyons, Very Rev. John V. G., Wilmington, Del.
184	Murphy, Rev. J., Decatur, Ill.

185 186	Morrissey, Very Rev. Andrew, C.S.C., Notre Dame, Ind.
187	Moore, Rev. R. T., LL.D., New Britain, Conn.
188 189	Murray, Rev. M. J, Riverdale on Hudson, New York City
190	Matutaitis, Rev. W. V., Grand Rapids, Mich.
191	Mahoney, Rev. T., South Boston, Mass.
192	Mahoney, Rev. P. J., D.D., New York.
193	Moran, Rev. Francis T., Cleveland, Ohio
194	Moffitt, Rev. James A., Taylor, Pa.
195	McGuire, Rev. Hugh, Chicago, Ill.
196	McEvoy, Rev. H., Pittsburg, Pa.
197	McInerney, Rev. Patrick, Kansas City, Kans.
198	McGivney, Rev. P. J., Middletown, Conn.
199	McClean, Rev. Peter, Milford, Conn.
200 201	McQuirk, Rev. John, D.D., New York
202	McQuaid, Rev. W. P., Boston, Mass.
203	McCall, Rev. M. J., Salem, Mass.
204	McAdam, Very Rev. W. J., Brooklyn, N. Y.
205	Noll, Rev. J. F., Hartford City, Ind.
206	Nihil, Rev. John B., Bridgeport, Conn.
207	O'Malley, Rev. Peter, Dubuque, Iowa
208	O'Brien, Rev. James J., Somerville, Mass.
209 210	O'Reilly, Very Rev. Jas. T., O.S.A., Lawrence, Mass.
211	O'Grady, Rev. Jas., Louisville, Ky.
212	O'Keefe, Rev. Thos M., New York.
213 214	Price, Rev. John, Pittsburg, Pa.
215	Pyne, Rev. William, Providence, R. I.
216	Power, Rev. Jas. W., New York
217	Phelan, Rev. R. W., Bath, Maine
218	Phelan, Rev. James, Kansas City, Mo.
219	Plamondan, Rev. W. A., Burlington, Vt.
220	Pfeil, Rev. Nicholas, Cleveland, Ohio
221	Philipps, Rev. M., Buffalo, N. Y.
222	Ryan, Rev. D. J., Auburn, Ill.
223	Ryves, Rev. John, Terre Haute, Ind.

224	Rosensteel, Rev. T. W., Sharpsburg, Pa.
225	Randall, Rev. W. E., St. Louis, Mo.
226	Smith, Rev. J. T., Omaha, Neb.
227	Stapleton, Rev. John H., Hartford, Conn.
228	Shaw, Very Rev. J. W., Mobile, Ala.
229	Stephan, Rev. J. L., Buffalo, N. Y.
230	Orosz, Rev. Frederic, Elmhurst, Providence, R. I.
231 232	Van Dyke, Rev. Ernest, Detroit, Mich.
233 234	Van Antwerp, Rev. Francis J., Detroit, Mich.
235	Walsh, Rev. James, Kansas City, Kan.
236	White, Rev. William, Brooklyn, N. Y.
237	Wheeler, Rev. Jas., Detroit, Mich.
238	Salter, Rev. J. B., Spring Valley, N. Y.
239	Savage, Rev. D., Montgomery, Ala.
239a	Scullin, Rev. Felix, Niagara Falls
240	Gavisk, Very Rev. Francis H., Indianapolis, Ind.
241	Hurley, Rev. Geo. Auburn, Mass.
242	Fitzgerald, Rev. Robert J., Minneapolis, Minn.
243a 243b 243c	Coyle, Rev. Denis F., New York
244	Sweeney, Rev. Edwin M., New York
245	Tracy, Rev. Joseph V., Boston, Mass.
246	Quilter, Rev. P. J., Pittsburg, Pa.
247	McRae, Rev. K. J., Brechin, Ont.
247a	Drumm, Rev. Thos. W., Dubuque, Ia.
247b	Kittenhoffen, Rev. F. J., St. Johns, Ore.
247c	Kelty, Rev. Wm., Crafton, Pa.
247d	Mulcahy, V. Rev. D. J., Anderson, Ind.

Patrons among the Religious Orders

248	Franciscan Fathers, Very Rev. J. B. Stark, New York
249	Passionist Fathers, Rev. Bertrand, West Hoboken, N. J.
249a	Benedictine Fathers, Julius, Rev. O. S. B., Bristow, Va.
250	Benedictine Fathers, Rt. Rev. Nepomecene Jaeger, O.S.B., Chicago, Ill.

251	Benedictine Fathers, Rt. Rev. Frowin Conrad, O.S.B., Conception, Mo.
252	Benedictine Fathers, Rev. Leonard, Walter, O.S.B., Manchester, N. H.
253	Benedictine Fathers, Rt. Rev. Abbot Bernard, O.S.B., St. Bernards, Ala.
254 255	Benedictine Fathers, St. Mary's Abbey, Richardtown, N. D.
256 257	Benedictine Fathers, Rt. Rev. Innocent Wolf, O.S.B., St. Benedict's Abbey, Atchison, Kan.
258	Benedictine Fathers, Very Rev. I. Hitmann, St. Procopius College, Lisle, Ill.
258a	Benedictine Fathers, Rev. P. J. Sittenauer, O.S.B., Atchison, Kan.
259	Benedictine Sisters, St. Mary's, Elk Co., Pa.
259a	Benedictine Sisters, Erie, Pa.
260	Benedictine Sisters, Bristow, Va.
261 262	Benedictine Sisters, Villa Sancta Scholastica, Duluth, Minn.
263 264	Carmelite Sisters, Cor. Caroline and Biddle, Baltimore, Md.
264a	Carmelite Sisters, Roxbury, Mass.
265	Carmelite Sisters, Cor. 18th Street and Victor, St. Louis, Mo.
266	Carmelite Sisters, 1808 Howell Street, Seattle, Wash.
267 268	Carmelite Sisters, Discalced, 1236 N. Rampart St., New Orleans, La.
269	Dominican Fathers, Rev. B. F. Logan, Minneapolis, Minn.
270 271	Dominican Fathers, Rev. F. A. Linahan, Springfield, Ky.
272 273	Dominican Fathers, Rev. C. H. McKenna, Lexington Avenue, N. Y.
274 275	Dominican Sisters, Corpus Christi Monastery, Hunts Point, N. Y.
276 277	Dominican Sisters, 13th Avenue and 9th Street, Newark, N. J.
278	Dominican Sisters, Park Street, Fall River, Mass.
279	Dominican Sisters, Sacred Heart Academy, Grand Rapids, Mich.

280 281	Dominican Sisters, Aquinas Academy, Tacoma, Wash.
282	Dominican Sisters of Perpetual Rosary, Hale's Corners, Wis.
283 284	Dominican Sisters, Jersey City, N. J.
285	Dominican Sisters, St. Mary's of Springs, Shepard, Ohio
285a 285b	Dominican Sisters, Detroit, Mich.
286	Franciscan Fathers, Very Rev. Edw. Blecke, Paterson, N. J.
287	Franciscan Sisters, Maryland Avenue, Baltimore, Md.
288	Fathers of Blessed Sacrament, Rev. F. Letellier, E. 76th Street, New York
289	Helpers of Holy Souls, E. 86th Street, New York
290 291	Jesuit Fathers, St. Louis University, St. Louis, Mo.
292	Jesuit Fathers, College of Sacred Heart, Denver, Col.
293	Religious of Sacred Heart, Rev. Mother Dupont, Chicago
294	Religious of Sacred Heart, Lake Forest, Ill.
295 296	Marist Fathers, Dr. Gunn, S. M., Atlanta, Ga.
297	Marist Fathers, Rev. J. Guinan, S.M., All Hallows, Salt Lake City
298	Norbertine Fathers, Very Rev. Pennings, West de Pere, Wis.
299	Oblates of Mary Immaculate, Very Rev. H. A. Constantineau, San Antonio, Texas
300	Oblates of Mary Immaculate, Brownsville, Texas
301	Passionist Fathers, Brighton, Mass.
302 303	Passionist Fathers, Normandy, Mo.
304 305 306	Passionist Fathers, Very Rev. Stanislaus, Grennan, West Hoboken, New Jersey
309	Paulist Fathers, W. 59th Street, New York
310	Paulist Fathers, Austin, Texas
311	Paulist Fathers, San Francisco, Cal.
312	Redemptorist Fathers, Very Rev. Caspar Ritter, New York
313	Redemptorist Fathers, Very Rev. Francis Klauder, Annapolis
314 315	Redemptorist Fathers, Very Rev. J. J. Frawley, Brooklyn, N. Y.

316   Redemptorist Fathers, Very Rev. Jas. Hayes, Mission Church, Boston, Mass.
317   Sisters of Mercy, Sister M. de Sales, Xavier Park, Chicago
318   Sisters of Mercy, Manchester, N. H.
319   Sisters of Mercy, Freeman Avenue, Cincinnati, Ohio
320   Sisters of Mercy, Sr. Rosalia, Cincinnati, Ohio
321   Sisters of Mercy, Mother M. Vincent, St. Bernard's Hospital, Council Bluffs, Iowa
322   Sisters of Mercy, St. Joseph's Academy, Sacramento, Cal.
323 ⎫
324 ⎪
325 ⎬   Sisters of Mercy, St. Mary's Hospital, San Francisco, Cal.
326 ⎪
327 ⎭
328   Sisters of Mercy, Altoona, Pa.
329   Sisters of Mercy, Sister M. Antonio, St. Xavier, Beatty, Pa.
330   Sisters of Mercy, Sister M. Louise, East Oakland, Cal.
331   Sisters of the Visitation, Brooklyn, N. Y.
332 ⎫
333 ⎭   Sisters of the Visitation, Wilmington, Del.
334   Sisters of the Visitation, Cabanne Place, St. Louis, Mo.
335 ⎫
336 ⎭   Sisters of the Visitation, Mount de Chantal, Wheeling, W. Va.
337   Sisters of the Visitation, Riverdale on Hudson, New York
337a   Sisters of the Visitation, Elfindale, Springfield, Mo.
338 ⎫
339 ⎭   Sisters of the Visitation, St. Paul, Minn.
340 ⎫
341 ⎬   Sisters of Charity, Mount St. Vincent's on Hudson, New York
342 ⎭
343   Sisters of Charity, Mount St. Joseph, Cincinnati, Ohio
344   Sisters of Charity, Mount Seton, Greensburg, Pa.
345   Sisters of Charity, St. Mary's Academy, Leavenworth, Kans.
346   Sisters of Charity of Blessed Virgin, Mount St. Joseph's College, Dubuque, Iowa
347   Sisters of Notre Dame, Dayton, Ohio
348   Sisters of Notre Dame, Grandin Road, Cincinnati, Ohio

349 350	Sisters of Providence, St. Mary's of Woods, Vigo County, Ind.
351 352	Sisters of St. Joseph, 4th and Jackson, Troy, N. Y.
353 354 355 356 357	Sisters of St. Joseph, Carondelet, St. Louis, Mo.
358 359	Sister of Presentation, Holy Family Institute, Fitchburg, Mass.
360 361	Sisters of Presentation, Sacred Heart Academy, Fargo, N. D.
362 363 364	Sisters Poor Clare, Sr. M. Coletta, Abbess, Chicago, Ill.
365	Sisters Poor Clare, Omaha, Neb.
366	Sisters of Holy Names, Webster Street, Oakland, Cal.
367	Servants of Mary, Mount St. Mary, Cherokee, Iowa
368 369	Sisters of Good Shepherd, Gravois Avenue, St. Louis, Mo.
370	Sisters of Precious Blood, Putnam Avenue, Brooklyn, N. Y.
371 372	Sisters of Loretto, Nerinx, P. O., Ky.
373	Sisters of Holy Childhood, Mother Ethelburga, New York
374 375	Ursuline Sisters, Columbia, S. C.
376	Ursuline Sisters, Mother Jerome, Paola, Kan.
377	Resurrectionist Fathers, Rev. Michael Jaglowicz, C. R., St. Mary's, Ky.
378	Josephite Fathers, Rev. Justin McCarthy, Baltimore, Md.
379	Les Religieuses Dominicaines, Billancourt, France
380	Visitation Sisters, Mobile, Ala.
381	Carmelite Sisters, Philadelphia, Pa.
382 383	Dominican Sisters Mission, San Jose, Cal.
384	Sisters of Mercy, Pittsburg, Pa., Mother Gertrude
385	Paulist Fathers, Winchester, Tenn.
386	Dominican Sisters of the Sick Poor, New York

387 Bentley, Rev. O. L., Copenhagen, New York
388 Huber, Rev. L., C.P.P.S., Dayton, Ohio
389 Delany, Rev. Joseph F., D.D., New York
390 Kelly, Thos. B., New York
391 Gerest, Rev. Regis. O. P., Cienfuegos, Cuba
392 Dooley, Rev. Patrick, St. Louis, Mo.
393 Fenlon, Very Rev. John F., S. S., Washington, D. C.

Patrons among the Laity

400 Burritt, Miss Mary L. St. Regis House, New York
401 Boyle, James J., Mauch Chunk, Pa.
402 Brown, Edward Osgood, Chicago, Ill.
403 Campbell Napoleon, Northampton, Mass.
404 Coyle, John G., M. D., New York
405 Coyle, John A., Attorney at Law, Lancaster, Pa.

406
407
408 } Caffrey, J. J. 1320 S. Floyd Street, Louisville, Ky.
409
410

411 Daly, Daniel, New York
412 Dunphy, James W., Roxbury, Mass.
414 }
415 } Emmet, Thos. Addis, M. D., New York
416 Finlay, Miss Alice, New York
417 Frawley, Hon. James J., Senate, Albany, N. Y.
418 Fahy, Thos A., Philadelphia, Pa.
419 Fenton, T. E., Boone, Iowa
420 Griffiss Mrs., Baltimore, Md.
421
422 } Gallagher, E. P., Philadelphia, Pa.
423
424
425
426 } Grady, Hon. Thos F., New York Senate, New York
427
428
429 Healy, Mrs. Martha E., Preston, Minn.

430	Hartigan, John J., Troy, N. Y.
431 432 433 434 435	Hirst, A. A., Philadephia, Pa.
436	Haas, Michael S., Baltimore, Md.
437	Horstmann, Ignatius J., Philadelphia, Pa.
438	Kelly, J. F., North Tonawanda, N. Y.
439	King, James W., Philadelphia, Pa.
440	Lally, P. E. C., Denison, Iowa.
441	Meighen, Thos. J., Preston, Minn.
442	Murphy, The John Co., Baltimore, Md.
443	Murrin, Jas. B., Carbondale, Pa.
444	McAleer, George, M. D., Worcester, Mass.
445	McNamee, John, Brooklyn, N. Y.
446	Mahoney, Daniel H., Philadelphia, Pa.
447	McPartland, John E., New Haven, Conn.
448	O'Halloran, D., St. Paul, Minn.
449 450	Prendergast, James M., Boston, Mass.
451 452	Prendergast, W. A., Comptroller, New York City
453	Quinn, P. H., Providence, R. I.
454	Roesch, Hon. Geo. F., Municipal Court, New York
455 456	Routt, Harvey John, Jacksonville, Ill.
457 458	Storer, Miss Agnes, Newport, R. I.
459	Sloan, Peter Elendorf, Greystone Park, N. J.
460	Scanlan, P. B., El Paso, Texas
461	Shriver, C. C., Metropolitan Savings Bank, Baltimore, Md.
462	Smith, Thos R., Philadelphia, Pa.
463 464	Sullivan, Alexander, Chicago, Ill.
465	Thompson, Katherine Beach, New York
466	Reilly, Richard M., Lancaster, Pa.
467	Roe, J. A., Detroit, Mich.
468	McCusker, Bernard E., Troy, N. Y.

TABLE OF CONTENTS

TABLE OF CONTENTS—Continued

TABLE OF CONTENTS—Continued

TABLE OF CONTENTS—Continued

TABLE OF CONTENTS—Continued

The Sermons and Conferences of John Tauler

OF THE

ORDER OF PREACHERS

Surnamed "The Illuminated Doctor"

FIRST COMPLETE ENGLISH TRANSLATION

WITH INTRODUCTION AND INDEX

By REV. WALTER ELLIOTT

Of the Paulist Fathers

APOSTOLIC MISSION HOUSE
Brookland Station
Washington, D. C.

INTRODUCTION.

John Tauler was born in the city of Strassburg about the year 1290. His family was in easy circumstances, his father, as it is surmised, having been a member of the city council. At eighteen years of age, or even earlier, John entered the Dominican novitiate in his native city, a young man full of religious fervor, and endowed with high intellectual gifts. His order gave him the best possible education, sending him to their greater house of studies at Cologne, and perhaps to their famous school at the University of Paris. Besides profiting by the usual scholastic training in the spirit and letter of St. Thomas Aquinas, Tauler, it is noted, became well versed in the Fathers of the Church, especially St. Augustine. He merited and obtained his order's highest diploma, that of Master of Sacred Theology. He soon manifested a taste for the mystics, studying St. Dionysius, St. Bernard, and Hugo and Richard of St. Victor with characteristic ardor.

This mystical tendency was strengthened by personal association with men of like tastes, some of them of the highest degree of spirituality, mostly members of his own order. On his return to Strassburg at the end of his studies, Tauler entered into familiar friendship with Master Eckhart, a leading spirit of that day, and also with Blessed Henry Suso, one of the most beautiful religious characters of the era. Both were distinguished Dominicans. Their influence on their young friend and brother was powerful and permanent.

Tauler's lot was cast in troubled times, the epoch of the papal residence at Avignon, to be followed not long after his death by the Great Western Schism. Churchmen, monarchs and statesmen, of every degree of sincerity or of treachery, kept the whole Christian world in a state of conflict the most tremendous, perhaps, the Church ever experienced. Their good deeds and their misdeeds monopolize nearly every page of the history of the times. But the activity of the humble saints, missionaries and mystics of this era, including such various types as Tauler, St. Catherine of Siena, and St. Vincent Ferrer, accounts for the final settlement of the Church's difficulties more adequately than all the expedients of statecraft. In the supreme work of preaching Jesus crucified, and of enforcing the maxims of

the Gospel, Tauler's place was very important.   He was one of many
great preachers in the Rhine country, members of the religious orders
and of the secular clergy, who labored incessantly to divert men's
gaze from the perplexed external condition of religious affairs, to the
serene glories of the interior life of God in their own soul.   Though
preaching in Latin to an occasional audience of the educated, Tauler
usually preached in the rough German dialect of his day to all
classes of the people, and with a power seldom equaled.

His field of activity was all lower Germany, especially along the
Rhine between Basel and Cologne; and his opportunity was given him
by his great and learned order, which was everywhere venerated, and
which had houses and churches in most of the larger towns.

The least acquaintance with Tauler's sermons shows him to have
been the ideal preacher.   With soundness of Catholic faith and its
simplest spirit he combined real learning, gentleness of heart, and
dignity as well as fearlessness of address.   It is true that his denun-
ciation of the vices prevalent at the time verged on the extravagant
and excited hostile criticism.   On one occasion some of his violent
sermons caused his Dominican brethren of the convent in which he
was stationed—no cowards themselves, we may be sure—to forbid
him their pulpit.   But the people, including many whom Tauler had
scourged for their vices, petitioned the friars to remove the prohibition.   They did so, gladly enough, we venture to say.   But this incident is fine testimony to our mystic's mingled kindliness and boldness.
In fact, he or any other preacher could do little good in those
desperate days, without giving offense to the timid and time-serving.
Such is the fate of all who assail popular errors and vices.

But these sermons on popular themes, with some exceptions of
doubtful authenticity, have not come down to us.   What we have
are Tauler's ascetical and mystical discourses, a priceless treasure
for souls who are seeking by the more interior methods to make
themselves wholly responsive to the divine guidance.

These are the only ones that critics generally will allow to be his.
They treat of the life of the counsels of perfection, the virtues to be
practiced if one would become entirely pleasing to God, the spirit
of holy living as well as the various methods to be adopted.   They
were addressed to religious communities, mostly in convents of
Dominican nuns.   But it is plain that they were not strictly private
conferences, but rather sermons delivered in the public oratories of

these communities, in the main room of which were assembled congregations of the people, including both clergy and laity, the sisters meanwhile being inside their cloister whose grating formed one side of the sanctuary. To the zeal of these nuns principally, if not wholly, we are indebted for what is known as Tauler's sermons, meaning his spiritual doctrine. They made notes of his preaching and afterwards compared and arranged them. This was done with much intelligence as to ordinary ascetical and mystical matters, though with some defects as to theological terms and passages of Scripture.

As to Tauler's life, the reader is referred to the brief History which precedes his Sermons in this book. Therein is given an account of the most important event in his spiritual career. Perhaps he himself would call it his second conversion to a life of perfection. There also will be found a touching account of his death.

Tauler has been accused of being a forerunner of Martin Luther; of having openly disobeyed the Pope and defied his authority; and of having joined an heretical association called the Friends of God. But he is held guiltless of all these accusations by the best critics, especially by the more recent historical students, including both Catholics and non-Catholics.

Tauler's activity in later life centered at the Dominican house at Cologne, in which city he preached incessantly for many years, the "eight years" mentioned in the History, referring only to the last eight years of his life. He was also confessor and spiritual director of a convent of Dominican nuns in Cologne. But at the end he returned to Strassburg. He died there June 16, 1361, and was buried in the Dominican convent.

Tauler's fame rests solely upon the solid and magnificent foundation of the sermons here given for the first time in English.* The little

---

* Twenty-five of them were translated into English by Miss Maria Winkworth, a Protestant lady, and published in England in 1857. These are less than one fourth of all the sermons, and the translator expressly excluded the more distinctively Catholic ones. As to the spirit and tone of that translation, it is enough for Catholics to know that Charles Kingsley was chosen to write the preface to the book.

A translation of thirty-five of the sermons has lately been procured and published by an Anglican clergyman, Mr. Arthur Wallaston Hutton. It is conceived and executed in a true spirit of fairness. The little book is useful, and the editor and translator are worthy of thanks and praise.

For a very able vindication of Tauler against the claims of Protestants and the suspicions of certain Catholics, our readers are referred to a masterly and learned article by the English Oratorian, Father J. B. Dalgairns, Dublin Review, March, 1858.

book known as Tauler's Imitation of Christ, is undoubtedly spurious. A few brief spiritual letters to nuns and some little ascetical instructions, together with some short devout poetical pieces, may rightly be ascribed to him. The Divinæ Institutiones so often quoted as his, are but a collection of maxims drawn from Ruysbroek and other mystics no less than from Tauler's Sermons. A book of Meditations on our Saviour's Passion, attributed to him, has recently been given an English dress under the learned and sympathetic editorship of the late Father Bertrand Wilberforce, O. P. The book is worthy of our great author and has some of the characteristics of his powerful style. But its authenticity lacks extrinsic evidence.

In the spring of 1904 we engaged a friend to make an English version of these Sermons; but when that failed to give satisfaction we ventured upon the task ourselves, constantly being drawn nearer to Tauler by the attraction of his wisdom and force. And now with God's favor we offer the result of many delightful hours of labor to the devout Catholic public. We have used Dr. Julius Hamberger's modernized German edition (Frankfurt am Main, 1864), adhering as closely as possible to his rendering. Sainte-Foi's fine French translation (Paris, 1855) has also been consulted, together with a very early edition of Surius's Latin version (1553).

It must be understood that a translator of these Sermons is sometimes compelled to interpret them. Not any part of them was published by Tauler himself, for, as we have seen, they are an assortment of notes taken down by some of his auditors, persons zealous and intelligent, indeed, but plainly lacking in theological training. This has left us with occasional awkward statements of doctrine to deal with and misplaced quotations of Scripture. Besides this general difficulty, Tauler occasionally is made to use terms open to misunderstanding on various other grounds, especially in view of the errors of quietism condemned by the Holy See in the seventeenth century.*

---

*The reader would do well to begin this book with the sermon for the first Sunday of Lent, for in that, especially the second half of it, will be found Tauler's singularly explicit adherence to the approved doctrines on the subject of contemplative prayer. With that sermon in his mind one may go from beginning to end of our volume with a perfect safeguard against misunderstandings on the score of quietism.

All of which necessitates interpretation. This has always been done by his translators and editors, and in different ways; sometimes by foot notes, again by sentences of their own placed in the text in brackets, and at other times by incorporating Tauler's own words used elsewhere but in the same connexion—his exact words or their equivalent. Some passages of the original German are so obscure, even meaningless, that they are usually entirely omitted in the translations. Now and then Taulers' extravagance in assailing evil doers does not suffer literal translation into English, however much one may admire his sincerity and his splendid vehemence.

No effort has been spared to make this English version as perfect a reflex of the German original as our literary deficiencies allow. It may be added that in Dr. Hamburger's edition there are a few sermons which he agrees are not Tauler's; we have not translated these.

A reader not familiar with the mystics may object that Tauler constantly repeats himself—if not verbally, at least substantially—in these discourses. So he does. But so does the medical professor repeat his instructions as he walks the hospital wards with his class. Over and over again does he explain the same disease, symptom for symptom—but yet rarely suggesting identically the same treatment and remedies. For though the malady is the same the patients greatly differ one from another, and each requires some change of treatment, each case affords something new to be learned about the common disease. It is so with Tauler in teaching us the cure of spiritual ailments, and the building up of the newly recovered soul into perfect holiness. No doubt there is frequent repetition of the chief means of perfection, but with an infinite variety of personal application and of illustration, enlisting the renewed and unfailing interest of the student of the soul's welfare.

We heartily recommend these sermons to all who aspire to wholehearted service of God, whether they are led into mystical states of prayer or not. They will find Tauler a master of the entire course between repentance from grievious sin and ecstatic union with God. He is as serviceable a guide in the ordinary degrees of the ascetical life as in those of high contemplation, ever coupling the two states together into an integral Christian career.

St. Paul of the Cross was certainly a competent judge of the worth
of all kinds of spiritual writings; for besides being (as every saint
must be) a contemplative, he was also a most practical leader in the
devout ways common to all fervent souls.   And in advising one of his
Passionists about bearing the stress of care and disappointment incident to the office of rector, St. Paul says of our author: "My dear
Father rector, now is the time to dwell in the depth of Tauler.   I
mean in interior solitude, and to take the repose of love in sinu Dei.
There you will learn to perform well the duties of your office of
rector, and to become a saint."   And much more praise of Tauler is
added by the saint. (Oratorian Life of St. Paul of the Cross, Vol. II.
Ch. XI).   The same testimony is borne by many other devout writers—
that Tauler is a most enlightened and trustworthy guide to Christian
perfection in all its grades; and that he is especially helpful in
showing the simplest and shortest way, namely steadfast self-abnegation, joined to restful acquiescence in God's outward good pleasure,
as well as ready responsiveness to the inward touches of divine
grace.

THE TRANSLATOR.

The Apostolic Mission House,
Washington, D. C.

THE HISTORY OF THE REVEREND MASTER JOHN TAULER.

CHAPTER FIRST.

In the year of Christ 1340, a certain Master in sacred theology was engaged in preaching in a certain city. He was listened to gladly, and his teaching was spoken of for many miles around. Now it happened that a layman, a man rich in grace, was admonished in sleep that he should go to that city and hear that preacher; and this message came to him three times. The city, however, was thirty miles away, and was in a different country. But this man said to himself: Thou shalt go there and wait upon God as to that He wills thee to do. So he went and he heard the Master preach five times. Upon this God gave him to understand that the Master was of a sweet disposition, kindly and good hearted by nature, with a good mind, and well versed in Scripture; but that as to the light of grace, he was dark. This deeply aroused the man's pity for him, and he went to him and said: "My dear good Master, I have journeyed thirty miles for thy sake, for I wanted to hear thee preach. I have heard thee five times; and now I beg thee for God's love to hear my confession." The master said: "Gladly." Then the man made his confession very simply, and as he wished to receive the Lord's body, the Master gave it to him. Twelve weeks passed away; and then the man said to the Master: "Dear Sir, I ask thee, in God's name, to preach, and to explain to us the closest place to God and the highest perfection that a man may have in this life." The Master said: "Ah, dear son, what is this thou asketh? Why should I speak of such high things to thee, for I well believe that thou understandeth little of them." Then the man answered: "Ah, dear sir, even if I may learn little or nothing of this doctrine, yet I may at least be moved to lament my ignorance. Many people run after thee; and if among them all only a single one should understand thee, thy work were well done." Then the Master said: "Dear son, if I shall do this, I must first study hard to get the material together." And the man did not give over, but begged and insisted so long, that at last the Master promised him to do it.

So the next time he preached, he announced to the people that they should come again three days afterwards, for he had been requested to preach how a man could arrive at the closest place to God, and reach the highest and best spiritual state possible in this life. When the day arrived a multitude of people came to hear the sermon, and the man took a good place for hearing. The Master began his address, and spoke as follows.

CHAPTER SECOND.

Dear children, I have much to tell you in this sermon about what I promised; therefore I cannot explain the Sunday's gospel to you to-day, as my custom has been. Nor shall I use much Latin in this sermon; but what I have to say I will prove by holy Scripture.

Dear children, you should know that there are many men who reach a clear knowledge of spiritual things and have an intellectual understanding of them, but this they have by means of forms and figures imparted by men's instruction and without Scripture. And we meet with others, who, when they have learned something through the Scripture, stop there contented. Such men are far off from their supreme good. Dear children, when such a man has broken through and gone beyond all that, and when he has thereby died to himself, and when he has passed through forty years of such contemplation and of the reasonings and imaginings and figurings of his soul—then he has gained a place dearer to God than that of a hundred thousand men, who have never got out of self and who live in a state of self approval. Into these God cannot come, nor in them can He act. The reason is their self will, and because their simplicity of spirit is self chosen; it is on account of their self approval, their resting in the forms and figures of their intelligence. But the men who have gone beyond this, giving themselves up to God in the dying spiritual way and by renouncing all things, attaining to a state above the contemplation of the forms and images of the mind—in such men, let me assure you, children, God finds His place of rest; there He dwells and there He works as He wills. St. Dionysius says of such a one: "The light of faith demands that a soul shall transcend the power and scope of its own reason." When God thus encounters no resistance, He does His own will in the soul, drawing it to Him-

self and into Himself. You must know that these men are exceptional, for their spiritual life is hidden to all but those whose inner
experience has been like their own; and these, alas, are not numerous.
Another thing to bear in mind is that this noble degree of perfection
no man can achieve without boundless humility; and he must also
have a clear head and sound reasoning faculties. By lack of humility
several learned doctors have fallen, and other dignitaries in holy
church. And how many brilliant spirits of the angelic choirs went
astray, and fell away eternally from divine truth, though by their
very nature they were beings of the highest endowments of reason.
Thus it happens to all who trust to their own reason, who would make
themselves like unto God in their obstinate self opinionatedness. On
account of all this, it is necessary to understand what kind of a man
the right, true, reasonable, enlightened, contemplative man should be.
And this, dear children, is what I will tell you, as far as I can gather
it from holy Scripture. And there are twenty-four qualities which
such a man should possess.

The first is placed by the sovereign teacher of all teachers, and
the source of all science and wisdom, our Lord Jesus Christ: "This
is My commandment, that you love one another, as I have loved you"
(John xv:12); as if He had said: If you have all wisdom and
knowledge and high reasoning power, it is all in vain unless you
have mutual trust and love along with it. One might think that
Balaam was very intellectual, knowing as he did many things that
God was to do for hundreds of years. That, however, helped him
little enough, because he did not follow up what he knew with fidelity
of heart and great love.

The second trait of a truly reasonable and enlightened man, is
that he must be detached from self. And when he has come to that,
he must in no wise be proud of it, but must strive onward to a greater
and greater degree of self renunciation; he must banish from his
soul all love of created things.

The third is this: he must give himself up to God that He may
work His will in him; nor dare he ascribe to himself any of the
results of that divine operation, but on the contrary, he must esteem
himself incapable of it.

The fourth: searching carefully within his soul, in whatsoever thing
he finds his own self to be his aim and object, from that he must

depart for time and for eternity. This exercise of the spirit will give him much increase in virtue.

The fifth: he should consult his own interest in no manner or matter whatsoever or in any creature, either for time or for eternity; and this ministers to true content of heart.

The sixth: he should constantly attend upon God to learn what His will may be about him, and then with the divine help fulfill it, nor in any wise claim the merit of it.

The seventh: it should be his daily practice to surrender his will to God's will, saying: O God I will naught but what Thou dost will.

The eighth: he should so adjust his mind to God, and so steadfastly apply all its force and love to God, that God cannot act in him without him, nor can he act in God without God.

The ninth: he must profit by God's presence in all his activity, at all times and in all places, just as God disposes, whether for sweetness or bitterness.

The tenth: he must feel neither pleasure nor pain from any creature, but only from God. Although God often works through creatures, yet a perfect man receives their influence as from God direct.

The eleventh: he shall not be fettered by any pleasurable emotions received from creatures, nor be influenced by it beyond reasonable necessity.

The twelfth: no mishap shall force him out of the path of truth; let him tread closely and faithfully in it.

The thirteenth: he must not be betrayed by the deceitful attractions of created things. Let him take things kindly and quietly as they come, and make the best of them for his own perfection, nor be in any wise worried. This spiritual trait is a sure sign of the presence of the Holy Ghost.

The fourteenth: in order to oppose vice within him with all his might and to win the victory over it, he must be armed with every virtue and always ready for the conflict.

The fifteenth: he must look directly at the naked truth of things, just as truth is in itself, according as God guides him and as far as is humanly possible, and live perfectly up to this knowledge.

The sixteenth: he should be a man of few words, and much given to the interior life.

The seventeenth; he must be a perfect man, and yet by no means think himself perfect.

The eighteenth: his life must be open and sincere with all men, and he must preach better by his life than by his words.

The nineteenth: he should seek God's honor in all things, nor have aught else in view in his daily conduct.

The twentieth: in contending with others he shall suffer himself to be corrected and shall yield his rights, unless indeed he is contending for God's rights.

The twenty-first: he shall look for no personal advantage in anything whatsoever, esteeming himself worthy of not even the lowest place.

The twenty-second: he shall esteem himself the least instructed and the least deserving of all men; and yet he shall hold in his heart a great treasure of faith. He shall lay no store by his mental acquirements or his intellectual powers, and in regard of such things he shall rank himself beneath all men. For it is the author of all wisdom who is doing His supernatural work in him, but only on condition that his soul shall be found humbled to the very depth; and it is God Himself who goes before to prepare the soul for His coming, as He did with St. Paul. But it seems to me that in our days. alas, little heed is given to this.

The twenty-third: he shall set before his eyes the life and doctrine of our Lord Jesus Christ, to be the model of his own life, words and works. Into this he shall constantly gaze as into a mirror, striving always, to the best of his ability, to lay aside whatsoever is inconsistent with this divine rule of life.

The twenty-fourth and last: he shall always reproach himself with being a slothful servant of God; he shall always set to work as if he were a beginner in a good life. And if this draws on him the contempt of his fellows, let him value it more than the favor of the whole world.

And now, you dear children, these are the marks of a well seasoned and prudently grounded spiritual life, enlightened and instructed by rules of all truth. Any man who cannot show these spiritual signs then neither he can consider himself nor can any one else consider him a reasonable man.

May God the eternal truth, Father, Son and Holy Ghost, help us all to be thus formed upon the pattern of our Lord's truth and humility. Amen.

CHAPTER THIRD.

At the end of the sermon the man returned to his lodgings, and there he wrote it down word for word, just as the Master had preached it. He then took it to the Master, and said: "I have written out thy sermon, and if it will not weary thee, I will read it over to thee." The Master answered: "I will hear it gladly." When the man had done reading it, he said: "I ask thee, dear sir, if I have left out a single word." The Master answered: "Dear son, thou hast written it down exactly as it came from my mouth. I assure thee that if I could have been paid a high price to compose it anew from the holy scriptures and to write it out again, I could not do it as exactly as thou hast done it. And let me confess that I stand in much admiration of thee; I marvel that thou hast been so long with me and yet remain hidden to me, and that I have not observed thy great intelligence; and that thou hast often made thy confessions to me, and yet held back from me thy real character, so that I have not known thee for what thou art." When the man made as if he wanted to go away, he said: "Dear sir, if God pleases I will return home." Upon which the Master said: "Dear son, what wilt thou do there? Thou hast neither wife nor child to care for, and thou canst fare as well here as there; for with the blessing of God I intend to preach more upon the subject of a perfect life." And the man answered: "Dear Master, you should know that I did not come here on account of thy preaching. I came here with the thought that by God's help I should offer thee some advice." The Master said: "And what advice couldst thou give me? Thou art a layman, thou dost not understand the Scriptures. It is unbecoming that thou shouldst want to preach. Stay here longer; perhaps God will grant me such perfect preaching that thou shalt gladly listen to it." And the man answered: "Master, I would willingly have said something to thee, but I feared that thou mightest not willingly bear it." And the Master said: "Son, say whatever thou wilt; I pledge myself to bear it patiently." Upon this the man spoke as follows: "Thou are a great clergyman, and in thy sermon thou has given a good doctrine; but thou thyself dost not live up to it. And yet thou talkest to me about it, and asketh me to stay longer and hear yet another sermon. Sir, be sure of this: thy preaching and thy outward talking, and all like things that anyone can say in the whole world, can have no effect in my soul; but on the

contrary it has hindered me rather than advanced me. And the reason is this: when I came away from the sermon I found that it
caused me various distracting thoughts, which I was scarcely able to
get rid of after long continued efforts. The fact is thou hast
preached thyself. But when the sovereign Master of all truth comes
into a man, his spirit must be empty of all transitory things. Be sure
that when that Master comes to me, He teaches me more in one hour
than thou canst ever do, and all other teachers from Adam's time to
the end of the world." Then said the Master: "Dear son, I beg thee
as thou dost reverence our Lord's death that wouldst remain with
me." Upon which the man answered: "Dost thou adjure me so
solemnly to stay with thee? Well, then, if I remain here out of
divine obedience, it shall only be because thou shalt promise me, that
what I have said to thee and shall say to thee, shall be held by thee as
sacred a secret as that of confession, and shall never be told." The
Master said: "Dear son, that I will do gladly, if thou wilt only stay."
And the man said: "Thou hast imparted much good instruction in
that sermon; but as thou didst preach, a thought came into my mind.
It was that thy sermon was just as if someone should take good
clear wine, and mix dregs with it till it was all muddied·" Then the
Master said: "Dear son, what meanest thou?" And the man answered: "I mean that thy vessel is unclean, and many dregs adhere to
it. That is to say, thou hast allowed thyself to be killed by the letter
of thy doctrine, and dost continue so daily and hourly, although thou
knowest well what the Scripture says: 'For the letter killeth, but the
spirit quickeneth' (ii Cor. iii: 6). Now thou mayst be certain that
the same letter that killeth thee will make thee alive again, in so
far as thou wilt allow it. But in that life in which thou now dost
live, thou shouldst know that thou hast no light. Thou art in the
night, in which thou mayst indeed know the letter, but the sweetness
of the Holy Ghost thou hast not yet tasted, and on that account thou
art as yet but a Pharisee." And then the Master said: "Dear son, I am a
man of mature age, and believe me that such words have never before
been spoken to me." Then said the man: "Where is thy preaching
now? Dost thou now preceive how thou dost stand? And although
thou thinkest that I have spoken too hard against thee, yet thou hast
only thyself to blame. And I will prove that to thee." Then said
the Master: "I beg thee to do so, for I have never been considered a
Pharisee." And the man answered: "I will first show thee how it
happens that the letter killeth thee.

"Dear sir, thou wilt remember that when the time came for thee to know the difference between evil and good, thou begannest to learn the letter of religion, and therein thou didst seek thy own interest; and now up to this very day thou art of the same mind. That is to say, thou hast given thyself up to thy own intelligence for guidance. Thou dost not have in view God alone, nor love Him alone, but resteth in the letter, seeking thy own self and not God's glory alone, to which end, notwithstanding, the holy Scripture directs us. Thou art inclined to creatures; and especially to one creature art thou inclined, and that one thou lovest inordinately; and that is the reason why the letter killeth thee. And when I said that thou art an unclean vessel, I said true; for thou dost not take God into account in all things. When thou shalt come to know thyself, thou shalt find lodged in a portion of thy soul vain and frivolous things. These disturb thy soul and adhere to it as the dregs and lees do to a vessel of wine. When the clear, pure wine of divine doctrine passes through the unclean vessel that thou art, then it comes to pass that pure souls and loving hearts find no divine flavor in thy words; thou impartest no grace to them. And I further have told thee, that thou art in the night, and that thou hast not the true light; now that is also a fact. And that is easily seen, because so few receive an increase of the grace of the Holy Ghost from thy preaching. And when I said that thou art a Pharisee I told but the truth. Of course I do not mean that thou art one of those false wretches of our Lord's day. But was it not a trait of the Pharisees, that they were dear to themselves in all things, that they kept themselves ever in view in all that they did, rather than God's glory? Now study thyself carefully, dear sir, and see if thou art not a genuine Pharisee in God's eyes. Dear Master, thou oughtest to know that there are many people now a days, great and small, who are Pharisees in God's eyes because He knows their hearts and their lives."

As the man said these words, the Master took him in his arms and embraced him and kissed him. And he said: "Thou hast shown me a true picture of myself. I see myself as the heathen woman saw her image in the waters of the fountain. I confess to thee, dear son, that all my sins and imperfections have been manifested to me by thy words. Thou hast told me the things that I had hidden away in my soul, and especially that I am inclined particularly towards one creature; but thou shouldst know that I was not aware of this myself.

and I believe that not a soul in the whole world knows it. And I am at a loss to know who has told thee of it. I doubt not but that thou hast got it from God. And now, dear son, I beg thee as thou honorest the death of Christ, that thou will become my spiritual father and take me for thy poor, sinful son." Then the man said: "Dear sir, if thou thus speakest against the right order of things I will not stay with thee—I will go away at once; thou mayst be sure of that." Then spoke the Master: "Ah no, I beg thee for God's sake do no such thing; stay with me for a while; I promise thee willingly not to speak like that again. I have the will to become a better man, with God's help and with thy counsel; what thou approvest that will I gladly be guided by for the improvement of my life." Then the man said: "I declare to thee that the letter and the science of things mislead many great Masters, bringing some to an awful purgatory, and others into hell, according to the life they have led. And I declare to thee furthermore, that it is no trifling matter that God should give a man such great knowledge through the holy Scripture, and that neverthe-less he should not put it in practice in his own life."

CHAPTER FOURTH.

Then the Master said: "I beg thee for the love of God to tell me how thou camest to thy present manner of life, and how thou hast begun; and what has been thy custom and way of spiritual exercise." The man answered: "That is a simple enough request, and I will answer with the exact truth. And if I should write down the wonderful things that God does for me, a poor, sinful man, during the past twelve years, it would make a bigger book than any thou hast; at any rate on this occasion I will tell thee something of it.

"What first helped me was that God found in me a real state of detachment and a fathomless humility. Now I think that there is no need of my telling thee what were my external and bodily devo-tional practices, for men's natures differ greatly. But when a man has humbly resigned himself to God with interior sincerity, then God begins and never ceases to give him inward discipline by allowing certain temptations to afflict him; by that and other like means which He knows to be useful and which the soul is able to bear—if it only will—God tries it well. But thou shouldst under-

stand that any man who seeks many counsellors is very likely to go
astray; for each one will advise according to his own devotional
customs. One man may benefit by one kind of spiritual exercises
the like of which would be of no help to another. The devil sometimes excites a man to severe penances, thinking that thereby he will
break down his health and lead him into imperfections, or hurt his
brain and make him an imbecile, or the like of that.

"And I will tell thee what happened to me in the beginning. I read
the lives of the saints in the German language; and thought within
myself that they were only men as I am a man, but that they had not
sinned as I had. And at that thought I began to imitate the saints
in various ways; and soon I was brought so low in health that I was
at the point of death. One morning at daybreak, after I had practiced hard austerities, I became so weak that my eyes closed in spite
of myself and I fell asleep. And then it seemed to me that a voice
spoke to me saying: O thou simple-minded man, what art thou about?
Thou wilt kill thyself with penances, suffering dreadful pain. Let
God exercise thee in the spiritual life; He can serve thee better than
thyself, or the devil's counsels. When I heard the devil's name I
woke up, very much frightened; I rose and went into a wood near
the city. Then as I found myself alone, I recalled how I had begun
those austerities without seeking advice, and I said that I could seek
counsel about my condition from the old hermit living there. I did
this, and I repeated to him the words that I had heard in sleep. I
begged him for the love of God to give me his best advice. Then
the hermit said. to me: 'Thou must tell me what thy customary exercises of piety have been, before I can advise thee.' I told him what
they were. He said: 'Who has counselled thee to do these things?'
I said: 'I did them of my own will.' He said: 'Thou must know
that it was at the devil's suggestion that thou didst them; and thou
must no longer be ruled by him. Thou must give thyself wholly up
to God; He can better practice thee than thyself or the devil.'
Behold, dear Master, how it was I quit those austerities, and yielded
myself and all my doings with deepest sincerity to God. Now besides
all this, thou shouldst know that by nature I am a sensible, capable
and kindly disposed man, although I have had no training in divinity
as thou hast had. Thus I began to know myself according to my
reasonable intelligence, and sometimes it happened that I was so

highly exalted that I was astonished. Once it happened that I
thought within myself: Thou hast so intellectual a gift, that if thou
shouldst apply thyself earnestly to study, thou wouldst comprehend
something. But as this thought took shape, I saw at once that it
was a suggestion of the devil, and detected its utter perversity.
Then I said: O thou wicked spirit, what false and filthy counsel hast
thou given me—treacherous counsellor as thou art. For if we had
a God who could be comprehended by our reason, I would not give
a straw for Him. At another time, when at midnight I began to
recite matins, a great longing took possession of me, so that I said:
O eternal and merciful God, I would that thou shouldst grant me
to experience something above and beyond the power of reason. But
as soon as I had thus spoken, I was terrified at this eager desire, and
I exclaimed: Alas, my God and my Lord, forgive me in Thy boundless
mercy for acting thus—that I a poor worm of the earth should allow
such a thought to enter my heart, desiring so rich a gift and one so
full of Thy grace—I, a man who, as I fully confess, have heretofore
by no means lived as well as I ought. I confess, dear Lord, that in
all things I have been ungrateful to Thee. Therefore I am convinced
that I am not worthy to tread the earth after harboring such a pre-
sumptuous desire for Thy rich favors:—the earth is burdened with
my worthless carcass. I then flogged myself till the blood flowed
upon my naked body. The words I spoke to God burned in my heart
and were on my lips till day broke, and meanwhile my blood flowed
in my penance. Then did God show me mercy, and to my reason he
granted a much clearer light than before. But presently I was
ravished out of my reason into an ecstacy, and the time of it seemed
exceedingly short. When God permitted me to return to myself, I
beheld a marvellous supernatural sign, so that I could say even with
St. Peter: 'Master, it is good for us to be here' (Luke ix. 33). Let
me assure thee, dear sir, that I learned more truth in that short hour,
and was given clearer perception of spiritual things, than all the
teachers in the world could bestow with all their natural learning.
And now, dear sir, I have said enough to show thee how thou standest
before God."

CHAPTER FIFTH.

Then the Master spoke: "May God give thee grace to say more to me, for that would be very welcome, for I am telling thee the simple truth, when I say that I have heard thee gladly. Go on and do it, dear son, and do not leave me but stay with me. If thou needest money, I will not let thee suffer want, even if I must pawn one of my books." Then said the man: "May God reward thee, dear sir. But I do not need thy gift, for God has made me his steward to the extent of five thousand florins. These are God's, and did I but know some one who needed them, or any other purpose God had for them, I would give them away." Then the Master said: "Dear son, thou art thus a rich man, a very great steward of the Lord. But I am astonished at thy saying, that I and all other teachers till the day of judgment, could not teach thee as much as thou didst learn in one hour. Explain this to me, I will gladly listen. And is it not true that the Scriptures have come from the Holy Ghost?" The man answered: "Sir, it seems incredible that thou shouldst talk so childishly after all that I have told thee. And I will ask thee a question, and if thou shalt answer it with all thy intelligence, with or without the help of Scripture, I will give thee ten thousand florins." The Master asked: "What is it?" And the man said: "Canst thou instruct me how to write a letter to a heathen, one buried deep in a heathen country, in such style and language that the heathen can read it and understand it, and that the letter will have such an effect on him as that he will come to the Christian faith?" The Master said: "Dear son, that is the work of the Holy Ghost; tell me where that has ever happened, if thou knowest anything of the sort. Did it ever happen to thee?" The man answered: "Yes. Although I am a miserable sinner, through me the Holy Ghost has done that work. It would take too long to tell how it happened—one could fill a book with an account of it. The heathen was a well meaning man, and he often cried out to heaven, and implored Him who had created him and all the world besides, saying: O Thou creator of all things, here am I born in this country, and I find that the Jews have one faith and the Christians another. O Lord, thou art over us all and thou hast made all creatures: I implore Thy light to know. Is there no faith better than the one in which I was born—none whatever? If there is, I beseech Thee to show it to me that I may believe it—show it in what_ soever way it pleaseth Thee. I will gladly obey Thee and believe. But if it should happen that Thou dost not grant my prayer **nor** showest me a better faith, and that I shall die in my present faith because I know none better and because Thou hast not revealed **a** better one to me, then shalt Thou have done me an injustice. Now understand, dear sir, that a letter was written and sent to that heathen by me, a poor sinner, and by its means he came to **the** Christian faith. And he wrote me a letter in answer, in which he told me what had happened to him, and his letter was written in good plain German, so that I could very easily read it. Dear sir, much more might be said about this, but enough for the present; and thou wilt understand the meaning of what I have said." Then the Master spoke: "God is wonderful in all His works and gifts. Dear son, thou hast told things that are strange indeed."

The man said: "I fear that some of the things I have said may have distressed thee, and that is because I am a layman and thou a great master of sacred learning; and yet have I presumed to say so much after the manner of the learned. But I meant it all affectionately, seeking thy soul's welfare and wholly for God's honor, as He bears me witness." Then the Master answered: "Dear sir, if it will not anger thee, I will tell thee what has really distrssed me." And the man said: "Be assured on that point, thou needest have no fear of angering me." The Master said: "My mind is in a state of amazement, and I do feel distressed, that thou being but a layman and I a clergyman, I should receive instruction from thee. And it furthermore annoys me that thou didst call me a Pharisee." Then spoke the man: "Does nothing else weigh on thy mind?" The Master said: "I can think of nothing else." And the man said: "May I inform thee on both these points?" The Master said: "Yes, dear son, and I ask it of thee in all friendliness, and for God's sake." Then the man said: "Tell me, dear sir, how did it happen, that dear St. Catherine, who was but a young girl of fourteen years, yet vanquished by her discourse fifty of the greatest professors, so that they were ready to die for the truth? Who worked that wonder?" Then the Master said: "The Holy Ghost did that." And the man said: "Think you not that the Holy Ghost still has that power?" The Master answered: "Yes, I believe it firmly." Then said the man: "Why then wilt thou not believe, that the same Holy Ghost here and now speaks to thee through me, all unworthy as I am and a poor sinner; even as

He spoke the truth by the mouth of Caiaphas, who was also a sinner. But thou mayst be sure, that since thou receivest my message thus evilly, therefore will I be careful to have no more speech with thee." Then said the Master: "Dear son, say not so. I hope, if God wills it, to improve my soul's state through thy words." Then the man spoke: "Ah, dear sir, it distressed thee that I said that thou art a Pharisee. And yet when I did so, I added enough to prove to thee that I did thee no wrong; thou shouldst have rested content. But as thou art not satisfied, I must go on further, and I will show more plainly that I am right, and that thou deservest the name Pharisee. Dear sir, thou knowest full well that our Lord Jesus Christ Himself said of the Pharisees: 'They bind heavy and insupportable burdens, and lay them on men's shoulders; but with a finger of their own they will not move them, (Matt. xxiii: 4). Now, dear sir, thou hast in thy sermon bound together twenty-four burdens, and thou takest little account of them for thy own self. Our Lord also said: 'All things whatsoever they [the Pharisees] shall say to you, observe and do: but according to their works do ye not; for they say and do not' (Matt. xxxiii: 3)." Then the Master spoke: "Our dear Lord said those words for that occasion and time." And the man answered: "He speaks them yet, now and forevermore, and to all men. Dear Master, look into thyself and see if they are not to be applied to thee or to thy way of living: God knows if that be the case, and so dost thyself. And I avow to thee, as regards thyself, that I had rather be guided by thy words than by thy life. Lay it to heart as to whether or not thou mayst be called a Pharisee in the sight of God; but I do not mean that thou art one of those false Pharisees whose portion is the fire of hell." The Master spoke: "I know not what to say. I confess freely that I am a sinner, and I declare that I will reform my life; I will do it if it kills me. Dear son, I can no longer postpone this holy work, and I beg thee sincerely and for God's sake, to tell me how I shall take hold and begin. Teach me and guide me how to reach the highest perfection that man can reach in this life." The man spoke: "Dear sir, I beg thee not to be angry with me; but I must tell thee in all truth that thou art hard to advise. For if thou art to be converted, it will be a woeful thing to thy established manner and custom of living, for all the old ways must be given up; and now thou art nigh fifty years old." Then the Master answered: "That may all be so. But ah, dear son, remember that to him who came at the eleventh hour the same penny was paid as to him who came at the first. And I will tell thee this, my dear son: I have thought it all over, and I have set it firmly in my heart that with God's assistance I will give up the life and enjoyment of my senses, and also my intellectual way of meditating; and I will follow thy direction, and consider it all one if it costs me even my life. I beg thee for God's sake to delay me no longer, but to tell me at once how I shall make a beginning." Then the man said: "Since thou hast now received grace from God to wish to be humbled beneath a vile, poor, worthless creature, and to be subjected to him and bend under his yoke: let us give praise to God for all this, for this grace comes wholly from Him and must return again to Him by our thanksgiving. Dear sir, inasmuch as it is wholly on God's account that I will guide thee, I will call Him into help. I will instruct thee in divine love, and I will give thee a lesson to learn, as is done with children in school; it is the twenty-four letters of the alphabet. And so I begin with A."

CHAPTER SIXTH.

"A. Make a beginning of a new life in the spirit of a man and with no childish timidity.

"B. Give up all wickedness; and do good with thy mind made up, and all diligently.

"C. Be temperate and moderate in everything; learn to hold the safe middle course.

"D. Be humble in everything, in word and deed.

"E. Thy own will must thou renounce in the most thoroughgoing spirit, steadfastly and earnestly clinging to God and abiding in God.

"F. Be zealous, obedient, and willing for all good works, and be wholly free from murmuring.

"G. Diligently practice thyself in all divine works of mercy, both corporal and spiritual.

"H. Look not backwards, neither towards the world, nor creatures, nor thy own affairs.

"I. Deep in thy heart recall thy past life with entire truthfulness, real repentance, with bitterness of heart, and tearful eyes.

"K. Boldly and sturdily withstand the temptations of the devil, of the world, and of the flesh.

"L. Learn to overcome idleness courageously, and all delicacy in bodily matters, and the devil's suggestions of personal comfort.

"M. With burning love, with assured hope, with mighty faith, live in God; and bear thyself towards thy neighbor as thou wouldst towards thyself.

"N. Covet no man's goods, be they bodily or spiritual.

"O· Make the best of all things as they happen, never borrowing trouble.

"P. Penances, come they from God or from thy neighbor or from any creature, thou shalt willingly accept and suffer to atone for thy sins.

"Q. Whosoever shall harm thee in thought, word or deed, acquit him and pardon him in all sincerity.

"R. Purity of body and of soul, destitution of goods and of honors, thou shall cultivate with all earnestness.

"S. Be gentle-minded in all happenings, and find a way of improving thyself under all circumstances.

"T. Fidelity and truthfulness shalt thou cherish in thy dealings with all men, shunning all double dealing.

"U. Zealously learn to refrain from all and any kind of excess in eating.

"X. Follow the example of our beloved Lord, guiding thy every step thereby, as far as thou art able.

"Y. Ceaselessly beseech our dear Lady's intercession that she may help thee to learn this our lesson.

"Z. Hold thy will and thy senses in an even balance, so that thou mayst enjoy peace in all things, whether it be those between God and thee, or between thee and all created things.

"Now this whole lesson must be learned and observed without contradiction, with a free heart, and a good will."

CHAPTER SEVENTH.

"Now, dear sir, take this lesson of a child, without any objections, as if it came from God to thee for thy good, through me, a poor unworthy man."

Then the Master spoke: "It may please thee to call this a child's lesson, but to my thinking it will be a manly exploit to observe it all. And now tell me, dear son, how long a time wilt thou give me to learn it?" The man answered: "We will take five weeks, to do honor to the five holy wounds, so that thou mayst the better learn thy task. Thou shalt be thy own master; and when one or other of these sentences arranged by the alphabet is not observed, and thou thinkest that thou canst not master it, then strip thyself naked and chastise thy body, so that it may be reduced to submission to the soul and to reason." Then the Master said: "I will gladly be obedient."

At the end of three weeks the man asked the Master: "Dear sir, how stands it with thee?" The Master said: "Let me tell thee, dear son, that during these three weeks I have been whipped harder on account of this lesson, than ever I was whipped before in my whole life." Then spoke the man: "Dear sir, thou must understand that before one goes onward in a lesson, he must learn perfectly what goes before—namely, the first lines." The Master answered "If I should say that I now knew them well, I should say what is not true." Then the man said: "Go right on that way, till thou hast learnt thy task well." At the end of three weeks more, the Master sent for the man, and said: "Dear son, rejoice with me, for it seems to me that with God's help I now know the first lines well. And now, if thou wilt, I am ready to recite the lesson to thee." The man said: "No, dear sir; but I will gladly rejoice with thee, and fully credit thee that thou knowest thy lesson well." And the Master answered: "I tell thee in all sincerity, that I have something heavy on my mind. And dear son, I beg thee to teach me yet further." Then spoke the man: "I can teach thee nothing more, as far as I am personally concerned. But if it pleases God to teach thee through me, I will gladly do my part, willingly acting as the instrument by which our Lord will act upon thee.

"Listen, dear sir, for I will counsel thee about divine love and brotherly fidelity; so that when the Lord's call shall come to thee, as it did to the young man in the gospel, I shall have no responsibility: 'If thou wilt be perfect, go sell what thou hast, and give to the poor, and thou shalt have treasure in Heaven: and come follow Me'" (Matt. xix: 21). Then the Master spoke: "Dear son, thou needst not care for that, for I have already yielded myself to that call, and with God's help I will go forward obedient in it to God and to thee." Then spoke the man: "Because thou hast made that secure, giving thyself entirely over to God to have a care of thee, then will I earnestly counsel thee ever to be obedient to the rules of thy Order and to thy superiors; for it may easily happen, that if thou wouldst tread the straight, narrow way, thou shalt be oppressed by others, and especially by thy own brethren. And when that happens, thy thoughts will be bent on the words by which thou didst vow thyself to God, being tempted meanwhile to find some way of loosing thyself from the cross. But that must not be. For thou must willingly be obedient, suffering gladly what happens to thee, from whomsoever it may come to thee. Thou must tread the way the Lord pointed out to the young man, namely, thou must take up thy cross and follow Jesus Christ, imitating Him in very truth; in all humility and in patience. That proud, cultivated intelligence of thine, which thou hast gained by study of sacred learning, thou must let pass from thee. During this thy time of preparation thou must neither study nor preach. But toward thy penitents, both men and women, thou shalt bear thyself very simply when they make their confessions. And when they are done, instead of giving them thy usual advice, say to them: I am now anxiously learning how to give myself good advice, and when I have succeeded in that, I will then give you good advice. If any one askest thee when thou wilt preach, refuse to tell him; but say to him in all truth that thou art not idle; and thus the people will excuse thee." Then the Master spoke: "Dear son, all this I will gladly do; but what occupation shall I have meanwhile?" The man said: "Thou shalt go into thy cell and read thy breviary, and attend in choir and join in the singing; thou shalt celebrate thy daily mass when thou canst do so. Whatever time is left over, take it up with the passion of our Lord, and meditate how thy life stands in comparison with His. Think also on the lost time of thy life, namely that in which thou didst have thyself in view as thy aim and purpose. Think, too, how very small has been thy love compared to His love. These things shalt thou study and that very humbly, so that thou mayst attain to some degree of real humility, thereby becoming rid of thy old habit of mind and quite departing from it. And when our Lord decides that the time is come, then will He make a new man of thee, supposing that thou shalt have been born again of God.

"But be sure that ere all this happens, thou must sell all that thou hast, and humbly give it up to God. And that means all that thou dost possess in thy proud intelligence, whether of Scripture learning or other learning, whereby thou mightest achieve honor in this life, or that has before this ministered to thy joy. All this thou must now let go, and thou must with St. Mary Magdalen fall at Christ's feet, and earnestly undertake all these ways of perfection. Then without doubt the King of Heaven will look upon thee with favor. But He by no means allows things to rest thus, for He will push thee further yet, so that thou mayst be purified still more, even as gold in the furnace. And it may well happen that He will offer thee the bitter draught that He offered His only begotten Son. And I surmise that by God's will all that thou doest and all that thou leavest undone, and indeed thy whole life, shall be brought to contempt and made nothing of in the eyes of the people. All thy penitents will leave thee, thinking that thou hast not good sense any longer. All thy good friends and brothers in thy monastery, will take offense at thy way of life, and say that thou hast adopted a preposterous kind of devotion.

"But when all this comes to pass, do not be affrighted, but rather be rejoiced, for just then thy salvation is at hand. To be sure thy human weakness will be terrified and sickened by it. But nevertheless, dear sir, do not give up, but trust God steadfastly, for He in no wise abandons His servants; and thou knowest that full well from thy knowledge of the lives of the dear saints. Now, dear sir, if thou wilt indeed undertake this way, realize that nothing in the world is better for thee or more useful than great detachment—boundless and humble, extending to all things, as well sweet as bitter, whether for weal or woe, so that thou shalt be able to say truthfully: Ah. my Lord and my God, if it were thy will that I should stay in this pain and in this anguish of heart till the end of the world, yet would I not depart from Thee and I would steadfastly continue in Thy service. And now, my dear sir, I know that in thy heart thou sayest, that this is indeed a heavy task that I have conferred with thee about. And for that reason it was that I begged thee to dismiss me, and that I said that if thou shouldst fall short of thy purpose, I should not be to blame."

Then the Master said: "Thou hast spoken truly; I own that it seems to me somewhat hard to undertake this way." The man spoke: "But thou didst beg me to teach thee the shortest road to the highest state of contemplation. Now I know no shorter, no surer way than this, if one would model on the true example of our Lord Jesus Christ. But, dear sir, I counsel thee by all my truth, that thou take time to think over all this; and what God then gives thee to do, that do in His name." Then the Master said: "I will do that; and I will wait and see if with God's help I may overcome my repugnance."

CHAPTER EIGHT.

After eleven days the Master sent for the man and said to him: "Ah, dear son, what martyrdom have I suffered, and what interior battles have I fought day and night, ere I could vanquish the devil and my own flesh. But with the grace of God, I have now concentrated all my faculties of mind and powers of body to this decision: I will cheerfully undertake this way, and I will remain in it fast and firm, come weal come woe." Then the man said: "Dear sir, dost thou recall the words I used with thee, when thou didst ask me how thou shouldst make a beginning?" The Master spoke: "Yes, for the moment thou hadst gone from me I wrote thy advice down word for word." Then the man said: "Dear sir, that thou hast received this bold spirit from God, I am heartily glad, and value it for thee as if it were for myself, and of this God is my witness. And now in the name of our Lord Jesus Christ make a beginning." Then the man said farewell, and he took his departure, and the Master did as he had been directed.

And it came to pass ere a year elapsed, that the Master was held to be good for nothing in the monastery, even by his most trusted friends. And his penitents all left him; they were gone from him as if they had never seen him. All this was a heavy blow to him and caused him much suffering. Meanwhile his head began to grow weak. And now he sent for the man, and told him how things were with him, and how his whole body was almost in a state of sickness, and especially his head. Then the man said: "Sir, do not be alarmed. Humbly cleave to God, and trust Him implicitly. I assure thee that I am well pleased with thee; all goes well with thy life, and will daily go better.

"Dear sir, thou knowest well, that whosoever will take the right road and travel onward, must imitate the sufferings of our Lord Jesus Christ. Therefore stand thy ground, and give thyself wholly up to God. I assure thee that thy experience was also my own. And meanwhile, as thou art now undergoing those interior trials, treat thy body with some consideration, giving it wholesome food. As to thy head, I will have made for thee a decoction of herbs, the same as strengthened me when I was in thy situation. But bear in mind that I ever gave both body and soul to God, to do with them entirely as he pleased."

Then the Master spoke: "But thou toldst me before to avoid good food and drink." And the man answered: "Yes, sir; but that was in the first beginnings, while as yet the body was robust; but now that it becomes dry and thin and would be all submission to the spirit, therefore thou mayst come to its help and build it up somewhat, or otherwise thou wouldst be tempting God by excessive austerity. Whilst thou art in thy present weak state thou dost a service to God if thou dost discretely nourish thy body; but by no means shalt thou inordinately indulge thy appetite—that must not be. Dear sir, call in God to thy help and go forward cheerfully. Give thyself up to God in trustful and entire self renunciation; rely confidently on his infinite mercy, and wait for His grace. Whatever God may demand of thee, sweet or bitter, prove thyself equal to it with His help. And now I beg thee for God's sake not to take it amiss that I must return home, for thither I am called by an affair of great importance; my interest is much involved—that I say to thee in all sincerity. But if it should happen that thou canst not get on without me, send to my city for me, and I will willingly come to thee. But if thou canst endure to suffer without the help of any creature, that is everyway the best for thee." Then the Master spoke: "Dear son, say no such thing to me, for I cannot and will not get on without thee for any length of time. If thou goest away it will be excessively painful to me, for I can have no comfort in this world now." The man answered: "Dear sir, I will tell thee of a better comfort, and that is the Holy Ghost, who has called thee to this way, lovingly invited thee, and brought thee so far onward, by means of me a poor sinner. His is the work done in thee, not mine; and I have been but His instrument, gladly serving Him in it, to God's glory and to thy happiness." Then the Master spoke: "Dear son, may God be thy eternal recompense. And because thy affairs are so urgent I must let thee go. I will resign myself to God to suffer as best I may." The man spoke: "Dear sir, now that thou art subjected to the divine discipline, and hast entered a life of true spirituality in obedience to God, and inasmuch as this is thy free act, I now admonish thee to bear thyself discreetly, and care for thyself prudently, lest thou shouldst regret that thou art forsaken by all creatures. But if it should happen that thou fallest into want and money fails thee, then I advise thee to pawn a part of thy books, and to avoid suffering excessively. But on no account shalt thou sell the books, for the time is sure to come again, when good books will be useful to thee, and indeed necessary." Then the man made his farewell and took his departure. But as to the Master, his eyes overflowed and he began to weep.

CHAPTER NINTH.

So it happened that the Master suffered great trials and temptations for two years, and these included disgrace in the eyes of all his friends. To this was added such destitution that he was forced to pawn a portion of his library. Meanwhile his body was reduced to great weakness. But he bore it all, and found himself sincerely humble. And it came to pass in the night of the feast of St. Paul's conversion, that he was assailed by the worst temptation that could be imagined. And at that moment all his natural force was so weak, that he could not so much as walk to the choir to attend at matins, and must perforce sit idly in his cell, giving himself up to God most meekly, void of all comfort and help from creatures. This was his sorest trial. Now amid all that feebleness, he meditated on the passion of our Lord Jesus Christ, and on the great love He had for us. And then he considered his own life, and how petty a thing it was, compared to the love of God for him. Upon this he entered into a very deep sorrow for all his sins, and of regret for all the time he had wasted, and he spoke to God with heart and mouth: Ah merciful God! In thy boundless mercy take pity on me a poor sinner, for I am unworthy to walk the earth. And as he sat there in his utter helplessness and sadness, and being quite wide awake, he heard with his bodily ears a voice that said: Stand fast in thy peace, and trust in God. And remember that when He was on earth in His human nature, when He cured men of bodily sickness, He also made them well in their souls. The moment these words were spoken, he lost all sense and reason, and knew not whether he was carried away nor how. But when he came to his senses again, he found a great change had taken place in him. All his interior and his outward faculties were conscious of a new strength; and he was gifted with clear perceptions of matters that before had been very strange and alien to him. He greatly wondered from whence this change had come; and then he thought: Thou canst not rightly place thyself now, and thou wilt send for thy friend and tell him of this.

So he sent for the man, and when he came the Master told him all that had happened. Then spoke the man: "These thy words I have heard with joy from the bottom of my heart. Dear sir, thou must understand that now for the very first time thou hast found the true, the great grace in God. I say to thee that now for the very first time thou hast been touched by the Most High. And this thou must know: as formerly the letter had somewhat killed thee, so now shall the same make thee alive again. For now thy teaching comes from God the Holy Ghost, whereas before it was from the flesh. Now thou hast the light of the Holy Ghost, received from the grace of God, and thou hast the holy Scriptures in thee. Therefore hast thou now a great advantage, and in the future far more than formerly thou shalt understand the Scriptures; for thou knowest full well that the Scriptures in many places seem to contradict themselves. But now that in the light of the Holy Ghost thou hast received divine grace to possess the holy Scripture in thyself, so wilt thou understand that all Scripture has the same meaning and is never self-contradictory. And now thou wilt go on right, following the example of our Lord Jesus Christ. Thou must begin to preach again, teaching thy fellow men the right road to eternal life. The time is come when good books are useful to thee. And be sure that now one sermon will profit the people and give them good fruit more than did a hundred formerly. For the words that thou shalt speak go forth from a purified soul, judging and weighing all things in simplicity of spirit. Hence just in proportion as thou hast been good for nothing in the people's estimation, thou shalt now become all the better appreciated and loved.

"But it is of particular necessity that thou shalt keep thyself truly humble. Thou knowest that whosoever carries a precious treasure openly in his hand, must be on his guard against thieves. I assure thee that the devil is greatly frightened, when he finds that God has confided to a man so dear a prize, so noble a treasure as thou possessest. He will exert all his skill and cunning to rob thee of it. Therefore be prudently on thy guard. And thou canst in no way baffle his scheming so well as by boundless humility. Now, dear sir, there is no longer any need of my speaking to thee by way of instruction, as I did before. For now thou thyself hast that Master right and true, whose instrument I have been. Hearken to Him and be obedient; that do I counsel thee with all my faithful heart.

"And now I on my part wish to be instructed in divine love by thee, for with the help of God I have done thee the favor that God led me here to do. So, if God wills, I shall stay a good while with thee and hear thy preaching. For if God grants it, I am of opinion that thou shouldst begin preaching again." Then the Master spoke: "Dear son, what is thy advice? I have placed many good books in pawn for thirty florins." Then said the man: "I will give thee that sum of money for God's sake; and if after thy books are redeemed aught remains over, thou mayst give it to God; for all that we have is His, whether goods of body or soul." And thus did the Master redeem his books.

He then announced publicly that he would preach the third day following. The people were amazed at this, because he had stopped preaching for so long a time, and a great throng came to hear him. When he saw that the crowd was so great, the Master mounted a high pulpit so that all could hear him better. He knelt and covered his face with his cowl, and he prayed silently: Merciful and ever-lasting God, if it be Thy will, grant me the grace to speak so that Thy divine name may be praised and honored, and these people thereby advanced in Thy love. And as he said these words, his eyes overflowed with tears so abundantly, welling up from his heart, that never a word could he utter from the power of his feelings. That lasted so long that the people were much annoyed. And a man in the crowd spoke: "Sir, how long must we sit here waiting for thee? It is already very late; if thou art not going to preach, then say so and let us go home." But the Master yet remained weeping and in deep recollection, and again did he speak to God: Ah my Lord and my God, if it be Thy divine will, then take this weeping from my eyes, and grant that I may preach this sermon to Thy praise and glory. But if Thou dost not do this, so is it a sign that thou deemest that I have not yet been despised and scorned enough. Now, dear Lord, perfect Thy divine will upon poor me, to Thy praise and to my need. But this prayer helped nothing, for the weeping grew harder and harder. Then did he understand that God would have it thus. And so he addressed the people: "My dear children, it is a deep pain to my heart, that I have detained you so long, for I can say not a single word for weeping. Pray to God for me that He may help me. And I with His grace will preach for your benefit another time—the soonest I possibly can." And so the people went away, and this occurrence was noised abroad over the whole city. He was greatly ridiculed for all this, and made nothing of by everybody. People said: "It is now plain enough that he has become a veritable fool." Then his own brethren in the monastery strictly forbade him to preach again, for this occurrence gave much scandal in their community; and they said that he made the Order a scandal in the people's eyes, by the foolish spirituality which he had adopted, and which hurt his brain and made an idiot of him.

Then the Master sent for the man, and he related all that had happened to him. The man said: "Dear sir, do not be alarmed at this occurrence. The Bridegroom is accustomed thus to try all His best loved friends, and this is a certain sign that God is thy good friend. Without doubt there was something of pride hidden in thy soul unknown to thyself. This is why thou hast been scorned and ridiculed. And it may be that hereby thou hast received some great gifts from God, of which thou art thyself as yet unaware—granted thee through the exercise of patience in this trial. Therefore be at peace, and be cheerful and humble. Nor needst thou take this for so very strange a thing, for I have known the same and worse to happen to others. Thou shouldst not be ashamed of the burden of this cross that God has sent thee, but rather value it as a great treasure, a very precious gift of God. I counsel thee to stay by thyself for five days, shut off from speech with all men, to the praise and honor of the five holy wounds of our Lord Jesus Christ. And when the five days are passed, beg thy Prior for leave to deliver a sermon in Latin. If he will not permit that, then pray him to try thee in class, and permit thee to deliver a lecture to the brethren."

Now this last permission was granted him. And he lectured to the community in so deep-searching a way, that they never heard the like in their whole lives, so great and profound a divine doctrine did he teach. Then they allowed him to deliver a sermon to the people. One day after one of the brethren had preached to the people in the church—the same in which the Master had formerly been accustomed to preach—that brother announced: "I have been directed to announce that the Master will preach in this place tomorrow. If what happened to him lately should occur again, then I am not to be blamed for it. But this much I can truthfully say, that in our convent school he has lectured to us with such great and deep doctrine and such divine knowledge as we have not heard this many a day. How he will succeed with you God knows, not I." The following day the Master came to the church of that convent (it was a convent of nuns) and he began to preach as follows:

CHAPTER TENTH.

Dear children, it may well be two years or more since last I preached. I then spoke to you of twenty-four points of the spiritual life. It was then my custom to use much Latin in my sermons, and to divide them into points. But it is now my purpose not to do so any more; and when I do speak in Latin, it will be when the educated are present who can understand it. And now let us say an *Ave Maria* and beg God's grace.

Dear children, I have chosen a text for my sermon, and I will discuss it and adhere to it. In German it is as follows:

"Behold the Bridegroom cometh, go ye forth to meet Him" (Matt. xxv: 6). The Bridegroom is our dear Lord Jesus Christ, and the bride is Holy Church and Christianity. Ah, dear children, we are thus all spouses of Christ, and we should all gladly go forth to meet Him. But in that, alas, we are found wanting. Dear children, the right roads and the plain ways on which we should go forth to meet the Bridegroom, have become deserted and overgrown,, and we are even beginning nowadays to have little knowledge of them at all. The road to Christ is strange enough to many a one among us—that road on which we should gladly meet our true Bridegroom. Of this, with God's help, I will speak on another occasion. But now, knowing that we are all chosen to be spouses of Christ, I will have something to say, showing how the bride should act if she would really go forth to meet the Bridegroom.

My dear children, a faithful bride should strictly avoid all that is against the Bridegroom. That is all vainglory, pride, envy, together with all the sins of this world, all the concupiscence of the flesh, whether of delicate and luxurious pampering of the body or any other such thing: everything indeed except what is of real necessity. And when that happens, that is when the bride for sake of the Bridegroom detests all this and forsakes it totally, then does the bride begin to be somewhat pleasing to the Bridegroom.

But if she would become yet more pleasing, then must she humbly bow down and say with heart and mouth: Ah my dear Lord Bridegroom, Thou knowest all hearts well; and now with all my heart I say this to Thee—that I will do all that lies in my power to learn from Thee through my heart's reason, what is pleasing to Thee. Now when the bride pays these vows to the Bridegroom, He turns and looks upon the bride. Then she requests Him to give her a jewel for a keepsake. And what is that jewel? It is that she shall be visited with many inner and outer trials, according to the way He is accustomed to try His special friends.

But if it happens that the bride is as yet unused to suffering, then will she say to Him: "Ah, dear Lord Bridegroom, this is very hard upon me, and I feel most anxious lest I shall not be able to endure it. Therefore, dear Lord Bridegroom, I beg thee to make my sufferings somewhat lighter, or to take away a part of them. Then the Bridegroom says: But let Me ask this, My dear bride: should the bride be now better off than the Bridegroom once was? If thou wilt go forth to meet the Bridegroom, thou must in some degree imitate Him; and it is altogether proper that a faithful bride should suffer somewhat out of sympathy with her Bridegroom.

And when the bride thus heard her Bridegroom's will and perceived His earnestness, she was much frightened, and said: Dear Lord. Bridegroom, Thou must not be angry with me, for I will gladly be obedient. Visit me with what trials Thou pleasest, and I will gladly suffer it all with Thy help and in Thy love. When the Bridegroom heard this, the bride was somewhat more dear to Him than before. Therefore He would give her a better cup to drink. Now the draught He gave was that she should be quit of all her thoughts, that all doing and not doing should become entirely tasteless to her because it had ceased to please her in the least degree. No matter how good things might be in themselves, as she did them she could only think how much she angered her Bridegroom by doing them; and she greatly forboded how much punishment she must perhaps suffer for it all. As this showed itself outwardly, she was scorned and derided by everybody, and whatever she did was accounted nothing but foolishness.

Now, dear children, all this time the bride was worn and feeble in all her natural powers; she constantly dreaded that she could not hold out but must finally die during her trial. Therefore she was affrighted. This was because she was still cowardly and weak-spirited. So she invoked her Bridegroom anxiously, and said: Ah, dear Lord Bridegroom, how Thou hast terrified me, oh so dreadfully. I cannot suffer long this way; I am about to die. Then the Bride-groom spoke: If thou wilt go forth rightly to meet the Bridegroom, it is fitting that thou shouldst first go after Him a part of the way He has gone over. Now the Bridegroom suffered for thirty-three years—much shame, hunger, thirst, cold, heat, and bitter torments. At last He suffered a cruel death. And all this he bore out of true love of His bride and entirely for her sake. Is it not then proper that the bride should risk death for His sake, and out of heart's love for Him? Surely, if thou hadst right trust and true love for Him, all thy fears would vanish away.

When the bride heard these words from her Bridegroom, she was much frightened and her whole heart trembled; and she said: Ah, dear Lord, I confess most sincerely that I have done wrong in mur-muring; and on that account I am exceedingly afraid. It cuts me to the heart that I have not given myself up to Thee most trustfully unto death. Dear Lord Bridegroom, I will now most truthfully promise Thee all that Thou wilt have me: Whatever Thou dost will, that do I will also: sick or well, for weal or woe, for sweet or bitter, cold or hot, dry or wet—just as Thou wilt so do I will. I will give my will up to Thee entirely. I will be wholly and gladly obedient to Thee. Apart from what Thou dost will, I will never desire anything what-soever. Do with me, a poor worthless creature, all that Thou wilt in time and in eternity. For, dear Lord, when I consider what there is in me and of me, I feel that I am not worthy to tread the earth.

When the Bridegroom saw this true heartfelt loyalty of the bride, and the deep fund of humility in her, what did He do? He was moved with pity; and He bestowed a present on the bride, namely, a blessed sweet draught. And what draught is this? It is that He caused her yet greater trials, and afflicted her with yet greater anguish than she ever before had suffered. Now when the bride became aware of this, when she knew His stern purpose and His will, she suffered all this willingly on the Bridegroom's account. And she bowed down humbly before Him, and said: Ah dear Lord Bridegroom, it is indeed right that Thou shouldst not will as I will, but rather that I should will as Thou dost. From Thy divine hand will I receive this new present, all willingly and gladly, and wholly for the sake of Thy love, whether to my flesh come weal or woe: for to Thy love and Thy will have I most lovingly given myself up.

When the Bridegroom in His eternal wisdom knew this purpose of His bride's soul, knew the downright earnestness of this humble bride, then she became very dear to Him. And out of true love **He** left her this present of his—namely to suffer in all her natural powers so long as was necessary to cure all her imperfections, and to cleanse away all the stains of her former sins, until she should be all pure and beautiful. And so He spoke: All hail my well loved bride. so beautiful and so well pleasing to Me; for now thou art all clean and without spot, and thou art most acceptable to Me. Then did **He** gaze upon her with an immeasurably great and divine affection. And presently to the joys of the marriage feast comes the Bridegroom's eternal Father, and He says to the bride: All hail, my well loved chosen friend. It is now high time that we should go to the church, to solemnize the espousals. And then He takes the Bridegroom and the bride, and leads them to the church, and He plights them to each other, and binds them together in divine love; and God binds them in a union so fast and firm, that the bride says that neither in time nor eternity shall they ever be separated. And when they have thus been made one in the divine espousals, the Bridegroom says: Dear, eternal Father, what shall now be our wedding gift to the bride? The Father says: That shall be the Holy Ghost, for that office is due to Him as standing for the Father Upon this was poured into the bride the overflowing divine love, so superabundant that it seemed to overflow upon even the Bridegroom. And now the Bride was ravished out of herself, and was wholly inebriated with love, and became forgetful of self and of all creatures in time and eternity.

Now, my dear children, whosoever has been invited to so noble a spiritual espousals, and has accepted the invitation and come to the marriage feast, the same shall begin to taste the true, the solemnly promised, the richly gifted sweetness of the Holy Ghost. This bride is then a true adorer, for she prays to the Father in the Holy Ghost. At this marriage feast is joy upon joy. Here in one hour more peace and joy is had than all creatures in time and eternity can ever bestow.

The joy of the bride with the Bridegroom is greater than any human mind can ever comprehend.

As the Master reached thus far in his sermon and spoke these words, a certain man cried out very loud: "It is true!" and he fell down as if he were dead. And then a woman cried out from among the people: "Sir, stop speaking, or this man will die on our hands." Then the Master said: Ah, dear children, the Bridegroom then took the bride and led her away to His home. Let us gladly leave her to Him. And thus will I make an end of my sermon. Dear children, let us all call out to heaven to our God and Lord for His help. For there is sore need to do so, since we have grown so dull and foolish that we have no compassion one for another, although we know that we have been named by God brothers and sisters. There are few enough among us who are willing to crucify their flesh in imitation of the Bridegroom, and in order to obtain a better joy and have an espousals rich in graces.

You should know that in our days there are not many who have in all sincerity gone forth to meet the Bridegroom, as many a one did in former times. Hence the need that every one of us should study his soul, and take earnest account of himself. For the time approaches and is indeed now come, that most of those living here have eyes and see not, have ears and hear not. Dear children, let all of us strive to win to this most blessed, loving and joyous marriage feast.

Now after the bride had taken her departure from the espousals and was left to herself, and found herself still living amid this life's misery, then she said in her soul: Alas, poor me, miserable me; am I yet in this life? And so she was somewhat sad within herself. But she was so entirely detached in her inmost soul, and so perfectly humbled towards her Bridegroom that she dared not so much as think of or desire her Bridegroom's return, esteeming herself wholly unworthy of Him. But therefore did the Bridegroom by no means desert her, but He looked upon her from time to time, for He knew full well that no one could comfort her except Himself alone.

Now, dear children, do not be astonished that I have not told you how affectionately the Bridegroom conversed with the bride. It is possible that men would not believe me (except it be one here and there who has tasted this sweet union), if I told them the strange and marvellous words the bride speaks with her Bridegroom. We find such things in the Scripture; for when the inner soul speaks with its beloved the words cannot be perfectly uttered. And even in these days, it happens that when the espoused soul speaks out loud with its Bridegroom, those who listen say that the soul is drunk, or silly.

Now, dear children, I fear that I have held you too long. But it did not seem long to me; and I meant it all very kindly. Nor could I on this occasion be easily more brief, if I would rightly explain this matter. So I beg you to take it in good part. God grant us all to become true and perfect brides of our Lord Jesus Christ; that we may go forth in real and boundless self-abandonment and humility to meet our blessed Bridegroom; and that we may ever and eternally remain espoused to Him. To this happy lot may God the Father, and God the Son, and God the Holy Ghost lovingly assist us. *Amen.*

CHAPTER ELEVENTH.

When this sermon was over, the Master went and offered mass, and he gave God's body in communion to several good souls. But fully forty men staid behind in the churchyard lying as it were in a swoon. Now the man who had previously given counsel to the Master, when he learned of this, told the Master of it, and when mass was over he led him to the churchyard that he might see these people and consider what ailed them. But while mass was being said they had risen up and gone away, all but twelve, who still lay there. Then the Master said to the man: "Dear son, what thinkest thou we should do with these men?" Then the man went from one to another of them and touched them. But they moved very little, and lay there almost as if they were dead. This was a very strange thing to the Master, for he had never seen the like before. So he said to the man: "Tell me; what dost thou think? Are these people dead or living?" The man smiled and said: "Were they dead, the blame would be on thee and the Bridegroom. How canst thou bring them back to consciousness?" The Master spoke: "If the Bridegroom is with me in this undertaking, then can I indeed restore them." Then the man said: "These men are still alive, and I beg thee to request the sisters' leave to have them carried under shelter, lest by exposure to the night air and by lying on the cold earth, they should catch cold." And so the Master had them carried into a warm place. Then the sisters said: "Dear sir, here is one of our sisters to whom the same thing has happened, and who lies in bed as if she were dead." The Master said: "Have a care, my dear children, for all these sick people for God's sake, and as soon as any of them returns to consciousness, give him something warm if he is able to take it." And the sisters said that they would gladly do so. And now the Master took his departure, and the man also, and they went to the Master's cell. Then the man spoke: "Now, dear sir, what thinkest thou? Didst thou ever see the like of this in thy whole life? Thou now seest plainly what wonders God will do by one who is a fit instrument of his work. Dear sir, I foresee that this sermon will move many people, and they will discuss it one with another. If it be thy will, I would advise that thou leave these weak children awhile in peace, for they must have a long time to deal with this discourse. And if thou thinkest well of it, and God is favorable, then thou mightest give a sermon to people of the secular state of life, for it is now the time of Lent. The Master willingly complied, and he preached very well to the people living in the world, several of whom were greatly improved.

The next year it happened that the Master went to a certain monastery of nuns, and five of the sisters begged him for the love of God to give them a sermon, instructing them how a true religious should pass her life. Then the Master said: "That I will gladly do, with God's blessing, next Sunday." And when he arrived, many people attended the sermon, and the Master entered and began as follows:

CHAPTER TWELFTH.

Dear children, St. Paul gives us good instruction in this day's Epistle, from which I make this extract: "I know a man in Christ above fourteen years ago (whether in the body, I know not, or out of the body, I know not; God knoweth), such a one caught up to the third heaven" (II Cor. xii: 2). Now we notice that our dear apostle, who is speaking of himself, had kept these wonderful things secret for fourteen years, nor would he ever have revealed them but by God's permission. He did not do as people do nowadays. For if some little grace is granted them, they forthwith blazen it abroad without

God's leave, telling it to others who know as little as themselves what it may signify. This is very foolish, and is an injury to themselves. Therefore be on your guard against such an indiscretion. We find few men, alas, in our time who have correct judgment in such matters. Therefore, dear children, no one should without God's permission publish around the graces he may have received. God granted leave to St. Paul to tell us his wonderful experiences, and this was for our improvement. And also to teach the doctrine that when God gives a man the antecedent and unmerited graces, he should not shrink from any heavy task God may lay upon him; as He did in the case of St. Paul.

And, dear children, you must know that God's gifts are to come to us through suffering; and if they come before suffering, then are they none the less to be preserved by suffering. And because suffering so greatly ennobles the soul, and is so fruitful of good to it, therefore does God give great suffering to his dear, holy friends, and He did especially to His only begotten Son. Men suffer in this life by God's will, and this is on account of the fruitfulness of suffering. This is why God granted leave to St. Paul to tell us of his sufferings, and also of his graces. In this day's Epistle he says: "In many more labors, in prisons more frequently, in stripes above measure, in deaths often. Of the Jews five times did I receive forty stripes, save one. Thrice was I beaten with rods, once was I stoned, thrice I suffered shipwreck, a night and a day I was in the depth of the sea. In journeyings often, in perils of waters, in perils of robbers, in perils from my own nation, in perils from the Gentiles, in perils in the city, in perils in the wilderness, in perils in the sea, in perils from false brethren" (II Cor. xi: 23-26).

These and many other pains and miseries did the apostle suffer, and why? Further on in this Epistle he tells us why sufferings were sent him: "And lest the greatness of the revelations should exalt me, there was given me a sting of my flesh, an angel of Satan to buffet me. For which thing thrice I besought the Lord, that it might depart from me. And He said to me: My grace is sufficient for thee; for power is made perfect in infirmity." And then St. Paul adds: "Gladly therefore will I glory in my infirmities, that the power of Christ may dwell in me" (II Cor. xii: 7-9). Now, dear children, it behooves us to believe St. Paul when he says suffering is useful and fruitful, and imitate his example in bearing all kinds of inflictions.

For be sure that if ever we come to a fruitful Christian life, there
is no other way but this: a voluntary renunciation of our nature, so
that a man shall take leave of all natural joy, and do it from his
inmost heart, providing only for reasonable necessity and that solely
because it advances him nearer to God. Whatever provision for
nature is over and above that, he must renounce wholly and be totally
stripped of.

Be sure that nobody can possess and taste God's sweetness, until
he has put away from him and totally rooted out the inclinations of
the life of the senses, and the concupiscence of his entire nature.
Hence did St. Paul again say: "For if you live according to the
flesh, you shall die: but if by the Spirit you mortify the deeds of the
flesh, you shall live" (Rom. viii: 13). My dear children, we must
frame ourselves into the sweet image of our Lord Jesus Christ. Here
again St. Paul teaches us to put off the old man and clothe ourselves
with Christ: "Put ye on the Lord Jesus Christ, and make not provision for the flesh in its concupiscences" (Rom. xiii: 14).

But even beyond all this there is a much nobler and greater self-
denial. For after the spirit has fully vanquished the flesh, and has
suppressed all the lower, sensual, fleshly uprisings of nature, then
does the spirit leap upward into things eternal, and the spiritual life
becomes full of sweetness, and the former works of nature are heartily
hated. Now when that happens, when a man's spirit begins to enjoy
supernatural things, all very high and noble, another step must be
taken. As first of all he renounced all the sweetness of nature, it
now remains for him to renounce his own will. And he must give
up joy in spirtual things; he must renounce the superfluities of the
spirit as he did before those of nature; he must give up to God, and
let Him do His work in him just as He pleases. And herein does he
first come to real self-renunciation, real and true, arriving at that
poverty of spirit which is rewarded with the kingdom of heaven.

Now, my dear children, it happens that some souls, drawing themselves inward, place their joy in themselves, picking and choosing
what pleases them in the spiritual life. They do not abandon themselves to God, but all in self-will they follow their own self-chosen
devotional methods. The souls that act that way enjoy God's gifts
and graces inordinately, receiving little fruit, and sometimes none at
all. Now God knows that if He should cast a brighter light upon

such people's faults, and if He withdrew from them their devotional sweetness, they would not remain faithful to Him. That is why He gives such spirits the sweet solace of religious feeling, lest they should quite give up His service. They are yet petty and weak of character; and the reason is because they are full of self-will. They are very dear to themselves. As to perfection, they mistake the show for the reality. They are essentially outward characters, having little interior life. Hence they are all too readily led astray.

But there are other souls, who have given up to God in a state of most interior detachment, receiving everything from God with equal indifference whether it be bitter or sweet. And if spiritual joy departs, that loss moves them not one whit farther from God. These souls prefer the reality to the show of perfection; they lead spiritual lives fruitful of the essentials of religion. They are the true, interior spirits.

And you should know this: the man who has thus freely given up everything in the body and in the soul that is not God has made great and indescribable progress. What he now needs is the counsel of the wise and the good. And he must also very carefully cultivate a deep, a boundless humility, and in that constantly abide, for the evil beasts of hell never give over their purpose to destroy him.

Dear children, deep resignation—that is to say, a sincere detachment from all our natural inclinations—is a good beginning. But that should be inspired with real humility, as St. Peter teaches: "Be you humbled, therefore, under the mighty hand of God, that He may exalt you in the time of visitation" (I Peter v, 6). Dear children, could we but learn how to be gladly and totally free from desires, that would be good. Upon this subject St. Dionysius speaks: "When it happens that God actually and truly *dwells* within my soul, then is my spirit so exalted that it seems to me that nothing in the world is lacking to me, and if He at the same moment made all created things subject to me, it would not be a favor done me. But when it happens that God is in my soul only by His presence and by way of satisfaction in Him and perception of His sovereignty, then do I yet have a longing for Him, and that long-ing can only exist because of some imperfection of which I am guilty; for, as Solomon teaches, we should have peace in all Divine works." Thus does St. Dionysius reckon interior longing to be in a kind of a way a defect, for it is self-evident that if one longs for entire detach-ment he has not yet fully attained to it. The most perfect detachment is to be detached from one's very detachment, if we may say so. But this will seem a strange doctrine to certain men among us, who are advocating novel and erroneous views, for they have beheld God only according to their own spiritual joys.

But I must now grant the request of these Sisters and tell them what are the virtues proper to their state of life. And I say this: A true nun should all her life long be purified from all creatures and be detached from them. She should have so pure a soul that it may be fit and able to help to eternal salvation all who hold the faith of Christ. But one of the Sisters might say: I have so much human weakness that it is necessary for me to be now and then recreated and refreshed with human company, and I must spend some time conversing with people. I answer: Alas, thou poor creature, in this thou art under the guidance of the devil! Make up thy mind that whosoever seeks in the cloister anything else but willing suffering through God enters there very unadvisedly. Some enter the cloister with such motives that it seems a sin for them to live on the alms given to their order, for they would be very unwilling to practice actual poverty; that is to say, to lead the life of those poor people on the streets who are in actual want and subsist by begging. Besides this, when a Sister joins the community she should set about becoming free from all imperfections of the bodily and of the spiritual life. She must willingly go along with Jesus Christ to Calvary and be crucified with Him for the salvation of all mankind. For Christ exclaimed from the cross: "My God, My God, why hast Thou forsaken Me?" (Matt. xxvii, 46). And as God the Father did thus forsake His only begotten Son for men's salvation, so must all true monks and nuns forsake all created things, all worldly and fleshly desires. Otherwise, they have their labor for their pains. Holy Mary Magdalen was a true nun, for she willingly gave up all self-love and gladly chose to be deprived of all human help.

The Heavenly Father sent His only begotten Son in human nature, that He might endure suffering, and we would fly from all suffering. I tell you emphatically that, do what we may, if we would find the safest and the shortest and the most reasonable way to perfection, then we have no choice but to set our Lord's life and passion before us as our pattern and follow after Him by suffering.

But I must tell you something else: The Heavenly Father is not so hard with us as He was with His only begotten Son. If we will but give ourselves to God in a state of suffering and do it with all our powers;

if we but gladly accept sufferings because He so wills it; if we do not seek to escape from suffering when He visits it upon us, but stand fast and firm: when the Heavenly Father finds us at last thus disposed toward Him, then, in due time, He will withdraw all suffering from us and He will bestow on us a comfort divinely joyful. When a man experiences these happy and gracious joys in his espousals with God, he will never again think of earthly joys. The joys even of Christmas and of Easter seem to him to be all merged in the unbroken happiness of his perpetual marriage feast, as God ever comes to him with overflowing supernatural graces. Whatever day that first happens to him is the great day of his heavenly jubilation.

Dear children, these are the reasons why we should gladly suffer all that our tender Father inflicts upon us. We know full well that the man who through suffering attains to the Divine espousals is made a wise man, and his life is a well-ordered life. He overflows with the influence of the Holy Ghost, giving him plain guidance what to do and what to leave undone and making all his activity spiritually fruitful. But, meanwhile, such a man makes nothing of himself. He is profoundly humble, and he feels a continual fear, dreading lest he is falling short of his duty to his well-loved Father. God grant us to learn how to suffer in all our life. May God the Father and the Son and the Holy Ghost help us to enjoy the Divine espousals. *Amen.*

CHAPTER THIRTEENTH.

Dear child, if thou wilt finally come to thy perfection and to God, thou must observe three things: Firstly—Thou must make God thy one and only motive and meaning, seeking God's honor in everything and by no means thy own honor—His will and not thy own. Secondly—In all external activity thou shalt keep a close watch on thyself. Gaze down into thy own utter nothingness and take good heed of that. Look carefully to thy relations to persons and things around about thee, and to thy own sentiments and feelings about them, looking inward toward thy most secret thoughts. Thirdly—Meddle not with what does not concern thee. Let things be as they are, if they are not committed to thy charge. What is good, is good; what is bad, is bad, and thou canst not help it. Turn inward to thy own soul and there abide, waiting for the tones of thy Father's voice calling thee to be and remain steadfastly in Him.

And, O dear child, if thou wilt but observe these two other things, thou shalt win a great victory. Firstly—Thou must in all sincerity be little in thy own esteem, whether thou considerest thy outward or thy inward life. Nor should this sentiment be in words only, but in thy heart's truest sincerity. Reckon thyself as of small account, yea, of no account at all, and let this be the clear persuasion of thy mind and the strong feeling of thy heart, with not the least taint of hypocrisy. Secondly—Have true Divine love. And this is not to be what we call love in our life of the senses, but rather that essential manner of loving by which our intention is fixed singly and wholly on God in our inmost soul.

O man, thou shalt be void of all attention, understanding and activity of the senses that is not directed to God, because the Lord God Himself is empty and void [to thy apprehension] in order that the spirit may be assimilated to the infinite, absolute Divine essence. It is necessary that thy soul should thus stand free and detached if it shall ever be able to comprehend the hidden mystery of familiar union with God. Thus must a man renounce all things in which he detects any trace of self-love. *Amen.*

CHAPTER FOURTEENTH.

And now you must know that this Master increased in a godly life and became, by the grace of the Holy Ghost, so wise that he was often called on to preach both to the clergy and the laity, following the way we have described. He was much loved in both town and country. Whatever weighty matter was to be settled, he was called on for guidance, not only in spiritual, but also in temporal affairs, for his advice was implicitly followed. When the Master had passed eight years of these fruitful labors it was God's will to leave him no longer in this state of exile. And He would have him come to Him without any purgatory. God then sent him the decree of death. He was attacked by a severe illness and lay abed for full twenty weeks, a most painful time and full of deep sorrows. Finally he knew, in the grace of the Holy Ghost, that he was about to bid farewell to this world, for God would now reward him for his labors. Therefore did the Master send for that holy man, his beloved friend, telling him that he had not long to live. The man was obedient and came to the Master, who received him very affectionately. The man was glad to find him yet alive, and he said:

"Dear sir, how art thou?" The Master answered: "I believe that the time is at hand when God would take me out of this life. Therefore, dear son, it is a great comfort to me that thou shalt be with me at my end. And I pray thee to take the books lying there. Thou shalt find written in them all the conferences that thou gavest to me and my answer to thy words. Thou shalt also find there some account of my life and of what God has done for me, His poor, unworthy servant. Dear son, if thou thinkest well of it and God grants thee the grace to do it, thou wilt make a little book of all this." Then the man spoke: "Dear sir, I have written down thy five sermons, and if thou approve of it I will add them to the little book thou askest me to make about thee." Then the Master said: "I admonish thee with all the earnestness I am capable of, and for the love of God, that thou shalt write nothing about me and shall not mention my name. For thou shouldst certainly know that my way of life, the words, the works that have been done through me, a poor, unworthy, sinful man, are not mine, but Almighty God's—they are His alone, now and forevermore. Therefore, dear son, if thou shalt write the little book for the benefit of our fellow-Christians, so write it that neither my name nor thine shall once be mentioned. Thou mayst, however, use the words—the Master, the man. Again, permit not this little book to be read or to be seen by anyone in this city, for they would easily know that I was the Master named. Take it with thee into thy own country, lest my interior life should be be revealed in this place."

During full eleven days the Master conversed with the man. And then the time came when he must die. And he said: "Dear son, I beg thee, for God's sake, that thou wilt consent, if God is willing, that after my death my spirit should appear to thee and tell thee how it is with me." Then the man said: "Dear Sir, if God pleases, I will gladly consent."

And it came to pass that when he was dying the Master had a manner and appearance the most shocking and fearful, so that all the brethren in the monastery, and, indeed, others from without, were distressed and amazed, such was the anguish that he seemed to endure when he died. His death caused universal sorrow, both in his community and in the city generally. When people were told of the long and confidential friendship between him and the man, many came to see the latter and wished to show him honor, inviting him to visit them. But when this happened he instantly left the city and returned home. And while he was yet on his journey, the third day after the Master's death, he and his servant were overtaken by nightfall at a little village. Seeing a nobleman going along the road, he said to him: "Dear friend, is there an inn in this village?" The nobleman answered: "No." And the man said: "Wilt thou be so kind, dear friend, to give us a night's lodging for the love of God? and we will pay thee what thou wilt." The nobleman answered: "If thou will put up with our accommodations I will gladly lodge you as best I may.' And he led them to his house. And so he lay down to sleep in a room, and the servant lay on the straw in the barn.

Now, it happened during the night that the man awoke, and presently he heard a voice speaking, but he saw no one. Then he began to be frightened, and he made the sign of the cross on himself. The voice spoke: "Fear not, my dear son, it is I, the Master." Then spoke the man: "My dear Master, is it thou? Then I do beg of thee from my heart's depths to tell me, if such be God's will, how it is with thee and how it happened that thou hadst so distressful a death? For thy brethren in the monastery almost despaired for thee; thy own fellow-religious, it would seem, were much shocked at the manner of thy death." Then the Master's voice spoke: "Dear son, I will tell thee, and thou must know that the Lord God willed me to have so painful and anxious an end in order that the holy angels might receive my soul instantly after death and bear it away to Heaven. And I must tell thee, besides, that thou also shalt, for the same reason, have the same distressful kind of a death. It was necessary for me to suffer that trial in order to escape the pains of purgatory. I must tell thee, too, that the evil spirit caused me grievous pain and tempted me with great cunning, so that I was much alarmed lest I should fall into despair. But, however dreadful was my suffering at death, I now see how little it was compared to the additional joy granted me on that account by the Almighty, Eternal and Merciful God. The instant that my soul was parted from my body the blessed angels took it and they bore me away to Paradise. And they said to me: 'Here shalt thou tarry five days; but have no anxiety, nor the least fear that the evil spirits will harm thee more; nor shalt thou have any toil. Only this: Thou shalt be postponed here for five days from the everlasting and blissful company of Heaven. At the end of that time we will come to thee again and we will lead thee into the unspeakable joy of Heaven.' Now, dear son, more than this I dare not tell thee, nor mayst thou lawfully ask to know. I pray God to reward thee for thy good spiritual teaching of me and thy most profitable counsel. For this I can never give God and thyself sufficient thanks."

Then the man spoke: "Dear sir, I beg of thee from the depths of my heart that when thou shalt come to God thou wilt pray for me." What the man said after this received no answer. And then, being tired out, he would gladly have slept, and turned now on one side and then on the other, but all in vain. He could rest no more that night, and he was so anxious that he could scarcely wait the break of day. At daylight he instantly wrote to the Prior of the monastery and to the brethren there all that the Master's spirit had said to him. He then returned to his home, and in due time he made a good and happy end.

May we all follow the sweet example of our Lord Jesus Christ, so that we may pass through this miserable life and all its transitory joys and enter the ever-enduring joys of Heaven with God and His elect. May God the Father, and God the Son, and God the Holy Ghost, grant us that unspeakable favor. *Amen.*

END OF THE HISTORY OF MASTER JOHN TAULER.

THE INTERVIEW OF MASTER JOHN TAULER WITH A BEGGAR.*

There was once a famous Master of holy learning who for eight years prayed God to send him a man able to teach him the way of truth. It happened one day that this longing was more than usually earnest within him, and presently he heard a voice from on high, saying: "Go forth to the church door and thou shalt find the man thou hast been looking for." Going to the church door, the Master met a beggar there. He was in a miserable plight, his feet covered with mud and all his tattered clothes not worth three pennies. The Master said: "Good day, my friend." The beggar: "I never remember to have had a bad day my whole life long." The Master: "May God grant thee prosperity." The beggar: "I never have known adversity." The Master: "Well, then, may God make thee happy." The beggar: "I have never been unhappy." The Master: "At any rate, may God save thee. And I beg thee to speak more plainly to me, for I do not catch thy meaning." The beggar: "Thou didst bid me good day and I answered that I have never had a bad one.

---

*The authenticity of this incident is more than doubtful. It is not given in the German critical edition of Tauler that we have followed in our translation. But we give it here because it is inseparably associated with Tauler's name and career, and is in itself very instructive.

In fact, when I am hungry, I praise God; when I am cold, or it hails, or snows, or rains, if the air is clear or foggy, I praise God. If I am favored by men or despised, I praise Him equally. And all this is why I have never known a bad day. Thou didst wish me prosperity, and I answered that I have never known adversity, for I have learned to live with God, and I am certain that all that He does can be naught but good. Therefore, all that happens to me that is pleasing, or the contrary— sweet or bitter—I receive from Him as being very good for me. Thus I have never been in adversity. Thou hast wished me happiness, and I answered that I have never been unhappy, for I have resolved to fix my affections only on the Divine will. Hence it comes that I desire only what God desires." The Master: "But what wouldst thou say if God would will to cast thee into hell?" The beggar: "God cast me into hell? If He did it, I would embrace Him with my two arms. With the arm of humility I would embrace His sacred humanity, and with the arm of love I would embrace His divinity, and I would thus force Him to descend with me into hell. For hell with Him would be more happy than Heaven without Him." The Master concluded from this that resignation, united to profound humility, is the shortest road to God. Then he asked the beggar: "Whence comest thou?" The beggar: "From God." The Master: "Where didst thou find God?" The beggar: "Where I left all creatures." The Master: "Where is God?" The beggar: "In hearts that are pure and in men of good-will." The Master: "Who art thou?" The beggar: "I am a king." The Master: "Where is thy kingdom?" The beggar: "In my soul; for I have learned to order and govern my interior faculties and my exterior senses in such a way that I am master of all my affections and of all the powers of my soul. Now, that kingdom is certainly to be preferred to all the kingdoms of the world." The Master: "By what means hast thou gained this degree of perfection?" The beggar: "By silence, meditation and union with God. I have never been able to find rest in anything, be it what it might, that was less than God. I have found my God, and in Him I have found rest and peace eternal."

Advent and Its Lessons

Synopsis—Mortal sin—Uses of suffering—Interior life—Our Saviour's three motives.

SERMON FOR THE FIRST SUNDAY OF ADVENT.

It is now the hour for us to arise from sleep.—Rom. xiii, 11.

Today we celebrated the beginning of Advent, the coming of our Lord. A precious time has begun for us, and we find during this season words of joy and devotion in the lessons and songs of holy Church. Even as the month of May is the most delightful and beautiful part of the year, so the season of Advent has a holiness and sweetness all its own. It is the time toward which the prophets and saints of the ancient covenant during four thousand years sighed with incomparable ardor, crying out to God: "O that thou wouldst rend the heavens and come down!" (Isaias, lxiv, 1.) to deliver those that sit in darkness and in the shadow of death. All the happenings, all the symbols of the Old Testament, had the one end of setting forth the grandeur of Him who was to come, and who now has come. Let us, then, thank God and always praise Him, that He has created us at this time and under this law of grace, that He has willed to give us His gifts and His riches in such abundance, if we will only take them. The Holy Apostle exhorts us to awake from the sleep of sin: "The night is passed, the day is at hand * * * let us walk honestly as in the day" (Rom. xiii, 12-13). We must, therefore, consider carefully how we have fallen and how we can rise again out of our sins and vices to our first innocence.

God created us to fill the places from which Lucifer and His angels were driven out. Through hate and envy of us Lucifer treacherously led the first man into disobedience and caused him to lose all the graces and virtues which made him like God and the angels. In this way was man poisoned and his noble nature stained. By his sin he wounded it mortally. And by this transgression has come upon us blindness of reason, perversity of will, disorder of the appetite of concupiscence and weakness in resisting evil. "Man when he was in honor did not

understand; he hath been compared to senseless beasts and made like
unto them" (Ps. xlviii, 21).

We thus have three enemies to combat, which triumph, unhappily,
almost universally, and rule in the breasts of nearly all men—the world,
the devil and the flesh. When these three enemies have worked their will
in man his soul is lost—that soul so noble, chosen out by God with so
much love—for he who allows himself to be wholly overcome shall most
certainly go down to eternal death. God's friends—those who seek in
all things His glory—can hardly keep back their tears when they behold
the hateful tyranny with which these three enemies hold sway over so
great a multitude of men, among whom they usurp the place of God.
And these souls are to be found both in the worldly state of life and in
the cloister. To God's friends the eternal destruction of their brethren
is a great torture. Their hearts wither away with sorrow as they consider that self-love is so rooted in the world that there are few who love
God purely and tend toward Him solely.

The world rules by pride—exterior pride or that of the spirit. How
many men belong to this order of the devil! They wish to be something,
to make a fine showing, and they could not count their sins and vices
if they tried. Satan excites his subjects to hate, wrath, bitterness, suspicions, rash judgments and revenge, to aversions and discord. His
disciples are glad to sow dissensions; they are without love for their
brethren. Our flesh seeks its own interest in everything, in all sensual
and voluptuous pleasures. Men ignore all the misery this surely brings,
those above all who suffer from it. By these three enemies is the
greater part of men drawn into hell. If one wishes to recover his first
glory and the dignity which Adam lost by sin and which we have lost
with him; if one wishes, I say, to make a place in his heart for the
coming of Jesus Christ, he must flee from the world, triumph over
demons, overcome his flesh with sound reason and in all discretion, and
carefully exercise himself in the virtues which I shall explain to you.

In the earthly paradise man fell by two things—sensuality and pride.
Now we must rise up and regain the early force of our nature by two
things. Firstly—We must resist courageously and with judgment, even
unto death, every ill-regulated pleasure. Secondly—We must humble
ourselves in deep abasement, not only under God, against whom we have
risen in pride, but even under all men. Wouldst thou rise to the first
place, choose always the lowest. By these two means it is that nature
wins back her first energy.

Man must become like the angels in two ways. Firstly—He must willingly pardon all who have offended him and love his enemies sincerely, as do the angels in our case when we vex them by our sins. Secondly—He must render willing service to our neighbor, even as the angels serve us for the love of God. In two ways we should become like God—in the practice of obedience after our Saviour's example, who obeyed His Heavenly Father even unto death, and by growth and perseverance in that virtue and in all others. Thus do we become heavenly men; thus are we made one spirit with God through deep humility, by entire yielding up of self, by patience full of sweetness, by poverty of spirit and by warmth of charity. All who do this—and their number, alas! is very small—shall triumph over their foes. God will free them from the heavy burdens which weigh them down and help them in bearing the trials, many and painful, which He sends; for he sends trials in order that men entering within themselves may consider the reasons of these trials, so that being, as it were, thrown back on themselves by suffering, they may be kept in a state of recollection. He wishes them to ask themselves why God crushes them beneath so heavy a weight; for whithersoever God shall lead them by these trials they must follow, submissive to His Divine will. Again, God sends trials so that men may depart from themselves and from all creatures, and likewise that by suffering they may have patience.

But in what does this patience consist? Is it that a man is inaccessible to all external emotion? No; certainly not. To be truly patient is to hold for certain that no one can do us wrong; nay, far more than that, we feel that those who make us suffer are right in what they do against us, that they ought, indeed, to torment us yet more, and that we ought to feel a tender gentleness toward them. Such patient men follow Jesus Christ in His humility, who says: "If you continue in My word you shall be My disciples, indeed; and you shall know the truth, and the truth shall make you free" (John viii, 31-32).

There are two ways of hearing the Word of Jesus Christ. Some hear it with joy, as far as they can; reason and the senses listen to it with pleasure; but this is only a natural light. What they cannot feel nor taste they reject, and, since such food cannot satisfy them, they cease not running about looking for something new, something more that they can hear and understand. They do not perceive that they must stop these useless searchings and adopt another way if they would become better. The others, on the contrary, enter within themselves and dwell in the remotest depth of their being, observing simply by their reason, enlightened by grace, the commands of God, and they wait until He calls them and invites them directly and without any perceptible intermediary whither He wills to conduct them. Whatever Divine influence comes by such exterior means as perishable creatures has little flavor; is, as it were, wrapped up in multiplicity and contains a seed of bitterness. One finds herein a certain savor of the creature, from which the possession of God must be freed if the spirit shall truly taste Him and if He shall sink into the deepest depths of the soul. Those who look within themselves for the gifts and decrees of God partake of them at their very fountainhead, and there they give them back again. They draw and taste at the very fountainhead, whilst the former class are self-seekers in everything. And yet nowhere can they find their own selves in a way so certain and so simple as in that innermost depth, where we feel the immediate presence of God.

Perhaps you will ask me how we can do and observe without hindrance what God requires of us? It is by being careful to dwell within ourselves. Let each one dwell within and give over all seeking on the outside. So shall a man soon and surely learn what he should do, what God wills of him interiorly and exteriorly; and, when he knows it, let him yield himself to God and follow along whatsoever road He shall conduct him, whether it be in the active life or the contemplative or the unitive, in suffering or in joy. If God gives him nothing, let him resign himself simply to His will, and, for love of Him, agree to be deprived of His gifts. And let him sink yet deeper into his inner life, having ever before his eyes the dear image of our Lord. Our Lord had three motives in all His actions; He sought only His Heavenly Father's glory, with no thought of anything else, great or small, and He referred all to His Father's glory. Secondly—From the depths of His being He willed our salvation and our happiness. He willed the salvation of all, and to bring all to the knowledge of His name; even as St. Paul says that God "Will have all men to be saved and come to the knowledge of the truth" (I Tim., ii, 4). Thirdly—In all His words and deeds and life our Lord willed to leave us in an eminent degree the true pattern and exemplar of a perfect life. His followers are the noblest and most lovable of all men. Those who are born spiritually with Him are the choicest treasures of the Church—always striving after perfection and having no care if their works be great or small, but in all things seeing only God, and therefore it is that their works are perfect. They do by no means consider whether God shall set them very high or very low, for they have taste only for the Divine will.

May God grant us these dispositions! . *Amen.*

Going into the Desert to Find God

Synopsis—Spiritual direction—Self-knowledge—Brotherly love—Loving God—Growth in love—Imitation of the saints—Beholding Christ—Sensible devotion.

SERMON FOR THE THIRD SUNDAY OF ADVENT.*

What went ye out into the desert to see?—Matt. xi, 7.

Our Lord asks the Jews: "What went ye out into the desert to see? A reed shaken by the wind?" We find in these words three matters for consideration—the going out, the desert, and what they went to see. Let us first speak of the going out. This is done in four ways, for we must go out from the world, that is to say, from its concupiscence, by contempt for it, according to St. John's words: "Love not the world, nor the things which are in the world. If any man love the world, the charity of the Father is not in him" (I John, ii, 15). Those who renounce the love of the world depart truly out of Egypt; they leave King Pharaoh's service in renouncing pride, vainglory, presumption and all other sins; and those who would go out of the world have great need of finding a Moses who will serve them as conductor—one who will be like the first Moses, full of gentleness and compassion. They need a guide—sweet, kindly and patient—who will make their going forth, which costs so dearly, more easy to them. There are others who go forth out of Sodom and Gomorrah, that is to say, from avarice, intemperance and impurity, and who have still to suffer dire assaults from these vices. They should have an angel for director and counsellor; that is to say, a man compassionate, grave and of an austere manner of life. He who allows himself to be thus directed or led will surely escape pride, avarice and sensuality, according to the words of Isaias: "For you shall go out with joy and be led forth with peace" (Isaias lv, 12). Or, according to our Saviour: "In the world you shall have distress" (John xvi, 33), and in Me, peace.

We must go forth from all exterior things, useless preoccupations, self-love and self-will, and enter into ourselves if we would know our-

---

*Tauler has left no sermon for the Second Sunday of Advent.

selves and distinguish clearly the nature and origin of the motives which actuate us. Whosoever does not go forth from himself, whether on account of self-love or some other motive, cannot learn to know himself, according to the teaching of St. Bernard: "There are plenty of men who know many things, but who yet know absolutely nothing of themselves. Now, to know oneself and to realize how sick one is and full of defects is of more worth than to possess all sciences. Says Solomon in the Canticle: 'If thou know not thyself, O fairest among women, go forth and follow after the steps of the flocks and feed thy kids beside the tents of the shepherds'" (Cant. i, 7). That is to say, look at thyself in the lives of the saints and follow their example, instead of following thy own will.

Thou must depart from thy own ease and sense and thou must give thyself up wholly to the service of thy neighbor, helping him with all thy might by good advice, good works and pious example, by a deep and constant charity, in order that he may the more easily attain to eternal happiness. For such is our Saviour's precept: "A new commandment I give unto you, that you love one another. * * * By this shall all men know that you are My disciples, if you have love one for another." (John xiii, 34-35). And St. Paul says: "Bear ye one another's burdens, and so shall ye fulfill the law of Christ" (Gal. vi, 2). And in Genesis we read that Joseph said to his brethren: "You shall not see my face unless you bring your youngest brother with you" (Gen. xliii, 3). And again in the Canticle we read: "Come, My beloved, let us go forth into the field, let us abide in the villages; let us get up early to the vineyards" (Cant. vii, 11).

We must go forth from all that is not God; in such a manner that our love for Him surpasses all other love, and that we love Him with all our soul, all our heart and all our strength. Of old God said to Abraham: "Go forth out of thy country and from thy kindred, and out of thy father's house" (Gen. xii, 1). That means fix not thy heart on perishable things, but on God alone; seek Him and love Him in all that thou dost possess. The Canaanitish woman had thus gone forth, as her words testify, and, therefore, she got from Jesus all that she asked. In the Canticle God invites the faithful soul and its companions to this going forth, saying to them: "Go forth, ye daughter of Sion" (Cant. iii, 11). It is right that He should give them the name of daughters rather than that of sons, for their spirit is yet weak, troubled by the fears and distresses of women, for they are not yet strong enough of resolution to undertake to give up all, and they have still the weakness and delicacy of a young girl.

Let us now speak of the desert. Scarcely have we quit worldly desires and sin than we encounter the desert, an image of that life, spiritual and detached, that we must lead here below. But there are two kinds of desert—one good and the other bad. The latter is that in which the heart of man fills itself with vanity, stripping itself of charity and of heavenly longings. In the temple of the soul are no longer heard the chants of divine praise; and the sheep of the house of Israel, that is to say, good thoughts, are scattered and go forth each on his way. The fertile desert is that wherein a man has driven down into the lowest depths of his heart the stormy disturbance of passions, the irregularity of worldly desires and the love of created things. He still sometimes experiences, it is true, in his body or his senses the first movements of the passions, but his will remains inaccessible to their attempts. There is the good desert—storm without and the sweetness of peace within. It is of this desert that God speaks to the prophet: "I will lead her into the wilderness and will speak to her heart" (Osee ii, 14), for no one hears or understands what is within himself or what God says within until He reaches that desert.

It is called a desert, this life of detachment and separation, because of the small number of those who go into it after being separated from the world. These are few enough when compared with the great number of those who continue to yield to their sensual desires. We must drive out of our hearts the world and its images and advance into the interior of the desert, to dwell there with Moses. There can we the more easily guard our flocks; that is to say, free ourselves from our interior temptations and the caprices of our imagination. When Moses had led his flocks into the interior of the desert God showed Himself to him in a burning bush, which signifies that the fire of charity and holy desires shall fill our heart, and then it is that we can follow God whithersoever He calls us.

There is to be found that delightful desert of which it is written: "Who is she that goeth up by the desert as a pillar of smoke of aromatical spices?" (Cant. iii, 6). St. Gregory says that the nature of love is to rise each day higher above oneself toward God by holy desires and never to rest until one has reached the supreme good. For upon the earth there is nothing that can attract a loving soul's glances; but his whole effort is to go to God, raising himself above himself. Such is the heritage of God's friends, and the more they are united to Him by the fervor of their longings, the more wearisome and painful becomes all that smiles on them in the world. It is of this desert that the angels speak in the Canticle, saying: "Who is she that goeth up by the desert?" And to them the fervent soul makes answer: "I found Him whom my soul loveth; I held Him, and I will not let Him go" (Cant. iii, 4). For whoever penetrates into this desert knows how to savor and how to express interior and mystical things. Charity by its good works renews and increases all the virtues, and this our Saviour well showed us when he clothed himself with glory on Mount Tabor and discovered to us the fruits that we gather in the desert when we are sincerely converted to God. Thus St. Paul tells us: "We all, beholding the glory of the Lord with open face, are transformed into the same image from glory to glory, as by the spirit of the Lord" (II Cor. iii, 18).

We find, besides, in the desert a multitude of beautiful flowers on which the foot of man has never trodden. It is even so with a life of renunciation and separation; by pious practices, hard to nature, the habit of Christian virtue is acquired. But, as these practices cost much effort and pain, there are but few who make up their minds to adopt them. In this desert we find lilies and other flowers of shining whiteness, namely, purity of soul and body. There we also find deep red roses, namely, mortification, exhausting to flesh and blood, triumphing over sin and causing us, if necessary, bravely to suffer martyrdom. Ah, there are things there which one can hardly get in the world. This desert grows also the violet, the symbol of humility, and many other precious plants and flowers; that is to say, the example of the saints. Choose, then, for thyself a spot in that desert by living piously, by imitating the purity, poverty and obedience of the saints and their other virtues, according to what is written in the Canticle: "The flowers have appeared in our land" (Cant. ii, 12), which means that many men have departed this life full of virtue and of merit.

But one must not expect to find his ease in the desert, and it is on this account that the lovers of this world cannot endure it. The children of Israel murmured against Moses because of the very many privations to which they were subjected. Those privations are a symbol of the sober, severe and recollected life necessary for every Christian; for, had we the whole universe at our command, we ought yet to use only what is needful, and we ought ever to dread going beyond the just measure of necessity; it is thus that the soul strengthens itself. This desert ministers, it is true, very little that is pleasing to the senses, but in compensation we find abundance of spiritual comforts, much surpassing worldly joys. "The Lord will comfort Sion.   *   *   *   He will make her desert a place of pleasure and her wilderness a garden of the Lord" (Isaias ii, 3). And again the prophet says: "That which was dry land shall become a pool, and the thirsty land springs of water" (Isaias xxxv, 7). The solitary soul shall be granted a more numerous posterity, that is to say, a greater number of merits, than the soul that is wedded to the world. God had commanded Pharaoh to let the people of God go into the desert to sacrifice to the Lord, for they were to receive spiritual consolations in place of the worldly consolations of Egypt.

When we have penetrated into this desert we shall, with the eyes of the soul, see the King and His bride, namely, God and the soul; and that sight is a fountain of delights for us. So it is written in the Canticle: "Go forth, daughters of Sion, and see King Solomon" (Cant. iii, 2); that is to say, Christ, of whom Isaias says: "A child is born to us, and His name is Wonderful" (Isaias ix, 6). Behold, indeed, how much God is wonderful, since He has even willed to become man for the sake of His bride. This is the marvel that Moses saw and of which he tells: "I will go and see this great sight—why the bush is not burnt" (Exodus iii, 3). That bush is the human nature of Christ; the flame is His holy soul, burning with love, and the light, that is His divinity united to His mortal body. Come, then, and behold Christ, this Solomon into whom is poured the infinitude of wisdom and who understands all things. He is the truth that has shown us the road to Heaven. The soul should contemplate Him without ceasing, in order to be able to imitate Him by living according to the Spirit and not according to nature. And even nature will be greatly strengthened in her struggles, if she will hold her eyes fixed on her King, and meditate how it was that He accomplished His pilgrimage here below. It is a great consolation for a loving soul to consider in Jesus Christ at one time the infirmity of human nature, and again the spiritual life that He led so superior to human nature.

According to an illustrious teacher, an abundance of consolations weakens our energies, and spiritual joys even wholly devour the soul when they are excessive. A very lively happiness cannot last long, and a prompt change is made necessary, for here below the soul is not admitted to serve God in the holy of holies: "Thy chalice, which inebriateth me, how goodly it is!" (Ps. xxii, 5). The soul should, therefore, consider in Jesus Christ sometimes the glory of His divinity, sometimes the excellence of His humanity. As to souls estranged from God, whom He has not yet visited, in them we should arouse faith; but interior souls, well proved and rich in experience, them we must lead to contemplate this King in His beauty. Souls consumed with love should also study with the inner eye how they may guide other souls; or, if need be, how to resist them for their own good.

"Lord," exclaims St. Bernard, "come to me and reign from Thy throne in me, for, alas! it too often happens that I occupy it myself." Pride, covetousness, lust and sloth would reign in me; wrath, hate and calumny make deadly attacks upon me and claim control of my will. I resist them, I mourn over their assaults and I cry out: I will have no king but Jesus Christ. O peaceful King, come and reign in me, for I desire no other king but Thee! I await Thee, O Lord, with wonder, with prayers and burning supplications, with many changes of grief and joy! O, how can we for an instant leave off preparing to receive so great a King—a God who has made our poor nature capable of receiving His Divine Being. who has taken it and united it to Himself, and clothed Himself with its shades and colors and displayed its beauty to us. He loves us much more than we love Him. I shall, therefore, be without excuse if I do not love Him above all things, for He asks nothing else of us but that we love Him. We should, therefore, go forth entirely from ourselves, and enter into that blessed solitude, and long to know and to contemplate the true King and spouse of our soul. For this we need Moses—that is to say, a good will to conduct us even to that mountain where God dwells.

The people taken out of Egypt by Moses are our old habits, for after our conversion we easily go back to our accustomed ways and, with our fleshly desires and our unclean or worldly thoughts, make, as it were, a golden calf, that we may live according to the flesh and enjoy creatures rather than God. On this account we have great need that the true Moses, Jesus Christ, should lead us and guide us on our way; that He may draw us after Him, in order to make us enter into the interior desert of our soul, in which is the mysterious dwelling place of the Lord. May He grant us this grace. *Amen.*

Unity and Multiplicity

Synopsis—Definition of simplicity—Three classes of created things— Abandonment—Purity of heart—Unquiet souls—Perfection defined—Souls abandoned by God—Contemplating Christ.

SERMON FOR THE FOURTH SUNDAY OF ADVENT.

I am the voice of one crying in the wilderness, Make straight the way of the Lord.—John i, 23.

We are close to that festival, so full of charm, in which the Eternal Word took birth in human nature, in order that He might ceaselessly be begotten in every one of us. Speech, or word, and the voice are closely related to each other. Yesterday I explained to you how we should sincerely abandon ourselves to God, and annihilate ourselves before Him from the depth of our soul. Would it not be a great help if, in order to reach that end, we could find a road shorter than all others? That road is simplicity. And to obtain simplicity one must close his senses, empty his mind of every image, and despise himself. Amid the infinite multiplicity of our outward actions we should remain masters of our senses, for without this they will carry us outside of ourselves, and bring back into us a thousand foreign images. We read of a father of the desert, venerable for the holiness of his life, that, being obliged to go outside of his cell in the month of May, he covered his eyes with his hood. When asked why he did so he said: "So that my eyes may not look at the trees of these country places, and that I may be nowise hindered from seeing my soul." Ah, my children, if the sight of a lonely forest was a hindrance to that holy man, what an injury to us shall often be the worldly and trifling things which surround us. The second means to lead us to that simplicity, is to love God above all things.

Now, we can make three classes of the things amid which we live. One class is injurious; the other is vain and fleeting; the third, though consisting of good things, is yet capable of being made a hindrance to us. Outward things are hurtful to us when they draw creatures to us with pleasure and content and we are happy with them, and when we seek or enjoy in them ill-regulated or blameworthy delight. Ah, children, no one can tell how disastrous such things are to us, for they force God to draw away from us to make room for them, even when we have no intention of sinning, in clinging to them. Why rob that sweet friend of our souls of the happiness and pleasure He would love to enjoy in His own palace? Why defile this precious vine of His as if by a poisonous vapor; and we while in that state can no longer say, with the spouse in the Canticle: "Our bed is flourishing" (Cant. i, 15).

But here a distinction must be made. A man who loves God sincerely and who would love Him yet more, sometimes experiences the influence of creatures pressing upon him against his will and inflicting on him a kind of martyrdom, even unto death. What, then, should he do? Suffer them with patience and in abandonment to God—providing, always, that he is himself in no manner the cause of these temptations by his attachment to creatures. Happy, children, a thousand times happy, is the man whose purity shall never have been soiled by any image alien to purity. He will possess a priceless treasure.

Besides bad things, there are those that are vain and useless. As to these, we should be no more disturbed by them than by flies flying about, or the Rhine flowing along; these are no real hindrances to us, and no one here below is quite free from them; only it happens that by them some are more disturbed than others. "When the heart is full of the love of God," says St. Bernard, "vain things no longer find any room in it." What we should do in such a case, is to drive out one nail by driving in another on top of it, which means the sinking deep into our heart of thoughts of Divine things, so as to drive out thoughts of vain things.

Finally, there are things which, in spite of their usefulness, are yet for us a hindrance. We meet with people who make as much anxiety and uneasiness for themselves as if the river Rhine flowed over their soul. Their heart never can enjoy a moment of calm. If they try to taste a little outward peace and rest, they are prevented by the multitude of thoughts and cares that trouble them, as the wind tosses the leaves of a tree. They cannot free their hearts of the things they have undertaken to do, and they carry them on with such struggles of mind, that they are never happy, and enjoy no interior peace. Beloved children, when one wishes for many things he loses unity. I know that there are men who are quiet and restful by character. These more easily avoid these anxious preoccupations than the others do. But if men of a lively and eager disposition, had a little persistence in overcoming their restless nature, and would but do violence to themselves, thus conquering and winning peace of heart, they would become very superior to the others.

These unquiet and agitated souls should watch themselves closely and unremittingly; they should renounce and avoid all frivolity, put under the ban certain recreations and amusements, if they would reach a perfect way of life and fulfill God's will. Like brave and loyal knights, they should behave with honor on the field of battle and fight generously. They should break down nature, triumph over the images which usurp their mind, and act like a man who has a chain entangled in his hair and cannot remove it without pain—cut off and cast away what enslaves them. If a schoolmaster had among his pupils a child who, instead of learning his lessons, went gadding about and playing, he would correct him once or twice; then, if he saw that all this was useless, he would turn away from him and leave him to become what he willed. That is what our Saviour does with those whom He has deigned to invite into His Divine school, that holy state in which one enjoys His familiar company, learns to love Him tenderly and tastes His sweetness. His disciples—these are members of communities or others who are striving for perfection; his school—it is the spiritual life in which, by leaving the world, one frees himself from a multitude of sorrows and cares in order to love God sincerely and in the most perfect way, fixing one's glances ever upon God and oneself, and dying wholly to nature, to the senses, and to the world. There we are under the eyes of God; He warns, punishes, strikes us; and if, in spite of this, we run away to play instead of attending to His lessons, He expels us from His school and gives us up to our own will. From that on warnings cease, and so do chastisements; and thus without love and, so to speak, without grace, yea, without God, we are content to live in a deceitful calm, for now our Master deigns no more to chide us, to strike us or to be concerned about us. O children, how disquieting and perilous is that state? Guard carefully against falling into it.

A spiritual man should long only for God, forgetting self and creatures, acting as worldlings do who, if they can but obtain the earthly goods for which they strive, are indifferent to the pleasure or pain it costs them. Our Lord complains that the children of light are less wise in seeking their ends than the children of darkness. A spiritual man should be so aflame with Divine fire, and become so Divine inwardly and outwardly, that we could only see God in him, and that no heart would be so cold but it would be warmed in His company, as we see dead coals lighted up again by a burning one placed among them, receiving from it their light and heat. Be sure of this, children; there is not a single instant in which God does not pour into us some Divine influence, which we would plainly feel if we were but more attentive; for God is borne on by His nature to communicate Himself unceasingly, and all the nature of our spirit is formed to receive Him. God is all act, and the soul is all receptivity. The soul should be to God, who is our origin and our end, what the stream is to its fountainhead. But, alas, poor creatures that we are, we are ever going out of ourselves and remaining in the life of the senses! Therein we deceive and injure ourselves, even though we know that Jesus Christ has said: "God is a spirit, and they that adore Him must adore Him in spirit and in truth" (John iii, 24), and, therefore, not externally alone with the senses and the imagination.

But do not fancy that I wish to strip thee of all images; there is one which I would engrave deeply in thy soul. Enter, then, into thy interior, and from thence take thy flight, even to the heart of God; there possess thyself of that supreme image which is eternally being formed, and which God is ever drawing forth from the abyss of His Divinity, namely, Jesus Christ, God's only begotten Son. Go yet deeper into that Divine abyss in order to sink that ravishing image yet further down into the depths of thy being, as if in a mirror, until it penetrates all the powers of thy soul. Whether thou dost walk or stand still, dost eat or drink, sleep or wake, let not that beloved image be absent one instant from thy mind and thy imagination. According to it, guide and arrange all thy being and all thy life, whether inward or outward. Do as a painter does who would copy a masterpiece; at every touch of his brush his eye is carefully fixed on the model before him, which he reproduces as exactly as he possibly can.

Enter thou, therefore, into the Divine depths; contemplate there unceasingly that Divine and enrapturing image and all that it has received of the Father, and make after that picture the copy thou desirest; fix thy gaze upon both its Divinity and its holy humanity; study its humility and kindness; but stay not for any fixed form; rather elevate thyself above all forms and use them all vaguely, according to circumstances, having everywhere and always thy mirror before thy eyes, as well amid the throngs of men as alone in solitude. If thou art even the busy porter of a convent, or occupied in other outward works, let that sweet image be none the less familiar to thee than if thou wert seated quietly in thy chamber or in the church; act and speak as if thou wert ever in its presence. When thou eatest, moisten each mouthful with the precious blood of the heart of Jesus; if thou drinkest, think that it is He who giveth thee His blood to drink out of His sacred wounds; if thou sleepest, rest upon His bleeding heart; if thou speakest, realize that He is very close to thee and hears thy words, that He is present with thee and sees all thy movements and all thy thoughts, and thus busy thyself in the contemplation of this Divine model.

And He will draw thee yet further, and will lift thee up to that image without form, without mode, which nothing can picture or describe as it is revealed to devout souls interiorly. Go ever onward and upward, for whosoever halts and sits down before God has ordered him to do so, shall be expelled from his place. Sometimes we have many purposes in our mind, and when that is the case we lose unity with God. Formerly and in happier times a master of spiritual life said: "Watch well the depths of the soul, what works and observances raise thee up most quickly to that Divine image above all forms, and choose them instead of others, until thou shalt be stripped of thyself and of all images and absorbed into the Divine being." May God grant us that grace. *Amen.*

The Three Births of Christ

Synopsis—The three Christmas masses—The birth of Christ in our soul. The eternal generation of the Son of God—His generation in us. Interior emptiness and fullness—Practical suggestions— Detachment—Relation of virtuous acts to the inner life—Interior silence and retirement.

FIRST SERMON FOR THE FEAST OF CHRISTMAS.

For a Child is born to us, and a Son is given to us.—Isaias ix, 6.

Today the church celebrates three births, each of which is such a source of joy and delight that we should break forth into jubilation, love and thanksgiving, and whoever does not feel such sentiments should mistrust himself. The first birth and the most sublime, is that whereby the Heavenly Father begets His only Son in the Divine essence, and in the distinction of the Divine persons. The second birth is that which made Mary a mother in virginity most pure and inviolate. The third is that by which every day and every hour God is truly and spiritually begotten in our souls by grace and love. These three births are shown forth by the three masses of Christmas Day. The first is sung at midnight, commencing with the words: "Thou art My Son; this day have I begotten Thee" (Ps. ii, 7), that is to say, in eternity.

This brings home to us the hidden birth accomplished in the darksome mystery of the inaccessible Divinity. The second mass begins with these words: "Today light has shined upon us" (Isaias ix, 2). It figures the glory of human nature Divinely influenced by its union with the Word. That mass is celebrated partly in the night and partly in the day, because the birth it represents is partly known to us and partly unknown. The third mass is sung in the daytime, and begins with the words: "A Child is born to us and a Son is given to us." It figures that mysterious birth which should happen, and does happen, every day and every instant in holy souls, when they dispose themselves for it by deep attention and sincere love; for one can never experience that birth except by the recollection of all one's powers. In that nativity God belongs to us and gives Himself to us so completely, that nothing what-

ever is more our own than He is.   And that is what those words say to
us: "A Child is born to us, and a Son is given to us."   He is, therefore,
our own; He is ours totally and everywhere, for He is always being
begotten within us.

Let us speak first of the ineffable birth represented by the third mass
of Christmas, and let us explain how it may be brought about in us in
a manner the most perfect and efficacious.   To that end let us consider
the qualities of that first generation, by which the Father begets the Son
in eternity.   The ineffable riches of the Divine good are so overflowing
that God cannot contain Himself, and by His very nature He is forced to
expend and communicate Himself.   "It is God's nature to expend Himself," says St. Augustine.   The Father has thus poured Himself out into
the other two Divine persons; after that He communicated Himself to
creatures.   The same saint says further: "It is because God is good
that we are good, and all the good that the creature has is good with the
essential goodness of God."   What, then, is the peculiar character of
the Divine generation?   The Father, inasmuch as He is Father, turns
inward to Himself and His Divine intelligence; He sees Himself and
penetrates Himself with a gaze which wholly embraces His Divine
essence, and then, just as He sees and knows Himself, so does He utter
Himself completely; and the act whereby He knows Himself and the
Word whereby He utters Himself is also the act whereby He begets His
Son in eternity.

Thus the Father Himself remains within Himself in the unity of His
essence, and goes out of Himself in the distinction of persons.   Again
He returns into Himself, and therein He rests in unspeakable self-
delight, and that self-delight goes forth and overflows in ineffable love,
which is the Holy Spirit.   Thus does God dwell within Himself and go
forth out of Himself to return again into Himself.   Therefore, is all outgoing for the sake of ingoing again.   And hence in the material universe
is the movement of the heavenly spheres most noble and most perfect,
because it unceasingly returns again to the origin and beginning from
which it first set forth.   And so also is the course of man ever noblest
and most perfect, when it returns again upon its source and origin.

The quality which the Heavenly Father has in this His incoming and
outgoing, the same should every man have who will become the spiritual
mother in this divine bringing forth.   He must enter wholly into himself, and again go out of himself; as the soul has three noble powers,
wherein it is the true image of the blessed Trinity—memory, understand-

ing and free will. Through these powers is the soul capable of receiving and clinging to God, and all that God is, has and can bestow, and in this way it can gaze upon Him in eternity. For the soul is created between time and eternity; with its superior part it belongs to eternity, and with the inferior—the sensitive, animal powers—it belongs to time.

But both the higher and lower powers of the soul wander away into time and into the fleeting things of time, and this is because of the kinship between its higher and lower powers. Very easy is it in this straying thus to go astray from eternity. If we would be born again with the Divine birth, then we need to start back again, earnestly struggle inward and there gather up all our powers, lower and higher, if we would restore all dissipation of mind to unity, since united forces are ever the strongest, and they become united when drawn back from multiplicity. When a hunter would hit the mark he shuts one eye in order that with the other he may look straighter; when one would think deeply about anything, he closes all his senses and unites all his powers in his inmost soul, out of which, as branches from a tree, all the senses go forth into activity. When all our powers of sense and motion are thus by an inward movement assembled together in the highest power, which is the force and foundation of them all, then happens an outward, yea, an overflowing movement. beyond and above self, by which we renounce all ownership of will, of appetite and of activity. There remains for thee then only a pure and clear intention to be of God and of God's purposes, to be nothing whatever of self, or ever to become anything of self, to be for Him alone, to give room to Him alone, whether in things high or low, so that He may work His will in thee and bring about His birth in thee, and therein remain unhindered by thee to the end.

If two are to be made one, then must one stand passive and the other active. If my eye is to receive an image, it must be free from all other images; for if it already has so much as one, it cannot see another, nor can the ear hear a sound if it be occupied with one already. Any power of receiving must first be empty before it can receive anything. Hence St. Augustine says: "Empty thyself if thou wouldst be filled. Go forth, if thou wouldst enter in." And elsewhere he says: "O noble soul, O noble creature of God, wherefore goest thou outside thyself in search of Him who is always and most certainly within thee, and through Whom thou art made a partaker of the divine nature? What hast thou to do or why dost thou concern thyself with creatures?"

When a man thus clears the ground and makes his soul ready, without doubt God must fill up the void. The very heavens would fall down to fill up empty space, and much rather will God not allow thee to remain empty, for that would be against His nature, His attributes; yea, and against His justice. If, therefore, thou wilt be silent, the Word of this Divine birth shall speak in thee and shall be heard; but, if thou speakest, be sure He will be silent. Thou canst not serve the Word better than by being silent and by listening. If thou goest out of self, He without doubt goeth in, and so it will be much or little of His entering in, according to much or little of thy going out.

An illustration of this going out of self is given in the book of Moses, how God made Abraham go forth from his country and his kinsfolk, so that He might show him all good things. The Divine birth in the soul of man—that means certainly all good things, and that alone is its meaning. The country or region out of which the soul must go—that means the body, with its lusts and concupiscences of whatever kind. The friends he must have—these are his inclinations and the sensitive or sensible powers with their images, which draw him on and fasten him down. These set love and pain in motion, joy and sorrow, longing and dread, care and frivolity. These friends are very near akin to us; against them we must be strictly on our guard if we would wholly elude them, and if we would have born in us the all-good that this Divine birth really is for us. A proverb says: A boy kept too much at home behaves like a calf when away from home, which means that men who have not gone beyond their natural life, nor raised themselves above what the senses furnish to be seen, heard, tasted, moving about—men who have thus never gone forth from this the native home of all sensible life, are veritable animals when there is question of understanding the high things of God. Their interior being is like a mountain of iron, in which no gleam of light ever shines. When outward things and images and forms are gone, they no longer know and feel anything. They are, indeed, at home; but for that very reason they do not experience this wonderful resignation. Therefore did Christ say: "If any man come to Me and hate not his father, and mother, and wife, and children, and brethren, and sisters, yea, and his own life also, he cannot be My disciple" (Luke xiv, 26).

We have so far spoken of the first and last births, and how by the last we learn a lesson about the first. And now we shall instruct you about the second birth, in which this night the Son of God is born of His mother and becomes our Brother. In eternity He was born a Son without a mother, and in time He was born a Son without a father. Now, Saint Augustine tells us: "Mary is much more blessed because God was born spiritually in her soul than because He was born her fleshly Son." Now, whosoever would experience this spiritual and blessed birth in his soul, as Mary did in her soul, should consider the qualities of Mary, that mother of God both fleshly and spiritual. She was a virgin, all chaste and pure, and yet she was retired and separated from all things, and so the angel found her. It is thus that one must be who would bring forth God in his soul. That soul must be chaste and pure. If it has strayed away from purity, then must it come back and be made pure again; for the meaning of virginity in this teaching, is to be outwardly unfruitful and inwardly very fruitful. And this virgin soul must close its outward senses, having little external occupation, for from such it can have little fruit. Mary thought of nothing else but of Divine things. Inwardly the soul must have much fruit; the beauty of the King's daughter is all within. Hence must this virgin soul live in detachment in all its habits, senses, behavior, in all its speech. Thus will it bear many and great fruits, namely, God's Son, God's Word, Who is all in all and contains all things in Himself.

Mary was a wedded virgin, and so must the soul be wedded, as St. Paul teaches. Thou must sink thy fickle will deep into the Divine will, which is immovably steadfast, so that thy feebleness may be strengthened. Mary lived retired, and so must the soul espoused to God be in retirement, if it will experience the interior regeneration. But not alone from those wanderings after temporal things which appear to be faulty, but even from the sensible devotion attached to the practice of virtue, must the soul refrain. It must establish rest and stillness as an enclosure in which to dwell, hiding from and cutting off nature and the senses, guarding quiet and interior peace, rest and repose. It is of this state of the soul that we shall sing next Sunday in the introit of the mass "While all things were in quiet silence, and the night was in the midst of her course, Thine Almighty Word, O Lord, came down from Heaven, out of Thy royal throne" (Wisdom xviii, 14-15). That was the Eternal Word going forth from the Father's heart. It is amid this silence, when all things are hushed in even eternal silence, that in very truth we hear this Word; for when God would speak thou must be silent. When God would enter in, all things must go out. When our Lord entered Egypt, all the idols in the land fell down. However good or holy anything may seem, if it hinders the actual and immediate Divine generation in thee it is an idol. Our Lord tells us that He has come bringing a sword, cutting off all that clings to men, even mother, brother, sister; for whatever is intimately joined to thee without God is thy enemy, forming, as it does, a multitude of imaginations covering and hiding the Divine Word.

Although this tranquillity may not as yet wholly possess thee, nor last all the time within thee, yet thou shouldst so constantly cultivate interior silence as a means of experiencing the Divine birth, that it shall finally become a spiritual habit. What is easy to a well-practiced man may seem impossible to an unpracticed one, for practice makes perfect. May God grant us all the grace of inner stillness, and thereby the birth of His Divine Word in our souls. *Amen.*

The Four Dwelling Places of Christ

*Synopsis—Christ upon the altar—In the pulpit—In the literal flesh—
In the human soul—Conditions for interior union with God.*

SECOND SERMON FOR THE FEAST OF CHRISTMAS.

In the beginning was the Word.—John i, 1.

Learned men say of the Eternal Word, that God never spoke it but
once, and that in a certain sense it is yet unspoken, which means that
the Eternal Word is the speech of the Father, even His only begotten
Son, our Lord Jesus Christ. In Him, without beginning and without
end, has the Father uttered all created things. Nor can we say, in every
meaning of the terms, that the Word has been uttered, since He has
never come forth out of the Father.

And, mark well, dear children, that we may understand this Word in
four ways. The first is His place on the altar in the hands of the priest;
there shall we know and love the Eternal Word, just as we shall be
known to the Father in the same Eternal Word. Again shall we know
the Eternal Word in what we are taught by the preacher from the
pulpit, uttering His Divine truth. And we must receive Him thus
properly, for, as water flows through the stream, so comes the Eternal
Word through the lips of the preacher. We must not be hindered by
the preacher's defects; we must rather look at the Eternal Word in His
very essence, as He floweth forth eternally from the depths of His being.
Thirdly, we must recognize the Eternal Word in all our Lord's friends,
who, having imitated Him here on earth, are now joined to Him in
everlasting life, or who are yet His disciples here below. These are all
they who are in living union with our Lord Jesus Christ. Fourthly, we
must know the Eternal Word as He is uttered in our very souls by God
Himself; and this is a revelation of Him not to be described, for the soul
has no words that can tell it.

You must know that the Eternal Word is self-begotten in the soul and
that the soul itself, when favored with the Divine generation within it,
knows the Eternal Word better than all teachers can describe Him.
What one can put into speech is all too little, and, therefore, the Word

itself quickly teaches the soul. Hence we are instructed to hurry gladly to that school in which the Holy Spirit is the schoolmaster. And be sure, dear children, that when He is the schoolmaster, He wants to find His scholars very well prepared for Him, so that they may be able to understand the precious lessons which He draws for them from the Father's heart.

Hence the soul which would experience this birth of the Word must stand forth in great purity, and its life must be a noble one and wholly interior, not running after the pleasures of the five senses, nor absorbed in multiplicity of created things; but it must live in the utmost purity of heart. Says Master Eckhart: "What God does in a soul which He finds free and stripped of all things, so detached from creatures that He can be spiritually born in it, is both more pleasing to Him and more communicative of His own self than the creative act by which He drew all things out of nothing."

And why is this? Because God has no creature with so great a capacity as a soul in which He is spiritually generated, for in none can He express Himself so perfectly; into none can He pour Himself out so entirely and in all the force and essence of His being. Now, we have already said that the birth of God in the soul, is nothing else than that He reveals Himself to the soul with a new knowledge and after a new manner of communication.

It may be asked if the greatest blessedness of the soul is to be found in this work of God in it? I answer: Although God has more joy in this than in all His other works among creatures, whether in Heaven or earth, yet the soul's supreme joy is rather in its own work of receptivity while this birth of God takes place in it. It is not the soul's supreme joy that God is born in it, but rather that, with intimate love and union, it responds to the knowledge God imparts by this generation, whereby the soul is born again and restored to Him who is its origin. In this the soul departs from self and cleaves to God, and is thereby blessed not by self-blessedness, but by God's. The soul now has, if it will, the Father and the Son and the Holy Ghost. Now is it dissolved into the Divine Unity; now shall be revealed God alone to the soul's self alone. Hence a famous doctor teaches, that no one may come to this state who has so much of earthly taint on him as could be held by the point of a needle. Into the pure Godhead can no man enter except he be as pure as when he came forth from God. Thus teach spiritual writers, and they wisely counsel us to yield the victory to God, and

receive everything from Him direct and nothing from creatures. And
it is thus we give God His best glory, and, being detached and empty,
we await His action, when and how He wills it; for we must own that
God does all things best. Our part is to help God, as far as in us lies, to
advance His glory.

A certain teacher says that a king pays little heed to those of his
underlings who do menial service, but he is attentive to those who are
his personal associates, and these he always favors. God acts thus with
His chosen friends—souls that are in His company in His hidden retirement; God refuses them no petition. Some teachers tell us, however,
that many souls reach the Kingdom of Heaven, who on earth enjoyed no
more familiar intercourse with God than a man buried in a dark forest
enjoys the sunlight. But let us in our lives and in our purposes earnestly
strive after the highest privilege; and may God grant us His help.
Amen.

The Generation of the Word in a Perfect Soul

*Synopsis—What part of the soul is made conscious of the divine gen-
eration—The soul's inner sanctuary is God's holy place—Union
effected without similitudes—The soul's preparation is silence
and quiet—Reference in footnote to another sermon of Tauler's—
Teaching of St. Augustine—Fruits of this divine generation are
heavenly wisdom and increased assurance of perseverance.*

SERMON FOR THE SUNDAY AFTER CHRISTMAS.

While all things were in quiet silence.—Wisd. xviii, 14.

We are to speak today of the eternal generation, by which in eternity
and without cessation God the Father begets the Eternal Word, and now
in our Saviour's person born in time and in human nature. Says St.
Augustine: "What is it to me that the eternal generation of the Word
ceaselessly takes place if He is not generated in me? All depends on
whether or not He is born in me."

Thus it behooves us to speak of this generation, begun and perfected
when God the Father utters His Eternal Word in a perfect soul. Herein
understand me to be speaking of a perfect man, one who has walked in
God's paths, and that steadfastly until now, and not of men who are
natural and unexercised in a devout life; for these are far removed
from and unknowing of this Divine generation. The wise man Solomon
says "While all things were in quiet silence * * * Thy Almighty
Word leaped down from Heaven from Thy royal throne." This Word is
the subject of our sermon. Of it we remark three things. First, we ask:
Where in the soul does God the Father utter His Word? What part of
the soul is made conscious of this Divine operation? That must be the
part that is purest, noblest and most delicately sensitive. Indeed, whatever of nobility God, with all His power, has implanted by creation in
the soul's nature, and whatever of nobility the soul has afterwards
received from Him, upon all of this must God work in imparting this
Divine generation. Therefore, the soul must keep itself all purified
and high-minded, living in simplicity and wholly interiorly, restraining

itself from sensible things and the multiplicity of creatures, for God's
work is done in the purest, simplest and most recollected state of the
soul.

The second question is this: Just how should the soul behave toward
this Divine generation? Should it labor in co-operation with it, so as to
facilitate the Divine birth, forming images in the understanding and in
the thoughts, saying to itself such things as God is wise, almighty,
eternal? Or is it better to assist the Divine fatherly act by withdrawing totally from all thoughts, words and acts, and from all images of the
mind, resting quite passive under God's influence, as far as this may be
done, and letting Him alone to act? Which of these two ways best
serves the Divine birth in the soul?

Thirdly, we are to consider how great are the benefits of this Divine
generation.

And now, reverting to our first question. And I will herein use ordinary and natural language, easily understood. For, although I believe
the Scriptures more than I do myself, yet ordinary terms will be better
understood. Our text tells us that a secret word was uttered amid quiet
silence. O Lord, where, then, is that silence, where is the spot in which
that word is uttered? As I said before, so now say I again: It is the
purest place the soul can offer and the noblest; it is in the soul's very
renovated depths; yea, in its most essential being. That place it is that
holds the quiet silence ministering to this Divine birth. Never does
any created thing or any image enter there; nor in that innermost soul
is there any action, or understanding, or knowledge; no, nor any figure,
whether of herself or of any creature. Everything the soul does it does
by its faculties. If it thinks, it is with its reason; if it recalls the past,
it is with the memory, and if it loves, it is with the will. Thus, it is ever
with the soul's faculties and not with its essential being that it acts;
all its activity depends on some intermediary. The power of seeing
works not without the eyes; without them, seeing is not. And the same
is true of the soul's activity through all the other senses; it always
depends on an intermediary. But in the essential being of the soul there
is no action, for the faculties with which it works flow out of this very
essence. In this alone abides that silence, that perfect quiet, that
proper condition for God to operate the Divine generation and speak
His Eternal Word. In this depths of its being the soul is by its very
nature incapable of receiving anything but God's own essence, and that

without any intermediary. God enters here Himself alone, Himself wholly and not partially, and God enters into the soul's very essence.

None but God alone can have access to the soul's essence; creatures cannot, for they must stay outside among the soul's faculties, in which it beholds their image, by means of which it gives them entrance. When the soul's faculties come into touch with creatures, these faculties form an image of them and present it to the soul, which in that way knows them. No deeper than this can creatures sink into the soul. Nor does the soul ever approach creatures except by willingly receiving an image of them, and by the presence of the same it is brought in contact with creatures. The soul forms the image from the thing itself by means of its own faculties; knowing, for example, and being joined to, a stone, a horse, or a man by the image thus made and perceived, the knowledge necessarily coming into the soul from outside through the senses. Hence it happens that nothing is so little known to the soul as its own real self. And hence a certain teacher says that the soul is unable to form or receive an image of its own self, for the reason that all images enter through the senses, and these cannot perceive the soul. It knows all other things, but itself it knows not. Of nothing is it so ignorant as of itself, and this is for lack of necessary intermediate image.

And be assured that when the soul is freed from all images and intermediaries, God can for that reason join it to Himself directly and without the interposition of anything whatsoever. Consider that whatever power thou dost claim for any human master, thou must own God to possess the same, and that beyond all measure. Now, the wiser and mightier such a master is, the less does he need means and instruments to influence thee and the simpler is his power. But man needs many means and instruments for his outward works, and between his planning and his performance there is much preparation. On the other hand, the moon and sun in their masterful work of illuminating the world, need no longer than the twinkling of an eye to fill all the ends of the earth with light. And an angel needs even less means and uses fewer images; while the very highest seraph has but one single figure in which he knows and acts his part, though lesser spirits need a multiplicity of such aids. But God needs no aid of images or instruments at all, not even of one. God acts upon the soul directly, without image or figure; yea, upon the soul's deepest depths, into which no image has ever penetrated, nor any being other than God's self. This can no created thing ever accomplish. God the Father thus begets His Son in the soul, and not as creatures act, by showing figure and likeness, but just as He begets Him in eternity.

And how is this Divine generation accomplished in the soul? Remember that God the Father has a knowledge of Himself which penetrates His being perfectly and without the interposition of any image; and it is thus that God the Father generates His Son in true unity of Divine nature. Now in no other manner does God the Father beget His Son in the essence and being of the soul, and in doing so unite Himself with the soul. But if in this Divine work there were any intermediary of figure or image, there could be no true and perfect union, and upon such a union depends all the soul's happiness.

But you may object that by nature the soul is ever full of images. I answer no; for if that were true the soul could never be happy, nor could God ever make a being capable of perfect bliss; nor would God be our greatest joy and last end—God, who is the beginning and the end of all. No creature can ever be the bliss of another creature, nor its perfection. The perfection of all virtue in this mortal life is followed by the perfection of immortal life hereafter, which consists in immediate union with God. If thou wouldst, therefore, enjoy here below a foretaste of thy future bliss, thou must needs retire inward and dwell in thy soul's depths and essence. There must it be that God will touch thee with His most simple being, without medium or similitude. No image is for its own sake, but only to show its original, coming from without by means of the senses acting on creatures; and as no creature can ever make us happy, much less can any image of creatures.

And now let us consider our second question, namely: What shall one do to win and merit that this Divine generation shall take place within his soul? Shall we co-operate by meditating on God, and that by means of similitudes? Or shall one rather rest in mental silence and wait for God in quiet of mind, leaving to Him alone all active working? And now let me repeat what I have said before: Such a matter as this concerns only perfect souls, who have already won to themselves, as it were essentially, all virtuous living, doing good without any effort— men who are living examples of the life and teaching of our Lord. Let such as these know that if they would be granted this divine life, their best and highest part is to be still and let God act and speak.* When

*Tauler's teaching here and elsewhere about the prayer of quiet, is to be supplemented and explained by that in the Sermon for the First Sunday of Lent. Therein he exposes and condemns the quietism of the false mystics. There, too, he explains the restful and passive receptivity of real contemplation, just as it has ever been

all the powers of a soul are withdrawn from all activity and all similitudes of creatures, then in that soul shall the Divine Word be uttered. According to our text: "While all things were in quiet silence the Almighty Word leaped down from Heaven." Therefore, in proportion as thou dost earnestly gather inward all thy faculties in forgetfulness of all created things and of all their similitudes, being recollected wholly in thyself in obliviousness of creatures, the nearer art thou to receive the generation of the Divine Word.

O, if thou couldst but forget all things! Yea, if thou couldst but be unconscious of thy own very life, and be able to say, with St. Paul: "Whether in the body or out of the body, I know not, God knoweth" (II Cor. xii, 2). In him had the spiritual part so entirely absorbed the natural faculties that he forgot his bodily existence; memory and understanding no longer acted, nor did the senses and powers whose office is to regulate corporal life. His bodily heat was suspended, and yet without hurt to his physical condition, and he suffered no injury from being for three days without meat and drink. The same was the case with Moses; he fasted during the forty days he was with God in the mountain, and was no weaker, but just as strong, the last day as the first. So must one withdraw from the life of the senses and, turning inward all his powers, forget everything, even his very self. Hence a teacher says: "Quit the unrest of external activity, fly and hide from the storms of outward things and inward thoughts, for these breed disturbance." If God shall utter His Word in the soul, the soul must be in peace and tranquillity. It is then that He, indeed, utters His Word and His own self in the soul; it is not any resemblance, but it is His very self. St. Dionysius says: "God has no similitude or image of Himself, for He is essentially all good, all truth, all being." He does all in the twinkling of an eye, whether He acts in Himself or out of Himself. Do not imagine that when God made the heavens and earth and all things, that he made one today and another tomorrow; for, even though Moses thus writes, he does so in order that his readers may the more easily understand God's creative act, for He Himself was better informed. God's act of creation was only this: He willed and it was done. God acts without means or figures; and the more thou art freed from them, the more apt art thou to receive His influence; and, being the

---

taught by approved mystical writers. He shows that it is a relative and not an absolute cessation of mental action. While the ordinary activity of the faculties is suspended, the soul is gazing into God with a distinct longing, intensely reaching onward into deeper and deeper joy of contemplation.

more introverted and self-forgetful, thou art all the nearer to Him. About this St. Dionysius counsels his disciple, Timothy: "Chasten thy senses, elevate thyself above thyself and all thy powers above speech and reason, above works and methods and existence, and abide in hidden, quiet darkness, and it is thus that thou shalt come to the knowledge of the unknown and all-good God." There must be withdrawal of the soul from all things; God feels it beneath His dignity to act by means of images.

You might ask, Where does God act without any image? It is in the depths and essence of the soul. I cannot know it in the ordinary way of knowing, for my soul's faculties perceive nothing except in images, each object being necessarily known by its proper image; for example, the soul cannot see and recognize a horse in the figure of a man; and, because all images enter the soul from without, the Divine generation is hidden and mysterious to it, and that is all for the best. This Divine act within the soul being so unaccountable, it sinks it deep in amazement. Then it forthwith studies this event within its depths, and that very eagerly, and knows better and better that it is most real, though it cannot tell how it is, nor exactly what it is, only it soon knows that it is God. When a man knows the cause of anything, forthwith he tires of it and looks about to find something else to investigate, ever striving after knowledge and never resting content. But in this obscure knowledge of God acting within it, the soul is fixed fast and keeps on constantly enquiring. Hence the wise man's teaching in our text, that His hidden Word was uttered amid quiet silence of all things, in a very secret way, stealing into my soul unawares. But you may ask how can this be a hidden Word, since the very nature of every word is to reveal something. And I answer that this Word, as it flashes forth in my soul does, indeed, reveal something, for it is a witness of God, and only therefore is it called a Word. But that it was the Divine Word, was at first hidden from me by reason of its stealing into my soul in secret and in stillness.

And the benefit of this is that it makes us search for it, since it is hidden and yet with us, appears and yet is concealed, and so perforce we must yearn and sigh after it. So St. Paul urges us to follow after it and never give over till we have possessed it; for he had come back from the third heaven, having there beheld all Divine things; yet he forgot them, and this was because he had been rapt so deep into God that his reason could not act there. When he would seek to tell of what happened, he found it concealed from him; and so he looked for it within his very soul, and not by mental exertion toward what was outward; for such things are within and not without, absolutely within; and because he was interiorly sure of this so did he say: "I am sure that neither death nor life shall be able to separate us from the love of God" (Rom. viii, 38-39); namely, that love he felt the Divine Word had generated within him.

A heathen sage said this beautiful word: "I see something true within me, shining before my spirit. I know full well that it is something real, but what it is I cannot understand, only I believe that if I could but grasp it I should know all truth." And then another sage answered him: "Ah, yes, keep up thy search for this hidden thing; for if thou canst but grasp it thou shalt have all good, thou shalt have eternal life."

St. Augustine likewise teaches: "I have discovered something in my soul which lights it up and which, if it could but be perfected within me, I would be life eternal. It is hidden and yet revealed, coming in secretly. And its meaning is that it will steal all things away from the soul. What it reveals to me is that it is come to gain entrance to my soul and lead it away, and cause it to strip itself of all things." In the same sense the prophet prayed that the Lord might take from him his spirit and give him the Divine Spirit. And so spoke the love-stricken soul in the Canticle: "My soul melted when He [my beloved] spoke" (Cant. v, 6). As if to say, when He entered my soul I fainted away with love. And such is Christ's meaning when he tells us that whosoever leaveth father or mother for His sake shall receive a hundred-fold (Matt. xix, 29). And in St. John's Gospel (xii, 26): "He that would minister to Me, let him follow after Me," and not after his senses.

Perhaps thou wilt say: Oh, Lord, wilt thou reverse the soul's natural life and work against its nature? For by our senses and their image-making must we live. Art thou going to turn back this our soul's order of life? No; by no means. But dost thou know what nobility God hath implanted in this same nature, yet all unknown, all hidden? Those who have written about the soul's nobility have never come nearer to it than their natural reason could carry them. They have never entered into the depths, and hence much has been hidden from them and remains unknown. Hence the prophet says: "I will hear what the Lord will speak in me" (Ps. lxxxiv, 9). It was because of this hidden nobility of the soul that the Word came down in the darkness of night. And St. John says: "The light shineth in darkness." And he also tells us that the Word, coming among His own, they yet received Him not, but that "as many as received Him, to them He gave power to become the sons of God" (John i, 12).

Let us now consider our third point, the point of the Heavenly Word, and of the darkness which is His peculiar accompaniment. In brief, it is that thou shalt be born as the heavenly Father's child and nothing less, for herein He gives thee the power to be made a son of God.

Mark well this fruit. For all the truth that those teachers who follow reason alone have ever taught, all that such will ever teach till the last day, is nothing in comparison to the wisdom in the depths of this soul. Although this interior life is darkness and ignorance, yet it has more wisdom than all external knowledge whatsoever. It strips us of all knowledge of things gained by reason; it even strips us of self. As Christ says: "If any man cometh to me and hate not his father, and mother, and wife, and children, and brethren, and sisters; yea, and his own life also [and all the external things else], he cannot be My disciple" (Luke xiv, 26). It is as if He would say, whosoever does not give up all that is outward in creatures is incapable of this Divine inward generation. If thou wilt divest thee of thy own very self and of all that is external to thee, then God will in very truth give thee His Divine generation. And I firmly believe that the man who thus stands inwardly upright with God, would rather suffer the most shameful death than commit the least mortal sin. I will even affirm that as long as he continues thus joined to God, he will not be guilty of ordinary daily venial faults against himself or others, as far as these are wilful, whether by act or permission. He is so strongly drawn to God that he feels as if he cannot turn away from Him, and always sighs and yearns after Him.

May God help us to obtain this Divine birth within us—God who is now born unto us a Man—so that we poor, weak men, as we are, may be divinely born unto Him. *Amen.*

Lessons for the New Year

Synopsis—Causes of relapse into sin.—Lack of thoroughness, and of humility, which is defined—Lack of the interior spirit, and of resolute purpose—Examples of two virgins—Lack of recollection, which is defined—Practical suggestions.

SERMON FOR NEW-YEAR'S DAY.

On this happy New-Year's Day should every pious Christian cut himself off from his former transgressions and his evil habits, and over and over again renew his good resolutions. For many a one, warned by God or his own friends, begins a new course; but he quickly falls away again from his good manner of life, and before he knows how or where it happened, he has slipped back, and this comes mainly from the following causes:

The first is that one is not loosened from his inclinations and tastes for created things. It may be love of thy own self that holds thee down, or it may be some other transitory good. Whatever is not God, whether small or great, fetches thee down, even without thy knowing it, so that thou mayst not stay in the right way, or with God.

The second cause is that one is not rooted in humility. Whoever will have his tree grow must sink the roots deep in the earth; otherwise, no matter how the sun shines and the water is poured upon it, it all avails nothing to make it grow and bear fruit. Once it is well planted, and the deeper it is sunk below, the higher it grows up above. Just so then, supposing the soil to be good, it grows well and bears much fruit. with thyself. Are thy roots, that is to say, thy intentions, not planted in the good, fertile soil that God alone is, in real and submissive humility, and that without any doubt? Then all light and teaching and all the waters of devout sentiments help thee nothing. Thou must even be withered and dried up before thou canst come to anything. And true humility is not such talk as this: I am a good-for-nothing creature. But rather that one is in all reality totally subjected to God, not in outward show, but in his deepest heart, in the renunciation of self in all things and separation of soul from all creatures, until one clings to nothing but what God gives, cleaving to Him with steadfast earnestness, in humble fear, ever lying prostrate at His feet in constant prayer. True humility is to wait on God's blessed will in joy and sorrow, in plenty and want, living in detachment and interior conformity to God; giving up one's own will to the eternal will of God, which one waits on with patient trust, accepting everything from Him, and in turn offering all to Him again, with a willing soul stripped all naked and in poverty; appropriating to oneself not a hair's weight of all the gifts God grants him; everything of this done in deepest spiritual silence, the innermost soul sunk in humble recollection, without the least self-consciousness, without sitting in judgment on other men.

The third cause of failure is a man being too much occupied with his outward senses, not abstaining enough from efforts of his own, acting as if God could do nothing without his help. A man must in all things turn inward, wait inwardly, watch there for God, let God act, and be to God nothing but an instrument in His hands. Let him do God's will simply, passively and not actively, acknowledging as God's his every effort, act and word. Surrender thy will to God in all things, and live and act interiorly. Draw thyself in to the innermost recesses of thy soul, for it is there that God dwells; gather there unto Him all thy faculties and senses, all will and all activity, and busy thyself only with longing for the all-lovely will of God. And if thou hast no longing, yet long to have a longing; be God's bondsman, not in name, but essentially, by an act beyond power of words to tell, or thought, or understanding, in a manner all passive, mysteriously sunk down in the darkness of thy inmost being, and in pure faith. Only then it is that one prays most perfectly in the spirit, and seeks the heavenly Father with a prayer that is always heard and granted.

Take an example. There were two virgins in a convent, one versed in high learning and deep questions; the other had no thought of such things, but in simplicity of soul was absorbed in God, and ever gave herself up to Him. This latter was powerful with God, who at once granted her all she asked. And whatever others asked her to pray for, God forthwith granted it to them, even when she had forgotten to pray for it. When they thanked her she said to God: Ah, my dear Lord, how has this happened, for I forgot to offer the prayers which Thou yet hast granted! And He answered her: There was no need of thou thyself begging these favors; it was enough for Me that thou wast asked to do so, and that I knew thy good purpose to pray. I must always make it good, because thou hast given over to Me all thy will. And so we affirm that those who are entirely abandoned to God pray better without words, and, as it seems to them, even without thoughts or desires, than others do with long prayers full of tears; for the former pray in God and with God; all their conduct and their life is purely a prayer.

Any man who gives himself to God essentially determined always to remain His prisoner, to him will God in turn deliver Himself entirely, and, as it were, become his captive. And then God leads him ineffably above all captivity into Divine freedom in His own self, and makes him, in a certain way, rather a Divine than a human being. They who approach such a man come near to God, and they who would know him well must know him in God. Herein are all his wounds healed, all his debts paid, and he has passed out of creatures into God. His natural state has in a manner been changed into a Divine state. This blessed exchange is beyond comprehension, beyond sensible perception and feeling, for it is beyond natural conditions. Whosoever have found this interior way have found the shortest and happiest; and the most perfect and eternal enjoyment of God is theirs. We had better be silent about this than discourse of it, better experience it than comprehend it.

These souls are ever abandoned to God in their will and in all things as God desires, keeping always a close guard over themselves. God is constantly present to them in their perceptions and feelings; at no time or in any act do they lose touch of Him or He of them; they always mean God and seek Him in what they do, never themselves. And if it ever happens that they lose the sense of God's nearness, whether in their souls or in outward nature, then they immediately suffer. Multiplicity, unrest, darkness, dissipation of mind, afflict them and cause dissatisfaction in their labors. This is the test as to whether or not one works for God alone. Thus easily and strongly does Nature seek herself in all things, even, alas, in the things of God.

O, if a man will reach the possession of the Supreme Good, he must labor as hard and as skilfully as one who would master a difficult art! Let him always lie prostrate at God's feet as a poor little worm, as being nothing and good for nothing, actually realizing the words of the prophet: "I have become as a beast before Thee, and I am always with Thee" (Ps. lxii, 23). And again the Holy Spirit says to the bride: "If thou knowest not thyself, O fairest among women, go forth and follow after the steps of the flocks!" (Cant. i, 7). This means:

Learn a lesson from the patient beast, who eats nothing and does nothing except as guided by his owner and according as the heavenly bodies influence him.   O, if any one will but give himself up to God and follow Him, he will always be with God and with the prophets, and will, indeed, be happy! If you strike an ox, he does not resent it; if you caress him, he regards it not; he neither rejoices nor mourns, but leaves all things to themselves.   If we shall ever come to that state on account of absorption in God we shall, indeed, be perfect men.   Whosoever is really detached from himself and savors God alone, to him God makes a plain response in all things, in pleasure and in pain, in plenty and in want.

If one will arrive at this state, let him fly away, be still, wait and repose.   Whosoever has gained these four helps easily overcomes any affliction.   He who thinks always of his last end, and with a yearning heart awaits eternity, easily despises all earthly things.   Thou shalt never taste the Divine sweetness, until thou dost reject earthly sweetness as if it were the taste of death.   Whosoever will be saved must be saved by means of great care and watchfulness.   If thy thoughts shall dwell in Heaven, Heaven shall be granted thee on earth.   Whatever virtue is thine without interior silence it will be impossible for thee to keep. Know thyself, for many men know many things and never know themselves.   He who has mastered his thoughts, and keeps them hidden from men and the world, is secure from the strokes of the enemy.   He who is happy when all alone, is secretly visited by God, and the enemy disturbs him not in his inner life, while his outward life rests in much peace.   But he that is involved in multiplicity must suffer many wounds.   Whatsoever man begins to disregard the little things in the spiritual life and to heed not his trifling faults, loses courage and zeal little by little, and at last comes to nothing.   May God save us all from this. *Amen.*

The Holy Trinity in the Soul's Essence

Synopsis—The divine generation is continuous in the perfect soul—Explanation of natural spiritual activity—Examples drawn from Christ's dealing with His Apostles—Interior and exterior quiet necessary—How compatible with duty—Union of action with contemplation—How contemplation is superior to action—How the intelligence acts during contemplation—Zeal, when inordinate—Vows and other obligations, how related to higher states of prayer.

SERMON FOR THE SUNDAY AFTER NEW YEAR'S.

Did you not know that I must be about My Father's business?—Luke ii, 49.

These words serve our purpose well, for I am going to speak of the eternal birth, which yet happens in time and does happen every day, in the innermost depths of the soul, far from all outward things. If anyone will receive this Divine favor, it is before all things necessary for him to be about the Father's business.

What, then, is peculiar to the Father? We give to Him among the three Divine persons the attribute of power. If, therefore, the Divine generation is surely felt, it must be with great power, both in overcoming one's outward self and breaking away from the senses in all things. It takes strong force to throw back and subdue all our faculties, suppressing their activity. Force must be applied; only by force can this ever succeed. Christ says: "The Kingdom of Heaven suffereth violence, and the violent bear it away" (Matt. xi, 12).

And now a question arises. Does this Divine generation take place continuously in the soul, or only at intervals? I answer that that is according to our dispositions, and whether or not one applies himself earnestly to God's work, for that end striving day and night to forget all things. And now we must make a distinction. Man is endowed with active intelligence, passive intelligence, and that which is only possible intelligence. The first is always at work upon something present to it; the second works by accepting the action of another; the third remains in readiness to act and holds possession of what it may act upon. For example, what things one spoke ten years ago he now holds in memory, and although he does not at present speak them, yet are they as close to him as what he now does actually speak. The past things (not yet recalled to mind) he holds by virtue of what is called habit; that is to say, a power seated in him and ready to act; the latter he holds under actual consideration. It is thus with the Divine generation. Our Lord said: "Yet a little while and you shall not see Me, and again a little while and you shall see Me" (John xvi, 17). And so it is with our good God; sometimes He reveals Himself, sometimes He hides Himself. Our Lord took the three apostles with Himself into the mountain and showed them the bodily glory which was His by His union with the Godhead (and which shall be ours after the resurrection); and immediately Peter would gladly have remained there forever. And, in truth, when a man finds good things he cannot give them up, in so far as they are good. And, therefore, when the intelligence has found good things, so must the memory afterwards recall them with love. Nor can our love be withdrawn from anything good unless we feel that there is some evil mixed with it. Our Lord, knowing all this full well, must sometimes hide Himself away from us or we should lose our freedom of accepting or rejecting Him.

Notice, besides, that the active intelligence is always busy with some object, whether it be God or creatures. And when it acts reasonably upon creatures, that is to say, referring them by well-ordered reason to their first cause, namely, to God's glory and praise, then all is well with the intelligence, which is then rightly said to be active. But when God Himself undertakes to act within it, then the soul must hold itself passive. Meanwhile the possible intelligence co-operates with both the active and passive, so that while God acts and the soul receives His action, the best possible effect may be produced. The soul is active when it busies itself with its work; it must be passive and tranquil when God alone works within it; and ere this is begun and perfected the soul looks to God and to itself that it may possess a perfected work. In this position the intelligence is called the possible reason; and this, taken by itself, is of little value and produces no fruit. But in so far as the soul acts up to its possibilities in all fidelity, in so far does God's Spirit rule the soul and its activity; then does it see the power of God and receive His Spirit. But since the sight of God in this corporal life is oppressive, therefore at intervals He withdraws Himself. Hence: "Yet a little while and you shall not see Me, and again a little and you shall see Me," which is as much as to say that the good God sometimes shows and sometimes hides Himself to our understanding.

Call to mind what I have said about Peter and the other disciples at the Transfiguration, and how we cannot give up any good, as such, when we find it. Wherever the intelligence perceives good, the will and memory follow after, and the entire soul cleaves to it until it finds in it something evil. Hence if our Lord, Who is the Supreme Good, did not at times hide His glory from the soul, it would so turn inward to Him and therein fixedly remain, that it could not care for the body, of which it is the single indispensable form and the actual life. Hence St. Paul's words about his vision: "Whether in the body or out of the body, I know not" (II Cor. xii, 2). If he had been thus rapt away in the spirit during a hundred years, contemplating the infinite good, he could not come back to his body, and he would be meanwhile totally forgetful of it. That this Divine influence does not belong to this earthly life our gracious Father knows full well, and hence He imparts it to us only at intervals and in a way most fitting our weakness, just as a good physician gives a sick man medicine. It is all God's work, not thine; and He acts or He acts not by turns, for thy best interests. His hand is ever upon thee to guide thee to much or little of His Divine influence, holding thee away from Him when His Divinity becomes intolerable to thee. He is no destroyer of nature; rather He perfects it; but only according as thou art by degrees prepared for Him.

And now here is a difficulty. Since one must, in order to prepare for God's visit to his soul, be quite stripped of all interior images and freed from all activity of his mental faculties, which is yet ever man's natural condition, what shall we say of outward works of brotherly love? Is it not certain that these must sometimes be performed, such as instructing the ignorant and comforting the unfortunate? Must all these be quite given up, the very works that the Lord's disciples so often gloried in doing? A father of the church says that St. Paul was so filled with love of the people that he seemed to bear the whole world of humanity in his heart. Must one be deprived of this great good for the sake of a lesser one? In answer I bid you to observe this: The one good is in itself the nobler; the other the more beneficial. Mary was praised for choosing the better part, and yet Martha's part was in a certain sense the more useful, for she ministered to our Lord and His disciples. St. Thomas teaches that the active life is better than the contemplative, as long as one's activity springs from that very love which one has gained in contemplation. Thus the two kinds of holiness are one; for the active man is only fruitful when he holds fast to the

contemplative state as to the root of his activity.   Herein is placed the
fruitfulness of the active life, namely, that it fulfills the purposes of
the soul's contemplative state.   One kind of life may seem wholly active,
and yet it is in reality of a piece with the contemplative.   It is as if one
entered in and came out of a house now by one and then by another
door.   The doors are different; the house is one and the same.   Therefore, in active holiness one has nothing that is preferable to contemplative holiness; for one kind reposes in and is founded on the other and
carries out its designs.   In God's sight there is thus perfect unity
between the two states, in one of which He shows the principle of action
and in the other shows how to carry it out in the same spirit.   In the
one thou ministerest good to thyself; in the other the same ministry is
extended to the brethren.   This manner of life Christ our Lord perfectly
illustrated in His own career, and He enforces it upon us by His teaching
and example.   This is most plainly shown in His whole life, as well as
in the lives of all His disciples, all His saints whom He sent forth to
serve the common good of all.

St. Paul writes to his dear son, Timothy: "Preach the Word" (II
Tim. iv, 2).   Does he mean the outward word that beats the air?   No,
by no means; but rather that inwardly given word which lies hidden in
the depths of the soul.   He is to preach it in such wise that the powers
of his hearers' souls shall receive it and be fed with it.   He shall possess
it so that he may be enabled to announce it to other men in all plainness.
And a further grace is added: He shall so live outwardly that whatever
his neighbor stands in need of, shall be found revealed in his outward
conduct.   The word he preaches shall thereby light up men's thoughts,
reason, will and senses.   According to our Lord: "Let your light so shine
before men that they may see your good works, and glorify your Father,
Who is in Heaven" (Matt. v, 16).   This teaching is against certain
men who value contemplation and at the same time do not value active
virtue.   They say we have no need of the practice of virtue, we have
progressed above that.   Of these our Lord did not speak when He said:
"Some fell on good ground and brought forth fruit a hundred-fold"
(Matt. xiii, 8).   And elsewhere He says· "The tree that bringeth not
forth good fruit shall be cut down" (Matt. iii, 10).

Thou mayst ask: What, then, becomes of the hush and silence of
which thou hast told us before?   For to the active life belong many
images, every act having its own, either within or without; as, for
instance, that I teach this or do that, causes figures and forms in my

mind. And what, then, becomes of my interior quiet? Whatever the reason knows or the will determines or the memory recalls—all makes forms and images. I answer thus: Doctors, as I have already stated, tell us of a working or active intelligence, and of a receiving or passive intelligence. The active intelligence observes the forms of outward things and strips them of what is material and accidental; these images are then deposited in the passive intelligence as spiritual images. When the passive intelligence has thus become fertilized and impregnated, it knows outward things in these their images; but after this has happened the mind can only recall them with the further co-operation of the active intelligence, shedding new light upon the passive intelligence. Now, understand that all this work done by the active intelligence in the natural man, God Himself exclusively and completely does in a man wholly and supernaturally detached from all things. He suspends the active intelligence and puts Himself in its place; and then He does directly Himself the work that belongs to the active intelligence. This man has subjugated himself and reduced his active intelligence to inactivity. Therefore, God, if He wills him to work actively, must Himself be the worker and act directly on the passive intelligence.

Bear in mind that the active intelligence cannot contain two images at the same time; one must be before or after the other. Two colors may be in different quarters of the heavens, but thou canst see only one at a time. Now, mark well that this is not so when God Himself directly impregnates the mind in the stead of the active intelligence doing so, for He then conveys many forms and images to the passive intelligence at the same moment. When God inspires thee to one good work, immediately all good works are before thee; thy spirit is lifted on high a thousand times more swiftly than before, and is directed to all good. In one instant all the good thou canst do is displayed before thee; and this shows that the work is not of thy reason, but rather of Him Who has all forms and images in Himself at one and the same moment. Hence, says St. Paul: "I can do all things in Him who strengtheneth me" (Phil. iv, 13) ; not only this or that thing, but all things whatsoever. Learn by this that, when thou comest to this high state, the forms according to which thy work is done are not thine nor nature's; they are His, Who is nature's master; He it is Who has placed the forms and done the work. This has happened to thee in time, but it is generated and done by God in eternity and in a manner above all forms.

Thou mayst ask: Since my intelligence is herein stripped of its own natural activity, its own natural works and images, upon what support

shall it then rest? for some support it must have.   Can one's faculties
now have any basis from which to act, either of memory, reason or will?
In answer I say that the soul has for its basis of action not the acci-
dentals of being, but being itself.   When it perceives real being it immediately is drawn to it and rests in it, and therefrom does the soul reasonably speak its word or do its act.   Until it finds the very truth of being,
and touches the essence of what it knows, and can say it is precisely
this and nothing else, it refuses to rest, but ever searches further, ever
longing and seeking.   Thus does the soul labor sometimes a whole year
in the study of even some natural truth.   Yet a longer time will the
mind work at separating the non-essential from the essential, resting on
no basis and making no decision.

This is true of the soul's relation to natural truth.   As to knowing
supernatural truth, that is to say, God, never in this life can the soul be
without longing and laboring, always remaining in greater ignorance
than knowledge of Him, even in the highest spiritual states; for He
never reveals Himself very much to His friends here below.   What they
are given to know of Him is nothing compared to what He really is.   Yet
it is really God in His very essence that is in the soul, but to the reason
known only in a dark and hidden manner.   And the soul is, therefore,
ever without rest, struggling to know more, searching for what is concealed and yet is to be revealed of Him.   Thus it is that we cannot know
what God is in Himself, but we learn more of Him by unceasingly
abstracting from our thoughts of Him whatever He is not, always seeking Him as matter seeks form.   Matter never rests till filled with all
forms; nor does reason, until it has possessed that truth which informs
and enfolds all things; and that it must have in its essence.   God withholds this, drawing the soul on, exciting its longing and its endeavors
in search of greater and yet greater good.   And the soul is by its nature
never content with trifling things, but ever strives after the highest.

Thou mayst say: Master, thou hast told us before that all our powers
must be still, and yet now Thou hast taught us that in this stillness there
is a knowledge of and longing after all things in God.   Is not this a
loud cry and an eager speech after what one does not possess, an expecting and a longing—not stillness and rest?   Is it not absence of real
repose, and rather studying and wishing, seeking, thanking and praising, filling the mind with images?   I answer by pointing out a distinction.   If a man is stripped naked of self and all things else and that
in his every faculty and in every way, then whatever happens in his soul

is no longer his, but it is God's, to whom he has given himself up. Let me insist: The word or action of which we speak, whose word is it? Is it His Who speaks or his who hears? Although it is in a certain way his who hears, yet it is essentially the Word of Him Who generates it and utters it, not of him who hears it. Take an example: The sun sheds its light into the air, which receives it and gives it to us, so that we can distinguish colors. And yet the light, though as to its form it be in the air, yet in its essence it is in the sun. It comes from the sun and not from the air, which yet receives it and distributes it to everything that is capable of it. It is thus with God's generation of His grace in the soul. Thy soul receives it in its powers in many ways—in aspirations, in intentions, in newness of life, in thanksgiving. Although action thus affects thee, it is all God's and not thy own. Take, therefore, all that happens within thee as His and not as thy own, as it is written: "The Holy Spirit breathes very softly even amid the tempest (III Kings xix, 12). He does not pray in us, but we pray in Him, as St. Paul says: "No man can say the Lord Jesus but by the Holy Ghost" (I Cor. xii, 3). It is thus before all things necesary for thee not to cling to anything, but to surrender thyself totally to God, that He may act within thee according to His will. The task is His; He generates His Word within thee and thereby generates all thy activity, and, indeed, all else that concerns thee. If thou hast yielded thyself with all thy faculties to God, offering up all thy being and its attributes, then must God enter into thy being and into its faculties, because thou hast renounced all self-ownership and made thy soul like a desert waste before Him. Then happens what is written: "The voice of one crying in the wilderness." (Isaias xl, 3.) Let this voice resound within thee just as loudly as may be pleasing to God, who sounds it, and for thy part guard thyself with all carefulness.

Dost thou complain and ask how shall a man behave who is despoiled and cut loose from self and from all things else? Shall he stay waiting perpetually for God's action? Or shall he do some things that belong to a devout life—pray, fast, watch at night, read pious books—as long as he takes nothing from without, but all from God, who is within him? If a man does nothing, is he not a sluggard? Mark my answer: He must by no means neglect outward works, for these are commanded of him for the sake of good order; they lead him to God in a spiritual life, and they are for praiseworthy ends. Good works hinder his slipping downward into an irregular way of living, and, as they become habitual, they guard him from straying into eccentricities. By such means does

God prepare him for His more interior life, hindering him from that grossness of life which He cannot tolerate.

But remember that thou must guard against the inordinate longings of zeal; for the greater one's longing for outward things, the farther removed is one's happiness. Also, the greater one's love of God, the more bitter is one's pain, for love leads to detachment, and that is painful. Be assured that all good works are rightly practiced if they lead a man captive to God and preserve him from strange, foolish and ungodly conduct; and this applies to all such works as prayer, reading good books, singing God's praises, fasting and kneeling. Hence, if one perceives that God is not actively working His will within him, then he can do nothing better than practice any and all virtues, choosing those that are most needful for his soul, never seeking any advantage that is not truly spiritual. Let me caution such a one against all spiritual rudeness, for he must do nothing but what unites him closer to God. And then, when God once more visits him in high, supernatural ways, He will find Himself at home in his servant's interior life. Well-grounded interior life is the exclusion of outward unrest. Now, it may happen that God will ravish thy soul out of itself into a state of ecstasy, and then, perforce, thou must be totally passive. As to such pious practices as are imposed on thee by thy vows, even those thou shalt be for a while wholly unable to observe; for in that state God elevates the soul above all and into a state higher than all—into Himself. Consider an illustration: Suppose that a layman has vowed prayers, pilgrimages and fasts; now, as soon as he enter a religious order these vows are dispensed; for in his new state he is bound to all virtues and to God by a new tie; and this shows what I mean in saying, that when a man is rapt in God rightly and truly, he is released from all such obligations, for he cannot fulfill them, because he is absorbed and immersed in God in ecstasy. And if the soul thus remains wholly inactive a week or a month it is not time lost as God sees things, for the soul must be entirely faithful to Him.

But as soon as a man returns to himself from his rapture he must at once apply himself to fulfill all obligations, without imagining, however, that what has been omitted of rule and duty should be now made good. God is responsible for all that, because He it is that had made thee incapable of observing it. Nor shouldst thou wish that He would have enabled thee to perform all those holy duties, for the very least thing that God does is greater than all things else. And now be it well understood that all this teaching refers only to men who are by God and Holy Scripture well instructed and fully enlightened.

But what shall we say of an ordinary layman who knows nothing of this state, and is instructed only in external observances of piety, but who has made a vow to pray or to fast? If in an enlightened conscience he is convinced that the fulfillment of his vow interferes with his certain and ordinary duty to God, then he is dispensed from his vow. Whatsoever leads thee to God and places thee closer to Him, whether it be a vow or anything else, follow that earnestly, being sure that it is best for thy interior life. According to St. Paul: "When that which is perfect is come, that which is in part shall be done away" (I Cor. xiii, 10).

Vows differ one from another. Some are never dispensed, as the marriage vow, which, though made in the hands of the priest, is yet as sacred as if vowed to God in His open Divine presence. As to other kinds of vows, it is good to bind oneself to God to accomplish what one believes to be some better work. But if later on one finds his conscience oppressed, as often enough happens, and is convinced that to keep his vow would be injurious to God's honor and his soul's welfare, then he should release himself from his vow and find a surer way leading to eternal happiness. Nor is this a hard matter, for we have only to regard the fruit likely to result and the intrinsic truth involved, rather than the outward work. So St. Paul says: "The letter killeth;" that is to say, the external observance viewed entirely in itself; "but the Spirit giveth life" (II Cor. iii, 6), which means an interior perception of the actual realities of the case. Be earnestly watchful of thyself; whatever duty lies before thee, do it at once and in preference to everything else; cultivate an ardent and elevated spirit within thee and not a cowardly one, and all this in a state of interior tranquillity. Meanwhile take counsel with thy superior or some other enlightened friend of God, so as to avoid vain self-reliance. If thou canst not find such a one, consult at least thy father confessor; and in this course thou shalt be safe and secure. Remember that God guards thee, knowing well all thy wants before thou dost tell Him them. And, therefore, let thy prayers be simple, unlike those of the Pharisees, of whom our Lord Jesus Christ said that they trusted to be heard by reason of their long prayers, and meanwhile they were the enemies of God and man (Matt. xxiii, 14).

May the Blessed Trinity—God the Father, and God the Son, and God the Holy Ghost—bestow upon our spirit this blissful stillness, in which the Eternal Word shall be generated within us. *Amen.*

The Way of Perfection

Synopsis—Be not hasty or premature in beginning—Overcome world-liness—Bravely repress sensuality—Resist all envy and bitterness—Pray for divine guidance and wait for it—The part that patience plays; and obedience and holy fear—Finally pattern on Jesus in His life and death.

FIRST SERMON FOR THE VIGIL OF THE EPIPHANY.

Take the Child and His mother, and go into the land of Israel.—Matt. ii, 20.

If one reads the Holy Gospels a thousand times and preaches and meditates them as many, he will ever find some new truth unperceived before by any man. "Take the Child and His mother and go into the land of Israel, for they are dead that sought the Child's life." Dear children, as soon as some men are conscious of an inward striving toward a new life, they are rash and over eager. The newness of the Holy Spirit within them leads them to a sudden resolve to do great things for God. Meanwhile they have not considered whether their nature is such, or the store of grace in them is such as to make a success of what they are undertaking. Therefore, let every one look to the end before he embarks in such a work, considering his inner state and his outer surroundings carefully. Interiorly he should at once place himself in touch with God's Spirit, so that every work begun may in Him and by Him be happily ended. Yet some start away instantly, begin with untried methods, venturing this or that scheme blindly; and hereby many injure themselves in soul and body. They build upon their own foundation both in things natural and spiritual. Often one thinks he is guided by God, while he is but following his natural bent.

Our dear St. Joseph, abiding in his exile with the Child and His mother, received the angel's message that Herod was dead and that they were to return to the land of Israel; but he learned by human means that Herod's son, Archelaus, reigned in his father's place, and he feared that the beloved little Infant would be killed by him.

Dear children, what shall we understand from this? Herod, who had hunted the Child and would have killed Him, may be compared to the world, which would kill the Divine Infant in our souls. From the world we must flee if we would preserve the Child alive within us. Indeed, our own soul is the Child. And when one has fled from the world externally and gone into a convent or monastery, presently Archelaus rises up and begins to rule interiorly in the soul. It may be that this Archelaus can never conquer thee; but that is because thou shalt by the strength of God, fortify thyself with great and earnest industry in devout practices; for I assure thee that thou hast many fierce enemies arrayed against thee and ready to assail thee.

The first enemy is the world. This attacks thee with spiritual pride, leading thee to walk before men's eyes and be esteemed holy by them. Thou shalt be tempted to please others by thy dress, thy manners, lofty speech, wisdom, friends, wealth, honors; and all these things are nothing else than the devil's uniform.

Another enemy is a man's own flesh, which assails him with bodily and spiritual temptations to impurity, with evil suggestions of word and deed. In these ways are all those men guilty who wilfully indulge sensuality in any way whatsoever. Let every man subject to these attacks, guard himself most carefully in all his senses, and in all those irregular emotions wherein one is likely to suffer uncleanness. Any man whose mind is tenderly inclined toward creatures, whether lay people or religious, cherishing tender sentiments about them in his heart day and night, such a one is being drawn into that vice whose ugly name is impurity. And just as external unchastity deprives the body of its purity, so does interior unchastity smirch the beautiful purity of the soul. And as the soul is nobler than the body, in the same degree is interior impurity fouler than external.

The third enemy is bitterness of heart, that evil spirit which poisons thy soul with bad wishes, judgments, hatred, revenge; so and so has done thee this injury and has said such and such things to thee; these injuries thou wilt by no means tolerate and thou givest him angry looks, a scornful bearing, bitter and violent words. Hence come dissensions, mutual mistreatment, and other vicious things. Children, this is without any doubt the inspiration, seed sowing and actual work of the devil.

Be sure that if thou wilt ever be blessed thou must fly from all this and must, for God's sake, yield thyself up to suffer all things kindly and meekly, whether men treat thee justly or unjustly. Leave thy vindication to God and the truth and do not defend thyself; and then will the peace of God be born within thee, and be spread around thee in all patience and love. But if thou failest to do this with zeal and earnestness, then is thy Archelaus present and he will surely slay the Child, namely, the precious grace of God, within thy soul. We know how carefully the humble Joseph enquired, in order to discover if there was any one near who sought the Child Jesus to kill Him.

And even when all these vices are overcome there yet remain a thousand bands to be broken asunder, and these no one knows but a truly converted man; for Joseph's example teaches us an earnest perseverance in a godly and blessed way of living, together with an ever-growing love of God's will. By such virtues did he most faithfully guard the little Child and his mother from those who would have killed Him.

Joseph was warned by God's angel and led back by him into the land of Israel. Now, Israel means the land of vision. And, children, you must understand that many men are ruined, because they would prematurely break through the numerous cords of imperfections which bind them; that is to say, before God's mercy has graciously released them, before God's angel has warned them and led them forth. They fall into the grievous error of trying to perfect themselves before God really wills it. They think to succeed by their intellectual gifts and their eloquence about high things, and because they can meditate deeply and discourse loftily upon the Holy Trinity. It is a great misery that this delusion has now become so prevalent and grows worse day by day. Such men will not patiently endure the restrictions of God's Providence and the darkness of Egypt, for Egypt signifies darkness; for it must be well understood that no creature that God ever made can be released from the bonds of spiritual imprisonment by its own strength; the eternal and all-merciful God, and none other, can release us. Turn thee this way or that way, it must be so if all shall be well with thee. Run through the whole world, seek up and down everywhere, nowhere and from no one shalt thou find this release but from God alone. An instrument for His work He may choose, whether it be angel or man, but, none the less, He Himself does the work, and none other can do it. Therefore, search inwardly for God in the depths of thy soul, and give over outward searching. Suffer willingly for God's sake; dwell in the darkness of Egypt until thou art plainly invited by God's angel to come forth.

Joseph was warned in sleep. He that sleeps sins not. Thus the devout man should repose in peaceful sleep, indifferent to all the afflictions and oppositions that may come upon him, bowing meekly and in all patience under every sorrow, nor adverting to them unduly, willingly resigning himself and gladly suffering for God's sake. Surely in no other way canst thou set thyself free than thus to remain, as it were, in this sleep of patience without sin, until, like Joseph, thou shalt be rewarded for thy humble submission by the heavenly invitation to come forth.

Understand, too, that Joseph, the Child's guardian, represents the rulers of holy church, parish priests, bishops, abbots, priors, and father confessors. These are placed for ruling men and for directing them for God's praise and according to His will. But many among them are, alas, blind; and the blind thus leading the blind, it is to be feared that both will fall into the pit of eternal damnation. Now, each of us has many superiors. Thus I have over me a subprior, a prior, a provincial, a bishop and a pope; and suppose that by an impossibility each and all of them wished to do me evil, were all turned into wolves striving to bite me; yet I ought, none the less, meekly to resign myself and be submissive under them, and that without any murmuring or contradiction. If it happens that they do me good, I ought to receive it humbly, as from God; if it happens that they do me evil and wrong me, I ought to accept it in all good will and cheerfulness, and suffer it for the sake and love of God.

Notice, again, dear children, that Joseph was in constant fear until God's angel announced that they were dead who sought the Child's life; and then with all diligence he enquired who reigned in the land of Israel. Children, some men err by giving up all fear, for you must know that we should not ever be without fear as long as life lasts; for thus speaks the holy prophet: "The fear of the Lord is holy, enduring forever and ever" (Ps. xviii, 10). So, then, even when the angel calls thee forth, thou oughtest still to fear and diligently enquire what it is that reigns within thee, and whether it be truly God or only thy own nature.

Then holy Joseph took the Child Jesus and His ever-blessed and humble mother. The Child Jesus represents a pure, clean man. A man should be wholly clean and pure, quite unsullied by taint of outward things. And he should also be lowly minded, subject under God and under all creatures for God's sake in deep humility. The blessed mother of Christ represents to us godlike love in all sweetness and purity, for such love is the unfeigned humbling of a man in his own esteem, joined to entire subjection to God's will in all sincerity. Children, a man thus placed is a little child and ought not to stray away foolishly into the land of vision. Upon occasions he may enjoy some relaxation there, but only on condition that he shall betimes come back again into the land of Egypt; and.this continues until he has grown up to perfect manhood under the watch and ward of our Lord Jesus Christ.

He it is who truly teaches us the way of perfection in all things, giving us the pattern of His pure and guileless life. And if we could not so much as have God's word, yet in His pure and holy life we should find all that is necessary to possess eternal happiness. He went to Jerusalem when He was twelve years old, but He did not remain there; He came away again because He had not yet perfectly arrived at man's estate. He stayed away till that time had come, and then in His perfect manhood He was daily in Jerusalem teaching the Jews the way of truth. He went throughout the land of Galilee; He was in Capharnaum and in the city of Nazareth; He was everywhere in the land of Juda as a mighty teacher, doing signs and wonders. And thus must every devout man act. He must not dwell in the holy land of contemplation, but only go there from time to time and quickly withdraw again, for he is not perfectly grown up to manhood; he is a young and unpracticed and imperfect spirit. When he has become a strong, perfect and manly spirit, then let him enter into the land of Juda—I mean the perfect knowledge of God. Then let him in all freedom go up to Jerusalem, the true city of peace. Thou mayst then, at last, joyfully and plentifully teach others and correct them and journey to Galilee, which means a passing over.

Children, when one has thus gone onward, and has passed over all things created, he finally arrives at the city of Nazareth, the sweet flower-garden of joy, in which grow the beautiful and fragrant blossoms of eternal life. There he finds unspeakable peace, solace, and comfort, tranquil rest in God alone, all beyond the power of human tongue to describe.

Children, into this depth of God's being all those men are absorbed, who for God's sake have humbly and with good will borne the assaults of the passions, in inward and outward conflict. They have meekly bowed under God's yoke; they have been submissive to all creatures, and they have persevered till the ever good God has Himself released them and led them forth by His grace into His holy peace. Then it happens that it is given them often to enjoy for a brief moment, a sweet foretaste of the happiness that shall be theirs in God for all eternity. May God grant us all this in His infinite bounty. *Amen.*

Seeking for God

Synopsis—The natural yearning for God and its defectiveness—By grace one is drawn to God in the depths of his own soul—Effect of the inner finding of God on one's mind and heart.

SECOND SERMON FOR THE VIGIL OF THE EPIPHANY.

Where is He that is born King of the Jews?—Matt. ii, 2.

The soul knows that God exists, and that even by the light of natural reason; but as to who He is it has no knowledge; this is hidden from it. Now, there arises in every guileless soul a sweet yearning for more knowledge of its God; it seeks earnestly and enquires anxiously for Him; how gladly would it find Him Who is so hidden away from it. In this diligent search there appears to the soul a star, which is a gleam of the light of Divine grace. This light speaks to the soul and says, He is born today; and at the same time it points out His birthplace. Now, this cannot be any natural guidance, for all who follow nature's light in seeking God's birthplace will but go astray. God's birth would not be known but for the shining of a Divine light, telling us what that birth is, and where it has taken place. Foolish men cannot wait for the light of grace to shine and guide them on till they find the Divine generation; they break away and seek for it by the natural light of reason, and all in vain; they must bide their time, which has not yet come. This yearning for God works strong within them; in some it becomes so violent as to pierce flesh and blood; yea, to penetrate even to the marrow of the bones. It is true that our natural reason has a part to play and must use all its powers, if the soul's longing for God shall be satisfied; but natural reason does not know God's generation in us, and cannot, therefore, reveal it.

Herein are three things to be considered. One is the yearning, another is the seeking, and the third is the finding out of the Divine birth. Consider, too, three other things in the soul of man. One is what cleaves to his fleshly nature, his bodily senses and sensibility; another is his reason; and the third is the naked and essential substance of the soul. All three differ one from another, each one acting unlike the other and according to its own nature. The sun's light is one in itself and simple; but when shining through glass it is various, being black, yellow or white, according to the glass's color. Black glass may stand for our sensible life, yellow for that of reason, white for the essential spirit's very self. Now, when the senses enter the reason and the reason penetrates the purely essential spirit, then the black has become yellow and the yellow has become white. Thus a purely simple state of light results, and in that, and that alone, the light of the Divine birth shines forth. When rightly received all images, forms, and resemblances vanish away from the soul, and the light of the Divine birth alone beams in very truth within it. The natural light of day may be obscured by darkness, but when the sun rises in all his splendor, he triumphs over darkness, and all lesser luminaries disappear from sight. It is thus that the clear beams of this supernatural light shine in the soul, all forms and images disappearing. And hence wherever it shines natural lights are quenched, for the star that showed the three kings the Divine birthplace was not like other stars; it was not naturally fixed in the sky like them. The senses of man take from material things their images, and these are fairer than the things themselves. Then the understanding in turn strips these images of their sensible grossness, and retains only the heavenly forms that are in them by making them reason's images—the yellow glass acting upon the black. And finally the understanding itself may become the white glass; that is to say, if it will cleanse itself by self-renunciation, and thereby be made a purely spiritual faculty. Into this soul alone does the star of the Divine birth brightly shine. Toward this happy lot does all human life constantly tend.

Now, these three answers that I have given to the three questions, may be compared to the three gifts of the three kings; and this shall be the subject of tomorrow's sermon.

How Bitter Myrrh is Turned into Sweet Incense

*Synopsis—Spirituality is a bitter task—Even innocent joys must be
chastened—The bitterness that is sent specially by God—This
leads us to great things, the chief being power to suffer for God's
sake—Danger of seeking pain out of self-will—The crowning bitterness is inner anguish caused by God's testing the soul's fidelity
—Patience herein—The joy finally resulting.*

FIRST SERMON FOR THE FEAST OF THE EPIPHANY.

And opening their treasures, they offered Him gifts: gold, frankincense and
myrrh.—Matt. ii, 11.

Let us first consider the myrrh. This means the bitterness that one
must taste ere he finds God; for in turning to God one must turn away
from the world; and, besides that, he must banish away all pleasure and
concupiscence. It is a matter of necessity that whatever a man holds
dear must be given up, and that is a task bitter in the extreme. Whatever was sweet before must become just as bitter to thee now, and this
calls for a strong and diligent effort; the greater the pleasure before,
the greater the bitterness now.

Thou demandest how a man can live without pleasure, joy or desire.
If I am hungry, I eat; if I am thirsty, I drink; if I am drowsy, I sleep; if
I am cold, I warm myself. All this is nature's law, and how can I
change it as long as nature is what it is? How can what is sweet
by nature be turned into bitterness? I answer that these joys,
pleasures, savors, satisfactions, complaisances, when they are not sinful, may not be totally destroyed; but, at least, they ought not to enter
into the inner depths of the soul nor have any place there. These feelings should come and go with the acts which caused them, and leave
behind no trace of their existence. Thou shalt take no pleasure in them,
but let them pass off and away. Whatever of the world and of created
things thou findest lingering in thy soul, thou shouldst not consider as
thy own to possess, nor permit thyself the least satisfaction therein.
Creatures and the pleasure arising from creatures, must be to thee some-

thing thou hast overcome and put to death. And this applies even to the joys thou findest with men who are friends of God. Whatsoever of this kind of joy thou findest thyself inclined to must be totally overcome. Thy soul is the child, and until Herod and all his court who seek that child are really dead to thee, thou deceivest thyself if thou imaginest that thou makest any progress. Be not without fear; be not too eager; see how things stand with thee.

There is yet another kind of myrrh, whose bitterness goes far beyond the first kind. That is the myrrh that God gives. It is trouble and suffering, whether interior or exterior, sent especially by God. Oh, if thou canst but receive that myrrh with the same deep-hearted love with which God gives it, what a happy state shall be generated within thee— joy and peace and elevation of soul! Yes, whether God sends thee suffering little or great, it is from the depths of His unspeakable love; and in this He but gives thee something greater and more useful than any gift; namely, His very love itself. If God has numbered the hairs of thy head, so that not one of them falls to the ground without His knowledge and will, much rather has He foreseen from all eternity the least suffering He gives thee to endure, and hast loved it; and He has willed it for thy advancement in perfection.

Hence if thy finger pain thee or thy skin is hurt, if thy feet are cold or thou art hungry and thirsty, if someone annoys thee by word or deed, if anything whatever distresses thee with want or pain, it is all a preparation for the joyful time to come. It was all foreseen and ordered by God, as if weighed out and measured and numbered by Him for thy perfection. That my eye rests sound in my head, God has eternally foreseen. That its light goes out and I become blind, or that I become deaf, the heavenly Father has foreseen it eternally, decreed it in His eternal counsels. And shall not I, though blind and deaf outwardly, lift up my soul's glances and thank my God that His eternal decree has been fulfilled in me? Instead of my misfortune afflicting me, it should wonderfully excite me to thanksgiving. It is the same with the loss of friends, goods, honors, the comforts of life; such calamities are given by God to prepare thee for the truest interior peace if thou but knowest how to receive them. And if thou sayst: These afflictions have come from my harboring an evil thing in my soul and I have deserved them as a punishment, then I answer: Dear child, whether these painful things are deserved or undeserved, they equally come from God. In either case thank Him for them, suffer them and be resigned.

All the myrrh of suffering that God sends, is by Him intended to lead thee to great things. It is that we may be privileged to suffer, that God

arrays all things in opposition to us. It were as easy for God to have
bread ready baked grow in the field as raw wheat; but in this and all
other things God wills that man must be tried. Everything that happens is thus foreseen and prearranged by Him. We know how carefully
the painter calculates the strokes of his brush, broad or narrow, short
or long, mingling the red and the blue with all foresight to produce a
masterpiece of his art. God is a thousand times more intent than this
upon making a man the masterpiece of His Divine art; and He does this
by His strokes of suffering and His colors of pain. O that we would
accept and use the Divine gift of myrrh in the same spirit in which it is
given!

And there are some men who are not content with the myrrh that God
gives; they seek and find other pains out of self-will, injuring their
brains and breeding illusions, suffering much and long from this indiscreet mortification. Little grace comes to them, for they build upon
their own foundation, whether in penances, fastings, praying or other
devotional practices. In such cases God must wait till their meddle-
some interference is over and done. It has brought them no good. It is
God's way not to reward any works other than His own. In Heaven,
He will bestow on thee a crown for His works and not for thine. Whatsoever work of thine God does not work in thee, counts for nothing.

The third kind of myrrh is very bitter; it is God's gift of inward
anguish and darkness, aridity and distaste for spiritual things. Whosoever recognizes God's hand in this and resigns himself to it, will find
flesh and blood and human nature consumed in him; the Divine artist's
inward work changes the colors far more than all one's own outward
practices. God tries us herein with dreadful tests, and in amazing and
strange ways, unknown to all save those who have experienced them.
There is a wonderful store of the myrrh of suffering in man's nature,
which, if it were set loose, we could scarcely endure; but God knows how
to use it for our good. If one does not understand this, then when the
trial comes he is more deeply injured than can be imagined; for no heart
can measure God's love for us in giving us this myrrh of inner sorrow.
Given to us for our profit, we may yet get no good from it by bearing it
with sleepy indifference or with murmuring of spirit. And if thou com-
plainest: O, I am all dry and dark within my soul, I answer thee: Dear
child, bear it patiently, and thou shalt be much better on account of
it than if thou hadst been full of sensible sweetness.

Now, the bitterness of this myrrh is felt both in the senses and in the
mind. When felt in our sensible and external life, a man will sometimes

venture to relieve himself of it, being wise in his own conceit. He attributes his misery to external happenings, and seeks to avoid pain by remedying adversities; and, indeed, he may succeed in doing this; but all the time he is thereby setting himself up as wiser than God, Whom he would presume to guide and correct, being quite unwilling to accept any-thing and everything from His Divine hand. In the end these suffer the bitterest woe.

Others would manage their interior distress and sweeten their myrrh's bitterness, by using the resources of natural reason. They take refuge from their inward sorrow in the occupations and images of their intelligence. It, therefore, often happens that uneducated persons are sooner granted a solace than the learned. These uneducated souls are more single-minded and follow God's guidance more implicitly, knowing no other method than that of perfect trust in Him. Would that the more intellectual would do the same! This way would bring them to an elevated and free state of soul even sooner than it does the others, because they would be aided by their mental endowments. O that thou wouldst give thyself thus up to God, not a drop of blood in thy body but would help thee to thy perfection!

Out of this soul is breathed forth the frankincense of the magi—a little vapor from the fragrant grains of incense. Incense has a sweet odor. When the fire takes hold of its grains, it sucks into itself the sweetness concealed in them, and then gives it forth in its fragrant fumes. By the fire is meant nothing else than the burning love of God which blazes up in prayer. Prayer is the smoke of incense, arising from our souls to God during our devout exercises; for prayer is defined as the elevation of the soul to God. External devotion, however, is like straw; its whole use is for the wheat, and after the grain has been thrashed out of it, it is good for nothing better than to make a bed, or for kindling a very smoky fire. So outward devotional exercises are of no other use than to excite interior devotion, which is the sweet perfume of the soul before God. When thou feelest thy soul rising upward in interior aspiration, then cease the external practice; but this ought not to be done when holy Church commands us to observe outward devo-tional exercises, or when our father confessor imposes them by way of a penance.

May our Lord Jesus Christ, the King of Glory, help us thus to benefit by these gifts of frankincense and myrrh, and may He draw our hearts' prayers thus upward to God. *Amen.*

How Ignorance Leads to Wisdom

Synopsis—Difference between God's presence in the natural order and in the supernatural—His presence by grace is a divine birth in the soul—How this is hindered by sin—Rules for discovering God's interior guidance in ordinary things—God's deeper visitation baffles the soul's faculties and makes it stupid, alienates friends, and shrouds it in darkness—In due time this state of ignorance and misery is changed for one of God's own wisdom and power.

SECOND SERMON FOR THE FEAST OF THE EPIPHANY.

Where is He that is born King of the Jews?—Matt. ii, 2.

Consider this birth attentively as to where it takes place. And as I have many times told you before, so now I say again: This eternal generation is in our souls, and that in no other way than it takes place in eternity. It is thus in the essence and depth of our souls. And this gives rise to some questions.

The first point is this: God is present in all things, and that more intimately and naturally than they are present to themselves. Now, wherever God is, He must act; that means He must know Himself and thereby utter His eternal Word. How, then, is the soul of man to be compared with other created things in reference to this Divine birth? In this way: God is in all things by His essence, His action and His power; but in the soul alone is He born. We find a trace of God and His footprints in all creatures; but the soul is by nature made after God's likeness, and that likeness of God is perfected by this Divine birth. No other earthly creature is capable of experiencing it. Resemblance to God is the soul's perfection, whether in form of light, or grace, or happiness; and this is bestowed only by the Divine generation. Await this in thy interior life, and thou shalt obtain all that is precious, consoling and joyful, most truly and most essentially. Neglect it, and thou neglectest everything good, and everything happy. It will bring thee pure and essential blessedness. Whatsoever joy thou seekest apart from it, will

ruin everything, no matter how thou shalt manage it.   This birth alone
gives essential life; the other way destroys it.   Herein thou art made
partaker of the Divine influence, with all its gifts.   No creature not
made in God's image and likeness can be capable of receiving it, for it is
that Divine likeness in the soul, that has reference properly and peculiarly to the eternal generation, which, at the entrance of the heavenly
Father into the soul's deepest depths, is therein accomplished, no other
image but God's ever having penetrated there.

The second question is this: Inasmuch as the Divine birth is accomplished in the soul's depths, why shall it not be in a sinner's as well as
in a good man's? for the essential nature of one soul is the same as that
of another.   Yea, even in hell a man's natural nobility of soul still sub-
sists.   And to this I answer, that it is proper to the Divine birth always
to shed a new light upon the soul, pouring forth God's own self in that
illumination—first in the interior and essence, and then overflowing into
all the faculties of the spirit, and finally into a man's external life.   It
happened thus to St. Paul at Damascus, when God's light smote him
and spoke to him.   A reflection of that light shone outwardly round
about him and was seen by his companions.   It is ever so with pious
souls; God's light fills their inner depths, and then its overflow is seen
in their bodily existence, which is thereby made lightsome.   Of all this
the sinner is wholly incapable, totally unworthy, for he is filled with
sin and wickedness, which holds his spirit in darkness.   As St. John
says: The darkness did not comprehend the light.   This is because the
path of the light is blocked up by falsehood and darkness.   Light and
darkness cannot exist together in the soul.   Nor can God and the creature rule there together; before God enters in, the creature must be
driven out.

How does a man first perceive this light?   When he is converted to
God a light glimmers and shines in his soul, giving him to understand
what he ought to do and what he ought not to do; many a plain guidance
shall be thine which thou hadst not any notion of before.   And if thou
askest, How shall I know it?   I answer that thy heart shall be touched
by God and led away from worldly things.   How can this be done
except by enlightening thee?   And it will be so gentle and so sweet,
that everything that is not God or inclining thee to God shall distress
thee.   This enlightenment of soul will enrapture thee with God.   Thou
shalt become conscious of many good admonitions within thee, not
knowing from whence they come to thee; only it shall be plain that this

interior inclination does not come from any created things; it is plainly none of their influence. Whatever a creature works in thee comes always from without. But God's light touches the inner depths of thy soul, and that alone, and the more fully thou art freed from creatures, the more distinctly dost thou perceive, that it is the light and truth of God that reigns within thee. Therefore, one never goes astray if he keeps to this true way. But he does wander blindly if he leaves it and trusts for guidance to outward things. Hence St. Augustine teaches that many, indeed, seek the light and the truth, but only toward the exterior, where it is not, and they often go to such a length as never to turn their eyes into their own souls at all. They have not found the true path, because the guide is within and not without. Whosoever would learn how to find and to recognize the true light, let him wait and watch for the Divine birth in his inmost soul; soon all his spiritual powers will be lighted up, and also his outward faculties. For as soon as God touches the interior with His truth, all of a man's forces are filled with light, and by that light he learns more than anyone can teach him. Hence the prophet says: "I have understood more than all my teachers" (Ps. cxviii, 99). But since such a light as this cannot shine in a sinful soul, it is impossible that the Divine birth can be accomplished there. This light can have no fellowship with the darkness of sin, for it acts not in the faculties, but in the essence of the soul.

It may reasonably be asked why this regeneration does not take place in the soul's faculties. Now, consider that every act is done for a certain end, which has first place in intention and last place in fulfillment; and God intends a most blessed end in all His works, namely, His own very self. And He would bring the soul, with all its powers, to that same end—union with Himself. With this end in view, God does all His works; and He generates His Son in the soul so that all its powers may be made partakers of the Divine birth. All that the soul has and is, God gathers up, and He leads it all to this Divine entertainment. If, meanwhile, the soul turns its powers into the outer life, the eyes distracting it with their gazing, the ears with hearing, the taste with eating, and the like, in just that degree is it incapable of acting interiorly, for every mental power that lacks concentration is acting imperfectly. If the soul will have a forceful life it must call home all its powers, and all the bodily senses, and concentrate them upon an interior life. St. Augustine says: "The soul is more really present with what it loves than with its own body." A certain heathen master was absorbed in a mathematical calculation to that degree that he forgot to eat and drink. A soldier rushed into his room and brandished a sword over his head, knowing nothing of who he was. "Tell me who thou art or I will kill thee!" he shouted. But the mathematician was so absorbed in his problem that he neither saw nor heard his enemy, nor was he able to utter a word. The soldier called and threatened loud and long without any response, and at last he cut off the master's head. And this absorption was the fascination of purely natural science. How much rather ought we to withdraw ourselves from all things, and assemble all our mental forces to contemplate and to know the eternal and immeasurable truth that is God. Gather, therefore, all thy reason, faculties, and senses into the depths of thy soul, for there is thy hidden treasure. Freed from all action and holily unknowing of all things, thou shalt surely find God.

Thou mightest say: Dear brother, would it not be better that each of the soul's powers should maintain its own peculiar activity, each one not interfering with the others? I answer that I can in no wise know created things without suffering some hindrance therefrom. How, then, does God know all things without hindrance, and His blessed saints also? It is because the saints behold God Himself; and in Him it is that they behold all things else, even in one single image. And so does God behold all things in Himself, having no need to turn from one thing in order to behold another, as we must do. If in this life we could have a mirror, in which with one glance and in one image we could see and know all things, then our activity and our knowledge would work no hindrance in our spiritual life. But since we must always turn away from one thing if we would know another, therefore our knowledge of the one must hinder our knowledge of the other; for the soul is so bound up with its faculties that, withersoever any one of them goes, the soul goes forth with it. It is present with every faculty in all its activity; if it is not with them thinking, then they cannot be acting. Hence if it is poured out with them in the care of external things, so much the weaker must it become for the care of interior things. And for the Divine generation God will and must have a soul free and unencumbered, a spirit in which there shall be naught but Himself alone. He demands a soul which waits on nothing and nobody but Himself alone; and thus did Christ teach: "If any man come to Me and hate not his father, and mother, and wife, and children, and brethren, and sisters, yea, and his own life also, he cannot be My disciple" (Luke xiv, 26). He came upon earth not to send peace, but the sword" (Matt.

x, 34), cutting off from thee sisters, brothers, mother, children and friends. Whatsoever is near and dear to thee becomes really thy enemy. If thou wilt see all things and hear all, and if in thy heart thou wilt consider all things, then in very truth thy soul shall be wasted and scattered among them all. Hence a certain master says: "If a man would lead an interior life, let him draw all his powers, as it were, into a corner of his soul and hide himself with them there, far from all forms and images, and then he may act." Now, that man must forget all things, ignore all things, and rest hushed in stillness, in order that the Divine Word may be born within him. Let him know that he can now serve God's Word in no other way, except by being still and tranquil. He hears the Word speak amid his own silence; he sees the Divine light amid his own ignorance; when he has come to know nothing, then does the Word reveal itself to him.

You may say: Sir, thou placest all our perfection in a certain kind of ignorance, and ignorance is a fault, for God has made man to know, and the prophet prayed God to make men know. Ignorance is the cause of sin and vanity; an ignorant man is a fool, and is like an ape. And I answer thus: What thou sayest is all true if a man continue in his ignorance. But mark well that from the ignorance I speak of, a man emerges into a knowledge high above all forms and images. Again, this ignorance is not the continuance of a previous ignorance; it is from motives of wisdom that a man herein makes himself ignorant. We ought to make ourselves ignorant for the sake of having Divine wisdom; whereupon our souls, unknowing and empty, are presently adorned and ennobled with supernatural knowledge. In this process, if we but rest passive, we are made more perfect than if we actively worked. Hence the saying of a certain master: "We learn more wisdom by hearing than by seeing."

It is related of a heathen philosopher, that as he was about to die his disciples told him of a great discovery in science. He raised his head and said: "Let me know about this, that I may enjoy it in eternity." Hearing brings things into us; seeing gives us out to things. Hence in eternal life we shall have more joy in the faculty of hearing than in that of seeing, for my act of hearing the Eternal Word is all within me, and that of seeing goes forth out of me. By hearing I am made passive; by seeing, active; and our happiness does not consist in our activity, but in what we passively receive from God. As God is greater than all creatures, so is his action greater than mine. And it is by His infinite love that He has made our blessedness depend on His action and not on our own. For our capacity to receive is greater than our capacity to give forth, and every gift we receive increases our capacity for the reception of other gifts, deepening our longing for yet greater things. And hence certain teachers say: "In this is the soul like unto God, that as He is boundless in giving, so is the soul boundless in receiving; and as God is all-powerful in action, so is the soul all-capable in its passiveness; and thus is it transformed with God and in God. Let God work, let the soul suffer His working." Then it shall know itself with His knowledge, love with His love, ever be happier with His blessedness than with its own. And hence the soul's happiness is placed not in its own activity, but in God's. St. Dionysius was once asked why his disciple Timothy surpassed all his other disciples in perfection of virtue. He answered: "Timothy is more perfect than all other men, because he is a man who is passive under God's action."

All this explains how this kind of ignorance is not a defect, but a perfection; and how thy not doing is thy highest work and far above thy doing. Cease from all activity, be silent in every one of thy powers and faculties, and thou shalt in very truth experience the birth of the Divine Word within thee, and find thy new-born King within thy soul. Whatever else besides Him thou now findest there, thou must give up and cast away from thee. All whatsoever that is not pleasing to Him may He help us totally to reject—He Who was born a Child unto us that we might be made children of God. *Amen.*

God's Light in the Soul

Synopsis—How men mistake the light of human reason for the light of grace—Shown by persistence in sinfulness—The right way is the preparation of self-denial—The darkness of suffering goes before the dawn of God's light—Outward activity, how regulated in view of God's inner activity and the coming of His light.

THIRD SERMON FOR THE FEAST OF THE EPIPHANY.

Arise and be enlightened, O Jerusalem.—Isaias lx, 1.

God desires nothing upon earth but one thing, and that He has set His heart upon—that He may find the deep abyss that He has created in man's spirit empty and ready for the perfect work He will do there. In all earth and Heaven He has full power; one thing alone is lacking Him, the accomplishment of His all holy will in man's soul. And what is man's part, that God may light up and take possession of his inmost soul? He should arise, says Holy Writ: Arise, O Jerusalem! This is as much as to say, that a man has his own part to play in the Divine work, and that it is to arise from all things whatsoever that are not God—from all creatures, including himself. It is in this rising up that the soul's depths are quickly stirred with longing for God. The more all inordinate desires are shaken off, the stronger and stronger grows the yearning for God, until it seems to pierce flesh and blood and bones and marrow, and enter into the soul's very essence.

This movement toward God is managed in two different ways. One class of men work with their natural activity of mind, using the images and high thoughts of reason, with the result that they confuse the soul's inner life and stifle its yearnings, substituting their own efforts at understanding things for the longing after God. They imagine that by reason's activity they have made their souls God's city of peace. Others, men of the same class, think that they can prepare their souls by arrangements and methods of their own selection in prayers and meditations and the like, and thereby secure tranquillity. That this is a false peace is proved by their continuing in their defects, their pride, their sensuality and self-indulgence, in suspicions and rash judgments; they are irritated by reproof; easily moved to excuses, to hatred and to other wilful faults. From all this it is plain, that in taking in hand their own preparation for God's work they have hindered Him from doing it; that they have not arisen to be enlightened in the right way. Let them not fancy that their soul has been made God's holy city of Jerusalem, the abode of peace. They should rather resolve to overcome their vices, follow our Lord's pattern in their daily lives, do humble works of holy charity, die to themselves in all things; that is their way to learn how to arise and be enlightened.

But the others, they who in very truth arise and are enlightened, yield to God the task of preparing their souls' depths. These renounce themselves in everything. They are attached to neither words, methods or acts, totally content in joy or in sorrow. To them all things are acceptable as coming from God, and are received in humble fear. They stand before Him in entire self-abandonment, bowed down in willing submission. Whatever may be God's good pleasure is welcome. Be it peaceful or the reverse, it is all one to them, for all things are from God. To them may be applied our Lord's words to His disciples when they asked Him to go to Jerusalem to the festival day: "My time is not yet come, but your time is always ready" (John vii, 6). These men's time is all the time, for waiting and suffering is always ready for them; but God's time is not yet. When and how He will act and enlighten them they leave wholly to Him, in entire self-renunciation and the spirit of long suffering. It is thus peculiar to these men that to God is given over the preparation of their souls, and by no means do they assume the task themselves. Doubtless they occasionally feel the first movements of vice within them, from which, indeed, no one is exempt. But at the first evil suggestion, whether of pride or lust or worldliness, anger or hatred, they immediately and most humbly turn to God, and give themselves up to Him for protection. Such souls do most certainly arise, passing upward above all things, including self; they are, indeed, a city of peace, a real Jerusalem, enjoying tranquillity in the midst of unrest, and happiness in the midst of pain, having relish only for God's will in all happenings. The whole world is powerless to deprive them of their peace, nor could all men and devils together disturb it. They are assuredly enlightened by God, who shines in their souls brightly and powerfully, even more brightly and powerfully amid seeming darkness.

O, these are gentle souls, supernaturally guided by God, without Whose will they do nothing whatsoever. And, if we dared say so, they are in a kind of a way nothing of themselves, but God is all in all within them. O, it is these beautiful souls who are the pillars of the world! Blessed is he who is so fortunate as to be one of them.

These, then, are the two different classes. One class presumes to get their souls ready for God by their own efforts rather than His, with the result that they remain fettered by their sins, powerless to free themselves; or they sink into self-content and self-will. The other class are blessed souls, full of utter self-detachment, elevated in spirit, watching their lightest defects, and at once flying to God for pardon, and receiving from Him a Divine freedom of spirit.

It may be asked: Shall not these men whom God is thus preparing do any outward works? Is it not, indeed, a necessity for them? because the command is: Arise, O Jerusalem! and to arise is itself to do something. I answer: Yes; one work is theirs to do, and that they ought to be engaged in as long as life lasts, if they would come to perfection. They must rise up constantly; they must be constantly lifting up their souls in God and in a spirit of entire detachment, asking, in holy fear, Where is He that is born King? They must be ever searching what God's will is for them in their outward conduct or inward, and what they should do to please Him. Does God require them to be quietly passive, they rest still; does He bid them be active, they set to work; does He grant them contemplation, they enjoy its privileges. Their own inmost soul bears witness what He wills them to do, for His light is shining there, and that is God's chosen abode, which He will not share with any creature. And of those other men, those overactive and self-guided spirits of whom we have before spoken, it must be said that God works within them also, but not directly and without means and images, as He does in the nobler and really detached spirits. In these last God's influence is felt without figures and images, and, as far as they can perceive, immediately upon the essence of their souls. And it is not possible to describe or explain His work in them, nor does anyone understand it except one who has himself experienced it, and such a one can only say that God has taken possession of the center of his spirit. He soon finds himself freed from being absorbed by external activity, and at the same time his realization of God's life in his soul grows ever stronger. When, finally, by his own great earnestness and God's blessed graces, he has attained to the highest perfection, his self-renunciation is complete according to our blessed Lord's words: "When you shall have done all these things that are commanded of you, say: We are unprofitable servants" (Luke xvii, 10). This shows that, however perfect a man becomes, he should, nevertheless, stand in humble awe and fear of God. Yea, if he reaches the very highest point of holiness, he should say to God with deepest sincerity: "Thy will be done!" (Matt. vi, 10). He ought to maintain a sleepless watch over himself, examining whether he clings to even one single earthly thing, whether God finds in the interior of His soul, even the very least hindrance to His immediate influence upon his spiritual life.

May God help us all thus to arise and be enlightened and to experience His Divine action within us. *Amen.*

God is Gained by Detachment from Creatures

Synopsis—Human activity must yield to divine—The passive state is receptive of God—The pain of the soul's solitude and silence precedes the joy of God's coming—The soul must be empty of creatures before being filled with God—The good use of penances in this regard.

SERMON FOR THE FIRST SUNDAY AFTER THE EPIPHANY.

And when He was twelve years old.—Luke ii, 42.

We read in the Holy Gospel that when our Lord was twelve years old He went with His parents to the temple, and that when they started homeward He remained there and they knew it not. Then when they missed Him on the journey and could not find Him among their kinsfolk and acquaintance, they must go back to the temple seeking Him. And so they found Him.

We may use this event to show thee, that if thou wouldst find the Divine generation thou must quit all men, and go back to the source from which thou hast sprung. All the powers of the soul, intelligence and understanding, memory and will, lead thee into multiplicity. Therefore, thou must give them all up in so far as they lead thee into the life of the senses and of images in which thou seekest and findest thyself; then and not otherwise shalt thou find the Divine generation. It is not to be found among kinsfolk and acquaintance, but, on the contrary, the search for it among them only leads thee astray.

And now it may be asked: Shall a man find this birth in certain works which are in themselves Divine, but which give us representations of God contributed by our senses, showing God's goodness, wisdom and mercy—framed by our own reason and yet Godlike in very truth? I answer no. Although these are good and Godlike, yet they come from our outward life of the human senses, and the Divine generation must come from within us and direct from God. When this Divine illumination shines within thee in actual reality, then thy activity must all cease and thy soul's powers must minister to God's and not to thy own

activity; or, rather, God must alone be active and thou must rest passive. When thou hast given up thy own willing and knowing, then does
God enter in, and He then lights up thy soul brilliantly with His presence. Wherever God would know Himself, there must thy power of
knowing thyself cease to act. Do not imagine that thy reason may ever
be so highly developed as to be able to know God by its native power
in this Divine generation. If this light shines within thee, it borrows no
rays from thy natural knowledge, but rather both thy reason and thyself must be brought to nothing before God, and His light shall possess
thee. And when He thus comes to thee, He will bring with Him everything that thou hast renounced for His sake increased a thousand-
fold, to be known and enjoyed by thee in a new and all-embracing form.
An example of this is given us in the Gospel, where our Lord conversed
with the Samaritan woman at the well, and she left her pitcher and ran
into the city and announced to the people that the Messias had come,
and they believed her. But when they hastened out to the well and saw
our Lord Himself, then they said to her: "We now believe, not for thy
saying, for we ourselves have heard Him and know that this, indeed, is
the Saviour of the World" (John iv, 42). And so in very truth, all
created things and all sciences, added to thy own wisdom, cannot give
thee the knowledge of God as God is divinely known. Wilt thou gain
this knowledge? Then thou must give up all knowledge and become
oblivious to all created things, even to thyself.

Alas, then, thou mayst complain, what will become of my poor mind,
standing thus vacant and inert? Can such a way be right, since it
directs my thoughts to an unknown knowledge? And how can this
really be, for I cannot know at all without knowing something? If I
know anything I am not, according to thy teaching, rightly prepared for
God. Must I actually be in utter darkness? Yes, I answer, undoubtedly; thou art never better off than when thou art sunk in the darkness
of unknowing. And if thou askest: Is this to be my final state, from
which I shall never return? I answer: Yes; certainly yes. Again, if
thou wouldst know what this darkness is, what name it has, I answer
that it is thy soul reduced to a state of pure and simple receptivity,
which alone can fit thee to attain to perfection. Out of this thou art
not to come forth, except it be by a way that is not the way of truth.
Thou mayst, indeed, do so, but it must be by the way either of the
senses, the world or the devil. And that path will lead thee necessarily
into transgressions; perhaps it may lead thee so far from God as to

cause thy eternal downfall.   Let there be no going backwards, therefore; thou art to press ever forward with thy longing for God, until all thy capacity for Him has been filled by His blessed presence; thy soul's longing will never cease until it is entirely filled with God.   Unformed matter never rests till its form is granted it to the extent of its capacity; nor does the soul of man ever find repose till it possesses God according to the fullness of its capacity.

A heathen philosopher has said: "In all nature nothing is so swift as the flight of the heavenly bodies, and yet the mind of man overtakes and passes beyond them."   If our spirit were only true to its original power and unfettered by lower and degenerate influences, it would transcend the highest heavens, and would never be content till it had touched the remotest goal, and fed upon the most perfect food.   Such was its original capacity, which it should long to restore.   This it will do by entering upon a state of entire abandonment to its nobler impulses, in a state of entire self-renunciation, and never returning from this salutary darkness.   In this way it will finally win possession of Him Who is all in all, and its progress toward this end is in proportion to its emptiness and to its obliviousness to all created things.   Hence God speaks of the human soul by the prophet Osee: "I will allure and will lead her into the wilderness and will speak to her heart" (Osee ii, 14).   The true and eternal Word is spoken only in that solitude of heart, in which a man has laid waste his affections for creatures and for his very self, being quite alienated from self-love and all multiplicity.   This solitude and self-alienation is spoken of by the prophet David: "Who will give me wings like a dove, and I will fly and be at rest?" (Ps. liv, 7).   Where shall we find rest?   Assuredly in the rejection and alienation of all created things.   Hence David says again: "I have chosen to be an abject in the house my God, rather than to dwell in the tabernacles of sinners" (Ps. lxxxiii, 11).

And now thou mayst ask: Must one of necessity be spoiled of all things and alienated from them inwardly and outwardly, including his own natural faculties and their operation?   It is a grievous thing that God should thus leave a man wholly without support; as the prophet says: "Woe is me, that my sojourning is prolonged!"   (Ps. cxix, 5.) When God prolongs my waiting in a state of self-spoliation, not lighting up my soul, nor speaking His Word, nor being anywise active within me, as thou hast here been teaching me; when, in a word, a man is sunk in absolute nothingness, is it not better that he should do something to relieve the gloom and desolation of his spirit? Should he not say prayers, read good books, hear sermons, or resort for help to other pious means of relief? And to all this I answer no. These are all good in their place and time, but now God offers thee what is better. Be assured that to endure to the uttermost in thy patient silence, is in every way the best for thee. Out of that state thou canst not withdraw thyself without injury, no matter to what solace thou mayst resort. Thou art being made ready for God's coming, and thou wishest to have thy own share of this work of preparation, which cannot be; it belongs all to Him. Thou hast not, seemingly, so much as the power to think it or desire it. God alone must prepare thy soul. If, by an impossibility, thou couldst have for thy part the preparation and He have for His part the entering in and possessing of thy soul, yet be assured that when thy part were done and thy soul prepared, God must at that moment enter in and possess thee. But all this is impossible. Do not dream that God acts upon thy soul as a carpenter does his task, now working and again leaving off, all just as He pleases. No, but on the contrary, the moment God finds thy soul prepared, He enters in and dwells there. It is like the shining of the sun—shine it must if the air is clear. It would be attributing a grave fault to God to suppose that He would not do His great work in thee, as soon as He finds thee capable of receiving it; that is to say, wholly resigned and detached.

Learned men tell us, that the instant a human body is materially formed in the maternal womb, God imparts to it the spiritual soul, which is that body's living form; the readiness of the flesh and the pouring in of the spirit being simultaneous in this case, as in every other. When nature has been brought to its highest point of perfection, then and in the same instant God grants His grace. As soon as thy spirit is prepared for Him, God enters in without a moment's delay. In the Apocalypse we read our Lord's words: "Behold, I stand at the gate, and knock! If any man shall hear My voice and open to Me the door, I will come in to him and will sup with him, and he with Me" (Apoc. iii, 20). Search not here nor there for Him; He is not far from thee; He is even at the door. There He stands and waits. Whomsoever He finds ready, He inspires to open the door and bring Him in. Thou needst not call loudly for Him, as if He were far off, for He is at hand and eager to have thee ready for His coming—a thousand times more so than thou art thyself. The very instant thy soul's door is opened to Him, He is within thee.

If thou objectest that thou dost not feel His presence, I answer that thy feelings are not thine, but His, to control as He sees best. When He is with thee, He may show Himself or conceal Himself, as best suits His purpose. Accordingly our Lord said to Nicodemus: "The spirit breatheth where He will, and thou hearest His voice, but thou knowest not whence He cometh and whither He goeth" (John iii, 8). He has often spoken to thee, and thou hast heard Him and yet hast not understood Him. But God, whether as master of nature, or of grace, will not permit a vacuum. And when thou thinkest that thy soul is empty, having no feeling of God's presence, in truth it is not empty; God is there. Emptyness of soul cannot continue; it must be filled by heaven coming down into it, or by its own self returning to its earthly fullness. God never permits a vacuum. Therefore, stand thy ground in all tranquillity; suffer thy soul to be emptied; for if thou departest from this detachment thou canst not again easily recover it.

And now thou mayst ask an explanation about the Divine generation of the Son of God, of which we have been treating. May I, thou wilt ask, have a sign given by which I shall know it has happened? Yes, certainly; and the sign is threefold. Men often ask me, if one may ever attain to such a spiritual state that nothing hinders his perfection— neither the lapse of time, nor the oppressive weight of material existence, nor the distractions of the multitudes about him. And in very truth a man has reached that freedom, when this Divine generation has come to him; all created things after that are instinctively referred to God, and to His birth within the soul. Take an example from a stroke of lightning. Whatever object is struck it is instantly turned toward the lightning. A man may turn his back away from it, but when struck he is quickly swung around again; the tree's leaves are all drawn toward the lightning that strikes it. So when this Divine birth strikes the soul it is instantly turned toward it, carrying with it all the conditions and circumstances of its existence, even the most unfavorable ones being transformed into benefits, by the soul's new relationship to God. No matter what thou seest or hearest, it all comes to thee sanctified by the Divine generation in thy soul. Everything becomes, as it were, God to thee, for thou knowest and lovest naught but God. It is like a man who has been gazing straight at the sun in the sky; when he turns to look at other objects he sees the sun's disc shining in them. And if thou shouldst fail in this, and dost not seek and love God alone in everything, even the least, then instantly know that this Divine birth hath failed within thee.

Thou mightest ask: Ought not a man to continue to practice penance? Is he not to blame if, on account of this Divine state, he ceases his penitential exercises? I answer that all such practices, including vigils, fasts, tears, sorrowful prayer, disciplines and hair shirts, are good, because the flesh lusteth against the spirit and the body is grown too strong for the soul, producing an unceasing conflict. Here in this life the flesh is bold and strong, for this earth is its native home, and the world around us is allied with this fleshly uprising. Food and drink and all the comforts of life are injurious to the spirit, which is in exile in this mortal existence. But in Heaven everything favors the spirit. There is its fatherland and its home, and Heaven's freedom from fleshly hindrance is granted the soul, if it would but direct its thoughts and its love to Heaven's inhabitants, who are its real friends and kindred. Here below in our exile we must weaken the fleshly instincts and appetites, lest they overpower the spirit. This we succeed in doing by painful penances, putting a curb on the body's ease and comfort. Thereby the soul holds its own against the uprising of fleshly passions, and finally reduces them to captivity. Only lay on the appetites the curb and the fetter of heavenly love, and thou shalt most quickly and most overwhelmingly subjugate them. Hence about nothing does God complain so severely as about our want of love. Love is like the hook on a fisherman's line; the fish must take the hook or the fisherman can never catch him. After the hook is once in his mouth, the fish may swim about and even swim away from the shore, but the fisherman is sure to finally land him. And this I compare with love. Whoever is caught by love is held perfectly fast, and yet in a sweet captivity. Whoever has received the gift of Divine love, obtains from it more freedom from base natural tendencies than by practicing all possible penances and austerities. He it is that can most sweetly endure all misfortunes that happen to him or threaten to overwhelm him; he is the one who most readily forgives all the injuries that can be inflicted on him. Nothing brings thee nearer to God; nothing makes God so much thy own, as the sweet bond of love. Whosoever has found this way never seeks any other. Whosoever is caught by this hook is so entirely captive, that feet, hands, mouth, eyes and heart—everything that is himself—becomes God's own. Therefore, if thou wouldst conquer these enemies, namely, corrupt natural tendencies, and render them harmless, love is thy best weapon. Therefore, it is written: "Love is strong as death, [its] jealousy hard as hell" (Cant. viii. 6). Death cuts the soul from the body, but love cuts all things from the soul. When the soul loves, then whatsoever is not God or God-like, it suffers not to rest with it for an instant. Whosoever is enlisted in this warfare and treads this path, what he does or what he does not in active good works, or what he is not able to do, makes no difference— whether something or nothing, all is for love. The work of perfect love is more fruitful to a man's own soul and to the souls of all other men with whom he deals, and it brings more glory to God, than all other works, even if these be free from mortal sin, but are done in a state of weaker love. The mere quiet repose of a soul with perfect love, is of more worth to God and man than the active labors of another soul. Therefore, do thou but cleave fast and firm to this hook of Divine love and thou shalt be God's happy captive, and the more entirely captive, the more perfectly free shalt thou be. That this captivity and liberty may be vouchsafed us, we pray God the Father, and God the Son, and God the Holy Ghost. *Amen.*

How Men Thirst After God Differently

Synopsis—Beginners long for God amid trials and temptations—They gain Him by meditation on Christ's passion—Proficients seek for Him in correcting the least defects—This is followed by the joy of jubilee with God—Perfect souls now experience a torment of thirst, for God seems lost and gone from them forever—These find God again by groping through darkness into their deeper spirit.

SERMON FOR THE SECOND SUNDAY AFTER THE EPIPHANY.

And on the last and great day of the festivity, Jesus stood and cried: If any man thirst, let him come to Me and drink.—John vii, 37.

What is the thirst of which our Lord Jesus Christ here speaks? Nothing else but this: When the Holy Ghost enters a soul, that soul feels a fire of love; indeed, a very conflagration of love burns in that soul, causing a fiery thirst after God; that is to say, an interior longing to possess Him. And it often happens that such a soul is mystified and cannot account for its condition, knowing only that it suffers interior emptiness and anguish, and that it loathes all created things.

Three kinds of men experience this thirst, and each kind differently, one kind being beginners, the second those who are making some progress, and the third are perfect, as far as may be in this life. King David says: "As the hart panteth after the fountains of water, so my soul panteth after Thee, O God!" (Ps. xli, 1). When the hart is driven by the hounds through forests and over mountains, he is burnt with a consuming thirst and longs for water more than any other kind of animal. Now, beginners in the spiritual life, much more than any other class, are pursued by heavy trials and temptations, and they are like the hart hunted by hounds. When a man first turns away from the world and repents of his gross sinfulness, then the seven deadly sins assail him like so many horrible dogs, tormenting him more now, perhaps, than while he was yet a worldling; he was then tempted, indeed, but now he is fairly hunted by his vicious tendencies. Therefore, Solomon teaches: "Son, when thou comest to the service of God, stand in justice and fear, and prepare thy soul for temptation" (Ecclus. ii, 1). But remember that, according to the violence of thy temptations, so should be the fire of thy thirst for God.

Now, it often happens that the hounds overtake the hart, spring on his flanks and fasten their teeth in him, and he cannot shake them off; and then he runs under the outspreading branches of a tree, which strikes them and breaks their heads, and thus he is released from them. This shows what a devout man may do against his temptations. When they fasten on him, let him run with all his might under the tree of the cross, meditating piously on the passion and death of our dear Lord Jesus Christ. This it is that breaks the heads of his enemies; that is to say, enables him to overcome all temptations. And, again, it may happen that when the big hounds are shaken off, then the hart is attacked by little ones, which snap off little pieces of flesh; and if their attacks are neglected they may cause serious hurt; that is to say, a spiritual beginner, having overcome heavy and grievous temptations, must be watchful against trifling faults, for venial sins can mislead him to this side or that, distract his heart from God, hinder his devotedness to the interior life. These hindrances are such things as idle recreations, vain companionship, vanity in dress, human solace and comfort. Unless he carefully abstain from them, soon his devout way of living grows less earnest, and he loses grace and the spirit of recollection. It often happens that this petty warfare injures a soul, as far as perfection goes, more than did the heavier conflict; in the latter he was energetic in his resistance, for he knew that his enemies directly sought his life; whereas now he fancies he may disregard his lesser foes, because they allure him only to venial faults. Under cover of this delusion they assail him unawares, and we know that a disguised enemy is more dangerous than an open one, though the former be much weaker than the latter. So, therefore, let a man resist all kinds of temptations with equal courage and vigilence. And as the hart, the more he is hunted, the hotter grows his thirst, so the fiercer a man's temptations are, the more do all and each of them consume his heart with a burning thirst after the love of our Lord, in Whom he shall at last find all truth, all joy, all comfort and all righteousness.

When the hunters perceive that the hart is worn out, then the hunt grows tiresome to them, and they call off the hounds and feed and rest them, letting the hart roam at will till his strength is restored and he

can afford them better sport. And thus does our blesed Lord deal with
men during this period of trial; when He perceives that it is too much
for them, He calls off the temptation, He gives the wearied soul a
refreshing draught from His sacred heart, a taste of the sweetness of
Divine things. All that is not God now seems very bitter to the soul,
which imagines that the victory is finally and forever won. But it is
not so; this is nothing else than an interval of refreshment, granted in
preparation for further temptations, all unexpectedly assailing a man,
like hounds springing suddenly upon the neck of a hunted beast.

But if the trials are now more severe than ever before, so is the soul
stronger to resist them than in previous conflicts. Now, dear children,
it is only because of God's faithful and unbounded love for us, that He
allows this terrible ordeal; for it is plain that by so fearful a conflict a
man is made glad to run to God, as the hunted beast runs to a fountain
of water. A man's heart, by constantly struggling against his enemies,
becomes tormented with yearnings to possess God's joy and grace in
perfect truth and entire security. And all the thirstier he is, all the
sweeter shall the waters of life be to him, even here below; and then
also hereafter, as he drinks his fill at the fountain head of all joy in the
heart of his heavenly Father. Hence all his sufferings seem trifling, in
comparison with the comfort he feels in bearing them for God's sake.

And now that the hart has shaken off and distanced all the hounds, he
comes to a clear stream of water; he joyfully plunges down into it and
drinks all he wants and is fully refreshed. So it is with the soul at the
waters of Divine consolation. When, without Lord's help, he has driven
off his temptations and at last comes to God with all confidence, what
shall he do but drink deep of God's love and joy? And then he is so
filled with God, that in his happiness and peace he forgets himself and
thinks that he can work great miracles; he is ready joyously to go
through fire and water for God, and to face a thousand drawn swords;
he fears neither life nor death, neither pleasure nor pain. And so it
would seem that he is intoxicated with God's love.

This is the joy of jubilee. Sometimes such a one weeps for joy; sometimes he laughs, and again he sings. Men about him, whose only guide
is natural reason, cannot understand all this, knowing nothing of the
wonderful ways of the Holy Spirit with elect souls. Look at this
strange conduct, they exclaim; and they at once sit in judgment upon
these chosen spirits and harshly condemn them. But meantime these
enjoy unspeakable happiness; happiness comes to them from everything

that occurs. Do what you please to them, visit them with good or evil, it is all one. They rest wholly unconcerned, free and contented. Whatever happens without, the joy of God glows bright within them, a delicious thirst for God rules their souls without intermission, and is as constantly gratified. Some of them die of jubilation, their hearts quite overcome with love for our Lord. For, dear children, it is a mark of God's greatest work in their souls, that they can no longer endure its bliss and live in the body. Many a one of these favored men has yielded up with such entire abandonment to this wonderful visitation of God, that poor, weak human nature has given way and death has followed.

Dear children, when our Lord sees men thus intoxicated with His spiritual gifts, He acts like a prudent father of a family, whose children, taking advantage of their father's being in bed asleep, go down into his cellar and drink to excess the good wine he has stored there. When the father wakes up and sees what has happened, he goes out and cut a good, strong switch, and he comes and gives his children a severe whipping, and afterwards he gives them nothing but water to drink till they are perfectly sobered again. So does God deal with His chosen ones. While they drink to excess the delights of His love, He is, as it were, asleep. But presently he punishes them by withdrawing the strong, sweet wine of His joy, for their want of moderation has hindered its benefiting them. And now comfort and peace, and the sweetest sense of God's presence are gone, and they are as sad as if they never had been joyous; they are now as sadly sober as before they were wildly intoxicated. And when this state begins to darken upon them, they yearn mightily after our Lord; but by this deprivation He leads them once more out of themselves, and frees them more than ever before from all captivity to created things. They are restored to their sober senses and reason; they are moderated and brought down to their own proper level; they learn just what they are and what they can do when left to themselves. A while ago and they were ready to suffer such things for God as anyone might name and away beyond that; and now they cannot undertake the least little thing for God without the greatest difficulty, and if you say a cross word to them they can scarcely bear it, even for God's sake. In this state of spiritual collapse, they see with perfect clearness just what little good they are capable of, while acting with their own forces and following their own lights. Another effect is this: The abstraction of God's sensible graces makes them so humble, and so takes away their self-conceit, that they grow amazingly kind and well-disposed toward all men.

and in their outard activity they become very unassuming, all of which is quite peculiar to souls who have been chastised by God.

And yet you must know that all that God has thus far accomplished in such souls, causing these stormy times there, has happened among the lowest spiritual powers. My dear children, God's chosen dwelling is not there, nor will He there tarry long, for it is all too narrow a place for Him if He would do a perfect work. His proper place is only in the superior part of the soul, both to dwell and to work. There alone does He find His image and likeness. See Him there and nowhere else, if thou wouldst surely find Him.

And there it is that in all truth, and very quickly, too, an earnest soul finds what it has been seeking with so much unrest. There, in a sort of rapturous ecstasy, the soul's very self is lifted above all its powers into a spiritual wilderness quite impossible to describe, in whose hidden obscurity it discovers the unspeakable Good, and is absorbed in the Divine unity, so completely as to lose all sense of diversity; multiplicity is lost in unity. Children, when these men return to themselves, they find that God has granted them a most joyous knowledge of diversity, a wisdom otherwise unknown in this life, and born only in souls who have been thus absorbed in the Divine unity. All of the articles of holy faith now shine clear and distinct one from another. Bright light beams into the soul about the Father, and the Son, and the Holy Ghost, one true and eternal God. No one knows the Divine Trinity better than these souls, taught by God's Divine unity. Such is this indescribable darkness, which is yet God's essential light; such is this desert waste wherein no man finds road or path, for it is traversed in a Divinely supernatural manner.

This obscurity is, therefore, in reality a light; but because it is essentially superior to the nature of the human intelligence it is darkness to it. It is a desert because it is naturally inaccessible to us, and its paths are ways unknown to our nature. Into the midst of this state is the spirit of a man led by God, in a manner wholly incapable of his comprehension. There he drinks deep of the waters of life flowing from the well-spring of the very Deity. Heretofore the waters were bitter and tepid, for they were in the common, open stream; now, like the waters of any bubbling spring, they are sweet and cold. O how sweet are the waters drunk from the fountainhead of God! Into those waters the soul longs to cast itself, to be wholly filled with them and to be immersed in them. But it finds that this is a boon not to be granted in this life.

Meanwhile the soul is absorbed in God, as a summer shower sinks into the bosom of the earth.

Now, dear children, suppose a man arrived at this state; in case he allows his lower spiritual faculties to be idle and useless, then the higher life will profit him nothing. He must use his ordinary faculties according to their nature; otherwise the Spirit of God will depart from him, resulting in the return of the reign of pride, ill-regulated liberty, and intellectual self-conceit. Let such a man continually humble himself in subjection to the will of God, practice entire detachment from created things, hush all sounds of earth from within and without, and, in fact, abound in all the virtues of the ordinary Christian. Then will God continue His intimate union with him and transform him more and more into a Godlike man.

Children, behold in what marvelous ways God leads souls, and how strange a play he makes with them! First, He introduces Himself into their inner powers, so that He gradually absorbs them and they Him, and then they cannot restrain themselves and fall into singular and foolish ways. After that He draws them deeper into Himself and imparts His very Deity, quite differently from His former way, and this sets them rightly ordered in all things. And now the soul may truly say, in the words of the Canticle: "He brought me into the cellar of wine, He set in order charity in me" (Cant. ii, 4). He hath ordered all things well in the soul's life, leading it across a wonderful desert deep into its own self, showing it there what surpasses all sense and all reason, and what is quite above human experience, because it is a veritable foretaste of life eternal. Behold, dear children, how the gentle, kindly goodness of God is able so to hide His dealings with His chosen ones that, as He makes them perfect, He performs a most marvelous work. His aim is always to draw us to union with Himself in a holy and happy life. He would have us all athirst after His everlasting peace and love, calling to us with a loud, resounding voice: "If any man thirst, let him come to Me and drink" living water. He Himself, as it were, thirsts to find a true thirst in our souls, which He quenches by filling us with such sweet and heavenly fullness, that out of us "shall flow rivers of living water" (John vii, 37) unto life eternal. It is as when we are nourished with bodily food; it passes from the stomach into every member of the body, giving strength to all. So does the soul drink a Divine nourishment in this interior communication with God, which spreads Divine love everywhere throughout our faculties, making our works, our life and our very existence, rightly ordered in God and all devoted to the welfare of our fellow-men.   In such wise it is, that from the interior operation of God our outward life is well ordered.   Thus our labors blossom and bear great fruit in God's own way, making for eternal happiness.   To attain to this blessed end may God mercifully grant us His help.   *Amen.*

The Five Porches of the Pool of Healing

Synopsis—The first is humility—The second is recollection of spirit, especially needful for active spirits—The third is repentance deep and true—The fourth is joyous voluntary poverty, forming a noble and elevated character—The fifth is referring all gifts of God back to the giver, being opposed to spiritual gluttony—The waters of the pool of healing are the most Precious Blood of Christ.

SERMON FOR THE THIRD SUNDAY AFTER THE EPIPHANY.

After these things there was a festival day of the Jews, and Jesus went up to Jerusalem.—John v, 1.

This part of the Holy Gospel tells us that Jesus went to a festival at Jerusalem, and that He visited a pool of healing there enclosed by five porches. "In these lay a great multitude of sick, of blind, of lame, of withered, waiting for the moving of the water. And an angel of the Lord descended at certain times into the pond, and the water was moved. And he that went down first into the pond after the motion of the water, was made whole, of whatsoever infirmity he lay under." Our Redeemer there saw a man lying on a mattress who had been sick for thirty-eight years. Moved with pity, He said to him: "Wilt thou be made whole?" The infirm man answered: "Sir, I have no man, when the water is troubled, to put me into the pond; for, whilst I am coming, another goeth down before me." Then said our dear Lord to him: "Arise, take up thy bed, and walk!" And immediately the man was made whole, and he took up his bed and walked, not knowing who it was that had healed him. But "Afterwards Jesus findeth him in the temple, and saith to him: Behold, thou art made whole! Sin no more, lest some worse thing happen to thee."

The pool of healing, what is it but the sweet and noble person of our beloved Lord Jesus Christ Himself? And the health-giving water, is the adorable and most precious blood of the eternal Son of God, true God and true Man, Who has washed and cleansed us in that bath of love, and Who, out of His own tender love, will thus wash and cleanse all men who come to Him with real sorrow for their sinful lives, together with a sincere resolve to be better for the future. The sick who lay around this healing pool in such great numbers, waiting for the angel to come down and stir the waters, may be called the whole human race, who, before our Lord's coming, lay in captivity under the law of the Old Testament while they lived, and after death waited in limbo for the moving of the waters; that is, till our Lord's precious blood was poured out at His blessed and bitter death, giving them eternal health and salvation. And so also in these last days, which are the time of salvation, no man can ever be healed and saved except by the adorable and precious blood of our Lord Jesus Christ.

And you should know, too, that all sick souls that will not pass through our Lord's pool of healing will, without doubt, perish everlastingly. But there are yet other souls who feel the stirring of these waters only outwardly; they are influenced by the admonitions of their fellowmen, threatening them with the punishments of hell, or painful visitations of Providence afflicting soul or body; or, again, they are moved by the Word of God preached to them. All such come, indeed, into these healing waters, but only half-heartedly. And these are much to be pitied; for, although they are made whole of their sinfulness, yet they hold off as much as they dare from true and entire conversion to God. Let us pity them, I say, for they live and die but half-cleansed, and are finally cast into the bitter pains of purgatory, there to remain till they are entirely purified.

The pool of healing had five porches, before which lay a great number of infirm persons, each and all waiting to be first in the waters as the angel stirred them, and thereby to be healed. This means the proud, the wrathful, the vengeful, the covetous and the unchaste—all these, let us well remember it—are washed in the blood of Jesus and are made whole if they will but accept the cleansing.

We may also consider the five porches as representing our Lord's five holy wounds, by the overflow of Whose precious blood, we are healed and saved from the mortal sickness of sin. Yet another meaning may be given, for the five porches are like the five virtues of very great prominence in the Christian's life, all needed for every soul, but this one or that especially necessary to each, according to his peculiar spiritual sickness.

Humility is the first—humility, deep and unfeigned. By this a man rates himself as worthless; bows himself down beneath the hand of God and of every creature; meekly accepts all adversity and prosperity, sorrow and joy, no matter from what source it comes, as allotted him by God alone; is ever in fear and shame before the face of God; never repining.

The second portico of the pool of healing, is diligent attention to the interior life—recollection of spirit. O, how necessary is this virtue to many simple, well-meaning men! They do not wait for God's signal, but, wholly self-guided, they rush outwards to the showiest kind of teaching, preaching and the like, little realizing that they are influenced only by the human motive of sensible and natural satisfaction. St. Augustine tells us, that it sometimes happens that men who thus abandon a recollected life and unguardingly mingle with the joys of creatures, never more return. Be assured, dear children, that whoever would engage in external works should keep a careful watch over his interior, earnestly inspecting his motives. Laboring externally with this safeguard, he ever preserves peace and security both within and without. Imprudent activity breeds unrest, the soul being guided by the attractions of sensible joy and the casual happenings of life, instead of God's interior leadings and admonitions.

The third portico is repentence for sin, deep and true. It is turning away in all sincerity from everything that is not God, or that does not come from God. The very marrow of true contrition consists in this— that a sinner returns absolutely to God with all that he is inwardly and outwardly. That a man is wholly absorbed in trustfulness of God's goodness, that he ardently longs to possess Him and Him only, that he is resolutely determined to cleave to Him forever in all love, that he has the purpose clear and distinct to do God's will alone to the utmost of his power: My dear children, this is what repentance essentially is. Whosoever has it in that spirit, his sins are without any doubt forgiven him wholly, and the deeper the intensity of his earnestness, so much the more perfectly is he cleansed.

The fourth portico is a joyous voluntary poverty. You know, children, that there is a poverty arising from outward conditions, and an interior, that is to say, a real and true poverty. To outward poverty all men are not called; but to interior poverty all are called who would be true friends of God. By this virtue God alone is our riches; in our inmost heart we value Him and Him only. Whatever else we may have, is possessed only because we are sure He wills us to have it, and it is held in sincere poverty of spirit. St. Paul tells us of this poverty: "As having nothing and possessing all things" (II Cor. vi, 10). And we must understand this to mean, that we do not wish to possess anything in this life that God would have us be without; that we yield up to Him quickly and gladly our goods and our friends and our honor, our very body and soul, if He so wills it, for His love and glory. This should be our mind every hour of our lives, even though we have to overcome the resistance of mean, cowardly human nature; for this is essentially the poverty required of all good men. And this forms a noble character—one set at liberty from all attachment to creatures, and elevated in spirit above the vicissitudes of life, whether of joy or sorrow, ever ready to give up all earthly things as God wills it. If such a one were monarch of a kingdom, he would in spirit be no different from a literally poverty-stricken man, nor would his royal riches in the least degree hinder his soul from profiting fully by any of God's graces. Being incapable of resting for peace and joy upon perishable things, he constantly stands in spirit before God like a beggar asking for an alms from a kind, loving Father; and that alms, the only gift that can ever satisfy him, is nothing less and nothing else than God Himself. It is true that when some temporal gain or loss happens, such men are momentarily glad or sorrowful; but this is only felt in the lower part of the soul, is not yielded to, and is followed instantly by an elevation of the spirit to God.

The fifth portico is giving back to God the glory of all His gifts, a steadfast reference of all graces and favors to the Divine origin from which they have flowed forth. Many men, when God bestows special spiritual favors on them, regenerating them into His wonderful light, begin to felicitate themselves. They riot in spiritual gluttony; they never think of humbly attributing their good fortune to its only origin, but appropriate God's graces to themselves in a feeling of personal ownership. And this is very perilous to their souls. We should so steadfastly look to God alone in all happenings, that we shall scarcely perceive the gifts which he is showering upon us. Consider a man gazing at something through a narrow opening in a wall; if he fixes his attention wholly upon the object he is inspecting, the wall serves him well; but if he begins to examine the wall itself, asking how thick or thin it may be, then the wall is a hindrance to him. It is thus with the soul and God's gifts, little or great. Rest thy mind on them, study how noble and beautiful they are, indulge recklessly in all their joys, and then art thou hindered from possessing God, Who alone is to be praised and glorified in His graces. Thou oughtest instantly to refer back to God all the favors He bestows on thee, sinking thyself deep into the glorious depths of Divine love, from which they all have come forth.

Children, many infirm men lay in the porticos enclosing the pool of healing, and whichever one of them first entered the waters after the angel stirred them, was made whole. And what meaning has this stirring of the waters? Nothing less than the descent of the Holy Spirit into a man's soul, stirring up with a powerful movement of grace his whole interior life. Thereby is he so totally transformed, that things which once he loved have now become absolutely tasteless to him. Once he fairly dreaded and strenuously avoided what now he covets with all his heart—to be stripped of all things and to live like a banished man; to retire into inner silence; to be humiliated and to be cast off by all men. Such things become sweetest joys to him, when God's Spirit stirs the deep waters of his soul. All this happens to the sick man; that is to say, the man whose spiritual powers have been absorbed in the outward things of life; these faculties of his soul are now washed and completely cleansed in the adorable and precious blood of Jesus Christ. Only by this deep searching and cleansing process can he be cured of all his soul's ailments, as it is written: "As many as touched Him were made whole" (Mark vi, 56).

And now, dear children, sometimes when our beloved Saviour has cured a sick soul it does not know it, and it may even go on during its whole life hardly aware of it. But this is permitted all for the best; for our Lord knows full well, that if that soul thought itself all cured and safe and sound, it would quickly yield to self-complacency. It is, therefore, only out of special affection that He allows it to remain in ignorance of its happy condition, being all its days securely fixed in holy fear and anguish of spirit, and quite humiliated in God's sight. Such a soul is perfectly safeguarded against offending God, even if the whole world were offered it, and this is a high degree of holiness. Rather than arouse the wrath of God by sinning, such a soul would gladly and joyfully be put to death. And, indeed, it dies daily for God's sake within its inmost self, being entirely self-abandoned to His blessed will, and that in the darkness of a holy ignorance of what may be its standing with Him. One only purpose actuates such a soul: To be bound captive to God's and in their outward activity they become very unassuming, all of which will in time and in eternity, and without the least shadow of contradiction on its part.

And what is the termination of this devout resignation to a state of ignorance of God's love or hatred? It is this: When, at last, the beavenly Father comes to lead that soul to its eternal home, He dispels all ignorance and darkness and gives it a foretaste of the everlasting joys of Paradise.   And such a well-tried soul dies full of joy and confidence; and, having been so loyal to God during the long years of darkness and desolation of spirit, it is led instantly and without any interval of purgatory into His Divine embrace.   This is what is meant by the words of Scripture: "And I heard another voice from Heaven, saying to me write: Blessed are the dead who die in the Lord" (Apoc. xiv, 13).

It is related in the Gospel that our Lord found a man at the pool of healing who had been sick thirty-eight years.   Mark well that this sickness, however long continued, was not unto death, but that the glory of God might be manifested.   O, dear children, may God grant us to learn this lesson well—the example of a man who, because for thirty-eight years he so patiently waited on God, was at last rewarded.   God Himself came to him, made him sound and well, bade him take up his bed and walk.   This teaching, dear children, is a sharp admonition to many spiritual men of our day.   I refer to those who have, indeed, repented of their sins and entered on a pious life, but who say that all is lost if it happens that our Lord gives them no extraordinary graces; they act as if they thought God had treated them unjustly.   They are by no means content humbly to retire into themselves and patiently to wait on the Divine will.   O, how few there are who possess that beautiful virtue!   How few who sweetly and in perfect good-will give themselves up entirely to God's blessed guidance.   Such souls little know how pleasing they are in His sight, and therein they are very fortunate. May God teach us how noble and profitable a thing it is to surrender oneself captive to His will, never for a moment wishing to be released from His blessed bonds of ignorance and darkness, until His own appointed time.   May God grant us this grace, giving us steadfast confidence and courageous long-suffering under His guidance, even amid misgivings and anguish of heart.   *Amen.*

Marks of a Truly Converted Soul

Synopsis—As Israel of old fell away from God, so do many Christians now—This often happens from imperfect conversion to a devout life—First mark of a true conversion, low opinion of self; second, brotherly love; third, bearing wrongs patiently; fourth, compassionate kindness; fifth, humble subjection to others; sixth, alacrity and exactness in well doing; seventh, strict abstemiousness; eighth, rigid observance of the rules of chastity.

SERMON FOR THE FOURTH SUNDAY AFTER THE EPIPHANY.

Return, O Israel, to the Lord thy God.—Osee xiv, 2.

We read in this day's Gospel, that Jesus went up into a ship, and that His disciples followed Him. So should all Christians do; repenting of their sins, they should follow Christ, according to the teaching of the prophet: "Return, O Israel, to the Lord thy God!"

Out of all the races of the world our Lord chose one, upon which He bestowed many favors, covenanting to give them yet more, if they would turn to Him and would not follow the ways of other people who, in willful blindness of heart, lived only to gratify their sensual passions, led astray by their love of the vanities of the world, and by the deceits of the evil one. God visibly guided His own people by His servants and prophets, giving them His holy commandments. He showed forth His Infinite power by fighting for them against their enemies. He lavished His loving kindness upon them, by bestowing innumerable benefits on them, and promised to continue to favor them, if they would but turn to Him and love Him and keep His commandments. He bade them never forget the day on which He had delivered them from bondage and toil, and that they should set themselves with all diligence and earnestness to observe His law. But this people were stiffnecked, shortsighted and ungrateful. They would not obey the precepts God gave them by His servants, but, on the contrary, showed themselves self-willed, rebellious and light-minded. Therefore, our Lord punished them; many of them

He caused to be put to death, and He permitted all of them to die in the wilderness. To their children He continued to send His messengers, saying: O, my chosen people, return to Me and be converted with all your heart; wander not off in the devious ways of sin, but follow after Me, returning from the paths of Egyptian darkness and of wickedness and of damnation, and I will bring you into the land of promise and will give you all good things there.

These events happened under the Old Testament and in very ancient times and amid many wonders. But therein are to be found various signs of what was to happen after the incarnation of the Son of God, and even in our own days; for God uses the self-same words to cause us to turn to Him and to do so with all earnestness, giving us many reasons, warnings, instructions and inducements; leading us, if we will but follow, with signs and wonders and mighty power, exhorting us to depart out of the Egypt of this world and out of the bondage of Pharaoh, its king. All this does God do, both secretly in our souls and openly before our eyes, in order to work our conversion to Him. Would that we received it with thankfulness and were sincerely converted. But it is with us as it was of old with the people of Israel. We follow God in body and we remain in Egypt in our heart's desires. We all march after the pillar of cloud and the pillar of fire, but our joy is in the comforts of the world and the pleasures of the flesh. We are very earnest about external religious practices, about how to be religiously dressed, when to sing and when to be silent, when to bow down and to genuflect; if all this be exactly observed we are sure that we are delivered out of Egypt. Not so, my dear children, not so; this is only the pillar of cloud and of fire; these observances, if they lack this interior meaning, are but the leaves of the fig tree, and not the fruit that can nourish our souls and make them a fit offering to God. A man who thus acts is like the tree that God cursed and condemned to eternal barrenness. O, how often have you been taught that you must not trust to the appearances and shadows of religion! These things are good, and even punctilious practice of them is necessary for beginners in the spiritual life; but, considered apart from the essence and truth of holiness, for the sake of which they are instituted, they avail nothing. Unless a man is on his guard he will stick fast in these purely external practices, and in his heart will remain as wicked and corrupt as those who have not even this appearance of virtue; and, finally, he will fall into yet worse vices, sinking back into the Egypt of this world. Indeed, it would have been better to have remained in undisguised worldliness and sin, for the final condemnation of these external Christians will be all the greater, because their sins have the added guilt of being done under the garb of holiness, and in the outward profession of a sacred state of life.

Children, I know of nothing more necessary than that beginners, while taking their first steps in the spiritual life, should be carefully instructed in what is most essentially required; namely, that, being practiced in sound and useful external devotions, they should by no means stop at these, which, if emptied of their true meaning, are of little help, and are at best only given us as a good preparation for a perfect life. If this wisdom is implanted in youthful souls, quick and ardent for perfection, many of them will doubtless earnestly resolve to go forward to better things. But, alas and alas! How sad it is to see those who began with such fervor of spirit that they were once very guarded in their choice of company, finally absorbed in the society of worldlings! At first they could hardly bear to listen to a frivolous word, and now they are never done with conversation about profane things, early and late engaged in silly speech and foolish disputes. Once they longed for quiet retirement and were glad to follow their pious exercises undisturbed, and now the more distracting occupations they can have the better they are pleased. O, this and the like of this is all a plain sign, that such souls are held in captivity by their fleshly passions, and, as far as their hearts' desires are concerned, are wandering backward into Egyptian darkness. Children, for the love of Christ, let each one of you be on his guard. Once you have begun a good course, do not stop short; all may be lost again if you are not extremely vigilant; our inconstancy is beyond belief.

Consider how some fall away from a state so perfect that at first they are scandalized by an idle word; yet no long time afterwards they feel not a qualm of conscience for much flippant and even malicious speech, greatly to the injury of others, making nothing of the guilt of such conduct. We meet with men who in the beginning patiently endured opposition and contradiction, prepared, if need be and in spite of the very devil, to suffer martyrdom itself. And behold them now, after living for a while with even very pious people! You never saw or heard of men so perverse, self-willed and obstinate.

Others, again, in their first fervor are hot and eager for austerities; all the hard mortifications they see around them are little and trifling to them. But wait a while, and you find that they cannot bring them-

selves to perform such moderate acts of self-denial as are common to all
Christians.   And they incessantly complain, if their demands for ease
and comfort are not instantly complied with, making themselves in every
way burdensome to others, no matter how much is done for them.

Very different are those devout, interior men, who, though they must
struggle hard to make a beginning, and can only move forward slowly
and step by step, yet resolutely keep on until they become an edifying
example to all others, while the overeager spirits, who at first promised
so much, have finally come to nothing.   Let us be very regardful of our
want of steadfastness, for we know not what the future has in store
for us.

And now, dear children, I will tell you how one may know whether
or not he has been truly converted to God, and has really renounced the
evil one and all his works and pomps.   When we were baptized we made
our vows to God and holy Church never to commit sin, and to practice all
Christian virtue.   But we were afterwards led astray by the evil spirit
and fell into sin, losing thereby the grace of God conferred on us in baptism.   And then God, in His unspeakable mercy, called us back to His
friendship, and on our repentance He restored all His favors.   But now
many allow themselves to be again deceived by the evil one, for he cunningly endeavors to make the soul's contrition for all past sins more
apparent than real.   Let us consider this matter attentively, so that we
may the better avoid such a misfortune.

A truly converted Christian stands humbly persuaded of his own
nothingness, and to be so regarded by everyone is his only desire.   He
would by no means hold authority over anybody, but in all lowliness of
heart he is pleased to be subjected to others, and glad to do their will,
whosoever they may be.   He despises himself, regards himself as a
thief, chooses the least and lowest of everything, is readily guided by
others, and makes the best of whatever happens to him.   Thus, standing
toward men in all gentleness and toward God in all fearfulness, he
accepts with thanksgiving all that is commanded him or advised him, or
even wished.   The contrary is the case with those who are but superfi-
cially converted.   They stand high in their own opinion, and they set a
high value on their words and works.   To be subjected to others is to
them a disgraceful thing, and they will not suffer the rule of a superior.
They volunteer instructing others with a flood of talk, discoursing boast-
fully of high spirituality.   And all this they do with a show of holy
humility, lest their real condition should be suspected.   If you pay them

no regard they are immediately up in arms against you, and if you differ with them they defend themselves vigorously. They are rash, boastful and quarrelsome. All these are under the hand of the enemy of souls.

How different are the truly converted, who are ever affectionate to their neighbors, praising them with all brotherly love as far as truth will allow, rejoicing in their prosperity, aiding them in adversity, and overflowing with pity for all in distress—quite unlike the falsely converted, who are offensive to others, envious of their welfare and even of their piety, given to railing and contention, vindictive, contemptuous, self-assertive.

Rightly converted men patiently bear oppression and injustice, as trials permitted by God for their spiritual benefit. With peaceful hearts they suffer on, always gentle in speech, gladly and easily reconciled to those who have done them injury. Half-converted souls, on the contrary, blaze up quickly with anger, are sorry at the good fortune of others, are backbiters, double-dealers and gossipers; they murmur against their superiors; they complain about their inferiors.

The truly converted are ever kind and compassionate, ready-handed to give and to help; for they make little of earthly goods, even rejoicing in poverty and humiliations, for which they return unfeigned thanks to God, to Whom alone they look for their daily support. Their aim is to be delivered from temporal things and the care of them, so they may be wholly absorbed in eternal things. The falsely converted are afire with love for the good things of this life, ever seeking after personal convenience and pleasure. They misuse their time, deceiving their superiors if they can, and if that be not possible, then acting in defiance of them. They must be well praised for all they do and amply rewarded; for if they are made little of they are like men possessed, and secretly or openly they set about doing all the harm they can. For every work of religion they expect temporal gain. They often practice gross deceit to procure worldly honors.

Men who are right-hearted, diligently devote all their time to doing good to their neighbor or advancing God's honor, finding much spiritual joy in such a life. They are very careful to do everything exactly right, trusting with all their hearts for God's blessing on their labors. And the wrong-hearted are ever slothful to do good and inclined to evil, bitter-minded in dealing with others, petty, deceitful—as becomes barren-hearted men.

The right-hearted are ever temperate and self-restrained in ministering to their natural wants, and much averse to all superfluity. If they experience excessive craving for anything, it is precisely that thing that they deny themselves. They keep themselves in good discipline by meager diet, and with all precaution they guard against excess in drink. On the contrary, the evil-inclined are given to excess in eating and drinking, are overindulgent to themselves and thankless to God. Severe sickness often results from their shameless conduct in this respect. After their banquets they give themselves up to silly talk and mirth, jokes and idle stories; or they are inclined to quarrel; they are easily enraged, and when angered they shout and roar like jackasses; or, again, they are totally stupefied and can only lie down and sleep, not able to say so much as a *Pater Noster.* All this comes from heavy drinking and gluttonous feeding. Hence the extreme care taken by all holy men against overeating and drinking, in order to safeguard themselves and their disciples against such wickedness. But, alas, it has now come to such a pass that even some clergymen—and this is most of all to be regretted—cannot and will not be content with what suffices even rich worldlings. The men who thus behave are spiritually blinded and are seldom able to resist the temptations of the devil, who leads them, before they are aware of it, into foul impurity, smirching their souls with unclean thoughts and desires. Finally, they fall into detestable sins, calling down on their heads God's maledictions beyond anything they can appreciate. These wilful impurities unfit them for any good and useful works, and make them offensive to all devout people. And now, blinded by their passionate desires, they rush into low company and give themselves up to vice and the pleasures of the table. Their language is flippant, their minds totally averted from any pious practice; they no sooner begin any exercise of devotion than they are filled with the evil memories of their sins, the devil playing the ape in their thoughts and acting over again the orgies of their bad companionship, causing them to laugh aloud when they should be absorbed in penitential thoughts.

How different are men who have been truly converted! They stand before God and His angels so chaste and so timid and cautious, that they had rather suffer death itself than wilfully harbor a single unchaste thought. They keep so close a watch over their hearts, senses and members, that they hardly presume to look even upon themselves, being greatly distrustful of their own virtue. They chastise their bodies with fasts and vigils and hard labors; they constantly lift their souls to God, placing their confidence in Him alone—all to safeguard holy chastity. Those, on the contrary, who are only seemingly converted, care little whether or not they are thinking of impure things. So, then, it happens often enough that gross, sensual emotions of mind and body run riot in them. They are brought to the very gate of hell; nay, they overstep the limits of mere temptation and would fall heart and soul and body into open carnal wickedness, if they had but the means of doing so. Such is the end of their self-love; such the end of their tendency to gratify their love of bodily ease. Some of these men fall into such a besotted state of mind, that they are ready even to hate God because He has forbidden them the lusts of the flesh. They are so blinded by their vicious habits, that they would be glad if He had no knowledge of their sins and no power to punish them, which is equivalent to wishing that God did not exist.

O, dear children, consider earnestly how you stand; bear in mind what dangers surround us all. Let none of you be self-trustful; let each and all stand in holy fear. No matter how good you may now seem to be, by no means rely on that. And, on the other hand, no matter how sadly you may before this have fallen and gone astray from virtue, take courage and come back to God, this time by a true conversion. As long as God spares your life His favor is always ready to be bestowed. God help us all to that happiness! *Amen.*

The Yoke of Christ is the Soul's Thought of God

Synopsis—The inner man is the yoke upon the outer man—The soul is driven inward by all of God's creatures—Yet any of them may be made a hindrance—At least once a day we should seek God's light yoke by holy thoughts—Example of an ancient hermit— Christ's burden is the misery of this life—Sorrow is turned into joy by submissiveness to God's will.

SERMON FOR THE FIFTH SUNDAY AFTER THE EPIPHANY.

My yoke is sweet and My burden is light.—Matt. xi, 30.

It is eternal truth itself—our Lord and Saviour Jesus Christ—who utters these words. And yet men contradict Him, men who live according to mere matter; these by act and word affirm that God's yoke is bitter and his burden is heavy. But the right is with God.

Anything that crushes a man and drags him down is a burden. Now, we understand by the word yoke, as here used, the inner man; and by the word burden, the outer man. The inner man has come from God, and he is a noble being, made after God's image and likeness. And as he comes from God, so is he invited and urgently called back to God, so that, being drawn into the Divine life, he may become partaker of all good. The blessedness that belongs to God by nature the soul may hereby obtain by grace. Now, dear children, the treasures that God has hidden in the depths of our souls, whosoever discovers them and contemplates them becomes, indeed, a happy man. And, although a man may allow his spiritual insight to be for a time diverted from Divine things, yet he is incessantly drawn again to consider God's interior presence; he can never otherwise be at rest. The whole universe is not enough to content him. All outward things only turn him back into his inner life, whether he perceives it or not; for there is God, his final end and the only purpose of his existence. As all material things rest on their proper basis, as a stone on the earth; or as they rise upward into their proper element, as fire into the air; so does a devout soul rest upon God and rise into God as its only salvation.

Now, to what men is this yoke sweet and light, as they accept it and bear it along? Surely only to those whose thoughts are turned inward in search of God, and quite turned away from all created things. Children, our souls ever stand on the boundary line between time and eternity. If we turn toward time, we shall without doubt forget eternity, and soon be led far away from the things of God. Whatever we see from a distance looks small; whatever we see close at hand looks large, for there is but little intervening space. Thus the sun is many times larger than the earth, but if reflected in a cup of clear water on a summer's midday it seems no bigger than a little bean, and any little object that should come between the sun and that mirror, would be large enough to entirely take away the image of the great luminary. So it is with a man's soul. No matter how trifling may be the earthly image he places in the depths of his soul, it is enough to interfere with God's light shining there; the infinite good that God is may easily be hindered from entering and possessing the soul of man. And this is equally true when it happens that the image in the soul is not an evil and a little thing, but a great and really good thing; it may hinder the entrance of God, Who is without any image or intermediary whatsoever. Know, therefore, for a certainty, that in whatever soul the infinitely good God shall be mirrored, it must be totally freed and emptied of all images; if the soul reflects a single created thing, that is enough to exclude the reflection of God. All souls who have not established in their very depths this freedom from creatures, who have not uncovered and laid bare before God their innermost recesses, are as yet only scullions in the Divine service, and to them God's yoke is bitter. And, says Origen, the man who has not looked into the deeper depths of his being has a plain sign, that as yet he has not tasted of the eternal sweetness of God.

Let it be well understood, therefore, my dear children, that at least once in the day we should turn inwards with all possible recollectedness; for if we do not even that much for the interior life, we are without doubt unworthy the name of Christians. And all who cleanse the mirror of their souls perfectly clear of the images of created things, so that God may pour in the sunlight of His divinity quite unobstructed, to them His yoke is sweet beyond all other possible sweetness. To such souls whatsoever is not God is tasteless; yea, it is bitter and loathsome to the taste, whether it be within them or come from without, and the

very remembrance of the sweetness of creatures is bitter as gall.   The
sweetness of God enters so deep, that it seems to have become the marrow
in the bones and the blood in the veins of the truly converted man.
God's eternal image expels completely from the soul every other image
whatsoever.

But let us ask, children, why it is that the things amid which we live
here below hinder us spiritually?   It is because thou clothest thyself
with them as if with thy own proper personal qualities; for if thy mind
were in very truth unencumbered with their images, thou mightest be
master of a kingdom and suffer no spiritual harm.   Be but free from all
images, and all sense of ownership of creatures, and all is well with thee.
What thou needest, thou mayst in humility and in fear of God without
doubt possess and use, and God is thereby pleased.   If thou fallest short
of thy needful substance, trust God confidently, for He will provide for
thee, even, if necessary, by means of His dumb creatures; He no more
forsakes His children than He gives up His own eternal life.

There was once an ancient hermit, whose soul was so free that no
created thing encumbered his thoughts.   Now, it happened that a certain man knocked at the door of his cell, and when the hermit opened it
and went out to him, the man asked him to give him a certain object inside the cell, and the hermit turned and entered to do so.   But when he
would seek for it he found he had, meantime, forgotten what it was.
After a while the man knocked at the door again, and then the holy
hermit came out, and bade him go inside himself and take what he
wanted: "For," said he, "my dear son, I cannot retain in my mind what
it is thou dost want me to give thee, for I am entirely stripped of all
thoughts of created things."

Children, in such imageless souls, the light of God shines without hindrance.   They are elevated in spirit and set at liberty from creatures,
even detached from their own selves, and their wills in all joy and sorrow, in all work and rest, are entirely united to God.   They are most
joyfully enveloped by God's will, as if they were caught in a net.   To
them pain and pleasure are all one, or rather are instantly forgotten, for
God's yoke is sweet to their souls.   All creatures, considered in themselves, look far off and seem petty and contemptible, for they behold
them from the Divine bosom, into which they have sunken away; and
eternal things are close at hand and most wonderfully grand, for them
they behold in their own souls with God.   If men hate them or love
them their peace is equally untroubled, for the sweetness of Divine love

imparts a calm that can be disturbed by neither friend nor foe. The sweetness of our Saviour's yoke safeguards them from all bitterness of creatures.

Now, we are to consider that other Word of Christ: "My burden is light." This refers to the many sorrows we suffer in our external life. O, good and merciful God, who are those that nowadays find Thy burden light? For, alas, men no longer want to bear the burdens of life, even those that are unavoidably necessary for our welfare. And yet whichever way thou turnest thou must bear burdens, in spite of thyself. Fly from the heat and thou shalt fall into the deep cold snow. O, give thyself up willingly and joyfully to suffer, commending thyself piously to God's protection in whatever may happen to thee. Consider how bitterly our Lord Jesus Christ suffered, and how it was by suffering that He entered into His glory and into the bosom of His heavenly Father.

And what, dear children, shall a servant of God suffer? Thou must suffer all the visitations of God's providence, and that in entire submissiveness, without arguing about their justice or injustice, whether they are allowed to come to thee from men or come direct from God—the death of thy friends, the loss of thy property or of thy good name, the privation of consolations, whether exterior or interior, from God or from creatures. My dear child, these burdens must thou take up cheerfully and bear joyously. And, besides these, thou must bear with thy own defects, however painful they may be to thee, and however miserably thou hast failed to overcome them. Put thy shoulder meekly under thy burdens, and trust to God for strength to suffer; let God's blessed love be thy guide for time and eternity. Take an example from horses in the stable. Their manure is filthy and it is offensive to the smell. But the same horse that makes it, draws it with great labor into the fields and there it makes fine wheat and rich wine—all the better wheat and wine for the filthiness of the manure. Thus mayst thou use those disgusting faults of thine which thou canst not quite overcome. Scatter them upon the field of God's holy will, and abandon thyself very humbly to His loving care; rich fruit of virtue thou shalt without doubt gather to the honor of God and the edification of His servants.

Whatsoever man bows his back humbly under God's dispensations, and yields himself joyfully to His holy will in weal and woe; whatsoever man looks to God for everything in steadfast hope, receiving all from Him and returning all to Him in sincere detachment of spirit; whatsoever man sinks himself deep down into his own soul, seeking only for

God's will in entire renunciation of self and of all creatures; whatsoever man, I say, does all this with a true heart and perseveres steadfastly in it, to him will God's burden in very truth be made light.   Yes,
children, so light that if it were possible to lay on that man alone all
the burdens of the world, they would seem so light to him that it would
be a joy to carry them—a joy that would seem like that of Heaven.   For
you must understand, that it is God Himself who bears such a man's
burden; God has entered into him and taken charge of all that he does
and all that he endures.   May the eternal God do the like in us.   May
He thus make His yoke sweet and His burden light to us, God the
Father, and God the Son, and God the Holy Ghost.   *Amen.*

Signs of a True Scholar of Christ

Synopsis—That one is a diligent pupil of Christ is shown by not fear-
ing or avoiding disgrace; by readily blaming himself; by esteem-
ing all men his superiors; by holding rich friends in no higher
favor than poor strangers; by readily seeing God's will in all
circumstances of life, and finally by patient endurance of suf-
fering.

SERMON FOR THE SIXTH SUNDAY AFTER THE EPIPHANY.

Learn of Me, because I am meek and humble of heart.—Matt. xi, 29.

Christ, our beloved Lord, true master of all wisdom and virtue,
example of all perfection, came down from Heaven that He might teach
us poor, ignorant men.   And in doing so He did not use great subtility,
nor did He address us in mysterious ways.   No; He taught us our lesson in short sentences, and very plain words, at the same time giving
us in His own blessed humanity a pattern to go by.   He is Himself our
book—open, easy to read and written with plainest letters.   And His
lesson—it reads thus: "Learn of Me, because I am meek and humble of
heart."

What lesson could be more easily taught; what lesson more easily
understood and learned than this? So, let us study it diligently, reading
it over and over again, putting it in practice in our daily lives, keeping
ever before our eyes as our model the life of Christ, so rich in the virtues
He would teach us.   His whole life was kindly and gently humble, and
all His words ever taught this same holy lesson.. It was for the sake
of this virtue that he chose for His disciples and pupils men in a lowly
state of life, apt to learn meekness and humility.   Especially to elevate
this lesson to the highest place, did He choose for His beloved mother one
who, as she conceived Him in her womb, could say: "He hath regarded
the humility of His handmaid."   (Luke i, 48.)   And in today's Gospel,
He thanks His Father for this same virtue: "I confess to Thee, O
Father, Lord of Heaven and Earth, because Thou hast hid these things
from the wise and prudent and hast revealed them to little ones" (Matt.

xi, 25) ; that is to say, to the humble.   From all this we conclude, that to the humble-hearted alone is the hidden wisdom of God revealed. Therefore, dear children, that we may the better learn our Lord's lesson and acquire this beautiful virtue of His, let us consider certain signs of real humility, bearing in mind that gentle kindness is ever its close companion.

The first sign is this: A truly humble man never is ashamed to do any outward act because worldlings will think that it disgraces him, for it is a true sign of conversion from a sinful life, and of real pain of heart for past bad conduct, if a man is ready and willing to be thrust backward to the lowest place, so that this may help him to be advanced to true humility of heart and interior subjection of soul.   Whosoever would make progress in God's happy way of perfection, must keep a close watch on himself and avail himself of such opportunities, and for this God will give him such graces as he never had before.

The second sign of real humility, is that one is ready to blame himself to others, to look on all men as his superiors in virtue; one effect of which is to draw men's hearts to him, enabling him to lead them onward in the practice of humility.   And if it sometimes happens that a man is accused of what he is not guilty of, still let him bear himself meekly, and confess that if he happen to be guiltless, it is God alone that has saved him from this sin, as He had forgiven him other sins—the same grace both in pardoning and preventing.

The third work is this: The truly humble soul loves all men alike, showing no partiality for near friends or relatives over poor strangers. All men he loves in God; all are given him by God as his neighbors, and, according to their needs, he loves them all, whether good or bad, not from natural inclination, but rather from Christian principle.

In the fourth place, a truly humble man contents himself with a free and detached spirit; he is content with all circumstances of life.   The merciful God may join him in closest union with another whose heart is entirely given to the world.   In such a case, indeed, we see a man's humility, for he is sunk under God and all creatures, self-effaced in spirit and in act, entirely resigned to his lot for God's sake.

The fifth sign of true humility is patient endurance of suffering, offering everything up for God's glory, and in deep love of God, in single-hearted trust entirely submitting to His will.

Herein you will perceive that progress in humility is marked by patience, by loving abandonment to God in all faith, and by steadfast confidence in Him. In this way the soul grows into a sense of the state of exile that this life really is. A man gains a brighter and brighter consciousness of God as his Creator; and he is granted a complete subjection of his will to God's holy will—all this for the Divine honor and for no selfish ends of his own. That we may thus learn our Saviour's lesson of humility, may God aid us. *Amen.*

The Different Degrees of Spirituality

Synopsis—Beginners are absorbed in external good works, and easily are led astray—Others are quite detached from earthly things, but yet absorbed in the sweetness of devout feelings, and thereby are much hindered—Still other souls rise above this, but are liable to a more subtle spiritual self-indulgence; this is shown by indiscreet mortifications—The real work of perfection is wholly God's, and is done in the hidden life—Examples drawn from vine culture.

SERMON FOR SEPTUAGESIMA SUNDAY.

The kingdom of heaven is like to an householder, who went out early in the morning to hire laborers into his vineyard.—Matt. xx, 1.

Dear children, this householder went out at the first hour, the third hour, and the sixth, and hired laborers at a penny a day. And even when evening was come, he still found men standing idle, and he said to them: Why stand ye here all the day idle? Go ye also into my vineyard and I will give you what is just. Now, dear children, this householder is our Lord Jesus Christ, and His house is eternal life, this earth, purgatory and hell. The heavenly Father saw that human nature had gone astray, leaving His beautiful vineyard sterile and desolate—that vineyard which He had created man to cultivate and make fruitful. To call human nature back again into His vineyard the heavenly Father now goes forth "early in the morning."

Dear children, our Lord Jesus Christ goes forth from the heavenly Father's bosom and yet remains there; and this is one meaning of the words goes forth "early in the morning." But He may be said to go forth also in another sense, namely, in His human nature, that He may again hire us into His holy vineyard. This He does variously at the first, third, sixth and ninth hours. And yet once again He goes forth into the market place of the human race, namely, at the approach of evening, and He finds other men standing there idle. To these He speaks sharply: "Why stand ye here all the day idle? And they answered Him: Because no man hath hired us." Now, these men whom no man has hired, are those who still retain their natural innocence and guilelessness. They may well be called happy, for the eternal God finds them yet unhired; that is to say, unfettered by the world and by created things.

Again, dear children, there are some men who have once been enslaved by the world and by creatures, but have been liberated and are now free; and these are standing idle and unhired from spiritual tepidity and coldness of heart, without love and without grace. And whosoever is without grace stands in nature alone. Let such a one (by an impossibility) do all the good works in the whole world, yet will he, all the same, stand idle and fruitless and empty, helped thereby in no manner whatsoever. Going out "early in the morning" means the going forth of God's grace to men; for the morning puts an end to the darkness of night, and the coming of grace into the soul of man is the dawning of God's day: "Why stand ye here all the day idle?" Go into my vineyard and I will pay you what is right.

It is plain, children, that all these men go into the Lord's vineyard quite variously. Some are beginners. These labor for God with external religious works and according to their own plans, and they continue in that course, doing what they consider great things, fasting, keeping vigils, reciting prayers; at the same time paying little regard to the strictly interior religious life and resting wholly in sensible sweetness of devotion, thereby judging whether they are in God's favor or disfavor. From this state flow evil results—injustice to others, rash judgments, many faults of vanity and pride, bitterness of spirit and obstinacy, enmities and many other defects besides. Thus are they led astray from Divine grace and soon break forth openly into sinful words and deeds. Whosoever finds himself resting on this false foundation should at once take measures to change to the true foundation, which is interior, before he suffers further injury or inflicts it upon those who are his associates.

The second kind of laborers, dear children, who have gone into the Lord's vineyard are those who despise all transitory things and who have quite overcome their sensual appetites; and by these means they have attained to a good degree of virtue. They are absorbed in the joys of interior spiritual exercises, cleaving close to the supreme truth. But they are defective in this; they rest content with these their present consolations; they do not press onward through and beyond all consolations to the possession of God Himself, in Whom alone, and not in His gifts, they should find their resting place.

The third kind of laborers in God's vineyard are those most noble souls, who pass over and beyond all things in search simply of God— men who think of nothing, strive after nothing but God Himself, and God for His own self's sake alone—neither Divine consolations, nor any other outpourings from God, but His own very essential Deity, into which they sink their own existence in single-hearted devotedness. God's honor and praise, the perfecting in them and by them of God's own will—this, and this alone, is the end and object of all their strivings. To suffer all things for His sake, to stand in total abandonment to His providence in all events of life, and to attribute no good thing to their own power or merit, such is their invariable and universal purpose. As water seeks its level, so in their heart's allegiance do all of God's gifts return to Him. They will not tolerate the thought of receiving any gifts from God for their own joy or profit in any wise whatsoever; God alone, God alone is the starting point and the returning point of everything they receive from Him, whether it be a favor for their inner or for their outer existence.

And it is thus that such souls are lifted out of and above themselves into God, their intentions and purposes being singly and solely for Him. But meanwhile human nature must be reckoned with, for a man cannot be totally separated from his natural self; and therefore, whether he will or not, he longs with a natural longing to be happy, even while he would be absorbed in God alone. But this inclination of nature should not be strong in such elect souls; it should be reduced to the smallest possible degree of influence. Effecting this causes suffering in very spiritual men, for they can hardly help being pleasurably absorbed in the good works to which they devote themselves. Hence they are apt to seek for new ways of practicing virtue, with a view to the spiritual joys to be found therein—prayer, meditation, holy tears and many long vigils. And herein, often without realizing it, they go to excess, never getting enough of spiritual sweetness; and when that goes from them, as it surely will, then they are afflicted. They now have an aversion for devout practices and become cold-hearted. The blame is all their own; they have ceased to think of God alone and to seek Him alone; they have drifted back into an attachment to the sweetness of His service. A man must never seek joy in God's gifts; neither in methods of piety, in words and prayers, or in works of zeal. It is not God's gifts, but God's own self that we should seek.

Yes, children, there are some who cannot abide being empty of all spiritual solace and comfort. From this holy emptiness of soul they take refuge, for instance, with the saints and angels of Heaven, whom they appropriate to themselves without due regard to God, and from them they look for spiritual joys. They say, in effect, this favorite saint of mine, this beloved angel, shall be my comfort in preference to all others. Now, this is unfair to God and really gives little rest to the soul, but rather breeds much unrest. Endeavor to be detached entirely from all creatures, whether in Heaven or on earth, except clearly in view of God; lean upon God and upon none other. Once thou hast done that honestly, then thou shalt have learned how rightly to honor all of God's saints. For our beloved saints, are they not continually immersed in the depths of the Divine immensity—in the most holy Trinity?

I say to thee in that truth that God is: If thou wilt become a man after God's will, then all things to which thou cleavest must perish within thee. And this means that thou must not cleave to the graces God grants thee, nor to His Saints as something apart from Himself, nor to anything else; for whatsoever ministereth to thy spiritual joy must be cut off. Before God can perfect within thee His Divine work of light and love, thou must be unencumbered from everything that gives thee comfort except God's own very self.

Children, you are not to suppose that we are forbidden to venerate our dear saints in Heaven, but only to cling to them with a sense of proprietorship—with a selfish purpose of enjoying them. I say to thee that if thou wert enriched with all heavenly graces, and, in addition, wert granted all the merits of all holy men, the moment that thou shouldst appropriate these to thyself in spiritual joy, that moment they would be tainted with thy own personal sinfulness. The true and faithful servant of God goes ever right onward—consolation or no consolation, pleasure or pain, plenty or want—ever right onward through all these things to God's own self. It is by forgetfulness of this that a man will, all unconsciously, stray apart from the true path of Divine wisdom and love, and by returning again to this the only right way, does he attain to perfection.

Children, a really devout man should imitate a laborer in a vineyard who works all day long; and if he must stop to eat at certain intervals, the whole time thus taken up is hardly an hour, while the work absorbs the entire day. He eats because he must have food, for that makes his blood and flesh, bones and marrow, which, as they are consumed by working, must be renewed by eating; but much work and a little eating is his rule for laboring in his vineyard. And in like manner in God's vineyard. When one feels a yearning for the heavenly joy of Divine grace, let him indulge himself a little in it, so that he may be strengthened to work on more courageously, ever giving back to God in thanksgiving the joy that he has received from Him; and repeating this process from time to time, as he feels the yearning for God's joy and the need of its nourishment to strengthen him in his holy labors. The spiritual men who thus deal with God in their interior and external life, humbly accepting and gratefully returning to God all His gifts, constantly become more worthy of them. Such Godlike men would be worthy to feed upon the finest pearls and gold and silver, if these could be turned into food. The best that the world possesses is but their family inheritance—theirs and no one else's. But all worldly treasures are as nothing at all to them, and they are often the poor men of God, trusting, as they must, with all confidence in their heavenly Father's care of them; and He does provide for them—if they were hidden away in the heart of a rock he would provide for them.

Such men are like a vinestock, which outwardly is black, hard, dry and ugly, and, if one went by appearances, would be only fit to chop down and make into firewood. But under this unfavorable appearance are hidden the channels of the sap, and the rich natural forces that give life and sweetness to the noblest fruit of any plant that grows. It is thus with those recollected souls that are at all times sunken so deep in God. Outwardly, they seem dry and dull and useless creatures, for they are humble and retiring, and they appear very insignificant, with neither fine words nor showy works, nor elaborate devotional methods, in every way appearing the least among their fellows. But concealed within their souls are the veins of God's grace. They no longer belong to themselves, but God has made them and their lives and their innermost being His own portion among men.

And now, children, consider how the vine-dresser goes out and prunes his vines, cutting away the wild growth; for if he let it grow on with the useful branches, then the unpruned vine would give him only sour wine. It is thus that true spiritual men must do; they must cut out from their ways and inclinations, and their joys and sorrows, all whatsoever is ill-regulated. Thou must exterminate from thy heart all thy defects; thou canst do it and yet not break thy head or thy bones, for thou shouldst hold back the knife until thou art well advised what thou shouldst prune away. If the vine-dresser is not skillful at his trade, he may cut the wood that bears the grapes instead of the useless and barren branches, and thus injuring, instead of benefiting, the vineyard. Thus act imprudent and ignorant men in the spiritual vineyard. They cut and wound our poor, innocent human nature, while they pass over untouched the evil tendencies rooted in our corrupt human nature. Our nature is in itself noble and good. Why, then, wilt thou hack at it as if it were essentially evil? I say to thee that it may happen, that when thou hast come to the time of gathering the spiritual harvest, namely, when thou hast the grace of a devout, happy and pious life, thou shalt find that thou hast by thy indiscreet mortifications in earlier days destroyed the forces of nature within thee.

After the vine-dresser has pruned his vine he ties it carefully, bending it toward the ground, and then fastens it securely to a stake. And in all this we have the sweet figure of our blessed Lord Jesus Christ in His life and passion, which must be made our only support. Bound fast to Jesus crucified, the superior faculties of our mind are sunk in lowly humility, in His sufferings and death. Our whole interior and external existence is by this means subjected to Him, and that not in mere mechanical imitation, but in true and hearty conformity to His death, each one, according to his state of life, giving Him his senses and his thoughts in entire and constant abandonment. This is the taming of an overfree will under the rule of God's will, in all things inward and outward, exerting every effort to be truly obedient to God, and to respond to His grace, in all work and rest. Then one's humility is so true, that if he had done all the meritorious works of all mankind, and possessed all the inner graces of all saintly men, he would not be spoiled by any sense of proprietorship; his virtues would seem no different to him than if they were the virtues of someone else, and would all be readily attributed to God. In such a soul as that, will God the Father quickly and without hindrance complete His hidden work of perfection. And those who fail to acquire these dispositions will without doubt fail to experience God's perfect regeneration within their souls.

And, again, the vine-dresser digs up the soil about the vine and roots out the weeds; that is to say, the devout man vigilantly searches his soul's very depths, and if he finds spiritual weeds there, imperfect tendencies, whether great or small, he puts in his spade and cuts them out by the root. He thus gives the bright sun of God's grace free entrance to the inmost depths of his being, enlightening and vivifying all his powers. God's grace thus draws up into active fruitful life all the forces of the soul. Ah, dear children, how sweet and nourishing is the fruit of

Divine grace, when we thus give God's sunlight full entrance into our souls by cleaving away all that may hinder it! How beautiful its light and how sweet the fragrance of the flowers it produces, a fragrance which is the antidote to all spiritual poison, and fatal to the presence of the tempting serpent. O children, children, when the beams of God's sunlight are allowed to fall directly on the human soul, they draw the soul's whole life, inner and outer both, upward to Heaven! All that such a soul thinks and does, now tastes of God, so that the evil one and all his poisonous efforts come instantly to naught. If all the devils in hell conspired against that soul, and if all the evil men on earth joined them, they could not harm it, for it thinks and loves and acts only in God, and deeper and deeper into God's life would their machinations drive it. Nay, if such a man were (by an impossibility) sunk even into the pit of hell, he would bring down Heaven there, with God and all His blessedness. And in practical daily life, he is perfectly safeguarded against all dangers that may beset his path.

Now, as the sun of God's holy presence in the soul shines clearer and warmer as time goes on, so the virtues of that soul become riper, and the fruit of holy living is more and more filled with spiritual sweetness; for the hindrances to the Divine influence are lessened continually, just in proportion to the earnestness and discretion of the soul's co-operation. A man's entire spiritual conduct is in a way then made Divine, his chief, and we might say his only, inner conception being God. But this is a state of soul too far beyond ordinary human existence to be capable of description.

Finally the vine-dresser trims away the leaves, to allow the sunlight to complete its work of ripening the grapes. In like manner various devotional helps become after a time of little aid to the soul, such as the usual pious practices and prayers, and remembrances of the saints. But this only happens when God has drawn the soul very deep into Himself, and His grace influences it in a way quite above its natural comprehension. For the glory and the sweetness of God's communion, transcend all purely human methods and mediums of spiritual life, and the soul hardly knows how to distinguish its life from that of God. That the soul's very being should be penetrated through and through by God's sweetness, is His special purpose in this work of sanctification, just as if He were a cask of wine absorbing a little drop of water, until the soul is, as it were, unconscious of a separate life from that of God, unconscious of the lowly human existence to which it belongs. A secret and silent unity of man and God, quite beyond the power of description, is thus produced. Children, one hour, even one moment, of this blissful state of union, is a thousand times more beneficial to the soul and more useful to its fellow-men, redounds a thousand times more to God's honor and glory, than fifty years spent in self-chosen spiritual exercises, even the most approved. May God grant us grace to give Him place for His work within our souls. May we die to all that we should die to, live for all that we should live for, and do everything that His grace demands, in preparation for His Divine regeneration within our souls. *Amen.*

Not Our Own, but God's, Activity Makes Us Perfect

Synopsis—Going out of self and into God—Giving up the joy of virtue for the sake of virtue's self—Danger of self-inspired activity— Christ's passion a meditation safe against pride—Vigor of external zeal not lessened but increased by interior quiet.

SERMON FOR SEXAGESIMA SUNDAY.

The sower went out to sow his seed. And as he sowed, some fell by the wayside and it was trodden down, and the fowls of the air devoured it. And other some fell upon a rock, and as soon as it was sprung up it withered away, because it had no moisture. And other some fell among thorns, and the thorns growing up with it choked it. And other some fell upon good ground, and being sprung up, yielded fruit a hundred-fold.—Luke v, 8.

Dear children, take things as we may, the beginning of a spiritual life is a going forth; thou must undoubtedly go out if thou wouldst ever amount to anything in the Christian state—go forth and out of all self-content, self-conceit, and self-will. Thou must strive to have dear to thyself nothing whatever but God's honor and glory. Mark well: In whatsoever condition of mind or body thou findest thyself, out of that thou must go, whether it be a multitude of companions, or any other comfort of creatures. And this going forth must effect something more than a bodily change; it must be a deep-seated change in thy very soul. If God is ever to do a fruitful work in thee, thy spirit must be cut off and separated from all multiplicity. There is no escape from it; thou must forsake thy own activity, all thy natural faculties, forcibly break asunder the hard bands of nature; go out from thy manners and thy habits and all other such things; for it is clinging to these that especially hinders thy spiritual progress. Do as the ants do; when they have gathered the grains of wheat, they eat away and destroy the living kernel of each grain, lest it should sprout, and thus they save up their store of food. And so must thou destroy the kernel of joy that is in all thy inclinations and affections, lest when thou thinkest thyself making good spiritual progress thou art really near to complete failure. Thou must thus go forth out of all things.

Philosophers tell us that a man's power of going forth lies in his will, though the intelligence invites him to do it. As soon as my mind perceives something good, then the will is informed of it, and forthwith starts away to obtain it and to enjoy it; for it is on account of the good contained in anything that we love it and seek to possess it. Now, this means the good that is in one's own self, as well as that which we may find in other creatures. This is the better activity of the will. For if one's love is false and narrow, one's will does not go out, but would by a bad activity appropriate the desired good selfishly and slothfully. And it is certainly thus that all those persons act who seek themselves in serving God, calculating simply on their own spiritual profit. Their love is untrue and narrow and I would not give a penny for it all.

Dear child, thou must, in the love of thy God, so go out of thyself that thou shalt love Him alone, thinking as little as possible of joy or profit or reward, but only of His goodness and His glory. And, although thou knowest full well that He will recompense thee, yet on that thou must not allow thy mind to dwell, hiding it away as carefully as if thou didst not know it at all. Let nothing whatever but God's honor influence thee; let thy heart melt with zeal for that; forget thyself in that, adverting little to thy own profit in what thou dost for God in soul or body. Otherwise what thou dost is thine and not God's, for thou hast done it and not God. Consider Him always and seek to please Him, never anxiously asking whether or not or how much He will reward thee. Meantime be sure that all that thou thus givest exclusively to Him He will turn back upon thee. The less thou thinkest of thy glory and profit and recompense, the more will He think of thee in regard of all such things. Therefore does St. John say: "Perfect charity casteth out fear." (I John iv, 18.) Men who act in this way know not fear, for they never think of themselves, whether for gain or loss; all such things are shut out of their souls, which know nothing but love. And they are finally rewarded as Simeon was, to whom it was granted to take the infant Jesus in his arms.

But one might object: Is it really right that I should go out of my own activity and become void of all doing, thinking and willing? Is there no danger of my neglecting my bounden duty in this? Should I not even meditate on our Lord's life and passion? On how God in His goodness created me after His own image, and bore my sins on the cross?

And on the joys of eternal life? I answer that this is all good, and well calculated to arouse the love of God in one's soul, and elicit acts of thanksgiving.   But beware lest with these devout thoughts other thoughts and mental images intrude themselves.   St. Paul bids us walk in faith. and his meaning is that we should know God and truth by the feeling of faith.   The very essence of truth must shine into our souls, and that requires that the soul should be totally free from all images of created things.   God forbid that thou shouldst make little of our Redeemer's passion, or draw away thy mind from thoughts of His crucifixion; but rather and on the contrary, having out of supreme love and gratitude stripped thy mind of all images for His sake, then and in that state shouldst thou contemplate Him crucified.   If a man owes me five shillings, he pays me best in one single coin equal to the five shillings. Martha, Lazarus and Mary all knew the same Christ, but each one very differently from the others, and each received Him differently.

Now, take all this teaching, and act as a skillful artist does in painting a picture.   He has skill in coloring, and in drawing and in other branches of his art, but they are all joined by him in a single united effort to produce the figure upon his canvas.

If thou wouldst return God the thanks most pleasing to Him, then keep thy soul void, in order that He may do His perfect work in thee, and that work is to give thee to know Him and love Him disinterestedly. A skillful artist and a rude peasant may stand together gazing upon a picture; but how differently do they appreciate it.   The artist feels at once the full general influence of beauty and power; the peasant carefully counts and names the various figures.   So wilt thou be better thankful to God, if thou wilt empty thy heart to receive Him in all loving simplicity, rather than distract and disturb thyself with studying and numbering thy devotional acts.   What the lower orders of the angels behold in many images, the higher ones enjoy in a single act of contemplation.   Choose for thy meditation those subjects which are most familiar to thee and which profit thee best, for our Lord approves that simple way, meanwhile ever ministering His joy and peace to thy soul.   He seems to forego His own rights for a time, doing so in the interests of brotherly love among His children.   Thus He says in the Gospel: "If thou comest to the altar to offer thy gift, and there thou rememberest that thy brother hath ought against thee, leave thy gift at the altar, and going, first be reconciled to thy brother; and then come and offer thy gift.   (Matt. v, 23-24.)   Nor needst thou fear lest thou shalt lose anything by resting still in contemplation. Give thyself wholly to God in interior abandonment to His will, and be sure that thy external activity shall lose none of its vigor. What better canst thou do than work for God out of the single motive of love? Some think that everything in the spiritual life depends on their own exertions, and they constantly strive to absorb the Divine light into that of their natural reason. Far be this from thee, for that would be to change the uncreated wisdom into that of a poor creature. But do thou just the contrary; by an effort of perfect love cast all thy wisdom deep into God's—the lowest must not presume to master the highest. That we may go out of ourselves in all sincerity of detachment, and thereby prepare our souls as good soil for the seed of God's Word, may God impart to us His grace. *Amen.*

Suffering a Condition for Interior Progress

Synopsis—Interior degeneracy is in pride, in routine and in ingratitude—Progress is seen in earnestness, in humility without limit, absorbtion in Christ's passion, universal love of God's creatures, all crowned by steadfast perseverance—Progress becomes perfection by peculiarly painful trials, a very filial love of God and entire abandonment to Him.

SERMON FOR QUINQUAGESIMA SUNDAY.

With Christ I am nailed to the cross. And I live, now not I, but Christ liveth in me.—Gal. ii, 19.

The holy apostle St. Paul, whose life was a spectacle of suffering for Christ and of conforming to God's will, shows us how a spiritual man should bring forth the fruit of eternal life. It is by being joined close to Christ: "With Christ I am nailed to the cross. And I live, now not I, but Christ liveth in me;" and he adds: "And that I live now in the flesh, I live in the faith of the Son of God, who loved me, and delivered Himself for me." This is salutary counsel. The apostle bids us so to live that Christ may appear in us and be honored in us; that His passion and death may be exhibited in our mortal bodies, to our own profit and that of our neighbor. Now, although we have many afflictions to suffer, and each of these crosses has its length, breadth, depth and height, yet we should clearly understand, that it is only by the cross of Christ's holy humanity that we are saved. To this cross is joined—if we may so express ourselves—the cross of Christ's divinity, all painless and elevated in heavenly joy. And on either side of the cross of Christ stood two others—on the right that of the penitent thief, on the left that of the impenitent thief. These three crosses will serve to illustrate how our sufferings may be made to advance our spiritual welfare.

By the cross of the bad thief, we may understand those persons who belong to some holy state of life, and who are therefore obligated to certain painful outward observances. They have well deserved their sufferings, and yet they are not spiritually helped by them, for they obstinately continue in their wicked self will and fall into other sins. Although nailed to their cross, such persons may suffer eternal loss with the impenitent thief. So that, having borne a heavy burden here, they may bear an infinitely heavier one hereafter.

The height of this cross is spiritual pride and self-sufficiency. They set themselves arrogantly over other men; they are insufferably vain of their austerities. No one is good euough to be their equal in virtue, so they think; and they look with contempt on all who do not practice their manner of life. To such as these St. Augustine wrote: "Dear brothers, rather than have you say or even think that you are better than other men, or any way different from them, I would prefer that you went back into the world. You should say, with Christ, as represented by the prophet: 'I am a worm and no man, the reproach of men and the outcast of the people.' (Ps. xxi, 7.) And you should say, with the poor sinner: I have sinned; Lord, have mercy on me, a sinner."

The depth of this cross is the depth of sinfulness in such a man. His motives are essentially false, and he has never seriously been converted to God, never realized his unmortified state, nor really desired to change for the better. He has rested wholly upon his external observances, and even that very unwillingly and under compulsion. He knows nothing at all of intimate union of the soul with God—thinks and enquires about such things and longs for them as little as does the Grand Turk. To him the real spiritual life is as if it did not exist. If he hears devout men speaking of such things, he understands it as little as an Italian does German. He mumbles his *Pater Nosters,* and he mechanically recites his psalms, and he performs his barren routine of observance of rule, and so he is quite content. As to God uniting Himself intimately to men's soul, what does he care or know about such a thing as that? If by some outward religious practices one may gain some profit or attract some attention, then, indeed, he takes a living interest in the matter. Cross his will, if you dare; he at once is revealed as an ordinary senseless worldling. Hence St. Augustine says, that he knows no man worse than one who falls from a holy state of life, for it often happens that he ends in rejecting the true faith and impugning the teaching of Holy Scripture. Thus deep does such a man sink with the cross to which he is nailed.

The breadth of this evil cross is that it points to the broad and well-trodden road that leads to hell. Men fixed to it live according to the

flesh, caring naught for the sweetness of the spirit. Whosoever lives in
the flesh cannot be pleasing to God. Whosoever treads not the narrow
way that leads to eternal life, will surely go astray and jeopardize his
eternal welfare. These men are self-seekers, and they are self-opinion-
ated in everything. They must be favored in everything; they must be
continually dispensed from the Lord's counsels of perfection; in one
word, their whole object in life is never to suffer. But this cross they
must suffer, whether they will or no—sharp pangs of conscience. For
they can have no trust in God, because they have rejected and despised
Him; nor in the world, for the world, in turn, despises them. Ah, dear
children, they have, indeed, a hard life and carry a painful cross! They
would be without any suffering, and yet they have the bitterest kind.
Add to this the forebodings of eternal suffering if they do not return to
God.

And that brings us to consider the length of this cross. This is shown
when its votaries persevere in vice even to the end, which comes from
their ingratitude. They have received many great graces from God, the
like of which, if given to persons living in the world, would have been
gratefully received by them. But all these graces they have wilfully
rejected; they have disregarded God's many inner admonitions, even
sometimes being themselves amazed at their own hardness of heart.
They have not turned to God, and have finally reached that dreadful
state spoken of by St. Paul: "It is impossible for those who were once
illuminated, have tasted also the heavenly gift, and were made partakers of the Holy Ghost, have moreover tasted the good Word of God,
and the powers of the world to come, and are fallen away; to be renewed
again to penance; crucifying again to themselves the Son of God, and
making Him a mockery." And the apostle adds a comparison: "For the
earth that drinketh in the rain which cometh often upon it, and bringeth
forth herbs meet for them by whom it is tilled, receiveth blessings from
God. But that which bringeth forth thorns and briars, is reprobate, and
very near unto a curse, whose end is to be burnt." (Heb. vi, 4-8.)
Which all means this: These men who have been given so many graces,
who have been favored with so many marks of God's special love, and
who have wilfully refused Him their heart's allegiance and persevered
in their wickedness—it is to be feared that they will finally suffer God's
eternal anathema. See to it, my dear children, that you do not allow
yourselves to be fixed to this cross of eternal condemnation, lest you
remain hanging there till the end.

The cross of the thief at the right hand is good, for he has made it fruitful unto eternal life. It serves to illustrate the resolute earnestness of those who have entered upon a life of penance, turning away from the world and from all sinfulness with heartfelt sincerity. They have regarded it as a favor to suffer very painfully for their former sins, thus atoning for the free rein they once gave to their fleshly passions and to their proud self-will. All this they have now quite and entirely given up for the sake of God, and they are content to suffer whatever penalties God may inflict on them. To them the cross is not only salutary; it is also comforting, sweet and well beloved. The cross brings to them, as it did to the good thief, strong faith joined to an unshaken confidence in God's unspeakable love and mercy. Ah, my dear children, what greater good could the dying thief ever have gained in this poor, fleeting life than to hear those welcome words: "Amen, I say to thee, this day shalt thou be with Me in Paradise." (Luke xxiii, 43.) And what more consoling words could a soul so well disposed, so truly converted, ever hear than these: "Come to Me all ye that labor and are heavy burdened, and I will refresh you?" (Matt. xi, 28.) Which means that I will receive and embrace you by My grace, assist you in times of trial, and aid you to bear your burdens; and after brief intervals of spiritual toil, will continually and sweetly strengthen you.

The depth of this cross represents humility without limit. By this virtue a man never rates himself higher than others, and sees no one's faults but his own. He is like the good thief, who freely confessed that he suffered justly for his crimes. A good man, therefore, amid the acutest pains, willingly owns that he deserves yet more for his sins. All the sufferings of earth and hell, he really thinks, are not enough to atone for his former wickedness. Such a man can despise no one but himself, nor judge and condemn anyone except himself. And this humble state of the soul is the blossom and fruit of this tree of the cross.

Its height is elevation of spirit, withdrawal from outward things, and contemplation of heavenly ones. This means that we should train and direct our souls upward to thoughts of the eternal life, steering clear of all bodily delusions. We should meditate on the life and character of our beloved Lord, the soul's rich mine of all virtues—His sufferings and His bitter death, His resurrection, His ascension and His glory in the Kingdom of Heaven. This occupation of mind it is that makes our cross very light, as it did that of the good thief, who was thinking of Heaven and longing for it when he prayed: "Lord, remember me when Thou shalt come into Thy kingdom." (Luke xxiii, 42.)

The breadth of this cross is universal and true-hearted love of God and creatures; by which a man is ever inspired to pray, not only for himself, but for all men, even for his very enemies.   His prayers know no bounds. His kind feelings are lavished upon all men.   And his special task is to appease the wrath of God aroused against men who have dishonored Him.   This is the love spoken of by St. Peter (I Peter iv, 8) and by our Lord about Mary Magdalene as covering a multitude of sins: "Many sins are forgiven her, because she hath loved much." (Luke vii, 47.)

The length of this cross is perseverance and the increase of good works, for such men are never done doing good.   And they practice their virtues in such good order and with such prudence, that in all things they may put off the old man and clothe themselves with the new man, newly created by God in the righteousness and holiness of truth.   By this means their inner man is from day to day renewed, and they press onward through all sorrow, pain and opposition, so that they may truly say with St. Paul: "That which is at present momentary and light of our tribulation, worketh for us above measure exceedingly, an eternal weight of glory.   While we look not at the things which are seen, but at the things which are not seen.   For the things which are seen are temporal; but the things which are not seen are eternal." (II Cor. iv, 17-19.)

The third cross is the cross of Christ.   This means the perfect man, to whom the heavenly Father imparts a peculiar glory and honor in union with His only begotten Son.   To such men He sends many peculiar sufferings, contradictions, troubles and various other crosses. To them he grants the privilege of drinking the same chalice that His beloved Son drank, as our Lord foretold to His blessed apostles John and James: "Can you drink the chalice that I shall drink?"   They say to Him: "We can."   He saith to them: "My chalice, indeed, you shall drink." (Matt. xx, 22-23.)   As if he would say (for they had been contending about the first places in His kingdom) : If you would become God's best and most favored friends, then make up your minds to endure the greatest opposition, for the disciple is not above his Master.   If it was necessary for Christ to suffer and to carry the cross in order to enter into His Father's kingdom, so without any doubt every friend of God must endure suffering.

The depth of this cross is a filial fear of God, by which these men give themselves up wholly into His hands, and have an anxious care lest they may offend Him.   Its height is the true hope of finally coming to eternal bliss.   This is no vain trust in their own merits or in their devout life, but is rooted in the humility of a firm faith in God, and entire surrender to His infinite goodness—a trust that shall never be confounded, for it is such as St. Paul describes: "The charity of God is poured forth in our hearts by the Holy Ghost, Who is given to us." (Rom. v, 5.) The breadth of this cross is charity unfeigned toward God, toward self and toward every man for God's sake. Such men diligently cultivate unity of spirit in the bonds of peace, being ever on the watch against bitterness of heart, anxious to serve everybody and to be hurtful to none. Gladly do they bear adversity, if they can but thereby lead souls back to God. The length of this cross is the lifting upward of their thoughts to eternal life, for which they will cheerfully suffer every pain. Whatsoever God shall allot to them in time or in eternity, that is the most pleasing to them—let Him do or not do, place them here or place them there, it is all one; repining or contradiction is quite unknown to them. They can in all sincerity make Christ's words to His Father their own: "Not as I will, but as Thou wilt." (Matt. xxvi, 39.) Their sharpest pain is the thought that they cannot totally uproot their own will, being yet subject to some human weaknesses. O, how happy are these men! And how fruitful a tree is their cross, not only for themselves, but for all Christendom.

This cross leads them on to the ineffable cross of the Divine nature, as St. Paul wished his converts: "That Christ may dwell by faith in your hearts; that, being rooted and founded in charity, you may be able to comprehend with all the saints what is the breadth, and length, and height, and depth." (Eph. iii, 17-18.) The length is God's endless eternity; the breadth is the immensity of His goodness and gentleness, poured out and to be poured out upon all men and creatures; the height is His infinite power; the depth is the abyss of His eternal wisdom. But whosoever would attain to the cross of God's Divine nature, must first be conformed to the cross of His humanity. Round about this cross are gathered all those who lead a truly spiritual life, as we have already explained. They must strictly abstain from all works of the flesh, which God abhors, and they must have an earnest love of all holy living, their souls' hands being, as it were, actually nailed to God's Divine cross. They must, furthermore, constantly strive to fulfill God's will, steadfastly fix their thoughts upon Him, and most carefully avoid whatever they perceive to be displeasing in His eyes. And this will stand for the nailing of their right foot to the cross of God's nature. Again, they must learn to choose between two joys; namely, never to be drawn into the unhappy joy of this world, and never to refuse the joyful misery of God's service. If they choose wisely, then are they fastened by their left foot to the cross of the Divine nature. Yet again, they must have a profound sympathy for God, on account of the dishonor that has been done Him from the beginning of the world until now, and that shall yet be done Him even to the end by all mankind, including the wickedness of those whose state of life has called for the highest virtue. And they must include in this their compassion for God's dishonor; namely, that which is suffered for His sake by His beloved friends who have rallied to the side of Christ crucified; for them also must they wish to suffer, that God's glory may be increased in their lives. Such as these will He guard as He does the apple of His eye, for whosoever does injury to them does it to God Himself. That we may thus be nailed to the cross of Christ's humanity, and that we may finally be brought to the eternal vision of His unveiled divinity, may the almighty and the all-holy Trinity mercifully grant. *Amen.*

Gradations of Merit

Synopsis—Remarks on the perverse ingratitude of sinners—First grade of merit is religious fear of hell, forming an unstable condition of virtue and beset with many dangers—Second, fear of purgatory, and is far in advance of the first; but is mercenary and lacks whole-heartedness—Third class is made up of souls determined to win heaven by entirely generous devotion to God—Some of these unconsciously are self-interested—Perfect gratitude finishes their course.

SERMON FOR ASH WEDNESDAY.

Convert us, O Lord, to Thee, and we shall be converted.—Lamentations v, 21.

God is very pitiful of poor human nature, and He never ceases His endeavors to convert us, always looking out for our acceptance of His loving invitations. Some He calls by such visitations as sickness or poverty, or the like misfortunes; others He would draw to Him by the teaching and example of good men; some by His interior admonitions; some by force, as in St. Paul's case; now it is a severe way; again it is a gentle way that He uses to arouse men's consciences.

As to what hinders men's turning to God, we notice three things: Love of this transitory existence, greediness for worldly possessions, and desire of sensual indulgence. For some are infatuated by the honors of this world and set their hearts on temporal riches, so that they may gratify the lusts of the flesh. After they have persisted a while in this wickedness, they become hard-hearted and unresponsive to grace, even ready to undergo any toil or suffering to satisfy their passions. St. Gregory bids us look at the example of the people of Israel: They yearned for the flesh-pots of Egypt, which they had enjoyed only after most painful labor. They preferred this, with slavery, to the heavenly bread God gave them in the wilderness, full of every sweetness. Ah, my dear children, how sad a lesson is this! God had lovingly led this people out from bondage, showing forth for their sake His great power, and working many wonders, all His affection and all His mighty works having no other object than to turn their hearts sincerely to Him, and to cause them to observe His commandments. And behold, children, all this they regarded not, but quickly went back to their former evil ways and sinful pleasures. They revolted against Moses, God's friend and their appointed leader; they murmured and resisted him, now in one way and again in another. Until, at last, our loving Lord became impatient with them, and scourged them with serpents and with fire, and gave them over to the will of their enemies. And of all those who had journeyed into the wilderness, He allowed but two to enter the land that He had promised them.

Ah, how many are there among us, whom God with all power and mercy has delivered from the slavery of sin and evil habits and led toward a true conversion, so that we might lead a Godly life, according to His teaching and His Son's example! And we have but put on an appearance of conversion, outwardly doing things that might make one think that in all truth we were sincerely turned away from our former vicious practices. But how pitiful it is that this is all outward show. Inwardly we still long for the flesh-pots, secretly and weakly yielding to our bodily appetites, and if these enjoyments are now less accessible than before, we give ourselves up to murmurings wholly unworthy of religions men. And what is yet worse, we will not be content with the worldly goods that belong to our state of life, but whatever luxuries we hear of the rich enjoying, we, poor beggars, must crave to possess. Nothing pleases us. Our heavenly Father feeds and clothes and shelters our bodies; He gives our souls sweet and nourishing spiritual food—all in vain. He cannot win our love; we will not give ourselves up to Him in a deep and true conversion. But, on the contrary, we become too often a scandal to our brethren by our perverse discontent. And as we read that God destroyed from the earth certain leaders of the discontented Israelites, so does He sometimes similarly act among us.

These are often no better than openly wicked men, as is shown if you cross their will. They seem to be really possessed and driven onward, in their evil course, by Satan. Sometimes it happens that they get all that they want and rest quite satisfied with their success; and that is a plain sign of their final loss; the evil one has been given entrance, their hearts are hardened. No real peace or joy can be theirs, however, for their souls are sick with sin, and the enemy casts his fatal net about them. But let them make a mighty effort—naught else will suffice; let them painfully enter into themselves, cast away all that they have wrongfully possessed or coveted of this world's joys; let them humbly crave pardon of all whom they have injured; let them beg the prayers and the help of all who are fit to instruct them how to be freed from Satan's slavery; and thus, with hearts full of contrition, let them return again to God's service.

Alas, my dear children! What can we say of our conversion to God nowadays? It is for the most part only in external signs. Taking us all in all, we are like the fig tree that the Lord cursed: We bear leaves, indeed, but not fruit—not more than one in a hundred is a thoroughly converted man. We are self-seekers; we enjoy all sorts of material conveniences and the pleasures of this life, sometimes more abundantly than if we were still living among worldlings; for those who live in the outer world must, with all their luxuries, suffer besides many anxieties. We have become so spiritually enfeebled, that we have no will to suffer pain of any kind. If we can but imagine a new comfort, we must forthwith have it. If the superiors of the community will not give it, then we go to our friends and relatives outside. Complaints by letters and by word of mouth, every species of endeavor for a soft and easy life—all this goes on endlessly. Alas! shall we never ask ourselves why we came into religion? Shall we forever remain in this childish self-indulgence? But we now conclude our lament over this sad state of things, lest it should detain us the whole day long.

There are three things that make sin a most detestable evil. The first is that offending God is monstrous and shameful—the only thing that can possibly be offensive to Him is sin. The man who lives in sin, if he would but look into his condition, would be overwhelmed with horror at the intolerable and disgraceful state he has brought his soul into. The second is the shortness of the sinner's time—the swift approach of his death. The third is the horror that must fill him at the thought of the eternal death of his soul in hell. As to the reasons for a sinner's conversion, they are one of these three: His sins grievously afflict him because he dreads eternal damnation; or because he begins to long for the happiness of Heaven; or because his heart is touched at the thought of God's infinite love for him. These are the inner sources of all conversion to God.

The sinner recalls to his mind the principles of his Christian faith: There is a God, and He is all powerful and all just, and the dread of His judgment fills the sinner's soul with anguish. And, again, his faith tells him that God is all merciful, and that a virtuous life is rewarded with a blissful eternity; and now a joyous hope begins to glow within his soul. But, furthermore, he remembers our blessed Redeemer, and how God, pitying our fallen state, became man for man's salvation. This lights the holy fires of love and of gratitude in his heart, and he longs for the privilege of eternally serving and loving so good a God. When this noble sentiment inspires him, neither the fire of hell nor the joys of Heaven are the motives of his repentance. The fire of love devours every other feeling, and carries every thought upward into union with the Divine will. It is to heavenly love that he turns as the one source of all his happiness. And herein is found love rightly so called. The other two motives of conversion—fear of hell and longing for Heaven—have some mixture of self-love in them, and are not so pleasing to God as the third. Let us now consider each of these three motives more in detail.

Three kinds of men are converted by fear of hell. The first kind fear its pains taken by themselves, without fearing the God whose penalties they are. These are gross and bad natures, and if they should die with no better mind than this, they cannot be saved. The fear of death, sure to come, but the time of it never known beforehand, haunts them and tortures them with inward anguish, and finally drives them to repentance and reform of life. Feeling that the ordinary life of this world is too dangerous for them, these men sometimes enter religious communities. And their fatal error is that they think that if they but refrain from mortal sin in their holy order, they will surely escape eternal loss; that is the whole basis of their conduct, namely, to avoid mortal sin. All sorts of venial faults, however, they do not dream of avoiding, and have no sorrow whatever for committing them. Nor do they for a moment think it necessary to atone for their past mortal sins by true-hearted works of penance. No desire to advance in the practice of virtue actuates them, the reason being that there is little love in their souls. When they go to confession and perform the penance imposed on them, they think that they may now dismiss the fear of hell, and that gives them content. They thus continue cold and slothful, vain, neglectful, and frivolous, self-indulgent and ever seeking after superfluities; consulting their personal advantage in everything, only limited in careless living by the need of keeping up good appearances. Interiorly their thoughts and affections are ruled by self-will and pride, holding them back against all generous impulses, meantime showing an exterior decency of behavior. If one opposes them, they are irritable and impatient. If you would advise them, they are obstinate and act ugly toward you. They can talk wisely, and often have good mind, and this they would have to take the place of virtue. If things go well with them, they yield to excessive joy; if ill, they are sunk in despondency. They sit in judgment on other men, pointing out their defects very freely, and this they do by way of justifying their own. Such, then, are the characteristics in heart and in conduct of this class of souls. They are, nevertheless, on their guard against committing mortal sins, and yet ere they are well aware of it they fall into them most miserably.

Such men, all content as they are with an exterior conversion to God, are, as we have said, found in some religious communities and are an intolerable burden to them. The fervent members would rather have savage lions and bears living among them. It is by their means that our mortal enemy, the devil, can work his purposes, for in reality they are his slaves, no matter how many holy vestments they may wear. But, as they are very unstable of purpose, it is always doubtful whether or not they will continue in the community. The evil one keeps them in or sends them out, as suits his ends. If it happens that they return to right reason and would then wish to remain in the convent, they soon begin to realize, that they run as much risk of grave sin and of an unhappy death in a religious community, as they did when living in the world. Then they grow doubtful and undecided, exceedingly impatient and distressed. And now if they have no friends who will plead for them with God, none to help rescue them, they will surely fall into deadly sins, and will finally forsake their devout associates. They say to themselves: When I was in the world and in my sins, I had at least good hopes of salvation by entering a religious community; but now that I am bad in spite of these holy surroundings, what is to become of me? Some of them, fallen thus into despair and mistrusting God's goodness, leave the community, and are immediately sunken into their former vicious conduct; for they are too proud to reveal their temptations to anyone, and thus they act hastily and without good counsel. And now they go on from bad to worse, they rush headlong into the embrace of the enemy of their souls, giving themselves up to every evil propensity, at first secretly, but soon openly, until some of them are beside themselves with the resistless torrent of their vices and temptations. It may be that they escape the very worst consequences of their sinfulness and receive the sacraments at the point of death; but at the last it is extremely doubtful whether their end is good or bad. Perhaps an all-merciful God, will grant them an altogether unusual grace of sorrow and love during their last hours; then they, indeed, escape hell; but their purgatory will be long and bitter; thank God that it is not everlasting. And when Heaven is reached, their spirits will be placed below the least of the angels; for it was not out of love that they returned to God. Those who are saved, as it were, by mere compulsion of anguish and dread, must be content to be placed in the company of the least in the Kingdom of Heaven. Those who turn to God merely out of fear, and who do not serve Him for love first or last, should not enter a convent. It is better for them to remain in the world in some worthy state of life. The visitations of Providence will there chasten them and elevate their motives. Meantime they bring no shame on a devout community, nor inflict any injury on its religious observance. It is a mighty and a difficult task to change such creatures into men of interior spirit. And now if this is the sad condition of men who would, indeed, keep out of grave sin, but yet only half-heartedly, what must we think of those unhappy souls who constantly wallow in wickedness, and never give a thought to repentance?

The other class of men not only fear hell, but they have a lively dread of the fires of purgatory. They, indeed, avoid mortal sin very carefully, but they go beyond that; they diligently avoid committing venial faults. They sigh and weep over their former wickedness; they do painful penance. And yet if they die in no better state of virtue than this, they will suffer a long and painful purgatory, for they have so far been actuated only by self-love and not purely by the love of God. Yet we must know that their purgation will be a hundred times less painful than that of the cowardly souls above described. But how much better is it to do penance out of love and not by constraint of fear only! The souls we are now describing have not been loyal in all single-heartedness to the Supreme Good that God is; their inspiration has not been a pure-motived trust in the goodness and sufferings and merits of the Son of God. This lack of whole-heartedness they must painfuly make up in purgatory; that done and over, they shall be introduced into the second choir of the blessed spirits of Heaven. And one reason why they are a hundred-fold more generously rewarded than the others, is because they have left edifying examples of virtue to their neighbor.

The third class not only fear the pains of hell and purgatory, but they earnestly purpose to go straight to God without any purgatory at all.

They, therefore, dread and avoid not alone grave sins, not alone venial sins—our daily petty transgressions—but they anxiously watch against the very least imperfections. How earnestly do they not strive that the searching fires of purgatory shall find no material in them upon which to feed! To the very best of their power they conquer depraved nature, now by penitential exercises, again by accepting thankfully all painful happenings, and also by applying themselves to every sort of good works. These are more pleasing to God than the former class. And yet they, too, must suffer purgatory, for there has been a mixture of self-love in their motives. Their only and all-controlling motive was not God's honor. But their purgatory shall be much shorter, because real love has had a place in their virtuous lives. When their purgatory is done and over they shall be enrolled in the third choir of angels; namely, those that are specially called the Powers or virtues, for they have labored hard to overcome their self-indulgence. Hence their place is higher than that of the others. So far we have been considering only the first degree of conversion to God—that of souls moved by some sort of fear or anxiety for themselves. Of all of these it may be said that they enter into external bliss by the left-hand gate of Heaven.

Another class of men are converted to God by desire of eternal glory, and these enter Heaven by the right-hand gate. They are in general of a naturally joyous disposition. To them the joys of eternal life are a more powerful inducement to virtue than the pains of eternal loss. If the happiness of this transitory life, they say, is so sweet, what must be the everlasting bliss of Heaven? Such thoughts draw them away from earthly pleasure. They readily forget the allurements of the world, and soon begin to serve God earnestly, moved by nobler motives than the other classes we have considered, whose primary motive is fear. Once they have turned to God and have joined a religious community, or entered some other worthy Christian state, they advance immediately in virtue. They not only avoid all sin, whether mortal or venial, but they eagerly embrace every opportunity of serving God, determined to become perfect. As to heavy labors or deep afflictions, nothing of all this can hinder them, for they are ever absorbed in the thought of eternity. They are very receptive of Divine grace, and grow more and more so every day; and if they persevere until death, they are given a place among a yet higher choir of the heavenly spirits; this is the reward of their great earnestness. And yet they do not entirely escape the pains of purgatory, for they have sought their own happiness rather than the honor of God purely and simply, even though this was more or less the result of inexperience and inadvertence. If ever they emerge out of this imperfect condition, it will be by means of temptations manfully resisted, and sufferings patiently endured. Only these sore trials can reveal to them how much they have sought themselves, and how unconsciously they have forgotten God as the one only motive of their lives. Their painful probation must be long and wearisome. It is a tiresome and interminable task to leave oneself, to renounce self incessantly. It is indescribably hard to love God above one's own self, and to love one's neighbor as one's self; that is to say, in the meaning of those words when applied to a perfect life. But if they approach this state closely, and die in the full ardor of this love, then are they enrolled in the fifth angelic choir, that of the Principalities. Still, even these must suffer some small detention in purgatory, for their love is hardly quite and entirely pure.

If before death they progress yet further in God's righteousness, suffering many miseries and the contempt of men in a yet greater degree, and with motives still more purified, until at last they are unmoved by any and all pains and temptations, and if they finally are able completely to renounce all selfhood, all spirit of proprietorship, O, how happy are they! Penance is perfected; peace reigns supreme; they are masters of all temptations. And at death they are introduced into that choir of the angels called the Dominations.

The third kind of conversion is that of souls who realize how very good God has been to them, all undeserving as they are. A powerful impulse of gratitude possesses them, and an admirable yearning to serve God perfectly and forevermore. Not knowing what to do that God may best be honored by them, they cry out to God in deep anguish of heart, saying, with St. Paul: "Lord, what wilt Thou have me to do?" Acts ix, 6.) Ah, how gladly would I know Thy will, what I am to do or suffer or give up for Thy sake! O, grant me that knowledge, for I promise Thee that I will not spare myself any trial or pain to fulfill Thy purpose! Hell has no terrors for such souls, Heaven has no joys, until they know God's designs with them. Deep sorrow they have for their sins, yet not on account of the pains of hell, but out of downright love of God—that love to which they know they once were faithless. They cannot forget their past infidelity to so good a God, and they are at a loss to find penances severe enough to offer in atonement. They even imagine that if they had God's power over themselves, they would cast themselves into hell. Now, it must be affirmed of such souls, that God will not condemn them to any punishment in purgatory whatsoever, for the reason that they have so upright a purpose to condemn themselves with absolute justice, doing penance to the uttermost limit of their ability. If such a man had been guilty of the sins of all other men put together, God would forgive him everything the instant he had attained this state of perfect love. If he dies in these dispositions, we repeat that he shall have no purgatory, but shall be quickly transported into the seventh choir of the angelic host, that of the Thrones, for he is become, indeed, a throne of God and a vessel of election.

But, supposing these men to make yet further progress in holy love before death, then they are placed among the Cherubim. They can praise God with the prophet: "My heart is ready, O God; my heart is ready." (Ps. lvi, 8.) I am ready for joy or sorrow, to do or leave undone, according to Thy will—everything for Thy will and nothing for mine, in time and in eternity. And if death is yet further postponed, and such a soul makes yet greater progress in Divine love, then is he fit for the company of even the Seraphim. He exclaims, with St. Paul: "Who shall deliver me from the body of this death" (Rom. vii, 24), that I may live with Christ? As to their neighbor, such men say with the same apostle, and in all sincerity: "I wished myself to be an anathema from Christ for my brethren." (Rom. ix, 3.) This refers to the fruit of Divine grace they would help their brethren to enjoy, even at their own expense, and it is a disinterestedness of soul exceedingly pleasing to God. For now God, seeing them so ready to advance His kingdom in men's hearts, descends into their own in a most intimate union, so that the apostle's words may be made their own: "And I live, now not I, but Christ liveth in me." (Gal. ii, 20.) May God grant us to be thus converted. *Amen.*

True and False Spirituality Compared

*Synopsis—Piety to men's eyes and self-indulgence to God's—Hot and
cold by turns in endless succession; this results in final forgetfulness of God—The worst state is a false quiet of souls, cherishing
a state of mental blindness and stagnation as that of a divine
prayer—What supernatural quiet of soul is, as compared with
the false and natural—The errors and delusions incident to the
latter.*

SERMON FOR THE FIRST SUNDAY OF LENT.*

Thou shalt walk on the asp and the basilisk; and thou shalt trample under foot
the lion and the dragon.—Ps. xc, 13.

Thus does the Holy Spirit address devout, spiritual men; and we may
use these four beasts to typify four great delusions, four subtle temptations in the spiritual life.

The asp, or snake, represents the devil and his more secret attempts
to ruin the soul, which are also signified earlier in the same Psalm:
"Thou shalt not be afraid of the terror of the night," referring to the
nocturnal terrors which beset beginners in God's service.

By the second beast, the basilisk, we may understand impurity. For
the basilisk of fable was so venomous that even to look upon it was to
die instantly—just as the soul dies that dallies wilfully with the occasions of unchastity. Again, the prophet in the same Psalm says that
the true friend of God shall "not be afraid of the arrow that flyeth in

---

*This sermon serves to refute all accusations made against Tauler of favoring
false quietism. Whatsoever he says in other sermons about the passive state of
the soul and the inopportuneness of external works in the highest contemplative
state, is to be understood in the light of these explanations of false passivity. No
doubt some of his expressions are in other sermons obscure and capable of being
misunderstood, but not in this sermon. It covers the whole debatable ground; it
is as plain as day, and the doubtful passages found elsewhere in his discourses
must be adjusted to what is given here, which is incapable of any meaning but
the Catholic one. And in saying this of Tauler we say what might apply to all
or nearly all the orthodox mystical authors, nearly every one of whom, including
St. John of the Cross and St. Teresa, stands in need of similar adjustments and
reconciliations of meaning.—(*Translator's Note.*)

the day." He means that those who enter upon a devout life will be assailed by open enemies of chastity, striving first to corrupt their heart, and then to sully their outward conduct.

By the third beast, the dragon, we mean love of money, elsewhere called by the Psalmist "the business that walketh about in the dark"—the specter of greed. For this ugly vice may take a spiritual form, as when God's truth is sold for a price by its teachers or by learned men. By the fourth beast, the lion, we understand spiritual pride, "the invasion, or the noonday devil." St. Paul thus describes him: "For satan himself transformeth himself into an angel of light." (II Cor. xi, 14.) Under this disguise the evil one openly and grievously deceives men, watching till they have gone on well for a while, and then leading them astray by some wickedness under the appearance of good—good works done against good order, or fasting and vigils obstinately persisted in against obedience, and thereby turned into evil.

Let us consider the significance of each of these beasts; and first, the asp, or snake, a creature naturally hateful, creeping silently to its deadly work. This means the insinuating temptations that afflict devout men, who are self-indulgent in eating and drinking and lodging and all personal comforts. These will not tolerate a hard manner of living. Both to themselves and to others they are soft and good-natured, and in a scheming way manage to enjoy all sorts of conveniences. But, like a snake, they turn venomously on those who are different-minded, and who hinder their self-indulgence; they condemn them for singularity; and, while pretending to a kindly disposition, they yet violate charity. They gratify every natural inclination, secretly if need be, ever obstinately following their own will. Because they may happen to belong to a devout community and can count many years of external piety free from gross sinfulness, they imagine that God will condone their enjoyment of worldly relaxations. Nearly all Christians living in the world are in our days subject to this delusion, and the same is to be said of not a few living in the religious state. But alas, they slip almost unknowingly into mortal sin, open or secret, doing deadly harm to their own souls and to those of their soft-natured associates.

By the basilisk we may understand men outwardly spiritual, but interiorly addicted to impurity. In dress and manners they are classed as edifying Christians, but God sees that their minds are filled with unchaste desires. This state comes from their performing good spiritual exercises without the right interior dispositions. The devil, therefore, finds the door open. They now and again fall into impurity, sometimes secret, even sometimes open. Notice in them that they are variable in their moods, and that they are keen observers of other men's sins. How different is a true Christian; steady-minded, simple-hearted, disinclined to watch his neighbors, and drawn by God's interior light to an intimate union with Him—a condition wholly unknown to the other class Notice in them, again, a fertile imagination, dressing up their musings on high spiritual matters, in pretentions and winning words; meanwhile void themselves of inner taste for such things, while vainly trying to create it in others. The really devout man has an infused wisdom; he knows truth easily and teaches it fruitfully, all in simple words; treating not of lofty and difficult things, more calculated to mislead than enlighten, but giving plain and useful instruction for an interior life. The false spirit is the reverse of simple; it is, besides, quarrelsome, and readily attacks the teaching of others, no matter how admirable it may be. Such men do little that is praiseworthy, for they are quickly wearied with works of zeal. And, whatever they may do, they are puffed up with spiritual pride. See the difference: The right-minded Christian ever blossoms out into universal love for all in Heaven or on earth; the false-minded has some favorite or other; but at the bottom he loves but one single man, and that is his own beloved self, whom he esteems the wisest and best of mankind. He would have everybody follow him in all he teaches and does, and no one else, and if he notices that you follow anyone else, he is full sure that you are wrong. He yields to his appetites in excess; makes little of venial sins; he is not fair toward his neighbor; he has no real humility; toward the poor and unfortunate he is not kind or pitying, and in his heart of hearts he has no real virtue nor love of God. But let us be on our guard, lest we look around us and judge anyone to be thus miserably placed; let us rather sit in judgment on ourselves. Let us fix our eyes on Christ as our model, who offered Himself up, body and soul, for all mankind. So far have we considered the kind of temptation typified by the basilisk, namely, that of interior and external impurity. It is rooted in a false spirituality, fair-appearing outwardly, but with no Divine spirit within, being infected with sensuality in the inner springs of life.

The dragon may be taken to mean a yet worse condition, namely, that of men whose piety is infected with a sort of spiritual avarice, shown in four different ways. Some of these have an inordinate desire for bodily relaxation and creature comfort, which consumes them like a fever.

They must also know about everything, talk about everything, oblivious only of themselves. They encumber their souls with the care of things which concern them not at all; you may distress them with any trifling matter; their minds teem with useless anxieties—now about this, again about that. All the day long they are entangled in other people's affairs; sleeping and waking, they are distraught with cares. All this may not mean mortal sin, but it is yet seriously hurtful to the interior spirit.

A second kind of spiritual avarice is like a fever which returns every other day; that is to say, an alternation of too much fervor and too much indifference. It is the disease of men who, having received God's grace, presently feel the lack of the sweetness of devotion. Then they waver in fidelity, and beat about for one and then another practice of penance to recover it. They resolve to keep silence; that failing, they will try pious conversation; they resolve to join a certain order, and soon they would choose a different one; at one time they purpose to practice poverty, at another to retain their earthly goods; they plan a long pilgrimage; they aspire to become hermits; they purpose to prepare for holy communion, and presently forget all about it; now they will devote themselves to pious reading, and soon will change it for meditation. All this endless change comes from inconstancy of heart; it results from an extravagant esteem for the temporal and external side of religion, instead of the simple love of God in all things inward and outward, for that would free the soul from all inconstancy.

And even when the thought of God is present in such minds, it is too often held subordinate to that of self-chosen pious observances, and this is a yet worse sort of inconstancy of heart. Corrupt nature may easily mingle its influences with really religious ones, and that so imperceptibly that they remain for a time unobserved. Such men choose now one, and again another confessor. They are forever seeking advice, but very seldom do they follow it, often quickly forgetting it. If you reprove them they resent it; and yet they are habitually reproving themselves. They have fine spiritual talk, with no interior fruit. They gladly welcome praise for their virtues—even great praise for trifling virtues. All the good they do they publicly parade. Thus they are interiorly vain and empty and lack the savor of virtue. They presume to instruct and guide others, but to be guided themselves they will not tolerate, least of all to be admonished for their faults. Just commonplace self-love dominates their conduct, and hidden pride. This explains their inconstancy.

They ever tread on the brink of grave sinfulness; a single false step casts them downward into hell.

The fourth kind of spiritual avarice arises out of the other kinds, and is yet worse than any of them. From inconstancy of heart toward God comes forgetfulness of Him, disregard of one's self, obliviousness to all truth and virtue, and finally such a condition of error and doubt as to know not what to believe or what to do. Forgetfulness of God soon results in disregard of all devout practices. The least thought of reforming one's life is oppressive. The grossest sins are very likely to follow; soon it is as if God were not known at all. Nor is it easy for such a one to recover grace, unless it may be by taking refuge in thoughts of the passion and death of the ever-merciful Saviour. A man of this sort may stand his ground against open sinfulness, and may even make a career in studies, may be chosen for various offices and the management of business affairs, having an appearance of spirituality and apparent firmness of character. And all this is hurtful to the really interior spirits who may happen to be subject to his jurisdiction. Men like these are often overstrict in enforcing outward observances, and they are harsh to their inferiors. They love to play the master over others, but not to move them upward to God. They are always full of pride and self-conceit—true dragons, devouring all that approach them and resist them.

The lion, the king of beasts, typifies the highest grade of sin and error; namely, spiritual pride. It means religious men, members of communities, who follow their devout practices without having really given themselves up to God. Absorbed in themselves, making the object of life earthly things, the end they have in view cannot be good. All men by their very nature seek peace and joy—good men in God, the wicked in themselves and in other creatures. And these last are often little aware how great is their delusion. Joy and peace seem to be their possession in a sort of natural quiescence of soul, and it becomes extremely difficult for them to perceive that they are blinded by spiritual pride. It is good, so they are persuaded, thus to rest and be content in peace and quiet of soul, and from this dangerous state they cannot easily recover. It is young men, inexperienced and unmortified, who are mostly subject to this delusion. They imagine this false peace to be a true and good spiritual condition. Now, nature cannot be content with any natural repose, for God alone can content us; hence this counterfeit tranquillity is presently an occasion of sin.

A man may, indeed, be detached and recollected from things of the senses, and settled in a sort of rest and quiet of mind, freed from all activity; but in this he has arrived at a merely natural state of tranquillity; namely, that of his sensitive nature. Any man may attain to this without the aid of God's grace; he has but to empty his mind of all imaginings, and at the same time cease from all external activity. But no good man can continue in that mental and bodily sloth; Divine love cannot rest indolent. This is but a form of self-seeking. This natural quiet, this resting in complete emptiness of mind and stillness of body, with the sole object of being at peace and unhindered by all things, is nothing less than sinful. It makes mental blindness and ignorance and stagnation the object of the soul's endeavor taken in themselves and separated from all good works. Such a quiet is nothing but a false recollection of soul, in which one forgets God and oneself and all else, as far as the real duty of life is concerned.

On the contrary, the holy quiet of the soul in God is a loving seclusion from all things for the sake of God, and it is joined to single-minded contemplation of the incomprehensible glory of God. This means that the soul seeks this union with God by an interior activity of desire which never is at rest. This holy quiet is only acquired in the form of a longing altogether energetic, is enjoyed in an ever-burning love, and, when wholly possessed, it is none the less ardently and energetically longed for. This shows the deception in the other and false state of quiet, in which men by mere natural effort sink away into natural repose of the mental and bodily powers. They do not yearn for God; they do not seek Him with positive aspirations of love, and do not, of course, find Him. The quiet of soul they reach leads but to detachment from self, and from what by nature and habit they are inclined to; but this by no means is to find God. It is an emptiness of soul that a Jew or a heathen might attain, or any wicked man; they have only to cease questioning their conscience, live wholly self-absorbed, and withdraw from all active life—a state of quiet very enjoyable to a certain class of men. Taken in itself, it is not sinful, for it is only what all men naturally are when entirely void of active exertion. But it is far otherwise if one positively seeks to have it and enjoy it to the exclusion of the good works of a Christian life. Then it becomes sinful, and produces a state of spiritual pride and self-assurance from which the soul seldom recovers. Such a man imagines at times that he possesses God, nay, that he has been made one being with God; whereas he is in reality in that state which is most absolutely incompatible with union with God. In this false quiet and false detachment, he considers that all our devout religious exercises only hinder him in his inner peace, which delusion is but in reality to resist the entrance of God into his soul. It was thus that the bad angels acted; for what else did they do but turn away from God to themselves and follow their own natural lights? That was the cause of their blindness; it was that which led to their expulsion from the light and the repose of heaven into the eternal unrest of hell. But the good angels, from the first instant of their creation, turned absolutely to God as the only end and object of all their existence, and thereby were granted everlasting happiness. Now, as the lion is the king of beasts, so do these falsely guided souls imagine themselves the masters of all virtues; whereas they are the worst enemies of virtue, and in God's sight are hypocrites. Such is the state of souls whose spirituality is based upon a merely natural detachment.

This delusion leads to yet another evil, namely, a kind of spiritualized impurity; for spirituality without a sincere yearning for God lays one open to all sorts of errors and temptations. A man is herein averted from God and devoted to self; hence he instinctively seeks pleasure and solace in natural ways.

This soul is like a merchant who thinks of nothing but gain; all his spiritual labors and sufferings are for his own selfish profit, which soon leads to seeking satisfaction in forbidden pleasures. They sometimes practice severe mortifications, but always in a selfish spirit and that they may be honored as holy men. It may happen, too, that they do austerities with a view to the eternal reward; self-love craves praise, and works for a recompense in time and in eternity. They demand great favors from God, and are deluded with the thought that they have received them, for sometimes the evil one serves their ends, thereby puffing them up with yet greater pride, in which they remain fast fixed, God's grace meanwhile being absent from their interior life. They are elated by trifling feelings of apparently spiritual joy, little dreaming of the real inner comfort their selfhood has cost them. The interior sensuality, the spiritual lust of our fallen nature, quite absorbs them, being totally enamored of self, always passionately addicted to self, seeking their own selfish interests in everything. None can be more obstinately self-willed; if they fail to get what they want, even from God Himself, they are almost bereft of their senses, and sometimes say and do abominable things. And it has happened that some have suffered themselves actually to be possessed by evil spirits, in order to obtain what neither God nor man was willing to grant them. Alas, how manifestly do they live in contradiction to the Holy Spirit! How different are they from a good, humble Christian, who unceasingly offers to God all that he is and all that he has, and who can only be content with the possession of the supreme and incomprehensible good that God alone is!

Natural love and Divine love are as much alike as two hairs of a man's head, as far as outward activity and appearances go, but totally unlike in the interior of the soul. The good spirit seeks God's honor within and without the soul, seeks and longs for it alone, and with ever-increasing earnestness. Natural love invariably seeks self in one form or another, and when it has grown so strong as to dominate Divine love in the soul, four vices enter into possession—spiritual pride, avarice, gluttony and impurity. Such was the fall of Adam in Eden, and with him fell all human nature. It was because Adam made himself the object of his natural and inordinate love, that he turned away from God and in his pride contemned the Divine law. His craving for knowledge and wisdom was his sin of spiritual avarice; upon this followed his indulgence in gluttonous eating and drinking; and then came impurity. But behold Mary, the mother of God! She recovered the grace that Adam lost, and a greater grace besides. Hence she is called the mother of fair love, for all her works of love were directed straight to God. She conceived Christ in her womb in all humility; from the depths of her soul she offered to the heavenly Father all her trials and sufferings; she coveted neither knowledge nor wisdom; no, nor even any virtue in a spirit of selfishness or avarice; she sought not any joy or solace in the consciousness of her virtues, any more than in earthly comfort; in all her life and in all her soul and body she was unspotted. She alone, therefore, has overcome all heretics and hypocrites.

Out of these two illusions comes forth a third, and in every way the worst that can mislead men who are considered to be contemplatives. It is detected in their state of natural quiet and detachment; for they have the presumption to claim that they are exempted from the liability to sin; that they are united to God directly and without any intermediation whatsoever, understanding this in a perverted meaning; that they are emancipated from obedience to holy church; that they are not bound by God's commandments; and that they are no longer required

to practice virtue. They justify these errors by saying that their detachment is so noble a state, that nothing whatever must be permitted to
interfere with it. Thus, then, they stand free from all authority, without a single good work in things high or low—as idle as a workman's
tool waiting for his hand to take it up and use it. They fancy that if
they do anything, God will be hindered from acting through them, and
thus they are vacant and empty of every virtuous act. They go to the
extent of ceasing to thank and praise God; they must have nothing,
know nothing, love nothing, pray for nothing. They already have all
they could pray for—such is their delusion. They think that they are
truly poor in spirit because they have renounced all will and all proprietorship, whether present or future. They have arrived, as they imagine,
at the complete and final possession of the holiness which the church
was instituted to bestow, and no one can give them or take from them
anything whatsoever. Nor can God Himself increase their sanctity, so
they dream; for they consider themselves as placed high above all pious
practices and all virtues, maintaining that perfect detachment consists
in detachment even from all virtue, and that men should labor more
diligently to be detached from virtue than to acquire virtue. This
accounts for their assertion of a false liberty and their refusal of obedience to every authority, whether of pope, bishop or parish priest. If
they do sometimes obey, it is only outwardly, for interiorly they consider
themselves subject to none, either in soul or body; and they are determined to be exempt from all church authority. They say openly that
as long as a man strives after virtue he is still in a state of imperfection,
knowing nothing of spiritual poverty and spiritual liberty. They rate
themselves above all angels and men, above all human merit and faith,
incapable of further increase in holiness, incapable of committing sin;
for they live, as they think, in a state devoid of the action of the will,
in spiritual quiet and detachment so perfect as to amount to self-
annihilation and total absorption into God. Meanwhile, what nature
craves, that they may freely grant themselves, all without sin; for they
have reached the highest grade of innocence—no law can bind them.
Hence when nature yearns for any self-indulgence, they yield without
scruple in order that their liberty of soul may not be hindered. As to
fast days, festivals and commandments, they pay no heed to them,
except in order to keep up appearances; for they are no longer guided
by conscience.

Let each one of us examine himself carefully, lest he may be tainted
with these delusions. These falsely spiritual men are worse than any

shameless sinners, even murderers, for the latter own that they are wicked and the others know it not. It is extremely hard to convert them; sometimes they have even fallen under control of the devil. They are clever reasoners, and it is almost impossible to silence their arguments, except it be by the life of our Lord Jesus Christ and His holy Scriptures—a plain mark that they are under deception.

And now we are to consider the fourth kind of illusion which affects certain men calling themselves contemplatives, who resemble, but yet differ from the class we have just been treating. This fourth class consider themselves as mere passive instruments of God, set totally free from all activity of their own. God works within them; and they have thereby, so they claim, more merit than others who do good works and whose personal activity is ever inspired by Divine grace. They call their state a Divine passivity. Although they do nothing, they yet merit reward, so they affirm, and are by no means to be blamed for their inactivity. They live a life of perfect interior rest in God, as they think; and, cultivating a very humble demeanor, they pay no regard to anything whatsoever, and are quite patient with whatever befalls them—as bright souls which are mere instruments of the Divine will. They have many points of resemblance with men of sound spirituality. But here is what proves that they are wrong: Whatever they feel themselves interiorly moved to do, whether it be good or bad, they are persuaded is the work of the Holy Ghost. But the Holy Ghost never inspires men to be idle and useless, least of all, to do evil things, nor to do anything against the life and doctrine of Christ and His holy Scriptures. And this demonstrates that such men are under deception. But it is not easy to detect them, for they are cunning in concealing their vagaries. However, they are betrayed by their obstinate self-will. They will rather die than yield the least point of their infatuation. They are greatly opposed to those who tell them that they are not in a way of perfection, for they hold that they are in a most meritorious state. Be assured that all such men are forerunners of anti-Christ, preparing the way for the spread of unbelief and the eternal loss of souls.

And now let us briefly consider how we may escape these fatal snares. No man can be dispensed from keeping the commandments of God and practicing virtue. No man can be united to God in a state of detachment from creatures without having the love of God and the desire of God. No man is holy or can be made holy without good works. No good man shall cease doing good works. No man can rest in God without loving God. No man can be raised to any state which he does not desire and which he does not experience. No man shall cease to do good works under the pretext that his works hinder God's work in him, but rather he must co-operate with God in all thankfulness. No man shall serve God except with gratitude and with praise; for God is the creator of all men, Who alone has the right to give and to withhold—infinitely rich and powerful. A man may advance in virtue and in merit and in the practice of religion as long as he lives; but no one will receive more reward than he merits, however vainly he may imagine that he lets God work within him while he himself rests passive. God's work is in itself eternal and changeless, done by Himself alone and not otherwise; and in this respect His work receives no increase from any creature, nor gains any value; for it is of God alone, than Whom there can be nothing greater or better. But creatures are granted by God to have activity of their own, and this is placed in works of nature, of grace, and, finally, in the glory of Heaven. And if it were possible (as it is not) that our spiritual nature should be totally deprived of its activity, and should be, as it were, annihilated in itself and absorbed into oneness with God, as it was in God's mind before being created; if, in a word, a reasonable creature could bring about such a state of existence, then what would follow? Simply this: Such a man could merit nothing whatever, any more than he could before his creation. Such a human being could no more be holy nor happy than wood or stone.

Let it be well understood, that without our own activity in knowing and loving God we can never be happy. What does it avail us that God is happy, and is so from all eternity, unless we shall know Him and love Him? Hence this emptiness of spirit, of which we have been treating, is undoubtedly a deception. But the souls thus led astray are very hard to undeceive, so subtle is their spirit; indeed, they are not unlike the souls of the damned. The damned have neither joy in God, nor do they want to know Him; they have neither thanksgiving, nor worship, nor praise for Him, and they are lost eternally. The deluded souls whom we have been considering, have only this same fate awaiting them in eternity, when the justice of God shall be revealed in them.

Against them stands Christ and the example of His life. He lived His whole life long constantly loving, desiring, thanking and praising His heavenly Father, with Whom in the Divine essence He was most closely joined; and yet He never had the emptiness of soul these deluded men boast of. And all the saints of God incessantly hungered and thirsted with love for Him, always longing to possess Him, never having enough of Him. The blessedness of Christ and of all His saints was to enjoy God, in a union beyond all power of heart to conceive or tongue to tell; to attain to this has ever been the object of the striving of all elect souls. They worked and struggled for that as their only bliss. And such must be the perfection of every good man—a state of virtue which is measured by the extent of his love, finally bestowing on him a righteousness which shall never pass away.

And how shall we be safeguarded against all such delusions? By adorning our lives with interior and exterior virtues, and by good Christian living, docile in all such things to the guidance of holy Church and the teachings of Scripture, and constantly offering ourselves to God with that end in view. Thereby do we meet God with His own gifts, and these He makes use of to touch our hearts with love for Him, a love active and energetic, resulting in the fullness of fidelity to Him. And now we overflow with love for all mankind; and presently, entering into our souls, we are filled with loving thanks and praise toward God in our interior life, rooted fast and firm in simple-hearted peace, well pleasing to God. It is by a love thus active, and by God's light thus clear in our souls, that we are enabled to advance toward that union with God which is direct and without any intermediary influence, in the proper meaning of the words, in the enjoyment of perfect repose of spirit. Thus, besides, do we learn how to live a life always interior, readily and constantly withdrawing into our soul's depths to be alone with God—the truest means of acquiring and maintaining virtue. That we may have such a life, and be freed from all danger of delusion, may God mercifully grant. *Amen.*

The Rudiments of Perfection

Synopsis—Every man is called in a way peculiar to himself, yet all have a common road to travel—First, all must learn to hate mortal sin by studying Christ's passion—Second, all must suppress the evil tendencies of nature—Third, all must adopt a rule of life which makes sure of needful devout practices and penances— Fourth, all must patiently bear the painful happenings permitted by providence—Perfection of both motive and act surely results in God's good time.

FIRST SERMON FOR THE SECOND SUNDAY OF LENT.

For He hath delivered me from the snare of the hunters and from the sharp word.—Ps. xc, 3.

Thus spoke the great prophet and king, David, of those who give themselves up to the will and the protection of God. By the word snare, we must understand the poisonous temptations of the devil. And by the sharp word, we are to understand the day of doom and judgment then to be visited upon sinners: "Depart from Me, you cursed, into everlasting fire." (Matt. xxv, 41.) The man who has not often pondered these awful words is no servant of God; for it is by this means that we escape the snare and the hunter of our souls, and it is by a good life that we guard against the dreadful fate of the wicked.

Now, it can be said of every saint: "There was not found the like to him in glory who kept the law of the Most High." (Eccli. xliv, 20.) Every man called by God to repentance is called in a way peculiar to his own outward circumstances; but interiorly it is to one and the same love all are invited; they—all, without exception—love justice and hate iniquity.

If we are going to serve God, God must give us His grace of conversion. And now, if you will bear a little with my dullness, I will, to the best of my ability, show you a plain way by which to advance in perfection, if you will but follow it.

The first point is, for the love of God to renounce all mortal sin; and then for the sake of both penance and perfection, to meditate carefully on the passion of Jesus Christ the Son of God, especially on His five holy wounds: Jesus crucified must a man study daily, with particularly fervent prayers and devotions.

The second point is to suppress the gross concupiscence of nature, overcoming it from hour to hour; and this we should do by means of all the penitential exercises that we can endure. For this end one should gladly be much alone with God. As for the rest, one must seek every opportunity to do good to others and practice himself in all virtues.

The third point is this: A man must shut out all inordinate human love; his heart must be emptied of love of any creature in preference to God or on an equality with God. The better to accomplish this, he should make a beginning with such a desire as this: That God would punish him for his sins in this life by sending him suffering. And he should also undertake penitential works of his own prudent choice, lament and weep for his sins, and have at least a sincere longing to atone fully for them. For the better doing of all this he should adopt a rule of life, and begin at once, and with some severity, to hold himself as firmly as possible to his virtuous practices, having constantly before his eyes the example of Christ's humanity. And let him live in obedience to the precepts of holy church to the very best of his ability.

The fourth point concerns the bearing of trouble and adversity. For when this man has acquired some virtue and become pleasing in God's sight, He sends him many sorrows, both interior and exterior, and soon all devotional practices cease to attract him. Now is the time for him to be patient; he must by no means lessen his diligence in spiritual exercises; if all interior comfort be withdrawn, let him go right on without it, for thus does he become truly poor in spirit. Let him understand that now God is giving him lessons how to love, not for the sake of his own profit, but wholly for that of his beloved. Finally, he must not be actuated, as his chief motive, by the hope of reward in doing his good works; nor should he fear any suffering, looking upon all that as a form of self-love; God's honor alone should inspire him.

After a time such a one wonders how a spiritual man can serve God mainly for any reward, temporal or eternal. He seeks no interior comfort in this life, nor does he advert to reward hereafter as the motive of virtue; no thought of his personal profit enters his mind. He wills simply what God wills; and this state of soul is sweeter to him than the thought of any recompense can ever be. May Almighty God grant us these happy dispositions, whereby we may escape the snares of the hunters of our souls, and may never hear the sharp word of condemnation spoken against us by the Supreme Judge. *Amen.*

Steadfastness as an Element of Devotion

Synopsis—The danger in self-chosen devotional methods—The divine method breeds patience with delays on God's part—Exposition of the Cainanitish woman's steadfastness in prayer—To stand one's ground when hope seems gone is an indispensable requisite for perfection—Disinterestedness of spirit—Example of a holy nun.

SECOND SERMON FOR THE SECOND SUNDAY OF LENT.

And Jesus went from thence and retired into the coasts of Tyre and Sidon. And behold a woman of Canaan who came out of those coasts, crying out, said to Him: Have mercy on me, O Lord, Thou son of David; my daughter is grievously troubled by a devil. Who answered her not a word. And His disciples came and besought Him, saying: Send her away, for she crieth after us. And He answering, said: I was not sent but to the sheep that are lost of the house of Israel. But she came and adored Him, saying: Lord, help me. Who answering, said: It is not good to take the bread of the children and to cast it to the dogs. But she said: Yea, Lord; for the whelps also eat of the crumbs that fall from the table of their masters. Then Jesus answering, said to her: O woman, great is thy faith; be it done to thee as thou wilt: and her daughter was cured from that hour.—Matt. xv, 21-28.

Ah, dear children, this passage of the Gospel shows us the noblest, most profitable, surest and deepest conversion to God that a man can ever experience. And be assured, besides, that any conversion that is not, some way or other, effected after this manner, will be of little or no benefit, no matter what we may do or leave undone.

"Our Saviour went from thence," says the Gospel. And from whom did He depart? From the scribes and the hypocrites. Mark well that the scribes were the wise ones of this world, who trusted in their own knowledge and went according to their own plans. Children, this points out the most injurious condition in which spiritual men can be placed; many a noble soul is in this way brought to total failure, sometimes by one, sometimes by both of two different errors. Indeed, there are few who wholly escape. By scribes we mean intellectual men, who value everything according to the standard of their reason and the observation of their senses, and they have a great store of this kind of knowledge. Presently they are much admired; they discourse with beautiful and stately words. But in the depths of their souls—that interior source of all true science—there is nothing but an empty and barren waste.

The hypocrites, or Pharisees, are those who rank themselves good spiritual men, and yet are full of self-esteem. Their own plans and customs are the only rule they follow, and their one aim in life is to be praised by men. They hotly condemn all who venture to differ from them. Mark well, that our beloved Lord went forth from among such men as these, for they had demanded of Him: "Why do Thy disciples transgress the traditions of the ancients? For they wash not their hands when they eat bread." But he gently reproved them: "Why do you also transgress the commandment of God for your tradition?" (Matt. xv, 2-3.) So do these men of whom we are speaking value their own methods and practices above the interior admonitions of God's Spirit, condemning God's real friends because they will not be guided by their inventions, but prefer to be directed by the hidden impulses of grace. Yet these or any other kind of misguided men, should not be condemned openly in a monastic community, for that would not be in accordance with religious discipline.

Let everyone be on his guard privately against such men. There are always religious men who are totally absorbed in the external side of a good life, and who yet interiorly are miserably held captive by love of created things. They have many prayers to recite, many readings of the Psalter. As much may be said for the poor, deluded Jews of our time, devoted as they are to reading the Psalms and the other Scriptures, and yet the true knowledge of God is entirely hidden from them. These men take the discipline, they pray and fast and watch, and yet God is not purely and simply the motive of any of these practices, but only poor, deluded human nature. All this parade of spiritual exercises is entirely directed by their self-love. This Phariseeism excludes the eternal God from their souls. This vineyard was never planted by the heavenly Father, but will be disowned and destroyed, as our Lord Himself declared: "He that is not with Me is against Me; and he that gathereth not with Me, scattereth." (Matt. xii, 30.) When the time of the harvest has come, then God will gather in His corn, that is to say, His elect; and those who do not gather with Him shall be rejected; in whatsoever souls He finds a harvest that He has not planted, those also shall be rejected. Beware, then, of the influence of this false devotional spirit. The tendency to be guided by natural motives, after the manner of the scribes and Pharisees, running into the excessive use of external and showy exercises of religion, prevails greatly nowadays among all classes. Many are so much affected by the spirit of the scribes of old, that a conscientious father confessor can hardly hear their confessions, so obstinately are they rooted in their purpose to persist in their delusion. Out of the company of such men Jesus goes forth, and ever will go forth.

But whither goeth our blessed Lord? He goes into the land of Tyre and Sidon. Now, Tyre may be taken to mean somebody suffering from anguish of heart, and Sidon, one who is hunted. Alas, dear children, how few men there are who appreciate the value of interior suffering and of interior persecution, or being hunted! Yet nothing in the world is so honorable or so precious as that both these trials should meet together in our souls. When one has safely gone through such an experience, then alone can he understand what nobility of soul and what fruit of virtue result from these bitter struggles.

But what do I mean by a man who is hunted? I mean that an interior man must insist on being always close to God as the only true state of his soul, and this forces him incessantly to hunt and drive himself inward to God's presence in his interior consciousness. Now, this provokes the violent resistance of the outward man that is in us all; we would ever and again seek to return forcibly to the outward things that minister to our natural weakness. Here, then, is the conflict. The inner man's proper place is with God; of this he ever thinks and for it he ever yearns, and toward that union with God our Lord is ever driving and hunting him. Now, to our outward man this is always offensive and against nature, and he always fights against it. St. Paul tells of this struggle: "I am delighted with the law of God according to the inward man, but I see another law in my members fighting against the law of my mind." (Rom. vii, 22-23.) And hence the apostle complains that what he wills not that he yet does, and what he wills he is not able to do. This is the war between nature and reason, into which God enters with His grace, and hunts and drives both before Him. And be it well understood, children, that when this is rightly appreciated by you, then all is well; for whosoever is thus hunted by God's Holy Spirit is one of God's elect.

You can easily understand, children, that from this constant hunting of a man's soul bitter anguish results. But when at last he is content to abide, for God's sake, without any consolation, then will Jesus surely come to him and possess him. But if he will not patiently suffer the anguish of the conflict between grace and nature, then will Jesus not come to him. All who have not experienced this interior distress and sincerely accepted it—even unto the very death of nature—from them nothing good can be expected; they are bound captive to the world. Sometimes such men never realize the meaning of what has been going on within their souls, for there are many trials of body and of soul whose end and purpose is little observed by us, and which, if humbly and thankfully received from God and patiently endured, will end happily with the inpouring of Divine grace. Sometimes, again, the world, that is to say, our fellow-men, conspire to mislead us, and do even violently assail us. Add to this the cunning of the evil one, and the uprisings of fleshly passion, and the poor soul seems beset with fatal outward difficulties, while interiorly God Himself seems to oppress her and she is tormented by her naturally inordinate impulses—altogether a sad and bitter state of suffering.

Children, what can this poor, belated and desolate man do that he may hold his own, and not be driven to extremities in this dreadful hunted condition? No otherwise than the Canaanitess did in her deep sorrow—run to Jesus Christ and call out to Him with all his strength: "Jesus, Son of David, have mercy on me!" Ah, children, in this hunted state of soul, there is granted a voice to utter a holy call to God; the answer will be the measureless joys of the interior life. Our prayer is a sigh of the spirit yearning for God, so deep and so sad that it flies through measureless space far over all the range of nature— straight to the Divine heart. Indeed, it is the Holy Spirit Himself that now assumes charge of and perfects this work in us; and as St. Paul says, it is His voice that pleads for us: "The Spirit Himself asketh for us with unspeakable groanings." (Rom. viii, 26.) And, dear children, when the Holy Ghost thus prepares us, no other preparation can compare with it.

But now something strange occurs; for occasionally it happens that the soul's cry seems to be unheard by God. After bravely enduring the inner anguish and the outward tribulation, after crying aloud with a strength of yearning that seems to pierce Heaven itself, then, yea even then, God sometimes acts as if He would have nothing to do with this afflicted soul. This is the cruelest trial of all. Ah, children, how deep must be the self-denial of that soul, and how disinterested its loyalty to

God, if it now turns all the more resolutely to Him and relies wholly
upon Him, and upon none other, and suffers simply and purely for His
very sake, in this its hour of unspeakable desolation! Oh! it exclaims,
how can it be that God has shut against me the door of infinite mercy?
And yet that soul remains true to Him.

But so it happened with the Canaanitess—as she cried out her prayer
after Christ, His mercy seemed shut against her. And when His
disciples pleaded for her, His answer was a cold and stern refusal: "I
was not sent but to the sheep that are lost of the house of Israel." Then
when she came and adored Him and implored Him to grant her prayer,
He said these harsh words to her: "It is not good to take the bread of
the children and to cast it to the dogs." To His refusal He added the
sting of most bitter words, calling her not only an unworthy creature,
but even a dog. Could He have dealt more severely with her? Could
He have crushed her down more pitilessly? And, now, what did this
poor soul do in her agony of woe? She suffered everything meekly and
patiently; she let herself be hunted like a dog by the Lord her God
according as He willed. Nay, she more than accepted his dreadful
chastisement. He had called her a dog, she called herself less than a
dog—avowed herself to be only a dog's whelp, a pitiful and miserable
little puppy. By this entire self-annihilation, she proclaimed her true-
hearted and steadfast trust in our Lord Jesus Christ. How beautiful
are her words: "Yea, Lord, for the whelps also eat of the crumbs that
fall from the table of their masters."

Ah, dear children, happy is the man and holy, who can strike so deep
down into his heart to find the will of God there. This is not a matter
of words or of any pious use of the senses, but of truest earnestness, for
it annihilates us in a self-renunciation deeper than anything else in us,
human or Divine. Anguish, suffering, shame are at their worst in that
man's soul, and yet he trusts God with unshaken constancy, and his
confidence in the Divine loving-kindness grows stronger and stronger, as
God's abandonment of him seems to grow more certain—just as was the
case with the Canaanitess when rejected by our Lord. The harder He
treated her the more confidently did she beg His mercy; and it was for
this reason alone that she got all she asked from Him. Dear children,
this is the right and the Divine road to true spirituality. The man that
can thus stand his ground meekly under all God's visitations of inner
and outer affliction, looking to nothing but God's will for guidance,
awaiting God's time of relief most patiently—the man who will thus

stand his ground until death without the least repining—ah; children, he has found the straight road to union with God without any intermediation. That road is total self-renunciation, in mind and in heart, in the face of God and of all creatures; the soul willingly suffering ban ishment from all joy, and maintaining that self-renunciation with all confidence in God, even to the end. To such a true and faithful soul the Lord will, at last, speak words similar to the ones He addressed to the Canaanitess: "O, woman, great is thy faith! Be it done to thee as thou wilt."

Children, I tell you the everlasting truth when I say, that all who tread this path will one day, without doubt, hear such words as these: My beloved, whatsoever thou shalt ask of Me, shall be granted thee in all fullness, for thou hast for My sake gone out of thyself and away from all that is thine, whether in mind or in body. Enter, now, into My inmost spirit and be joined to Me without any intermediation, to be made one with Me by My grace, as I am one in My nature. Children, such an entrance into Infinite Good, is granted only to one who has given up all things, all selfhood in soul and body. For just in proportion as a man gives up self in all things, so does he enter into God by the help of Divine grace. He that voluntarily loses all things for God's sake, finds all things in God.

And now I will give you an example of a maiden whose case is like that of the Canaanitess; she is still living, and the incident occurred within four years. Once it happened that she was rapt out of her senses so far and high, that she seemed to behold God and our Lady and all the saints in their glory; but as to herself, she seemed to be separated from this glorious company by an immeasurable space. And this banishment gave her a pain so inexpressibly bitter, that it could be compared only to that of hell itself; for we know that the pain of hell is essentially this—the lost souls know that they have wilfully cut themselves off from God and His saints, never more to see Him and to love Him. Our good maiden in her anguish, now humbly besought our Blessed Lady and the saints to intercede for her. But, alas, they were all so deeply absorbed in the joy of God that they could not grant her a single instant's attention; her cry for relief was unheard. Then she turned to Jesus crucified; she implored Him by His bitter passion and cruel death to have pity on her. An answer came reproving her for praying to Him: Thou hast never yet proved thyself worthy of the favor thou asketh. Upon this, seeing that neither our Lady, the saints, no, nor even our

crucified Saviour, would help her, she went direct to God and said:
O Lord, O my everlasting God, no one will help me, Thy unhappy creature, in my misfortune! And now, O my Lord and Creator, my Eternal
Father, I humbly accept Thy righteous judgment upon me! If it be
Thy will that this awful pain, seemingly like that of hell itself, shall be
mine eternally, then may Thy will be done upon me in time and eternity;
to Thy disposal I meekly abandon myself. Whatever shall please Thee
in me and from me, heavenly Father, to that I give myself up for all
eternity. Thus did she offer herself to God absolutely and without
any reserve. And instantly she felt herself carried away from her banishment and absorbed, without any intermediation, in the abyss of
God's being. And since then not a day passes but that she is again
drawn in that manner into union with God. I am firmly convinced that
she has never in her whole life committed a mortal sin; and yet see
what dreadful pain she has had to suffer. Ah, dear children, what
manifold suffering must not we undergo before God grants us that perfect union with Him—we who have often offended God grievously and
even now cling so tenaciously to created things! Learn a good lesson
from this pious maiden's case, who was so lovingly submissive to God's
holy will that (if such an impossible thing could be) she would eternally
endure the pains of hell, if that were His decree.

But that is precisely what we do not do when we enter upon the
spiritual life. We count upon making wonderful progress inside of
four or five years. We are accustomed to say to others: Dear brothers,
pray to our Lord for me, that I may become one of His dearest friends
both in time and eternity. But be assured of this: If thou wert in the
right way thou wouldst not think thyself at all worthy of any such
honor, or of being enrolled even in the lowest rank of the friends of
God. Therefore, sit thee down in the lowest place, as the Gospel
teaches, for then only wilt thou be sure of being raised up higher, for
all those who exalt themselves, will undoubtedly be humbled and cast
down lower. Beg God's guidance that thou mayest clearly know where
He would place thee, both in His own sight and in that of men. Be
content with that place and aspire to none other. .

Children, it is in entire self-renunciation for the love of God in all
our doings, in plenty and in want, as well in matters spiritual as corporal, that God enters the soul without any intermediation. Mark well,
my children, that even a little drop of such virtue as this, joined to only
a faint emotion of Divine love in the soul, is a better preparation for

intimate union with God in our soul's depths, than if we stripped ourselves naked to clothe the poor or fasted upon rocks and briars. A
single minute of this perfect self-renunciation is of more profit to a man,
than forty years following his own religious contrivances. It is the
most praiseworthy way to God, and the shortest; of all ways that can
be thought of it is the easiest, and the most beneficial. O, my God, how
many men are there forever circling about and losing the precious time
of Divine grace, instead of going direct by this way to the possession
of the Supreme Good, which would then be given them in a life wholly
regenerated!   Year after year they continue oblivious to the grace that
awaits their fidelity, as if they were lulled to sleep by their forgetfulness
of God.   After the better part of a lifetime, they still remain as far
removed from perfection as at the beginning—a lamentable evil among
spiritual men.   Did they but recognize the injury, great and perilous,
that they do themselves by following their own inventions and methods,
the marrow in their bones would wither up and the blood would freeze
in their veins.

That we may sink deep down into the abyss of God's life, and willingly yield ourselves to His eternal decrees, grant us, O Father, and Son,
and Holy Ghost. *Amen.*

Children of Abraham: True and False

*Synopsis—The test is whether self is sought or God alone in one's de-
votion—How this is revealed in the sacrament of penance—Piety
reckoned by observances practiced compared with that generated
by love of God and man—The soul captured by God is interiorily
directed straight to Him, and is patient in exterior adversity and
pain.*

SERMON FOR THE THIRD SUNDAY OF LENT.

Then Jesus said to those Jews who believed Him: If you continue in My word,
you shall be My disciples indeed. And you shall know the truth, and the truth
shall make you free. They answered Him: We are the seed of Abraham, and we
have never been the slaves of any man: how sayest Thou: You shall be free?—
John viii, 31-33.

Upon this angry reply from the Jews, Jesus told them that not only
Abraham, but the devil, was their father, for it was the devil's work
they were occupied with. "Whosoever committeth sin is the servant
of sin. Now, the servant abideth not in the house forever, but the Son
abideth forever; if, therefore, the Son shall make you free, you shall be
free, indeed. * * * My Word hath no place in you. I speak that
which I have seen with My Father, and you do the things which you
have seen with your Father."

Herein we may distinguish between the true and the false in the spiritual life. The false spirit does not seek God, but self, and that in
everything whatsoever—personal advantage or personal enjoyment in
all created things. And it takes all things not as leading to God or
coming from God, but in a selfish spirit. The master and the father of
this way is the evil one, who, when he has accomplished his purpose,
leads his victims into his own house. They are not sons of God, but
servants of the devil. They have been cast out of God's house and
rejected by Him.

The other spirit—and the only true one, because it is born of God—
is altogether admirable and praiseworthy. It would go straight to
God as a ray of sunlight darts down to the earth. It is as Jesus said:

"I came forth from the Father, and am come into the world; again I leave the world and I go to the Father." (John xvi, 28.) The Son returns to His Father with all that He brought out from the Father. And that man is Christ's in word and in doctrine, who holds back nothing from God of all that he has received from Him—no, not a hair's weight. As he came forth from God, so does he return again to God. In this is he the Lord's true disciple, full of love and of thanksgiving to His Father, reserving no joy in self nor approval of self, having no thought and no sentiment whatever, that is not veritably consecrated to the Father's honor.

But there are some in whom, together with this solid foundation, there is mingled a certain weakness, the soul thinking of other things and having other affections, together with those devoted to God. And this defect a man must cure by the sacrament of penance, nourishing deep contrition and performing penitential works. This requires that one should learn how to confess his sins with much intelligence, and in a very interior spirit of sorrow. The father confessor must, on his part, carefully point out to the penitent in what manner his dispositions are defective—a duty very generally neglected nowadays, either from lack of skill or want of time; or, as is perhaps more often the case, from lack of affectionate interest of the priest in the penitent. Meanwhile the penitent should enter deeply into his own soul, and thoroughly search and discover what his motives are for everything he does or even thinks. And then, whatsoever he discovers inordinate or faulty, let him resolutely set to work to correct it. Let him pour out all his imperfections into the very heart of God, consumed with deep interior sorrow. By this means a man soon learns how to know himself; purity of heart is acquired, and fear of God, and earnest zeal of virtue, especially to guard against future defects. And if it should happen that when he goes to confession he forgets some faults, he has, nevertheless, already repented of them fully and been pardoned. His constant and contrite confessions to God, should be so made as to bring him continually in spirit before God's awful tribunal. There let him prostrate himself at God's feet in the deepest humility, and so remain till he is at least all afire with the Divine love, and melted, as it were, with confidence in the Divine mercy. O how good a gift of God is this, and how deserving of heartfelt thanks! And if it happens—as, indeed, it may— that the soul still continues to suffer from the remembrance of past infidelity to God, let this be accepted humbly and fearfully as God's blessed will.

Many men, however, who have begun in this right way, give it up and exchange it for the wrong way, because they must have consolations and spiritual solaces. But what peace can there be between the temporal and the eternal? Can joy in transitory things exist in the same heart with joy in eternal things? Where the joys of this life dwell, there the joys of eternal life cannot abide. These deluded men say with the Jews: We are the children of Abraham; we are spiritual men; do we not sing hymns and read pious books and say fine prayers? Why, then, should we not have the comfort of created things? Do we not know by experience that these relaxations and consolations are not harmful? Are we not well-disposed and really pious men? Are we not always in the state of Divine grace? Dear children, listen to St. Paul's answer to all this: "If I speak with the tongue of men, and of angels, and have not charity, I am become as sounding brass or a tinkling cymbal. * * * And if I should distribute all my goods to feed the poor, and if I should deliver my body to be burned and have not charity, it profiteth me nothing." (I Cor. xiii, 1-3.) And tell me, I pray thee, how can that love be called God's love, which is given in all joy and self-satisfaction to created things? Ah, this is a false spiritual way! It is quite otherwise in the true way, in which all one's love is held captive to God alone.

This captivity is twofold—interior and exterior. The interior affects the higher faculties of the soul, directing them so resolutely to God, and binding them so fast to His will, that they shall not ever resist Him. The external captivity to God is best shown when heavy sorrows are borne in all patience for God's sake. When one's worldly goods, one's honor, beloved friends and relatives, are all lost; ah, then poor human nature weeps and wails to God and to all creatures in earth and Heaven for relief. And this painful experience must happen to all well-tried friends of God. They must have their inmost soul full of God and their outward life full of suffering. But the outward tribulations and pains can well be endured, if the interior life be only fast and firm in its union with God.

But, again, the inner man is sorely tried by temptations—those of pride, impurity, irritability, silliness, rashness and many others—as St. Augustine teaches: "For such is the misery of our poor fallen nature. O let us grapple courageously with these evil tendencies and ever keep God and His blessed law before our eyes, absolutely resigned to suffer all these trials, simply and entirely because such is the Divine will!" Not the slightest thing happens to us but that our heavenly Father knows it, and knows just exactly when and where and how it happens. Let us even be thankful to God that He permits us thus to suffer temptation, remembering that God allows the bitterest sufferings to fall on those whom he best loves. And this applies especially to those whom He has set over His people as their teachers or father confessors. Of that class, those who have had the hard lot of trial and temptation are the ones who are very compassionate in dealing with sinners. Others are not so much so, but are too often over-severe with them.

Whatsoever man, therefore, shall steadfastly endure this course of trial repeated over and over again, has become in very truth God's disciple. He will easily find the right path to perfection. Him the truth will in very deed make free from all subjection to sinful inclinations. And one effect of this self-renunciation will be that even his body will by God's grace be so freed from its weakness and fitted for all possible virtue, that it will become a proper companion for his soul. That we may thus be made God's disciples, and that we may thus be made free, may His blessed grace be granted us. *Amen.*

Jesus the Focus of Divine Light

*Synopsis—Man's tendency to truth and joy is the craving of darkness
for light—Hindrances the worldly spirit; self-conceit and self-
guidance—Helps; unfeigned self-abnegation; recourse to Jesus in
joy and sorrow alike; avowal of sinfulness; devotion to the humanity of Jesus.*

FIRST SERMON FOR THE FOURTH SUNDAY OF LENT.

I am the light of the world.—John viii, 12.

To these words of our beloved Saviour the Jews could only reply by
reproaches and contradictions. He insisted, and continued to teach
them that He was the light of the world and of all mankind.

And, indeed, He is the light of the world, even of the material universe, for He gives the sun its light, and the moon and stars; He is the
light of our bodily eyes; He is especially the beautiful light of reason
shining in our souls. And to this light, to God our Saviour, the source
of all light, must the light in every creature return again or it will lapse
into utter darkness; and He that is the light of the world hateth darkness. Now, Jesus says to thee: I am the true light, and I will give thee
My eternal light to expel thy darkness, and with My light I will give
thee My being, My life, My glory and My joy. He will join us to Himself, as He prayed His Father to make us one with the Father and with
Himself. He says to thee: I would that thou shouldst be in Me and
I in thee, not simply joined, but united in one—"that they also may be
one in Us" (John xvii, 21) ; not, indeed, by unity of nature, but by the
mysterious operation of grace. We know that all things tend toward
the original source of their existence, as even the rocks and the elements
of fire and air and water. What then, shall we say of man's tendency
toward God his Creator—man, for whose sake God made the heavens
and the earth and all things that are in them, so that they might minister to his wants and help him to serve his Creator the better. Is it
not a pitiful thing that man, full of the light of reason and God's noblest

creature, should of all creatures remain alone fettered and helpless, and should not return again to his heavenly origin—into the true and eternal light of God?

Let us study this matter and learn what hinders our making God the end and object of our life, and then what is the manner and method to follow to attain to our final destiny in God.

It must be something very strong, my dear children, that can hinder us from gaining possession of infinite good. With one class of men it is this: Their hearts are worldly. They live for the joy they find in created things, which they intensely love. They are wrapped up in the sensual enjoyment of creatures, in which they wear themselves out and squander their precious time. Children, these men are not only enveloped in darkness, but they resist the light that God is and they sin against it.

Another kind of men are, indeed, in a kind of a way spiritual—at least as far as name and appearances go. They fancy that they have soared high above the realms of darkness; but, as God sees their inner life, they are in reality but Pharisees, full of self-love and self-will; and they are themselves the only object of all their strivings. It is not easy to distinguish them from the friends of God, whom they often surpass in practicing external devotions, such as prayers, fasting, vigils and outward austerity of life. But if thou hast the true spirit thou canst detect them. Only one external difference from right-minded souls they all have, and that is censoriousness; they are addicted to judging and condemning, especially really devout men, and, of course, praising themselves. It is just the reverse with those who are in the right way; these readily condemn themselves and just as readily praise others. Self-seeking characterizes the others, whether in things human or Divine, a defect (peculiar to the Pharisees) so deeply rooted in our fallen nature that it tends to influence everything we do. The men whose false spirituality we are considering, are as hard to change in this as it is to pierce a mountain of iron; that is to say, by any natural influence or argument. No, children, one thing alone can overcome their obstinate selfhood: God must come with all His goodness and gain the upper hand in their hearts and thus possess Himself of them. But, alas, this happens but very seldom. The blame is not God's, it is ours; we all too willingly admit created things to have that place and power in our thoughts and affections which belongs alone to God.

A reasonable being should never give himself rest until he has struggled through all created things to the possession of God alone;

and it is an unspeakable misery, that the world is full of men whose lives show that they do not recognize this duty. God's friends are afflicted to the marrow of their bones, as they see and hear the injury done to God and the harm to immortal souls by men's affection for creatures, which is all too prevalent around them. Therefore, dear children, be zealous and diligent in acquiring the true spirit of detachment, for it involves a lifelong conflict. To be guided by one's own light and not by God's, is the chief cause of our not attaining to union with God. And, no matter how courageously we combat, the victory is never quite complete. There is an overmastering joy in self-guidance, even in spiritual matters; nature is intoxicated by this pleasure more than by any other; and, withal, it is deceitful, and its hurtfulness too often remains hidden. It was this natural self-guidance that the heathen philosophers knew so well and loved so dearly. In that they remained; they were powerless to go onward to union with God; and hence it was that they dwelt in eternal darkness.

And now let us consider the true way, and the shortest way leading into the very focus of this heavenly light. Briefly, it is unfeigned self-denial joined to boundless love of God—one's own self in not a single particular and God's honor in all things. Let there be no crooked, but all straight ways in thee; whatever comes to thee, accept it as immediately out of the hand of God, sweet or bitter, and refer it all back again into the same loving hand, in entire abandonment to His holy will. This is the straight road to perfection, even the highest. And it is this that gives the test, as to who are the true and who are the false friends of God. The latter look to self; they accept even God's gifts in a spirit of proprietorship. They are far from accepting His graces in a spirit of self-renunciation and entire thankfulness—by no means absorbed in the Divine Giver, in spirit and in flesh, inwardly and outwardly. The former are God's true friends, because their self-renunciation and their loyalty to God has become a personal trait, deep-rooted in heart and mind. Without this a man stands in self-love, and is addicted to created things, and while in that state he can never see the true light of God.

But, dear children, mark further, that the false spirit is often deceitfully mingled with the rays of Divine light in the soul, and this involves serious peril. Many a time one cannot tell whether or not he is seeking to do God's will only; and it often turns out that he has been but guided by natural impulses. Adversity opens his eyes; grievous suffering reveals the hand of God. When trouble comes, then God's true friends fly to the feet of Jesus, and there they suffer in all patience, lost in His love, accepting every pain from His hand. And their sincerity in this is so deep, and their love of God so true, that presently their sorrow is turned into joy, because they now suffer because God wills it.

Those whose spirit is not the right one, as soon as adversity falls upon them, are at a loss to know what to do and whither to fly for relief. They run to this one and that one for help, for counsel and for comfort, and are frantic even to despair. How sad to think that such men sometimes are overtaken by death in this condition of soul. In their whole lives they have never sought for God sincerely, never truly loved Him—God is not in their souls during their last moments. They have not built their lives upon Christ as the only foundation, and the building can now only fall to the ground. Such men are worse off a thousand times than mere worldlings, who make no Pharisaical pretentions. Ordinary sinners are conscious of their evil state, and are not devoid of some salutary fear of God, as was the case with the common multitude that always obediently followed after our Lord Jesus Christ. The Pharisees, on the contrary, and the elders and scribes—men with the external show of holiness—never ceased to contradict and to oppose Him, and at last they put Him to a cruel and shameful death. To the like of these you dare not say a word, for if you try to advise them about their sins, they resist you violently and scornfully, or they instantly fly from you—just as did the Jews when our Lord wrote their wickedness with his finger on the ground. They will not own to their wickedness; but they take to flight, beginning with the oldest and the greatest and including the very least among them, till the precincts of the temple are cleared of them all. Simple and commonplace sinners are far more easily led back to God, because they will not deny that they are sinners. Many a time, while they dread that they are yet God's enemies, they have in reality become His friends, because their humble-hearted fear has brought them to the feet of our Redeemer.

Amid all this distrss our heavenly Father has comforted us. Out of the love of His Divine heart for us, He has sent us His only begotten Son, our Lord Jesus Christ. Before our eyes stands His holy life, filled with divinely perfect virtue; in our souls is His glorious truth; we have the merits of His bitter suffering, His shame, His poverty, His death—all given to us with unspeakable love and all for our salvation. And, besides, it is all given to us as an example to follow with every possible earnestness, inward and outward, so that we may pass out of the dark-

ness of sin into His glorious sunshine of truth and love. And that this
may the more efficaciously be granted to us, God has given us His holy
sacraments, beginning with the grace of the true faith in holy baptism,
and then the sacrament of confirmation; holy penance, with its deep
sorrow for sin, humble confession and sincere satisfaction; our Redeemer's precious body and blood in holy communion; and in our last
moments the sacred anointing. All these Divine gifts has He given us,
in order that when we unhappily fall from His grace we may the more
readily be restored to His friendship.

These are all helps to guide us back to God's first love for us, as St.
Augustine teaches: "The infinite Divine light has placed a lesser luminary between itself and us, not to hinder, but to temper the over-brilliant
rays of heavenly influence." The great light is the heavenly Father,
and the lesser one is the humanity of God the Son, our Lord Jesus
Christ. Although in His divinity He is the equal of the Father, yet He
has humbled Himself and taken our humanity, not so much to conceal
His divinity as to temper its majesty, so that it might be possible for us
to look upon it. For He is the true light that enlighteneth every man
that cometh into this world—the light that shineth in darkness and the
darkness received it not.

No man receives this light who is not poor in spirit. He is a man
who is totally empty of self-love and self-will. But, alas, we meet with
men not a few, who for forty years have been poor, indeed, in the goods
of this world and yet have not an atom of poverty of spirit. In theory
and in external observance, yes; in the depths of the soul and in all
sincerity they are by no means self-denying men. True poverty of spirit
is unknown and strange to them, absent and distant from their souls.
Dear children, I beg you to bend all your energies, in principle and in
outward endeavor, to acquire the right dispositions and to do the right
things for enjoying the bright rays of God's light; for that will bring
you back to God, the source and origin of all light. Long for it
earnestly; pray and strive for it incessantly with mental and vocal
pious exercises; implore the Divine aid and that of all of God's friends
in earth and Heaven, that you may be brought to union with Him.
May He graciously grant us this favor. *Amen.*

The Soul's Festival Day

Synopsis—The sacredness of longing for God's joy—Need of energetic
purpose in spiritual affairs—Our baptismal vows bind us irrevo-
cably to strive for God's joy alone—Community vows and rules
are for the same end—And the joy of God is essentially in our
soul's deeper depths.

SECOND SERMON FOR THE FOURTH SUNDAY OF LENT.

My time is not yet come.—John vii, 6.

And when He had said this to His disciples, our Saviour added: "Go
you up to this festival day; but I go not up to this festival day, because
My time is not yet accomplished." As He had already said to them:
"My time is not yet come, but your time is always ready."

Let us enquire what this festival day is, to which our Lord invites us,
and whose time it is that is always ready. It is the greatest of all
festival days, namely, the feast of everlasting life, eternal beatitude in
God's unveiled presence. This cannot yet be ours; now our festival
day is but a foretaste of that eternal jubilee. It consists in the presence of God in the interior of our souls, to obtain the joy of which, is
the object of the seeking and the longing of all our time—the purpose
of all work and life and love. To obtain this festival enjoyment of
God in our souls, we must journey far beyond ourselves, we must go
beyond all that is not God, and this must be done with our whole
heart and in all sincerity. The time for doing this is always.

Now, inasmuch as men naturally desire to be happy, so, however
dimly, do they desire this festival day by an impulse of nature itself.
But such a longing is not enough; it by no means can be naturally satisfied. We must know God better; we must seek Him for His own sake,
and that will give us a foretaste of Him. To this happy state many
souls would gladly attain, and they complain that they are powerless
to do so. When they find no festive joy of God within them, they start
to pray, and they practice other devotional exercises, trusting thereby
to succeed in their wishes. But when they fail they lose courage, they

lessen their pious practices, they give up or but half perform their good works, and in their distress they complain that they have no feeling of God.

Now, no man should act that way. We should never relax our energy in well doing from any such cause, for God is really present with us, whether we feel Him or not. As Jesus did with His disciples, so does God do with us; He comes secretly into our hearts, and where He is there in very truth is the festival day. It cannot be otherwise; God must be with any soul that seeks Him and Him alone, and that in all things. He may be either secretly or openly present; He is none the less there. And whether we are consciously influenced by Him or not, yet must we ever turn inward to Him, passing over and beyond all selfhood. This is what our Lord meant when he said: "Your time is always ready;" that is to say, your time to pass interiorly beyond self and into God. His time is not yet come; that is to say, to reveal Himself to you; leave the choice of that time entirely to Him. Without the faintest doubt He is with you, right there in your soul, but in a hidden manner; pleased that you will think of Him as being there and that you will there commune with Him. Do not, therefore, relax your fervor in your devotions, for He will in His own good time most certainly discover Himself to you.

To this end serve all the pious exercises of our holy religious orders, and all their good works; all sacred laws and rules of what kind soever they may be have this object in view: That we may make ready our souls to hold high festivity with God in the interior life, unencumbered by any other thing whatsoever. In so far as our devout observances minister to this, just so far are they useful and praiseworthy, and where they fail in this the fault is our own; we have caused them to rank only with the observances of the Jewish synagogue. The Old Testament prescribed many things great and holy in themselves, and some of them difficult to perform, and yet all of them taken together could not bring eternal salvation; they were one and all no more than a preparation for the New Testament, to which alone the gates of God's kingdom were thrown open. So must it ever be with external observances; they are useful as a preparation; and, taken by and in themselves, no man can find in them the Divine festival day. The Old Testament led up to and was ended in the New, because the New alone reached into the depths of the soul. So all devotions and pious works must do, or they serve our spiritual life but little.

We have all vowed and sworn to God in holy baptism that we shall serve and love Him until death, an obligation from which no priest or bishop can ever dispense a Christian. It binds us more firmly than any oath taken in a human court; to break which, nevertheless, makes us liable to the penalties of perjury. How much blacker shall be our perjury, if wilfully and deliberately we forswear ourselves to God, by giving to creatures the hearts and souls that we have vowed to Him. When our holy father, St. Dominic, was about to die, our brothers besought him to tell them what was the distinguishing spirit of the holy order, the spirit that inspired him when he made all our rules. They wanted to know the essential reason of those external precepts, all of which they, like ourselves, knew perfectly well. And he gave them the essence of the rule: It is, said he, the love of God, humility and poverty both of spirit and of worldly goods. Thus he would teach us to love God with a whole-hearted love; that, and only that, is the foundation of all; and then to love one another as we love our own selves, being subject to one another in God, in all meekness of behavior; and, further, to be totally void of all sense of ownership, whether of ourselves or of all things else except God alone, our own will no less than the things of this world that may lead us away from God; all this in order that He may enter into our souls. God had made them in His own image, and He wills to take free and entire possession of them, for in that is placed all His content and all His joy.

Dear Sisters, this is the whole meaning of our order. And it is the same with all orders, all the rules and discipline, laws and observances, even of hermitages, as well as of every manner of living devoutly, no matter what its form or its name. The better they serve to bring God into His chosen abode, our interior life, the more useful are they and the more strictly to be observed. This is the meaning of our vows to God; this measures the extent of our guilt if we are unfaithful. If we fail from this point of view we are forsworn to God; if we are true, then we have the very essence of our order, just as our holy father, St. Dominic, taught, and also St. Benedict, St. Augustine, St. Bernard and St. Francis. One and all, their minds were ever preoccupied with this one essential order, for whose sake all their outward rules were made. Dear children, I bid you learn this rule well and thoroughly: to love God and to have Him ever in view, and to love all things only in so far as they actually help you to that end. Keep this rule, and our Lord will keep with you a great and a perfect festival day.

We must keep many rules. We must go to choir to sing and to read office; this we must do, whether we like it or not. Well, then, let us do this with a festive and joyous soul, rather than with a spiritless observance, dragging ourselves to the task. Let us be faithful to our rules in order not to forfeit the eternal festival day in Heaven. It is, indeed, very true that a man who lives a life free from mortal sin, doing nothing wilfully against God's law, will hold fast to the holy faith. But if you would enjoy the happiness of God's festival day in your interior life, then, by way of preparation, you must disencumber your soul of everything that is not God. All true piety of life must have this for its single purpose: That nothing whatsoever shall taste good to thy soul but God alone, whether in thinking or in loving. Such is thy glorious vocation; for that alone has God called thee into this order. For that has He called thee away and freed thee from a deceitful, wicked world, and drawn thee into this holy penitential life; because by our sins we are by nature children of wrath and of everlasting death and damnation. St. Augustine says: "Man is formed of corrupt material, as if he were made of rotten wood and vile earth, and his end is eternal death." Then, for his salvation, there is granted him a life of penance, the same to which God has called you, by no merits of yours, but only by His free and loving gift

And what is that life of penance in very truth and in its essential quality? Nothing else than a whole-hearted turning away from all that is not God, and an equally sincere turning to all that leads to God and means God. The more one answers to that requirement the more penance he does and the better. In this spirit, dear children, must you gladly thank God that He has called you to this order. Your vocation should fill you with confidence that He will finally bring you to His holy company for all eternity; for He has gathered you together here out of a deceitful world, that He might make you His own chosen friends and spouses, and introduce you into most intimate union with Him. It is the plainest sign that God is present in us, when in our early youth he has visited us by our vocation and touched our young hearts with His love. We were by nature inclined to worldly joys, and yet we bridled our appetites and passions, we turned away from the world and all created things, and we followed after God. What if we have no great sensible feeling of devotion, nor lively consciousness of God's indwelling presence! This one fact stands plain: I gladly suffer pain for His sake. Now, that could not be if God were not with me, in however hidden a manner it may be.

O, dear children, bend all your energies to make sure of the enjoyment of the Divine festival day in your souls, when God shall manifest Himself to your inner perceptions.   Let all prayer and work of yours minister to preparation for that close, personal possession of God; for in any other way you cannot feel that you possess Him.   He who possesses God in that true way, him also does God possess, and never does He allow him to leave His holy presence.   Is not this a happy lot?   Is not this the soul's festival day?   Is not our life blessedly happy when we are thus in God and God in us, as well in time as in eternity?   May God grant us this.   *Amen.*

Hearing and Bleeding for Christ

Synopsis—The way of Christ is that of His disciples: self-immolation and obedience to the Father—This is His teaching; how we hear it with the hearing of the heart—How Christ's word affects the various powers of the soul—Hearing His word with an inferior hearing, and the good that may come of it—Bleeding for Christ is by prudent, penitential works by suffering patiently all of life's ills, and by sadness for Christ's sake at the sight of sin—A joyful bloodshedding is granted in the bliss of divine interior union.

FIRST SERMON FOR PASSION SUNDAY.

He that is of God heareth the words of God.—John viii, 47.

I beg you, my dear children, to give me your close attention, and to turn your hearts and minds to this discourse, which will show you your present state of soul, and instruct you what to long for and what to strive after.   Our Redeemer says: "He that is of God heareth the words of God.   Therefore, you hear them not because you are not of God." And then He added: "If any man keep My word, he shall not see death forever."

Children, this is the time of year when we contemplate the holy passion of our Lord Jesus Christ.   Let none of us now give himself up to rest, but rather let him open and read this holy book of Calvary, in which he will find all comfort and all truth, all knowledge and all gift of counsel.   Be well assured that whosoever knows how to study the precious book of Christ's passion, is rightly learned and understands all books whatsoever.   And whosoever cannot do so walks in twilight.   Let our rule and our pattern be the life and death of Jesus Christ, whom we are called on by God to follow.   Therefore does St. Paul teach us in today's epistle: "But Christ, being come an High Priest of the good things to come, by a greater and more perfect tabernacle not made with hands, that is, not of this creation; neither by the blood of goats, or of calves, but by His own blood, entered once into the holies, having obtained eternal redemption." (Heb. ix, 11-12.) Children, let us follow right after this our High Priest, as you were exhorted to do yesterday. Let us seek His honor alone in all things, and with all our own heart and mind.

Our beloved Lord, our High Priest, has gone before us with both the higher faculties and the lower ones of His nature. With the high powers of the Divine nature, to which He was united, He never ceased to regard the entire race of mankind and all their words, works and thoughts. He never lost sight of any one of the human beings made by His heavenly Father, and all the happenings of their lives, whether past, present or to come. He heard the word of God that I now speak to you. He saw all our faces here, looked into our deepest souls and saw all our thoughts and all our inclinations, with every one of the differences that characterizes us. And all this, even of the entire race, did He offer up to His Father, from Whom He had received it all, not excepting the very least thing; for in everything without exception He sought but the glory of His Father. Now, in this our Lord's return to His Father of all that was His, His true friends should faithfully imitate Him. They should not make an exception of a single gift; no, not the very least; but they should give back to God for His glory alone, even though it may be a painful thing to do, everything whatsoever that is theirs, making no reservation at all.

The other way in which our High Priest has gone before us, is that of His inferior or human faculties. And this is the way of His practicing all virtues, especially that of suffering so bitterly for sins of which He was wholly guiltless, because He was determined to seek His Father's glory. It was for this cause that He patiently bore the persecutions of the Pharisees—men who esteemed themselves righteous. So must all of Christ's followers suffer pain, especially those who have sworn and vowed to seek Him and serve Him, suffering, as they must, from the persecution of those who have fallen away from Him. The followers of Christ seek after nothing, keep nothing in view in their conduct, but God. They do not confine themselves to particular ways of serving Him, but in every way that is God's, and always as He guides them do they go forward, making no choice for themselves. It is for this reason that they must suffer from those who seek themselves, and will hear of no way of serving God except their own chosen way. These do not understand men who, not in any particular or favorite way, but in any way and in all ways whatsoever serve God.

Notice that our Lord said: "He that is of God heareth the Word of God." St. Gregory comments on this in a lesson of this day's matins, bidding every one of us search his conscience as to where he stands and to whom he belongs, and whether or not he hears God's Word with the hearing of the heart. God commands us to cherish thoughts of our heavenly fatherland, and to banish the concupiscence of the flesh, and to shun the honors of this world. Hence, insists St. Gregory, each one should examine whether it is his heart that hears and heeds the Word of God; for, he says, there are some whose lives are so unworthy, that they are incapable of interiorly understanding God's word, and are hardly able to listen to it with their bodily ears.

God spoke two words for men's hearing: First, the heavenly Father spoke His eternal Word in the Godhead itself. How closely the human soul is related to that Word in that life of the soul which extends beyond space and time, no human understanding can grasp. The soul of man is exceedingly close to God and kindred to Him in the soul's deepest depths, hidden in that inner and Divine stillness. There it is that the heavenly Father utters His Word, a hundred times quicker than the twinkling of an eye. There that Word is understood, more plainly or less, in proportion as the interior ear of the soul is turned more or less intently to listen, in proportion as the soul abides in greater or less interior quiet and union of spirit with the Word.

But however deeply hidden in the soul that Word may be, it yet rises and spreads upward and outward into those powers of the soul that are above the imagination; that is to say, into the will and the understanding. Therefore might God say that His Word was not His, but ours as well as His. Now, when the will is made aware of the Word within the soul, it quickly starts up, but does not know what it has heard. And then it exclaims: I do not know what I should do, or whether I should do anything. But the understanding now comes to the aid of the will, for it also has heard the Word, and it says to the will: Follow me carefully, for I can teach thee and guide thee. And the understanding forthwith teaches the will what to do and what not to do. And then the Word is sounded within, deeper and farther; namely, into the soul's power of desire, teaching the soul detachment from all created things that can hinder God's work in it; teaching temperance in the use of all things innocent; not in restraint of nature's real necessities, but of superfluities. And then the Word is heard in what philosophers call the soul's irascible faculty, the faculty by which a man resents and avoids what is injurious; herein the Word teaches us patience and meekness, virtues which more than any others will transform thee into what God would have thee. Search thy soul diligently as to what effect God's Word has had on thee, first in thy innermost soul, and then in its different powers. This will be a sign to thee as to whether thou art of God or not, as truth itself has spoken: "He that is of God heareth the Words of God. Therefore, you hear them not because you are not of God."

How shall one continue in this Word, that he may always hear it and understand it? The first way is found in the interior of the soul, where it hears the Word in a state raised above time and space. Does the soul there obey the Word with inward detachment of spirit? That is the question. Those noble souls whose external life has been well trained in devout practices, never, as long as body and soul hang together, consider themselves well enough advanced in virtue. Such a one the moment he hears the Word spoken within him, must draw in to his interior consciousness all his exterior faculties, and, soaring above space and time, he must direct his gaze into eternity. Thus says St. Augustine: "When a man's interior spirit is turned toward eternity, forthwith he has nothing to do with time." Even the active life and that of the senses, to such chosen spirits as these, is almost wholly raised above this temporal existence, and it is only those who have arrived at this state, who hear the Word and receive it in their interior souls. As to the others, they hear the Word in their less spiritual, that is to say, their inferior faculties. Their response is given by a service of mortification and suffering, totally submissive to God's visitations and good pleasure. Yet be cautious; be not imprudent; thou are not allowed to overburden thyself. But yet bend thy back obediently under all afflictions coming from God, whether direct or through men, suffering with all willingness, as under His chastening hand. Carry all burdens back again to Him. Lay every sorrow at His feet with unfeigned gratitude. Our High Priest has not entered in without the shedding of blood; He shed His blood for us; nay, He poured it all out most generously; and there are four ways in which we can shed our blood for Him.

The first is by true penitential works, both of the spirit and of the flesh. When a man has departed from God by his disorderly pleasures and his indulgence in this world's joys, he must turn back and away from such things and wean himself from them, turning now to God;

and this is the essential thing about true penance—a true turning away from sin and a true turning back to God. This is, indeed, to shed one's blood; and it is hard and bitter in proportion to the joy we have had in creatures while we were turned away from God; our blood is now spilt in the death struggle against sin. As one begins this combat, his body is fair and strong; if his penance is genuine, his blood is gradually consumed in God's service, and his body becomes pale, weak and crippled.

The second bloodshedding is in the outward senses; for these are so tamed by penance, that their disorderly use dies out of a man, and pleasure in such things as are heard or seen quite ceases; a man then readily constrains himself to look and listen for inward joys alone. Part of this bloodshedding, is in the persecution God's friends suffer from those who live without taking God into account, and who pierce them through and through with their ill-treatment. This affliction, if they cannot escape it, they must suffer with all mildness. And now a question is asked by strong-souled men, at once pious and bold, but overeager in their own opinion: Should we avoid, should we endeavor to escape, any suffering that overtakes us? As to themselves, they never do so, for they are not rightly guided and do not know from what and when to fly, for their souls are full of impressions which have entered in from the outward world. But the true friend of God knows well what trials to fly from and how long to avoid them. For example: As often as my presence wounds my neighbor's sensibilities rather than helps to sanctify him, then I must leave him. How bright an example have we in our beloved Lord, as we have several times read in the lessons of this week, as He repeatedly fled from among the Jews and hid Himself!

The third bloodshedding is a great one. It is that God's friends must stand by and behold their God, whom they love better than life itself, grossly dishonored by His creatures, the very souls whom He purchased at so dear a price. Sometimes it seems to them—O, what agony!—that the whole world cares nothing for God or ever thinks of Him, not only laymen, but sometimes even clergymen dishonoring Him. This is a two-edged sword, and it cuts through their very heart and soul. They love their neighbor most sincerely, and literally as deeply as they love themselves, and here they behold them doing themselves deadly injury and caring very little about it. One longs to cry out: If thou art baptized a thousand times, and if thou wearest a hundred different religious garbs, it all avails thee nothing if thou dost those things that are not right. It is cause of the deepest sorrow that holy Church, God's blessed flower garden of virtue, is in many lands laid waste by such evil men. And it is a fortunate thing that so many of God's friends are not father confessors, for their hearts would be broken with the knowledge of this misery.

The fourth bloodshedding is very delightful. It happens when God, the Supreme and Blessed Good, takes possession of the soul in its innermost being, withdrawing it from its own self and from all created things and fixing it in Himself most blissfully. Then does a man at last behold the infinite and most sweet Good that God is, that no created being can fully comprehend. Then does he know that all the praise and love that is due to the saints and angels, is as nothing compared to the glory that is due to the Being that is now present to his soul. Ah, when the spirit of a man thus learns the superessential infinity of God, how utterly sinks away out of his sight the pettiness of self and of all creatures! Now, at last, he is able to say: I hold back nothing from God. The soul stripped of everything that is not God, is immersed in the abyss of the Godhead; self-existence is lost and gone, as it were, and the soul dwells in God alone, and God, in turn, loves and praises the soul and has His delight in it. This bloodshedding,—is it not, indeed, delightful when the creature is thus immersed in God the Creator? That we may all attain to this happy end, may our good God grant us. *Amen.*

Of Desiring to Be Perfect

Synopsis—The sin of disliking spiritual doctrine—Desire of perfection is in itself a grade of perfection—Contentment with present spiritual conditions is apt to be sinful—Unrest is often a sign of vigorous spiritual health.

SECOND SERMON FOR PASSION SUNDAY.

He that is of God heareth the words of God.—John viii, 47.

Dear children, although you may not live up to God's word, yet you should none the less hear it, and then you should speak about it. For as long as you continue to love it and wish to possess it, it is in a way yours, and you will yet be made eternal partakers of it. We meet with those who turn away from high spiritual doctrine, because they cannot comprehend it, and they think they have no concern with it; and at last they have an aversion either to speak about it or hear others do so. I have no notion of these things, one will say, and it is best that I have nothing to say or hear about them, for I am better without them, and so I wish to remain; and then they even try to turn others away from high spiritual thoughts, as if they, too, had better avoid them. But meanwhile, though pretending to be well satisfied with their own way, they know in their hearts that it is not the best. All this indicates plainly that they will never reach their best interior state, nor partake of the infinite Good, except God leads them through a season of grief and mental trial.

St. Bernard says: "O man, dost thou yearn for a noble and holy life, and dost thou beg this favor of God? If thou dost, then persevere faithfully in this state of soul, and thy prayer shall be granted thee a single day, yea, even one hour before thy death; and if God does not grant it thee in this life, then all the more surely will He do so in eternity in union with Himself." Therefore, never give up thy hopes and thy prayers because they are not immediately heard and fulfilled or are heard only for an occasional moment. And be not disheartened because this holy purpose easily escapes from thy mind. To lose it totally were a great misfortune, but that shall not, we hope, be thy sad lot. When thou hearest God's word cleave fast to it as if for all eternity, resolve to keep it and live by it forever and ever, sinking it deep into thy soul. It may happen that thou shalt afterwards quite cease to think of it; but, for all that, the love of it and the longing to observe it with which thou didst first receive it, shall always shine brightly in God's sight, and in His own good time He will make His word efficacious for thy eternal welfare.

What we can actually do may not amount to much, but we can always desire to do great things. A man may not play a great part in act, but he always can have great good will; and whatsoever he would wish to be, supposing that his whole heart and soul and mind are in his wish, that as a matter of fact—in some true way, at least—he actually is. We have little strength to do, much strength to desire to do, and that it is that constantly grows within us, and finally goes forth from us into the heart of God. Of course, we do not mean that a man should idly dream that he would like to be equal to such or such a saint or angel, but simply this: I long most earnestly to give myself entirely and exclusively to God—to God alone. If a man cannot be God's as much as he would gladly wish to be, yet let him be as much God's as he can be. Whatever a man is, let him be that to God wholly; and what he cannot be to God, let him wish earnestly yet to become, by God and in God. And it may well happen, that we have God more in this state of privation than in some states of possession. Therefore, be thou God's man; wait patiently on God; hold God to thee and in thee and with thee; nothing will now ever go wrong with thee.

Do not for a moment suppose that our Lord God will grant thee special favors, such as perfect spiritual contentment, enlightenment or warmth of love, as He sometimes does in the beginning of conversion. That thought is only a sort of alluring snare, such as the falconer uses to capture his hawk. Our Lord deals with His own thus: First, He teaches them, and then He lets them work for themselves. Just as He caused Moses to make his tables of the law after the pattern He Himself had set. So God allows a man to stand by himself, and, having awakened, enlightened and attracted him, after a time he does so no more; He leaves us now to utilize His graces. We must arouse our own slothfulness, awaken our consciences and perceptions, light up the fires of energetic action, and serve God diligently at our own cost. While children are yet quite young their father helps them in everything, giving them all that they need and turning them out to their play, happy and contented and well provided for—all at the father's expense and care. When they are grown, he gives them a share of his property and bids them care for themselves; all playtime is now over and done, and they must learn how to become rich men by their own exertions.

God treats us the same way. The beginning of a devout life is all joy and sensible devotion, for He is now alluring us by His gifts. He so manages that we find His will in everything that we do; His will coincides with ours entirely. But presently all this is changed. Now God insists that we shall give up our own will in spite of ourselves; in fact go against our own will—a very hard and unpleasant task, indeed. We must learn to suffer; and, besides, we must grope along in the dark; and, although we are quite willing, yet it is not by our natural will, but in spite of it, that we yield all guidance to Him. Thus did our Lord prophesy to Peter: "Amen, amen, I say to thee, when thou wast younger thou didst gird thyself, and didst walk where thou wouldst. But when thou shalt be old, thou shalt stretch forth thy hand and another shall gird thee, and lead thee whither thou wouldst not." (John xxi, 18-19.)

Thus in the beginning we fettered ourselves with God's will by the help of His loving and sweet influences, and we went by His leave whithersoever we would, our will and His being perfectly in harmony. And now it is altogether different; He will bind us all unwilling and lead us whither we do not want to go. Against all our natural inclinations He will lead us by dark paths into Himself. This He will continue till He has stripped us of our natural will, wholly brought it under subjection and totally consumed it. His purpose is that finally to will and not to will shall not any longer be considered by us, nor giving and keeping, nor having and lacking. The end will be to forget all things created, and let them go from us and let them stay away from us, and, instead, to accept and possess God alone, to have Him alone in all joy and sorrow. We become most dear children of God only when neither happiness nor misery, pleasure nor pain can keep us back from God. What all this means in the soul cannot be described, but this much is plain: It is incomparably better than if one were all afire with devotional sentiment, accompanied with a lesser degree of thorough-going self-renunciation, having more self-chosen spiritual methods with pious feelings, and at the same time less true-hearted loyalty to God. May God help us to the better state of His love. *Amen.*

Short Cuts to Holiness

Synopsis—One is the way of public shame; another is by a call to extraordinary penances, accompanied by deep humility—Herein is danger of self-righteousness.

FIRST SERMON FOR PALM SUNDAY.

It is expedient for you that one man should die for the people.—John xi, 50.

St. John adds that Caiaphas spoke not of himself when he said these words, but that he was moved by the Holy Ghost to prophesy; and you will notice, dear children, that this last prophesying was just before our Saviour's death. The chief priests had said: "What do we, for this Man doth many miracles. If we let Him alone so, all will believe in Him, and the Romans will come and will take away our place and nation." Children, let us admire the deep and unspeakable love of Jesus for us, shown by the wonderful sufferings He endured in all His powers of body and of mind, in His inner and in His outer life.

Now, children, many men enquire for the shortest road to the highest truth. Mark well that to answer this our Lord calls three kinds of men to perfection. One kind He calls to suffer public humiliation, in order that they may turn to God and maintain entire purity of intention; and such as these, if they but accept their lot humbly, will experience wonderful effects of Divine grace. To our outward senses such souls may seem deserving of condemnation, for appearances are often against them. But if we do condemn them, we shall only hurt our own selves.

Another kind of men God draws to Himself by works of penance. But let us ask, What is true penance? It is, for example, that when a man would gladly talk, he yet, for God's sake, keeps silence; and when he would with much pleasure enjoy looking at something or indulging any of his other senses, he yet will not allow himself to do it, but, for God's sake, shuts himself away from it. The third kind of men our beloved Lord draws by His own self.

Mark this well, children: Every man must die if all shall go well with him. And what "man" do we mean by this? We mean a man's own

will, his spiritual sense of proprietorship; that is what must die. And to what things must a man die? Be assured of this, children: If thou hadst suffered all the pains of the martyrs and of the other saints, and hadst done the good that all Christendom has done or shall do to the end of the world, unless this has entered into thy soul and has done its work within thee, it will profit thee nothing, and thou hast not died to thyself; no, nor unless thou hast wholly renounced everything to which thou hast cleaved for thy own satisfaction.

And what sign shall a man have, that he has thus spiritually and in very truth died? Be it known to thee that if thou wert dead and raised to life a thousand times over, and if thou hadst fed daily only on rocks and thorns, and been broken on the wheel, yet all this would not be the true sign of dying to self. But rather this, and this alone: If thou hast bowed thyself down beneath the infinite mercy of God with all humility and self-renunciation, yea, and under the feet of all creatures, then know for certain that Christ, entirely out of His loving kindness and compassion, has granted thee His gift.

And here shines forth Christ's teaching: "So you also, when you shall have done all these things that are commanded you, say: We are unprofitable servants." (Luke xvii, 10.) And if it should happen that a man comes to the end and expires fixed fast in his own will, then the Romans shall come and take away his place and nation. For, as the Empire of Rome was the greatest power in the world, so is spiritual pride the greatest among all the vices, holding possession, as it does, of the very highest powers of the soul—those that God alone should possess by His grace. It is this terrible enemy, pride, that destroys the whole virtue of a man in all his powers, from the highest to the lowest, as the Romans smote and destroyed the Jews.

Children, be on your guard, for there are many men who seem to be something wonderful, and who, with all their great knowledge and fame, go astray from this one only way to God. As long as self-guidance and self-will rules in us and is not exterminated, it will go right onward in its fatal course, till all that Christ has done within our souls is destroyed. How many men are there not—men of fair appearance spiritually, and with whom God in the beginning worked wonders—who have, nevertheless, finally failed? It was because they did not accept this truth in single-hearted sincerity, but rested upon self, inwardly and outwardly, in mind and body. Look at King Solomon as an example of this; God once spoke familiarly with him. Look at Samson, who received God's messages by a holy angel. And upon both of these fell God's wrath and condemnation, because they were not willing to die to themselves in spirit and in act, as they ought to have done. They rested and dwelt on God's gifts for their own self's sake; they took His favors with a sense of personal ownership, and with unbridled enjoyment of them; and they failed in thankfulness to God. And now how stands it with them in the final judgment of the Most High? Holy Church knows not whether they are saved or lost, and we must blindly leave them to the goodness of God.

And now come yet another class—men rich in the treasures of their own natural understanding and puffed up with self-importance, and they would boast that they have acquired all spirituality. No, children, their spirit is false; go not after them. For all that our poor fallen nature gives, it exacts again; and what Christ gives, He also exacts again. Yet these men often seem to bear pain more courageously than really spiritual men, to whom they speak and say: God have mercy on us! What an unmortified man art thou! Thus they mock a man who is really mortified in spirit as well as in outward behavior. But sometimes these really good men do not appear mortified, for God grants them, as a sign of their genuine and interior self-denial, the grace of being cheerful and hopeful toward God and toward all men, good and bad; they are gentle and kindly and happy in their manners. Creatures can neither give nor take, in their case; for what they long to possess, namely, God's holy will, that they ever have, whether in pain or ease, weal or woe. That alone they desire in time and eternity, whether they reckon for themselves or think of created things. Children, waste no time with self-righteous men, led only by reason's light. About them Christ has taught us: "Every plant which My heavenly Father hath not planted, shall be rooted up." (Matt. xv, 13.) This fate is visited upon them because they will not repent and turn to better ways. Thoroughly good men, on the other hand, are instructed by the example of our Lord in the garden. When His bitter agony came upon him, He sweat blood, so great was His anguish of soul; and in this awful pain of heart did He continue, till He lovingly gave up His life for us. Every man must do in like manner. He must suffer death in soul and body, in what he does and what he leaves undone. Children, learn our Saviour's lesson: It is to give yourselves up to all suffering for His sake; it is to be wholly subject to God and to all His creatures, even unto death, both in spirit and in body. God grant us this. *Amen.*

Christ's Cleansing of the Temple of the Soul

Synopsis—Who are the traffickers—All who deal with God not purely out of love—Danger of counting too surely on a recompense for virtue—Beauty of holiness all freed of mercenary motives—Revelations of Jesus to a soul devoid of selfhood.

SECOND SERMON FOR PALM SUNDAY.

And Jesus went into the temple of God, and cast out all them that sold and bought in the temple.—Matt. xxi, 12.

And when Jesus had done this He spoke to those who sold doves and said: "Take these things away." It was His will to cleanse His temple. It was as if He had said: I am the owner of this temple, and I alone shall dwell in it and be master of it.

And what is this temple in which God alone shall rule with all power and according to His own will? It is man's soul, which He has created in close resemblance to Himself, according to His word: "Let us make man after Our image and likeness." (Gen. i, 26.) And this likeness of man's soul to God is so close, that nothing else is to be compared with it for close resemblance to Him in Heaven or on earth. This is why God will have our soul free and clear of everything but Himself alone, and when that is done He is well pleased to make His abode there alone.

Who were those that bought and sold in the temple, and who are they that do so now? And take notice that I am to speak only of those buyers and sellers in the temple who are good people, and who are nevertheless scourged out of His temple by the Lord; not gross sinners or such as are consciously in a state of mortal sin; and yet they are buyers and sellers. They are souls who, indeed, guard against grievous sins, and would do good works for God's glory; they fast and pray and keep vigils and do other good things. But what is their motive? It is that God would in return do good things to them, bestow on them the favors they wish. They are, therefore, self-seekers; they are merchandisers with God, as anyone can see. They give that they may get. They must traffic with our Lord. And meanwhile in all their trading with

God they are self-deceived. For what is there of all they possess and trade with but God has given it to them? God owes them nothing, no matter what they may give Him or do for Him. Whatever they are, they are from God; whatever they have, they have from God, and are nothing and have nothing of themselves.

Hence I say again, God owes them nothing for all they may do for Him or give Him. He has given them all they have willingly out of His free grace, not on account of their works or gifts. They have nothing of their own to give Him; no power of their own bestowal wherewith to work for Him, as Christ says: "Without Me you can do nothing." (John xv, 5.) How dull and foolish are such men, to think that they really trade with the Lord! They perceive the truth of Divine things scarcely at all, and hence the Lord scourges them out of His temple. Light and darkness can have no fellowship. God in His very essence is truth and light, and when He enters His temple He drives ignorance and darkness out of it, revealing Himself in all His brightness. When truth enters in and is recognized, then trafficking must go out; truth can tolerate no trafficking with God. God is not selfish, but in all His works He is free, being directed wholly by perfect love. And thus acts every man who is united to God. In all that he does he is free and unselfish, acting purely from love, never asking why and wherefore; that is to say, never seeking his own, but only God and His glory; and in all this God is working in him.

And let me insist: As long as a man in all his good works seeks or desires as his controlling motive what God may give him as a recompense, so long is he like the traffickers in the temple. If thou wilt be quit and done with all such trafficking, then do all the good that thou dost for God's praise alone, and stand as entirely free as if there were to be no return made thee. Then thy good deeds become entirely spiritual and Godlike. Then are all traffickers driven out of the temple of thy soul. God alone dwells in the soul of a man that in his good works takes Him and Him alone into account. This is then the purifying of the soul from all self-seeking, God and His honor becoming the end and purpose of all.

But this Gospel points out to us a yet higher grade of distinterestedness. For there are some who have a pure intention in their well-doing, and yet are hindered from attaining a high state of perfection; namely, those who keep up a less blameworthy traffic with creatures, like those dealers in doves whose chairs the Lord overthrew in the temple. The traffic in doves was well meant at first, and yet it was unseemly; and it became the occasion of avarice rather than a help to the worship of God in the temple. So it is with some men, who have an upright intention and serve God without self-seeking. Yet they still yield to a feeling of ownership in their good deeds. They insist on doing them in a certain sense mechanically, and strictly according to time and place and number and routine, and according to specified plans, and this hinders their coming to the best spiritual state. They should hold their souls free from all such things, just as our Saviour Himself did, and be ever ready to begin anew, without waiting for certain times or going to certain places. They should give themselves over to the guidance of the heavenly Father just as Christ did; yea, obedient to the least intimation of His holy will, determined on one thing only— to be perfectly under the loving influence of His fatherly heart. Thus one is led to a life of the truest perfection, unhindered by methods and arrangements of his own, only anxious to yield instantly, and, as it were, to the beck and nod of God's will; and in the same spirit to return God's gifts back again into the heart of our Lord Jesus Christ with all praise and thanksgiving. Then it comes to pass that all hindrances to spiritual progress are taken away; from such a soul even the doves and their venders are expelled—all sense of proprietorship whatsoever, even that which is least blameworthy, is done away, and a man seeks himself in nothing at all. Our Lord is determined that no one shall make any disturbance in His temple; He will permit no running about here and there, as St. Matthew tells us. Which means that a spiritual man must purify his motives, until they are clear of every obstacle that may divert him from advancing even a single step in perfection.

And when this purification of the temple of the soul has been accomplished, and all ignorance and proprietorship are cleansed away, then God's work in it shines so beautiful and so bright that it excels the glory of any other of His creations. No beauty can outshine that of such a soul, save only the uncreated beauty of God Himself, whom it resembles more than any other creature can. No angel can be like it; not even the highest of them; for, though it have much resemblance to it, it is yet not quite like it. For to the progress of an angel there is now, in a certain sense, a limit fixed as to the beatific vision, whereas this soul can continue to grow more and more perfect as long as it lives in time. Suppose a man who is still in this life gifted with the virtue of a certain angel; his freedom and his opportunities are such as to enable him to advance every instant beyond the angel in perfection. God alone is free with uncreated liberty, and so is the soul free, but not in uncreated liberty; and herein is there a peculiar resemblance between God and the soul. And when the soul departs this life, it is absorbed in light uncreated—in God—then it must attain to union with Him by full knowledge of Him. And this, as we have already shown, is begun by our Lord Jesus Christ, when He enters the soul and drives out of it the buyers and sellers, and begins intimately to speak to it.

Dear children, rest assured that if any one undertakes to speak in the temple—that is, in our soul—except Jesus alone, then does Jesus immediately become silent. He no longer feels at home there; indeed, it is now not His home, for it entertains strange guests and holds converse with them. Not only so; but if Jesus is to speak, the soul itself must be silent, and do nothing but listen to Him. The moment it sits still and listens, He begins to speak. What does He say He says, I am: I am the Father's Word. And then in the same Word thus spoken the Father Himself speaks, the entire Divine nature is heard—all that is God, all that God's Word is to God's self, perfect in self-knowledge and infinite in power. God is infinitely perfect in His utterance to the soul, for the Word He utters is Himself; it is the Second Divine person of the Godhead, of the same nature with the Father.

And in speaking this Divine Word God utters all reasonable beings in created existence, thus forming them like unto His uncreated Word. as It ever dwells within Him. All the brightness of created intelligences, is made after the image of the glory of this uncreated Word of God. And this resemblance consists essentially, in the capability the created soul has of receiving by Divine grace God's uncreated Word; yea, even the very Word that is God, receiving It as It is in Itself. This was all uttered by God, when He divinely spoke His infinite Word in the Godhead. Now, one might enquire: Since the Father has thus spoken His Word, what does Jesus speak in the soul? Dear children, I answer you by recalling what I have already said of the manner of His communication: He speaks and reveals His own self, and that includes all that the Father has spoken in the Divine act of uttering the Word, all being now addressed to the soul according to its capacity to receive it.

First, He reveals the Father's supreme majesty in the soul, in His sovereign and immeasurable power. And when the soul feels and perceives this almighty power in God's Son—feels itself made a partaker of that power in all virtue and in perfect purification, so that neither joy nor sorrow nor any other created force can unsettle its peace; then in that Divine power it rests, strong against all adversaries, great or little.

In addition to this, the Lord reveals Himself in the soul in infinite wisdom—in the very Divine wisdom that He is Himself, that in which the Father knows Himself with His almighty paternity; and, again, the Word that is wisdom itself and is one essence with the Father. When this wisdom is united to the soul, all doubting and all straying away is stopped, and all spiritual darkness vanishes, and the soul is placed in the clear light that is God's self. It is now as the prophet said: "In Thy light we shall see light." (Ps. xxxv, 10.) That is to say: Lord, all light is seen in the soul in the light that Thou art. Thus is God known in the soul by the light that God Himself is. And thus is Wisdom known by the light of Wisdom Itself; and with it the soul knows itself and all things else that it knows. Thus, again, by this wisdom is known God's fatherhood in majesty, His essential unchangeableness, and His Divine and indivisible unity.

Thirdly, Jesus reveals Himself within the soul with infinite love, with sweetness and abundance of love welling forth from the Holy Ghost, and overflowing into the heart, all docile and receptive of its rich streams. Yes, it is by means of the Love that Jesus is that He reveals Himself to the soul and unites it to Himself. It is this sweetness that causes the soul to flow into itself, and then to overflow beyond all creatures—melted by Divine grace, given power to return again into God its first fountain and origin. Then the outward man bows down obedient to the inward man—obedient unto death; then are both the inward and outward faculties at peace with each other in God's service. May God grant us this happy state; may He expel and destroy all hindrances in us in both soul and body, so that we may be made one with Him in time and in eternity. *Amen.*

Lessons of Christ's Passion

Synopsis—His nakedness makes voluntary poverty a divine virtue—His being placed between two thieves shows the splendor of brotherly love—His pity for His enemies tells us of God's mercy to sinners—Obedience is taught by His resignation to His father's will even unto death—Holy friendship is illustrated by His treatment of His mother and St. John—Patience and perseverance are inculcated by the nailing of His holy body to the cross—Constancy in prayer is shown by His ending His life with a sigh of prayerful hope.

FIRST SERMON FOR GOOD FRIDAY.

With Christ I am nailed to the cross.—Gal. ii, 19.

Thus speaks the apostle, teaching us that we must never permit the sacred passion of our Lord to be absent from our thoughts, but that with deep emotion, sympathy and gratitude, we must ever meditate on it. There is no surer, easier or better way to be freed from our sins and to acquire all virtues, graces and joys than this devout practice. Nay, there is no other way to go to God; it is the one only way that all the saints have trodden. O, how much is to be said on this holy theme, one which surpasses the angels' powers of understanding: Of how God became man out of His great love for us, and then for such vile sinners humbled Himself even to the bitter cross!

And if the everlasting Lord and God of all, suffered such shame and such torment for us, should not all who claim to be His friends willingly suffer whatsoever God allots them, whether they be guilty or innocent? Should they not esteem themselves honored, thus to be made like Him and allowed to follow after Him in this His chosen way of the cross? Hence the holy apostle St. Peter admonishes us: "Christ, therefore, having suffered in the flesh, be you also armed with the same thought." (I Peter, iv. 1.) And so does our holy and faithful mother, the Church, tell us that this thought should never be absent from our hearts. This

she does not only by the holy scriptures and in her public worship, but
also she would help our weakness with pious pictures and statues of
our Lord's sufferings. She never ceases to exhort us to praise and
thank God for His infinite love, most perfectly proved by His blessed
death for our souls. This is also holy Church's reason for giving us
the pictures and other representations of her saints. These are offered
us to make us imitate their holy lives, to help us battle manfully against
evil, and suffer patiently for God's sake, to strengthen us in our faith,
to arouse our sleeping energies to the faithful service of God. Above
all these emblems is the figure of Jesus crucified—above all to be prized,
most often to be venerated, and interiorly to be contemplated. Let us
now study the lessons that our beloved Lord has written upon His crucified body, and let us print them indelibly in our hearts.

The first lesson is taught by the nakedness of His body on the cross;
it is voluntary poverty. So must we learn to be poor for His sake,
since He became poor for our sakes. Out of all His rich kingdoms, He
kept not so much as would serve to cover Him as He hung on the cross.
He had said: "Blessed are the poor in spirit, for theirs is the Kingdom
of Heaven." (Matt. v, 3.) Is not the Kingdom of Heaven a rich treasure to him who is so fortunate as to possess it? And it is a blessed
lot for more reasons than its riches. Voluntary poverty bestows more
upon a man than he can desire. What he has contents him; he is satisfied in his poor estate, so much so that he does not feel himself poor at
all. The covetous man ever covets to gain yet more, ever dreads to be
robbed; the poor man of Christ is ever thinking that he has more than
enough. Therefore is he rightly called blessed and happy, because he
has all that he desires; for all he desires is to be poor, and to suffer want
is his purpose—very willingly and for God's sake. Such men have,
indeed, learned by heart and in their hearts how to be poor. They have
always before their eyes the spectacle of Jesus crucified. His blessed
humanity, poor and in want all His days on earth, is printed on their
heart's tablets. Blessed are these men; no man can rob them, for they
own nothing worth stealing. Again they are blessed, because they have
been granted a foretaste of Heaven's blessed freedom, owning all and
more than all that is needful even in and by their poverty; for that
gives them a sweet contentment of mind, to be rewarded after death by
the Kingdom of Heaven itself.

The second lesson of Jesus crucified is perfect brotherly love, for you
know that He was hung between two thieves; and this was His own

choice, for He desired to bear the penalty of their guilt. How could He ever have better shown that His love was perfect, than by bearing the burden of the guilt of His enemies on His own shoulders, having it struck and cut into all His members? If He had but died for His friends alone, even so it were a mark of mighty love; but that He died for His enemies is a mark of perfect love. In this He teaches us that we should love our enemies, and that we should do so by serving them in all their necessities. Our Lord would be put to death not only for His friends and for good people; He would suffer all His bitter passion and His cruel death for the wicked and for His enemies. And if He showed such love to His very enemies, what, think you, must be His love for His friends, who have so faithfully followed Him? St. Paul tells us: "When as yet we were enemies, according to the time, Christ died for us; much rather therefore now, being justified by His blood, shall we be saved from wrath through Him." (Rom. v, 9.)

The third lesson of Jesus crucified is His overflowing mercy. See how He treated the thief that hung all justly for his crimes alongside of Him on the cross, and who had reviled and blasphemed Him. (Matt. xxvii, 44.) But when this malefactor repented and begged a grace of Jesus, He instantly pardoned him, and He granted him a greater boon than he had asked. He said: "Lord, remember me when Thou comest into Thy kingdom." Jesus gladly hearkened to him, and answered: "Amen, I say to thee, this day thou shalt be with Me in Paradise." Jesus not only thought of him kindly and spoke a good word to him, but He joined the poor wretch very closely to Himself, Who is the true and living paradise of eternal joy. And you know how our Lord, as soon as He died, descended in His human soul joined to His Divine nature into the Limbus of the just, and announced to all those God-fearing souls there the near approach of their eternal happiness. In that happy journey the good thief was our Lord's companion, and his paradise was to see Jesus then amid His chosen friends. Was not this a proof of a heart overflowing with mercy? And if He treated an enemy thus, will not His love overflow yet more generously toward His friends? But, besides adoring His mercy, let us be sure to imitate it in our conduct toward friends and foes, and especially the latter.

The fourth lesson learned beneath the cross of Christ is, perfect and devout obedience. Obedience it was that nailed Him to the cross, and that virtue did He especially show when He bowed His head and gave up the ghost. Herein piety and obedience are both shown forth. For it was an act of absolute obedience to His Father, when He accepted death and gave up His soul out of His body; and that He reverently bowed down His head, was a mark of the devout feeling with which His heart was filled. And listen to His last words: "Father, into Thy hands I commend My spirit." (Luke xxiii, 46.) As if to say: Father, I have obeyed Thee even unto death, and all of Thy holy will I have completely accomplished: "It is consummated" (John xix, 30); and, bowing His sacred head, He gave up the ghost. Learn from this to be not only obedient, but devoutly obedient, as our Lord was. Whatever is commanded us, or advised, or counselled, let us receive it with a devoutly bowed head. Thus will men know that we have gentle hearts and a devout spirit in our obedience; for the devotional spirit is always gentle and yielding.

Let me tell you what is true piety toward God. It is that one interiorly realizes for whose sake we give up our body and our goods in holy obedience—namely, for God's sake. And when one receives directions from a superior, let him say in his own mind: My Lord and Father and Redeemer, I gladly accept this obedience out of love for Thee; receive this the submission of my will as a sacrifice to Thy glory. And let us maintain this devout obedience to the end, even unto death; for St. Paul teaches what Christ did for us: "He humbled Himself, becoming obedient unto death." (Phil. ii, 8.) We should often meditate on Christ's obedience, gaining thereby strength to practice obedience ourselves. For whosoever comes to the end of his life and is not found in a state of holy obedience, cannot hope to share in the merits of Christ's obedience on the cross.

The fifth lesson of Jesus crucified is that of respect and friendship. Mark well His treatment of His beloved mother. As she stood beneath His cross, He would not allow her to suffer her dreadful sorrow without any solace. However sad His own desolation as He hung there, He yet did not forget her. He could not speak much with her, so great was His pain. But the few words He did say, proved to her how boundless was His love and His respect for her. All sweetly did He address her, as best He might in His state of torture, being nigh unto death, His bodily forces wasting fast away: "Woman, behold thy son!" How mindful was He of His beloved mother, even amid such bodily torments. He committed her to the care of His beloved disciple St. John, as if He would say: You perceive, dear mother, to what a pass I, thy only Son, am come. I know that My sufferings pierce thy soul with a sharp sword of agony, beholding Me hanging here before thy eyes, all dripping with blood; but behold John, thy son! Let him comfort thee in My place. How well this teaches us to honor and reverence our father and mother, and not only our natural parents, but also our spiritual parents—our fathers and mothers in religion; yea, and our brothers and sisters, too— all for the sake of God and in God, just as our Lord has commanded us, so that it may be well with us in the land He will give us.

The sixth lesson of Jesus crucified is the virtue of patience. For our Lord, in allowing Himself to be nailed fast to the cross, as much as said to His torturers: Inflict on Me all the suffering you wish; I will gladly bear it all. In his whole life He never did anything that merited the least punishment. And yet, now that He is so cruelly treated, He is so patient that He has not a single bitter thought, not one word of reproach. For what did He say? "Father, forgive them"—these men who are torturing Me; "forgive them, for they know not what they do." This teaches us to willingly accept unjust punishment, to patiently suffer wrong, never forgetting how patient the Lord was as He allowed Himself to be nailed to the cross. What else does this mean but that we should suffer miseries visited on us rightly or wrongly, with equal and entire submission, accepting meekly whatever God permits to happen to us.

The seventh lesson of Christ's cross is steadfast perseverance. Mark that he allowed His feet to be nailed to the cross, as if to say: I will stand fast here in My obedience to My Father; I will not move one step away; here stand I till death. Thus should we stand fast in a good life, bearing the cross of penance to the end, hands and feet nailed to the cross of a dying life, never harboring a single thought except that of following Jesus crucified, crucifying all our vices and concupiscences with great good will, and so persisting even unto death. If Jesus finds us thus fastened to the cross, He will forgive us every evil thing that we ever did. To stand fast in good—that is our purpose; for if one had lived a good life for a thousand years, and afterwards fell away but for one hour and thus died, then in spite of all his former goodness he would be lost. Therefore, let us persevere with all steadfastness, and, as it were, nailed hands and feet to the cross, even unto the end; for as we are found at the moment of death so shall we be judged.

The eighth lesson of Christ's cross is constant prayer, for you know that our Lord, amid all his pains, prayed without ceasing. A certain teacher surmises that He recited a hundred and fifty verses of the psalms, a verse for every psalm in the psalter. According to this, He began with the twenty-first psalm, "O God, My God, look upon Me; why hast Thou forsaken Me?" and ending with the sixth verse of the thirtieth psalm, "Into Thy hands I commend My spirit." And with these last words He gave up the ghost. Now, just consider that Jesus the Son of God, who was all innocent and guileless, was so desolate in His last agony as to exclaim, "My God, My God, why hast Thou forsaken Me!" When we consider that, must we poor sinners not shrink in dismay from the thought of our own last agony? What shall we then say to God? Jesus prayed to His Father thus humbly, and as if He had been a life-long sinner, and He did so to set us an example, so that now and always until death we should meekly appeal for pardon to our Heavenly Father. Such should be our constant prayer, for prayer is always nec-essary, and if diligently persevered in, as death comes, when it is most necessary, we can easily turn our heart, with all its emotions and affections, perfectly to God. Then shall we be granted deep and humble confidence in God's blessed mercy; we shall be enabled with this prayer to beat off all evil spirits, who will then assail us more fiercely than ever before, in order to bring us to eternal ruin. May God grant that they shall have no power to hurt us. *Amen.*

How God Draws Souls to Himself

Synopsis—This drawing is essentially inward—Need of detachment if this drawing is to be felt—How adversity and suffering should turn us towards God's inward drawing, and even more the sense of desolation.

SECOND SERMON FOR GOOD FRIDAY.

And I, if I be lifted up from the earth, will draw all things to Myself.—John xii, 32.

Our Lord Jesus Christ means that He will draw all men to Himself when He is lifted up; for man has a share of all things in himself—in common with the stones of the earth he has existence, life with the trees and plants, sense with animals, and reason with angels.

But someone might say, O Christ, Thou eternal truth, I do not feel Thy drawing, I am not attracted to Thee. St. Augustine answers: "Then pray that thou mayst be drawn to Him." The fisherman casts his baited hook that the fish may seize it, and if it does not do so, then the fisherman does not get the fish; if it does, then the fisherman is sure of it and draws it in to the shore. So has God cast his hooks and his nets toward us and all around us; they are His angels and all His other creatures, by which He would draw us to Him most gladly by our eyes and our ears and our hearts. By joyous things he draws us to Him, and by painful things as well. Whosoever is not caught and drawn to God has only himself to blame, for he has wilfully avoided the angels' drawing—he will not receive God's baited hook nor enter His net. If he had done so, God would have surely captured him; we have only to reach a hand toward God, and He will never fail to grasp it and draw us to Himself. Suppose you are at the bottom of a deep well and someone comes and lets down a rope to you; ought you not to grasp it and be saved?

The soul is like a feather blown about by the wind; but if a weight is attached to it, it rests idly on the ground. So does a soul freed from all weight of sinfulness easily soar aloft to God on the wings of holy meditation. Such a soul is lightened and cleansed of all thoughts about bodily things, and set at rest in all stillness of spirit. Its intentions and aspirations cleave close to the unchangeable Good that God is. God's praises are unceasingly sounded in that soul. And this happens because the soul is self-denying in all things, as far as its state of life will allow. Whosoever is for God's sake far removed from love of earthly things, becomes transformed, and, like an angel, he is drawn deep into God. And, being so closely joined to Him, then whatever happens to that soul in its outward life is received in God and on account of God—eating or drinking, sleeping or waking, or whatsoever else he does, that man does all for the best honor of God.

A man's highest perfection consists in interior tranquillity, all his faculties drawn in by an indescribably powerful detachment from created things, producing an angelic state of soul. Such a one is freed from what is offensively unlike God, and is granted a foretaste of that Divine union which he shall enjoy in eternity. Therefore, retire into thyself and be at rest from all outward and inward stirring, as far as God's law will allow thee; give thyself up to Him in that state of mind, receiving His communication with thee directly or otherwise, according to His good pleasure. And whatever then comes to thee from God, accept it in entire self-renunciation, as being wholly from His hand, and be sure to return it back to Him in deep gratitude; receive all as a loan from Him, for it is His and not thine, and ever so remains. Thus wilt thou give God His glory, and thy own nature and heart and mind will abide in holy poverty in His sight.

When a man is thoroughly detached from all transitory things, and is rightly ordered in self-renunciation, he is in the first degree of his progress toward God. The second degree is when his soul is established in peace and rest. The third degree is when he receives all things, pleasant or unpleasant, from God's hand in equal contentment of mind and is wholly resigned to God. This happens when a man lives in self-forgetfulness, in forgetfulness of all created things, and is lost in God. This degree is the highest perfection of purity of heart.

But let no man presume to take up this high and holy work of God of his own initiative. Rather let him humbly await God's guidance, abandoning himself in all peacefulness and in total detachment to the Divine influence, whenever and however it may come to him. This will be all that God requires of him—that he stand before Him meekly and as a poor sinner, and await in entire self-denial the working of Divine grace in his soul. The man who thus passively yields himself up to God's hidden operations of grace, him will the power of the Almighty Father visit, and the light of the only begotten Son will shine within him, and the infinite love of the Holy Ghost, proceeding from the Father and the Son, will be poured out upon him, and the heavens will rain down on him the dew of divine sweetness, and the earth and all creatures will minister to his happiness.

The lowest grade of these men are drawn close into God; those of the higher grade are illuminated and strengthened; the highest are elevated into union with Him. Yet be it known, that the entrancing joy and the quiet stillness of God's peace is not always perceptible to one's natural faculties; the soul is often placed in a state of poverty of feeling. In that state let one remain content in all self-renunciation, for God reveals Himself only in a supernatural manner. What if a man, who has given himself up entirely to God as the source of all his being and is lost entirely in the Divine will—what if he does not always experience the sensible emotions of piety and of love; he is none the less pure of heart, none the less pleasing to God. The more God leaves a man in a state of natural desolation of spirit, the stronger does He establish him in supernatural grace. The more a man is tried by natural feelings of dread and of anguish—as long as these are not quite intolerable—the more do these very sufferings become an element of security in his spiritual life by nourishing holy humility. They hold him back from ruin; they are like a stout wall built up between him and the danger of losing all the graces that have been granted him. These trials hinder him from rashness and over-security. May God's eternal love, overflowing and ever faithful, thus be given to us. *Amen.*

Union With God

Synopsis—Our natural yearning for unity—Multiplicity is a trait of fallen nature—Dying to self is followed by rising into union with God—Many ways shown of thus dying and rising again—After that created things may be more safely used—Marvellous effects on the deeper interior life.

SERMON FOR EASTER SUNDAY: FIRST PART.

That they all may be one, as Thou, Father, in Me, and I in Thee * * * **and** I in them, and Thou in Me; that they may be made perfect in one.—John xvii, 21-23.

To this union St. Paul had attained, for he says: "And I live, now not I, but Christ liveth in me." (Gal. ii, 20.) Let us ask how we, too, may be made one with God. Not otherwise than by losing ourselves and forgetting ourselves, and then by being made over again in God by God's spirit. For as long as a man is self-conscious, even though he have God and is even conscious of Him, just so long is He not one, but two—he has not become one with God: this is multiplicity and not perfect unity. In unity a man loses multiplicity. True unity is the state in which a man finds himself solely in One, the One that is called and is God. In this state a man has, as it were, lost his selfhood in God; so that he has no joy in self, no thought of self, no outward life of self. Nor does it seem to him that it is his own self that knows and loves either God or creatures —all seems done by God. Self is absorbed as it were in God.

All creatures seek after this unity; all multiplicity struggles toward it—the universal aim of all life is always this unity. Every creàture comes forth from this unity by an immediate creative act, and each one tends again to be absorbed in its entire existence into indivisible unity, according to each one's capability. All activity of mind and body, and all love, as well as all unrest, has an end and purpose; it all tends toward entire rest; and this rest is to be found nowhere but in the one, indivisible unity that is God. All that flows outward is to flow back-

ward into its source—God. And when this has happened, and not
before, do we find rest and tranquillity. When all that goes to make
up a man's being has become lovingly one with God, then all the soul's
cries are hushed, and the unrest of longing and of acting has ceased.
Nature itself universally craves this unity, and consumes everything,
even its own life, in its strivings to attain to it; but to true unity can
nature never come except in God, the only being wholly one. And O
how anxious, how uncertain is the soul of man whilst deprived of this
union! How can he abide out of it a single instant! How can he find
in himself aught worth knowing or loving as long as he is out of God!

What is the best way to enter into God and to be made one with him?
Certainly there is but one way: To die to self; to totally give up all
self-seeking, all multiplicity. If thou wilt be made white, thou must
wash off the black; the less black, the more white. The less thou art
multiplied, the more shalt thou be single-minded and single-hearted.
God does not work in thee rightly and by Himself alone, as long as thou
art multiplied; His living work in thee must be one. The more the
soul's powers are detached from outward things and gathered into one
in the interior life, all the stronger grows God's action inwardly, and all
the diviner and more perfect. This state no man can achieve except
by dying to himself. The sooner and the more truly and the more
perfectly he dies to himself, the sooner, the more truly and the more
perfectly will he find his life made one with God's. Therefore, Christ
died a physical death that He might show us the way to die a spiritual
death. That He might rise from the dead into immortality, He must
die to mortality. If we would reach a condition of unity, we must die
to multiplicity; we must die to all mortality, to all self-ownership, to
all divisibility. Unity has no division; division is lost and so is multiplicity—all made one in unity. Of Christ we read that, "Rising again
from the dead, He dieth now no more; death shall no more have dominion over Him." (Rom. vi, 9.) Out of death comes life that dies no
more. There is no true and undying life in us except the life that comes
forth from death. If water is to become hot, then cold must die out
of it. If wood is to be made fire, then the nature of wood must die.
The life we seek cannot be in us, it cannot become our very selves, we
cannot be itself, unless we gain it by first ceasing to be what we are;
we acquire this life through death.

In very truth there is, rightly speaking, but one death and one life.
However many deaths there may seem to be, they all are but one,

namely, the death a man dies to his own will, to his sense of proprietorship, to division and multiplicity and activity—in so far as this is possible to a creature. And there is one life, and only one, namely, the one ineffable, incomprehensible, uncreated, essential, divine life. Toward this life all other life hurries on, is driven forward, streams along, being irresistibly drawn to possess it. The nearer our life comes to this essential life, and the more it is likened to it, the more truly do we live, for in this and from this life is all life, and not otherwise. Any life that lives apart from this, to it may be said these words: "Thou hast the name of being alive, and thou art dead." (Apoc. iii, 1.)

Whosoever will have this Divine life living within him, made most essentially and most truly his own, such a one must most essentially and most truly die to himself. Whosoever fails to die will fail to live. And whosoever totally dies to self, such a one is wholly made alive in God and without any separation. And this death has many degrees, just as life has. A man, for example, may die a thousand deaths in a single day, and each is instantly followed by a joyous life in God—death is no longer death. This happens perforce, because God cannot refuse the offering of death nor resist its plea for life. And the stronger death is and the more complete, so is the life that responds to it all the stronger and more integral; just as death is, so shall life be. And as life succeeds to death, so does life prepare a man to die a more perfect death to himself.

And it is thus that a man dies to himself: if he meekly accepts an insult for God's sake, if he curbs his inclination for inner or outward joy for the same Divine motive; if in any way whatsoever, in pleasure or in pain, he bridles his wayward will for God's sake in words or deeds, in labor or rest, in seeing or tasting; if he bears unjust reproof in silence and in all patience; if in any of his unmortified tendencies he dies to self, he begins to live to God. At first he yields to this holy death of selfhood reluctantly and with much pain; later on he grows used to it, and to die to self and to live to God grows into a holy habit. No matter how small the death an earnest man dies to himself, it wins him a great life, and this great life heartens him to die another and a yet greater death. And soon it comes to pass that the most joyous thing in life is to die to oneself, far more joyous than any life that is lived for self's sake. For life is now found only in death, and light shineth only in darkness. In outward things a man may so constantly die to self, that in course of time there is nothing left in him of any inclination to

them that is not dead.   Then, indeed, he hath fought a good fight; and
yet in his interior life there is much that must die.

When one is truly mortified or dead to his selfhood, then all things
are his and he can use them moderately without danger.   Indeed, no
man has real and reasonable joy in created things, until he has first gone
forth out of all joy in them for the love of God—until he has died to
them and they have died to him.   Only after that canst thou turn again
to their use, without feeling anxiety lest thou misuse them.   No man
truly loves his father and mother, his sisters and brothers and all his
other friends, with the love that is in God, until he has first given them
up and wholly died to them out of love for God; until that happens they
are rather enemies to his spiritual welfare than friends.   Therefore, our
Lord teaches: "For I came to set a man at variance against his father,
and the daughter against her mother, and the daughter-in-law against
her mother-in-law.   And a man's enemies shall be they of his own household."   (Matt. x, 35-36.)

But it is only a lesser death when one has died to outward things;
for when a man has sincerely renounced the world and all its superfluities, and entered upon an interior and divine life, it is an easy matter to
be quite dead to external enjoyments.   To him the death he has yet to
die is hidden.   What bitterness can he suffer who is full of the sweetness of a devout life?   What battle can he have to fight who has escaped
from the clutches of his enemy, and is journeying safely along the way
of peace?   If a man be truly converted to lead a perfect life inwardly,
no matter what outward things cross his path, they do not touch his
interior life.   Mary was turned to Christ in all her inner faculties, and
hence she sat at His feet unconcerned about the many things that
troubled Martha, who complained about her.   Mary thought not at all
of justifying herself—quite other things absorbed her thoughts and her
feelings and her love.   So does it happen with any soul that is turned
inward to God and away from all transitory things—turned to God,
revealed within him, and by no intermediary, but directly.   Whether
such a soul wills it or not, it must forget everything but God.   All
images of things created are gone; such a man has within him that
which is the original of all things.   He is liberated from creatures; he
has no room in his soul for figures and types, and strange happenings
and contradictions make no impression on him.

Such men as these St. Paul may have had in view when he said: "For
you are dead, and your life is hid with Christ in God."   (Col. iii, 3.)

But now it is to be remarked, that they may progress to a yet closer union; for they are hid *with* Christ, and are therefore two and not one with Him. On the other hand, our Lord prayed to His Father that "they may be one, as Thou, Father, in Me, and I in Thee." As if it were not in what made Father and Son different persons, but rather in what made them one essence, one life, one Divine operation—as if He prayed that *this* union might be granted us and perfected in us, as far as we are capable of it. Is it not true to say that to bring about this unity with God's being, His life and operation, a thousand times more perfect death to self and to creatures must be experienced? If God is to go into the soul, nature must go out totally, even to the last atom; fire and water cannot dwell together in one. He whose life is to be made God's life, must quickly and entirely die to any other life. If a man be already averse to the things of this earthly existence, then he more easily dies to himself; but whether or not this be so, the man who will have God to live within him and be his only support and only comfort, must be dead to all transitory things and they dead to him, absolutely stripped of their support and void of their comfort. Life has its hiding place in death; consolation has its hiding place in desolation. When the outward man is hushed still, then the inward man begins to live; then does he begin truly to speak his happy words, according to the prophet: "My soul refused to be comforted; I remembered God and was delighted and was exercised, and my spirit swooned away." (Ps. lxxvi, 3-4.) The outward craves the outward life in everything. It is true that the outward life longs for God's help in some exterior form, as the Psalmist says: "It is good for me to adhere [that is to say, exteriorly] to my God." (Ps. lxvii, 28.) But even this comfort has a savor of self-seeking, and it, too, must die out of the soul.

The death of self and the union with God that we have been considering, affects all the powers of the soul, even the most interior ones. The will must efface its symbols and images and rest motionless; the understanding, including knowledge and memory, and, indeed, all mental powers, must set aside, as far as possible, the objects of their activity. Listen to our Lord's words: "He that findeth his life, shall lose it; and he that shall lose his life for Me, shall find it." (Matt. x, 39.) It is a hard death to the soul, when all natural lights in it and all its faculties go out in darkness; and a yet harder death when even the bright rays of light shed by God's own gifts, must be quenched in darkness; for these are not God, and God alone must finally content the soul. All these are, as it were, but a part of God and not God one and indivisible.

But in truth it is only when all that lives within a man, and all that gives him light has died out and gone from him—it is then, and only then, that he finds his real soul—never otherwise. Does he not find it? Can you say that in such a state he rather has utterly lost it? No, by no means; for freedom of the will yet remains, and responsibility for choosing to act or not to act. Does he not now stand in control of his spiritual powers to will and to act, and how to choose? See how our Saviour and our model acted in His agony: "Father * * * not as I will, but as Thou wilt." (Matt. xxvi, 39.) As if to say: I have no will; but Thou, Father, shalt have My will, for I am stripped of My will and dead to it, and now in Thy will I am absorbed and restored to life.

Union with God is not action, in the human meaning of the term, nor knowing, nor loving with diversity; for in God all is one and all is rest and peace. Knowing and loving, bringing forth and being brought forth, and all manner of simply human activity, is the product of diversity. In God, in this One, is all action ended and unified, and we are made one in God through Christ. *Amen.*

Union With God

Synopsis—Self-surrender precedes union with God—The light of God shines in souls united to Him—The scene of this union is the depths of the soul—It resembles and partakes of the union of the Persons of the Holy Trinity—The high kind of brotherly love it produces.

SERMON FOR EASTER SUNDAY: SECOND PART.

That they all may be one, as Thou, Father, in Me, and I in Thee * * * and I in them, and Thou in Me; that they may be made perfect in one.—John xvii, 21-23.

Herein our Lord and Saviour teaches that when a man has left all things of his outward life, father and mother, and, indeed, all multiplicity totally surrendered for God's sake, then must he turn inward and do in like manner in his inward life. He must surrender his soul to God in total forgetfulness of whatsoever is native to his inner life, his soul to be dismantled and, as it were, taken to pieces, that it may be rebuilt and newly adorned, in a life wherein all images find their prototypes, namely, in God. If one loves in a human spirit, there is danger of one's hating; if he hopes in that spirit, he can scarcely be entirely humbled. But if one willingly has nothing even that is lowly, he can scarcely be ambitious of the high things of this life. Let him, then, die to all and enter into God in search of the highest. This means, as I have said, that God will dismantle him, and then build and adorn him over again. All virtuous imaginings, may lead to selfish picking and choosing this or that way to gain virtue; but when the end is reached, the way is not needed and should be forgotten—the end is God. Virtues will never be so much our own, so true and so deep-seated in us, as when we have been stripped of their images and joined in unity with God. It then comes to pass that these virtues are not for this or that place or time, nor for any manner of self-seeking whatsoever; for they act within us for virtue's own sake and, as it were, by their own holy force. God is the essence of all virtues, which without Him are non-existent; possess Him in holy unity of life, and good is done in thee for the sake of the Supreme Good, with no other why or wherefore but that essential Good, and because of it. Thou shalt then love for the sake of love itself, be true for the sake of truth itself, righteous for the sake of this supreme holiness.

We ask why Christ did not answer Pilate when he inquired, "What is truth?" And the usual explanation is that Pilate was unworthy of an answer. So is it here. Whosoever departs from Divine unity of life, is not worthy to know what truth is. Such a one can say nothing but this: Truth is truth. He can neither take nor give on such a subject. The true, the good are indivisible and one in God—simple unity. A creature possesses good; as we say a good angel, a good man, a good heaven—all these have good in them, as they have also truth and being; but it is not with them as with God, for they have these as a manner of existence, all in place and measure and all with limitation. God has good because He is esential good.

But if thou wouldst have all the true and the good and all essential being, thou shalt find them in their fountain and origin, wholly without limitation. Pass over man and angel and Heaven into the indivisible and limitless good and true. All else may but hide God's unity of goodness and truth from thee, and may become a prison to thee. Unity looks not outward; it covets nothing foreign to itself whether far or near; it is not measurable as broad or long; it is one, it is God, who has all good in Himself, and there is none out of Him. It is He who gives being and its good to creatures—not they to Him. Any spiritual method, in so far as it is Divine, is not outside of God, for all that is indivisible and true and good is in Him.

A man in whom all manner of self-seeking has quite perished away and been replaced by love, and who has God in him and is himself in God—whatsoever that man does in and through God is the best and done in the most perfect manner. And this perfection is inherent in the work and not borrowed from without; it is not from length and breadth, but from the unity of purpose with God; and so little works and great ones become in a way equally good in such a state of soul, from the uniform greatness of their origin. Say an Ave Maria with God's holy unity, and it wins as much as a whole psalter less perfectly said; one step with God is equal to a pilgrimage beyond the seas without Him. Great works with upright intention shall be granted great reward; but the real worth of a good deed is in the disinterested love with which it is done; its value is intrinsic.   One grain of gold has all the nature of gold that a thousand golden marks have.   Therefore, if we desire more than one gold piece, it is because we desire something besides the essence of gold.   But as to Divine things, all the good in them is in their essential nature and not in their quantity, and there is as much good in the least as in the most that we do, when we act entirely united to God.

The external is but a symbol of the internal, as a sign may tell us that there is wine in a cellar; yet there may be wine where no sign is hung out, and it is then of none the less worth to its owner.   The main thing is to have a good will to serve God; that being made secure, my soul ranges free over the good deeds of all men, including the saints, all their sufferings for religion, their alms to the poor.   Of these I think with a longing heart to do and to suffer them all for God's sake, and that most gladly—but I lack the opportunity.   In God's eyes it is as if I had done them all.   I fail in none of the merit, if my good will is equal to the effort that would be required for their actual accomplishment.   And as I read of the holy men of the past, and keep my heart fixed on their marvels of virtue, my good will gives me a share in their merit; to God a thousand years are as a day that is passed.

St. Augustine says: "Turn into thyself; there alone shalt thou find God."   And as thou turnest—so we may add—thou turnest in God Himself, with whom thou hast been made one.   In God is life and all things; and, as St. John tells us, "He came into His own, and His own received Him not.   But as many as received Him, He gave them power to be made the sons of God."   (John i, 11-12.)   Now, God's Son is of one nature with His Father, and a Godlike man is not by nature, but by grace, one with Him, by Whom he is made Godlike; and if there be anything in him that is not Godlike, in just so far is he out of God.   Truly is he God's son, and one with Him after the image of the sonship of the only begotten Son; so that God out of him acts not, nor does he act out of God.   And as God does not separate Himself from His only begotten Son, so neither does He separate Himself from a Godlike man, unless because this man has first separated himself from God..   A certain master exclaims: "I do not envy all the good that God has given to His only begotten Son, because I can by the mystery of grace become unified with that same Son, out from Whom, through Whom and in Whom are all things—so truly one with Him that no part remains not united."

Philosophers say that God does nothing out of—that is, outside of—Himself. In the same way a man who is truly good and Godlike, does all things he does in God, having Him as the only end of all; yet further, we may say that a Godlike man never thinks of God outside of his own self, for when and where and in whatever manner he considers God, he finds himself one with Him.

Since God works all through the man with whom He is one, it follows that not the man, but God, does the works that the man seems to do. As Jesus taught: "The Father who abideth in Me, He doeth the works." (John xiv, 10.) To this Godlike man, therefore, his own works are very strange to him, and seem to him as if they were not his own; he is so deeply one with God that it is He who is in him and He who works in him, and not the man himself—so does he feel. If this fails and he appropriates his works to himself in distinction from God, so does he instantly cease to be enveloped in God's unity.

Our Saviour said: "I am not alone, but I and the Father that sent me" (John viii, 16); and again: "Believe you not that I am in the Father and the Father in me?" (John xiv, 11.) Therefore does St. Augustine teach: "God became man that I might become God; He became the Son of man that I might become the son of God." And David says: "I have said, you are gods, and all of you sons of the Most High." (Ps. lxxxi, 6.) What God gave to His only begotten Son made man, that is He ready to give to His Son's brethren, each in his place and measure. If they refuse to receive it, then God is not to blame; just as the sunlight is not to blame if a room is dark at midday—the owner of the house has shut the blinds.

The nature of man which our beloved Lord assumed, is as much mine as it is His; although the case is infinitely different in regard to His person, which is wholly Divine. He took to Himself my very nature, and thereby He took me to Himself wholly. Now, what remains for my part? That I give myself to Him personally. If I hold back, what can He do about my perversity? Did He not take our nature so fully as to be as truly man as He is truly God's own Son and the Eternal Word? Hence we must truly say that the virgin's Son is God, precisely as we say the same of the Only Begotten of the Father; and this comes from the unity of person in the Son of Mary and the Son of God. In this manner He has shared with me by grace all that the Father gave Him by nature, making it all mine, just as it is all His. But woe to me if, having been made one with Him by community of our human nature, I yet refuse to join with Him in a loving personal union. Do I not know that I am by nature one with all men and as near of kin to them as to my ownself—to the Sultan of Turkey as well as to my next-door neighbor—one with the wisest and with the simplest, the least and the greatest? Do I not know that all men stand together and alike one in nature? Thus does our Lord stand as near to me as I do to myself; and I stand likewise as near to Him as He does to Himself—all this in His human nature. But woe to me if I am far removed from personal union with Him by my own self-love and self-seeking, removed from Him and joined to self in His despite; or, again, if I am by my selfishness removed from a loving union with any man and all men, even if they be a thousand miles distant from me. For all of us men are of one nature and should be as one man in love; we should be one in personal union of love. To all men should my heart be given, and their welfare should be as dear to me as my own, their misfortune as bitter to me as my own. In this way do I go out of myself, if I am true to the unity of nature God has made among men; until at last I think of my own and enjoy my own no more and no less because it is mine, than if it belonged to a man whom I have never seen.

But from this we must not suppose that this common love is to be equally distributed over all men; for, though God loves all equally, He yet bestows His favors unequally. First come parents, children, friends and neighbors; begin to bestow thy love on these, and then go forth with thy loving service to others as best thou canst. One must consider those committed to his nearest care by Providence, as entitled to the perfect and immediate overflowing of love, not exactly because one is a father and mother and friend, but because God has made them such. For it might be that God would lead thee away over the seas, to serve with equal love men whom thou hadst before never heard of; love is equal within the soul, and shown by God's will unequally in outward act. It is the man who has gone out of self in all things, and been made one with God in Christ, who does all this wisely. Being one in God and with God, then it follows that whatsoever all men and angels have of joy and bliss, is also his in God; and whatsoever others may have of badness or punishment, that is not his, but their own, for it is not in God.

In very truth, in proportion as a man goes out of selfhood does he enter into oneness with God. Yet he must not have regard to himself in this relation, for the less he regards himself the more does he find himself in God. Whosoever totally gives up self achieves total union without any doubt. All things now come to him consciously from God, and all are alike to Him, whether for joy or sorrow. Hence our Saviour's teaching: "Take up my yoke upon you." (Matt. xi, 29.) That means that His will shall always dominate ours and be infinitely dearer to us than our own. It was in giving up His will to His Father that Jesus saved us, for nothing is dearer to a man than his own will.

Thus it is that a man stands in indifference to all things; it is because he has passed out of self, as if he were become quite as different to himself as to the Sultan of the Turks and had merged his selfhood in God's unity. Not, of course, that he is the equal of God, but that in uniting himself to God he has become oblivious to what equality means, so absorbed has he become in the Divine unity. It is unity and not equality that he has attained to in God. When emptying himself of all self-seeking, he has given himself up to God to be one with Him. Nor does he lose his natural existence; but in all his thoughts and deeds he does not perceive himself or consciously consider himself, but only God. As the prophet says: "For my heart hath been enflamed, and my reins have been changed, and I am brought to nothing, and I knew not." (Ps. lxxiii, 21-22.) He knows not how to describe this change of his soul into God's life, for it has no description, no image; all his interior representations are covered by the one uncreated being of God taking the place of all. He himself, so it seems to him, knows not, acts not; God knows and acts in him and through him, according to His Divine will and without any obstacles, in a manner above what the soul can understand. And now it is needful that I should cease to speak on this subject, recalling only our Lord's words, and begging Him to fulfill in blissful unity what He said to His Father: "That they all may be one, as Thou, Father, in Me, and I in Thee * * * and I in them, and Thou in Me; that they may be made perfect in one." *Amen.*

The Degrees of Love

Synopsis—The first is active love, full of pious exercises and good works—The second is persevering love, shown in Magdalene, who was faithful unto Calvary—The third is the fiery love, and is very fervent—The fourth is a penetrating love, which has a peculiar gift of understanding God—The fifth is overflowing love, which casts the soul out of itself into the Beloved.

SERMON FOR EASTER MONDAY.

And they said one to another: Was not our heart burning within us whilst He spoke in the way, and opened to us the scriptures?—Luke xxiv, 32.

Dear children, one of these two disciples of our Lord was named Cleophas, and the other, as some think, was St. Luke, the evangelist, who tells of this apparition of our Lord the evening of the resurrection. Their eyes were held as the Lord appeared to them, and He was disguised as a pilgrim; they did not recognize Him at first. St. Gregory says that He appeared to them because they loved Him, and that yet He concealed who He was, because they were still doubtful about His resurrection. Hence He upbraided them fo· their incredulity and hardness of heart and their want of understanding, and opened to them the hidden meaning of the scriptures. Their faith was mingled with doubt, and yet they had been speaking affectionately about Him; and when He joined in their conversation, His words made their hearts burn within them.

St. Dionysius tells us that love has **five** degrees. The first degree is the active one, and is less closely joined to God than the others. In this degree the soul begins to turn to God and to cherish Him with a kind of anxious love. It practices certain devout exercises very earnestly, is afraid that it will cool in its ardor, and would seek its beloved and ever follow Him. Its voice is that of the bride: "In my bed by night I sought Him whom my soul loveth." (Cant. iii, 1.) But the Bridegroom finds this couch of active love too narrow, and this state is not according to His will. But the soul does not give Him up; on the con-

trary, it seeks to possess Him with much distress of mind, as Zacheus eagerly climbed a tree in order to behold our Lord Jesus Christ. Such an undersized man is every lover of Jesus, when first he turns in all seriousness to the love of God. Like Zacheus, he avows himself a great sinner, overcomes his shame in a good confession and reveals all his wickedness. He says with St. Paul: "Christ Jesus came into this world to save sinners, of whom I am the chief." (I Tim. i, 15.) And this sinner is enriched with grace, for as in him sin did abound, so now does grace superabound. Let every one aspire to enter this first degree of love, as Zacheus climbed the tree to behold Jesus; let none despair because his sins are grievous. This is the degree of active love in which the soul diligently practices all sorts of meritorious works, its sins not only being forgiven, but, as St. Augustine teaches, many great gifts bestowed upon it.

The two disciples who journeyed toward Emmaus, had this sort of love, meanwhile conversing about their beloved Master with afflicted hearts. Although every lover of Christ is in this world like a sojourner in Egypt, and is bowed down under a heavy burden of fear and of anguish, yet he has the privilege of this degree of love. And the thought of the eternal life hereafter, now and again fills his soul with deepest joy. Yet there are brief intervals, during which he overflows with spiritual happiness and says with Sarah: "God hath made a laughter for me; whosoever shall hear of it will laugh with me." (Gen. xxi, 6.) But presently all is changed and the soul exclaims: "Woe is me, that my sojourning is prolonged!" (Ps. cxix, 5.) And again with Job: "Who will grant me, that I might be according to the months past, according to the days in which God kept me, when his lamp shined over my head and I walked by His light in darkness? * * * When I washed my feet in butter, and the rock poured me out rivers of oil?" (Job. xxix, 2, 3, 6.) What else is the soul's lamp but Divine grace, and what is its shining, but the bright rays of that same grace enlightening our mind? The lamp is over our heads and guides us forward in the darkness, till we pass out of and beyond this first degree, namely, that of active love. We may also compare the soul's faculties of desiring and seeking, to a man's spiritual feet, which are now to carry him into the more interior regions of the spiritual life. The oil that flowed from the rock, may be taken to mean the tears of sweet joy shed by the soul in its love of God.

The second degree of love is perseverance. By this love we continue
to hold fast and firm to God in joy and sorrow, nay, even when we are
groping in darkness; what we began with, that we keep on even to the
end, just as Mary Magdalene outstayed all the disciples at the Saviour's
tomb. And as her perseverance in love was rewarded with the first
apparition of the risen Lord, so shall we be likewise blest if we remain
steadfast in His grace. The worth of perseverance and the perfect
completeness of our task of love, was typified in the old testament by
the law that no beast that had been deprived of his tail was to be offered
in sacrifice to God. Joseph's coat, so long as to reach to his feet, had
the same signification of steadfastness in our devout exercises of love,
no matter what our darkness of mind. To the same effect is the word
of the bride in the Canticle: "My soul melted when He spoke; I sought
Him and found Him not; I called, and He did not answer me. The
keepers that go about the city found me; they struck me and wounded
me; the keepers of the walls took away my veil from me." (Cant. v,
6-7.) The veil is perseverance in love. And then the bride heartens
herself to renewed seeking for her Beloved: "I adjure you, O daughters
of Jerusalem, if you find my Beloved, that you tell Him that I languish
with love!" (Ibid., 8.)

The third degree of love is fervor, by which the heart receives a grace
which sets it on fire. Thus Job asks: "Art not thy garments hot when
the south wind blows upon earth?" (Job xxxvii, 17.) Then it is that
both of the soul's powers, those of loving and understanding, are
aroused and enflamed. Therefore, Hugo of St. Victor teaches: "When
thou dost not seek thy Beloved with ardor, thou remainest apart from
His true lovers, dull and heavy." And St. Augustine: "O love, ever
burning and never extinguished, how late have I come to know thee!
Thou wast within me and I sought thee out of me; thou wast with me
and I was not with thee." Love, like the burning bush that Moses saw,
is always burning and never consumed. For however much the lover is
tormented by his love, he is also comforted by it and well pleasea with
it, as witness the two disciples: "Was not our heart burning within us
whilst He spoke in the way, and opened to us the scriptures?" And
they partook of the second grade of love, for with strengthened faith
they turned back to Jerusalem; and also of the first grade, for they
showed the active zeal of love in constraining Christ, whilst they
thought Him only a pilgrim, to accept their hospitality.

The fourth grade of love is its penetration. This was granted to the
patriarch Jacob: "I have seen God face to face, and my soul has been

saved." (Gen. xxxii, 30.) This means that my soul has been granted love's gift of knowledge, by which I know my beloved by love's sweet way of understanding, and in the same way I know that I am known by Him. This was St. Augustine's petition: "Lord, help me, that I may know Thee and myself." And it was thus that the two disciples knew the Lord after their loving conversation with Him, in the breaking of bread. This penetration of love pierces through obstacles, and sheds so clear a light as to show forth its own glorious brightness in the soul, relieving the lover of many a bitter pain. St. Augustine says in his confessions: "O Lord, when I cling to Thee with all my might, I am unburdened of the heavy load that I am to myself; my life is full of Thee, and toil and distress are done. O, who will grant me to have Thee dwell within my heart and so to inebriate me with love that I shall forget all my pains!" Hugo of St. Victor says: "The fire of love bursts forth in flames strong and consuming; it burns until the lover is united to the beloved: 'I found him whom my soul loveth; I held him, and I will not let him go till I bring him into my mother's house and into the chamber of her that bore me.'" (Cant. iii, 4.) That happens when the penetration of love has entered into the deepest depths that can be explored, a state of love beyond what one can understand—love enters within and understanding remains without.

The fifth degree is love so overflowing as to obtain a gift beyond even that of penetration, namely, love's freedom. The heart is like a vessel of water boiling over in the fire. The fire of love in the heart casts the soul out of itself, so fierce is its energy—a force all hidden and known only by its mighty effects. In the Book of Job, Elihu said: "Behold, my belly is new wine which wanteth vent, which bursteth the new vessels" (Job. xxx, 19), meaning that his soul was overflowing with his message to Job. And thus the lover in the Canticles: "My soul melted when he spoke" (Cant. v, 6), as if to say: As molten gold is poured into its mold and takes its shape, so am I melted and poured into and shaped by my beloved. Hence St. Paul says: "For whom He foreknew, He also predestinated to be made conformable to the image of His Son." (Rom. viii, 29.) And, again, the apostle quotes from Moses: "Our God is a consuming fire." (Heb. xii, 29.) When at last the soul is thus melted by God and rests at peace in Him, it is united to Him and filled with His light. Love, then, gives a man power to say: All things are common with Him and with me, for I have nothing of my own; we two have but one house, one heritage, one table, one couch.

But if any weakness in such a soul happens to intervene between it and God, then it is instantly in anguish. Ah, it says, tell my beloved that I languish with love; for that soul cannot remain separated from Him. This painful visitation has happened to the soul because it still harbors some remnants of self-love. Yet, in all its pain, the soul is still faithful to its beloved, and this is shown by its diligence in keeping up its sweet exercises of devotion to God. Gilbert says: "Wheresoever love is, there is an active and powerful impulse toward the beloved, especially if it is withdrawn from it." The holy prophet Daniel suffered from this, for "He was a man of desires" (Dan. ix, 23); his yearning for Divine things made him weak and sick. And the two disciples on the way to Emmaus were likewise greatly distressed, till they had questioned the Lord and listened to Him, and finally were made sure of His resurrection; and then they were united to Him in the breaking of bread. God grant us the same favor. *Amen.*

The Qualities of Love

Synopsis—True love is without limits, as universal as Himself—It loves God without rivals, God and God alone—It loves Him unceasingly, either by praises or by good works—Meantime God constantly rewards such love with the gift of greater desire and power of loving—A summary of God's worthiness of our love.

SERMON FOR THURSDAY IN EASTER WEEK.

She turning, saith to Him: Rabboni (which is to say, Master).—John xx, 16.

When Jesus rose from the dead, Mary Magdalene longed with all her heart to behold Him. But He appeared to her in the form of a gardener, and she did not recognize him. Then He said to her: "Mary!" She, turning, saith to Him: "Rabboni!" (which is to say, Master.)

You will notice that as long as Mary stood gazing into the empty tomb and looked at the angels, Jesus stood behind her and concealed Himself from her. This means that our Lord God hides Himself from those who are busied with creatures, absorbed and distressed about created things. The moment the soul turns away from them and goes in search of God, then God reveals Himself. And the meaning of our Lord's word "Mary" is, literally, the star of the sea, or otherwise the queen—queen of the world enlightened by the Holy Spirit, shining like a star.

Whosoever longs for the sight of God must soar aloft like a star, and must have an aversion for all transitory things; he must be much enlightened by God if he would behold heavenly sights. Mary recognized her Lord when He called her name, and she answered instantly, Rabboni (Master). That was the name she and His other disciples usually addressed Him with, for He had approved it: "You call Me Master and Lord, and you say well, for so I am." (John xiii, 13.) He is, indeed, the Master of the supreme good, and as such we must love Him supremely and above all things. He is the Master of all truth, and therefore we must contemplate Him. He is Master of the highest perfection, and therefore we must follow Him without ever looking backward.

Master of the supreme good: such is his true name, and it entitles Him to our love above all things. But you might say: God being infinite good and the soul finite, how can the soul love Him or even know him? Ah, mark well that, although God be infinite good and the soul finite, yet the soul's longing is an abyss without limit; the human soul can never be content, except with the possession of an infinite good. And the more the soul longs for God, the more does it yearn for deeper longings; the more we love God, the more we yearn to love Him with yet greater intensity. God is a good without the slightest imperfection; He is the fountain-head of the living and exhaustless waters of love. The soul is created in the image of God, and even for that reason is made capable of knowing and loving Him as He is; and as Christ is the Master of the supreme good, so must the soul love Him supremely and above all things. He is love; out of Him floweth love into us as out of an overflowing fountain of life; the fountain of life is love. For, says St. John: "He that loveth not, abideth in death." (I John iii, 14.) Christ, the fountain of love and the master of the highest good, must have our perfect love. It is a characteristic trait of the soul to have a longing to love Him who is God, who is Supreme Good—to love Him without limits to its love, Him and none other except for His sake, Him to love with increasing praise.

Without limits. As St. Bernard teaches: "The reason why the soul should love God is God Himself; but the limit of this love is without limits, for God is unlimited good, without count and without end." And St. Paul says: "And this I pray, that your love may more and more abound in knowledge and in all understanding." (Phil. i, 9.) And St. Bernard again: "In loving God there is no other method or distinction, than that we should love Him as He has loved us." He has loved us unto the end in order that we should love Him unto the end, or rather without end. Hence all through our earthly existence, our desire to love God should constantly increase in our inner life. But bear in mind that, however the inner work of loving God should always grow stronger, yet the outward exercise of that love should be regulated with prudence; we should choose such devout practices of love as may not injure our spirit.

We must love Him without rivals—God, and God alone. This means that in that degree in which we love God, no created being shall be allowed to enter. Whatever creature we may love, it must be done for God's sake alone; that love must be some way a love for God and in God; for God's sake, since God is the origin and only reason of that creature's existence; a love of the creature, yet a love for God, who is the sole good that any creature possesses or may be loved for; in God, because He is the only joy that love of any sort can minister to our souls; and He is the term and end of all our love. This is, therefore, how we love creatures in God and God in creatures. Thus did our Saviour teach: "Thou shalt love the Lord thy God with thy whole heart, and with thy whole soul, and with thy whole mind." (Matt. xxii, 37.) St. Augustine says that our Lord by these words means that a man should have no idle and empty power in his soul, but all should be occupied with the love of God and filled with Him; and that whatever the soul cares for in its outward life, is to be referred to God's love and be used for God love. God loves the soul; and therefore should the soul love God without a rival.

In the third place, we must love Him with unceasing praise; our love must never be silent, but must forever call upon our beloved and beseech Him. St. Gregory said that our speaking to God is by the voice of the mouth and by the voice of good works, and that the latter has more power than the former. Listen to the Psalmist: "I have labored with crying." (Ps. lxviii, 4.) "It is a trait of lovers," says St. Chrysostom, "not to be able to conceal their love, nor ever to be silent while with their beloved, to whom they must entrust their heart's burning affections." So do God's lovers speak to Him, revealing to Him even their faults; they do this over and over again, because they love Him too well to hide their sins from Him; and because in doing so they are comforted and encouraged. The voice of the lover by outward works is the utterance of the inward depths of love. "The proof of Divine love," says St. Gregory, "is in good works. Wherever love is, love acts; if there is no act, there is no love."

Rightly did Magdalen exclaim, Master! For Christ is, indeed, master of all good, and therefore He must have our supreme love. But over love our Saviour has a triple sovereignty. For as our sovereign Master He rewards us for nothing but for our love for Him; he rewards us on account of nothing but His own love for us; and He rewards us with nothing but with the gift of His love for us. Every way we look at His reward to us it is love.

Now, one can serve God meritoriously with outward works, with inward contemplation, and with inward longings. Outward works are worthy of reward only when done from motives of inward love, for in themselves they are transitory, and therefore cannot win an eternal recompense. On the other hand, "Love never falleth away," says St. Paul. (I Cor. xiii.) Works done apart from love cannot merit eternal life, and hence whosoever loves God separates himself from all that is not God—craving the uncreated good, he despises all created good.

And God rewards us on account of nothing but His own love for us, and that reward is the gift of Himself; not partly, but wholly Himself, for He loves us with an eternal love. Remember what He said to Abraham: "Fear not, I am thy protector, and thy reward exceeding great." (Gen. xv, 1.)

Again, as we have seen, He rewards us with a gift of love or of loving, whereby a man clearly and without any medium contemplates God, a love which enables the soul to enjoy God and posses Him everlastingly. Hence, Christian soul, say to Him with all the fervor of Mary Magdalen, speaking from thy inmost heart: O my Master, Master of all good, and my God, draw me to Thee by the love which Thou Thyself art, for I crave to possess Thee, Thou infinite good, and to prize Thee above all things.

Let us return to my first affirmation, namely, that God is master of the supreme good, and that we must contemplate Him as such. Thou art aware that thou canst contemplate God in His creatures, even though they are made out of nothing, for thou canst learn herein that He is almighty. His infinite wisdom also is apparent in them, as thou studiest their laws of being and the admirable order that prevails in them; and this Divine wisdom is attributed to the Son of God. And when thou observest the gentleness and affection that exists more or less in all of God's creatures, thou mayst learn by them God's loving-kindness, which is attributed to the Holy Ghost. And this is what St. Paul teaches: "For the invisible things of Him, from the creation of the world, are clearly seen, being understood by the things that are made; His eternal power also, and divinity." (Rom. i, 20.) Divine grace, too, gives the soul light to see God: "and in Thy light we shall see light" (Ps. xxxv, 10), says the Psalmist, meaning God Himself, a light in which there is no manner of darkness. Finally, we shall see God in the light of glory, knowing Him then without any intermediary, as He is in Himself. Truly He is the master of truth, and He gives us all truth.

And He is master of perfection, requiring us to give up everything in order to follow Him alone. Man finds in God the complete and unified assemblage of all the excellences that creatures have in imperfection and only partially. O man, wouldst thou be perfect? then follow God. Hence our Saviour says: "If any man come to Me, and hate not his father, and mother, and wife and children, and brothers and sisters, yea, and his own life also, he cannot be My disciple." (Luke xiv, 26.) For does it not often happen, that one's very parents and brothers and sisters and all other creatures become enemies, when he loves them so dearly that they stand in the way of his serving God and his neighbor? Therefore do thou give up all created things and follow after the Master of Perfection, Jesus Christ, Who is blessed forever. May He grant us this privilege by His holy grace. *Amen.*

The Call to Peace

Synopsis—The first call of God is to give up the world, leading the soul from an outward to an inward life—The second call is to be transformed into the living image of Christ by meditation on Him, perfected by Holy Communion—The third call is more rare, and is the opening of a door which leads into a state of absolute abandonment to God—The privileges of this call.

FIRST SERMON FOR LOW SUNDAY.

Jesus said to them : Peace be to you.—John xx, 19.

"Peace be to you!" exclaimed our beloved Lord, as He appeared to His disciples after His resurrection. All men long for rest and peace by a law of their very nature. Toward this end are directed all their strivings, all their manifold labors, their devotions and spiritual exercises. But they will never attain to true peace, no, not if they struggled for it for all eternity, except they seek it where alone it can be found, namely, in God. What, then, is the way to this true peace, as it is in most perfect truth, in God? We may learn this by the threefold vocation of St. John the Evangelist, for in this way does God call all men to eternal peace.

The first, was when He called St. John from the world and made him an apostle. The second, was when He drew him close to him and made him rest his head on His breast. And the third and most perfect, was on holy Pentecost day, when He gave the apostle the Holy Ghost, and opened the door to his entrance to perfect love.

So shalt thou be first called, namely, to give up the world. This means to subject all thy lower powers and thy appetites to reason; to learn to know thyself thoroughly and remain at home with thyself, watching all thy words carefully, lest thou sayest anything different from what thou wouldst have others say to thee; also keeping guard over all thy emotions and scrutinizing them, as to whether or not they come from God, and are fit to be directed back again to God; over thy thoughts, never arboring evil thoughts or occupied with idle ones, and if they intrude hemselves against thy will, struggling manfully against them, and using his conflict as a preparation for better things; finally over thy works, o that in all of them thou hast God alone and His honor in view and he happiness of thy fellow-men. It is in this wise that the Lord calls hee from the world and makes thee His apostle; thus dost thou learn he change from being an outward living man to becoming an inward iving one. Of such a kind is the beginner in the spiritual life.

The second call is to repose on Christ's bosom. If thou wilt enjoy his privilege with St. John, thou must be transformed into the holy and iving image of our Saviour. It means that thou shalt cultivate very iligently the study of His blessed meekness, His burning love for friends nd foes, and His wonderful and most self-denying indifference to all hings except His Father's will, in all methods, states and ways of life.

Consider His unbounded kindness to all our race, and also His lessed poverty. Heaven and earth were His and He owned it all, but He was in it as if He owned nothing of it. Every word He spoke, everything He did, was for His Father's honor and the happiness of all mankind. Look yet closer upon Him, look deeper into His heart, study Him with perfect attention, and then look upon thyself, and behold how different thou art from Him; acknowledge thy pettiness. Now it is when thou has honestly done this that our Lord draws thee to Himself, and makes thee rest thy head upon His bosom. For this end there is nothing so useful as the holy sacrament of our Saviour's body and blood. And thou shalt be also aided by the counsel of one whose soul has been enlightened by Divine grace more fully than thine own. Thou shalt hereby be so filled with the sweetness of heavenly consolation, that thou canst easily renounce all the sweetness of this world.

These two calls to God are common enough among men, and many sincerely resolve to persevere in them. But it often happens that a certain rashness of temperament hinders them from going forward in answer to the third call of God. For, although St. John reposed on our Lord's bosom, yet when Christ was seized by His enemies he deserted him and fled away. So let it not be with thee. When temptation tries thee, resist all self-seeking, resolutely stand fast by thy Saviour; and, on the other hand, do not allow any impetuosity of temper to cause thee to make a false step. If thou hast done well in these two ways and wilt not allow the love of created things to lead thee astray, God will then draw thee closer to Him. When thou feelest this drawing, let no pious method or practice of thine own devising hold thee back, but yield thyself without form or image lovingly to Him as an instrument in His hands. If He is allowed His way, then in less time than it takes to say a Pater Noster He will sanctify thee, and thereby give honor to Himself—more than thou canst do by a hundred years of thy devotions in the two former ways. But one might at a certain point begin to ask himself: Hast thou not now passed beyond thy former state and come into the higher one? Always answer: No! For no man can go forward otherwise than after the pattern of our Lord Jesus Christ. Rather ask thyself this: Hast thou progressed beyond the spirit of self-love in the pious exercises that thou hast practiced? Diligently examine thyself in this regard, and then accept God's good pleasure as He leads thee forward from one devout way to another.

The third call was when St. John received the Holy Ghost, and the heavenly door was opened in his soul. This happens to some in the form of an ecstasy, to others simply by absolute abandonment to God. Thus speaks St. Paul: "Eye hath not seen, nor ear heard, neither hath it entered into the heart of man, what things God hath prepared for them that love Him." (I Cor. ii, 9.) But one must never presume to think that he can reach his highest degree of perfection; it only happens when the outer man is absorbed in the inner, for only then is a man fully mastered by God, and the Divine marvels and riches are revealed in him. And you must understand, children, that those who are partakers of this privilege, must often lie abed quite enfeebled and helpless, for nature cannot endure such a strain; nay, one has, as it were, died a painful death many times over before reaching this state—death within and death without; but a death that means eternal life. Nor does one day bring it all about, nor one year of preparation. But be not frightened; for if it takes time and self-denial and purification of heart, it is also the most perfect way of all.

By these three processes does a man acquire that purity of heart that St. John had in a superior degree, and of which our Lord taught: "Blessed are the clean of heart, for they shall see God." (Matt. v, 8.) A clean heart is more highly prized by our Lord than anything on earth. That heart is very noble, splendidly adorned with virtue, the golden temple of the Holy Ghost in which God loves to dwell; it is the oratory of the Divine Son in which He intercedes for us with His Father, and in which He daily offers His Divine sacrifice. A purified heart is the chair of the highest judge; it is the chamber of rest of the holy Trinity;

the light of eternal glory shines within it; it is the secret council hall of the three Divine persons; it is the treasure-house of all Divine riches; its banquet is a foretaste of the sweetness of everlasting joy in God; it is the symbol of eternal wisdom; it is the trysting place of Divine love and confidence; it is the dispensation of all the graces of Christ's life and passion; it is the heavenly Father's tabernacle with men; it is the spouse of Christ; it is the trusted friend of the Holy Spirit; it is the envy of the saints above; it is a beloved sister of the angels; the expectation of the celestial army; the brother of all good men; the terror of evildoers; the complete victory over temptation; a weapon to resist every assault of the enemy; an assemblage of all good gifts; a treasury of all virtues; an example to all men; a restoration of all that was ever lost.

Who, then, has such a heart as this? He—we have already described him—who is wholly and absolutely content with God and intent on God; who has no taste for anything but God; who fixes his thoughts ever and always on God; to whom all that is not God or has not God for its inspiration, is strange and remote and unwelcome; who holds himself aloof from all intruding forms and images, all joys and sorrows of the outer life, as far as he may, and who for this end makes the best of everything that happens; for to the clean all things are clean, and to the meek and humble of heart nothing is bitter. *Amen.*

Prayer: Outward and Inward

Synopsis—Prayer of every kind must begin by an act of retirement into God—How vocal prayer is joined with this—An illustration drawn from a church edifice—How we may pray the Father for the Son.

SECOND SERMON FOR LOW SUNDAY.

And now glorify Thou Me, O Father.—John xvii, 5.

As our beloved Saviour uttered these words, the evangelist tells us that He lifted up His eyes to Heaven, thus showing us how we should raise our eyes and hands and hearts and all our powers upward to Heaven, and with Him and in Him and through Him offer our prayers to God. The homage that the Son of God paid His heavenly Father was the greatest of His works on earth—an incomprehensible mystery, far surpassing all human understanding, known only to the Holy Ghost. St. Anselm and St. Augustine say that prayer is an ascension of the soul in God.

Children, rich men come to you and give you—as you may be poor and needy and sick—five or six pennies, and agree with you for many genuflections and perhaps a hundred Pater Nosters in return. What the eternal God thinks of this kind of barter I know not; only this I say: When you pray, turn away from yourself in all sincerity, lift up your soul above all created things, and turn your thoughts to God alone; do this in the inmost depths of your being. Sink thy soul into God's infinite spirit, abandoning thyself to Him in all thy faculties, high and low, all thy senses and understanding, in order that thou mayst be entirely united to Him; and do this very interiorly. By this kind of prayer thou shalt attain to something beyond all methods and practices of devotion. And when thou art placed thus with God, then offer all the prayers to which thou art obligated, or that others have asked of thee and that God wills thee to offer. And be well assured, that as one penny is to a hundred ⁄ thousand golden marks, so are all external forms of prayer compared to this prayer of thy inner soul.

or it is real union with God; it is the absorption and melting away of he created spirit of man into the uncreated Spirit of God.

Children, if this kind of prayer may be made in company with prayer of the lips and tongue, then join them together without hesitation; and, besides, thou mayst have promised to offer vocal prayers, or thy vows may require thee to do so. But as thou prayest with thy lips, be sure to do with thy thoughts what Moses did with his flocks—lead them all into the wilderness. But if any of thy particular methods of prayer hinder, or any outward occupations interfere with this interior prayer of the spirit, set them all on one side, and I will take the responsibility; unless, indeed, these happen to be appointed thee by lawful authority. Vocal prayer of all kinds is good, just as the straw is good to ripen the wheat. Thus Christ taught: "The true adorers shall adore the Father in spirit and in truth." (John iv, 23.) It is in the spirit of a man that all his outer devotions are perfected; and if that perfecting of the external prayer by the interior spirit has not yet taken place in thee, then begin diligently to bring it about; for one moment of sincere and inward prayer is worth all external devotions whatever that are devoid of it—all that ever were offered from the time of Adam till now.

Behold this church and the many parts that go to make it compelte— foundation and walls and stones—and you know that it is all built for the interior life of prayer, to aid men in offering real and fruitful prayer to God; and if it served not that purpose it might as well in- stantly be swept out of existence. Our Lord once said to His Father: "I have finished the work which Thou gavest Me to do." (John xvii, 4.) And He did not refer to His work in time, but rather in eternity, for He had yet much to accomplish in time: He was to suffer and die and rise again from the dead. He meant His work for all time and for all eternity. It is so with men whose spiritual life is rightly guided; for their outward work in time is extended in spirit into eternity, namely, in God's Spirit, in whom they pray and live and labor, and in whom they have died to themselves. No man can be transformed until he ceases to be what he has been. If he would pray and work in the Spirit, he must be born again where the Son is born of the Father, namely, in the inmost depths of the Deity; there he is absorbed, without form and image, his soul, as it were, stripped of forms and images and all meth- ods. Such a state of prayer obtains all things, and such men pray the Father for the Son—that is to say, for the extension of His kingdom; just as before the Son had prayed His Father for them.

You ask: How can they pray the Father for the Son? I answer that our Lord taught us to pray that God's name might be hallowed. These man, therefore, pray that it may be made known and reverenced every-where and dearly loved on earth, just as He wills it to be honored in Heaven and in all eternity, and that His precious passion and death and merits may be made fruitful. And they pray, besides, for all the Christian people, and their prayer is always heard. They accept, furthermore, all happenings of life as sent from God, and receive them with all peace of mind; they feel neither prosperity nor adversity. Joy or pain is all the same to them, one as gladly accepted as the other. And in this there is great merit.

Our Saviour also prayed: "That they all may be one, as Thou, Father, in Me, and I in Thee." (John xvii, 21.) Now, this union is brought about in two ways, for it is external and internal, by intermediate influences or without them, in spirit and in nature. But this is some-times erroneously understood, for the Divinity has no accidents; nor can we understand how we are united to It. But this is no wonder; for can we understand how the human body and soul are united? How can the soul act in the hands and feet? If this is incomprehensible, no wonder we cannot understand how the human soul is joined into unity with God.

But we know that those who come to the state we are considering act in time and outwardly, and yet their act extends into eternity. Their created life is projected into the uncreated life, their multiplicity into simplicity of being. Amid unrest they enjoy peace, and with deep longing they pass into the depths of God, drawing with them all things that concern them, being thereby made eternally in Him as He would know them and love them to be. This is to come nearer to God than ordinary prayer can bring the soul—very much nearer. But to this state those cannot attain, whose spiritual life has been developed in exercises framed by natural reason alone; nor those who have been foolishly self-guided; least of all those who have lived in the enjoyments of the senses. A venerable spiritual teacher formerly discoursed to you on this subject, and you have misunderstood him, for you took his meaning in a temporal sense, and he was instructing you from the eternal point of view. Perhaps I have gone beyond bounds; though as God sees it, it is not so. At any rate, you will forgive me, dear children, and I will endeavor to do better in future. God grant that all this be so. *Amen.*

The Winter of the Soul

Synopsis—Turning inward, the soul sometimes finds a wintry land: the heart has really grown cold towards God—Warmth is restored by courageous penance and fervent prayer—Sometimes the cold is but an illusion: the soul is being tried by withdrawal of sensible fervor—This is restored by patient waiting upon God—Remarks on the friends and foes of Jesus among the Jews, and in our own day.

SERMON FOR THE SECOND SUNDAY AFTER EASTER.

And it was the feast of the dedication at Jerusalem, and it was winter. And Jesus walked in the temple. in Solomon's porch. The Jews therefore came round about Him, and said to Him: How long dost Thou hold our souls in suspense? If Thou be the Christ, tell us plainly. Jesus answered them: I speak to you, and you believe not. * * * My sheep hear My voice, and I know them, and they follow Me. And I give them life everlasting; and they shall not perish forever, and no man shall pluck them out of My hand.—John x, 22-28.

All this took place in the temple of Solomon, of which the Psalmist spoke: "His place is in peace." (Ps. lxxv, 2.) The name Solomon means peaceful, and Christ is the eternal Solomon, whose abode can be none else than that of peace, interior peace.

The temple into which the loving Jesus enters is the purified soul, the soul of the man given up to the interior life. Upon that soul God lays more store than on all His other creatures, and is more occupied with it than with all else. In this temple is the feast of dedication, namely, of renewal. And how does this renovation take place, the renewing of that temple in which God so loves to dwell; yea, rather than in any temple of His that was ever built?

We call anything new whilst it is not long after its beginning; and a man is made new when he turns inward, and enters into the temple of his own soul with all his faculties. There he finds God in all His eternal truth, dwelling and acting there very perceptibly—not as the bodily senses perceive, nor even as the mind reasons, nor yet according to what one may have read or heard. No; but the Divine action in the soul is perceived by the soul's spiritual power of tasting and experiencing the Divine influences, welling up in its depth as out of their own fountain—not introduced from without. A fountain is better than a cistern; the latter is easily muddied and is liable to dry up; but the fountain ever bursts forth fresh and pure, and its water is always its own. Now, in the temple of the soul there is a true feast of dedication—that is to say, of renovation, as often as a man enters his interior soul—even a thousand times a day, if that were possible. And at every dedication there is new purity of intention, new light, new grace and new virtues bestowed. O, this turning inward is a beautiful act; to do it and to do it right, all external devotions and all good works serve to assist, receiving from it in return all their perfection. Indeed, without this interior movement external religious practices are of no great worth. However active one may be in all pious practices, above all other things he should constantly practice this turning inward to his soul's renewal.

"And it was winter." Now, when is it really winter? It is when the heart has grown cold; when it has within it neither grace, nor God, nor any Godlike things. Snow and frost are those miserable, pitiable created things which hold the soul fast bound in love of them and pleasure in their use. They quench the fire of the Holy Ghost there; they freeze up the fountains of grace with a dreadful spiritual coldness. They destroy all spiritual comfort and sweet familiarity with God.

But there is yet another winter. This is suffered by a really God-fearing man. He is mindful of God and loves Him, and is careful to avoid all sin. But God seems to have forsaken him. As far as his feelings go, he is dry, dark and cold, devoid of all heavenly consolation and spiritual sweetness. Our Lord Himself suffered this spiritual winter, being deserted by His heavenly Father and deprived of His help. Although He was united to the Divine nature, yet His poor human nature received no drop of comfort from the Godhead during His unspeakably bitter passion—not an instant's consolation in His sorest need. He was the most forsaken and helpless and agonizing of all men. Now this is a lesson to His chosen friends. These must with all joy and entire good-will endure this state of abandonment in union with Christ. For He is their shepherd; they are privileged to be His sheep; they must suffer patiently in their interior souls, and show all patience in their outward behavior, in imitation of Jesus Christ. If they are but overjoyed to follow Him into this His winter time of desolation, abandonment by God and all creatures, then will God in actual reality be

present with them, and in a manner far more to their advantage than
if they experienced the brightest possible summer-time of His sensible
favor. No one can fully understand all the good that lies hidden in this
stern trial of desolation of spirit, this dark and frozen spiritual winter—supposing always that one holds his mind steady and firm in
patient endurance.

The gospel tells us, further, that "the Jews came round about" Jesus.
There were among them, as among us, some good and some bad. Now,
the word Jew may be taken to mean one who confesses God. And when
the soul's powers turn into the interior, down to the very roots of life,
using natural and supernatural means of perfection, then the soul confesses or truly acknowledges God, and does so in a manner full of feeling and spiritual enjoyment. This is an act of faith so true and living
that it wins all that is born of faith. Its power is so great that pro-
claiming God in all sincerity absorbs the soul's entire life: Interiorly,
in the understanding and the will; outwardly, in every external human
faculty; in deeds and words, in doing and refusing to do, and in all
sufferings. A man now feels and knows nothing in act or in contemplation except the confessing of God in perfect truth. This may have been
Christ's meaning when He said: "Every one, therefore, that shall confess Me before men, I will also confess him before My Father Who is in
Heaven." (Matt. x, 32.) Be well assured of this: Whatsoever work
thou dost in which thou settest before thee any other end but God, in
doing that work thou forgettest God. God by His very nature must
be the end and object of all things, and of all thoughts and intentions;
and if thou placest any other object before thee, it is as if thou didst
deny God, for thou givest to a creature what belongs to God alone and
that by prerogative of His very nature.

And there were bad Jews round about our Lord, hearts full of bitterness, men who could not endure to look on Him or suffer Him for a moment. They were stony-hearted against Him. Alas, do we not see the
like of this among Christians today? We meet with some men who are
enraged against God's friends; who cannot behold their good deeds
without the bitterest opposition; who do their utmost to hinder their
good works and destroy the good effects of them; who are totally
opposed to their ways and their lives, and are ever seeking to misin-
terpret them—in a word, they act toward good Christians as the bad
Jews did toward our Lord. This is a very dangerous state to be in.
No sign is as plain of having no part with God and His friends in

eternity, as when a man has within him no favor for what is good and pleasing to God in other men's conduct. Therefore did Christ teach: "He that is not with Me is against Me." (Matt. xii, 30.) On the other hand, it is plainly a sign of God's friendship when men are like the good Jews, who were kind to our Saviour. These praise the virtuous lives of fervent Christians in all candor and good will, without false interpretations, full of affection, favor and uprightness of intention—a true sign that God dwells in their inmost souls, and that they shall finally possess eternal joy. The others are altogether different. Of them did He speak on that same occasion, saying: "Ye are not of My sheep, for My sheep hear My voice."

Now let us ask why our Lord so often calls His friends sheep. Because sheep have two qualities that our Lord especially loves, namely, innocence and gentle meekness. We read in the Apocalypse that the pure and guileless "follow the Lamb whithersoever He goeth." (Apoc. xiv, 4.) The meek and humble of heart are near to God, and they hear His voice; proud and haughty men never hear it. When the wind howls and the doors and windows clatter, one can hardly hear the voice of man. As to the voice of God, that fatherly, whispered, secret word, uttered in the inmost depths of thy soul—if thou wilt hear it, thou must be deaf to all the roar of the world without, and hush all the voices of thy own inner life. Thou must yield thyself up like a meek and gentle little sheep, confess thy sins, and, all humbly hushed and quieted, hearken to this voice of God; it is denied to all who are not thus made like unto sheep. It was to His sheep that the Lord spoke, as we read in the lessons of this night's office: "I will give thee a lovely land, the goodly inheritance of the army of the Gentiles. And I said: Thou shalt call Me Father and shalt not cease to walk after Me." (Jer. iii, 19.) And what is this lovely land which He has promised His chosen sheep, His beloved friends? That land is their own body. Our bodies are by nature full of concupiscence and rebellious, but He enables His friends to reduce them to obedience, and they find much joy in compelling them to do their will. What was once waste and barren is now become a fertile and well-tilled land, in which one sows and reaps in all abundance.

And what is the goodly inheritance? O, it is nothing less than our Lord Jesus Christ Himself, for He is the heir of His Father and we are co-heirs with Him, as St. Paul tells us: "Heirs, indeed, of God, and joint heirs with Christ." (Rom. viii, 17.) The Son has received from the

Father all that He is and all that He can do; and into His hand hath the Father given all things. And, in turn, the Son hath given back to His Father all that He received from Him, even to the very least, seeking the Father's glory alone in all things. And in this we are to imitate God's Son. For if He is to be made our inheritance, we must restore to His Father everything without exception that we are and that we have power to do, holding back not a hair's weight of all that is ours in our interior or our exterior existence. No matter how it has come to us, direct or indirect, everything must go to Him Who is its owner: do thou make no exception whatever. And then seek God Himself. Our miserable nature is greedy and selfish, seeking its own in everything, and hereby our lovely inheritance is obscured; for to appropriate to self what is God's alone, is to debase the Godlike to the state of the creature, and is to obscure the glory of our heavenly inheritance.

And what does He mean by the words: I will give thee the exercise of the heathen? This means that the soul shall receive God's grace with the humility of a converted pagan. Those converts received grace as grace, having no pious practices to help them, nor any holiness to begin with, and starting without any merits; whereas the Jews were more fortunate in having their law and their ceremonies and their good works, and many other helps. The heathen had nothing whatever to build on but God's grace and mercy alone. Now in that spirit should thy devout practices be offered up, trusting to God's great mercy and kindness and nothing else.

Thou must not place too much confidence in thy own good preparations, or take much account of thy worthiness. Many men follow the Jews in this respect, building on their own methods, and trusting (however secretly and unconsciously it may be) to their own works. And if it happens that they miss doing certain pious things, they think that all is lost, and forthwith they lose trust in God and man. By saying this I do not mean that one should give up his devout practices; no, let him do them well and punctually, but without making them— rather than God's blessed grace—the foundation of his hopes. Such men depend wholly for their union with God upon the boast that they have worn haircloth and chains, fasted and prayed and watched, been poor men for forty years; and apart from these things they would have no solid trust in God. But if a man has done all the good works in the world, then it but gives him the occasion to be detached from them in his soul, and to stand before God as if he had never done a single good deed his whole life long, whether great or small, accepting God's grace for its own sake alone and as a gift of His loving mercy, rejecting every thought of trusting in his own personal preparation for it. This is what we may call the exercise of the heathen. May God help us to what He has promised in the prophecy of Jeremias: "I will give thee a lovely land, the goodly inheritance of the army of the Gentiles. And I said: Thou shalt call Me Father, and shalt not cease to walk after Me." *Amen.*

The Paraclete's Judgment Against the World

Synopsis—We here mean by the world our own heart—The Holy Spirit will condemn the hidden wickedness of refusing to avow our sinfulness—Also for secret self-righteousness on account of our good works—Again, for sitting in judgment upon our neighbor—If we meekly accept the Paraclete's judgment, He will enlighten us and cleanse us unto perfection—How this is done.

FIRST SERMON FOR THE FOURTH SUNDAY AFTER EASTER.*

It is expedient to you that I go; for if I go not, the Paraclete will not come to you; but if I go, I will send Him to you. And when He is come, He will convince the world of sin, and of justice, and of judgment.—John xvi, 7, 8.

Children, note carefully this teaching, which tells us that if God's well-loved friends and followers shall receive the Holy Ghost, then Jesus must first depart from them. Depart? And how depart? It is nothing less than leaving us in utter abandonment, void of comfort, incapable; so that we become dull, heavy, cold and dark in regard to all good deeds. That is what is meant by Christ's going away from us. Whosoever is thus placed by God, and shall learn how to take advantage of his state will find it exceedingly profitable, a blessed and a Godlike gift. If he but wisely abandons himself to God's will, then all his multiplicity is turned into unity; in the midst of suffering he finds joy; he is patient of all shame, peaceful amid strife, and he extracts sweetness out of bitterness.

When our Lord says that the Holy Ghost at His coming will condemn the world, He means that He will show us clearly whether or not the world lies concealed in the depths of our soul. If He finds it there, He will expose it, convict it, and condemn it. And what is the world in us but its methods and works and images; or again, its comforts and joys and sorrows, its fears and hopes and cares? Hence St. Bernard tells us: "With what thou art made joyous or sad, with that thou shalt be judged." Children, this is what the Holy Spirit will condemn in

---

*Tauler left no sermon for the third Sunday after Easter.

us—that we would never have rest nor peace except when possessed by the miserable and wicked influence of the world. In whatever man this tendency is found unrepressed, that is to say, joy in creatures, in the same man, whether living or dead, is found what our Lord means by the world. And this is, again, a plain sign that in such a soul the Holy Ghost has not taken up His abode. For Christ has declared that when He comes He will condemn all such things.

He will also condemn the world for its sins. And what sins? Now you know, children, that the eternal God made all things, and that He hath rightly ordered all things to their proper end, just as fire is made to go upward and the stone to fall downward. And in our own nature He has made our eyes to see, our ears to hear. our hands to work, our feet to walk, and these and all our members to be obedient to our will, whether hard or easy, bitter or sweet; yea, even for life or death. And this will power is perversely used by many lovers of this world, who gladly give up all their goods and their honor, that they may possess and enjoy what ministers to their fleshly indulgence. Now sinners, to excuse their sloth, seem to address the Lord and say: Who is there nowadays, Lord, that obeys Thee truly and keeps all Thy command- ments, who does it willingly and is content in his inmost soul to give up all self and all transitory things at Thy behest? Children, this sin will the Holy Ghost punish when He comes; it is the sin of resisting the Divine will, stifling God's warning voice within, and doing it over and over again—this will He punish, and many a hidden wickedness besides. This judgment produces in the soul a sudden sense of being condemned by God, a pain so sharp, a woe so unbearable that it is like the torment of hell, a feeling the like of which is almost unknown to the worldly minded, or to men who blindly follow their natural instincts. This feeling is the plainest sign that the Holy Ghost is, indeed, present in the soul; and it gives us a cause of real confidence in God, for it shows the true state of things. For if a man has committed a thousand sins and knows them and sincerely confesses them, it is infinitely better than to be guilty of one single offense that he will not avow, that he does not admit to be sinful, and to which he continues to give himself up. O, dear children, be assured that any so-called spiritual man who rests in total self-content, who is well pleased with his state of soul and his manner of living, is really in great danger and is committing offenses perilous to his salvation. He is a self-willed man from whom nothing good can be expected.

And then the Holy Ghost will convict and punish us for the sake of justice or righteousness. O merciful God, how poor and contemptible is our justice in Thy sight! Therefore, says St. Augustine: "Woe to all justice and woe over again, if God, when He comes, will not judge our justice according to His mercy." And Isaias says: "All our justices are as the rag of a menstruous woman." (Isaias lxiv, 6.) And our Lord thus taught His well-loved disciples: "When you shall have done all these things that are commanded you, say: We are unprofitable servants." (Luke xxvii, 10.) What deception is plainer, children, than that by which a man reckons himself to be what in reality he is not. Many a one is so infatuated with his own way of acting, that he will yield to neither God nor man; indeed, such men very carefully guard against giving themselves up to God. When the Divine warnings overtake them, whether coming from God direct or through some intermediary, they pay no heed to them—unmortified men, pleasing neither to God nor to His creatures. But it may happen that the Holy Ghost visits them with the judgment and condemnation of their spiritual exercises and methods; and then such a man confesses his faults in all sincerity, learns in his own heart the lessons of self-denial, humility, and all other virtues that fit him for eternal happiness.

Children, the Holy Ghost, as our Lord tells us, will convince the world of judgment. And this applies to any man who, blind to his own faults, sits in judgment upon other men's faults. Our Saviour teaches: "Judge not, that you may not be judged. For with what judgment you judge, you shall be judged, and with what measure you mete, it shall be measured to you again." (Matt. vii, 1-2.) Children, it has come to pass nowadays, that everybody, without exception is wanting in this respect—clergy and laity, bishops, priests, monks, provincials, abbots, nobles and common people, these are ever judging and condemning one another, and thereby building up a high wall between themselves and God. Be on your guard against this failing, as you love God and His eternal bliss. On the contrary, judge and condemn yourselves. That will be of much benefit to you, and will save you from being condemned by the eternal God and all His blessed saints.

Children, never condemn anything whatsoever, unless it is manifestly and openly a grievous sin. Bite your tongue till it bleeds rather than speak words in condemnation of others, be it in matters great or small. What seems evil to thee, do thou silently recommend to God's eternal justice. From the practice of judging one's neighbor grows up a habit of self-righteousness, pride and contempt for one's neighbor, the seed of Satan, by means of which many a heart is defiled. This is a sign that the Holy Ghost is not really present, Who would guide the soul to right and timely judgment, as necessity and one's office would require. It sometimes happens that in healing one wound, a man by his violent temper inflicts three or four other wounds. Hard words should not be used in correction, but rather those of affection. One should not crush another's heart; love, all kindly and meek, should be the invariable rule in administering correction, whether among clergy or laity. By this spirit one keeps his own soul in meekness; he never loses self-control, but knows in all calmness of mind what he is about, whether he be addressing many or few; never failing to treat others in all single-mindedness as he would be treated by them; setting aside in silence all that does not strictly belong to the duty in hand.

Children, assume no airs of superior wisdom. Look in all simplicity into your own hearts and study yourselves in body and soul. Go not astray after God's deep secrets, such as Divine emanation and Divine immanation, the difference between being and not being, or essence of being in the soul. Christ has taught that the secret things of God are not for us to know. Hold fast by the faith, the true and simple faith; believe in one God and three Divine persons without a multiplicity of fine distinctions. Sabellius and Arius had wonderful imaginings about the Trinity, and Solomon and Origen have transmitted to Holy Church wonderful disquisitions—and what has been their eternal fate? We know not. Take heed to yourselves; permit no one to answer for you except yourselves. Have regard to God and His holy will; stick to the calling in which God has placed you, and fulfill it truly and with a pure intention.

If you do not know what God's will may be in any matter, then seek counsel of men more enlightened by God's Holy Spirit than you are. If none such are at hand, then go direct to God, and doubt not but that He will give you all needed direction; stand fast by that. But if even this leaves you doubtful, then diligently seek out the way most unpleasant to flesh and blood and to which you have the least inclination; follow that to begin with, for God most certainly dwells and His grace increases in a heart that is dead to self.

Now, children, since God's well-loved disciples cannot receive the Holy Ghost until Christ Jesus has in this way departed from them, it behooves us also to willingly prepare ourselves for that departure.

Give up all things for God, and without doubt God will give you Himself in all things. Do that, children; do it earnestly, resting your thoughts in the inward life in very truth, and your reward even in this world will be wonderfully great.

Our Saviour also teaches, that when the Holy Ghost comes He will teach us all things, even future things. This does not mean that we shall be taught beforehand whether the corn harvest will be great or the price high or low; but that He will teach us all that is necessary for a perfect life. He will teach us the secret wisdom of God: that this world is false, our natural lights are misguiding, that the evil spirits are crafty. Children, go forward steadfastly in God's paths and with all discretion; look well to the duties of your state of life as being God's merciful vocation—be ever-faithful in this course. Do not act as some do: if God would have them by their vocation cultivate the inner life, they forthwith turn away to the outward life; and if He calls them to the outward life, they turn obstinately to the inward life—spirits hard and perverse.

Now, children, it is in this wise that the Holy Ghost teaches us all truth when He comes to us: He reveals to us our sins as they are in reality, and He annihilates us in our own eyes; He shows us how to live purely and simply for truth and according to truth; He teaches us how to sink down with true humility in subjection to God and all of God's creatures. Is not this real knowledge? Does it not embrace in itself all the knowledge and all the wisdom a man needs for perfection and happiness? namely, genuine humility, deep seated in the soul. This is very different from the humility of some men, who humble themselves in words, and if you use the very same words about them, they will not tolerate it for an instant. This meekness is not well grounded; there is little good back of it, for such people are self-absorbed. Nor can a man's life ever amount to anything with our Lord, unless he has real and heartfelt humility. May God grant us sincere subjection of soul under His hand and under all His creatures. May He draw us into entire conformity to His holy will. May His Holy Spirit come to us and possess us with His grace, teaching us all the truth of His holy way of life. *Amen.*

Hindering the Coming of the Holy Ghost

Synopsis—The wilfully wicked are the first class who reject the Spirit, being slaves of vice—Good men lessen His influence in their souls by using mechanically the outward parts of the confession and communion, nor fully adverting to the interior graces—Some suffer themselves to be deluded by fancied visions.—This often comes from mistaken thoughts about our Lord's humanity—The true way of meditating on Christ's humanity.

SECOND SERMON FOR THE FOURTH SUNDAY AFTER EASTER.

It is expedient to you that I go; for if I go not, the Paraclete will not come to you.—John xvi, 7.

Mark well, dear children, to how high a place a man must be conducted if he shall achieve perfect happiness. That can only come to pass by his sincerely renouncing all those things that are most pleasing to human nature. From all these he must be mortified; he must let them all go, no matter how good and precious they may seem to him, nay, even holy and spiritual. The disciples of Christ—were they not required to give up their Master in His humanity, so full of grace, so holy and so beloved? And this was expedient to them, in order that they might be made capable of receiving the Holy Ghost. Therefore, no man shall be fit to receive Divine grace whose heart is in possession of creatures. Three kinds of obstacles in as many kinds of men hinder the coming of the Holy Ghost.

The first class are wilfully wicked men, having their pleasures in creatures against God's law; far away from God's paths are these. Of these the Psalmist speaks: "Cursed are they that depart from the way of the Lord" (Ps. cxviii, 21); that is to say, go away from God to creatures. And there are others who are really good people, but who are anxious about their needs, or who take over much pleasure in outward things. Therefore does our Lord oppose them, saying: "He that loveth his life shall lose it." (John xii, 25.) He means carnal love of life; and He immediately adds: "He that hateth his life in this world, keepeth it into life eternal." These latter are the ones who resist and suppress their disorderly appetites.

The second hindrance of good men to attaining real spirituality, is misunderstanding the seven sacraments, fixing their soul too exclusively upon the outward signs therein, and thereby failing to obtain the full inward grace; for the holy sacraments are instituted to lead us to single-hearted truth. Thus the married life is a sign of the union of the Divine and the human natures in Christ, and also represents the espousals of the soul with God. Hence those who rest wholly upon the outward sign in this sacrament, through their sensual understanding of it prevent its helping them to the eternal truth; they do not live rightly in the married state.

Again, some men lean too much on the outward part of the sacrament of penance, on the saying of its prayers and on the confession of sin, not going down into its very truth. To admonish these our Saviour said: "He that is washed, needeth not but to wash his feet, but is clean wholly." (John xiii, 10.) Which means that when a man has washed his soul once by a good confession, being deeply penitent and honestly confessing all his sins, he need not suppose he must keep on repenting his old sins, already repented of, already confessed. Let him tell his daily venial sins; let him, as it were, wash his feet from the petty faults of life as his conscience reproves him, and thereby he shall be made clean wholly.

And good men are often burdened by the outward customs they observe in receiving our Lord in holy Communion. They have so many outward devotions that these consume their interior fervor. The true sacramental state is an interior longing for God and an interior union with Him, and not a union in appearance only. Hence some do not receive this sacrament properly, for this and all sacraments lead us to God in all simplicity of truth.

We must realize that God is to be rightly adored by all men, in all states of life, and at all times. Now whosoever would rightly adore the heavenly Father, must set his soul into solitude, and give himself up to his longing for God, and have steadfast confidence in Him; and this condition belongs to the highest part of the soul. When thus placed, the spirit of a man rests oblivious to time and to bodily life. St. Paul bids us ever to rejoice, give thanks to God without ceasing and always to pray. To pray without ceasing is to do all one's works in God's love, meanwhile renouncing all self-gratulation in them, and at the same time to bow down humbly before God, and give up our souls freely to His influence. When these dispositions are united together in the highest faculties of the soul, then is the soul spiritualized. It then cleaves to God with perfect union of its will. It becomes, as it were, divinized, and then a man begins first to have the right and true adoration of God, for he has attained the end for which he was created.

Now there are some, yes, there are many, who do not adore the Father rightly and in truth. For as often as we pray to God on account simply of benefiting by creatures, we pray to our own injury. The creature is what it is—a creature, and can only bring with it bitterness, hurt and evil. Men who pray for created things, without any spiritual intention, are rightly served when they suffer misery; they have implicitly prayed for the infliction they now endure. Whosoever seeks God and seeks anything else with Him, will not find Him. Whosoever seeks God alone in all sincerity, will find Him and all besides that God may give.

Many good men are hindered from their perfection, because they rest in a deluded spirit upon the humanity of our Lord Jesus Christ, by which means they give themselves up too much to visions. They see in spirit angels or men, or the humanity of Christ; and they believe the words they think are spoken to them, assuring them that they are God's favorites, or that certain persons have committed sins or practiced virtues, or that God is going to do something by their means. By all of which they are often deceived, for whatsoever God does, He does by His goodness; he has no need of creatures. Hence our Lord said to His disciples: "It is expedient to you that I go." This was because He would lead them to higher perfection. Even His humanity was a hindrance to them, because they cleaved to it with inordinate pleasure. They must follow God in all their ways, and His humanity should lead them to His Godhead. Christ said: "I am the way, and the truth, and the life. No man cometh to the Father but by Me." (John xiv, 6.) Hence those men are much mistaken who flatter themselves that they can do anything good of themselves. Jesus Himself said: "From God I proceeded and came; for I came not of Myself." (John viii, 42.)

We must adore the humanity of Christ only on account of its union with the Godhead. The man Christ is truly God, and God is truly man. Let us not concern ourselves with any creature; let us be absorbed in God, in our Lord Jesus Christ, who alone is our way to the Father. And yet even where we have entered mentally upon the way of truth

that Christ is, even yet. I say, we are not perfectly happy, although we
have caught sight of Divine truth. For as a matter of fact, when we
only contemplate an object we are not yet made one with it, nor can
this take place while it remains in our understanding associated with
anything else. Because where there is only one, then only one is seen;
and hence we cannot see God except in blindness, nor know Him except
in unknowing. "No soul can come to God," says St. Augustine, "except
it goes to Him without creatures, and tastes Him as an incomparable
sweetness."

Because the soul is a creature, therefore must it give itself up and go
out of itself in the moment of contemplation; yea, even give up for the
moment the contemplation of all the angels and saints. These are all
but creatures, and taken in themselves can only interfere with the
soul's Divine union. When the soul stands free and in need of nothing
whatsoever, then it can come to God, as it were, resembling Himself;
for nothing helps union so well as resemblance. As soon as the soul
takes on the Divine colors, as it may be expressed, so soon does God
grant Himself to the soul's powers, and then the soul grows in a Divine
resemblance, and is, if we dare say so, tinted and shaded with the
colors of the Divinity. The image is in the soul's powers, the resemblance is in its virtues, the Divine coloring is in the union. And thus
what we may call God-coloring becomes so intimate, that the soul seems
no longer to act in the form of a creature, but in the divinely colored
form of its union with God. And while the soul is in a state of contemplation of God and has grown into this yet closer union with Him, and
after He is yet more deeply poured into the soul's depths and has drawn
it wholly to Himself, then it happens that there remains no power in the
soul to know what sort of a being it is now to consider itself to be;
yet meanwhile God holds it in its place as a creature. Thus it is that
the light of grace expels from thee the light of nature; for the higher
the soul is elevated in the knowledge that the light of grace gives, the
darker grows the light of nature. If the soul will know the very truth,
let it consider whether or not it be withdrawn from all things, whether or
not it is lost to itself, loves God with real love, and is not hindered from
Him by anything whatsoever; and finally whether or not He alone
lives within it. If the soul can answer rightly to all this, then it has
lost Christ, as His mother Mary lost Him in the temple, as He tarried
in the school of His Father's highest doctrine, and seemed no longer to
think of even His mother—only to find Him again, as she did, in greater

joy.   Thus it is with that noble soul that goes to school to the Godhead, there to learn what God is in relation to the humanity of Christ.   There, too, it learns to know the most adorable will of God.   That man is most perfectly God's man, who does all and loves all and wills all in the will of His heavenly Father.   That we may all come to this happy state and be freed from every hindrance thereto, may God grant us. *Amen.*

Why Prayer is Without Fruit

Synopsis—The first and greatest gift we should ask is love; and then guidance as to how to pray; after that we should calmly but closely look into our good thoughts—Prayer is made fruitless by disordered interior affections—Before God's love comes in all other love must go out, or be ready to be sanctified—Interior resentments hinder good prayer, and often stifle even the graces of Holy Communion—Discouragement after faults is a serious hindrance to fruitful prayer—The example of the prayer of Lazarus, the beggar.

SERMON FOR THE ROGATION DAYS.

Which of you shall have a friend, and shall go to him at midnight, and shall say to him: Friend, lend me three loaves; because a friend of mine is come off his journey to me, and I have not what to set before him. And he from within should answer, and say: Trouble me not, the door is now shut, and my children are with me in bed; I cannot rise and give to thee. Yet if he shall continue knocking, I say to you, although he will not rise and give to him because he is his friend; yet, because of his importunity, he will rise and give him as many as he needeth.—Luke xi, 5-9.

This is part of our Lord's teaching about how we should pray. And he immediately adds: "And I say to you: Ask, and it shall be given you; seek, and you shall find; knock, and it shall be opened to you. For every one that asketh, receiveth; and he that seeketh, findeth; and to him that knocketh, it shall be opened." Now let us consider the difference between asking, seeking and knocking. Asking means the turning of a really interior man to God, begging some favor with deep sincerity. Seeking is praying for something because we have a particularly earnest longing to posses it more than other things. Knocking means constancy in one's petition, never giving up till one has obtained what he asks for.

Venerable Bede explains this teaching thus: "The friend spoken of by our Lord is the soul of man, which, having strayed away into distant and foreign lands of unspiritual thoughts, returns again and again to itself hungry and thirsty after all good, and finds nothing granted to it. Then that soul turns to its friend, namely, God, and, standing before

His door, prays and knocks, begging three loaves of Him, meaning the knowledge of the Holy Trinity. He that is within excuses Himself, and says that He has gone to bed and so have His servants; and these servants mean God's appointed teachers, who are absorbed with Him in a state of holy contemplation. But the soul, standing without at the door, perseveres, and it continues to knock, until He that is within at last arises and gives him what he desires." He gives him His answer by means of teachers, or by directly teaching him without any intermediary. And this is why Christ said: "Ask, and it shall be given you; seek, and you shall find; knock, and it shall be opened to you."

Here we may remark God's unspeakable goodness; for He grants us gladly just for the asking, and He earnestly bids us ask, exhorts us to do so, and teaches us how. But His gifts are not granted to the slothful, but to earnest askers and to those who persevere in their petitions.

And what shall we ask? Love. When one sets himself to pray, when he calls home his wandering thoughts and banishes all distractions, then let him with genuine humility cast himself at God's feet and crave love as an alms from the Divine charity; let him knock at the door of his Father's heart, and beg as a gift the bread of love. If one had all the food in the world except bread, his meals would be tasteless and unprofitable. So is it with regard to all things without Divine love.

Again, let a man beg God's guidance as to how he shall pray. Ask of God that prayer that pleases Him best, that kind of interior exercise that will serve thy soul's best interests. After having done that, accept whatsoever devout thoughts come before thee, whether they be of the Godhead simply, of the blessed Trinity, or of the sufferings and the wounds of our Lord.

Remember that all are not able to pray wholly with spiritual acts of the mind, for many must pray with words. Dear child, pray to our Lord as thou canst, with all possible pious and Divine words, and thou shalt find thy heart and mind enraptured with joy. And pray to thy heavenly Father, that through the merits of His only begotten Son He will present His own blessed self to thy soul as the object of thy worship, in whatever manner is most pleasing to Him. Then when thou findest any manner or method of praying very productive of devotion and most pleasing to thee, stick to that—whether it be the sorrowful thought of thy sins, or anything else whatsoever. Our Lord's way for us to seek and to find, is seeking and finding the grace to do His will and to best serve our neighbor. Knock at that door with all persistence: he that perseveres shall be granted the crown.

Our Saviour says: "And which of you, if he ask his father bread, will he give him a stone? Or a fish—will he for a fish give him a serpent? Or if he shall ask an egg, will be reach him a scropion? If you then, being evil, know how to give good gifts to your children, how much more will your Father in Heaven give the good spirit to them that ask Him?" (Luke xi, 11-13.) Now, the gift of a fish may be taken to mean confidence in God, and the gift of an egg may signify living faith.

But if truth itself says, "Ask and you shall receive," how does it happen that so many men are asking their lives long and the living bread is never given them? And yet we know that God is unspeakably kind and a thousand times more ready to grant than man is to receive His favors. They utter the same devout prayers every day—Pater Nosters, the psalter, and other prayers taught us by the Holy Spirit, and yet they are not heard. There must be some great cause for this, and it is a wonderful thing. Children, I will reveal it to you: Your inmost hearts, your love and your intention are all in the possession of some alien affection. Whatever it may be that you expend your love upon, the living or the dead, yourself or your kindred, that holds possession of your heart, it occupies the place that true Divine love should occupy, that love which is God's bread of life. Pray and ask as you like, and as much as you like, and it is all in vain. Hence Hugo of St. Victor teaches: "That a man can live without some love or other is as impossible as that he can live without a soul."

Let each one study carefully his own case. Remember that before one love can come in, the other love must go out. See to it at once, says St. Augustine, that thou art filled with the right love. Men come with their worldly hearts to God, hearts preoccupied in their inmost depths, and when they pray and ask, the heavenly bread is not given them. Is this God's fault? If they get a stone instead of bread, is it not their own stony heart, dry and cold, from which all devotion and grace are absent? They read many good books, and they enjoy them, but what they read does not open the springs of grace in their souls. As a man does his daily task of work and sleeps and wakes and works again and over again, so does he pray, and all in the same routine spirit; and he thinks that that is enough. Meanwhile his heart is as hard as a millstone, and is not any more capable of being softened or broken. If you happen to propose anything to him that he does not like, whether to do or not to do, you soon find that you are beating upon a heart of stone. Dear child, beware of this hardness of spirit. And have little to say to such a man; deliver thy message in one word and fly from him; let it

be our Lord's: Yea, yea, or no, no. Take care lest such a one cast
his stone at thy head—avoid it, be on thy guard, never answer him with
hard words, shut thy lips tight and raise thy heart to God: Do this, I
beseech thee, and do it for God's sake. Always be like a meek and
gentle lamb in dealing with those who oppose thee. Be silent, be
patient, keep a close watch on thy feelings. Stoniness of soul often lies
hidden for a long time, until in some way or other one becomes conscious of it.

Let me assure you that when I find these men harboring hidden hate
and resentment and refusing to give it up, I will not allow them to
receive the Lord's body. There are many who go to confession for
twenty or thirty years, and never do it rightly, nor are every rightly
absorbed, and yet always afterwards receive the blessed Sacrament—
a most distressing, a most terrible thing. The Pope himself, who has
the highest power in Christendom, could not validly absolve such men.
The oftener they receive holy communion, and the more they pray and
do good works, the harder and stonier grow their hearts, and the blinder
and duller do they become; they fancy that all is well with them, for
they are trusting to the outward good deeds they do. Better do no
good thing, than to approach our Lord in communion without quitting
their sinful state and curing the cause of it. Be sure of this: God will
never allow such conduct to go unpunished; He will visit it with penalties, not only for the soul's pain, but also for the body's—they will
receive a serpent instead of a fish.

Children, another bad trait in these men is their tendency to rash
judgment. The serpent instills his poison into them, and they spit it
out upon their neighbor by making little of his good deeds and by
destroying his reputation, their evil work extending in all directions.
They never consider their own state of sin, but watch and count their
neighbor's sins, often playing their snake-like part by injecting their
poison secretly. Be on your guard against this; judge yourselves, and
judge nobody else.

And, again, such men have received a scorpion instead of an egg;
that is to say, they are deluded about themselves and cultivate a false
confidence in their supposed virtue; and they despise others. Why, they
ask, shall not I get on as well as such and such others? Do not I pray,
and read pious books, and sing pious hymns, and live as well as they do?
Just as the scorpion shows no venom with his mouth, and yet stings with
his tail. Such is the case with those whose confidence is misplaced and
falsely grounded. And what happens when they begin to realize that

they are wrong? They fall into despair, and they are stung with death's poisonous sting, and are lost eternally.

Children, this comes from the dreadful failure to take true account of what is going on in the interior of the soul, and what offenses against God we have committed. Children, it is for this reason that some sins are reserved for absolution to the Pope, some to specially appointed confessors and to bishops. This is by no means done foolishly, but that men may learn the difference between various kinds of sins, think of them more intelligently, and thereby have greater sorrow for them and guard more carefully against committing them. Children, did you but know how horrible a sin it is to drink the precious blood of Christ our God— blood poured out for love of us—while the soul is in this wicked state, you would be ready to expire with grief. It is for this reason that in some monasteries it is the rule to receive communion only once in three weeks, so that each one may have full time rightly to prepare for this great banquet, and that it may have full opportunity to complete its good results within him. But as to you, you should stimulate your hearts to ardent longings to receive holy communion, and establish a custom of often doing so. Pray to our Lord that He take this preparation of thy soul into His own hands. Live kindly disposed toward all, be inclined to the interior life, be humble to all men, and be detached from created things.

A certain master was once asked, how it pleased him that certain persons wished to receive our Lord oftener than was the custom in their community. He answered: "May our Lord God be praised, and may we rejoice in our hearts that there are any who long and yearn after God in this manner; the inmates of whatever monastery that has them, should most earnestly help them to enjoy this privilege." But such as these should carefully abstain from thinking that those who act differently are worse than they are. For others there are who often abstain from motives of humility, deeming themselves unworthy of so high a favor. And if it should happen that anyone sits in judgment on thee, and, as it were, throws stones of condemnation at thee in the shape of hard words, let this be to thee as if it came direct upon thee from God Himself.

And there are other stones: As when a man is sincerely detached from this world and longs for God with all his heart, and yet his soul remains hard and dry, cold and dull. If thou art thus afflicted, then I bid thee stand carefully on thy guard, suffer this spiritual dryness patiently, and willingly continue in it. Take heed lest thou seek a solace for it in

some alien comfort, which, indeed, can only result in interior disorder.
Stay at home in thy desolate heart. Attack thy faults, condemn thyself
severely for them with resolute courage, chastise thyself hard. And if
this judgment of God rests on thee a whole year long, all the better.
Keep on stoning thy guilty self in God's presence.

And just the same shouldst thou do immediately that thou art conscious of having committed some fault. Confess it to God without any
delay. And if this defect escapes thy mind when thou dost make thy
confession to the priest, be sure that thy sincere repentance more than
compensates for this lapse of memory, for the sacrament of confession
is given to Holy Church primarily for the remission of mortal sins; and
one should not be distressed with doubts in any venial matters. It
may be that thou shalt imagine that the devout exercises of thy vocation hinder thy spiritual progress; such exercises, I mean, as assisting
in choir, and the usual works done by obedience to rule. But this is a
delusion. Be by no means diverted from keeping thy rule, for disorder
in this respect would be the real hindrance to thy progress. If thou
shouldst yield to this error, it would show that the actual cause of thy
trouble is that thy love of God is not disinterested, that thy resolutions
have not been made with purity of intention, and that thou art in reality
preoccupied with alien things, and art become thy own real hindrance.

Jesus once said: "I am the door. By Me, if any man enter in, he
shall be saved." (John x, 9.) Now it is on three parts of this door
that a man must knock if he would be surely let in. First, he must
knock at our Lord Jesus Christ's heart, which is invitingly offered him,
and which was cut in two after His death. And when he enters in, let
him do so with profound reverence, avowing his utter poverty, his absolute nothingness; let him take pattern by poor Lazarus who lay at the
rich man's door; let him crave the crumbs that fall from the table of
God's grace. The grace that will be granted thee will change thee into
a divinely supernatural being.

The second knock must be on the holy wounds in our Redeemer's
blessed hands, wounds ever open to thee. This knock is to obtain real
Godlike knowledge, which will be like His wounded hands guiding thee
and lifting thee upwards. Then knock on the door of His holy feet,
begging the gift of true Divine love, whereby thou shalt be united to
Him, sunk into Him, enclosed within Him. That we may all pray thus,
asking and seeking and knocking, and that we may all be called within,
may God grant us. *Amen.*

Why Christ Upbraids Men

Synopsis—Both by outward authority and interior voices Christ re-proaches us for our shortcomings—Slowness to believe Him im-plicitly is one fault: men believe without relishing the truth—This arises from ill-ordered affection for created things—Another fault is preferring the outer to the inner ways of serving God—Disdain of weaker brethren is also offensive to Him—Richard of St. Victor's four degrees of love.

FIRST SERMON FOR THE FEAST OF THE ASCENSION.

At length He appeared to the eleven as they were at table; and He upbraided them with their incredulity and hardness of heart, because they did not believe them who had seen Him after He was risen again.—Mark xvi, 14.

This reproach of our dear Lord is spoken every day, and it is directed against men of all conditions who have hard and unbelieving hearts. But it is especially meant for members of approved religious orders, or others in like state of life. The message sometimes comes to them from our Lord through His appointed teachers, sometimes by the inner voice of conscience, if men would but hearken to it. All persons in this state of life well deserve to be reproached, if they are hard of heart and unready to believe, for it is a favor exceptionally great that they should be called by God to so high a spiritual vocation; it is something for which they should thank God sincerely and love Him fervently.

Our Saviour upbraids these men for their hardness of heart and in-credulity, but they receive His reproof ungraciously. Would that they acknowledged their fault; then they would be open to good advice. St. James teaches: "Faith without works is dead." (James ii, 26.) If they, in answer, quote our Lord: "He that believeth and is baptized shall be saved" (Mark xvi, 16), and add that they make professions of their faith with their mouth, they are silenced by St. Paul: "Know you not that all we who are baptized in Christ Jesus are baptized in His death?" (Rom. vi, 3.) And St. Augustine teaches: "That is not true faith which stops at the mouth alone, and does not go on to God with

living love and good works." Our lack of faith clearly appears if anything suits us better than God, or if we cannot truly say: Thou art my
God, and nothing is well with me except in Thee. These men have, in
fact, fallen off from a real and living faith; and this is true of them,
though they have the name of spiritual men and have been under God's
influence, even supernaturally, sleeping or waking, and have been
admonished by Him in their inmost soul.

It is an awful thing that when our Lord has upbraided them for
hardness of heart and has called out unto them, they yet do not relish
Divine things. They have no taste for their prayers and spiritual practices, whereas other things give them great pleasure. Their hearts are
soft to many things, but are stony enough to God. Of such as these—
if God will save them—the Lord spoke by His prophet: "And I will
take away the stony heart out of their flesh, and will give them a heart
of flesh." (Ezech. xi, 19.)

And let us ask what makes these men's hearts hard? Why are they
so dry and cold about all good works, or only do them by a sort of outward observance? It is because their heart cherishes something that
is not God, and continues in that state in spite of our Lord's admonition. Of this He spoke by Jeremias: "Be astonished, O ye heavens, at
this, and ye gates thereof be very desolate, saith the Lord. For My
people have done two evils. They have forsaken Me, the fountain of
living water, and have digged to themselves cisterns—broken cisterns,
that can hold no water." (Jer. ii, 12-13.) What comes into the cistern
of their heart is foul and dirty rain water. They have nothing of God
in their hearts, and that is the great evil that God, through the prophet,
laments in the sight of Heaven and earth.

And of what people does he complain? Alas, it is of His own people,
men in spiritual states of life. These are the ones who have forsaken
the fountain of living water that God is. In their interior they have
little left of light and life. They remain in their external observances
and methods, clinging to the outward part and not at all penetrating to
the inner meaning, from which alone all good must spring forth. And
even their external conformity slips away from them as soon as it ceases
to please. At best, all their spirituality consists in their observances,
and these they have undertaken according to their own way of thinking.
They never turn to the interior life; for that they have no thirst, and
in their souls its waters do not spring up. If they go through their
outward routine, they are content and all is well with them, in their

Conferences

own opinion. They are satisfied with their broken cistern; its waters are good enough for them, but God is not sweet to them, and they drink not from His living waters. They lie down at night, they rise in the morning, always following their old-established devotional customs—in them they rest, for with them they are pleased. The Lord says of them by the prophet that they have done unchastely and have become unclean, because they have forsaken Him, the fountain of living water, and digged to themselves broken cisterns. The foulness of these cisterns is in their adhering to external practices without the inward spirit— inward, indeed, are found only pride, self-will and stiff-neckedness.

As to their neighbor, they have no love nor any kindly feelings for him, and they speak injurious words, uttering them against him regardless of circumstances of time and place. Many of them would, indeed, help their neighbor, but it is with rash zeal; like one who, in striving to put out the fire in his neighbor's house, sets fire to and burns his own— he has enough of destructive zeal in him to burn two or three houses if he had the opportunity. If some poor, afflicted soul comes to them, they call him a bad man or a silly creature. Ah, you are good cisterns, indeed! If your desert waste of hearts flowed with living waters, you would make no distinction of persons. There would be no belittling of others, nor harsh judgments, nor oppressive treatment, if God's love were in your souls. And in all these cisterns the muddy waters are ever growing more foul.

It sometimes happens that these cisterns are men of cultivated minds, speaking high things, having fine intelligence. As those just treated of are self-satisfied with their outward appearance of good works, so are these proud of their noble words and their elevated thoughts. What, think you, will be their fate when the storm of wrath overtakes them and sweeps them away, them and all their vain conceits—these miserable plagues of humanity? Then will be heard such lamentation as is almost incredible; and it will come from men who made a parade of external holiness in works and words, and within were void of all living virtue, cisterns into which all filth had been cast. One blow from Satan's axe and the ruin is complete; all is scattered abroad, not a drop of good is found within, and the outward show is broken to pieces.

Children, you will one day remember what I have said to you, though it be only in the other world. I know perfectly well that this false show of virtue is common enough among all those men who, though in devout states of life, cling to external virtue only, blindly practicing the out-

ward good without the inward spirit. And I know that many Christians living in the world in the state of matrimony, as well as many
widows, far surpass in virtue such pretended spiritual men. May God
in His mercy convert them in their last hours. And if He does, then
doubtless they will suffer an incredibly severe and prolonged purgatory,
far removed from the joy of God's presence. I beseech you for the love
of God, children, to examine your soul's interior motives with every
possible vigilance. Be kind and gentle, be subject to God and to every
creature, for of you does God complain to earth and Heaven and all His
creation. To Heaven—that means all good and heavenly hearts; for
every good man is God's paradise. The wicked come close to Heaven
and never enter in. The greatest torment of the damned, is the certainty that they shall never enter Heaven.

Our Lord says to the soul through His prophet: "Thou hast prosti-
tuted thyself to many lovers; nevertheless return to Me, saith the Lord,
and I will receive thee." (Jer. iii, 1.) This means: Come to Me, O
soul, and I will pour into thee the living waters of holy sorrow—if thou
wilt only come to Me in whole-hearted sincerity. Adore the boundless
and unspeakable mercy of God. See how gladly He helps us, if we are
but willing to be helped, how affectionately He receives us, if we will
but return to Him. But the Lord has said to those who will not
return: "Therefore will I yet contend in judgment with you" (Jer. ii, 9).
Is not that to be a fearful contention; and do we not know who will
get the upper hand? Take care lest He does not at the last say to thee
that thou art not of His sheep. For His sheep hear His voice, and the
voice of strangers they hear not nor go after them.

And what is the "prostitution with many lovers" of which the Lord
speaks? Taken in a spiritual sense, it means—if it be no worse—
delivering one's soul up to a sort of devotional sensuality, being quite
seduced by the sweetness in the external forms and figures of religion.
For the sake of all this does the soul depart from that chaste service of
God, which alone is sincere because it is interior.

But return to Me, He says, and I will give you living water. This
He tells of in two places in the gospel: "If any man thirst, let him come
to Me, and drink. He that believeth in Me, as the scripture saith:
Out of his belly shall flow rivers of living water" (John vii, 37, 38); and
again to the woman at the well: "He that shall drink of the water that
I shall give him, shall not thirst forever;" He had previously said to
her: "If thou didst know the gift of God, and who He is that saith to

thee: Give me to drink; thou perhaps wouldst have asked of Him, and He would have given thee living water" (John iv, 10, and 13, 14). And now when the woman asked Him for this water, He refused her. And He showed her why, by revealing to her His knowledge of her living in unlawful union with a certain man. As if to say: Before I give thee the waters of Divine grace, cleanse the cistern of thy soul from sin, study thy wickedness, and come to Me and confess thy sin humbly and completely—only then shall the waters of life be thine. When He told her that she had lived unlawfully with five men, it was as if He spoke of the five senses, which the sinful soul uses for forbidden purposes. This makes it unworthy of the living springs of God's love. As thus: Be converted from thy disorderly life, return to Me, and I will receive thee.

The Lord spoke thus by the prophet: "My Beloved had a vineyard on a hill in a fruitful place. And he fenced it in, and picked the stones out of it, and planted it with the choicest vines, and built a tower in the midst thereof, and set up a wine-press therein; and He looked that it should bring forth grapes, and it brought forth wild grapes" (Isaias v, 1, 2). God addressed this to the people of Israel, but it applies to all people to the end of the world. To every unfaithful soul He says: Thou hast become bitter to Me; I planted thee a vineyard of choicest vines, and from them only sour wine has come forth—bad deeds are the result of all my care for thee. And therefore I will contend in judgment with thee—unless thou art converted to Me and ask for the living waters of My love.

Richard of St. Victor, a great master of spiritual doctrine, speaks of this living water as being four degrees of love. The first degree is wounded love. God wounds the soul with a stroke cf true love, and it is thus He grants it the living waters of grace. And then the soul in turn wounds God with its stroke of love. For the Lord thus speaks to the bride in the Canticles: "Thou hast wounded My heart. My sister, My spouse, thou hast wounded My heart with one of thy eyes, and with one hair of thy neck" (Cant. iv, 9). Here the word eye means an eager glance of the intelligence, resting on God and on Him alone; and the word hair means pure and unalloyed love. And it is thus that God may be said to be wounded.

The second degree is captive love, as it is described by the prophet: "I will draw them by the cords of Adam" (Osee xi, 4).

The third is a fainting love, described by the words of the bride in the Canticles: "I adjure you, O daughters of Jerusalem, if you find my beloved, that you tell Him that I languish with love" (Cant. v, 8). The fourth degree is a devouring love: "My soul hath fainted after Thy salvation; and in Thy word I have very much hoped" (Ps. cxviii, 81).

To illustrate wounded love, I ask you to consider a merchant sailing about in a ship, his heart all wounded with desire of profit; here and there and everywhere he gathers his cargo till his ship is filled. Thus acts the soul: it gathers into itself all imaginations of its beloved, and is filled with thoughts of Him, is absorbed in devout practices in honor of the beloved one. And thus laden, the ship of the soul starts homeward—a strong ship and able to withstand the storm. The wind that wafts the ship is love, driving it home into the Godhead, all prosperously and according to its longing desires. The rudder is deep down in the ocean that is God.

But the wound in the soul is ever aching—the more God is granted to the soul the more the soul longs for Him. What seems perfect love turns out not so; it creates new powers of loving and receiving and enjoying God, new emptiness to be filled; new wounds of love are ever opening. And now the second degree of love begins. The Lord cuts in twain the cable by which He drew the ship onward. That is to say, he casts the soul adrift and leaves it to the mercy of the storm, breaking the rudder and the oars and all that could steady it—leaving, in a word, a man imprisoned helplessly in love, yet abandoned seemingly by God, wholly unable to guide or help himself. And this is captive love. In the first degree He is like a knight sorely wounded in battle, and yet able to escape. But if he is too helpless to escape, then he is made a prisoner and is no longer his own master. And thus it is with love's captive in the second degree. He has no control over either thought or action: all this he must perforce yield up to the control of the beloved with no other law but love. May God grant us true love. May He enable us to give up all our own cisterns, so that into our souls the waters of true love may be generously poured. *Amen.*

The Soul's Five Captivities

Synopsis—Inordinate love of creatures is the first, which is ended only after remorse and painful penance—The second is the lamentable captivity of good men by self-love, self-interested motives and self-indulgence—The third affects bright minds, dazzled and often perverted by intellectual self-conceit—The going astray after the sweetness of devotion is another and a pitiful enslavement—The fifth is the delusion that increase in holiness is due to one's own exertions, not attributing both our activity and our power of suffering to God's grace alone.

SECOND SERMON FOR THE FEAST OF THE ASCENSION.

Ascending on high, He led captivity captive.—Eph. iv, 8.

There are five kinds of captivity in this life, and they are very hard; but Christ has taken us out of them all, if He has spiritually ascended in our souls.

The first is our enslavement to creatures, whether living or dead, unless our captivity to them be on God's account. This arises from human love, a very intimate power of our nature on account of our kinship to one another. The injury done us is quite beyond description, and is twofold. One class know themselves to be involved in it, dread it, suffer deep pain of mind, offer hard resistance and suffer keenly; all this is a good sign that they are not abandoned by God. God leaves such a soul in its misery day and night, whether eating or drinking. But when its ears are not shut to Him, soon a happier state is reached.

The other class of men are in this hurtful captivity of attachment to creatures, and abide in it with all security of feeling, wholly deaf and blind to their misery. They live on quite free from anxiety, and must have themselves reckoned as pious men. They do many good things, sing and read piously, or keep the rule of silence; they serve and pray much. Their purpose, however, by all this is that they may be approved as devout souls by their fellows, and may have some feeling of being right with God. How dangerous a state: for all the time it is the evil one who guides them, keeping them in captivity. And, besides, their natural vagaries mislead them, and they are assailed by grievous temptations. It were better for a man in this state that he quit praying as he does, for he prays for what is against his own best interests—far better that he sank into oppression of soul and woe and sorrow. This would much sooner lead him to a release from his deadly captivity; for he is under the power of Satan, and is in danger of dying so and being eternally lost.

The second captivity is that of men who have, indeed, been released from the slavish love of creatures and external things, but have then fallen into the slavery of self-love. And it is marvelous how virtuous this seems, and how complacently they regard it. No one reproves them for it, least of all do they reproach themselves. They are arrayed in seeming beauty of virtue—not a word can be said against them. And yet they seek themselves in everything—self-love guides them to seek their own personal advantage, enjoyment, consolation and honor. They are so deep sunk in self that they seek self in everything, even in God. Getting to the bottom of this evil, what shall we find in a state so false and yet so well-seeming? How hard it is to help men so self-indulgent, and yet so full of reasons and methods—how can they be freed from captivity? Who can help one who is piously absorbed in mere nature? Surely none but God alone. Such a man finds a thousand things necessary—his needs are everywhere and about everything, and his health is so delicate. Touch anything of his, his room, a friend, his goods, his honor, interfere in the least with his comfort, and he offends God with a furious outburst of passionate words or even deeds, sometimes by detraction and calumny. He is no longer a man— he is rather a snarling dog, a savage wolf. How lamentable is the captivity of self-love!

The third captivity is that of the intelligence, and some men are sorely injured by it. Whatsoever their brains can produce turns to their hurt. They glory in learning, in knowledge of doctrine, in their bright understanding, and their talent for speaking. It all lifts them up high and honorable—but it never changes for the better their mode of living, nor leads to good works. Even the sweet image of our Lord they view only from reason's standpoint. If they attempt to discourse in the supernatural spirit, it is in strong contrast with what is the real spirit. Their mind, compared to the spiritual mind, is like a candle compared to the noonday sun—so much less is natural light than Divine light. The former shines forth outwardly in pride, self-assurance, seeking the applause of men, judging others. The Divinely enlightened reason, on the contrary, is full of real truth, tramples all self-seeking under foot. A true man rates himself the least of all, the meanest and feeblest and blindest. And this is plain fact, for what else is man face to face with God? And such a man looks ever inward and away from the outer world, seeking God in his inmost soul, in which he is begotten to God, and into which he is ever ready to hasten with all speed. A Divinely enlightened man sinks down deep in search of the root of life from which he has sprung. And his quest is full of energy. Hence the great difference between those who live up to the scripture and those who just read it. These latter seek praise for their knowledge of it, and at the same time they despise those who live up to its maxims. They consider such souls foolish, even perverse. They go so far as to curse them, scorn them and condemn them outright. Those who actually live according to the teaching of the scripture deem themselves sinners, and as to the others, they have a kindly, merciful feeling for them. And as the lives of these two classes are so different, so also is their end different: one class finds life and the other death. This is according to St. Paul: "For the letter killeth, but the spirit giveth life" (II Cor. iii, 6).

The fourth captivity is sweetness of devotion, and many men go astray in this, yielding up to it and sticking fast in it. It seems a great good thing; but it is only poor human nature cleaving to its own self in much joy, meanwhile dreaming that it cleaves to God. Hence let us carefully distinguish between God and self in all our spiritual feelings. Here is a test: when the sweet feeling of devotion passes away, dost thou feel unhappy, unrestful and distressed? Dost thou find thyself less faithful and willing in God's work? If so, then it is plain that God was not the cause of thy sensible pleasure in His service. Forty years of sensible devotion may suddenly end, and thou shalt be in danger of gravely falling away from God. And if a man had the highest degree of these natural feelings in his religious practices, and died in them, God alone knows whether or not he would be saved—he might, indeed, be lost.

The fifth captivity is self-will. By this I mean the state of a man who is set on having his own way, and that in Divine things, nay, even as to God Himself. If by an act of my own will I could be freed from the guilt of my sins, and be adorned with all virtue and perfection, it would seem to be folly in me not to exert my will to this end. But a moment's thought makes me exclaim: No, Lord, no; not by my grace or gift or will, but by Thine alone; and, O Lord, if it were not Thy will, I had rather feel the want of Thy grace according to Thy will (if it be lawful to say so), than possess it according to my own. And by cultivating this sense of abandonment to God, a man gains more by far, than ever he could acquire from God or His creatures by virtue of his own will. Humble and voluntary subjection to the sense of deprivation, in a true spirit of detachment from one's own will, this is infinitely more profitable than any efforts inspired by one's own will. I had much rather see a man really detached from his own will and having no great show of religious works, than one less detached from self-choice and abounding in high and showy works of virtue.

While our Lord lived with His disciples, they so deeply and blindly loved His humanity, that it hindered their attaining to His divinity. Hence He said to them: "It is expedient to you that I go; for if I go not, the Paraclete will not come to you (John xvi, 7). And He must remain with them forty days longer, before He could win their entire souls to a heavenly state, and bear them with Himself upward to God; and even then they must wait ten more days before the Holy Ghost was sent them. What those ten days were to them, so many years must be to us; for since they were to be our foundation, their preparation was to ours as a day is to a year.

Let a man do what he pleases, he shall never have true peace, he shall never be essentially a heavenly man, until he has passed the equivalent of those forty days between the Lord's resurrection and His ascension—until he has finished, as it were, his forty years of preparation. He can never be what God would have him to be, before God's allotted time is passed and over. Such a one has much to do with men by necessity of nature, driven now this way and again that way, nature often ruling every motive; and yet he thinks that God is his motive—and this may be called his forty years' probation. This again is followed by ten years more of waiting—like the additional ten days' waiting of the Lord's disciples—before the Holy Ghost, the Comforter, is received; that Spirit that teaches the soul all things. When the disciples at last were given the Holy Spirit, it was after they had resigned life's dearest treasures for Jesus' sake. They had made the best preparation; they loved God above all things; He had carried their hearts and souls with

Him into Heaven.   This preparation having all been completed by their last ten days of patient waiting, the Holy Ghost came down upon them.

They were assembled together in deep seclusion, and thus they waited. So must we be, as we end, so to speak, our forty years of preparation, having meanwhile overcome depraved nature, and celebrated the festival of our heavenly transformation.   Even after that, we must wait ten years longer.   We must have a maturity of preparation equal to fifty years of self-renunciation, ere we shall receive the Holy Ghost in the most perfect manner, so that He may teach us all truth.   During that final period of probation, natural defects are at last quite overcome, and the soul enters upon a Godlike existence.   A man turns inward, and sinks into God, being blended with the one, pure, Divine Good.   The light of his life is now returned into the Divine flame from which is first flashed forth.   When this overflow of the soul into God is perfect, then all its debt of sin is fully paid, were it as heavy as that of all sinful men put together from the beginning of the world.   Then all the grace and joy destined for the soul is granted to it.   Then, in fine, the soul is made Godlike.   Such men as these are the pillars of the world, the mainstay of the Church.   May God grant us some share of this happiness.   *Amen.*

How to Ascend with Christ into Heaven

Synopsis—The road to heaven is shown us in the whole life and passion of Christ—Christ draws us upward after Him like a magnet —The force of this drawing differs greatly among men—The end of the drawing upward is hard, being the ascent of the Mount of Olives, that is the place of sadness and toil.

THIRD SERMON FOR THE FEAST OF THE ASCENSION.

And the Lord Jesus, after He had spoken to them, was taken up into heaven.— Mark xvi, 19.

The most blessed Son of God, Christ Jesus our Lord, after He had sat with His disciples on Mount Olivet, and had chided them for their incredulity and hardness of heart, ascended out of their sight into Heaven.

Ah, children, what think you were the thoughts in the hearts of those disciples, who loved their Lord so well? Must they not all have felt a bitter pain of heart after His departure? Indeed they had loved Him well, and we know that where one's treasure is, there is his heart also. Jesus Christ carries away with Him in His glorious ascension, the hearts and senses and all the faculties of His chosen friends. Never again can they feel at home in this world. All their goings and comings and all their life is now in Heaven—all is now with God. Dear children, how can it be otherwise? Must not the members be with the head? And our Head has this day most affectionately gone before us to prepare a place for us. Hence we can but echo the words of the bride in the Canticles: "Draw me after Thee" (Cant. i, 3). Who can prevent us following our Head, Jesus Christ? He Himself has said: "I ascend to My Father and to your Father" (John xx, 17). His principle of life, His final end, His eternal bliss, are all made one with ours in Him. We have come forth from the same origin as He, we are associated to Him in the end and purpose of His life—if we will but fit ourselves rightly for this high destiny.

Consider, children, that Jesus Christ has gone before us into the blessedness of His heavenly Father. Now if we would follow Him effectively, we must mark carefully the path He trod. And we find that for thirty years he laid out the journey to Heaven by enduring misery, poverty, shame, and finally the bitterness of death itself. Behold then the road we have to travel if we would join Him in Heaven! If all teachers were dead, if all books were burnt, the story of His life alone is doctrine enough for us. He is Himself the way, and there is no other. Let us press on after Him in this His path to the blissful end that awaits us; let us go forward with all our strength. As the magnet draws iron to it, so does Jesus Christ draw after Himself all hearts that He touches. And furthermore, as the iron itself receives the magnet's power of attraction, and is moved and lifted up and joined to the magnet in spite of its own nature, so it is with souls touched by the magnet of the eternal Son of God. Such men no longer feel the force of their own love, or joy, or consolation: they are drawn out of themselves upward to God. They forget the laws of their own nature, and follow the touch of God. And this they do all the more readily and perfectly, according as they are more deeply influenced by the Divine attraction.

So, then, let each one of us put himself to the test, as to whether or not he has been touched by God. Men who are not really drawn by God's magnet, start up with various fine methods and systems of devotion, lacking the interior spirit. They fancy they will gain great results, and before they are aware, it all comes to naught. For you must know that they soon fall back into their old ways, giving themselves up to natural joys and the love of created things. They act like good-for-nothing hounds in a hunt, which care nothing for the game or whither it runs; they only follow the good hounds lazily along, until they are distanced; and then they go astray and are lost. I say to thee in all sincerity: it may be but a little half hour during which thou dost grievously neglect thy duty, or cleavest to thy forbidden pleasures. And in that short interval the game has escaped thee, thou art not among those who have a share in its capture. Those who may be compared to the good and faithful hounds are God's true servants. These track the game and fiercely pursue it through fire and water, till they overtake and capture it. So do good men act who duly appreciate the Divine object they are striving after—they never give up till they have possessed themselves of it, they are hindered by neither the joys nor sorrows of this life. The others are wholly inactive, they rest slug-

gishly idle; and if they so continue till death, then they are in peril of
remaining so after death and through God's eternity.

Children, if a man is not moved by God, he must not lay the blame
on Him. Yet sometimes one says: Almighty God does not influence me
to good as He does this one or that one. Such talk is false. God
touches, influences and admonishes all men, and will bring all men, as
far as they will allow Him, to happiness. But His gifts, His admonitions and His touches, are received by men very diversely. When He
visits some, bringing His precious favors with Him, He finds their souls
occupied before Him by other gifts, and in a state of uncleanness. What
can He then do but turn back from us, since our souls are fixed upon
and love a rival lover? So then He carries His gifts to another soul,
who has kept its heart free and clean from love of all created things.
Thus it is that the cause and the guilt of our eternal misery is in ourselves and not in God. What utter folly is ours, thus idly to dally with
the poor creatures of this life, regardless of the presence of the infinite
God—doing ourselves thereby an eternal injury.

How shall we escape from this infatuation with natural joys? In no
better and surer way than by quickly and courageously turning to God,
and practicing prayer in an earnest and devoted spirit. Not otherwise
can we win a steadfast heart and obtain great confidence in God's
boundless mercy, as being all our hope of salvation. Add to this a
determined purpose to be absolutely subject to God's will in all things,
in doing and not doing, in things spiritual and things natural.

Again, children, remark that the spot from which Jesus Christ, the
Son of God, ascended into Heaven was the Mount of Olives, and this
may be made a threefold lesson of light. First, the Mount is raised
above the earth east of Jerusalem, and is lit up by the rising of the sun;
later in the morning, the brightness of the sun is reflected back on the
Mount from the shining pinnacles of the temple; finally, the Mount's
fruit, oil, is the food of light in our lamps. So is it with the soul in
which God's ascension sweetly takes place without any intermediary.
It must be elevated above earthly and transitory things if it will be
resplendent with God's threefold light, namely the Divine Trinity
shining and acting within it just as God wills.

Again, this Mount lay between Jerusalem and Bethania, and, children, be assured that whosoever would follow after Jesus Christ, must
climb up this Mount, no matter how bitter the toil may be. For there is
no hill in all this wide world so sweet and so beautiful—give to its

peril of
e blame
thence me
. false. God
f all men, as
His admoni-
When He
their souls
..ess. What
upon
..ther soul,
ings,
our
ly with
f the infinite

In no
...g to God,
otherwise
in God's
to this a
ll things,

hrist, the
and this

f the sun;
..k on the
..e Mount's
..e soul in
...mediary,

..e Trinity

and. chil-

..re to its

climbing all your hard pain and labor. Children, every follower of our Lord Jesus Christ must say good-by to his natural joys; for there is many a one who would gladly follow God, if it cost no toil or pain and caused him no bitterness. Many a one would gladly be on top of the Mount that is so near Jerusalem, the city of peace, if he could be there without overcoming difficulties. In truth it is in themselves that such men seek for peace and consolation and happiness; and nothng comes of it all. Yet, as they idly tarry on the Bethania side they are miserable, for there they find only obedience to others and suffering. Of one of these the Psalmist speaks as having an abode in "The vale of tears, in the place which he hath set" (Ps. lxxxiii, 6).

Children, be sure that whosoever does not struggle up this Mount, will always remain spiritually sterile and will amount to nothing. A devout man should keep his longing eyes fixed on his soul's spouse, Jesus Christ, ascended now so far above him and so hidden and unknown. Realize fully, that the deeper the touch of God in thy soul, the more surely is one side of thy life a vale of tears. If this served no other purpose, it would in thy direst need preserve thee from the sinfulness that lies concealed in thy poor human nature—those tendencies which hinder many a one from turning wholly to God. God's grace can and should rule in us continuously. And so it does, when one without ceasing makes sacrifices to God of all things whatsoever that may lead him away from God. These weaknesses too often prevail in the soul of man, where God alone should hold undisputed sway. And conquering them is winning up the side of the Mount of Olives that is toward Bethania.

Children, whosoever looks deep into his soul begins to draw near Jerusalem. And it were well that he should watch the different influences of God and of nature, in all that he does or does not. It were good that he nerved himself to suffer more bravely all sorrow and pain, and not weakly yield to nature in such visitations. When he seems forsaken by God, and stands in all bitterness and desolation of spirit, oppressed from within and from without, then let him diligently call to mind God's goodness. And in times of spiritual joy, let him anticipate sorrow; as the Wise Man says: "In the day of good things be not unmindful of evils" (Eccli. xi, 27).

Children, both sides of the Mount must be in our souls together. For if the word Jerusalem means a city of peace, yet in that city was God's Son Jesus Christ put to death. Our peaceful city must be the scene of many a suffering, for thou must without doubt suffer greatly, and in all peacefulness die totally to self: there is no escape. Ascend, therefore, high up into God's holy will, sincerely deny thyself in all things both of spirit and flesh. Thou must fall into the hands of, as it were, the malicious Jews, who will torture and scourge thee, and drive thee out from among them as a base and wicked man, condemn thee to the worst punishments they can think of, and put thee to death in the minds of all men, as far as they can do so. I say to thee that in thy inmost soul thou must die the death, if the eternal God shall become thy only life. As it happened to Jesus Christ, that when He was put to death the Jews thought their crime was a great honor to God, so shall it happen in thy case. All who despise thee and condemn thee and torment thee, will think that in doing so they have greatly served God. Ah, beloved children, how happy of heart shall such a man be, when he thus dwells in Jerusalem the city of peace, full of peace indeed, even in the midst of this dire unrest; for in his soul's depths the essential peace of God is born to Him, coming out of God's own abyss of truth and love.

Children, on this Mount grows the olive tree; and therein we can perceive what true religious devotion is. Real devotion is an interior clnging to God Himself, with a soul entirely ready to possess all things and to think of all things just as God does. A devout man is one who is in all things fast bound to God in his will and in his understanding. Such a soul is indeed a sweet olive tree to our heavenly Father and to all His elect. Hast thou this in thy inner life? This devout spirit must ever and again be renewed by the fire of Divine love; and it must be aided by earnest searching in the soul's depths, lest something that is not God in all truth, shall be hiding there. Therein must be nothing deceptive; for it is nature that sometimes inspires us when we think that all is being done for God. And this, also, is too often the case with men, both in communities and in the world: they do not think and love wholly and absolutely according to God, but rather according to self, whether in matters spiritual or corporal. Few are to be found who serve God for His own sake alone, having regard neither to consolations nor joys—no object but God alone, not even (if it were permissible or possible) His holy grace in time and eternity, but just simply God's own self alone. That we may thus ascend with the Son of God, and rise high above this land of exile, far above all creatures; that we may possess eternal life with Him—may God the Father, and the Son, and the Holy Ghost mercifully grant us. *Amen.*

How We Witness to Christ in Unrest and Suffering

Synopsis—Entire self-renunciation is needed for Christ's discipleship —Unrest of soul, borne patiently, shows our fidelity—How one may inordinately cleave to spiritual sweetness; its use and abuse —How an entirely detached soul stands between earth and heaven, his higher faculties resting calm in God, and his lower ones busy with God's external works.

FOURTH SERMON FOR THE FEAST OF THE ASCENSION.

You shall be witnesses unto Me in Jerusalem, and in all Judea, and Samaria.— Acts i, 8.

Dear children, since our Head, Jesus Christ, has ascended into Heaven, it is both possible and proper that we His members should ascend thither after Him. We should neither seek nor desire comfort or joy in this unstable life of ours, nor put up with any delay here. To follow Him always, to desire Him with a yearning heart and without resting, to love Him, to keep Him in view in everything, to urge others to follow fast after Him who with such bitter suffering led the way filled with love for their eternal happiness—all this should be our task.

It was necessary that Christ should die, and in that manner return to the glory of His heavenly Father. Let us ever follow our beloved Captain, Jesus Christ, the eternal Son of God. He has unfurled the banner of bitter pain, and borne it faithfully forward with heroic patience. With like patience should all His chosen friends grasp and hold aloft that holy standard of suffering, each one to the very best of his power. Wouldst thou be a true follower of God's eternal Son? Then humbly take up thy cross of pain, and suffer gladly for the sake of God, no matter whence may come thy sorrow, whether it be merited or unmerited, interior or exterior. And by this means thou shalt joyfully ascend to the Son of God and into eternal life.

Beloved children, you know that in our times many a man serves the world for the sake of its petty honor and fame. For this end he gives up all comfort of body and all his worldly goods, journeying often into a strange land to fight in battle in order to win glory and gain. In like manner must a man act if he would be a true follower of Jesus Christ the eternal Son of God. He must renounce everything for His sake, and he must do it freely and joyfully. All comfort and convenience of life must be given up and all honors, if he would come to union with the very truth and essence of life that God Himself is. For if there is any single member of the whole body that is not joined with the head, it is a rotten member and must be cut off.

Christ our Lord said to His disciples: "You shall be witnesses unto Me in Jerusalem, and in all Judea, and Samaria, and even to the uttermost part of the earth." Now Jerusalem, the city of peace, was to Jesus Christ also a city of unrest, for in that city of peace He had received inhuman torment and suffered a cruel death, all for the love of men. In that same kind of city shall we be witnesses unto Jesus Christ, not by words alone, but by works, by our life, by our imitation of Him to the uttermost of our ability.

You all know, children, that all would gladly bear witness to our Lord in peace, if only everything went on as they willed. They would gladly be holy, if devotional exercises were never distasteful and God's work was always easy. They would gladly proclaim God, if it were to be done always in sweetness and consolation, never amid powerful temptations or deep interior darkness. But when such men find themselves in interior desolation, and are at the same time outwardly forsaken, then they turn back to their old ways: they are not witnesses of God in very truth. All men seek peace in their relations of life; but, my dear children, we must die to this kind of seeking after peace, and go forth out of it. We must seek for peace in another way, namely, in the midst of unrest, and that with all earnestness; that peace alone can give us a supernatural, holy and Divine life. That peace alone generates in us true and Divine peace, always abiding, ever enduring within us. Any other peace causes thee self-deception. But if thou canst be willing to seek joy in sorrow, steadfast peace in unrest, single-mindedness amid multiplicity, comfort in bitterness, then veritably thou shalt be made a worthy witness of God. Jesus Christ promised His chosen followers peace, both before His death and after His resurrection. Yet as long as they lived they never found outward peace. But they none the less really found peace amid all their troubles, and they got it from all the unpeaceful men they met, essential peace. They stood immovably peaceful in all pain and pleasure. From death they received life; they rejoiced when they were hated and judged and condemned to death. And thus they became true witnesses of God.

There are many men whose souls and bodies are so saturated with Divine sweetness, that it seems to flow through their very veins and marrow. But when suffering comes, and when they are left in darkness, when they seem forsaken by God and creatures both interiorly and externally, then they are at a loss to know what to do with themselves; nothing good can be made of them. Dear children, when the tempest strikes men's souls, that is to say when interior abandonment oppresses them, and when opposition and temptations assail them from without; when the world, the flesh and the devil conspire against them—whichever one of them can stand up against all this with genuine patience, will find true peace. He will find essential peace in all trouble, a peace that no creature can take from him. And whosoever does not tread this path shall never attain to true peace.

Our Lord also said to His apostles: "You shall be witnesses unto Me in Judea." Judea may be taken to mean first confessing and second praising God. Children, we must be God's witnesses in such wise that we follow after our beloved Lord in all our works, ways and intentions steadfastly, without any intermission, and not because things go well with us, nor because of our spiritual consolations and devotional sentiments. While we enjoy these feelings, we flatter ourselves that we are right with God, and we imagine that we cannot yearn enough after Him, nor ever be satisfied with Him. But when the shock of spiritual adversity strikes us, then we do not know what to think of our former state, or of how we now stand with God. And this shows that formerly the interior foundation was not God alone.

Sweet feelings of devotion were the unstable basis on which our confidence in God was built—not just God alone, God in all joy and all sorrow. God's true witnesses ever rest fast and firm on God alone and on His most adorable will, come weal, come woe. God gives or God takes away—they remain always in peace, resting wholly on God, not at all on their own devotional contrivances. When all seems prosperous, and when they feel as if they could do mighty things for God, they nevertheless do not build upon that; distrust of self and real lowliness of spirit possess their souls. God often deprives them of all comfort, and He does so because He is true to their better spiritual interests. And so it happens frequently that such men can accomplish nothing. If they would gladly keep holy vigil, they fall asleep in spite of themselves; they try to fast, and cannot help but eat; they crave repose, and they are forced into the very opposite. All this happens because God would withdraw from them all support but Himself alone. On Him simply and solely must they rest, themselves being annihilated in all things of soul and body, their souls dropping deep down into pure single-hearted faith in God. For as worldly men do themselves harm by their excessive enjoyment of the pleasures of the senses and of their temporal goods and honors, so do spiritual men hurt themselves by excessive joy in God's spiritual gifts, whether in good works or in the sweetness of devotion. They rest with inordinate joy in God's ever-flowing spiritual favors, instead of resting simply on the only true foundation, namely God's own self, held and possessed in true poverty of spirit.

Judea also may be taken to mean the praise of God. Ah, children, if a man could but be guided to praise the eternal God in all things no matter whence they come, interior or exterior, for him or against him, then, indeed, would he be journeying along the right road. And if a man would but offer all things up to God with thanksgiving, then would he become a true witness of God. Therefore, dear child, render back into God's deep being all that has thence come forth to thee; do this invariably; and never tarry in thine own self, which is mere nothing-ness. Rather restore thyself habitually to thy source and origin, namely the abyss of God's love. Out of this thy act, be well assured, shall come forth a noble praise of God; from this will be granted thee a fruitful harvest of virtue. The blossom and the fruit are one, for herein God is in God and light in light. All that is outward thou shalt give to God, as created things affect thee in joy or sorrow; and all inward things, too, of whatever kind they may be, and thyself along with them.

Christ also said: "You shall be witnesses of Me in Samaria," and that name may be considered to mean union with God. This refers to the truest witness that man can bear to God in this life, namely when he is most perfectly united to Him. Then, as it were, there slips away from him his own spirit, and all creatures seem gone: in the Divine unity all multiplicity vanishes away. The highest powers of the soul are now drawn up to Heaven, where God the Holy Spirit dwells in God the Father and God the Son, in the Divine unity. The soul now finds its highest bliss in very truth, enjoying God with a delightful sweetness, drawing after it, too, its lower powers, as far as this is possible in our mortal life. And, absorbed into the Divine abyss of being, the soul need do nothing more than humbly abandon itself to enjoy all the gifts of

God's grace; for now it beholds them in God, and is entirely without self-consciousness concerning them.

After this, again, the soul is led into yet another heaven in the Divine being, in which it loses itself and sinks into God. No man can tell what happens there to the soul in the possession of God and in His enjoyment—neither tell, nor think, nor even understand. How can the soul tell or understand what has come upon it, while it was meted out of itself and absorbed in the Divine abyss, knowing nothing, seeing nothing, feeling nothing but only the pure, simple being of God? But after that experience, dear children, you may be sure that a man can look into the very essence of all his devotional exercises, even the littlest of them. And he can plainly discover all imperfections in his use of them, find out why they do not profit him, and how they may be freshened anew and made more fruitful.

Thus does the faithful and detached soul stand between Heaven and earth. With the higher faculties of his being he dwells always in God his Lord, elevated high above self and all things else; and with his lower faculties he is placed under foot of all things, sunk down in deep humility, not otherwise than if he were a mere beginner in the spiritual life. He can content himself in the lowest order of devout practices, for he is ashamed of nothing that is good, however contemptible it may seem to others. He keeps true peace with all creatures in spirit and in act, in joy and sorrow. Such a man is in very truth a witness of our Lord Jesus Christ, who first came down from Heaven, and ascended again into the Heaven of Heavens. And all who would dwell there must become one with Him, that in Him and with Him and through Him they may ascend to Heaven.

Whatsoever man shall earnestly endeavor after this end, and shall bid farewell to all the joys and pains of creatures, shall not go astray in his conscience. He shall not have a silly head; he shall not be found gadding about asking foolish questions, wasting his time and following delusions. May God make us His true witnesses in things spiritual and things natural; may He raise us up to Heaven with His eternal Son; may He grant us all this as He is God the Father, and God the Son, and God the Holy Ghost. *Amen.*

The Exchange of Matthias for Judas in the Inner Life

Synopsis—It is the enthronement of high motives in place of ignoble ones—The Judas within us is our self-appropriation of God's gifts —Our Matthias is the heartfelt and universal attribution back to God of all His favors, especially spiritual ones.

FIFTH SERMON FOR THE FEAST OF THE ASCENSION.

In those days Peter, rising up in the midst of the brethren, said, etc.—Acts I, 15-26.

On the return of our Lord's disciples to Jerusalem after His ascension into Heaven, Peter addressed them about choosing someone to take the place of Judas, who had fallen away. Two disciples, Joseph, called the Just, and Matthias, were then set apart, and the latter was selected to hold that high place of an apostle, and to become a witness of Jesus Christ.

Mark well, beloved children, that the disciples came to Jerusalem, which in our previous discourse today we have called a place of holy peace, and also a place of unrest. And we have explained how no one can come to true peace except in two ways—he must gain peace through conflict, as well as joy through sorrow; and he must learn to possess abundance through suffering want. The disciples returned to Mount Sion. And so must we go upward with all our powers and all our mind to the eternal festival of God, rising high over all lower and created existence, leaving all things as Abraham did, when he left his servant and his ass behind, and took his son up the mount of vision to sacrifice him. This upgoing is led by the will, which commands all the faculties of man as a prince in his kingdom and a father in his house. This prince, our will, should always command a man to go upward above all created things.

The disciples went to the cenaculum, which may be taken to mean a banquet hall, for *coena* means a supper. Now after supper there is no other meal that day, nor is there any real labor done; repose now has its place—a fact carefully to be noted. For as the disciples abide in the banquet hall, their minds and all their faculties should be at rest: the

soul's labors should know their end, for now, indeed, there is no longer
any meal nor any labor, namely in God, in Whom there is everlasting
repose.   The man who forces his attention toward anything whatsoever
it may be, does not mean the supreme good, God.   He is not waiting in
expectancy of receiving the Holy Ghost

When one's soul is in the cenaculum, then Peter rises up; and Peter
may be taken to mean a man who confesses God.   His purpose is to
choose a true witness to take the vacant place of Judas, for it much distressed Peter that Judas was a thief and a traitor.   And so we, too,
have a Judas within us, namely, our miserable tendency to appropriate
to ourselves by theft and treason all the good that God by His free gift
works within us.   This Judas-like trait in us would cause us to unjustly
assume ownership of God's work in us.   Now that distresses the sense of
right in us, which confesses God, inclining us to choose another state of
soul to take the place of the Judas-like one which is to be expelled from
within us.   Lots are cast between Joseph, who was called and really was
a just man, and Matthias.   Joseph was also called Barsabas, which may
be taken to mean obedient.   Against him is placed Matthias, and he may
be taken to mean a man who is little in the sight of God.   And upon
which of these two did the choice fall, in order to fill this holy apostolic
vacancy?   Not upon obedient and just Joseph, with all his merit, but it
fell upon him who was little before God.   Ah, children, this quality out-
weighed justice and obedience, great as may be the merit of these virtues.   The little and the humble surpass all others in worth.   And such
a man it was that was chosen.

And wilt thou reach the highest perfection by the shortest way?
Wilt thou be chosen God's disciple, and be made in the highest degree
His true witness?   Then thou must confess thyself before the face of
God the least and the littlest of all mankind, and sincerely hold thyself
to be so.   Then and not till then will the lot fall upon thee.   Let all thy
diligence be exerted, that thou mayst be considered little and mayst be
despised.   Then shalt thou be raised to the greatest place, and be set
nearest to God, and given the most honorable position God can bestow,
namely a place among the apostles.   To this thou canst never come
except by thorough-going belittling of self.

And this must be no mere apparent humility, or one of imagination,
for that delusion is but a sister of pride, and a mere play-acting of
humility.   In this condition pride is very deep-rooted; and the soul has
often the very reverse of a real sentiment of littleness before God, nor

does it **really** desire to be an object of contempt to both **God** and **man.**
Now, children, the man who is fully determined to make of himself **real**
nothingness before God, has entered on the truest preparation **for receiv-**
ing the Holy Ghost. He has begun to tread the shortest path to **God,**
and God's grace will meet him and conduct him forward. That we **may**
thus be made ready for the Holy Ghost, and that we may finally recei**ve**
Him in all reality, may God grant.   *Amen.*

Prudence and Praying

Synopsis—The sweetness of God's grace should lead us to watchfulness in prayer—Like the habit of using drugs is the intoxication of spiritual intemperance—The prayer of thanksgiving is an antidote to this gluttony—Some instructions about mingling good thoughts with good vocal prayers.

SERMON FOR THE SUNDAY AFTER THE ASCENSION.

Be prudent, therefore, and watch in prayers.—I Peter iv, 7.

Let every man now prepare for the approaching feast of the Holy Ghost, that he may receive Him with the best possible dispositions, keeping only God in view. Let each one search his whole way of life with all care, considering his interior soul, and whether anything dwells therein that is not God. This preparation will consist of four dispositions: detachment, self-renunciation, the interior spirit, and union with God.

A man should also be practiced outwardly in the natural virtues, and his lower spiritual powers in moral virtues. Then the Holy Ghost should be placed in possession of one's higher spiritual powers, to adorn them with the theological virtues. All this should be done with discretion and in right order in every respect. We should carefully examine if anything has found place in our life that is not entirely for God; and if so, then it should be at once condemned and reformed. We should imitate the farmer in the month of March; as the sun gains power he prunes his trees and he digs his ground and works his farm with great industry. So should we industriously dig up the ground of our soul and find out what is underneath the surface; we should prune the tree of our outward life of the senses, and we should clean out all weeds, as well as subject our lower powers to the higher ones. We must cut out the seven capital sins by the very roots. Pride should be exterminated inwardly and outwardly; and all avarice and hate and envy; all foul lust in body and soul, in heart and senses, in spirit and act must be totally expelled; no sloth of any kind must be allowed to lurk in the soul: all these evils must be cut away and totally rooted out. As yet the soul remains cold and hard, for although the sun grows warmer, it is yet far from summer's clear and genial light. But soon all is changed. The Divine sun begins to do its heavenly work in the well-prepared garden of the soul.

When, therefore, the genial sun of God's grace begins to shine brightly upon this well-cultivated garden, all the soul's inner and outer faculties being fully prepared, all its higher and lower tendencies directed towards Heaven, then indeed the sweet flowers of May begin to bloom, and all the welcome gifts of summertime. The eternal God causes the soul to blossom forth and to produce good fruit of virtue; and the joy in that soul no tongue can tell. For now the Holy Ghost is there, and His brightness shines directly upon the soul, yea, into its inmost depths. Well may He now be called the true Comforter, since His influence is so delicious. O how great a joy! O how rich a feast, the sweet odors of whose nourishing food excite the soul's deepest longing! These are granted in every plenty of enjoyment to the rightly prepared soul by the gentle Spirit of God. One drop of this Divine comfort is worth more than all the joys of created things put together; and it overpowers and quenches all longing for them whatsoever.

When a man feels this action of the Divine Comforter so wonderfully great and so unexpected, he would gladly sink down into its depths and rest and slumber in it forever. He feels like St. Peter at the Lord's Transfiguration; it is good for him to be there, and he would set up three tabernacles of joy out of one drop of the happiness now granted him, and there dwell forever. But such is not our Lord's will. When Peter said "It is good for us to be here," he was far from that degree in the spiritual life that his Lord would lead him to. So it is with souls in this stage: they think they have got all when they are in this brilliant sunshine of God's favor, and they would like to lie down and bask in it forever. And all the souls who actually do so, remain stationary in their career. They amount to nothing unless they rise up and go forward.

To some of these it happens that they slip down into unlawful liberty. Their poor human nature turns inward and regards itself with self-complacency, a weakness toward which we are above all other things inclined. It is with them as with sick persons who trust too much to medicines. I have heard physicians say that men, finding relief in drugs, trust to them entirely and not at all to their natural forces, and that this breeds indolence. If a man is doubtful of all help from others, then he energetically sets to work to help himself. Remark, children, how this poisonous longing for ease and convenience, penetrates every-where in our natural life. And it is a thousand times worse in our spiritual life. When this very unusual joy is felt, the soul forthwith counts upon being sure to keep it. Earnest and faithful labor is now thought unnecessary; a soft lethargy possesses the spirit—no more activity of virtue, no more zealous toil, all is to be rest and peace. And this is Satan's chance. He comes to this soul, thus indolently reclining, and he insinuates into it a false sweetness, hoping to hold it fast in this wrong state of rest.

What shall we do, then? Shall we run away from this happiness? No, by no means. But, receiving it with much gratitude, we must humbly return it again into God's hands praising Him in all sincerity, as we nevertheless protest ourselves to be wholly unworthy of such a favor. We should act like a young and robust traveler, but poor and hungry and thirsty as he starts on his journey. If he goes forward four miles and can only manage to get a meal to eat, he springs forward blithely and makes ten miles more. So let us do, when God feeds us with His sweet food of spiritual joy. Whatever good things such a man formerly did, he does more and better things now, loves God more, praises and thanks Him more. He is more upright, his heart is full of a more burning love, and thereby he becomes worthy of the gift of a yet deeper interior comfort. Just as we may fancy a man going to the Pope and giving him a florin, and receiving in return a hundred thousand, and getting the same exchange every time he gave a florin: so is the exchange between God and a rightly guided soul. As often as he goes to God in all love and gratitude and humility, so often does God meet him on the instant with gifts and graces a thousandfold more precious than before. Thus it is that sweetness of devotion is made a help to us, and leads to greater good: we must use our spiritual gifts and not enjoy them. It is like riding in a wagon: we are there for the good of the journey and for the progress made, and not for the enjoyment of the wagon's soft seat. So let it be with God's gifts; draw the good out of them, leaving to God the joy. Hence St. Peter's warning to us to be sober and watchful; not to sink into the slumber of sensual pleasure, a state in which the soul is but half alive and is incapable of activity. The sober-minded man works right on courageously and intelligently: "Be sober and watch: because your adversary the devil, as a roaring lion, goeth about seeking whom he may devour; whom resist ye strong in faith" (I Peter v, 8).

And again the Apostle bids us be "prudent and watch in prayers," that is, not to be so dull as to rest in anything that is not God; to keep the light of piety brightly burning; to keep a vigilant outlook over ourselves; always to long for God alone. It was on this account that our Saviour's disciples must give up the bodily presence of their Master, if they would receive the Holy Ghost. "If I go not," said He, "the Paraclete will not come to you" (John xvi, 7). These loving disciples were so possessed of the visible presence of the Lord, that heart, soul, senses and faculties were entirely absorbed—inner and outer life all taken up. This condition must be changed, if they were to arrive at the true, spiritual, interior comfort of God—they must be cut off from the outward presence, no matter how bitter the stroke. Otherwise they should have remained in the lowest spiritual degree, that of the sensible life of religion. When they rose above the senses, it was to enter the religious life of the highest powers of the soul, every way nobler and more delightful.

After that the soul enters further into its own deep interior, the very hidden shrine of God's presence within it. Divine sweetness is there and there only quite at home, there fully and essentially experienced. And there alone is the soul wide awake and watchful.

The apostle bids us be sober, watchful and prayerful, for our "adversary the devil goeth about like a roaring lion." What prayer does he mean? That of the mouth? Reading the Psalms over and over? All that is truly prayer, but he means a yet higher prayer. It is the prayer our Lord meant when He said: "The true adorers shall adore the Father in spirit and in truth" (John iv, 23). Saints and Divines teach us that prayer is the elevation of the soul to God. If thy prayer by word of mouth serves this purpose, well and good. But even so: if my clothing serves me, all the same it is not my own self. Thus does all prayer of the mouth serve true prayer; but in itself and taken alone it is not true prayer. For by true prayer the heart and soul of a man must go direct to God, and that is the esential thing. True prayer is this and nothing besides: a man's mind is totally subjected to God in loving desire and genuine humility.

Clergymen and members of orders are indeed especially bound at certain times to recite vocal prayers. But none of these prayers are so devout and lovely as the sacred prayer taught us by the supreme master of prayer Himself, namely the Pater Noster. That prayer approaches the nearest of all vocal prayer to the truest, the most essential. This prayer of spirit we lift up incessantly toward Heaven, and it lifts the soul with it straight up to God. And it is equally true to say, that the soul penetrates into its own most sacred and interior depths, where alone it may form a union with God. Thus St. Augustine says: "The soul has within itself a hidden abyss, and the things of time and of this world have no place therein, but only what is high above them and above all that concerns the body and its activities." In these heavenly abysses the soul finds all its sweetness, and there is the eternal abode of all Divine joys. In them the soul is still, fixed in God, cut off from creatures, and drawn into uncreated bliss. There is God Himself, acting, dwelling, ruling, granting the soul an incomparable Divine life. Into this life the soul melts away—into the infinite light and fire of love that God is by essence and by nature. Back and forth into this relation with God does such a man pass in prayer, as he pleads for every necessity of all Christendom, his holy petitions, his deep yearnings ever guided by God Himself. Thus does he pray for his friends on earth, even sinners, and for the souls in purgatory. The needs of every soul in holy Church are not beyond his help by counsel as well as by prayer. And yet such favored spirits do not always pray exactly for this or that particular person or object. But with a certain kind of wide-sweeping universal and yet most simple prayer do they embrace all souls of men, just as I stand here and behold with one glance all of you sitting before me. They see all in the same Divine abyss, God's love, as in a Divine contemplation, and in the fire of Divine love—viewing thus as with one glance the necessities of all Christians. They may seem to themselves to be in and out of God in their soul's movements, and yet they are ever in Him, deep in the calm of fathomless love: therein is their life and being, therein all their life's activity. Nothing is to be discovered in them under any and all circumstances but a Divine existence; whether doing things or leaving them undone, everything tells of God. These are noble souls, necessary for holy Church, sanctifying and consoling all men, giving honor to God. Wherever they may be, God dwells in them and they in Him. May God help us to the methods and the devotion leading to such an end. *Amen.*

Preparing to Receive the Holy Ghost

Synopsis—The only right preparation is cutting off attachments to earthly things—This is the more nobly done in the higher powers of the soul by deep longings for God, and Him alone—Scruples and foolish misgivings are a hindrance—But reasonable self-suspecting is most useful—Example of the serpent changing his skin.

FIRST SERMON FOR THE FEAST OF PENTECOST.

Be prudent, therefore.—I Peter iv, 7.

Holy Church at this time celebrates the sending of the Holy Ghost upon the apostles, who received Him in a most interior manner. It was necessary for our sakes that they should make such a beginning of a new existence, for we are by their means to receive the same Divine gift. And it was good that they should be comforted, for they had languished comfortless and forsaken within and without. And it finally came to pass, that as long as they continued in this life the disciples constantly grew into deeper union with the Holy Ghost. So should every true friend of God celebrate this lovely festival every day he lives—yes, every day and every hour should he receive the Holy Ghost in his soul. The whole task of his life is to prepare a loving welcome for Him. And His coming again and again continuously fits the soul better and better for His ever-renewed entrance. As Pentecost day was the festival of the Holy Ghost's being sent to the disciples, so is every day of the year a Pentecost day to each Christian. If he will but thoroughly prepare his soul, the Divine Spirit will enter in with all His graces and gifts.

And now, Children, here is our dear apostle St. Peter to teach us what that preparation is. He says to us: "Be prudent, therefore." And this does not only mean wisdom, but experience also, by which a man knows how to do a thing all the better, because he has made trial of doing it over and over again. The apostle means that we should have the habitual knowledge and the foresight which come from practice, and that in all our spiritual affairs. He means that we shall thereby be made able to understand clearly the difference between God and creatures on all occasions.

Children, the men who rightly comprehend this preparation, and who understand the noblest manner of receiving the Holy Ghost, are those who cut off all things but God, who are made entirely empty, and thus attain to the interior life and Divine unity: these are rightly prepared for the Holy Ghost.

And what is this true and genuine detachment? It is voluntary separation from all that is not simply and purely God. It is the searching of the soul with careful scrutiny, to discover if there is even the least thing, though it be in its inmost depths, that is not simply God. It is constantly enquiring whether or not God and God alone is had in view in all things done or omitted. And when anything is found that savors aught else than God alone, it means cutting it off absolutely. And this preparation is the task not only of men whose lives are very holy and interior, but of every good man whatsoever.

Children, we meet with good men, well versed in excellent religious exercises, who yet know nothing whatever of the interior life. Yet these are bounden to search out all that may interfere with God's reign in their souls, and instantly to cut it off. This much detachment every one must certainly have; otherwise he cannot receive the Holy Ghost and His Divine gifts. It is taking God into account in all things, separating ourself from all that is not God.

But men differ much in way of this separation, and in their waiting for God's Spirit. Some receive Him in the way of the senses and of devotional feeling; others, more nobly, by way of the soul's highest faculties and in the reason, far removed from sensible emotions; others, again, while partaking of both these ways, receive the Holy Spirit in the hidden recesses of their soul, in that secret Kingdom of God, where the sweet vision of the Holy Trinity is enshrined: and this is the noblest way of all. Ah, children, how gladly does the Holy Ghost make such a soul as that His chosen abode, and how divinely are His gifts imparted there. As often as that man but glances intelligently into his interior life, so often does he renew his union with the Holy Spirit, each instant receiving new favors. Nothing more is needed than that he maintain his earnest purpose to be ever turned toward God alone, in all wisdom, and in all detachment of spirit. He scrutinizes all his doings and all his ways and words and works, eager to detect whatever may not have God alone for its meaning, instantly correcting himself when necessary.

By the Holy Spirit's light of grace, he guides his steps in all the moral virtues—such as humility, mildness, gentleness, silence and piety; watching his motives lest any of these good acts should be done for other intention than God only.   And the natural virtues of prudence, justice, fortitude and temperance, are all under this same Divine light, as he performs their holy acts.   This is indeed the good ordering of a man, a divine ordering, the establishing of purely Divine motives, all things arranged in God, all done for God's sake.

When the Holy Ghost finds that a man has done his part in this field of the natural virtues, He pours into the natural light of the soul His supernatural illumination, and with it the grace of the supernatural virtues—Divine faith, and hope, and love.   Now he is enlightened; now he becomes a virtuous man indeed, a Godlike man in his state of disengagement from created things.   But as to this, one must act with prudence, for it often happens that what appears to be God's action, is, when more closely considered, found to be not so, and hence one must be on one's guard.

And furthermore it sometimes happens that a man who has entirely given himself up to God, yet fancies with much anguish of mind that he has not done so sincerely.   He then thinks that all the good he ever did is lost and wasted.   Peace has now fled from his soul, all is trouble and woe.   Children, this anguish frequently comes from natural bodily causes; or, again, it is due to bad weather acting on the nerves; or it is the influence of the evil one, who would gladly distress the soul of so good a man.   And such an unfavorable condition one must meet in all quietness of mind and meekness of spirit.

Some would oppose it with violence, storm against it with forceful measures, and by such means make fools of themselves.   They run about to learned doctors and to devout servants of God begging advice. But they are asking for what they cannot have: no one can give them relief.   Children, when this interior storm strikes a man, he should do as one does when overtaken by a storm of wind, rain and hail—he should take shelter under a roof till the storm passes over.   Is a man conscious that he desires nothing whatever but God?   Then when this trial assails him, let him humbly bow to it, let him patiently suffer in all abandonment to God, in all painful detachment of spirit, and wait upon God in his deep affliction, his soul all calm and gentle.   Who can tell in what manner the loving God will come to him and grant him His precious favors?   Dear soul, remain under the sheltering roof of God's will in patient meekness, and this is more pleasing to Him a hundred times, than sweet spiritual joys in practicing virtue—thy stormy sorrows bravely borne are more welcome to Him than the beautiful sunshine and the bright blossoms of fair-weather virtue. In this anguish of spirit, a man cannot lose his upright intention so easily as when he revels in consolations and the sweetness of devotion. Among these nature can readily insinuate lower motives, and the taint of spiritual self-indulgence may unconsciously stain the soul. God's gifts are not God's self. Our joy must be in God alone, not in His gifts.

Children, human nature is ever greedy, ever selfish. We hinder God's work in us, we destroy his glorious gifts after they are granted us, because we allow selfishness to appropriate what is not our own, yielding to the poisonous influences inherited from original sin. Our nature looks to self in everything. St. Thomas teaches that by this infection of nature, man is inclined to love himself more than anything else, even the angels, nay, even more than God—not that God created us thus perverse, but it has all resulted from the original turning away from God in the fall of Adam. And this evil tendency is rooted so deep in us, that its traces baffle the search of all the wise men in the world. All the industry of man cannot correct this innate weakness of both his inner and outer life. It often happens, that when we fancied God alone was our motive, it turned out that it was only the poisonous influences of nature that guided us—we were but seeking self in everything. St. Paul was a true prophet when he said: "In the last days, shall come dangerous times. Men shall be lovers of themselves" (II Tim. iii, 1, 2). This is manifestly the case in these times; for the world is full of misery because men, both of the world and of the clerical state—how pitiful a spectacle!—are both openly and secretly striving to defraud one another. And father confessors are sometimes privy to this, by condoning it by means of their novel and pagan interpretations of holy scripture. Children, if any of you fall under my accusations in this matter, I beg him to amend at once, if he would come to God. O if one could but give up self in his outer and inner life, in spirit and in nature, it were a precious gain! It would be a small price to pay if he gave up gold and silver and castles and farms for this end. Even in our interior spirit and in our devotions, nay, in our closest approach to God, nature secretly insinuates selfishness, so great is the deordination of self-love; and herein God's way of having us act, is rightly given us by St. Peter: "Be ye prudent, therefore."

Our Lord Jesus Christ also admonishes us how to be wise: "Be ye therefore wise as serpents" (Matt. x, 16). Remark how the eternal Son of God has given us this very humble comparison, to teach us the wisdom of His Father, and His Own unspeakably glorious wisdom. As He was Himself always very humble, so is His teaching very simple. Now you should know the wisdom of the serpent in this: when it finds its skin grown old, it selects a place where two stones are close together, and by going between them it draws off the old skin, and soon is furnished with a new one. So must a man get rid of his old skin, that is whatsoever he possesses by nature, no matter how great or how precious—all that is not purely God he must lay aside. To accomplish this he must pass between two Divine stones, one being the eternal Godhead, which is truth itself; and the other is the humanity of our Lord Jesus Christ, Who is the way and the truth. Between these must be drawn a man's very life in its essence and its action, including all his virtues, both natural or moral. Of this stone that Christ is, St. Paul speaks: "Jesus Christ being the chief corner-stone" (Eph. ii, 20). And thou mayst be sure, that if thou dost not truly strip thyself thus most humbly between these stones, then nothing will avail thee, even if thou wert as wise as Solomon and as strong as Samson. Lose thyself in Christ's poverty, in His obedience, in His love, drawing all thy transgressions off of thy soul in detachment of spirit; and then take upon thee all His virtues, His doctrine, and His life. By this means will a man receive the seven gifts of the Holy Ghost, and more especially the three Divine virtues of faith, hope and charity, all perfection, and all truth, interior peace and joy in the Holy Ghost.

From this detachment is born kindness, and also separation from all worldly things; so that one now receives freely from God's hands and with entire thankfulness, joy or sorrow, or whatever else may befall him in the inner life or the outer: everything helps him to eternal happiness. Such a man has the grace to feel, that whatever happens him has been eternally foreseen by his heavenly Father, and in the very way it does happen, and, viewing all things as God does, he rests in peace of mind, no matter what occurs. This peace of soul is gained only in the practice of real detachment, and in solicitude of spirit; in that school and in no other can it be acquired. Let a man seek it in all sincerity, and it will soon be his, and become a virtue rooted in the depths of his being.

All that I have preached to you in this sermon is addressed to noble-hearted men; let such bear these rules continually in mind, and in word and work carry them out practically; then they will find it all quite possible for them to do. The result will be that they will keep God efore them as their single motive, stripping themselves of all hindrances to grace by means of our corner-stone, Jesus Christ, who liveth and reigneth eternally with God the Father, God the Son, and God the Holy Ghost. *Amen.*

Giving God Unhindered Liberty in the Soul

Synopsis—Seeming abandonment by God is often the prelude of high perfection—If we but let Him, God does the work of preparation Himself in the soul—Signs of this are dullness and self-disgust, despondency arising from self-contempt and a feeling of total emptiness of good—Delusions resulting from the first joys of divine union: self-appropriation of divine gifts, silly excess of spiritual enjoyment, forgetfulness of inborn weakness—On return to their good sense, these souls honor God by wisdom of speech, and by charity of act, and by invincible patience.

SECOND SERMON FOR THE FEAST OF PENTECOST.

And they were all filled with the Holy Ghost, and they began to speak • • •
the wonderful works of God.—Acts ii, 4, 11.

Beloved children, this is the day on which the precious treasure of Divine love, lost so sadly in the garden of Eden by Adam's disobedience, was restored to us.   The whole race of man had fallen into eternal death, had lost the sevenfold gifts of the Divine Comforter, and lay under the wrath of God in the bands of everlasting servitude.   Jesus Christ broke these bands on Good Friday, as He was bound fast in death to His cross. He made perfect peace between His Father and mankind; and today He confirms that reconciliation.   He restores the lost treasures of grace in the Holy Ghost.   Our hearts and souls and senses are incapable of understanding the superabundant wealth of love that is in our Saviour, and which overflowed the souls of His disciples when they received the Holy Ghost.   It was like a downpour of rain which overflows the streams and fertilizes the valleys and fields.   And as with the disciples then, so in all ages and without any intermission ever since then; the Holy Ghost overflows the inmost hearts of men with His graces, if only He finds those inner depths ready and open to receive His gifts.   And now suppose that this our land were like Palestine in the days of Elias, when for three years and six months the earth was parched with drouth and no man could sow or reap, and that then there should come a sweet plentiful rain, quickening the fields with new life—and one single man's farm were left dry: would not he and all his friends cry out with misery? In the same way, a man who feels himself parched with spiritual drouth in heart and soul about interior things and external things of religion, empty and loveless, entirely void of the overflowing comfort of the Holy Spirit—shall that man not mourn over his state of abandonment? Let us then consider what is to be done in order to obtain the Holy Ghost.

The first and most important preparation must be made by the Holy Ghost Himself, making ready a proper place for His abode; and that He does by two acts. One is to empty the soul, the other is afterwards to fill it. The emptying is the greatest preparation, for the more the soul is emptied of human attachment, the more receptive of God's Spirit does it become. If thou wouldst fill a cup with some liquid, thou must first empty it of any other liquid that may be in it. Of two different materials, one cannot be perfectly itself if it is to be blended with the other. If fire is to come in, water must first go out, for these elements are naturally opposed. Well then, if God is to come into the soul, creatures must first go out—all that is not God must go out. Thus, again, the animal instincts must yield place to the dictates of reason, if these shall hold sway. Thus, therefore, a man must surrender himself captive, be empty, detached, and ready. Nay, even this state of detachment itself—as far as any honor shall be due to it—must be surrendered to God in total self-annihilation; otherwise a man will prevent the highest activity of the Holy Ghost within him. But to go to this extent no one nowadays seems willing.

But when this emptying of the soul has been done, at once the Holy Ghost does His second work: He gratifies the soul's capacity to receive Him. Yes; if thou art truly detached thou shalt receive abundantly, and if thou art but partially detached, thou shalt receive but partially. Thou must be totally emptied of self-will, self-love, self-opinion. Consider that if Heaven itself stood open before thee, thou wouldst not dare to enter in, until thou hadst known if God would have thee do so—such must be thy detachment from self. This is the state and this alone, in which the soul must be if the Holy Ghost is to be given to it unto perfect fullness.

Ah, children, when a man feels himself dull, hard and slow, being oppressed by nature; when peace is gone; when he is become quite helpless; then let him detach his soul's affections from everything, yield himself up entirely to God, suffer these trials and all other evils patiently, and he will have obtained real poverty of spirit; and then the Holy Ghost will soon fill the empty void. Into such a soul He pours all His riches, overflowing with His presence the whole man both inward and outward, enriching the highest faculties and the lowest. In this the man's own part is to allow himself to be prepared by the Holy Ghost, and to make room for Him as He begins His Divine work. Few men do this, even of those whose vocation calls for it, and who show outward signs of spirituality. There is a widespread state of delusion and self-hood in such matters. This is owing to our acting in self-chosen ways, full of self-assurance. Nobody seems willing to yield simply up to the Holy Spirit's action; everybody must have his own plan of spiritual life—such is the rule in our perilous times. Let thy only rule be to allow the Holy Ghost unhindered liberty in thy soul. He will thereupon so possess thee with His Divine influence, that even in thy outward conduct every word and work shall be according to His will—all in due order and quiet. As to thy interior life, He will turn thee inward to achieve great spiritual things, even though thou shalt be hardly aware of His action. For just as the soul acts in the body, so does the Holy Ghost act in our innermost life, all without our easily perceiving it, until we turn again and bend our mental powers deep into those recesses of the soul in which the Divine Guest has taken up His abode.

And then a man is apt to become foolish. When he sees these great things of God in his heart, he appropriates them to himself. It is as if a great painter had begun a masterpiece and some fool should come along and meddle with it and quite destroy its beauty. Thus do we act when we meddle with God's work in our souls. This is done by the inordinate joy to which we give ourselves up, as we perceive how God is doing His holy work within us, for, indeed, that joy exceeds all other joys known to this life. But by means of this self-appropriation, God's work is destroyed. It is very true that as long as a man does not fall into mortal sin the Holy Ghost is not driven out, but his soul may meanwhile be far removed from self-renunciation.

Sometimes a man will be under the delusion that his inner life is all of God, and as a matter of fact it is all his own self, his own self-sufficiency. A man may receive high spiritual gifts, even revelations and knowledge of secret things, and yet it may remain very doubtful as to what will become of him in the end—it is quite possible for him to be eternally lost from the consequences of his self-appropriation of these supernatural things. Children, spiritual matters are not as you fancy. A man must go out of himself and stay out of himself, if the Holy Spirit shall have His way with him according to His supreme and infinite dignity: beware of placing obstacles in His way. If thou hast, however, made this mistake, it is not necessary for thee to run off at once and annoy thy father confessor with matters so hard to explain. Turn immediately into thy own heart's deep chambers, confess thy faults humbly to God there, and He will place His Divine hand on thy head and heal thee.

Thus said our Lord: "They shall lay their hands upon the sick, and they shall recover" (Mark xvi, 18). And again He says: "They shall cast out devils." God will thus grant thee power to detect the devil's deceits and to escape them—a reward for thy soul's self-renunciation. "They shall take up serpents," meaning an interior man's patience in bearing with snake-like men, with their overbearing manners and their usurped authority. These may sting and wound God's servants in their lowermost faculties, but they cannot touch the higher powers of their souls—be of good courage and never let them distress thee. Our Saviour says also: "If they shall drink any deadly thing, it shall not hurt them." Does not this mean suffering from bad men, in whom everything turns to poison? They make the worst of everything, spinning around all that comes near them a poisonous web of wickedness. If it should happen that thou art desirous of receiving the fulness of the Holy Spirit, and that on that account thy sister should assail thee with her scolding tongue, then if thou wilt only accept this patiently for God's sake, be certain that this is the work of the Holy Ghost. If thou wilt only be silent and bear with thyself sweetly, be sure that it is a preparation for the coming of the Holy Ghost. It hurts thy outward self, but it cannot injure thy interior self.

Children, would you be always happy, always at your best? Then hold fast to these two little points: Empty yourselves totally of all created things, including your own self, maintaining a well-ordered inner and outer life, so that the work of the Holy Ghost may be unhindered in you. Secondly, accept every happening of your existence, whether in the soul or in the outer life, as coming directly from God's hand: come from where it may, be it what it will, look upon it as given you to help you make ready for His great gifts and for no other purpose whatsoever, knowing that only by trial and hardship, whether coming from the evil one or from unruly men, you can attain the supernatural and marvelous perfection to which God has called you.

Our Redeemer also said of His apostles: "They shall speak with new tongues" (Mark xvi, 17). This means that a man must cripple his tongue—that is to say, he must restrain his natural tendency to talk. Children, learn how to guard your tongue, learn that art before every other art. Habitually take care what you say, or you will never amount to anything with God. See to it that your words are all to God's honor, or to your neighbor's good, or to your own peace of mind. Converse with God without ceasing. St. Bernard says: "I condemn and detest talking much with men; but we can never talk too much with God." Thank God loudly with your tongue, and praise Him continually. If thou hadst only this to thank Him for—that He has patiently borne with thee to this hour and silently suffered thy disorderly conduct before His face, thou oughtest to demand new tongues of Him to give Him proper thanks, even if He never led thee onward to the complete fulfilment of His holy designs with thee. And among yourselves, as often as you meet together talk about God and about a virtuous life. This does not mean disputations about the Deity or any other such things, nor does it mean subtle reasoning of any kind; for that will only help to damn your soul and the souls of those you draw into such controversies. But converse about God and virtue, out of a heart full of God and of virtue. Avoid subtle and disputatious men, who are the serpents of whom we were lately discoursing. They are externalized men; thou must not draw them into thy sacred interior life. By their means the evil one may manage to entrap thee, taking advantage of thy weaker tendencies.

Besides this, the Holy Ghost works His supernatural ends according to the good natural tendencies He finds in thee. As God's work grows in thee, He will draw under His influence both thy soul and body. When He finds a good and willing natural disposition, He works along its lines. Just as a copious rain produces a good harvest, so does God will that His gifts shall not be unfruitful—He develops all natural powers of soul and body, so that He may in due order act by their means for thy sanctification. But all this is on condition that God finds thee in true poverty of spirit. Hence thou must cast out of thy soul whatever thou hast cherished there that is not the effect of the action of the Holy Ghost; all hardness of heart, suspicious rash judgments—of all such things thou must be entirely emptied. But thou shouldst bear in mind that whatever happens to thee against thy will can do thee no harm.

Again, do not suppose that thou shouldst wait inertly for the Holy Ghost, ceasing to perform thy usual external works of religion, ceasing to observe thy rule of life, such as singing and reading thy prayers, serving thy neighbor, and doing works of charity. No, it is not thus that we must wait for the Holy Spirit—supinely letting everything slip away from us. The man who loves God and serves Him gladly, will do all things out of love, to the praise of God, for the sake of good order, in a becoming manner, according as God has arranged by His Providence. Let everything be done by thee in a kindly spirit, in all gentleness and self-denial, resolved to be at peace with thyself and with thy neighbor. It is not the work that hinders thee; no, but rather it is thy spirit of disorder in doing the work that hinders thy spiritual progress. Set that right, and keep God alone in view in all thy activity. Look carefully into thyself very often; take heed to what thy mind is occupied with; admit no confusion of motives there, whether about joy or sorrow; guard carefully thy external behavior. By these means thou shalt abide in contentment in all thy doings; the Holy Ghost will come to thee and fill thy soul. He will dwell within thee. If thou wilt but hearken to His teaching, He will work miracles within thee. To that happy state may God help us all. *Amen.*

The Gifts of the Holy Ghost

Synopsis—The scene and circumstances of the coming of the Holy Ghost—The first gift is Divine fear, which is a supernatural instinct of seeking safety from danger—Then comes the gift of piety, which is a Divine trustfulness in God amid all inward disturbances and outward calamities—The third is the gift of knowledge, by which we learn how to place reason in supreme control over sense and God over all—The fourth is fortitude, by which a a man does wonderful things and overcomes horrible obstacles to holiness—Counsel is a gift revealing our defects in their naked deformity, and showing us how to overcome them—Understanding and wisdom are the perfect gifts, and place the soul in close but indescribable union with God.

THIRD SERMON FOR THE FEAST OF PENTECOST.

And they were all filled with the Holy Ghost.—Acts ii, 4.

This is the blessed day on which the Holy Ghost was sent down upon the Lord's holy disciples, and upon all who were united to them in God's love. Today was restored to us by God's mercy that precious gift of grace, first lost to us in Eden through the evil counsel of Satan and human weakness. The outward manner of this high gift was wonderful, to say nothing of the hidden marvels enclosed in the apostles' souls, for this is incomprehensible to all reason and sense. The Holy Spirit is so immeasurable and so lovable a boon, that His infinite greatness totally surpasses all our powers of understanding by means of figures and mental conceptions. A little grain of dust compared to the whole bulk of the world, even this is more than all our power of thinking and imagining, compared to the task of understanding the Holy Ghost. And all creatures together are infinitely less than our least thoughts of the Holy Spirit. Therefore it is that wheresoever He shall take up His abode, He must Himself make ready all things for His reception. God's own deep abyss must be God's place of welcome, and that even in His creatures. The house in which the disciples were gathered was filled with God—"and It filled the whole house where they were sitting" (Acts ii, 2). Be sure of this: into whatsoever soul God comes, He fills every corner of it, according as it is receptive of Him.

The disciples were all filled with the Holy Ghost. This brings us to the consideration of their condition at the time; and it is that of all of God's followers when they are to receive Him. We find that they were all shut in and assembled together in one place, and that they sat in all stillness, when they received the Holy Ghost. And so with us. This beloved Spirit of God is given to each one of us, as often and as much as we are shut off from all creatures and turned wholly to God. The very instant this happens in a man, the Holy Ghost comes to him with all His graces, and He fills every desire; He takes possession of the very being and essence of the soul. And, on the other hand, the very instant the soul turns away from God—that is to say deliberately—and gives itself to creatures apart from God, having its own self and not God in view, that very instant the Holy Ghost takes His departure from the soul with all His treasures.

"And filled the whole House" where the disciples were sitting. And herein we may understand holy Church to be meant, which is indeed God's house; and in another sense it may mean each man among us. For each one should be a temple and dwelling place of God, well beloved by the Holy Ghost as being His chosen shrine. And as in every house there are many different living rooms, so in a man there are many senses, powers and activities, into all of which the Holy Ghost comes with His gifts. And the moment He enters in He lights up a man's soul interiorly with His brightness, He excites him to the practice of virtue. This entrance of God into the soul and His interior working is not always perceived, although He is thus present in all good men. If one would plainly feel that holy presence and taste God's sweetness, he must gather all his faculties together into one place, as it were; he must shut himself away from all outward thing, and give himself up in all stillness to His Divine Guest. Then will he feel Him in all his soul's activities, all the more in proportion to the increase of his fervor in turning wholly to Him, hour by hour adding to his first impulse of devoted allegiance.

The disciples of God were shut in out of fear of the Jews. O merciful God, how much more necessary a thousand times is it not for us in these days, to take flight and to be shut in and separated from the wicked

Jews whom we meet at every corner of our life, and who fill all our
houses. Ah, beloved children, beware of these hateful Jews, that is to
say the men who would rob you of God, of confidence in God, and of the
delightful communion of your soul with the Holy Ghost. The Jews of
old could do no more against the apostles than take away the life of
their bodies, but the men of the wretched world of today can deprive
you of eternal life, rob you of your soul and of God. Fly from these
Jews, shut yourselves safely away from them, put an end to your dangerous companionship with them, beware of dallying with them, whether
by words or deeds; for God's honor and praise is not with them. And
if you fail in this, be sure that you will lose the Holy Ghost and forfeit
all His gifts.

But someone might say: No, sir, this intercourse with men does me
no harm, because I mean no evil in it. And I must recreate myself and
enjoy some little relaxation. But O my God, how is it that Thou, the
sweetest and the only good, Thou eternal and infinite joy—how is it that
Thou hast no sweetness to our taste, while we can find peace and happiness in the enjoyment of miserable, perishing creatures, full of darkness
and destruction.   O man, how canst thou prefer the joy of creatures to
that of God, and drive from thy heart the blessed Spirit that made thee,
and is and must be thy truest consolation?

But, dear children, fly not the company of good men, those who long
for God's love alone, and who keep Him ever in mind with deep sincerity.
When such as these are engaged with outward things, they nevertheless
remain preoccupied with their interior life, where they are always privileged to enjoy the peace and happiness of the Holy Ghost.

The disciples of God were all assembled together; and this teaches
us to gather in to our hearts all our mental faculties and all our bodily
senses, so that the Holy Ghost may constantly act upon them, producing,
as He is sure to do, wonderful fruits of grace, when place and time are
found appropriate.

The disciples of God were seated when they received the Holy Ghost.
So must thou in very truth sit down submissive to God's will in all
events, whether joyful or sad, doing or not doing. And this is a necessary requirement on the part of God from all who would become spiritual men. For what is meant by spirituality, except to be intimately
united to God in one will? All Christians who would be saved are
bound to this—to will nothing against God's will.

And now one might enquire whether all men in the ecclesiastical
state are bound to become perfect. They are bound, answers St. Thomas,

to live and strive always toward perfection. You must understand that the Holy Ghost imparts seven gifts, through which He does seven works in the soul. By three of them He prepares a man for high and true perfection; by the other four, He finishes His interior and external work, granting the highest and most splendid achievement of all perfection.

The first gift is Divine fear, which is the certain entrance way to perfection even the highest. The gift of fear is like a solid wall of resistance against all transgressions and all hindrances. Holy fear causes one to flee from deadly snares, as well as to escape falling into the deep pit. The soul becomes like a bird that the hunter would entrap, but which flies swiftly away into safety. As God gives this instinct of safety to His inanimate creatures, so does He bestow His blessed gift of fear upon us, to enable us to escape whatever would hinder us from union with Him. This noble gift guards us from the world, from the evil spirit and from our own weakness—from every manner of means by which we may forfeit our peace of soul. Whatever man has really given place to the Holy Ghost within him, quickly flees from danger; and he makes no terms with evil, nor holds any middle place between what is for God and what is against Him, that is to say in what involves mortal sin. And in all this, the gift of fear is, as the prophet taught, the beginning of wisdom.

After the gift of fear comes that of piety, a gentle endowment, which leads the soul far in advance on the journey toward union with sovereign truth. This gift takes from a man all depressing influences that might result from fear, lifting him out of his heaviness of spirit, so that he may have Divine trustfulness in all that may occur, both in inward feelings and outward happenings. Piety cures spiritual weariness, remedies obstinacy, and softens bitterness against one's self. And it makes one kindly toward one's neighbor in word and deed, very peaceful in outward behavior: and as to rashness, that the Spirit of God by this gift banishes totally away.

The third gift follows after, elevating the soul yet higher—the gift of knowledge. These gifts lap over one another and partake more or less of one another, but each in turn places the soul nearer to God. Dear children, in God a man is enabled by this gift to hearken to the Holy Ghost's interior voice warning him and guiding him, according to the words of our beloved Lord Jesus Christ: "When He, the Spirit of Truth, is come, He will teach you all truth" (John xvi, 13); that is to say, all things that we need to know. The warning of God is like this: O man, beware of doing that, for such and such evil results may follow. Or again: Do not say that; go not that way. These are prohibitions. But God also bids us do things: Act in such and such a way; give up this and undertake that. All these things are the gentle leadings of the Holy Spirit. He would have our souls possess the mastery over our bodies in all things, ruling them with a noble spiritual supremacy. He would have our bodies live a worthy life, by practicing virtue and in steadfast industry. He would have us suffer disgrace patiently. He would draw every single one of us to Himself, that He may elevate us to a thousand-fold more perfect union, banishing inordinate fear.

They who are faithful to this gift of knowledge, God leads to the fourth gift, Divine fortitude. O children, how noble and how very superior a gift of God is this, for it lifts us high above our human weakness. This was the force in the holy martyrs, as they cheerfully suffered death through God's assistance. Fortitude makes a man great-hearted. He feels able to perfectly accomplish everything for God, to suffer everything for His sake, as St. Paul said: "I can do all things in Him who strengtheneth me" (Phil. iv, 13). To such a man neither fire nor water nor death itself has any terrors; as St. Paul again teaches: "For I am sure that neither death, nor life, nor principalities, nor powers, nor things present, nor things to come, nor might, nor height, nor depth, nor any other creature, shall be able to separate us from the love of God, which is in Christ Jesus our Lord" (Rom. viii, 38, 39). With this gift a man becomes so strong, that he goes far beyond abstaining from mortal sins; he would rather die than deliberately commit even a single venial sin. And this is a doctrine taught us by our dear saints; for if all will admit that we should give up life rather than wilfully commit a mortal sin, the saints, in addition to this by example and teaching, lead us to abhor venial sin.

With the gift of fortitude the soul can do wonderful things. You must know, dear children, that when the Spirit of God comes into our souls, He always brings great joy, bright light, sweet consolation, for He is called and He is the Comforter. And now what too often happens? When the silly man feels this happiness, he appropriates it to himself in a state of self-satisfaction. He diverts his mind away from God to the enjoyment of God's gifts. Quite the contrary is the way of the wise Christian. He ever reverts to the origin of his joy, restores all God's gifts back to God with clear-minded self-renunciation. Not this or that particular one; but all without exception that he is and has he refers straight back to God alone.

Upon this follows the Divine gift of counsel, the fifth in order. Ah, how great is the need of God's counsel now; for it will be as if He had taken away all that He had given before, showing a man in naked reality what he is and what he can do! But He will instruct him how he should bear himself in this sore trial of self-knowledge. A man is now left destitute; of God he knows nothing—so it appears to him,—has nothing of His grace, is wholly deprived of comfort. Whatever he had before is gone—gone, at least, out of his knowledge, snatched away and vanished. He stands desolate, at a loss what to do or whither to turn. The gift of counsel is now of essential necessity, if he would behave as God would have him, and yield himself up to God's holy will, dying to self, standing in utter abandonment to his heavenly Father, giving himself cheerfully up to the awful secret judgment of God, by which he has been despoiled— so he thinks—of those graces which were once his perfect salvation and joy and comfort. This gift is no less a grace than to be content to be robbed of one's very self—this utter abandonment to God's will, this sinking down into the abyss of the Divine sovereignty. Nor is it enough to be willing to accept this fate for a week or a month of dark suffering, but for a long thousand years, if God so wills it—nay (if such a thing were possible consistently with loving God), to accept the eternal pains of hell, if God so willed, so that one might at last be wholly conformed to the Divine decree.

Dear children, here is a grade of self-renunciation above all others. Compared to this, the giving up of a thousand worlds is nothing; or the offering of their lives that the blessed martyrs made, for they had God's comfort in their souls, so that they could laugh at tortures and could die joyously. But there is no torture to compare with the loss of God that is now felt by the soul undergoing this trial. And, besides, all the misery that the soul had previously endured with patience, all the temptations it had previously overcome, all the faults it had rooted out—all this together now returns upon it and assails it, and that with a violence far greater than when the soul was struggling out of a state of sinfulness. Now let a man suffer meekly, now let him give up to God's will, and that for as long a time as God pleases. Sometimes a good soul will be so self-weary as to find solitude an unbearable agony—not for one hour can he be alone. For relief he turns now to this solace and again to that, and ever in vain: his only recourse is to struggle meekly through it all and yield himself up to God. Why, think you, did the Lord say to St. Peter, that a man should forgive his enemy seventy times seven

times? except because He knows our weakness, and would instruct us
that as often as we turn again to Him repenting and confessing, so often
will He pardon us.   How great a boon is it, for a sinner to be taught
what it means to fall away from God and then to return to Him again.
Dear children, in this trial as in all things else, one must resign himself
into God's hands, and be guided by His gift of counsel, lifting himself
high above all created existence, and becoming united to the origin and
essence that is God's will.

Dear children, by the three first gifts of the Holy Spirit—fear of God,
piety toward God, and God's science or knowledge—a man is made good
and holy; but by those of fortitude and counsel he becomes heavenly, and
as it were Divine.   It is by these, in truth, that God sets a man in everlasting life.   After enduring the agony we have described, the soul
endures no other agony whether in earth or hell.   It is impossible that
the eternal God would ever give that soul up, any more than He would
give Himself up, for the soul has yielded itself totally to the Divine will.
That soul has placed itself safely in the one only origin of all things,
and if all the suffering in this world fell upon it, it would regard it not
at all, it would experience no manner of harm, nay, it would even turn it
into joy—such a soul seems to be in Heaven itself.   That man's conversation is in that blessed home of his soul, into which he has, as it were,
placed one foot; and now he has only to draw the other one after it in
order to be wholly in life eternal.   He is in direct communication with
everlasting joy, which, indeed, has already begun in his soul.

And now come the last two gifts, understanding and wisdom, which
lead a man directly into the abyss of God's being, and in a manner far
above any other means.   The way of these gifts is understood by God
alone, for they grant a savor of His own essential wisdom.   When the
soul is given them, it is forthwith lost to its own consciousness.   Self is
absorbed in God.   A man can think of nothing of his own, neither
works, nor feelings, nor knowledge, nor life.   All this has been absorbed
and centered in one simple infinite good, to which it is joined in the
unspeakable depths of God, joined in essential unity.   What God has
in Himself by nature, that He now imparts to the soul by grace, the
Divine being, unnamed and without form or manner of existence that
we can express.   And now everything that is done in that soul God
Himself does, acting, knowing, loving, praising, enjoying; all of which
the soul has and does as if it were passive instrument of God's activity.
One can no more speak of this state clearly than he can speak clearly

of the Divine life itself.　To men and angels it is far too high for expression.　The created mind is incapable of understanding God's life, whether in Himself in His natural activity, or in these favored souls, when it is a gift of grace.

And thus it is that the Holy Ghost leads those who prepare their souls for Him, who long to be filled with Him, who would entertain Him as their Divine Guest, who would yield themselves freely and loyally to His guidance.　How glad and more than glad should we not be to extend Him this welcome, giving up for His dear sake ourselves and all things else.　That is what the disciples did when He was granted them on the feast we today celebrate; that is what is done daily and hourly by all who make themselves ready for His coming.　May God the Father, and God the Son, and God the Holy Ghost, grant us the privilege of this noblest way of union with the Holy Spirit.　*Amen.*

The Good Shepherd and His Sheep

Synopsis—The sheepfold is God's heart—The sheep are all saints and angels—The thieves are those who try to enter, trusting to their own natural good qualities—The robbers are the envious and backbiters—Every man who would enter God's heart must try himself by these tests.

FOURTH SERMON FOR THE FEAST OF PENTECOST.

Amen, amen, I say to you: He that entereth not by the door into the sheepfold, but climbeth up another way, the same is a thief and a robber.—John x, 1.

Our Lord teaches in the same chapter that He is Himself the door of the sheep. And what is the sheepfold? It is the Divine Father's heart; of this our beloved Lord is the door, ever opening to admit us, ever closing to keep us in. For we know that till our Saviour came, the door of God's heart was shut against us. In that sheepfold is the assemblage of all the saints. The shepherd is the Eternal Word, the door is the humanity of Christ, the sheep in this beautiful house of the shepherd are the souls of men, and, we may add, that this is the dwelling place of all angelic natures. The Good Shepherd, the Eternal Word, has shown all reasonable creatures the road to the Divine sheepfold. And who is the doorkeeper? The Holy Ghost, as Saints Ambrose and Jerome teach: "All truth that is ever known or ever spoken comes from the Holy Ghost." As to how the Holy Ghost instructs our hearts, inclines them, incessantly compels and enraptures them, that is known by those who have entered deeply into their own interior life.

Ah, how sweetly does the fatherly heart of God shut to the door when we have entered in, how generously does He lavish upon us the hidden riches of His house of love. No one can fully understand how ready and as it were thirsty God is thus to receive our souls, meeting us every instant halfway and with all eagerness as we advance toward Him. O children, how does it happen that we hold back, and that we refuse this gracious invitation, that we do it so often and for such frivolous reasons? We read in Scripture that when King Assuerus invited Vasti, his queen, to a royal banquet, she refused to come; and then the king detested her and cast her off forever, and chose another queen in her place. Ah, children, how many invitations of God Himself have we not refused; for they come to us directly from Him in our hearts, and again through the medium of creatures. God would have us to be with Himself, and we refuse and insist on being joined to others.

Now the Holy Spirit, the Gatekeeper of the Sheepfold, calleth His own sheep by name. Some refuse to hear Him and go away, but others hear His sweet voice gladly, and follow Him faithfully, turning neither to the right nor left and following no other. He leads onward, and they follow loyally after Him into the fatherly heart, into their peaceful home, passing through the door of the Eternal Word in His beloved humanity. True sheep of God are these; no alien shepherds do they follow; only God and His honor do such souls regard, guided absolutely by the Divine will—true sheep of the one Good Shepherd. Our Saviour says that He knows them and they know Him and recognize His voice, the voice that calls them to the door that opens into everlasting life; for He is the way, the truth and the life. Whosoever cometh to the Father must go through the door that Jesus is. To strive to enter any other way is to be a thief and a robber.

And who, dear children, are the thieves? All who would enter into God's sheepfold trusting to their natural good qualities; those who do not keep God alone in mind and heart in humble self-denial, nor follow the lovely form of Jesus Christ in entire disengagement of spirit; those who will not acknowledge themselves worthy of rejection—all these men enter in by the wrong door. And who else is the thief? The bad man who seeks out other men to corrupt them, the treacherous man of the evil eye. It is the selfish man, wholly consumed with self-love, who would appropriate to himself everything, grasping after what is God's and his neighbors. This evil trait drives the soul to appropriate all to itself, and then selfishly to seek to enjoy the comfort of God's generous gifts, harboring ambitious thoughts of being holy. And this evil state is fastened on the soul, unless it be sternly resisted, and self-denial be practiced in all inward and outward things. For it is ever against nature for a man to be content with oppression, to be glad to die to his own will, and to make that the starting point. Self-interest is always the hidden thief in our hearts, stealing from the eternal God His due honor, and from ourselves the truth of God and our everlasting perfection. This spiritual thief within us, dear children, does more harm to men than those criminals who are hanged for stealing our natural goods.

Therefore I warn you against this secret thief; as you value your eternal welfare resist self-love, lest it steal from you the fruit of Heaven's joy.

So much for the thieves. And now, dear children, let us ask who are the wicked robbers. They are rash judgments of our neighbor. Some men—and you find them in all states of life—are full of the spirit of rash judgment; so much so that their condemnation of others prevents them from knowing and condemning themselves. Such a one inwardly exclaims: That man talks too much, that other talks too little; this one is overbusy, that one is too idle; one has committed that fault, another this fault. And thus injurious reflections are multiplied as well as heavy condemnations, and at last a pitiable and sinful state of interior uncharity results. This inner contempt for one's neighbor often breaks out in ugly words, and characterizes the whole outward demeaner. It spreads the deadly infection to other men, slaying souls right and left. Ah, thou poor, blind creature; why dost thou not sit in judgment on thyself? What canst thou know of the heart of thy neighbor, or the way God is leading him with His loving favors, or of the inspirations and drawings of the eternal God in his inner life? What! Wilt thou, poor wretch that thou art, sit in judgment on these secret things, known to God's eye alone? Wilt thou thus presume to decide about what is wholly God's work, to meddle with it and destroy it? Repent of this before God and His saints and angels, repent sincerely, for all judgment is God's alone.

This death-stroke of evil judging works great harm in religious communities. It is a pitiful thing that such uncharitable spirits should forget our Lord's words: "Judge not, that you may not be judged. For with what judgment you judge, you shall be judged; and with what measure you mete, it shall be measured to you again" (Matt. vii, 1, 2). One must never condemn anything except mortal sin. If it happens that a man must pass judgment because he holds an office, then the Holy Ghost judges and punishes through him, and he therefore should act with Divine gentleness, lest in curing one wound he inflict ten others. Divine love, brotherly charity, a meek and gentle heart—these are the right dispositions for a judge. Without these, a religious superior gropes in darkness and soon wanders away from the truth. Ever and always should we first sit in judgment on ourselves. As long as thou livest thou hast hanging about thy neck a sack full of thy own sins, calling out constantly for judgment. As to judgment and punishment of thy neighbor, leave that to himself and his God, if thou wouldst make sure of entering into the fold of eternal life. For I say to thee in all truth, that as many judgments as thou visitest on others, so many shall be visited on thyself.

Dear children, when a man turns inward, he discovers in his soul these two enemies, the thief of self-appropriation of God's graces, and the robber of rash judgment against his neighbor. These hidden enemies steal and destroy the treasures of God's grace, and lay waste His interior kingdom. Let a man turn one enemy upon the other. Let him force the robber of rash judgment to exercise true judgment upon the thief of spiritual self-conceit, and then follows what often happens: both suffer death, the robber and the thief destroy each other. O children, happy is the soul in which this happens. Blessed is the life of a man when nature's fierce tendency to condemn, is turned upon its greedy self to inflict punishment for appropriation of Divine gifts. Then he rests meekly under God's judgment, in his own case and in that of all others; then he soon finds himself at the door that is Jesus Christ our Lord; then the beloved Doorkeeper, the Holy Ghost, opens wide the portals of eternal life, and introduces the soul into the deep abyss of the Father's love, into and out of which it passes, always enjoying rich pastures of grace.

That soul sinks with unspeakable joy into the Deity, comes forth again with equal joy by union with the blessed humanity of Christ, fulfilling the word of our Saviour spoken through His prophet concerning His sheep: "I will feed them in the most fruitful pastures, and their pastures shall be in the high mountains of Israel; there shall they rest on the green grass (Ezechiel xxxiv, 14). Then shall the soul's work and rest be made one. May that be our blessed lot, by the help of God. *Amen.*

The Apostles Before Pentecost

Synopsis—Deserted by the world, the Apostles turned inward to God
—They went back to the city, recalling the teaching of Jesus—
They fearfully examined their souls and bitterly repented of their
sins—They grew in hope, and confidently awaited the Holy Spirit
—Reasons why He had not been granted them before.

FIFTH SERMON FOR THE FEAST OF PENTECOST.

Then they returned to Jerusalem.—Acts 1, 12.

When the eternal Son of God had finished the work His Father had
sent Him to accomplish, and His bodily presence had been taken away
from His disciples, they returned from the Mount of Olives to Jerusalem.

And there they did six things. First, seeing themselves deserted by
the whole world, seeing, too, that all Heaven's joy and consolation had
been taken away from them, they turned inward. They withdrew their
thoughts from all outward things, for this world was now wholly dead
to them, and with it all the joy of transitory things.

Secondly, they resolved on self-renunciation. Now they had as leave
die as live. As long as God's will were done and His honor saved, they
cared not what might happen to them. Hence it was that they went
back into the city, a place full of their enemies, because they had been
so commanded by the Lord, there to await what His will had in store
for them. This they did, although not without great fear.

Thirdly, they called to mind the sweet and holy teaching of Jesus by
word and by example; and how stupidly they had received it all; how
unworthy they had been to hear His words and to look upon Him; and
how feebly they had responded to His loving care. Recognizing all this,
they confessed it before God with bitter sorrow of heart, and upbraided
themselves with interior reproaches.

Fourthly, they now remembered how their beloved Master had in all
things practiced self-sacrifice; that in His whole life He never was a
self-seeker. They recalled, too, His words: "If any man will come after

Me, let him deny himself" (Matt. xv, 24). Upon this they inspected their own souls, and they owned that they were very far from true denial of self, and that they had copied Christ's example only in a natural way. They became aware that fear and other natural motives had not been displaced by higher ones. They sorrowfully confessed all this, and accused themselves bitterly, and despised themselves heartily.

Fifthly, they rose out of this humble state of mind, this candid avowal of dullness of soul and of disorderly inclinations, and they turned with sincere longings to their beloved Master. From the depths of their heart they implored Him to forgive their great imperfections, to cure all cowardice within them, to correct all the self-seeking of their perverted nature, and to utterly strip them of anything that could lead them astray from a true life, establishing in them the rule of His blessed humanity. All this they did with most hearty sincerity; otherwise, I do not believe that they would have received the Holy Ghost.

Sixthly, they aroused within their souls a gentle sentiment of confidence, recalling the word of their Master that He would bring them help and would comfort them. Although they saw themselves forsaken and opposed by all, and in the sorest necessity, yet were they full of a great confidence in their faithful Master and Lord. They were sure that He would not abandon them, even though they felt some misgivings on account of their unworthiness, and their lack of disengagement from worldly things.

And now you might ask this question: Since the disciples were dead to the world, and since they sincerely longed that all shortcomings of nature might be remedied by the Divine light, why was the Holy Ghost not given them immediately after the Lord's ascension? I answer that we cannot believe that the Holy Spirit was withheld from them during the interval between the ascension and Pentecost, and we may be sure that they received Him; but only in a preparatory sort of way. They were to receive Him in far greater fullness at Pentecost. The more they advanced in self-knowledge and self-annihilation, so much the more plentifully was He imparted to them. He was delayed till Pentecost as to the fullnes of His graces, because they were not as yet entirely emptied of self. Then it was that their souls were perfectly ready for Him because entirely disengaged from other claimants. Only then; that is to say when God's Spirit was poured into them and the Divine power finished the work of preparation: that preparation had been going on beforehand. but only then was it completed. God now was

in their souls content with Himself as He possessed them. And this
we will more fully explain in the next sermon. St. Gregory speaks of
the disciples and of souls similar to them, when he says: "In proportion
as the Divine power grows within us, so does our own spirit lose its
strength; and thus do we increase wholly in God, as we decrease wholly
in ourself." May this holy gift be granted us by the Father, and the
Son, and the Holy Ghost. *Amen.*

The Drawing of the Holy Ghost

Synopsis—The first drawing is through creatures, giving proofs of His existence—Secret and interior touches of consolation or of chastisement are a second attraction—The third is a drawing to a very close embrace of love—This is followed by entire self-renunciation, sometimes in joy, more often in sorrow—Another drawing is into a state of interior prayer without images or forms—The other drawings perfect all these and add new heavenly joys to the soul.

SIXTH SERMON FOR PENTECOST.

No man can come to Me except the Father, who hath sent Me, draw him.—John vi, 44.

These words apply to our Saviour's disciples after the ascension, for they were very wretched. They lay, as it were, imprisoned in the deep dungeon of their sinfulness, bound by their own inclinations as by fetters of iron. Conscious at last of their own powerlessness, they now cry out pitifully to the eternal Father. For St. Luke tells us that they were persevering with one mind in prayer—prayer to be set free from their heavy chains, to be released from their dark dungeon. And God their Father heard their fervent prayer. He struck off their chains, He drew them forth from prison, and set them in the Divine school of the Holy Ghost, in which they were to be filled with all truth. The cords with which He drew them forth were six in number.

The first is that He turned upon them His eyes of compassion. Nor was this in the way of His ordinary mercy, but with particular mercy for them. God draws men to Himself by created things, through which He reveals His existence in the created light of their souls. St. Thomas teaches that some of the heathen saw God's presence as He dwelt in the created world about them, which showed Him as its Creator and Master, so that men should pay Him honor in every part of the world. Thus God draws men through His creatures, thereby giving them proofs of His existence.

In addition to this, God manifests Himself to the soul of man by **His secret word of truth** within them. St. Augustine says: "The heathen have discoursed of certain truths that they know from the everlasting law of God, and not from their own natural knowledge." Such is the case with all men **who** utter truth, as St. Ambrose teaches: "Whatsoever is true, no matter by whom it may be spoken, comes from the Holy Ghost." Hence it happens that when the soul is deeply recollected, it often becomes sensitive to the words of eternal truth, a state that sometimes comes upon us in the night time toward morning. This influence may be either in the nature of a caress from God or of a chastisement.

Yet again God influences the soul when a man gives himself entirely up to Him, waiting solely upon God's blessed will, truly disengaged from love of self and of all created things. Then the eternal Father, finding his creature's will offering no manner of resistance, draws him in a way that causes his soul to adhere to Him in an especially affectionate manner. This drawing is called a union, an embracing. Its gift is the possession of the Supreme Good, Who made Heaven and earth and all things for our sake, Who came on earth and humbled Himself to the death of the cross. It is because man is dearer to God than all Heaven's glory or that of earth, that He seeks to possess him, and that He desires to guide him in all his ways. This attraction for man it was that turned God's gracious glances upon Christ's disciples, this is the reason of all the joys and sorrows with which He visited them. All was to fit them to respond to His drawing of their souls. And when at last the disciples allowed God to manage them after His own will, they answered His drawing perfectly. This will appear better as we go on.

One might enquire: Why did God prepare the disciples for this privilege and does not thus prepare me and other men, at least in this wonderfully special manner? I answer that there are two reasons. One is God's free choice, by which He prefers some men rather than others for the bestowal of His most familiar love, just as a king by his royal freedom of choice, calls to his privy council certain of his nobles rather than others. Another reason is that some men correspond better with God's invitation and more diligently co-operate with it than others do, using every means at hand, overcoming all obstacles. This extraordinary Divine drawing was given to our dear disciples, because they prepared for it by most hearty prayers for pardon. They lamented most sincerely their former dullness of heart, and their unworthy lives while their beloved Master had been with them. They painfully called to mind His holy life and bitter death, His boundless love for them, His giving up all that man holds dear for their sakes; and they despised their own stupidity and ingratitude. Then they set a watch over themselves, abandoned themselves wholly into God's hands, cut themselves loose from all attachments as far as they were able, and begged God's help to fully complete their disengagement from earthly things. And in that frame of mind they humbly waited on God's blessed will. This explains why they were so specially favored.

One might object that the disciples could not thus prepare for God by their own power, for it is written: "Without Me you can do nothing" (John xv, 5); it is God who has led them through these degrees of preparation, and drawn their wills to Him. In answer I say that it is true that without God's general sanctifying influence we can do no good thing, and that without the Holy Spirit's particular influence we can take no single step in advance. And yet it also stands true that we have our part to perform, for it is certain that we can resist the Holy Ghost and cling to self in spite of Him. God does not sanctify a man without his own free will. Our eyes cannot see without light shining; and yet when the light beams we must open our eyes, or we shall not see, in spite of our having the light. No matter how brightly the sun shines, if I bandage my eyes with a thick cloth, it shines not for me; in spite of all the sunshine I do not see. Thus, therefore, when the eternal Father cast His light upon the disciples, they stripped off all bandages, and set aside as far as they could all things else that intervened between them and Him. Then God did His work, and drew them to Him with a special attraction. This was the work of the beloved Son of God, the guide of all hearts. He pierced every obstacle with His light, He banished every hindrance to the full enlightenment of their souls.

The second drawing is now to be considered. By it the heavenly Father enabled them to answer His first attraction in a spirit of entire and permanent self-renunciation. This He had taught them by His beloved Son: "Do not possess gold, nor silver, nor money in your purses; nor scrip for your journey, nor two coats, nor shoes, nor a staff" (Matt. x, 9, 10). Anyone can see, that to obey this a strong drawing away from all bodily comfort is needed. It is a call to enter the school of eternal light, which teaches us to cast our heart's affections high above even the third heaven, to say nothing of all the things of time. Besides this, they must give no place whatever in their souls to any sense of proprietorship; and, joined to this, they are to cultivate a spirit of repose, withdrawing into the unchanging tranquillity of the secret depths of their hearts, far from the storm, that is to say, the imperfections, of the outward life. There they become, as it were, partakers of that light eternal that is God—a light clear and steadfast, different from the light of the sun and moon, which alternates with darkness. Thus did the disciples need to be released from the narrowness and the degradation and the unrest that is essential to created things, and to be freed from all bodily fetters. St. Jerome says: "As it is impossible that a stone can have the wisdom of an angel, so is it impossible that God can communicate Himself in time or in the things of time."

And now occurs a question. Since God draws some men to Him by means of joy and others by means of sorrow, by which of these did He draw the disciples? The answer is found in considering their life. It was passed in our Saviour's company in much hardship, ending in great shame and distress. So they were drawn to God more by sorrow than by joy. And especially after their Master's cruel death were they in a state of bitter suffering, until they had become entirely detached. And thus, by the special favor of their heavenly Father, they were made fit to receive the Holy Spirit by the way of suffering. The drawing through sorrow is a safer way than that through joy. And it is in this sense that St. Gregory understands the psalmist: "A thousand shall fall at thy side, and ten thousand at thy right hand" (Ps. xc, 7) ; meaning that a thousand helpers shall fail thee in time of sorrow and persecution, but ten thousand in time of joy and prosperity.

And the way to God through sorrow is more like Christ's way in all His life, and in His death. It is, besides, a better sign of God's love, for it is written: "Such as I love, I rebuke and chastise" (Apoc. iii, 19). It is, indeed, true that the disciples enjoyed a close familiar companionship with the Divine Master, but it was embittered by the knowledge that for every gift they got they must suffer the death of all self-love. And as fast as God relieved them of one suffering he sent them another just as hard—for God is always accustomed to thus treat his beloved friends. The disciples found this to be the case, and so must they keep on suffering to the end, according as their heavenly Father arranged for them. Until at last their sorrow was turned into joy, and they were glad to suffer for the name of Jesus.

The third drawing of the heavenly Father, had the effect of freeing the disciples from thinking of the humanity of Christ under gross bodily forms. God granted them deliverance from this and all other kinds of such mental images in their union with Him, just as if He had but now newly created their spiritual existence. This was necessary, if they were to enter the glorious school of the Holy Spirit. Four reasons may be given for this. The first is that truth and love—for about these is all teaching imparted—can, strictly speaking, have no images. Can any painter in the world picture truth and love, whether in the inner or outer order of existence? Whatever form comes forth into our minds from love is not the form of love's own self; and the same is to be said about images of truth. The second reason is that truth and love are not, in this high school, taught by the external images and figures found in books. For now the truth is imparted interiorly; it is spoken without words or figures or forms of any created kind, which, indeed, are not according to truth's essential nature. Therefore did the humble St. Francis exhort his brothers in his rule, that they should not busy themselves much with books and writings. If they were unlettered, let them not be too anxious to learn to read, but rather be absorbed above all things in striving after the spirit of God, and with pure hearts pray for His holy operation in their souls.

Thirdly, one is to renounce such images and forms in the mind, because in the holy school of God, wisdom is learned by humility, speech by silence, life by death, knowledge by forgetting. John slept when he gazed upon the fountain head of eternal wisdom. When Paul in his trance looked upon eternal truth, he knew not whether his soul were in the body or out of the body. In like manner must the souls of the disciples be imageless, if they would have places in such a school. Fourthly, when the mind is occupied with images, these run through the imagination in the order and succession of time. Now that is not the way with the Holy Spirit's highest school, wherein not images nor intervals of time, but the touch of God, quicker than a flash, moves the soul and enlightens it. St. Gregory says: "The Holy Ghost is a marvelous master workman. He takes up His abode in a fisherman and makes him a preacher; He takes up His abode in a cruel persecutor and makes him a teacher of nations; He takes up His abode in a publican and makes him an evangelist." Who is like this master workman? To teach everything that He pleases He requires no time—a single touch and all is taught the soul—nothing more is necessary.

Now from these four reasons, it is plain that the disciples' souls must be drawn away from forms and images. And yet in this drawing, they did not see all that St. Paul did when he was rapt into the third heaven;

for, as St. Augustine thinks, Paul and Moses on the mount saw the Divine Essence direct and without any intermediation. This was not granted to the disciples, because they still were conscious of being in their bodies. And yet in their inmost souls they were so flooded with Divine light, that they experienced essentially the same as St. Paul did, some more completely than others.

The fourth drawing was that whereby the heavenly Father drew the disciples out of themselves. He emptied them of self and self-seeking, so that they stood in entire freedom from self-enthrallment, and were wholly disengaged from self-interest. All complaint now ceased among them, and all anguish and pain was dead. Herein was perfected most highly the first drawing, in which they were started toward perfect Divine union, and of which we have already treated. For now the eternal Father shall not meet with any resistance from their natural inclinations in His designs for their sanctification. This drawing is to give God His place as master in their souls, a free and undivided and most loving supremacy. From it they shall learn His perfections and be made like unto Him. No wonder that they must be drawn out of and away from self, for selfhood is wholly inconsistent with Divine liberty, love and nobility.

And now one might inquire: Did the disciples' natural life now die within them, since all forms and images were drawn out of their minds? Is nature now entirely dead? The answer is, no, nature is not now dead within them. Nay, in this their self-renunciation they are more truly natural than ever before. For whatsoever the Lord of nature operates in his creature, that is to be judged most perfectly natural, and resistance to it is resistance to nature. Thus says St. Augustine: "That the rod was turned into a serpent in the Old Testament was not against nature, because it was done by the will of God." And so I say, that inasmuch as the disciples yielded themselves wholly to God's will, they were in the highest degree natural. Their nature did not die, but it was elevated into the right order of existence. As to mental images and forms, they still had them no less than before, but they did not direct them upon selfish ends nor any otherwise than according to God's will. When I said that they were emptied of all images, my meaning was, that these forms in the soul were now like a candle in the light of the noonday sun. The candle shines as much as ever, but its beams are mingled and lost in the sun's rays, which are now the means of distributing the candle's light. Thus do the mental images and the whole nature of the apostles, work through the illumination of the Divine light. They use that Divine light, and are made thereby truer to nature and have more forms and images than ever before.

The fifth drawing now took place. By it the heavenly Father, finding the souls of His disciples in all freedom of spirit and entirely set at liberty from self and created things, drew them into a proportionately close union with Himself. God had obtained His way and purpose with them, for He could have asked no more from them than entire self-surrender. And on their part, all their aspirations for the possession of God were now fulfilled. Nor was it that the Holy Ghost gave them Himself alone, but that God the Father and God the Son gave themselves also in the fulness of the indivisible Godhead. For when we attribute love to the Holy Ghost (as we do wisdom to the Són), so we must remember that in the distinction of the Divine persons it is proper to infinite love to unite the Father and the Son in the one Godhead.

And now you might enquire, as to whether or not God drew all the disciples to Himself in the same degree of love, and endowed them with the same degree of holiness, since they were all equally absorbed in Him and given up to Him. I answer that although all of them were equally detached in spirit, nevertheless they turned to God with different degrees of love and with varying ardor. It was with them as with the angels who remained true to God; they differed one from another in the greatness of their love, and God gave Himself in different degrees to them, although each and all partook of His union. Thus were God's gifts granted to all the disciples, but not in equal distribution. The beloved disciple John, for example, inasmuch as he gazed more profoundly into the Godhead, was the more richly gifted. But we must remark that God is wholly free in .the granting of His favors, and bestows them just as He wills, and for no other reason than his Own will. And we must bear in mind, that God gave Himself personally to the disciples not only on Pentecost, but on many other occasions. For Richard of St. Victor and other teachers inform us, that as often as sanctifying grace is given us, so often is the person of the Holy Ghost imparted. Therefore they had received Him personally many times before, but they had not then been entirely detached from creaturs, nor had they received the fullness of His gifts. And in this sense it was that they received Him for the first time on Pentecost.

The sixth drawing of the disciples into the Holy Ghost's high school, was a peculiar enlightenment of mind. By this grace the most secret meaning of holy scripture was imparted to them, and the truth of God was revealed nakedly to them, and that in a way wholly incomprehensible to all the doctors in the schools. God's greatness was first presented to their souls, implanting deep within them the gift of filial fear, there to remain till the end of their lives. Besides this, they were taught a universal power to do good, joined to a deep insight into God's being—the gift of fortitude. In addition, they were shown how to keep not only God's commandments, but also how to observe the counsels of Christ—the gift of counsel. Joined to these was the gift of piety, the enjoyment of the sweet familiarity of sons with their father, in their union with God. To this, again, was added a penetrating knowledge of God's creatures and all their mutual distinctions, with power to detect the difference between God's supernatural light and that of our natural reason—the gift of science. God also taught them to compare their present spiritual state with former conditions, granting them thereby the gift of understanding. Finally He bestowed the gift of wisdom, and with it gave them a most precious union with Himself, and a manner of life altogether Divine. This was what God taught in His high school of the Holy Ghost, namely His seven spiritual gifts; just as He teaches us in the school of nature His seven natural sciences, and in that of holy faith, the seven sacraments.

You might enquire whether or not the disciples, being thus taught in the sublime school of the Holy Ghost, learned all the knowledge learned in natural and human schools. I answer yes, in so far as human art and science conduces to God's glory and to man's eternal welfare: they were taught it all, from the course of the stars down to the simplest knowledge. But otherwise not; whatever does not benefit the soul they were not taught, nor did that leave them less happy, less perfect. Thus says St. Augustine: "How miserable is the man who knows all things and knows not God; and how blessed is he who knows God, and knows nothing at all about anything else." Whosoever knows God and all things else, is not at all happier from knowing what is not God: God alone it is that makes him happy. May God help us to this happy state; may He thus draw us to Himself, and thus cause His light of truth to shine in our interior souls. *Amen.*

Knowing God

Synopsis—God is known by our resemblances to Him—These are in our virtues—And He is known by contrast, when we consider our sins and our evil tendencies, which are directly contrary to Him— How our knowledge of God is increased by trials and contradictions, meekly born for His sake.

FIRST SERMON FOR TRINITY SUNDAY.

Amen, amen, I say to thee, that we speak what we know, and we testify what we have seen.—John iii, 11.

Dear children, this is the happy day when we celebrate the glorious feast of the blessed Trinity. And you should know that all our other festivals are to be valued on account of what we commemorate today, just as the blossoms of a tree are esteemed for the sake of its fruit. I know not what words to choose to fitly show its greatness, for it surpasses our power of expression, telling as it does of the reward of all our labors and giving them their perfect ending. As a seraph surpasses a beast in intelligence, so do the lessons of this day go beyond human reason. Therefore, St. Dionysius said: "Whatsoever a man says about the holy Trinity seems to be empty of truth, even like to a lie, for no man can in the least degree understand this Divine mystery." How then can one discourse about it, without saying things which in one's ignorance are, as it were, untruths?

Dear children, foolish men talk of the holy Trinity as if they had penetrated its mystery—a gift denied to all created beings. Let it be otherwise with you. Talk little of this sublime theme, as St. Paul admonishes us. Leave study of it and discourse about it to great doctors, who, however, can but stammer about it. Yet they must treat of it for the purposes of holy Church in refuting the errors of heretics. But such learned discoursing is not your privilege.

In my text Christ says: "We speak what we know, and we testify what we have seen." Applying this to the knowledge of the holy Trinity, dear children, then only Christ alone has seen it and known it. As to us here below, we can know nothing of it except through the witnessing of our Lord Jesus Christ. And He is a witness in two ways, one by similarity, the other by difference or contrast, namely in His lower and in His higher powers. If we lack either of these witnessings of His, we shall fail to reach a true knowledge. These two ways are like two sisters inseparably joined in their lives. It is not as if the knowledge in the lower faculties goes in advance and that in the higher follows after, but they must work together, inseparably associated. By this means the mind finds itself made ready for the knowledge to be gained by contrast, on account of already possessing the knowledge gained by similarities; and then *vice versa*. It is thus, too, one gains joy by sorrow, sorrow by joy; he gains honor by disgrace, comfort by misery. Dear children, these relationships cannot be achieved by the powers of our poor fallen nature, or in our outward life alone. But by the aid of Divine grace one may essentially reach the mutual effect of like upon unlike.

But nature must suffer many a bitter death, death inward and outward, before the soul stands absolutely indifferent to joy or sorrow. Ah, what fervent thanks do we owe to God for these many deaths, by dying which we gain possession of a glorious and Divine life—if we would only realize the gift of God. Children, we should carefully watch our souls, and yearn and long for, and sincerely pray for this death, which grants us so perfect a life. For by its means the enlightened spirit is indifferent to pain or pleasure, truly balancing like and unlike, incapable of disturbance by any happening whatsoever; hate or love of men, consolation and misery, being to such a soul, one in no wise different from the other.

We find many men, both of the clergy and the laity, who would gladly be perfect followers of Christ if all things were pleasant, if they met with no contradictions. But when opposition is met, inwardly or outwardly or from their fellow-men, then they turn off from God. And yet trouble would be much better for them, and more useful, than peace. Tribulation leads to the essence of truth and is its fruit, and peace is but its flower. Peace is serviceable to tribulation which it precedes, helping us to bear trouble. But only in the midst of tribulation is God born into our lives, all in a hidden manner. Hence must a man stand indifferent between the favorable and unfavorable circumstances of life. But alas, nowadays nobody wants to follow God on this road nor love Him in adversity—many would on this account almost hate Him and forsake Him.

These are by no means true witnesses of our Lord Jesus Christ, for He is truly typified by that brazen serpent which Moses hung up before the people, and upon which all must gaze if they were to be restored to health. Let us always look earnestly upon this symbol, and bear true witness to Him in all poverty of spirit and boundless self-denial. We should suffer all trials and all opposition with burning zeal, whether they afflict our inner souls or oppress us from without, coming from the evil one, from our corrupt inclinations, or from our neighbor. ·

And let me say in all truth, that if every trial were done and over, all contradictions passed and opposition overcome, then we should most earnestly invite them back again. For by suffering them again they might cleanse us from the rust that they had left after them. A true and enlightened man needs to suffer from the feelings and the tendencies to sin that lurk in his flesh and blood, in order to know himself thoroughly, and to hate his weakness and sinfulness. A great sinner, who stands amid his sinful inclinations, is sure to fall and is lost. A perfect man, on the contrary, struggling with his natural weakneses, is only made the purer, and from this painful conflict passes into eternal life. The bad man knows nothing of the steadfast resistance of virtue against vice, gladly if painfully maintained by a good man to the very end.

And now, children, let me ask why there is such a difference between these two men. both whose souls are nevertheless occupied with the forms and images of sin. I answer that they have an essentially different way of acting. The devout man suffers these imaginations for God's sake—God is exclusively his thought and his support; from God he accepts the sweet and bitter of life, giving himselt up to God wholly. The wicked man makes no account of God, and falls wilfully into sin; he would do so without any temptation. No matter how God would treat him, he would never be content. If he had his way, his whole life would consist in having much of everything without price or labor, and this state of mind is in the end his death. Therefore, dear children, if you seek God purely, and love Him in all your ways, nothing whatsoever can hurt you—if all the devils in hell pour all their malice and uncleanness through your soul and body and your flesh and blood, and if the wicked world joins all its baseness and filthiness to that flood of evil, as long as it all happens against your will, and if you had rather die than commit a single sin against God, then all this wickedness can do you not a hair's weight of harm, even though your temptation lasted ten years and longer. Nay, the very contrary. For this trial would undoubtedly merit a great reward, and would prepare your soul for incalculable good both here and hereafter. God works miracles in the life of such a man—a steadfast soul, that never falls away from the Divine friendship in word or work.

Therefore the Son of God teaches us in the gospel: "Unless a man be born again of water and the Holy Ghost, he cannot enter into the Kingdom of God" (John iii, 5). By the word ghost or spirit one may mean the joys of life, and by the word water, its sorrows. The ugly external aspect of adversity disguises its noble interior advantages. Be assured, children, that whosoever will persevere in patient suffering, to him will be unveiled a clear view of the unspeakably precious qualities to be found in suffering. This revelation is to be gained only by one who accepts adversity with a loving spirit, loving, that is to say, to suffer pain more than to enjoy pleasure, yea, even in all things and under all circumstances. The clearer the value of afflictions is understood, the deeper is the inner joy found in outward suffering. To this was Lucifer wilfully blind—he would be established in joy without passing through sorrow. And therefore did he lose all joy and was buried in unspeakable and eternal sorrow. But the good angels, faithful and true, were willing to suffer the sorrowful trial God imposed on them, and forthwith they were absorbed in the unspeakable joy of God.

Ah, children, how sweet is the fruit grown upon this soil—a spirit fully enlightened about adversity, and pervaded with Divine love. Such a man, entirely melted into God's will to receive all trials, is presently given a spiritual power far above his nature and rooted in the Divine life. He is cleansed from the imperfections of his inner and outer existence; he grows well accustomed to self-denial; and he is finally absorbed most sweetly in the Divinity. When a man does his own utmost, reaching the highest possible point of his striving, then does God's infinitude take up the work. In the innermost spirit of such a man the Divine light begins to gleam, and with it is imparted a supernatural force. Finally the soul is drawn out of itself into thoughts of God wholly beyond power of expression—a preparation on earth for the eternal happiness of Heaven. This is the work of God's power, a turning inward not to be told in words, not to be conceived in the mind. Although the soul is so far advanced beyond the previous time of suffering, yet that patient endurance has served to win it the grace of interior union. The steadfast uprightness of intention, the will all pliant to God's influence, the deep longings for God, all words and works offered for God, every pang of pain meekly borne for God's sake—this has all served to prepare the devout soul for the inward reception of God's heavenly visitation.

Children, this turning toward God is not the gift of angels or saints, much less of any earthly benefactor, but comes forth direct from the deepest heart of God Himself; by Him granted, by Him to be perfected. Into the Divine obscurity the soul enters, to be there joined to God in a Divine stillness. And now all sense of what is pleasant or unpleasant in life is quite lost, nay the soul's very identity seems gone, and its knowledge of God is so elevated, that it seems as if it were not knowledge, but just a perfect union.

You should know, children, that to find this happy lot, a man must die to all created things. Joy and sorrow, whether in body or mind, or in flesh and blood, must be indifferent to him. He must love God alone. He must diligently cultivate the interior virtues with a view to suffering gladly all adversity. He must behave himself very virtuously, be fond of a hidden life, never complain, never seek outward comfort—very different from those who have made little progress in virtue, who know little of God in their interior souls. Really good men fly from all the multiplicity of external human existence, are ever removing hindrances to virtue, offer up everything to God, and by this manner of life are brought to that blessed and ever-adorable Trinity of which I am wholly unworthy to speak, or even to have any knowledge. That such a grace may be granted to us, help us, O God the Father, and God the Son, and God the Holy Ghost. *Amen.*

The Trinity and the Interior Life

Synopsis—Definitions of the Trinity—Inner perception of the mystery—Witness of a pagan writer—How a detached soul is taught the divine generation interiorly—And also the divine procession —The imparting of the gifts of the Holy Ghost in this experience —Practical suggestions.

SECOND SERMON FOR TRINITY SUNDAY.

Amen, amen I say to thee, that we speak what we know, and we testify what we have seen, and you receive not our testimony. If I have spoken to you earthly things, and you believe not; how will you believe if I shall speak to you heavenly things.—John iii: 11, 12.

We read these words in the Gospel of this feast of the Holy Trinity, the most glorious feast of the year, the end and perfection of all others; just as the beginning and course and term of all creatures, especially reasonable creatures, is in God one and triune. We are at a loss for words to tell the glory of the Holy Trinity, and yet words must be used to endeavor to describe this overpowering mystery of the Godhead. To rightly discourse on this theme, is as impossible as to reach from earth to heaven; for as a needle point is compared to the bulk of the earth and sky, so, only a thousand times less, is all human speech and thought compared to the Trinity.

It is beyond all comprehension how God, who is so simply one in His essence, is yet with this essential unity three fold in personality. And, again, the distinction of the persons: how the Father begets His Son, and how the Holy Ghost proceeds from the Father and the Son, and yet remains in Himself, self-conscious; how the Father utters His eternal Word, and from the knowledge going forth therefrom there proceeds an inexpressible love which is the Holy Ghost; how this outflowing is also in turn an inflowing into inexpressible perfection of the deity's essential unity—all this is absolutely beyond our power to comprehend. So is the Father what the Son is and what the

Holy Ghost is in power, wisdom and love; and the Son and the Holy Ghost with the Father are all one; and yet is there great distinction between the persons, though one in nature mutually and formlessly inflowing and outflowing.

Many wondrous words may be uttered about this divine unity in distinction, but all must yet remain unspoken and uncomprehended, for it is better to feel this mystery than to speak of it. Nor is it pleasant to discourse about the Holy Trinity or even to listen to others discoursing, no matter from what source the words may be drawn, for everyone is unequal to the task. The mystery is a strange thing to us and far removed from us, deeply hidden, incapable of understanding even by the minds of angels. Men in high places must treat of it in order to defend it; let them do so, whilst we on our part shall be content to believe. St. Thomas says: "Let no man go beyond the teaching of the doctors of the Church; these have been disciples of the Holy Trinity in their lives, and therefore has the Holy Spirit guided them in their teachings." To feel the Holy Trinity is the sweetest experience; to err concerning it, is the worst calamity. Therefore refrain from disputation and hold your faith in all simplicity, giving your souls up to God, longing to have Him born within your souls, not after the manner of human reason, but in the essential depths of your being.

We shall experience the divine Trinity within us in proportion as we are conformed to it in all truth and reality. The resemblance to God is in our souls certainly by nature, though of course in no such noble manner as the resemblance of the divine persons one to another. Hence we need to cherish the determination to consider the divine image within us most attentively, the glory of which no man can rightly describe. For God is here formed in us in a formless way: truly is it formless, though spiritual writers often strive to picture this divine image to us by many forms and comparisons. All teachers say that He is in the highest faculties of our soul, memory, understanding and will, by means of which we are made rightly conscious of the Trinity. Yet all this is but in the lowest grade of perception of God's presence, for it is merely in the natural exercise of the soul's powers. St. Thomas gives us a plainer description: "The perfection of this divine image is rather in its operation in the soul and in the activity of its powers—the active memory, active understanding, active love." So far St. Thomas. Other doctors go much farther. They say it is in the most secret recesses of the soul that God is most essentially to be known, in which He acts, and exists, and enjoys His own divine life. And while that state continues a man can no more separate himself from God than from his own self. [This union is rooted in the depths; and therein has the soul by grace a participation of all that God has by nature.] As the soul yields itself to God, so is grace born in the highest degree within its interior life—there and in no other part.

The pagan writer Proclus says: "As long as a man is concerned with images of things beneath him, so long is it impossible for him to fathom the depths of his being." It seems to some of us a sort of delusion that men should think there is such an inner depth to our soul. Wilt thou realize its actual existence? Then renounce all multiplicity and observe thy inner life intelligently. Wilt thou have a yet clearer knowledge? Then renounce even thy reason's observation of the interior life—for reason's activity is beneath thee—and become one with the One. The same Proclus considers this state as a silent, insensible, slumbering and divine perception. Children, how great a shame it is that this heathen philosopher attained to such knowledge, while we Christians are so far from it and are so unequal to acquiring it. But our Lord teaches: "The Kingdom of God is within you"(Luke xvii: 21)—namely, in those interior depths, transcending all the operations of the mental faculties—there it is guaranteed by God's grace. But we do not search it out, as this day's gospel tells us: "We speak what we know, and we testify what we have seen, and you receive not our testimony." Alas, how can a brutish, sensual man, ever absorbed in outward things, accept this testimony of an interior life wholly incredible to him. Thus spoke the Lord by His prophet: "As the heavens are exalted above the earth, so are My ways exalted above your ways and so are My thoughts above your thoughts" (Isaias lv: 9). And thus our Savior reproached the Jews in this day's Gospel "If I have spoken to you earthly things, and you believe not; how will you believe if I shall speak to you heavenly things?"

Formerly, children, I spoke to you of the wounds of love, and you told me that you did not know what I was saying—and that was a discourse about earthly things: how then can you now understand

me, since our subject is the divine work in our interior soul? Your
life is wholly given up to outward occupation, all absorbed in the
activity of the senses, and this testimony of mine is not about that.
Our testimony is truly found in the depths of the soul, all formless.
There it is that the heavenly Father generates His only begotten Son
swifter a thousand times than the twinkling of an eye. It is done
in the swiftness of eternity, in an eternal newness of life, and in the
unspeakable glory of the divinity. Whosoever would experience this,
let him turn himself inward, abstract himself from all outward works,
suspend the activity of his faculties, and exclude from his imagination
all that it has drawn from the outer world. Then let him melt away
into the depths. And now the fatherly power of God will come and
call the soul through His only begotten Son. And as the Son is
begotten of the Father and returns again into the Father, so shall the
soul of this man be born of the Father in the Son, return into the
Father with the Son, and be made one with Him. It is thus that the
Lord would have us call Him our Father, and never cease to follow
after Him as He mounts upwards; as if to say: This day have I
begotten thee by My Son and in My Son. And at the same time the
Holy Ghost is poured into the inmost depths of the heart with unspeakable love and joy, bestowing His heavenly gifts of justice and
of knowledge.

A man then becomes most righteous and most gentle, and his knowledge of the path he must tread becomes entirely clear. But this
supposes that all virtues have already been acquired, for the gifts now
imparted lead the soul into a state of perfection beyond that of the
ordinary virtues. Then follow the passive virtues which work
together, namely, counsel and fortitude, to which are added the contemplative gifts. These are fear, which holds fast in all carefulness
the graces granted by the Holy Ghost; and understanding and
wisdom—the two highest—which give the taste of God's truth to the
soul. Children, the enemy of mankind antagonizes a man of that
kind more than all other men in the world.

Especially is he combatted by the more subtle demons, and hence
he is in special need of the gift of knowledge.

Children, a moment of this divine influence is better for the soul
than all the outward works a man can do. And the prayers of such a
man united so deeply to God, when offered for his friends living and

dead, are of more avail than the reading of a hundred thousand psalters by an ordinary Christian.

This is the true witnessing of the Holy Ghost within us that we are the Sons of God, as in this day's epistle it is spoken of. In this thy inner heaven there are three witnesses, the Father, the Word, and the Spirit, testifying to thee most truly that thou art God's child, and brightly illuminating thy soul's depths. This in turn reveals thy own self to thee with all thy defects in deed or omission, and that whether thou willest or not. All thy life is hereby manifested to thee if thou wilt but advert to it. If thou shalt heed this interior witnessing and be guided by it in thy outer and inner conduct, then shalt thou be exempt from the adverse testimony of the last day. If in word and work and life thou dost reject this hidden witnessing, then at the end of all it shall be thy condemnation, and thine the blame for it, not God's, for not God only but also thy own self shall be thy judge.

Therefore, dear children, keep a watchful eye upon your interior life, recognize God's witness there, and it will be a joy to you. Hast thou overcome thy external weaknesses? Then hasten home to thy interior soul. There thou shalt find thy real self—there more than in thy outward life, or in thy outward methods and devotions. We read in the Lives of the Fathers of the Desert that once a devout married man retired into a forest to escape the obstacles to his perfection, and that his wife in like manner went into a solitude. And soon this good man had two hundred brethren living under him and she had many women with her. This shows the value of single-minded and hidden retirement, a state of soul in which the senses with their methods are no longer in control.

But you might say: I am a help to interior souls, and I would gladly aid all those who are touched interiorly by God and have seen the divine light. And I answer that whatsoever external minded person forces good souls to accept his rude external methods in place of the interior ones, subjects himself to a terrible condemnation, for he thus hinders God's work more than the pagans and Jews did of old. Therefore, ye hard and censorious spirits, take heed to yourselves, with your bitter words and your scornful manner, how you meddle with these good souls.

And now, dear child, wouldst thou attain to the union of thy soul with the Holy Spirit, then must thou diligently do three things. One is to keep God and His honor in view in all that thou dost and in all that happens to thee, and make no account of thyself. The second is to hold a vigilant watch over thyself in all thy doings, keeping at home to thyself in thy thoughts, and recognizing thy utter nothingness; meanwhile cautiously observing thy surroundings. Thirdly, meddle not with what does not concern thee; what is not committed to thee, let it take care of itself—what is good, let it alone, what seems evil, trouble not thyself about it. Turn into thy interior life and therein abide, listening to the fatherly voice that there is calling to thee. If one were thus absorbed in the interior life, a great wealth of gifts would be bestowed on him, and he would be so enlightened that even priests would receive instruction from him.

Dear child, if thou wouldst forget all that has so far been said to thee in this discourse, yet hold fast to two thoughts. One is that thou shouldst be a little, insignificant thing in thy own estimation, and not in words but in the deep sincerity of thy soul, not in outward show but in the very truth of thy conviction. The other is that thou shouldst love God; and this should be not in the way of sentiment and feeling so much as essentially, and in the deepest interior life of divine love. Nor should this be simply an advertence to God in thy outward conduct, as we commonly understand when we speak of good intention. No, it is more than that. It is having God for one's end in one's very soul; just as a man racing towards a goal fixes his eye upon it; or one shooting at a mark never for an instant loses sight of it. That we may all obtain this interior spirit, that we may all totally annihilate self and find instead the Holy Trinity within ourselves, we pray the same Holy Trinity graciously to grant us. *Amen.*

On Holy Communion

Synopsis—God's goodness shown in the real presence—The process of assimilation between God and man—The bitter taste and the sweet nourishment—The inner change from the human into the divine—The good of frequent communion—Advice about preparation.

FIRST SERMON FOR THE FEAST OF CORPUS CHRISTI.

For My flesh is meat indeed.—John vi : 56.

This is a most blessed day, on which we venerate the precious body of our Lord Jesus Christ. Although the Sacrament of the Altar is honored every day of the year, and has a special festival on Maunday Thursday, yet our holy mother, the Church, sets this day apart that we may do particular honor to our Lord in the blessed Sacrament, thereby renewing our devotion to Jesus really present with us. Thus has holy Church done her part; and she has met with hearty response from her children, who honor our Lord in the blessed Sacrament by carrying Him in procession from one church to another, with splendid and costly ornaments, the sound of church bells and of organs and of loud musical chants.

Children, all this is good, because it helps the interior praise of Christ in our souls—everything even the littlest may be made to serve that end. Let us gladly do reverence to God every way we can think of— the humblest little earth worm, had it but the use of reason, would willingly lift up its head to God and then bow down in all reverence to Him. But as to man, he has a high degree of praise to offer, for he has the privilege to love and honor God out of the depths of a heart endowed with intelligence; and this far surpasses all that he can ever do without this in the external order of religion.

And he can reach a yet higher grade of praise, namely, by having so full a knowledge of God's greatness and of his own littleness, that he feels that he cannot praise Him enough—a veneration of God exceeding all speech, song, memory and understanding. A certain master teaches, that the man who discourses most beautifully of God, is the one who from his knowledge of the interior riches of God, can be content to remain silent about Him. Once a certain doctor praised God with many words, and another doctor bade him hold his peace, saying: "Thou blasphemest God." And both were right. It is a wonderful thing, that the unspeakable Goodness is so great that no one can rightly praise it. Right praise of God is infinitely beyond the two degrees we have mentioned, and exceeds all words and methods of veneration. Let a man be absorbed in God, blending selfhood into God, until in this man's soul it is God who praises Himself and returns thanks to Himself; and whosoever reaches this state, it can hardly be supposed that God will permit him to fall away from Him.

Our Lord says: "My flesh is meat indeed, and my blood is drink indeed," and He adds: "He that eatheth My flesh and drinketh My blood, abideth in Me and I in him." Behold our Lord's fathomless humility, in that He is silent about His infinite greatness, and speaks only of the least of His attributes. His greatness is His adorable Godhead, and yet he speaks only of His flesh and His blood. Yet in the Holy Communion His blessed soul and His divine nature are also present. His amazing and unspeakable love for us is shown in that He was not content to make Himself our brother and assume our poor human nature. No, He became man that man might become God— nay more: He insists that He shall become our food. Of this St. Augustine speaks: "No nation is so great as the Christian people, nor any to whom God has come so close as to us: we feed upon our God." How wonderful a love is His, to invent this way of union. This love overwhelms us; it should wound every heart of man with its overpowering greatness. No act in our material existence is so close to us, or enters so intimately into our bodily life, as eating and drink- ing. And this is the reason why our Savior chose this marvellous way of being brought into the closest and most interior union with us.

Let us consider the processes of taking bodily food; it may seem a gross thing, but it serves to illustrate the Holy Communion. St. Bernard says: "When we eat this food, we ourselves are eaten." When we take food we first chew it, then it passes into the stomach and is changed in the heat of our organs of digestion, which separate the coarser and useless portions from the good parts; sometimes out of a whole pound of food only a small portion really serves for our nourishment, and the rest is rejected, the good part passing through three processes of digestion. When the bodily powers have done their work, a higher force comes from the soul, making flesh and blood, and distributes the food into the head and the heart and every member, filling the veins with blood. It is thus with us and our Lord's body and blood, only differently in this: whereas our bodily food is changed into ourselves, on the contrary when we receive our Lord's body and blood we are changed into Him. Thus did He say to St. Augustine: "I shall not be changed into thee, but thou shalt be changed into Me." Whosoever receives this divine food worthily, it penetrates the veins of his most interior existence.

Let us explain St. Bernard's saying: "When we eat this food, we ourselves are eaten." For then God feasts upon us; as He enters He scourges us for our sins, which He reveals plainly to us—His divine presence scourges our conscience. As one turns his food over and over again in his mouth and continually bites it, so is a man cast back and forth under God's scourging, namely, in anguish, dread and sorrow about his sins. Dear child, gladly endure this biting of God's presence in thee, let Him eat thee and chew thee to pieces, seek not to escape His chastisement, and offer Him the deep sighs of thy heart: Oh, Lord, have mercy on me a poor sinner; and meantime keep close within thyself. Be sure that all this is more for thy profit than much pious reading or praying if these should take thee out of thyself. But be on thy guard lest the evil one cunningly afflict thee with excessive sadness about thy sins; for he would gladly sow in thy heart the seed of bitter sorrow. Our Lord sows the seed of a sorrow that is sweet and good.

After the chastisement comes a gentle softening of one's soul, loving trust, divine confidence, holy hope: it is now that God is absorbing and, as it were, swallowing thee. And just as well-cooked food when it is chewed, softly and gently sinks into the stomach, so shall it be with thee in Communion when thy conscience has been prepared. But thou must give thyself up to our Lord with all trust, and then shalt thou be gently absorbed in Him. If we have followed St. Paul's directions about the Eucharist: "Let a man prove himself, and so let him eat of that bread, and drink of the chalice" (I Cor. xi: 28), then our Lord will consume us as we consume our food. This is done by renouncing all our selfhood, and destroying out of our lives all attach-ment to created things. The more carefully food is masticated the more it becomes unlike its former self. Thou shalt find out if thou art absorbed into God as His food, if thou are so changed as to find nothing in thyself except Him, and findest thyself nowhere else but in Him. For does He not say: "He that eateth My flesh and drinketh My blood abideth in Me and I in him." Therefore must thou be stripped of thy old self, as it were, by the divine mastication of thy soul—just as thou dost change thy food by chewing it. If anything will be turned into what it is not, surely it must cease to be what it is—when wood is turned into fire it is perforce no longer wood. If thou shalt be changed, as it were, into God thou must cease to be thyself.

Again, our Lord says: "He that eatheth Me, the same shall live by Me." Hence, if thou wouldst gain the life of Jesus, thou must receive the blessed Sacrament often, for thereby the old Adam within thee shall be wholly destroyed. As the forces of nature fill our veins with the strength that is in our food, making it one thing with ourselves, so shall the divine food entirely change thee into itself. Thou shalt know if this is done, if after receiving this Sacrament thou feelest thy heart wholly detached from whatever is not God. And this new life within thee will work outwardly and be manifested in thy conduct and actions and conversation. This adorable Sacrament separates all that is bad, profitless and superfluous, casting it all out of the soul; and then God enters into all one's life, love, thought, intention, making all newer, cleaner and more divine.

This Sacrament cures a man's inner blindness and gives him to know himself, teaching him how to turn away from self and all created things. Thus says the wise man: "With the bread of life and under-standing, she shall feed him" (Eccli. xv: 3). This divine food so changes a man into itself, that his whole life is regulated by God. He is led by God, he is changed by God, through this food. Therefore, if a man goes to Communion and still remains empty of heart, vain and arrogant, his demeanor frivolous, if he be yet addicted to fine clothes, fond of amusements—if, I say, he wilfully adheres to these defects, then his going to Communion is a perilous thing. Better a thousand times that he stayed away. He goes to confession, indeed, but he does not give up the occasions of sin. Not the Pope himself can forgive the sins of an impenitent man; yet such a one goes to the altar along with the rest.

Prudent confessors will tell each one how often he should receive Communion, some every week, others every month; and these should be able to spend a week before and after each Communion very piously. Yea, yea, and nay, nay, should be their guileless rule of life, besides much moderation at their morning and evening meals. Others, again, may receive Communion at the great festivals, and some at Easter. These will do little enough if they spend all Lent in preparation. And some, alas, should never approach the holy table as long as they have no grief for their sins nor any firm purpose of amendment of life— such a óne would make himself guilty of the body and blood of our Lord Jesus Christ.

Children, you know not how serious a matter this is, for some seem to think going to Communion a sort of recreation. But I assure you that it is a matter of life and death as to what diligence one exercises in preparing for this Sacrament. Any man who neglects the teaching of the Church's ministry in this matter of preparing for Communion, falls into a state of the greatest possible danger. There is a class, besides, who will go to Comunion weekly, often actuated by no spirit of devotion nor moved by any divine impulse, but rather out of mere custom, or because they see others going. No, no—let none yield to such a tendency. If, however, a man would approach the altar weekly out of gladness of heart towards God, and with reverent fear, and in order to strengthen his soul against damnation—by no means to put on airs of perfection—a man, in fact, who is of good life and carefully guarded against the occasions of sin, then let him do it, after obtaining the counsel of his father confessor. Let me tell you this: if I found a man who had been a vile sinner, and who now has given up his vices and turned to God with all his heart, I had rather give him Communion every day for half a year, than do so a single time to a half-hearted and lukewarm man. For I believe that thereby I should drive the world out of my poor penitent's heart.

I have shown you the reasons why the holy Sacrament does these tepid men so little good—men who once had some trace of God in them, and who now after Communion remain cold-hearted. One reason is a secret sin, a deed of inner or outer wickedness. Perhaps it is the sin of unguarded speech. The harm thereby done is often incalculable—attend to that, for God's sake, or you will come to nothing. Another reason is going to Communion not out of real love but from custom.

Now there are some customs that are really good, such as that of staying home in one's interior self after Communion, the lack of which does much harm, and hinders the realizing of the good effects of this heavenly food. The immediate fruits of Communion are perceptible for three or four days, if one will but advert devoutly to them. Dwelling with one's interior self sweetly and happily, one will not fail to experience them, no matter in what circumstances he may be placed or in what company, as long as he avoids as much as possible what hinders his soul's solitude. Be sure that if thou keepest faithfully to thyself, the holy Sacrament will keep thee company and work its way in thee, changing thee into a noble being. Any priest whatsoever will serve thee for receiving this Sacrament, and it may happen to be better for thee than for himself. And every time thou hearest mass thou shouldst cherish a longing for Communion, a practice which tends to train one's thoughts towards God. And may God grant us that we may all worthily receive this adorable Sacrament. *Amen.*

Dispositions for Holy Communion

Synopsis—The four requisites according to St. Dionysius: freedom from sin, the virtues of Christ, devoted to divine things, and peacefully disposed—How the onslaughts of Satan may be made a help —And the persecutions of men—Preference of divine visitations over self-chosen austerities—Daily communion—Spiritual communion—The holy inner silence that should follow communion— How to use this Sacrament in periods of inner desolation.

SECOND SERMON FOR THE FEAST OF CORPUS CHRISTI.

He that eateth My flesh and drinketh My blood abideth in Me and I in him. —John vi, 57.

Dear children, rightly to praise the holy and adorable Sacrament is beyond the power of the tongues and hearts of men, and yet to that end are our devotions now directed, for in it is concentrated all our joy, all our hopes of salvation. Let us avail ourselves of St. Bernard's words (although they may seem somewhat coarse to us), as, by comparison with bodily food, he tells of the qualities of this heavenly nourishment—of the chewing and the swallowing, the digestion and the assimilating of the Son of God. Proud men and subtle minds may not be pleased with such figures of speech, but a humble spirit always loves simple ways of explaining divine things. Thus says our Lord: "I confess to Thee, O Father, Lord of heaven and earth, because Thou hast hid these things from the wise and prudent and hast revealed them to little ones" (Matt. xi: 25).

Dear children, we must view this glorious gift of God with both enlightened reason and ardent love. How humble is our Lord, to thus give Himself to us under such lowly appearances as bread and wine, so that all may partake of Him just as they do of their ordinary food. This can mean nothing else than His purpose to press in so close to us, to sink so deep within us, to be so entirely made one with us as

possibly could be—made one with us with all His gifts and graces.
He might, indeed, have chosen to come to us with greater outward
splendor, as He does sometimes miraculously appear in Communion,
according to St. Hildegrade. He was once seen by a sister of our
order with her bodily eyes, lighting up priest and altar with indescribable splendor, surrounded by His glorious angels, whilst He imparted
to her soul the most beautiful sentiments. But in this era of grace
nothing is more precious to us than receiving this adorable Sacrament
devoutly and humbly. Nor is there anything more frightful than
Communion received unworthily or without preparation. Hence,
says our beloved St. Dionysius: "Four things are necesary for receiving the holy Sacrament: first, to be free from all sin; second, to be
clothed with the virtues of our Lord Jesus Christ; third, to be emancipated from self and given over to God; fourth, to be God's temple."

As to being free from sin: that means clear knowledge of one's sins,
then Sacramental confession of them and acceptance and performance
of the penance imposed according to the rules of holy Church. After
that let a man interiorly sigh for a perfect knowledge of his sinfulness,
a spiritual exercise of far more benefit than vacantly reciting vocal
prayers. In addition to this one must have a firm purpose of amendment, including a determination to avoid all occasions of sin in the
future. These dispositions being posessed, one's soul is set free from
sin. The second is to possess the virtues of our Lord Jesus Christ,
namely, mildness, obedience, purity of intention, patience, gentleness
and mercy, readiness to be silent, and love for all men, friends and
enemies, good and bad, for the sake of God. The third is emancipa-
tion from self and subjection to God. This means that having become
possessed of the virtues of Christ, one cultivates peacefulness of soul
in God's inner presence. Then it is that one experiences the meaning
of our Lord's words: "He that eatheth My flesh and drinketh My
blood abideth in Me and I in him." One should with carefulness
preserve this peace, allowing himself never to be disturbed by any
word or deed, for it must not be mistaken for any natural state of
restfulness, but rather the inward peace that belongs to God's Spirit
alone, extending to all sorrow and joy, all things natural and spiritual.
For in so far as a man is in God truly, just so securely is he placed in
quietness of soul; and in so far as he is out of God, so is he in unrest,
And when he has thus entered essentially upon peace, he becomes the
temple of God in very truth, for the abode of God is in peace. Thereby

does he attain to the fourth holy state spoken of by St. Dionysius, in which God inspires all this man's works, he being now only God's instrument for both his interior and exterior activity.

But let us again consider St. Bernard's words about receiving our Lord in holy Communion: "As we have eaten Him, in like manner shall we be eaten by Him." Now by the word eating he means—as we have already said—the punishment and, as it were, the biting which the Lord inflicts on our conscience, and which He causes all created things to inflict upon it. Herein does a man find himself hunted like a wild animal that the emperor's huntsmen pursue, in order that their master can capture him. We know that the emperor is better pleased to have the animal resist so that the hounds shall bite and tear him, rather than if he meekly submitted. Dear children, the eternal God is the divine monarch who will possess Himself of our hunted souls, and, as it were, feed upon them. His dogs are the evil spirits, who pursue and bite the soul with many unclean temptations. Again they assail the soul with pride, avarice and various other evil suggestions; now from one side, again from another, striving to throw him into despondency and excessive sadness. I say to thee, stand thy ground. Nothing of this can hurt thee. If thou shalt ever succeed in the spiritual life thou must thus be hunted.

But besides the evil spirits, this world and thy fellowmen will hunt thee with their injurious words and their false accusations. And yet further thy own imperfection, thy tendency to yield to corrupt nature, will assail thee. And thus is a man hunted and driven by everything that is bad, if he is ever going to acquire patience by true humility and mildness in all things of soul and body. Meanwhile he must culti-vate a merciful and forgiving feeling for those dreadful men who have thus persecuted him, scoffed at him, tortured him, despised him, and maligned him to others as a wicked man. Let him now cry out from a heart all full of love: O eternal Lord and God of all creatures! Have pity upon them and upon me. Thus pray to God. Also be on thy guard by thy very soul lest thou endeavor to escape from thy trials— as if by running away from thy hunters across hedges and through the woods: our wild animal keeps to the straight, smooth road that lies before him, nor does he bite back at his hunters nor bellow at them.

Now the heavenly Father has His hunting hounds everywhere—in convents and monasteries; in our homes and in cities, and in the forests; and you may be certain that all chosen friends of God are going to be sorely hunted by all created things. As the hart is driven by the hunters, tormented with thirst, so must thou be driven on till thou findest thy refuge in God. To make us thirst for God alone in time and in eternity—that is the divine purpose in allowing us men to be thus hunted, each one according to his special circumstances of life. Go forward, then, in all humility, patience and mildness, for without doubt thou shalt at last come to our Savior's sweet fountains, which will refresh thee beyond the power of words to describe. Once thou hast truly gained His refuge, thou shalt attain the highest perfection, and then will flow into thy spirit all those noble virtues of which we have already treated, humility, merciful sympathy, divine love for God and thy neighbor.

Ah, dear children, how sad it is that the universal virtue of love of God is quenched out of the world, gone from all states of life. If we could find a man pursuing the course of divine love, we ought to revere him above all others, no matter what his condition in life. All creatures should do him service, for he has gained the eternal inheritance of the heavenly Father. And yet God sometimes withdraws His comfort from these elect souls, because He thereby advances them still further in virtue; they must yet again be willing to be hunted by all creatures, suffering in silence and in self-abnegation, complaining by no word or action.

Such an immolation of the soul to God is more pleasing to Him, and is more valued by all choice spirits, than any kind of self-chosen means of perfection, such as fasting, vigils, reciting prayers—yea, or a thousand strokes of the discipline every day, although it all be done for God's sake. The reason is because the trials sent by God work their good effects in the inner depths of thy soul—and there it is that God must be united to thee in very truth. Stand this test bravely, and God will make thee worthy to partake of His heavenly nourishment in holy Communion as often as thy soul desirest, were it even as often as every day. For the High Priest of eternal truth would thus permit, since He has at heart in everything He does for thee thy welfare for time and for eternity.

How perilous a thing for a man to approach this holy table unprepared and unworthy, especially if he be absorbed in the love of creatures living or dead, and unwilling freely to give them up for the love of God. How different is it with the soul that gladly gives up every creature of God for God's own sake, as far as he is conscious of loving them and realizes that God would wean him from them. Such a one, entirely resigned to God's chastening hand, wholly willing to be hunted by God and by all created things, is furnished with the great virtue of holy patience. If thou art such a one, then the oftener thou receivest Christ the better for thee.

Art thou conscious that God's work of purification is increasing within thee, and that thy soul is being softened to its influences and humbled beneath God's hand in real detachment? Dost thou perceive an increase of the love of God in thee? Dost thou also perceive the lessening and the quenching of thy desires after earthly things, with an increase of childlike and reverent fear of God? Are these thy dispositions in very truth? Then the wide world does not possess a more profitable thing for thy soul than to receive the body and blood of our dear Lord Jesus Christ. Dost thou inquire how often? St. Ambrose, in commenting on the words, "Give us this day our daily bread," takes them to mean daily Communion. But where shall we find a priest so kind as to allow us to be daily communicants? But be not distressed if thy priest, dear child, shall refuse thee this privilege. Earnestly endeavor to maintain thy detachment of spirit, keep thy soul in quiet peace, fall back upon the thought of thy own nothingness, and meanwhile do not doubt but that the Lord will grant thee in compensation spiritual gifts greater, perhaps, than those which thou wouldst have received in the holy Sacrament. Eat and drink of Him spiritually and in the Holy Ghost, for even then His words will be true: "He that eateth My flesh and drinketh My blood, abideth in Me and I in him." This kind of dwelling in Him is one of the degrees of holiness granted by this Sacrament.

And there are yet two more degrees, both of them higher and more glorious than any we have yet spoken of. By one we receive graces of both knowledge and feeling, bestowing on us the emptying of self unto its annihilation. The other is feeling without knowledge, an oppression of spirit born of this annihilation; for in proportion as selfhood possesses us, just in that degree must our anguish be bitter and sore.

Thus does St. Bernard teach us, when he says that we must be consumed as food by God in our process of detachment. For as food suffers a change into something not itself, so must we, if we would be truly united to God. All our preferences and our activities and our acquisitiveness and selfhood must be destroyed. Nothing less than this can happen to us, for two rival existences cannot be united into one, of that we may be sure. If heat enters in cold must go out. If God enters in all created life that is not sanctified must go out, and all created proprietorship. If God really acts in thee, thou must rest in a passive state, all thy powers being stripped of their own activity, their own initiative, placed in self-renunciation and, as it were resting in their own nothingness. The more perfect is that sense of thy own nothingness, the truer and the more essential is thy union with God. See the annihilation of self that happened to the adorable soul of our beloved Lord Jesus Christ. If it were possible (as it is not) that any man could show the same in his soul, his union with God would be the same.

If God shall truly speak within thy soul, then all thy soul's powers must sit in silence. This is not a case of doing but of undoing. If bodily food shall be changed into the natural man, it must be first annihilated out of its own self and be made totally unlike itself, as if it had never been the food that once it was. If this be true of the food of our natural life, it is a thousand times more true of the food of our spiritual life. But, dear children, I must tell you that hurt is herein done by the interference of the human reason, which too often insists on having a share in this divine work, wanting to know all about it, and refusing to be willingly undone by God. Be on your guard against this; I warn you for God's sake and for the sake of your eternal welfare. And if frequently receiving the holy Sacrament be an aid to thee in yielding willingly to God, thou mayst receive it, even two or three times a week. But do not run to it over eagerly, especially when thou art conscious that God is interiorly leading thee to the degree of self-renunciation proper for the best effects of Communion.

Dear child, thou must know that a soul so placed feels an intolerable inward woe in its self-destitution, so that the whole earth seems too narrow for it, until it is at loss to know what ails it, so bitter is the oppression upon it, for God seems gone from it never to return. It is all caused by the self-surrender to God: it is a dreadful thing to wish not to die and yet be compelled truly to die to oneself. In this state St. Paul's words about the holy Sacrament are applicable to the soul itself: "As often as you shall eat this bread, and drink the chalice, you shall show the death of the Lord until He come" (I Cor. xi: 26). This showing of the Lord's death is not simply in words telling of the actual fact of His decease—that is no difficult thing. No; it is rather to show the Lord's death in the dying of the soul to itself by the power of His death. And this is hindered by three things, all of which thou must overcome. One is clinging too selfishly to the adorable Sacrament; the second, clinging in the same spirit to God's word; and the third, over-attachment to thy own chosen devotional practices. For in truth everything that might be a help to thee in ordinary circumstances may during this trial be turned into a hindrance. Ah, dear child, if in this thy time of anguish thou wouldst but make up thy mind willingly to suffer, and positively resist the tendency to break away from the visitation of God, that would avail thee more than all that thou couldst possibly do. And that is just the trouble; for many a one runs about from one counsellor to another, vainly seeking comfort, and therefore remains uncomforted by the eternal truth. Stand fast and be patient, and the very essence of that eternal truth will be born within thee.

One cannot express the harm that is done souls by yielding to nature's weakness, and seeking, while in this process of purification, to be relieved from the inner distress that accompanies it. Reason rises up within thee and demands an object for its activity; and it says to thee: Alas, what art thou about? Hast thou no end in life? Thou art neglecting thyself in everything. And then thou fanciest that thou must say prayers; and forthwith the evil spirit says: What art thou doing here? Thou art wasting thy time; thou shouldst be engaged in some good work; get up at once and set to work. After that come rude men with their favorite pious devices, and these say to thee: My dear man, what art thou about? Thou shouldst go to Church and listen to God's word. Now let me remind thee that all these are God's hunting dogs, and thou thyself art a hunting dog teasing and barking at thyself along with them, and saying to thyself: What ails thee to be wandering about this way?—thou shouldst receive the holy Communion.

Now children, while one is thus interiorly tried he should not expect to be relieved by the holy Sacrament. If thou camest to me for advice about going to Communion while thus suffering, I should cross-question thee to discover whether it were God moving thee thereto, or only an impulse of nature, or the force of pious custom. If nature or custom guided thee, then I would refuse to allow thee to receive Communion, unless, indeed, thou wert reduced to a state of misery simply unbearable. Then, indeed, once or twice a week thou mightst receive Communion; but not to relieve thee of thy distress—rather to strengthen thee in bearing it.

God's generation within thee shall never take place—be sure of that—until thou hast passed through this agony. Whatever gives thee relief, that same and not God is born in thee. Be sure that thy distressed nature had rather journey to Rome than patiently suffer this trial to the bitter end—a trial of far greater advantage than any other possible gift; for it is better to suffer than to labor. And sometimes this poor man calls to mind his former sweetness of devotion at Communion and while hearing the word of God, and afflicted nature would gladly enjoy that comfort again. But it has been withdrawn, and to that withdrawal the soul must submit in its inmost depths, in misery, in death—yea, a death more bitter to nature than any other death.

But, dear children, thou must not misunderstand me, as if I had forbidden thee the Sacrament and the word of God. Thou art aware that in the first two degrees nothing is more profitable to a blessed, a divine life than Communion and sermons—these stand above all else. Only this: in the present degree of God's dealing with the soul, everything that ordinarily helps the soul is liable to become a hindrance. For in seeking help the soul, as it were, turns its back on God and seems to say to Him: I will not go by Thy guidance, but I will go by my own—and that is to our Lord as if He were crucified again; for His adorable will cannot now be effectuated in that soul. Alas, that this incalculable benefit should be lost to that soul, simply because it will not yield itself up to suffer the want of all comfort in body and in spirit.

And now let us consider these words of St. Bernard: "I am eaten by God when I am transformed by Him; I am made one with Him when I am conformed to Him." And we exclaim: O blessed Father, when shall this sorowful state of soul have an end?—with all its undoing, and anguish, and pain. But O how noble an end that shall be, when at last the soul is made over again and new-formed in God, united to God. St. Paul teaches us this, having himself learned it in the school of God, in the third heaven: "But we all, beholding the glory of the Lord with open face, are transformed into the same image from glory to glory, as by the Spirit of the Lord" (II Cor. iii: 18). Therein does God's Spirit draw a man into Himself, changing him into Himself. We have already recalled that St. Augustine heard God speaking to him: "Thou shalt be changed into Me, not I into thee." As to how this change takes place the man himself is made aware, but not by any manifold way of knowing, but rather in a very simple way, beyond words to describe.

You should also know that there are men who are only in the first degree of those who follow devout practices, and to whom, nevertheless, the new forming of soul is granted. It comes as in a flash of supernatural light, sometimes once or twice a week. It is granted wholly according to God's merciful will, for it is something that cannot be merited. Sometimes it comes with clear knowledge, at other times without knowledge and in darkness. Such a man is left in a state of soul all wounded by love. But those of whom we treated above are fettered by love, being conformed to love and drawn into it, and one can better feel this condition than describe it. This class is made up of men wholly self-abandoned, perfectly well ordered—far beyond spiritual men who lack this divinely established degree of holiness. May God prepare us all for this detachment of spirit. May God the Father, and the Son, and the Holy Ghost perfect His great work within us, removing all hindrances. *Amen.*

The Dignity and Worth of Holy Communion

Synopsis—Difficulty of explaining so divine a gift—It is known only to very detached spirits—Various comparisons to help understand this—The elimination of defectiveness natural and acquired— Heretical exaggerations—Delusions of certain imperfect communicants—Marvellous results of careful preparation for communion— Daily communion according to St. Augustine—Striking comment on a passage from St. Thomas.

THIRD SERMON FOR THE FEAST OF CORPUS CHRISTI.

He that eateth My flesh, and drinketh My blood, hath everlasting life, and I will raise him up in the last day. For My flesh is meat indeed, and My blood is drink indeed.—John vi: 55,56.

The more a man receives from God the more is he a debtor; the greater is his debt of thanks and praise, honor and service to God. All devout practises lead to God and prepare the way for Him, so that a man may at last come to God and be in Him. and herein is the holy Sacrament both the end and the reward, for it gives us God without intermediary. It unites a man to God directly, in simple unity—the most adorable and superessentially divine of all gifts, far surpassing all others. The celebration of Holy Thursday is, therefore, not enough for us, for Easter Sunday comes too soon afterwards. Hence has holy Church remedied this difficulty by calling us to celebrate this festival of Corpus Christi with all possible thankfulness, praise and love.

"My flesh is meat indeed, and My blood is drink indeed." If understood as an outward ceremony, this Sacrament is but drinking and eating wine and bread; and thus one knows nothing of the unspeakable sweetness, the heavenly fruit, hidden in the Sacrament. The food of our bodies is dead matter, and gets its life from the man who eats it, who thereby gives it a noble destiny. But this sacramental food is living bread; it is the very essence of life, and all who are fed by it receive from it everlasting life—as our Lord teaches: "He that eateth

My flesh and drinketh My blood, hath everlasting life." And as He
spoke these words, many of His friends went away from Him; they
did not understand what He meant. "This saying is hard, and who can
bear it," they said. They understood Him only in the outward way
of the senses, and that was why they left Him, whereas in truth this
gift is far above the senses, for the food that is given and the giver
of the food are one.

Three things may here be considered. One is the pre-eminent dignity
of this food; the second, its inestimable worth to all who worthily
receive it; the third has reference to the preparation one should make
for this divine banquet. Now in speaking of all this, as God's grace
guides me, I am at a loss for words, or even thoughts; for this marvelous Sacrament surpasses all grasp of human reason, aye even angelic
thoughts. Dear children, only a perfectly detached man, one given
over wholly to the interior life, can rightly understand and inwardly
taste the meaning of the holy Sacrament. But even he could not frame
right words for its description, for sense and reason are wholly at
fault in its contemplation. And yet, alas, we find not a few seemingly
spiritual persons, who, from childhood to old age, rest in themselves;
they are engaged in multiform religious activity, and yet know nothing
of the real nature of this precious treasure, never enjoy the real taste
of this holy food, however often they may partake of it. It can not
be otherwise with them, because they receive the Sacrament absorbed
in the life of the outward senses.

Whosoever would know the dignity of this marvelous banquet, must
be a man detached and set free from created things, and given up to
the interior life. But this must not be misunderstood. I do not mean
that one must literally separate himself from his state of life in order
rightly to communicate, nor adopt any peculiar ways and customs.
Some think that when they cannot do the like of that they must give
over, and therefore they turn away from Communion. Do not thou
act thus, dear child; do not imagine that this supreme good of our
life cannot be fully thine, because thou livest in a secular state of
life. Only be earnest, only be diligent and thou shalt possess God in
this Sacrament without at all interfering with the duties and customs of thy state of life. Thou must, indeed, acquire a true knowledge
of thyself; thou must keep a strong guard over multiplicity in all
thy doings, methods, devotions, for these should be mainly engaged
with the interior life. Seek God earnestly in thy soul's depths; for

this end leave on one side, as far as possible, certain very external devout practices, gathering together inwardly thy outer senses and thy soul's powers, all deep sunken in the soul.

Children, for me rightly to speak of and you rightly to understand the dignity of this Sacrament is not possible. We could not understand the dignity of Adam as he stood in Paradise, even while as yet unendowed with grace, but only full of the sweetness and beauty of guileness nature. How then can our poor little minds comprehend what takes place in the inmost depths of the soul, as it becomes united to this living food, changing man into its divine self. The human soul becomes like a drop of water lost and mingled in a cask of wine; like a pane of glass with the sunshine pouring through it; like the body united to the soul and made into one man, one being with it.

By this union our spirit is elevated above all its natural weakness and is cleansed and illuminated. It is raised above its natural forces. It is penetrated with God. It is led away from itself in a divine manner, and experiences within itself the divine generation, losing meanwhile its native incompatibility with God; and it is brought to divine unity. Compare this union to that of fire and wood. First the dampness and greenness is consumed, and gradually the wood grows hotter and hotter till it is made like unto fire; as the fire approaches nearer and nearer so does the resemblance increase, until in one short hour the fire has absorbed the substance of the wood. The difference between the fire and the wood is gone, for the wood has become fire— the two are not simply alike, they are the same thing. So does this spiritual food draw out of the soul and consume all difference, changing difference into resemblance, and changing resemblance into unity. That happens to an enlightened spirit, losing likeness and difference in unity with God. The fire of divine love has absorbed all the soul's foulness, all its unresemblance to God. In partaking of this food the soul is absorbed and lost in the Godhead. It is as St. Augustine heard our blessed Lord say: "I am the food of the full-grown; purify thyself and eat Me; thou shalt not change Me into Thee, but thou shalt be changed into Me."

O children, before this shall happen nature must die many a death. By many a wild and desert way does God lead the soul as He teaches it to die. But, O children, what a noble life is born of this death— noble and joyous and fruitful. O how precious a thing it is to be able thus to die. You know well enough how our bodily food must die to itself and be undone before it is absorbed into our nature and united to us, undergoing, so to speak, many a death in the process, ere it enters our vitals and receives a new existence, entering into our heart and liver and the organs of the senses, into close union even with the reason in the brain. At the end it is so unlike its former self that the sharpest eye could not perceive any resemblance, nor could the subtlest mind detect it. We know it to be the same food in substance, but we cannot perceive it to be so with our senses. Much less can we understand how in this Sacrament our soul is unmade and then remade and absorbed into divine union, itself being lost so entirely as to escape our power of understanding it.

Foolish men understand this in a fleshly way, affirming that they are changed into divine nature; and that is a heresy, false and wicked. For after the very highest union of our soul with God, closest and most intimate, the divine nature and essence is removed to a height far beyond us, higher than all height. That is a divine eminence unto which no creature can ever, attain. Let us not be too curious about the union of the soul with God in the holy Sacrament. Even the marvellous change of bodily food into our physical system is beyond the keenest search of our mind, so noble is human nature. And wilt thou intrude upon the hidden ways and deepest mysteries of the union of the Sacrament with a holy soul, superior as this is to its dull and cumbersome body? That union is a fathomless mystery. Give up thy disputations about it, for it is removed far from thy reach, being hidden in the depths of the illuminated soul and in God.

It happens to some, that if they experience the sweetness of devotion two or three times a day at their prayers, they are sure that all goes well with them. No, children, no—they are immeasurably far from what they fancy. We are all too ready to involve our souls in the excessive sweetness of the grosser kinds of spiritual joy, and that is evil in God's sight. He is not pleased that we should be content with the trifles of the spiritual life. Nothing is so pleasing to God as to give us His own very self, and that in the best and highest way. Therefore we should go forward beyond every gift. We should strive right onward with all our senses, powers, longings—with all our heart—directly to God Himself. We should be content with nothing less than God, and not simply in sensible mental forms, but in a way that is supernatural. This leads us into the divine depths, for one can never attain to so deep a place in God but that a deeper depth opens out before him.

O children, many men do themselves incalculable hurt by tarrying amid their senses' life and in prayer using only the lowest faculties of their souls. Nothing, therefore, comes of their spirituality; any more than bodily food helps head and heart and bodily members when it lodges undigested in the stomach. The food must change its nature or no good comes of it. We shall never secure the real good of this blessed food, to eat which God has invited us, until our whole interior life, with its powers highest and lowest, shall be conformed to God and delivered over to Him, far beyond natural effort, with single-hearted faith living in good works, and full of the practice of virtue.

For our faith must not be a mere pretence, but must be shown forth in our life. And when God sees that a man can do no more, then He Himself comes and works in a hidden way that nature knows nothing of, leading the soul beyond and above its natural ways. These aids of God are his who aproaches the adorable Sacrament best prepared, and with the most devout sentiments. To such a one God truly gives Himself in a personal manner and esentially. All who long with loving hearts to attain the highest perfection, should keep themselves well disposed often to partake of this living bread. Whosoever feels within himself an increase of divine love, nor yields to any disregard or belittling of spiritual things, the oftener such a one communicates the more profitable it is. St. Augustine plainly shows this. "Whosoever feels the love of God growing within him, and at special times knows himself to be not unworthy to receive the Sacrament, why should he not be made worthy to receive it every day?" Worthiness does not ever come from human effort or deserving, but purely from the grace and merits of our Lord Jesus Christ flowing from God into our souls. And if this happens once a year, or monthly or weekly, why shall it not happen daily, as long as a man yearns for it, and does his part to obtain it?

I knew of no shorter or surer way than this for an interior man to attain his best spiritual state. I make bold to counsel all my friends, that if God's fear does not lessen within them, and if God's love grows within them, then let them come often to Communion. Nothing prepares fuel for the fire so well as to bring it close up to the fire. Wetness and hardness gradually yield to the heat as the closeness of

contact continues, until at last the fuel is like the fire, and then it is
actually turned into fire—all in proportion as the fuel is apt and prepared. No man is so soaked with sin, so hard and perverse, so inclined
to the wickedness of the world or of creatures, but that this fire will
communicate its heat to him, melt his stony heart, and make him a
godly man—supposing he receives Communion with true devotion,
does all his part in preparation, and will keep his place close to the
divine warmth.

And as to preparation, none is better than what God Himself gives.
Suppose that to-morrow is to be some high festival; how better can I
prepare to celebrate it than to receive to-day, with all devotion, the
eternal and all-merciful God in holy Communion? How better can I
honor God than by offering God His own very self? How better can
I give a new life to my imperfect and unspiritual nature, how better
baptize anew, as it were, my old corrupt nature, than to receive God's
true and only Son, His living divine flesh, His all cleansing blood, His
Holy Spirit, His all-loving heart and His sweet human nature, even
the Holy Trinity itself, and all that God is and has and may do?
How can God refuse the least to one to whom He has promised to give
the greatest? What gift is too great for Him to give who has given
Himself wholly, and yet wills to give Himself again. God's purpose is
not gained by the mere outward granting of the Sacrament. But
rather in that He shall be with this child of the human race according
to His word: "My delights are to be with the children of men" (Prov.
viii: 31). And by this is meant men of loving hearts and souls. All
this have I spoken to you by the grace of God; but what follows is the
best that I have found in the writings of the masters.

St. Thomas says: "All the graces which our Savior Jesus Christ in
His humanity brought to the whole world, these brings He to each particular man with His holy body and blood. And He grants all the
fruit of His death, resurrection and ascension, together with the glory
and blessedness of His holy body and blood, soul and divinity." St.
Thomas thus embraces in his teaching about holy Communion the
granting of every grace that one may imagine. Take a commonplace
comparison, for worldly-minded men view things only after the manner of the senses. Suppose a mighty monarch to whom belonged all
the riches, dominion, beauty and pleasures of all mankind taken
together, his every heart's desire gratified perfectly; suppose him to

take a man who was the outcast of the human race, covered with the scabs of leprosy, offensive with foulest odors, blind and crippled, and to join him to himself, and that he should make the union absolute, so that he poured into this miserable man his own glorious heart, head, hands, feet and whole being, inner and outer, poured himself thus wholly into this man's body, so that the body and the members that were the monarch's have now become the unfortunate man's own body and members:—would not this be a great and marvelous act of love? But a thousand times greater, incomprehensibly greater, is the loving union that God gives us in the holy Sacrament. And now it remains for us to discourse of the fruit of this holy Sacrament. That we may well succeed in that task, let us beg our beloved Lord to remedy our deficiencies by His blessed grace. *Amen.*

The Fruit of Holy Communion

Synopsis—The purification of the heart and life of the worthy recipient—Grades of worthiness—Advantages of spiritual communion to highly devout souls—Venial sins: the many hindrances they place in the way of the fruitfulness of communion—A disquisition on venial sins, deliberate and indeliberate, with special reference to communion—Interior spiritual self-indulgence is the fault of spiritual men—God's painful way of curing this fault—Effect of communion in relieving souls in purgatory.

FOURTH SERMON FOR THE FEAST OF CORPUS CHRISTI.

For My flesh is meat indeed, and My blood is drink indeed.—John vi, 56.

Yesterday I spoke of the dignity of the holy Sacrament (though, indeed, no one can worthily do so); of its benefits; and finally of the preparation we should make to receive it. If this be too high for us, yet the words of St. Thomas, which I quoted, in some measure aid us— that all the glory, grace and happiness that our Lord Jesus Christ brought to the world with His humanity, living, suffering, dead, risen again and ascending into heaven, that all of this He bestows on every single man with His holy body and blood. There is no imaginable grace not embraced in this divine-gift. Think as deep or as high or as interiorly as thou mayst in thy devotions, whatever thou framest by thy own powers is all nothing compared to the holy Sacrament. Other devotions may be indeed divine, but this one is the divinity itself. Here the illuminated man is changed into God, as St. Augustine was taught by our Lord: "Not I into thee, but thou into Me."

What is thy pious purpose? Wilt thou overcome thy failings, win grace, acquire virtue, consolation, love? Thou shalt find all here, if thou seekest rightly. If a man had lived a hundred years, and had committed a hundred mortal sins every day, and if God should but give him a true conversion from sin, and if with that disposition he should go to holy Communion, then it would be but a little thing for our Lord to forgive him all his sins in the twinkling of an eye with this blessed gift of the Sacrament—as easy as to blow a grain of dust from off His hand. Yes, and the conversion thus wrought could be so efficacious that every penalty and penance due to the man's sins should be at once remitted, and he should be made entirely holy.

In the city of Cologne there is a good custom of receiving the blessed Sacrament quite often, but it is done with much difference of dispositions. Some receive it sacramentally, indeed, but not spiritually nor happily, and these do so in a state of mortal sin, as did Judas. Others receive it both sacramentally and spiritually in their souls, and yet gain little comfort, grace or fruit, for they are stained with many venial sins, and communicate without preparation and indevoutly. A third class receive it with great and holy fruit and incalculable advantage to their souls. A fourth class receive it spiritually without actual sacramental communion—good and clean hearted souls full of holy desires for Communion, more so, perhaps, than those who receive sacramentally. One may do that a hundred times a day, if he is a good man, and in any place, be he sick or well, whereas once a day is all he could receive it sacramentally. This spiritual Communion, if made with deep desire, secures incalculable fruit of divine grace. Many a man, receiving this Sacrament in his soul, will enjoy it in life eternal—supposing him to be free from grave sin. But not so if the priceless treasures of holy Communion are to him not in the depths of his soul, but are matters of outward observance, his life meanwhile being lukewarm, being full of venial sins, and graceless. Then is the soul cold and barren and grace inoperative, on account of these hindrances.

What then are the hindrances which do men such a harm, preventing this treasury of the riches of earth and heaven from benefiting them?—a misery that we daily behold around us. Mark well that it is all venial sin daily committed. This it is that cools the warmth of love, dissipates the heart's affections, lessens devotion, expels the consolation of the Holy Ghost, and makes God a strange thing to the soul. Venial sins do not destroy the grace of God, but this harm they do: they lay the soul open to dangerous occasions of losing His grace and to perilous tendencies to mortal sin. And these sins are of two kinds.

One kind of venial sin is obstinate and continued yielding to affec.
tion for created things—affection that has not God for its motive.
Love for creatures for their own sake, satisfaction in their possession
and joy in them, hinder the effects of Communion. Children, all sensi.
ble pleasures in created things enjoyed wholly apart from God are
venial sins; and these sometimes are so gross that ten years and more
of the fires of purgatory will not atone for them, if one dies without
having done proper penance. Of course this means that such affection
for creatures is for their own sakes, whereby they usurp the place of
God in our heart, hindering His supremacy and His action there.
Hence the need of closely observing our interior life, marking all dis·
orderly inclinations and joys, watching our self-satisfaction in what
we have or what we do.

Ah, children, how sad a state of transgression is this. And how
commonly do we meet men in all states of life, eagerly gathering
together all they can of this world's goods, going beyond all meas·
ure. No one has enough, everyone is planning to get more. They
build great houses, adorn them foolishly and furnish them with rare
things, consulting only their worldly taste, amassing silver table serv·
ice, rich bodily ornaments, and then luxuriously feasting. Pleasure is
their universal aim, and venial sins are their regular habit. Their
only pain is that they have so little of what they covet. They run
after company and recreations and all sorts of frivolity, neither seeking God nor thinking of Him, and of course never finding Him. Ah,
children, how close are these to mortal sin and its pitiable ruin. Ere
they think of it they fall into it and are sunk into its depths.

Venial sins, therefore, dear children, are the standard obstacles that
prevent men from receivng the graces of the body and blood of our
Lord Jesus Christ. Yet amid all this each one has his own particular
devotions, meantime refusing to give up his dangerous practices. In
Communion they feel neither God's presence nor enjoy His consolation.
They leave that on one side, clinging to their own consolation, namely,
the love of the creature. And yet sometimes they spend forty of fifty
years with a show of spirituality. They do not realize what their
state is, but it is a serious question as to whether or not they are
saved; for to the very end their hearts are entangled with created
things. And they are full of excuses: I must have such and such a
thing, they say; or, that will do me no harm; and again: this is not

sinful. They thus create their own hindrances to grace, until the evil goes so far that they have no conscience left about it. These powerful obstacles are built up like a wall against the action of God upon the soul. And yet the soul is often unconscious of them. Such a soul may do what it pleases to better its condition: so long as it is filled with the love of created things, so long does God turn away from it.

Besides this first kind of obstacles, namely, wilful venial sins, there is the other kind yet to consider. These are venial sins of weakness. There are men who are by no means enslaved by love of created things, who are ever ready to renounce what they are made aware is not according to God, whether it be affection for friends or for the goods of this life, and who are nevertheless not careful enough. They are not sufficiently guarded against their natural weaknesses. They do not readily enough repress anger, or it may be pride, sloth, frivolous talk. Nor do they search earnestly after the causes of these defects, such as excessive talk, excessive mirth, lack of restraint of appetite at table, too great absorption in wordly occupations. If such venial sins are due to ill health, or happen in moments of forgetfulness, the obstacle to grace is less serious than when they are more deliberate.

If these faults occur the day itself of Communion or the day before, the harm is all the greater, hindering union with God, distracting the mind, weakening confidence, making the soul unresponsive to the light and the sweetness of the Sacrament. If the faults were done yesterday and without wilfulness, and I sincerely deplore them to-day at my Communion, they do not hurt me so much as if they happened to-day, for the bitterness of my sorrow cleanses off the rust of my transgressions, at least in great part. It is different when one frivolously yields to distractions the very day of Communion, chats and gossips freely, is over occupied with secular affairs; this adds obstacle to obstacle and is a serious harm. But yet in such a case one should not omit his Communion, for he does not sin in receiving, and his weakness is a matter of regret to him.

Nature, again, puts an obstacle to grace by yielding to excessive sleep or eating. One should hardly eat a mouthful without questioning his soul about excess. Children, the soul into which God shall enter by holy Communion must be entirely detached, or the divine influence, the divine generosity, is hindered in its secret work.

But if honest self-denying men are dull and sleepy against their will, nature demanding much more rest than they like to yield, in such case they need not struggle against it.

Again, there are hindrances of a hidden kind which beset spiritual men. These are spiritual self-seeking, indulgence in sensible consolations and in devotional feelings. Some, if they do not experience these emotions, will not receive Communion. They unconsciously crave for something besides God. But God often intervenes and draws these men to Him forceably by outward painful visitations, and so violently that it seems as if He were striking them with a sledge hammer. Or, perhaps, inwardly He cures them by an anguish so dreadful that it is like the agony of hell. And if they are not thus visited, then will their purgatory be dreadful hereafter. They too often remain to the end of their days thus imperfectly disposed.

Others are good souls who are full of blind fear. If they do not feel a veritable fire of love within them or experience some great movement of God, they abstain from Communion, even though they are not aware of any real reason for it. And so they remain, making no progress.

But the ones who best receive the blessed fruit of the holy Sacrament, are they whose souls are cleansed of all sin and whose intention is wholly pure, who rest entirely upon God's mercy. To them it is all one if God gives or takes; they trust Him ever the same in abundance or in want. In holy Communion God is born in them and they are born in God. If they find any obstacle to God's grace, whether it be in their inner or their outer life, they are not distressed; they instantly reject and turn away from it. They recognize God's will in everything. They dwell upon Him and not upon His gifts—upon His very self alone. All that they have they accept from Him, and to Him they refer it all back again. Marvellously does the holy Sacrament do its work in men like these, flooding their souls with blessed light, and giving them the shortest road to perfection. A man may reach such an earnestness of devotion in communicating, that if he were to depart this life immediately afterwards, instead of attaining to the lowest choir of the blessed—to which he was destined—he would by this Communion be granted entrance into the second, perhaps into the third or fourth choir. Nay, by frequent Communion in such dispositions he would be made worthy of the highest choir, surpassing the seraphs and all the angelic natures. But of this he must not think, nor desire any such lot, but only long to do the blessed will of God and advance His honor.

The miracles of grace wrought by this Sacrament in a truly mortified spirit, are beyond the comprehension of angels, for it is now elevated above itself, drawn into God in its interior life, and closely united to Him. And if it happens that such a man is unable to receive Communion, he humbly resigns himself; he daily communicates spiritually, and this he does whether he can hear mass or not. Ah, children, what wonders of grace will not God work within us if we will but be converted sincerely to Him. We shall find all good things in His Sacrament, and heaven will be established in our souls. But, alas, we do not do our part. Dissipation of mind goes beyond all limits. We may go to a sermon and hear its lessons—and presently we forget all about it—wandering about from one preacher to another, like silly women, unstable of mind, to-day glad and to-morrow sorrowful.

I have been in a certain country, where the people are so manly and turn to God so earnestly and steadfastly, that the word of God produces more practical fruit among them in one year than here in Cologne in ten. There among that lovely people do we see marvels of divine grace. Some countries breed only effeminate characters: no matter what one may do for them, nothing comes of it. You do not find it pleasant to hear such things said about you; but, children, we must become men. We must make a free and vigorous start away from created things, and go forward to God. We must have God in mind in all our life as the final end—God, and not creatures. We must live in Him, not in self nor in creatures. How lamentable it is that the blessed grace of God is ignored among us: it is enough to break one's heart to think of it. Alas, even in many convents, it is what is the latest news that interests souls, filling them with foolish thoughts. There are those, to be sure, who gladly hear about divine things, but the others condemn them for it. Children, depart from them, and have nothing to do with their pretended piety. Hide yourselves away and wait upon the will of God. When that appears, follow it faithfully.

And if you are seeking to know the divine will, let me give you some good advice. When the question comes as to doing or not doing, then enter into yourself and earnestly consider. And bear in mind that the safest course is to choose what is most opposed to nature. Whatever nature is fondest of, that is the most unsafe. The more you live in nature and in its pleasure, the less do you live in God and in His will. The less of nature, the more of God. The more you live in the Spirit, the less you live in nature.

Such is my teaching about this Holy Sacrament. It is but a small part of what one should say of its worth and its holiness. It is God's honor, it is the joy of the blessed, it is the reformation of mankind, the conversion of sinners, the release of souls from purgatory.

It is related that once a friend of God had a vision. A soul appeared to him clothed in a burning flame, and said to him: "These intolerable pains, the agony of which words cannot tell, I suffer in punishment for having received the blessed Sacrament of our Lord Jesus Christ without due preparation." And the soul then added: "If thou wilt receive our Lord's body and blood once for me that will help me." The good man did this, and the next day the soul appeared to him again shining as bright as the sun; it announced that it had been freed from all its unbearable pains and taken up into eternal happiness. May God grant us thus to receive holy Communion, and to live a life in accordance with its graces. *Amen.*

Foretastes of Heaven

*Synopsis—The first is granted to those who turn away from the ban-
quet of worldly joy—This is not always accompanied by devotional
sweetness—the second is holy Communion—A doctrinal explanation—The various benefits of mass and communion—How these
are hindered by venial sins, and also by neglect of spiritual exercises—They are made permanent by detachment and self-abasement.*

SERMON FOR THE SECOND SUNDAY AFTER TRINITY.*

A certain man made a great supper and invited many. And he sent his
servant at the hour of supper to say to them that were invited, that they should
come, for now all things were ready. And they began all at once to make excuse.
The first said to him: I have bought a farm, and I must needs go out to see it:
I pray thee, hold me excused. And another said: I have bought five yoke of
oxen, and I go to try them: I pray thee. hold me excused. And another said: I
have married a wife, and therefore I cannot come. . . . But I say unto you
that none of these men that were invited, shall taste of my supper.—Luke xiv.
16-24.

St. Gregory says that we may understand this supper, to which we
are all invited, as a most interior self-knowledge, a most clear knowledge of that inmost depth of our soul which is God's kingdom. And
also the very taste of how it is that God dwells and works there,
experiencing the same knowledge and love. In another sense, this
supper means the holy Sacrament. In yet another meaning it is
eternal happiness, which is the true supper of our souls, and compared
with which all banquets of soul or body which the whole world could
set before us, would be no more than a single morsel of bread.

Whatsoever man would come to this last-named glorious supper,
must diligently take into account the other two. For devout writers
tell us that whosoever attains to the banquet of eternal life in heaven,
must have had a foretaste of it in this life. But inasmuch as the
foretaste is different in different men, so very truly shall the enjoyment

*No sermon of Tauler's for the First Sunday after Trinity is extant.

be. And yet during some good men's whole lives, God withholds all
savor of eternal joy, granting never a drop of sweetness until they
arrive at the very end. But these may be a thousand degrees higher
than others who have enjoyed much devotional sweetness. A man
may be granted supernatural revelations, and yet these may be of no
profit to him; while one who never had such privileges, may be placed
much nearer to God in the celestial banquet. God measures His gifts
with love's measure; He gives to each what is best for him. And if
any one will taste of this sweetness in his deepest life, he must turn
his heart away from all that is not God.

The second supper is that of the holy Sacrament, bringing such
grace and joy as no words can explain. And we should be all the
more gratified for it because it is a holy feast that we can enjoy
every day.

One might enquire how it happens to be necessary that we should
daily renew in the Eucharist the commemoration of our Lord's death,
since on Good Friday our Lord was offered up once for all, and for all
the world, and, if it were needed, for a thousand sinful worlds besides.
The answer is that our Savior devised this blessed way of daily renewing His death, out of pity for our human weakness and our daily
necessity. He would give us His adorable sacrifice of Cavalry newly
offered up every day for the sins and miseries of mankind. It is thus
that St. Thomas teaches: "All the fruitfulness, all the benefit that God
granted us the day He died, is found every day in every mass that is
celebrated; and all this grace is received by every man each time he
worthily receives the Lord's body and blood."

This holy Sacrament banishes sin. It puts sin to death, and causes
a man to grow strong in a virtuous life, imparting new graces. It
safeguards him from future dangers, and from the snares of the enemy,
snares incessantly being laid for us. Without its strong help one may
easily fall, either by inner or outer sinfulness. Besides this, the holy
Sacrament is a great grace when offered for the souls in purgatory;
many souls would suffer there till the last day were it not for holy
mass, especially when offered by very devout priests. This blessed
observance works wonders in purgatory, especially during this part of
the year. Each one should assist at mass with deep longings of spirit,
uniting his fervent intention with every mass offered in the whole
world, especially remembering those who are dear to him, whether
living or dead. We thus feel ourselves present not only at the mass

being celebrated before us, but at all the masses being said in the whole world. , I strongly counsel any interior man to hear mass every day,

What is the reason that so many who receive this holy Sacrament, full of graces as it is, show little or no sign of improvement, even though they remain in the state of grace? The blame is their own. They take no diligent account of their venial sins; they do not look on themselves with disfavor. These defects hinder the influence of grace. A man must scrutinize his life closely and watch his conduct strictly, and take measures to stop any habitual venial sins. Especially should he guard against idle words—and all words are idle that are not spoken thoughfully. This he should do to the best of his ability.

Another obstacle to the practical working of the grace of holy Communion, is when one interrupts and omits his regular and daily devotional practices. Many a one has no steady religious observance, runs after every distraction, will not wait with a recollected spirit for God's grace to work within him. But it must be remembered that the graces of this Sacrament often become active in a willing soul only after two or three days have passed.

Whosoever will experience these benefits, must journey out of the land of Egypt and out of the land of darkness, ere he can eat the bread of heaven, whose sweetness is proportioned to our heart's desires. The bread of heaven was not given to the chosen people, as long as the flour lasted that they had brought with them out of Egypt. But when that was gone, the manna came to them, full of every sweetness their hearts desired. So it happens to us.

When we have gone forth out of Egypt, out of the world and its ways, and when we have become spiritualized, we are fed with heavenly graces—but not before: not while we feast on the bread of nature and of creatures, that is to say, our evil and imperfect tendencies. For while that is the case we can never interiorly enjoy the divine nourishment of the Sacrament. All who would interiorly receive the fruits of Communion will not allow the world, creatures or their own weakness to cleave to their souls. They will not approach the Sacrament trusting to their own perfection, but rather to strengthen their weakness. They feel as weak as a man reduced so low by illness that his life is despaired of—who, if he were able, would purchase the medicine needed for his recovery with an immense amount of gold and jewels.

The wise Christian does not receive Communion for the joy of it, but out of dire necessiay, so that his very life may be preserved. In no other spirit should we receive Communion, than to strengthen our weakness and save ourselves from death, that is to say, from the love of created things. With some it is as if you poured water on fire—such is the effect of their conduct after Communion. For after receiving it they open their soul to the images, the fooleries of the world, which absorb it in thoughts of outward things. These cool the warmth of love. The soul is incapacitated to receive the graces of the Sacrament. It is incapable of waiting in recollection the action of God upon the soul.

But when one is in a frame of mind to give up attachment to creatures, then it sometimes happens that the enemy says to him: This is foolish; thou canst not keep this up. Then this deluded soul does what the people of Israel did. As Moses led them forth out of Egypt, they looked backwards and saw their pursuers coming with their six hundred chariots, and they exclaimed: "Why wouldst thou do this, to lead us out of Egypt? . . . For it is much better to serve the Egyptians than to die in the wilderness" (Exod. xiv: 12). Thus act these fainthearted men, men of little faith. As they hear the enemy coming on, hear the noise of his many chariots, as it were, rolling over the stones, feel the attacks of temptation, they begin to think: O, this is all foolishness; it is much better to be back in Egypt, in the world, busy with creatures, full of their love, rather than to lose it all. Thus it is with many a man who trusts not God. Fall at the feet of our Lord Jesus Christ, therefore, and beseech Him to plead for you with His eternal Father, that He may bestow on you great confidence in Him.

We shall draw lessons from the third supper when we come to consider it, and meanwhile may God help us thereto. *Amen.*

Three Foundation Stones: Humility, Love and Detachment

Synopsis—Our inborn frailty and our evilful pride reveal the need of humility—Look inward, look outward, and we behold only our sins and our tendency to sin—Difference between humility and despondency—Loving God: how natural it seems, and yet how easily hindered—From humanity and love springs the divine virtue of hope—An exhortation to earnestness and courage, springing from love and hope—Detachment, inwardly practiced, is entire obedience—Many reasons for praising this high virtue—Detachment also shown by patience.

FIRST SERMON FOR THE THIRD SUNDAY AFTER TRINITY.

Be ye humbled therefore under the mighty hand of God, that He may exalt you in the time of visitation. Casting all your care upon Him, for He hath a care of you. Be sober and watch; because your adversary, the devil, as a roaring lion, goeth about seeking whom he may devour. Whom resist ye, strong in faith: knowing that the same affliction befalls your brethren who are in the world. But the God of all grace, who has called us into His eternal glory in Christ Jesus, after you have suffered a little, will Himself perfect you, and confirm you, and establish you. To Him be glory and empire for ever and ever. Amen.—I Pet. v, 6-11.

Dear children, this is the teaching of St. Peter's very instructive epistle, giving us a perfect doctrine, by means of which we can complete all that holy Church has done for us the entire year past, with which, if we take it seriously, we shall find it to coincide perfectly.

"Be humbled," he says, "under the mighty hand of God," in which we see the essence, life and work that a man must have in all his devout practices. It consists in three things, all most essential, so that if any one of them be lacking, the essence, life and work of our piety comes to naught. The first is that we must be humble. Humility is the solid foundation on which the whole structure is to be built, if it is going to be worth anything in the sight of God. Whatever a man builds without this foundation falls down. The second thing is true and divine love for God and our neighbor. The third is genuine detachment from all things. With these three things a man reaches the perfection of a true and godlike life.

Dear children, God has by His grace implanted in us the beautiful virtue of humility, knowing how greatly we stand in need of it. In this he does us a great favor, for He thereby places in our souls a divine spark much closer to our nature than we may imagine. If humility seems an alien thing to us that is to be blamed on pride. If human nature be rightly ordered, we find matter for humility within us without fail. We cannot expel it from its place there, for as we look into ourselves we find two great causes for it. One is our natural frailty. Every man can see how miserably needy he is, how many things he lacks, and how all that he gets fails to satisfy him. Nothing is better known than the inborn deficiencies of the natural man, and that just as every man comes from nothing, so all ends in nothingness—all of which furnishes material for humility. The other reason for humility is our sinful frailty, something perfectly plain to anyone who searches his interior. He finds in himself a bottomless depth of natural depravity. Unless God guarded him constantly by his merciful graces, how unspeakably ready would he not be to commit sin, even to fall into mortal sin, and to be condemned therefor to eternally suffer in hell among all the devils. Tell me, dear children, is not this a great cause for true humility? Thus our own nature inclines us to the practice of this holy virtue. Looking inward, looking outward, we find there is nothing good in us, nor of ourselves can we do any good.

The second virtue is true love of God, and this has God rooted in our nature; for by a law of our nature every man must love. Even humility is not an interior growth, but comes from without, whereas love is inborn, as Venerable Bede teaches: "As it is impossible to live without a soul, so it is impossible to live without love." If a man, therefore, is naturally rightly ordered he must love God more than himself or all creatures. It is a pitiful thing that man should pervert so noble a trait, turning deliberately away from God, his creator and the creator of all things, and inclining towards creatures.

The third virtue is prudence or discretion, which belongs to reason itself. Mark well, children, that every act of man that is not guided by discretion comes to naught, and is not pleasing to God. Therefore does St. Peter say in this epistle: "Be sober and watch." This means that discretion should soberly guide our whole life, our words and

Conferences

: :enuine
: reaches

the beautiful

: souls a
imagine. If
.: pride. If

for as we
: natural
how many

.:ral man,

: : reason
: : anyone
: depth of
: his mer-
:mit sin,
: eternally
.: this a
:ees us to
:reward, we
:ery good.

:re. Even
: : whereas
:sile to live
: a man,
: more than
:d perrert
:restor and

: to reason
: : guided
: Therefore
: : means
: : : rds and

works, eating and sleeping and watching—let discretion direct all men in all states of life in all their conduct.

Dear children, let us return to the first virtue, humility: "Be ye humbled, therefore, under the mighty hand of God, that He may exalt you in the time of visitation." Ah, dear children, when the time of visitation comes and God does not find us humble, it will be an evil thing for us without doubt; for "God resisteth the proud, and giveth grace to the humble" (James iv: 6). Therefore, the greater our humility, the greater the grace of God. If He finds us proud, He will crush us down; if He finds us lowly minded, He will undoubtedly raise us up. The mighty hand of God is wise and good, aye, it is kindly and loving: "Casting all your care upon God, for He careth for you." If this loving watch of God over us were his only favor, His daily care for all our spiritual and bodily needs the only gift he were to give us; if His loving intervention against our heartache and all misery were His single benefit to us, it alone ought to be enough in our eyes to inspire a return of love. It should cause us ceaselessly to adore His Providence, to direct all our longings towards Him alone, and to enkindle in our hearts a deep love of His holy will in ordering our life.

Again, dear children, does St. Peter speak: "Be sober and watch, because your adversary, the devil, as a roaring lion, goeth about seeking whom he may devour. Whom resist ye, strong in faith." Now when the lion roars, all the beasts of the forest fall to the ground with terror, and he comes and tears them to pieces. And in like manner, when the evil spirit comes roaring upon poor, weak men, they instantly fall down helpless, and he comes and tears them to pieces. But St. Peter bids us be bold and vigilant, and bravely to withstand the assaults of the demon with the weapons of holy faith. One should act like the garrison of a beleaguered city which knows that the enemy's army is superior in number. On whatever side the ramparts are weakest, there is concentrated the strongest defense—or the city and its defenders and treasures are lost. So must each one of us carefully mark the weakest side of his character, for there without doubt the evil one will deliver his fiercest attack—that is to say, where he finds the greatest tendency to vice.

Sometimes the devil's readiest temptation is to despondency. He shows a man his native frailty and his sinfulness, and tries to make him heavy-hearted on that account. And then he, as it were, roars in his ear: Art thou so foolish as to spend thy life in anguish and in penance? No! No! Live in joy. Enjoy thy carnal pleasures. Almighty God will give thee time for penance at the end of life. Have thy own will, enjoy creatures whilst thou art young and strong; when old age comes, then shalt thou become pious and serve God. Ah, dear children, what treacherous counsel is this. Be on your guard. Diligently watch while it is day, for soon eternal darkness will enshroud you. Regulate your life by no such false confidence, but rather by a wise understanding of what is a really God-guided life. And let there be no turning back. See to it that God alone shall rule you. For it is our Lord Jesus Christ Himself who says: "Every plant which My heavenly Father hath not planted, shall be rooted up" (Matt. xv: 13)

Look into this matter, dear children, very carefully, for the evil one lays many a snare for you. One will say in time of temptation: O God, would that I had a father confessor in this my great distress; I wish I knew how I now stand with our dear Lord. Now, children, I know about this case, and I say to you, do not annoy your father confessor. Keep up good courage. Evil thoughts have come? Then let them come and let them go. Be at peace; think no more about it, but turn thy heart straight to God. Make no parley with thy temptation, but just let it alone. By debating about it in thy mind, thou shalt suffer more misery than the demon himself has caused thee. All this trouble comes from excessive despondency, which may end by his suggesting despair, and saying: Everything thou dost is vain and useless—thou art lost forever.

The thing to do in such a case is to cast "all care upon God" and rest in Him. Turn to the eternal God with unshaken trust in His goodness and mercy. Do as mariners do when threatened with shipwreck—cast thy anchor deep down to the bottom of God's love and grace. Place thy confidence firmly in God our Lord. If it comes even to the end of life, and a man in deep distress shall but anchor all his hopes in God and die in that mind, it is truly a happy and a holy death.

Children, be well assured that a really godly man must dwell in the practice of divine hope just as much as in any other of the divine virtues; and that is a great help to him when at last he comes to meet death. But this must not be a false and deceitful confidence in God, trusting in which a man presumes to lead a sinful life; for whosoever trusts in God and on the strength of that lives wickedly, sins against the Holy Ghost.   The confidence in God that I mean springs from the depths of true humility and love.   It is based on consciousness of one's helplessness; it is a most reasonable recognition of the need of God's help; it is part of a true and full and joyful conversion to God; for whosoever gives himself up to God loves and trusts God sincerely. Shalt thou not trust Him who has already done thee so many favors? Before thou wast created God foresaw thy weakness; knew that thou wouldst sin, foresaw in His divine wisdom how it was that he would redeem all mankind from sin, namely, by the bitter death of our beloved, innocent Lord Jesus Christ.

Therefore, dear children, turn away from sin with all earnestness. I say to you that any man under temptation, who does not courageously resist, but stands halting and hesitating, not turning from sin with his whole heart for the sake of God, such a man the evil one pursues with the object of dragging him down into everlasting damnation.   Dost thou really wish to overcome the demon?   Then do thy part manfully, fly from sin, and say in thy inmost soul: O Eternal God, come to my help with Thy divine grace, for I am firmly resolved never to commit mortal sin.   Thus by thy good will and by thy resolute purpose, thou shalt overcome the evil spirit and put him shamefully to flight.

Children, you should know what a disgraceful thing it is for a man endowed with reason to allow himself to be vanquished by the devil, to be led into greivious sin and to forfeit the grace of God.   A man gifted with reason who gives up to the evil one, is like a well-armed soldier who runs away from a fly.   Think of the powerful weapons with which we can withstand the devil—our holy faith, the blessed Sacrament, God's holy word, the glorious example of the saints and of all good men, the prayers of holy Church, and more besides—all strong weapons against the demon.   He has no greater force against these arms than a fly has against a big bear.   Let but a man bravely resist, and he never can be overcome.   Therefore turn away from thy sins and cheerfully and manfully fight thy battle.   See to it carefully that thou goest not into the next world without having fought and conquered the devil, nor without having sincerely repented of thy sins; for then thou shalt be the scoff of all those evil spirits, who will eternally torment thee.   It will be a deeper pain to thee then that thou hast followed the devil than any other misery connected with thy sins.

Futhermore, a man must examine his inmost soul, lest there should be aught there but just simply God and His eternal glory. For, alas, there are many men in all states of life who make a show of a good life, as if fancying that they can deceive the eternal God. No, not so; but in reality thou deceivest thyself, and thou losest the precious time of grace. Thou art so guilty before God that He permits the evil spirits to have power over thee, so that they will not let thee do any good work. Take heed, dear children, whilst it is day, lest the time of darkness overtake you, and the grace of God be withdrawn from you. Search deep into your hearts; have God there and only God, making him your only aim in life, whether consciously or unconsciously.

Such is not the way of men who follow not after God. Creatures are their object in life. And if they find sorrow for sin beginning to stir their hearts, they run away from it; they go into another country or city, they start new ways of wickedness, and thus they leap into everlasting death. Or acting otherwise, such a one is caught in a panic and adopts a life of poverty, or enters a monastery. Others, again, obtain a securer refuge by entering an approved order, even one strictly enclosed.

Now it may happen that some have entered an order from motives not divine; but finding themselves there they say: Dear Lord, I thank Thee eternally that I am here, and I will ever remain here, to love Thee and serve Thee. Blessed are all those who persevere in this holy state till death, for without doubt they will be saved. The least little work there done in holy obedience, is nobler in God's eyes and more worthy of reward than many great works performed by one's own will. I declare to you in all truth, that no lovelier offering can be made to the Almighty God than a truly humble and obedient heart. In a single instant a man can, by means of obedience and giving up of his own will to God, be made so humble that he will be led directly to God—more directly than if he spent ten years in practicing high devotions. Take an example: suppose a man so full of God's grace that God constantly dwelt with him, and was as personally present as He will be in heaven; and suppose him now to be required to pay a real obedience to God by some external act of charity. Such a one would humbly say to God: O beloved God, let me go out of Thy presence and follow Thy holy will in obedience; and this would please God more than to see that man enter eternal life surrounded by all the angels of heaven.

Children, this example is straight against all the religious men who go by their own will, and who do not quickly respond to God's will manifested to them in obedience. There are such men in communities; they lay out their devotions and other good works for themselves. When obedience would draw them out to the active labors of their order, then is shown how little liberty of spirit they have—self-conceited men, with a god to rule them who is a divinity of their own appointment. A man truly obedient is always obedient, cheerfully dropping everything, even prayers and meditations, at the voice of lawful authority. If God is really in his heart, then does he offer himself in all meekness to the disposal of his superiors. It is this that leads him to union with God; without this he will lack God's favor. Obedience is that very noble virtue which is more pleasing to God than any of the others, even when we obey in matters which are in themselves of little moment. The eternal Son of God was for our sakes made obedient to His heavenly Father, in His coming down from the Godhead to our poor human nature, and then in the embracing of His holy cross; finally in His cruel and bitter death. Therefore must we **one and all be** obedient men, in all divine things and human things, interiorly and exteriorly, without murmuring or contradiction—**if** God shall do His work of love unhindered and continuously within **our souls.**

Yet this doctrine is directly opposed to the practice of those pious men who obey unwillingly. These make interpretations and excuses in order to avoid this beloved virtue, and they cleave to their own customary opinions. They insist on having their own way. I **declare to you** that such conduct separates you from God, from His graces, from the sweetness of His love—all this you will lack as long as you persist in a self-willed course.

Therefore, child, when thou beginnest a good work, humbly approach the fountain of divine grace, and crave that thou mayst begin and end it wholly to the praise and honor of God, sinking deep within thy soul **till thou art** fully conscious of thy own nothingness when without God's grace. In the quiet of that interior life, search out very humbly what is God's all lovely will—rest upon that without further running about for motives. This is a better way than taking the whole world into thy counsel with a dissipated spirit. Any man who is conscious of having true humility of heart and real love of God, together with discretion, in such a man's soul God does a work greater than words **can describe.**

St. Peter teaches us that we suffer the same as do our brethren in the world. And, children, I say to you that we must suffer, whether we turn this side to escape or that side—we must suffer. We must be willing to suffer or go straight against God. Now there are many young people who risk life and limb in the service of the world, and whose whole reward is to pamper their wretched bodies, food for worms as they are, and commit their souls to the devil. Such are the only wages the world pays to its hirelings. How different with you. You gladly serve God and suffer for His sake, and He will give you as your wages His own very self, together with the kingdom of heaven and everlasting life. O how gladly should you, His chosen friends, suffer for Him, since for your sake He suffered shame, poverty, and all misery. Since the head of the human race, God's eternal Son Jesus Christ, has thus suffered, surely we His members ought to blush for shame that we are not always glad to suffer. Who in this world has ever endured the blasphemy, disgrace and shame that befell Jesus Christ God's eternal Son? He, indeed, would continue thus to suffer for us were it now possible for Him to do so. Daily and often in the day is He crucified in spirit by men's curses; constantly is He rejected and cast out, His wounds opened again and His innocent and precious blood poured out by every mortal sin that is committed. Think of the sacrilege, the blasphemy that is done Him by unworthy Communions, foul sinners taking Him into their filthy souls, all full of deadly sensuality. Could such a wretch feel the wickedness of that profanation of God, his horror would be worse than that of Judas. For these men confess the Godhead of Jesus Christ, acknowledging Him to be their God and their creator, whereas this divinity of our Savior was not known to Judas. If God's true friends could feel a pain equal to the guilt of this sacrilege, a pain of a bodily kind as well as the spiritual grief of a loving heart, their very bones would be pierced to the marrow, and their souls would be wounded to their very depths. If they could turn away from God this foul indignity by offering up their own lives, then death would be to them far more joyous than life.

Such then, dear children, is St. Peter's teaching of the right and the sure way: humility must be the foundation within us and with-out. Upon that, again, we build the house of the love of God, and we adorn it with the virtue of discretion. And all this God brings about by His days of visitation.   Hence I declare to you, children, that those who set out toward perfection by ways of high reasoning—not traveling by this humble road of St. Peter—every one of them will fall into the pit of hell: for the higher the mountain the deeper the valley. May God grant that we shall be found resting on the right foundation. May God grant us to go forward by the threefold virtues of humility, love of God and discretion.   *Amen.*

Four Classes of Sinners

Synopsis—First, coarse men, wholly and openly regardless of divine things—Their ways described—How timid confessors may be involved in their guilt—The second class are hypocrites—These are often self-deluded—Our Lord's anathema on this class—The third class are spiritual sluggards—These ever seek the easiest way, and never escape, falling sooner or later—They sin against the light, and by ingratitude—They are formalists in religious things, and excessively resent correction—The fourth class are penitent sinners—Marks of the validity of this happy and lovely state—Rules for their guidance.

SECOND SERMON FOR THE THIRD SUNDAY AFTER TRINITY.

Now the publicans and sinners drew nigh unto Him to hear Him. And the Pharisees and the scribes murmured, saying: This Man receiveth sinners, and eateth with them. And He spoke to them this parable, saying: What man of you that hath a hundred sheep, and if he shall lose one of them, doth he not leave the ninety-nine in the desert, and go after that which was lost till he find it? And when he hath found it, lay it upon his shoulders, rejoicing; and coming home, call together his friends and neighbors, saying to them: Rejoice with me, because I have found my sheep which was lost.—Luke xv, 1-6.

Dear children, we are sinners and sinfully inclined, and, as St. John teaches: "If we say that we have no sin, we deceive ourselves, and the truth is not in us" (I John i: 8).

And I will speak of four kinds of sinners. The first are coarse, worldly men, who lead a frivolous and proud life, forgetful of God, without the fear of God, regardless of divine things, a cause of sin to others. They neither seek nor love God, nor will they hear or learn anything of Him, for they are sunk in mortal sin all their days. If they happen to be present at mass, they are ready to spring up and be away—it is all too long for them. As to the divine honor, they are wholly unconcerned about it, or about the practice of virtue. They may, indeed, receive our Lord in Communion at Easter, yet it is for appearance sake, and without the purpose to give up their evil ways; they intend to go on with their sinful course. Such a man had better receive into his body a hundred thousand devils, rather than receive our Lord as Judas did; he is guilty of the body and blood of our Lord Jesus Christ.

Dear children, if we fully knew the peril in which such a man stands, it would wither up our very souls. If he knew it himself—the torment and horror, the awful doom and the dreadful agony that awaits him in his eternal punishment, his reason could not endure the thought. Some of them, as they reach the end of their days, and become aware of this misery, fall into despair, and they die distrusting God, being lost eternally. When such a one on his death-bed speaks out the anguish and horror of his soul, his friends say: He is raving. And hereby, in God's mercy, others may be warned against a bad life. How much better had it been if these sinners had had faithful father confessors, who, knowing how badly disposed they were, had refused to allow them to go to Communion, and had warned them of their danger: courageous teachers and confessors are most necessary for these stony-hearted sinners.

The second class are also great sinners. But they keep up an appearance of piety. They practice devout exercises, do good works and set a good example. But they are hypocrites, and they have the spirit of Pharisees. They are full of self-will and self-love, proud, unmortified and quarrelsome. These are secretly great sinners, quite unrestrained in their vices; they care for God and love God not at all—they are absorbed in self-love. Their road is a perilous one, indeed, for they are enemies of God. By the very good things they do with the delusion that these practices are leading them to God, they are really led only the farther away from Him. Their works have a show of virtue indeed, and are accompanied by outward signs and professions of humility, but they gain their authors great harm. But such men are corrupted by self-love and their motive is pride. We cannot be without uneasiness concerning them, for they are self-flatterers. Meanwhile they are harsh in their judgment of others, and our Lord's condemnation of the Pharisees falls upon them. They have no patience with those who will not adopt their ways, being tainted with spiritual pride, full of self-love—sins that of old thrust the highest angels down into the deepest hell. Avoid this spirit as you would eternal death. Judge no man but yourself. Even if you see anything that is plainly evil, excuse it as best you may. The Good Shepherd left the ninety-nine sheep to go in search of one that was lost. As to the perverse men we have been considering, it is of them that the Lord speaks in the Gospel: "Amen, I say to you, I know you not" (Matt. xxv: 12).

The third class of sinners are the cold-hearted and slothful. Holy baptism was given them by God that they might have grace to avoid mortal sin, according to His laws in holy Church. But they have rejected this grace. They have no earnestness for God or divine things. They may sing hymns and recite prayers with their fellow Christians, but it is only like turning over the leaves of the book; they have neither savor nor grace in these devotions—but much love and pleasure in creatures. To the utmost of their ability they seek for the enjoyment of created things, exciting all their energies to that end, gladly, habitually. This is seen in their manners, words, deeds clothes, and in the letters they write. Their conduct is without restraint, their conversation is idle chatter. Yet they fancy that they would not willingly commit mortal sin, especially of the grosser kind. God knows full well the state of these souls—would that they feared Him. They are like men with foul stomachs, belching forth offensive odors, incapable of digesting good food, or knowing the taste of it. Such souls find good actions bitter to their taste; they are like pregnant women craving unwholesome food. Their souls are surfeited with the joys of creatures, spoiled for the taste of divine food.

Spiritual teachers say: "The raw material of nature hungers and thirsts after its proper form." At first there is the mere unformed matter, then an animal form, finally the human form. This hungers and thirsts after an immortal, reasonable and godlike form, which can never know rest till it is made over again with that form which perfects all others, namely, the uncreated and everlasting Word of the heavenly Father. Every soul has a spark of light within it, or rather a thirst within it, which even God, who can do all things, cannot quench except by giving the soul Himself—if He gave the soul all that earth and heaven contains, it would not be content without Himself; and that thirst for God is implanted in the soul's very nature. It is this longing for God that these perverse men destroy in their souls. They gape with wide-open mouths after transitory things, as if they could be fed by the wind. Their taste is spoiled, they are filled with creatures—they draw nigh to eternal death. Dear children, what do you suppose such men will do as their end approaches? Then they will begin to realize that they have perverted their natural nobility of soul, injured themselves essentially, and rejected the priceless good that was offered them. Ah, children, one cannot describe the misery of their last hours.

You know, children, that all that we have has been received from God—the goods of nature and of grace and of Providence, all inner gifts and outer ones. And all are bestowed on us that we might offer them again to God with gratitude, love and praise. Now a soul that thus pays God His due, with difficulty accounts for the favors of a single day. What then of the incalculable debt of a whole life? Look into it, calculate the last farthing that we owe God: how much, think you, would it all amount to? See to it that your fate shall not be that of the foolish virgins, of whom it is not certain that they were guilty of greivous sin, but only that they were found unready for the coming of the bridegroom. Indeed, they would have made ready, for they had some sort of good will, but it was too late. And so they were shut out, and they heard the words: "Amen, I say to you, I know you not" (Matt. xxv: 12). Alas, it was not as they had hoped. No, no. Men are blind who fancy that they can trifle with the sacred passion of our Lord Jesus Christ with impunity, and with His precious blood. No, children, such cannot be the case.

They may say that they are in a holy order, are surrounded with decent companions, and are occupied with prayers and pious reading. Yes; but it is all without love, devoid of the true devotional spirit, with distracted hearts, cold and blind. They also go to confession, but only with words, lacking hearty good will; and in the same state they receive holy Communion. It is like inviting a king into one's house, and then lodging him in a filthy pig sty—it were a thousand times better not to go to Communion at all in such a state. And if any friends warn them of their danger, they laugh at them, and call them teachers of novelties. Such is their treatment of men who are pained at their evil course, and would set them on the right road—they treat them worse than Jews and pagans. Be sure that if they persevere wilfully and knowingly in their wickednesses, they will never see the face of God. They say that they would not wilfully commit sin. But (I answer) dost thou think it no sin that thou givest only

lip-service and religious formalism to God who died for thee, and that
thou bestowest on creatures thy free and loving service? God cares
not three beans for such an offering as thou givest Him. Thou art
indeed the sheep that the Lord had lost—thou hast gone astray from
His flock. Perhaps God will give thee the grace of repentance on thy
death-bed, though this cannot be counted on. But even so, thou shalt
have merited a terrible purgatory, lasting, perhaps, till the day of
judgment. And then, finally, thou shalt be placed in an obscure
corner of heaven, far distant from the special friends of God. Now
such men rate themselves anything but sinners. Outwardly blameless,
they would come close to our Lord; and inwardly their hearts are alien
to Him.

The fourth class are happy and lovely sinners, for they are penitents.
It is true that in former times they fell deeply, more deeply, perhaps,
and into greater mortal sins than all the other sinners of whom we
have been discoursing. I care not for that, for now they have with
utmost sincerity come close in to our Lord. They have turned away
absolutely from all that is not simply God. Him alone they love, and
above all things. To Him they yield instantly in all happenings of
life, no matter what. God will never reckon with these men's sins,
He will never know their offenses again : they are wholly turned away
from them, and so is God. Now what is the method and the mark
of such men? It is that of a man who with absolute sincerity and in
his inmost heart loves God and Him alone, and holds Him in view in
all His life and work. He is conscious of a will most ready to do or
not to do everything just as God wills. He searches the way God
would lead him, whether directly or by His representatives, and that
way he gladly takes, wholly detached from self-will.

The gospel tells us that the Lord went in search of the lost sheep.
How are we to understand this search? It is thus: God seeks and
searches for a humble, gentle and poor-minded soul, one that is detached from earthly things and rests indifferent—though that does
not mean a sluggard who sits down idly with his mantle over his
head. I bid you prepare for God's seeking by learning humility, by
suffering every kind of oppression. Now if anybody seeks anything
earnestly, it is not in one little corner only, but in every corner and
place till he finds it. And so God seeks thee—let Him find thee everywhere He may look, in all circumstances of thy life. Whatever shame
comes on thee, know that that is the place in which God is looking

for a gentle and meek soul; therefore suffer thyself to be constantly trodden under foot, until thou hast well learned thy lesson of meekness. God is looking for a poor man; therefore if anyone will take from thee thy money, thy property or thy friends, let him do so, that thou mayst be found poor by God, who is looking for thee in just such a state. Let thy inner life answer true to God's searching, in purity and in poverty, in all enlightenment and detachment of spirit, after no matter what struggles and combats. In every occurrence of life God seeks thee. What happens thee from friends or from foes, nay from thy very mother or sister—no matter how it comes or from whom, all whatsoever that comes to thee prepares thee for God's searching and finding.

Dear children, if one had a putrified wound, he would allow himself to be cut very cruelly and would suffer much pain, so that greater pain should not befall him—he would not spare himself until the corruption were cut away, so that he might recover his health. So must you suffer what God inflicts upon you, in order that your soul be healed eternally. When unforseen adversity comes upon you, say: Welcome, dear and trusted friend; welcome even though thy coming is all unexpected. Let us bow humbly down to such visitations. Be sure that God, who would make thee a self-denying man, will try thee in everything. God does not seek men exercised in great and peculiar devotions, any more than He looks for large horses or strong oxen. Nor does He look for men of mighty outward activity. No, He seeks only humble, gentle-minded and mortified men, men who are glad to be sought by God, and whom God finds as a shepherd finds peaceful sheep.

Wilt thou become the Lord's sheep? Then cultivate a peaceful spirit, no matter what may happen to thee. Do thy best, and then rest without anxiety as to how things will turn out. Remain quiet in mind, and recommend all to God our Lord. Place thyself in His hands in a heavenly spirit, even in thy imperfections, as long as thou art displeased with thyself and turned away from danger. Be not over-distressed at thy faults, argue not with thyself about them, for that is a serious obstacle to thy progress. And let this peaceful condition extend over God's gifts. The Lord giveth, the Lord taketh away. Let thy mind be equal and balanced towards God in joy and in sorrow, in things sweet and bitter, in true and perfect peace.

Children, such is the lovely sheep, sought after and found by the Lord. He is very different from that proud-hearted sheep that says: We are the ones who have gained such and such a prize, who have travelled to this place and to that; but who and what are you? What can you do? And other such proud words they speak, striking about them right and left like an unbroken colt. Ah, children, beware of striking about your neighbors with an unbridled tongue. The Lord left ninety-nine sheep; aye, and He would leave ninety-nine hundred arrogant and self-willed men in the wilderness, where there is little pasture, that is to say, little fruit of a good life; because such is the state of these men.

But when He had found the lost sheep, He laid it on His shoulders, and coming home He said to His friends and neighbors: "Rejoice with Me, because I have found My sheep which was lost." Friends and neighbors, that means the whole company of the angels and saints in heaven, and all His friends on earth, and their joy is exceeding great. But the joy of this sheep himself is inexpressibly great, for it sinks down into God's inmost being. And when the Divine Shepherd takes the beloved sheep on His shoulders, it is thereby placed between the Shepherd's head and body—that is to say, it is brought into touch with both our Lord's all-holy humanity and His eternal divinity. The holy humanity is the soul's stepping place, whereby it goes into the Lord's divinity. The Lord's humanity is united and blended with His sheep, and leads it on in all its works. Heretofore the soul did all its work with itself and by itself; and now God draws it so close to Him, that He works in all and by all its activities—speaking and eating and going is all done in God. This soul lives and moves in God. This sheep of God goes forth from the humanity to the divinity, and back again from the divinity to the humanity, always finding good pasture. Its joy and its content, even in this life, is unspeakably great, and above all joy of all creatures put together. This is the one penitent sinner, over whom the Lord said that the angels rejoiced more than over many just ones; for, in fact, God's honor is greatly advanced by his repentance. He is the sinner who has in very truth come nigh unto God. May God the Father, and God the Son, and God the Holy Ghost grant us the grace thus to be sought after, and as God's true sheep thus to be found. *Amen.*

God's Deep Searching of Our Souls

Synopsis—Qualities of sound spirituality—The interior and exterior virtues compared—The inner confusion that sometimes besets beginners and the good effects of it—Self-abasement and resignation to God's will overcome all inner troubles and outward afflictions— How cleansing and elevation of motives leads the soul to contemplative joys.

THIRD SERMON FOR THE THIRD SUNDAY AFTER TRINITY.

What woman having ten groats. if she lose one groat, doth not light a candle, and sweep the house, and seek diligently until she find it?—Luke xv, 8.

Our last discourse was about our Lord's seeking and finding the lost sheep. Children, however you may manage it, you must become like a sheep in meekness, in silence, in all self-denial and patience, and in subjection to all creatures. It is thus that thou shalt submit to God's seeking for thee and finding thee, when and how He will, directly by Himself, indirectly by thy fellowmen, whether friends or foes, by His creatures in heaven or on earth. Sometimes by very hard words He will search thee out, and thou must be still, not answering Him, no matter in what plight thou art placed. Imitate our Lord Jesus Christ, that meek lamb, who, when He was led before His judges, opened not His mouth. Men blinded by pride, men who for forty years have stood on their own self-love, will revile thee and call thee a dumb beast; never mind them, suffer what they inflict on thee. I declare to thee that when men persecute thee it is nothing else than God's visitation: hold thy peace and let them afflict thee. Follow the example of our Lord, that innocent and suffering lamb. Follow Him in His suffering till thou art brought to His infinite Godhead; there shall be thy place of perfect pasture. Self-willed men would have thee answer back, and not allow thyself to be oppressed. Not so; but do thou take Jesus Christ as thy pattern. That thou must do if thou shalt become holy.

And now thou must know there is something yet higher placed before thee, if thou dost aspire to greater perfection.

Our text tells us of a woman who lost a piece of money, and then lit a candle and looked for it. Consider the woman as the Godhead, the candle as our Savior's humanity, the groat as our soul. The groat must have three things, wanting any of which it is not good money; the right material, right weight, right form or stamp. Its material must be gold or silver. Ah, children, applying this figure of speech to the soul—how wonderful is the substance of our soul, far beyond our comprehension. And its weight: the soul if spiritual and has no weight, yet does it outweigh all earth and heaven, for God is contained in the soul, which thus weighs as much as God. And it is stamped, is this spirit of ours, with the very Godhead itself, which, indeed, has quite absorbed it. But this thou must attain to by coming much closer in thy life to God, quite otherwise than outward acting men. Thou must pass beyond the mere outward forms and observances of both active and passive life. Notice that the woman of this gospel lit a candle, and then turned her house upside down looking for her lost coin. Now it is the eternal wisdom that lights a candle in our soul, and its light is true divine love—it must be lighted in thy heart, and it must burn brightly in thy heart.

Dear children, you know not what love is. You feel great sensible devotion and spiritual sweetness, and that you call love. No, by no means; love is the burning and destroying of self, real self-denial, steadfast yearning for God in a spirit of abandonment to Him, the soul melted into God in a persevering state of resignation to Him; such is love, and such is the lighting of God's candle in the soul.

Then the woman turned her house upside down, looking for her piece of money. And how does this correspond with God's treatment of the soul? His searching of the soul is both active, in making it act; and passive, in making it suffer His act. In the active searching, God causes the soul itself to work; in the passive, He Himself does the searching. The first is in the external order, the second in the interior life; and the interior is as high above the external as heaven is above the earth. The active and outward life is in external devout practices and good works, according to God's guidance and the suggestion of God's friends. This is especially seen in the practice of virtue, such as humility, meekness, silence, self-denial.

The other is far above this, namely, our entering into our soul's inmost depths in search of God, according to His own words: "Lo, the kingdom of God is within you" (Luke xvii: 21). Whosoever would find God and all His kingdom, all His essence and nature, let him seek Him where He is. It is in the deepest depths of the soul that God is nighest to it, much nearer to it there than is the soul to its own self. Let a man enter that house, leaving outside all that is self, all that belongs to the life of the senses in forms and images and imagination; yea, he must in a manner transcend even his reason and all its ways and all its activity. When a man thus enters his interior house in search of God, he finds it all turned upside down, for God it is that is seeking him; and God acts like a man who throws one thing this side and another that side looking for what he has lost. This is what happens in the interior life when a man seeks God there, for there he finds God seeking him.

And now I will say something that not every one can understand, though I always speak good plain German; but only those can now understand me who have had some previous experience of such matters. For you must know that this turning inwards is not to last for only awhile, to be followed by turning back again to busy oneself with created things. No, by no means. For when one goes deep into his heart in search of God and thus finds God in search of him, and when all his interior life is thereby thrown into confusion, then it happens that all his pious practices seem set at nought, and the spiritual lights heretofore granted him seem to have gone quite out. And yet—supposing that nature could endure it—if a man could be thus day and night thrown into confusion by God's seeking for him seventy-seven times over, it would profit him more than any favor that had ever been granted him. He would hereby be advanced farther in perfection, than by all the good deeds and good purposes he ever could do or think of doing:—happy is he who is rightly guided in this, for everything will soon become plain and easy to him. As often as he wills he can elevate his soul far above all created things.

The trouble is that poor human nature is so tenacious of its own, that it cleaves obstinately to it. Like uneven ground, nature requires a sharp, heavy harrow to level it down; but when once leveled, even a feather duster will finish the work. So is the soul of some men full of lumps and clods, all crude, and quite unsubmissive to God. A sharp harrow must tear across it, that is to say, many temptations and much

suffering, so that it may learn to be resigned to the divine action.
Devout and self-denying men go straight against self always, and are
more quickly and easily transformed—are regenerated in a blessed
manner. They strip off and cast away all that nature loves, and they
stand before God truly poor in spirit, truly submissive, blindly led by
God in all His own chosen ways. Ah, child, when thou allowest thyself
thus to be sought after by God, and thy house turned upside down,
then art thou indeed found by Him, as the piece of money was found
by the woman in the Gospel. And thou shalt be led far beyond thy
own good works and self-chosen devotions, beyond all this world can
do for thee, whether inwardly or outwardly. And this was what our
Lord guaranteed when He said: "If any man will come after Me,
let him deny himself, and take up his cross daily and follow Me"
(Luke ix: 23). So must a man renounce all that hinders true spiritual
progress.

But when an unmortified man encounters severe trials and temptations, and when the sharp harrow cuts him deep, then he thinks all
is lost. He is tormented with doubts, he is haunted with terrors. He
says: Alas, O Lord, all light is gone, all grace is withdrawn, and all
is lost. And yet I say to thee that if thou wert but a well-practiced
and really self-denying man, thou wouldst know that thou never hadst
been in so good a state as now. When the Lord is searching for thee
in thy soul, then thou shouldst be well contented. Does He demand
of thee to be dark, cold, destitute? Yield lovingly to Him. Ah, dear
children, how do you suppose God is going to deal with a soul He
leads in this way? He will elevate it above all creatures. Beloved
soul, fortunate soul, fear nothing. As to those who do not aspire to
this high state, I bid them not to lose courage, for there are many
men who support life well enough, and who yet have no better food
than bread and water.

But the woman's piece of money must have its proper weight, and
also be rightly coined and stamped. The weight means the sinking
of the soul down into the abyss of God's being, out of which it first
came forth. This includes its stainless purity when it has become
entirely detached from creatures, all emancipated and uncontaminated,
having in itself but one image—not only that by which it is made
like God in its nature, but also an image which is a gift of grace,
even the uncreated God Himself in His very essence, in which God
loves it, knows it, enjoys it and is active within it. Here it is, then,

that the soul is as it were colored with the divine color, being in a manner by grace what God is by nature. And if it could see itself in this state of union and absorption. in God, it would value itself in a sort of a way as it values God; or, better said, it would see itself clothed with God, shining in God's colors, and living in God's being. All this is, of course, not by nature, but by grace. God and the soul are one in this union of grace—not simply the union of nature.

If, on the contrary, one could behold a soul in its real essence, a soul that had wilfully given up its entire love to the service and enjoyment of created things, and in them was clothed, by them colored, it would certainly behold something no less insufferably horrible than the demon himself. It would be a sight to wither one up with terror. Yet this is what a lost soul will behold in itself for all eternity. But the souls in Heaven will be seen by God as if He beheld Himself, so close will be their union with Him, drawing all their blessedness from Him, and beholding their glory as if it were His. O how happy are they who permit themselves to be sought and found by God, to be led into Him, to be made one with Him—happy beyond words to tell or mind to conceive. Whosoever will come to this glorious end must carefully follow the way we have pointed out; therein he cannot go astray. If he will not undertake it, if he will rest absorbed in the joys of his senses and in creatures, then he must eternally be excluded from this blessed lot. May God the Father, and the Son, and the Holy Ghost, grant us thus to be sought after and thus to be found. *Amen.*

Patience with Men and Patience with God

Synopsis—A merciful man is a favorite with God—The cure of harshly judging our neighbor is just judgment of ourselves—The relation of thinking and speaking in dealing with others—Why God seems over-severe in His interior visitations—Rules for the use of bodily mortifications during interior trials—Joy and sadness, how they alternate in the soul favored by God—The worst desolation of spirit must be met by patience, and that alone.

FIRST SERMON FOR THE FOURTH SUNDAY AFTER TRINITY.

Be ye therefore merciful, as your Father also is merciful. Judge not, and you shall not be judged. Condemn not, and you shall not be condemned. Forgive, and you shall be forgiven. Give, and it shall be given to you; good measure and pressed down and shaken together and running over shall they give into your bosom. For with the same measure that you shall mete withal, it shall be measured to you again.—Luke vi, 36-38.

In this Gospel two things are taught us by our Lord—one to be done, the other to be omitted, namely, to be merciful and not to judge others. Children, yesterday I instructed you how dangerous a thing it is and how distressing to sit in judgment on our neighbor, a sin to be most carefully guarded against, for the lips of truth itself tell us: "With the same measure you shall mete withal, it shall be measured to you again." Art thou very merciful? Thou shalt be very mercifully dealt with. Little merciful? Little mercy shalt thou receive. Not merciful at all? Thou shalt receive no mercy at all. This mercy one must cultivate in his interior soul, cherishing a deep-seated pity for his neighbor in his time of suffering, whether his pain be inner or outer, heartily praying God to grant him comfort. Canst thou give him bodily assistance? Do so generously, helping him with good advice and with material aid, as well with words as with works, as far as lies in thy power. Canst thou do little? Do that at least with a pitiful heart and with kindly words, and herein thou shalt have done thy part, and mayst expect to meet a merciful God.

Now as to the other lesson: "Judge not, and you shall not be judged." Children, the amount of harm done by this vice is amazing—it is simply lamentable. Do all the good works of outward religion thou pleasest, the devil laughs at them all if thou art addicted to this judging of others. No man should set himself up as his neighbor's judge without first sitting in judgment on himself. It is a miserable case of blindness of heart, that a man should insist upon another being subject to his will and pleasure, and meantime with all his endeavors he is unable to behave himself as he ought to, or even as he would wish to. One should not rate his neighbor's fault greviously, if he would have God rate his own fault mercifully; or in case he cannot help knowing his neighbor is bad, let him not be eager to judge him.

If we would adopt the right plan, it is to take the beam out of our own eye before noticing the mote in our brother's eye. Look at home; study thy own defects and no one else's. If it happens that thou art appointed judge over another by thy office, then administer justice affectionately and mildly, with gentle looks and kind words, as St. Gregory admonishes us. To priests especially, set, as they are, to be judges in Holy Church, it is strictly forbidden to punish with severity, bearing in mind their own accountability to God and to men. Bear in mind that thy own life and works are one day to pass under God's judgment; and take heed to thy sentence on thy neighbor lest God shall in turn pronounce against thee an awful sentence. Injurious gossiping is so common that it is a lamentable evil, men thereby losing God's grace and their eternal happiness. Think three times before thou operrest thy mouth to speak once, so that thy words may be for God's honor and thy neighbor's good, conducive to thy own interior and exterior peace. Do you know why the holy founders of religious orders have prohibited talking so strictly everywhere in convents except in one single place, and allowing it there only after special permission? It is because incalculable injury results from talking, far more than it is possible to reckon.

This Gospel speaks also of giving good measure. Now, the measure is a man's own soul. God is measured by our soul, if we will only have it so. Ah, dear children, that is indeed a noble measure. But it is too often sadly in need of cleansing, that it may be a fit receptacle for Him, for the foul things of this life pollute it. Wilt thou turn to God in holy prayer? Then must thou give thy soul to Him in pawn, and with such sincerity as no longer to have control over thyself. How can God enter in when the love of created things is the door-keeper and holds Him back? If thou prayest without sincerity it is all tasteless to thee, it wearies thee, and thy soul presently runnest away after distractions. Dear child, redeem thy soul from the pawn shop of creatures, by love, by intention, by occupation; then God shall enter in and creatures shall go out. Hold thyself free from vain occupations. Fire does not burn upwards so naturally, nor birds fly into the air so lightly, as a really detached soul ascends to God. If we would be absorbed in the depths of the Godhead, the least that we can do is to go down into our own depths to begin with. Sunk down with real humility, we then come forth bearing all our sins and imper-fections, and we lay them sorrowfully at the door of God's mercy, that He may melt them away and destroy them. As to what virtues and graces we may happen to find in our soul's depths, these also let us offer at the gates of His loving kindness, so that He may melt and absorb them into His gentle love.

And when thou hast with all thy might cut off the love of creatures and all entanglement with them, then thou must do more: thou must hinder even the thoughts and images of creatures from lodging in thy soul. If thou dost not at first succeed well in this, nevertheless keep up a constant endeavor, abandon thyself to God, stay at home with thyself, plead most humbly with Him: O dear Lord, have pity on me. Lord, come to my help. Lord, I beg Thee to force Thyself into my soul. And stand fast to that practice, begin no other, for I have no manner of doubt but that thy trouble will thereby right itself. I have noticed how silver is mined. The ore is pounded fine and all mixed with water, and then the water is poured through it and finally drawn off with the dust and dirt, leaving the precious metal behind, which pays all the expense of this process and gives great profit besides. So must it be with the dust and dirt of all foul images in thy mind, which are there against thy will. The waters of sorrow and suffering will finally cleanse them all out and away from thee, amply repaying thee for thy patience, and leaving great gain to thee. Our Lord will say to thee: O well-beloved man, thou art an honor to Me, and I praise thee for having been mindful of My passion and borne the weight of My heavy cross with Me; for in struggling with thy imperfections thou hast taken part in My sufferings. Behold, I shall now be thy reward exceeding great.

But if thou wouldst become an interior man, thou must give God an overflowing measure. Whatever outward thing hinders thy inward recollection must be given up. Study thyself. Carefully scrutinize thy conduct, affections, intentions, words, works, clothing, adornments, friends, property, honors, lodging, pleasure, manners. Look into thy whole life. Find out every single thing that hinders God's dwelling within thee; relentlessly cut it all off. For this is an absolute condition of thy becoming an interior man. So must thou also study over those of thy external religious exercises that are of the more showy kind—stop any of them that may interfere with thy interior spirit. And dost thou ask why I do not recommend thee severe fasts and vigils? I answer that these are of great help in the spiritual life it one has the necessary strength. But if one is of weak bodily constitution, or if he has a weak head (in this country men have very weak heads), and finds that watching and fasting injures and may destroy his health, then let him dispense with these practices, and when a fast day comes obtain dispensation from his father confessor, or if he is not accessible, let him presume on his permission and tell him of it as soon as possible. Holy Church does not mean that we should destroy our health by obeying her law of fasting. Dear children, my whole teaching is very simple: whatsoever hinders thee from the shortest road to perfection, get rid of it—whether it be in thy soul or in thy outward life, and no matter what name it may go by. Follow this rule steadily, and, dear children, be assured that you will become perfect souls.

Yet further, our Lord requires a measure pressed down and shaken together. Dear children, mind what I am going to say. When one has systematically taken up this way, when he has cut off all hindrances to his spiritual life, then it happens that many wonderful sweetnesses come to him, pouring through both his soul and body a joy far above any known to this earth. Then what follows? After some time has passed all this joy suddenly vanishes away. It seems to a man that he has gained nothing at all by his mortification and his love of God—the measure—that is to say, his soul—is pressed down so hard into its own very self, that all pleasure in life is quite gone out of it. Now, if one will attain to true peace, he must yield himself up to this spiritual destitution; he must make nothing of it; he must in all single-heartedness resign himself to the holy will of God, and suffer this oppression of spirit in all patience; yea, even if it were to endure to the end of the world.

But, O children, how unbearable is this oppression. The whole world is too narrow for that poor soul's misery. He seems to be withering up with this pain, the pain of losing a heavenly light so sweet and so perfectly happy. Well, there are some who fail, who will not be patient under this trial; for they are too deeply attached to their own spiritual joys. This lack of patience comes from two causes. One is that the soul is not essentially and at bottom dead to self. The other cause is that God is not absolutely trusted. Dear child, stand fast in thy confidence in God, stand fast in holy fear and in humility; for God will, without fail, release thee from thy sorrow. Lift up thy hands to God, to the very essence of God, thinking of nothing less than the infinite God. Do not act like one who receives a jewel from a friend, and forthwith becomes so absorbed in its beauty, and so vain of wearing it as to forget the giver. Hold thyself towards whatever may minister to thy joy like a man asleep—be awake only to God Himself. Whether thy joy be natural or supernatural, cleave not to it. Press thy measure down in all humility till it reaches thy own nothingness, holding fast to God's blessed will in all detachment of spirit. You know that our Lord's disciples were required to give up His blessed bodily presence among them, that presence so consoling and so divine. They were required to make that sacrifice in order to be transformed into new beings. So says St. Paul: "Brethren, I do not count myself to have apprehended. But one thing I do: forgetting the things that are behind, and stretching forth myself to those that are before, I press towards the mark, to the prize of the supernal vocation of God in Christ Jesus" (Phil. iii: 13-14).

But now our poor man seems hemmed in by high walls, denied relief or rest anywhere. Dear child, give up to God, try not to escape, all will yet be well with thee. Have no desire except that God's will be done in thee—let Him afflict thee as long as He pleases and in whatever manner. When our Lord perceives thy fidelity in the midst of misery and suffering—for on that everything depends—then will He come to thee with His overflowing measure of relief, namely, the gift of Himself. He will pour Himself into thy soul, Himself who is essentially all joy and all good, immersing thee in the abyss of the deity. He pours Himself out to thee, yet He remains filled with gifts to impart them continually to thee. Thy soul will be filled with Him as a cup is filled with the exhaustless waters of the ocean, filled beyond all that thou has ever desired.

When King Assuerus beheld his Queen Esther standing pale and frightened before him, he reached her his golden sceptre, rose up from his throne and embraced and kissed her, and then promised her to grant her wish, were it for half of his kingdom. So will God the Father treat the faithful soul bowed down before Him, blanched with fear, stricken with grief, totally desolate. He will, as it were, reach to it His divine sceptre of power and joy, and embracing it most lovingly, He will make room for it on His throne, instantly relieving it of all its misery. And now what wonders are wrought in that soul. The gift of the divine sceptre is the only begotten Son, and the kiss of love is the unspeakable sweetness of the Holy Ghost, making the soul queen of earth and heaven, sharing God's own royal sway, imparting to it by grace a share of the divinity that is His by nature. This overflowing measure of divine favor makes such souls as receive it the highest glory of all God's creatures. Without the presence of these elect souls amid the Christian people, the world would not survive one hour, for their deeds are much greater in God's sight than those of all the rest of the world put together, because it is in God Himself that they do them. As far as God is above creatures so far are His works in these souls above the works of all other men—yea, they are above the comprehension of men and angels. Here, then, is the truest peace and joy, that of which St. Paul said that it surpassed all understanding.

Dear children, to take lot and part with God is not so dreadful a thing as you have fancied. Whosoever treads this road steadfastly will at last come happily to the end of all his troubles; and whosoever goes not by this road will not arrive at the ever-living truth. He may attain to the knowledge of spiritual things that is gained by the strivings of human reason, but this is as far different from the divine reality as shining brass is different from precious gold. Such knowledge gives forth a deceitful appearance, but the living truth must be sought and found only as I have explained to you. The man that would plant his vineyard on the shady side of a high mountain where the sun never shines would be a fool, as would be the man who looked for the sun with his back turned to it. And among a hundred men, men, too, who would be thought good, you will find hardly one who squarely and honestly turns his face to the light of the living truth that God is. May God grant us the grace to turn ourselves full and direct towards the truth, so that we may be given good measure, full to overflowing. *Amen.*

Giving God Good Measure

Synopsis—This begins with an ordinary good Christian life—Sincerely done, it is all that God requires of many souls—Others are called to many additional works of religion and penance and a higher degree of virtue—These shall be judged by their inner fidelity rather than by their outward conformity—Nor does this mean a barren intellectuality of religion, but deeply-lying simplicity of intention —Various comparisons—the supremacy of loving God in a career of perfection.

SECOND SERMON FOR THE FOURTH SUNDAY AFTER TRINITY.

Be ye therefore merciful, as your Father also is merciful. Judge not, and you shall not be judged. Condemn not, and you shall not condemned. Forgive, and you shall be forgiven. Give, and it shall be given to you; good measure and pressed down and shaken together and running over shall they give into your bosoms. For with the same measure that you shall mete withal, it shall be measured to you again.—Luke vi, 36-38.

Children, it is a pitiable thing how alien to some men's hearts is the beautiful virtue of mercy. Every man is bound to be merciful to his neighbor in all his needs, and' that not only in temporal matters; for he is bound to have a pitiful heart for his moral and spiritual defects. But, alas, everybody strikes at his neighbor with his condemnation. If any misfortune happens him we add the weight of our accusation, attributing the basest motives we can think of. Blessed be God that He does not do the like. What untold misery comes from an evil tongue, which hurries in with its condemnations without a moment's consideration. I beg thee, my dear man, for the sake of thy eternal welfare, to pause awhile, and come to an understanding with thyself, carefully weighing both thy thoughts and thy words about thy neighbor. It is a shameful thing and almost blasphemous, thoughtlessly to sit in judgment on thy neighbor, and to launch against him injurious words, spiritually murdering him in the minds of thy hearers.

Hence those words of Christ: "Judge not, that you may not be judged. For with what judgment you judge, you shall be judged; and with what measure you mete, it shall be measured to you again" (Matt. vii: 1-2).

And now, children, let us consider the Lord's words: "With the same measure that you shall mete, it shall be measured to you again." Devout teachers understand four kinds of measures here—good, full, pressed down, and flowing over. The first means a pious Christian life with God's grace, ending in eternal life. The full measure means God's gift to us of a glorified body at the last day. The measure pressed down means the blessed companionship granted us among God's saints and angels in everlasting bliss. And the overflowing measure is our possession of God Himself in perfect happiness and in the fulness of every desire.

Such are God's measures to us. And now let us inquire what are our measures to God, given by that power of loving which we call the will, by which we weigh out all our words and works and life— the will, to whose properties we cannot add nor take away. And let us ever bear in mind that with what measure we mete here in this life, it shall be measured to us again in life eternal.

First, what is our good measure? It is a hearty turning to God, with a sincere purpose to observe God's commandments and those of holy Church; that we hold fast to the true faith; that we devoutly receive the sacraments; that we interiorly detest our sins and totally give them up; that we live a life of penance, trusting securely in God's mercy and grace. Alas! It seems as if nobody at all gives God this good measure nowadays, nor lives in His holy fear. But whosoever does follow this true Christian life will without doubt enter into eternal joy. And it is the indispensable rule of our religion for all and every one. There are men from whom God requires no more; it is their good measure. And it may, therefore, happen that some upright souls who thus conform to God in this life, shall go straight to Heaven, escaping all purgatory. And yet it is the very lowest degree of the divine service.

Other men God invites to a much higher degree; and these may, nevertheless, have their purgatory, because before their death they have not perfectly conformed to the will of God in their case—and their pains shall be great beyond expression. But that being done and over, they will be raised very high above the others in Heaven, for they originally had the courage to undertake a far more spiritual career, although death interrupted their progress in perfection.

And what is our full measure? It refers to those whom God calls to a life of holy observances, many prayers and kneelings, and much fasting, and other such devout practices. They give God a full measure, if they will but cultivate an interior spirit of real fervor together with their outward piety, seeking God within their soul and finding His kingdom there. This life is as different from the other two kinds as running is different from sitting.

Ah, dear children, how happy is the man whose outward piety is no obstacle to his interior progress in perfection—happy, indeed, and holy, for two good things are better than one. If, therefore, thou perceivest that any outward observance hinders thy inward recollection, give up the outward and concentrate thy soul upon the interior life with all thy might. This pleases God better. Do as we priests do in our monasteries at Easter and Pentecost; for then our vocal prayers are greatly shortened, in order that the holy interior spirit of these festivals may be the better enjoyed. Thus do you, when God invites you to the high festival of His inner visitation, so that leaving off some of your external devotions, you may be the more intently engaged with Him in your soul's inmost depths—there He will accomplish His dearest will with you. In such case thou mayest confine thyself to those outward exercises of religion that are required of thee, as, for example, by the rule of thy order, and boldly cut off all the rest—suposing them to impede thy interior recollection. I declare to thee that this interior life is most divine, most sweet, most fruitful of virtue, if thou wilt but hold steadfastly to it. To this end turn to account the best aid thou canst have. And that is to contemplate the blessed life of our Lord Jesus Christ. Study His bitter death and count His blessed wounds streaming with His precious blood. Or meditate even on the eternal Godhead itself and the holy Trinity, God's eternal wisdom, infinite power, and His merciful goodness to thyself and to all mankind in life and in death.

Whichever of these divine subjects arouses most thy pious sentiments, turn inwards and ponder it, full of humility and gratitude, sinking deep into the divine abyss, and there awaiting God's coming. Now this method, if followed faithfully, produces more aptitude for receiving God than all outward devotions whatsoever, for the interior life is far better than the exterior. All exterior virtues draw their worth from the interior life of the soul. A drop of the interior spirit will sanctify a whole cask of external exercises.

But it sometimes happens that men can think deeply of our Lord in their interior soul, but yet are spiritually superficial—like a wide stretch of water of scarcely a finger's depth. Now, the reason is that they are deficient in real humility, and they lack a universal love for their fellowmen. Says St. Augustine: "The blessedness of one's life consists not in the length of time given to pious exercises, nor in doing many good works; but it consists in the greatness of love." Take an example from poor farm laborers. They raise the best of wheat and of wine, but not for their own benefit—they eat only brown bread and drink only water. Such is the case with men who do good works without deep interior dispositions.

Let us now consider the measure that is pressed down and overflowing. This means superabundant charity, drawing into a great heart all good works, all painful trials, all that is good in the whole world, whether done by God's servants or by His enemies. A man of this degree of love is more truly the proprietor of the good works of others than they are themselves—as long as those persons are lacking in such high charity—so strong is the attraction of love. Consider the many recitations of the divine office, the many masses offered, the many sacrifices made for God—the good of all this is more theirs who have this great heart of love than the ones who actually did all these holy things—supposing them not to have this same fulness of divine love. For I assure you that God will not acknowledge any good works of which He is not both the beginning and the end; according to St. Paul: "And if I should distribute all my goods to feed the poor, and if I should deliver my body to be burned, and have not charity, it profiteth me nothing" (I Cor. xiii: 3).

The love of God is a virtue above all virtues, drawing into the bosom of love all the good deeds done by the grace of God in heaven and earth. The evil that is in a man is his own; all the good he has is to be attributed to divine love. As the grain that is poured into a measure is all pressed together and held into one mass by the sides of the measure, so does love press together into unity all the saints and angels in Heaven and all their merits, as well as all the pains suffered on earth for God,—which but for love we should have neglected and lost. Hence the teaching of certain holy commentators of Scripture: "In everlasting life so deep a love shall the elect have for one another, that if one sees another gifted with greater joy and higher contemplation than himself, this will be to him as much happiness as if he himself had merited it and were now enjoying it."

In proportion to one's share of this overflowing love in this life, so shall be his enjoyment of it in the life to come. Hence it is that the evil one hates these men. And he tempts such a one by insinuating a sense of self-righteousness, and by inducing dislike for his neighbor. The devil leads him to sit in judgment on his neighbor's conduct, to rate his good works and his devotions as hypocritical. If he consents to this uncharity, he has fallen from his holy state of love. He condemns others right and left, and his tongue shoots out poisoned arrows that wound the souls of men unto eternal death. And by the same stroke of false and rash judgment, thou hast stripped thyself of all the merits and virtues thou hadst gathered by thy overflowing measure of love. Thou art now distracted and distressed, peace has fled away from thy soul, and thou art come into a very dangerous state. O, I counsel thee in all fidelity, that thou guard thy tongue most vigilantly, if thou wouldst continue to be called and to be a friend of God.

It often happens that the evil spirit will cause thee to dislike a good pious Christian, and if thou yieldest to this and speakest it out, then God withdraws from thee thy share of that man's graces in the practice of virtue, as well as thy part in the enjoyment of His own holy love. As the prophet spoke of the oil of consecration flowing down from the head of Aaron even upon his beard, so does God's love in a holy man's soul flow out upon all who love Him—it is the overflowing of God's love and all the virtues that belong to it. Whosoever shuts out any one from the spirit of universal love, is himself deprived of his own share of God's love. See to it carefully, dear children, that you cling fast to this divine virtue; hold all mankind in good favor; be sure to avoid contention; profane not that temple of God that every man is, a temple consecrated by the Supreme Pope and Father of Christendom, namely, God; take care lest you fall under the ban of the eternal God.

Alas, that our poor human nature should be so turned against true brotherly love. If one happens to see his neighbor fall into mortal sin, he lets him lie there and perhaps says the worst things about him. Look carefully to your own faults. How do you stand before God in reference to love? And learn diligently the fear of God while you are in this life; for beyond this life all is over with you, and you can neither gain nor lose any degree of virtue—tears of blood shed for you (were it possible) by our Blessed Lady and all the saints will then be of no avail. But now God is steadfastly patient; He is ever ready to grant us more than we are ready to ask Him. Meanwhile the love of God is never idle: labor and suffer cheerfully for His sake, and the superabundant fulness of the measure will be given thee, so full and rich and abundant and sweet, that it will spread everywhere over thy life and fill every corner of thy soul.

And now God comes and touches with His finger the well-filled vessel of his graces, and immediately it overflows and is poured back again into the divine being out of which all its treasures originally came. The soul now is united to God without intermediary and loses itself in Him—will, knowledge, love all overflow into God and are lost in Him and made one with him. The eternal God loves Himself in this soul, all of whose works are done by Him. But this flow and overflow of God into the soul cannot be limited to itself alone, which most longingly petitions our Lord, and says: Ah, dear Lord, have mercy on all mankind, and forgive them their sins; and especially have pity on all those who once did good deeds and then fell away from Thy grace; give them, beloved Lord, the crumbs that fall from Thy table; convert them from their sinful ways and save them through the fires of purgatory; give them the well-filled measure of thy grace, that by Thy merits they may be saved.

These elect souls thus turn back again into God's bosom all their gifts whatsoever, their own selves included, and all created things. They embrace within their souls all that happens in holy Chruch everywhere in the world, offering all up in a happy, humble and self-denying spirit to the eternal heavenly Father, for themselves and for all men whether bad or good. Their love bars out nobody still living in this time of grace, for they constantly join themselves in spirit to the whole human race. And if we in our days did not have among us men of this godlike character, our lot would be an evil one indeed. Therefore let us pray the merciful God that we may be granted this overflowing measure of His love. *Amen.*

Prayer, Vocal and Mental

Synopsis—Elevation of the thoughts and affections to God is the essence of prayer—This involves thoroughgoing detachment from created things—How even good works may hinder prayer if done out of order or from defective motives—True prayer makes the active and passive life one—Examples drawn from our Lord's life.

FIRST SERMON FOR THE FIFTH SUNDAY AFTER TRINITY.

Dearly beloved: be ye all of one mind.—I Peter iii, 8.

In this Sunday's epistle St. Peter bids us be all of one mind, and that is chiefly fulfilled in prayer, which is the most necessary, and delightful, and fruitful, and honorable work that we can perform in this life. Now I would have you clearly to know what prayer is, and what its essence is, what its method is, and in what place we ought to pray.

What is prayer and what is its essence? The essence of prayer is the going up of the soul into God, as spiritual writers define it. And what is the place in which one should pray? It is in the spirit itself, as our Lord taught us. As to how we should pray, I will briefly explain. When any good man starts to pray, he should gather back into himself the life of his senses, and he should inspect his soul to find whether or not it be really turned to God. This method of praying a man can practice in the highest degree of recollection, or the lowest, or midway between these two. Let a man carefully note what form of praying arouses his soul most effectually to a devout feeling—and that let him use. But whosoever would acquire a prayer that is genuine and that God will surely attend to, must turn away from transitory things, and from outward things, and from all that is not of the things of God. He must relentlessly cut off everything that does not mean God to him truly and in its very cause, whether friends or joys or the vanities and ornaments and apparel of this life. He must sever the bonds of disorderly affection that hold him outwardly or inwardly, in words or behavior, to any created thing. Such is the preparation for the true practice of prayer. The soul must cleave to God alone; a man must turn his face towards God ever present in his inmost soul; he must meekly and affectionately cleave to God.

Children, everything we have little and great comes from God, and back again to God must it go, to be given with an undivided heart. So, too, we must collect together and offer to God all the powers of our soul and body. Such is the right method of prayer. Never imagine that noisy mouth-praying, hurried recitations of the Psalms, the heart meanwhile inattentive and straying off, is true prayer. So-called prayers and socalled good works may sometimes even hinder the soul from real praying; do not hesitate to give them up no matter how good they seem, or what people may say, if they distract thee from God—excepting, of course, the divine office and the devout exercises prescribed by holy Church.

It sometimes happens that a community is obligated to certain long vocal prayers, and that a member feels that hereby he is hindered from inward recollection: what should he do? He should both observe the outward obligation and take proper means to preserve interior recollection. While joining outwardly with his brethren, he should bridle all his faculties and senses, and he should turn his mind inward to God's blessed presence, making interior acts of conformity to the divine will, into which he should sink himself and all created things ever deeper and deeper. Thus does he faithfully perform every task imposed on him, begging God to show forth His honor and praise in those persons who have been commended to his prayers:—this is a better prayer than if he had a thousand mouths to pray with. Prayer in the spirit immeasurably exceeds in value prayer that is outward. All other prayer pays tribute to this. Thus the Father would have men pray; and when any prayer serves not this kind, then delay not to let it go. It is like the building of a church with which a hundred men are occupied in many different sorts of work, some making mortar, others laying stone; but it is all for one single purpose—to build a house of prayer. So let everything be made to help you in acquiring a true interior method of prayer. When this true prayer of the spirit is established, then all that helped to this happy result is perfected, extending far beyond the results of external methods, which, besides, are now blended with the interior spirit, one kind of prayer being no manner of hindrance to the other.

It behooves a thoroughly converted and enlightened man that his life of act and his life of joy should be made one, as they are one in God in their uttermost development, interfering with each other not in the least degree. God's act is in the divine persons and His joy we attribute to His most simple essence. The heavenly Father, as He is distinctly Father, is pure act, by which He begets in divine self-knowledge His beloved Son, and from the ineffable embrace of Father and Son the Holy Ghost proceeds,—He is their mutual joy and love. And this is the essential act of the divine persons. To the most simple essence of God is attributed the divine joy, and thus in act and in joy God is one, as in persons and in essence God is three in one. And all creatures, being made like unto God, are created to act; even the sun and stars and all other lifeless creatures. But far above these are angels and men, each active according to its laws of being. Not a little flower or leaf but is acted on by the heavenly bodies, and by God Himself. And shall not noble man, made in God's likeness, resemble Him in activity? As man is formed after God's image in his soul's powers and in his soul's essence, must he not have a much higher activity than reasonless creatures like stars and planets? There must be a close resemblance to God both in man's activity and in his contemplation; and this resemblance must be seen both in his higher and lower powers. And man's activity is characterized by its object, whether that be God or creatures. And whatsoever man makes all the objects of his activity heavenly and divine, turning his back resolutely on all transitory things, that man makes the life and activity of his soul wholly divine.

The glorious soul of our Lord Jesus Christ was ever turned towards the Godhead, as far as His higher faculties were concerned. This was always so from the first moment of His incarnation, just as much as it is now in the bliss of Heaven. But as to His lower powers, these were constantly moving in His life of work and suffering, at the same time that the higher ones were rapt into union with the divine nature. Even when He hung dying on the cross, His soul was with God in its more spiritual powers, essentially the same as it is with Him now. So must we be, if we will imitate Him: we must keep God deep and peaceful in our heart, while in our ordinary occupations we are

engaged with many different things. O, children, the man who neglects
this interior privilege, and allows his nobler spiritual powers to lie
idle, lives in constant danger. He wastes precious years of life, he
merits an intolerable purgatory, and his eternal reward will be the
least possible. He will feel in Heaven like a coarse rustic creature,
who finds himself suddenly thrust into the presence of the King surrounded by his court. As to a self-conceited man whose life is all
external, he will be unfit even to behold the happy place in which
God's friends will eternally dwell. And what of those sluggards who
are far worse, who live without God both inwardly and outwardly?
The evil spirits eagerly assail them with temptations and lay snares
in their path.

Let us return to our former statement, that man's likeness to God
is in his power of combining interior restful joy with exterior activity;
and that means the interior man's unalterable adherence to God in his
deepest consciousness, pure and perfect. This is a state quite different
from the outward methods of serving God, as different as running and
sitting down. The interior state is a perception of God's presence,
joined to the happiness of His possession. And it is from this that
an interior man goes forth to his outward activity as necessity or as
the good of himself or others may require—and again returns into the
same divine centre and source. Thus does the interior life supervise
the exterior life. A master workman, for example, has many servants
under him, all of whom do the work that he lays out for them and in
the way he points out, while he himself does no work, and does not
often go into the workshop, though he gives his men the rule and
form of their work; they call him the master workman, as if he
alone did all that they do, on account of his showing them how to
work and what to work. It is all his from his command over
them and his planning, for it is in carrying out his plans that their
work consists. So in the interior life the master workman set over the
exterior life; it is from his interior that a man enlightened by God
constantly guides his external faculties in their activity. In the depths
of his soul he is immersed in God, in whom he is absorbed in joy;
there he remains free and unhindered by his external activity. And
every external work down to the least and smallest, is in the service
of the interior. It is precisely so in the ordering of the spiritual
body of Christ, namely, holy Church, of which our Lord Jesus Christ
is the head. Or, again, in a man's body and its many members—the

eye sees all the other members and yet sees not itself. Mouth, hands and feet, and the other members, all have their peculiar offices, but are not for themselves, but for the whole body, under direction of the head. And so, too, in our Christian religious life, every act, even down to carrying a candle and ringing a bell, is done to serve the interior work of God in the soul.

And the unity between the different members of holy Church should be so close, that one should no more harm the others than he harms himself. If I find any member of this body of Christ worthier than I am, I must hold him dearer to me than I hold myself, just as a man's hand and arm protect the head and heart more carefully than they do themselves. So should be the instinctive love of God's members one for another, esteeming them according as their devout life and their virtue make them more precious to our divine Head. And whatever my neighbor would wish to have, or not have, should concern me just as if it were my own desire. If I love the good that is in him more than he loves it himself, then that good is more mine than his. If he has any evil thing, that remains wholly his own, whereas the good that I love in him is rightly mine as well as his. That St. Paul was rapt in ecstacy was granted by God to him and not to me. But if in this rapture of St. Paul I adore the will of God, then I had rather that the rapture was his than mine—and yet in loving it in him it all becomes truly mine. That and every other holy thing that God did in him is made mine, just as if it happened to me, supposing that I truly love it in him. And this would be true of me in relation to any man, even if he were beyond the sea, nay, even if he were my enemy. Thus strict is this coworking of God's spiritual body; and thus I am made rich with all the spiritual goods of God's friends on earth and in Heaven in God who is the head of all, all flowing from Head and members, from God and angels and saints, into me. This is because I am joined to this divine Head and to all His members by love, being made and formed like unto Him and them, and yet in them separated from myself and made unlike unto myself. But, alas, we sometimes seem to love God and His holy will, whereas as a matter of fact it is our own selves that we love or some of our possessions: sometimes what looks like gold is not worth as much as copper. But when a man has sincerely gone out of self and is detached from all his own belongings, has become truly poor in spirit, then to him all earthly things whatsoever are equal—he stands indifferent to them. Oh, children, an equal love for joy or sorrow is a rare thing to find among the generality of people.

It remains to describe the three degrees of perfection accessible to men. The first degree of an interior life, leading to God's high truth, is when a man turns inward in search of the marvellous evidences and the ineffable gifts of the hidden deity, and this results in a state of soul called jubilation. The second degree is destitution of spirit, in which the soul experiences a special drawing of God amid a terrible process of stripping and deprivation. The third is a transcending movement of the creature into a God-like form, uniting the created spirit with the uncreated deity; this may be named essential transformation. Of those who attain to this last degree, we can hardly believe that they will ever fall away from God.

To the first degree we attain by meditating on the evidences of divine love everywhere found in earth and Heaven. O how much has God favored us among all His creatures. The whole world blooms with the beauty of God, Who overwhelms all creation with His gifts for our sakes. How tenderly has He not sought us out, invited us and admonished us and waited long and patiently for us. For us He became man, suffered and died, offering His blessed soul and body to His Father for our sakes; and to how indescribably close a friendship has He not invited us. How long has the Holy Trinity waited for us, that we might share the divine joy eternally. Let a man but deeply ponder all this, and the interior rush of heavenly joy will overpower him, and his poor body will be too weak to endure the strain. It often happens that during the stress of this feeling, the blood will burst its veins and pour from the mouth; in other cases one is affected with serious illness.

Thus is this man granted a powerful influx of sweetness from our Lord, as he is embraced in entire and sensible union with Him. Thus does God forcibly draw a man out of himself and correct all dissimilarity. Let no man meddle with these gentle souls, nor impose on them their commonplace outward observances—be not guilty of such a thing. Nor need the Prior be disturbed if such a brother leaves the choir during recitation of office, for he cannot do otherwise, and he is not a vain creature who must be watched and corrected. Once our Lord offered a special friend of His to give him this kiss of jubilation. But he answered and said: "Beloved Lord, I do not desire it; for it would make me beside myself with joy, so that I should be a useless creature: how could I pray for the poor souls in purgatory and help them to Heaven, or for poor sinners who are but just now departed this life? And how could I pray for poor sinners yet in this life and who will not pray for themselves? For God has willed to help them only through our prayers in this time of His grace." Ah, children, how great love was this, that a soul would deny itself these heavenly joys for the sake of helping others.

The second degree is when God has drawn a man far away from created things. He is no longer a child to be fed with the dainties of spiritual sweetness, but he must be content to eat the hard rye bread of tribulation, as becomes a man; for a man he is now grown to be. Hard and strong food it is that this man needs—not the baby's bread and milk. Before him lies a desert road, dark and lonely, and as God leads him through it, He deprives him of all the solaces and joys that He ever gave him. The poor man is so confused that he knows nothing of God—he does not know whether there is a God above him or not. Woe is upon him deep and heavy, and the wide world is too narrow for him. And while he feels not and rightly knows not God, neither does he feel at home with created things. He seems to himself penned in between two steep walls, a sword before him, a spear behind him. What shall he do? He dare not go forward, he dare not go backward. He can but sit down disconsolate and exclaim: All hail to Thee, O pure and bitter pain, may God bless thee, for thou art full of all graces. If hell could be added to this purgatory of his, it would be—so it seems to him—a softening of his pain. To love so deeply and yet to be deprived of the supreme Good that one loves—such is his torment. Talk to him as thou pleasest of the comforting things of religion; it is as if thou offerest a hungry man a stone to eat:—and how mcuh less comfort shall he have in all creatures. The greater his spiritual sweetness was before, the greater is now the misery of his deprivation. O now behave thyself well, thou favored soul, for the Lord is surely nigh unto thee, holding thee fast by the link of living faith; be sure that all will yet be well with thee. But, alas, this poor soul is in anguish so deep, that he no more can believe that all will yet be well with him than he can believe that darkness shall be turned into light.

This trial prepares a man for God's higher work in him more than all the devotions and pious practices that can be thought of. And when our Lord finds him well enough purified by hanging upon this cross of insufferable agony, He then comes to him to introduce him to the third degree. Immediately He removes the bandage from his eyes and reveals to him the truth. Forth bursts the bright sunshine, lifting and dispersing every cloud; every sorrow vanishes away—he seems to himself to be a man risen from the dead. The Lord leads him back into his own soul, there to behold every anguish gone, every wound healed. For now out of a human he is led into a divine way of living, free from pain, fast fixed in security of spirit. Whatsoever he now is and does, that is God in him and that does God in him, being made by grace what God Himself essentially is by nature—as far as this may be. He feels lost to himself in God; he can find self nowhere; he knows nought but the simple essence of God.

Children, to be truly placed in this state, is to begin by being rooted in the deepest depths of humility and self-abnegation, a depth beyond our power to comprehend, for it involves a most perfect knowledge of one's own nothingness. It is the deepest immersion of the soul in humility; and the deeper the sinking the higher the rising, for deep and high are all in God. But if a man in this state should waver from the straight path, if he should resist God and strike about him, if he should return to self as a foundation, if he should depart out of this high festival and return into self-complacency, that would be like the fall of Lucifer. Herein consists the good of the single-minded prayer of which we began by treating, and which brings us into union with God. May the blessed Trinity grant us entrance into that single-minded prayer. *Amen.*

𝔉𝔦𝔰𝔥𝔦𝔫𝔤 𝔦𝔫 𝔇𝔢𝔢𝔭 𝔚𝔞𝔱𝔢𝔯𝔰

*Synopsis—Christ's net is a man's thoughts—The fish He catches are
holy desires and deeds and doctrines—To these are added useful
joys and sorrows—How ordinary good Christians are also helped
—A true test: What gives us pleasure or pain—When Christ
has a good catch our net breaks—This is the destruction of selfhood.*

SECOND SERMON FOR THE FIFTH SUNDAY AFTER

TRINITY.

And going into one of the ships that was Simon's, He desired him to draw
back a little from the land. And sitting, He taught the multitudes out of the
ship. Now when He had ceased to speak, he said to Simon: Launch out into
the deep, and let down your nets for a draught. And Simon, answering, said
to Him: Master, we have labored all the night, and have taken nothing; but
at Thy word I will let down the net. And when they had done this, they
enclosed a very great multitude of fishes, and their net broke. And they
beckoned to their partners that were in the other ship, that they should come
and help them. And they came and filled both the ships, so that they were
almost sinking: which, when Simon Peter saw, he fell down at Jesus' knees,
saying: Depart from me because I am a sinful man, O Lord.—Luke v, 3-10.

The ship that our Lord commanded to be launched out into the
deep may be taken to mean the interior life of our soul. It journeys
over the dangerous sea of this sorrowful world, which is so subject to
changes from storm to calm, from joy to sorrow. It makes one's heart
wither away with fear, when one realizes the dangers that beset those
whose hearts are entrusted to the custody of the world's stormy ocean.
How it will be with you in eternity, that you think little about, but
you voyage along blindly, concerned wholly with your bodily apparel
and adornment and nourishment, totally forgetful of the awful judgment that awaits you—when? You know not; it may be even today
or tomorrow. O if you but realized the danger of clinging to the
world, the danger that besets all who do not with deepest sincerity

adhere to God, or at least remain among the lowest grade of His friends. Not long since it was revealed to one of God's friends how dreadful shall be the fate of such worldlings. Ah, whosoever fully knew this could scarcely bear the shock of it—it would seem impossible of belief. Let all those to whom this applies remember the warning now given them.

Let us come to our subject. "Launch out into the deep," our Lord said. This may mean to us that the supreme need of a spiritual man is that his soul, with all its thought and love, shall and must be drawn away from everything that is not God. Whosoever would not be wrecked and drowned in the stormy sea of this life must be elevated above all creatures. St. Peter said: "Master, we have labored all the night, and have taken nothing." This was well and truly said; for all who are preoccupied with outward things labor in the night and take nothing. Then said our Lord: "Let down your nets for a draught," and forthwith they caught so many fish that the nets were breaking. This all happened before our Lord's resurrection; for after that, the Gospel tells us (John xxi: 6), that when He bade them let down their nets, they did not break, though they caught a great multitude of fish.

Children, what may here be meant by the net? It may mean a man's thoughts,—the net that he casts out to gather into his mind what will inflame it with holy desires, holy deeds and teachings, especially the divine life and passion of Jesus. Holy meditation fills the soul with Christ, all our mental powers and our senses being transformed by love and joy in Him, so that sometimes one cannot hide it, but must break forth into loud songs of jubilation.

This launching out into the deep is, however, but the first degree; and to be made a truly mortified man, or as Dionysius says, a God-like man, one must be guided to a yet profounder depth of divine influence. This means that all those things wherewith the lower faculties of the soul are occupied, must fall away and be lost to it—even holy thoughts and imaginations, joy and jubilation, all, in fact, that God had granted, now must seem out of place and something to be excluded from the soul. Such things have lost their savor and the soul can no longer be content with them. But here is the dreadful misery; for they are gone and there is nothing to take their place. The poor man craves something in their stead and is wholly unable to possess it—he is imprisoned within the walls of a narrow cell, and is overpowered with anguish. Now indeed is the ship of his soul tossed upon the deep sea of spiritual want, and he seems entirely abandoned by God. Every trial and opposition that man ever suffered is become his lot. The waves of a tempest of anguish break mercilessly over his little ship.

Dear child, I say to thee: Be not affrighted, for thy ship is too well anchored to be wrecked by any storm. That just man Job says: "After darkness I hope for light again" (Job xvii: 12). Rest tranquilly in thy own soul, depart not from thyself, be patient to the end. Some men, finding themselves, in this painful destitution, run away from it; but it is a hurtful thing to try to escape this suffering. Nor does this attempt to fly give them relief—the teachers to whom they carry their complaints help them not at all, and they but wander further away from joy. Stand thy ground. Be sure that after darkness comes light—await patiently the sunlight of the dawn. If thou wilt but wait, thy birth into God is nigh at hand. He says to thee: Have confidence in Me, for no trial is ever imposed upon a soul, but that he shall be granted a new spiritual birth if he bears himself bravely. It is for the sake of this that every tribulation from Me or from My creatures is sent to thee. But if thou permittest any creature whatsoever to interfere with this trial, be sure that it will prevent the divine regeneration within thee—and how great an injury is this. If thy soul be anchored fast to the rock of Christ, then what St. Paul said becomes true of thee: "For I am sure that neither death, nor life, nor angels, nor principalities, nor powers, nor things present, nor things to come, nor might, nor height, nor depth, nor any other creature, shall be ever able to separate us from the love of God, which is in Christ Jesus our Lord" (Rom. viii: 38-39). The more all devils and men conspire against thee or assail thee, the higher do they lift thy soul unto God.

Children, the man who yields his soul patiently to this oppressive sorrow, gives up more of self and takes on more of God than would be possible by a whole world of external devout exercises. Therefore, look nowhere for any help, neither from within nor from without. Let thy wounds bleed, seek no solace for them—God will surely relieve thee in His own time if thou wilt but commit thyself to Him absolutely. Children, this is the nearest way to the divine birth within the soul, which illumines it with God's unhindered light. It sometimes happens that an outward living man suffers an outward misfortune, such as a case of backbiting or other injustice, and now he clamors and protests incessantly, and he feels such an agony that he is tired of life. How different the case of our truly interior man. He never complains of his afflictions, whose sorrow yields him finally a harvest of joy. What is so sweet to him as entire surrender to God? Every pain that comes is to him nothing less than a visit from God Himself.

Children, would you have a true sign of what you really are in God's sight? Ask yourself what it is that gives you pleasure or pain? Art thou filled with God? Then the ship of thy soul cannot be endangered by the storms of created things. On such a man God bestows the priceless jewel of inward joy, which no other man can comprehend—the firm possession of divine peace. Many a time the storm of temptation beats fiercely on the little barque, threatening to sink it to the bottom—it can never disturb the interior tranquility, however much the outward man is moved.

As to those good souls who have never experienced this degree of perfection, I say to you, be not disturbed. There are fishermen who are rich and those who are poor, far more of the latter. And no matter how simple or lowly may be thy devotional life, if thou dost follow it with deep sincerity of heart, and if thou longest to be made a higher lover of God, rest in that with all confidence; allow nothing to interfere, keep God before thy eyes in all thy conduct—thou mayst be quite sure that the deep quiet of soul we have been considering shall yet be thine, if it should even be postponed to the hour of thy death.

And yet after all, this true friend of God has with his great peace of soul a mixture of unrest—a breaking of the net. For he is distressed that he cannot be so much to God as he would wish; and also that God is not yet quite perfectly enjoyed by him. We read of a holy man who lived in a forest for forty years, and he always went on hands and feet for God's sake, never feeling a moment of divine consolation. Now there can be no doubt but that he really had more comfort from God than a thousand others; but not enough to satisfy him, for he could only enjoy that divine consolation which was of the very highest degree. In that degree there is granted an essential peace, of which it is written: "Seek after peace and pursue it (Psalm xxxi: 15)—the peace that passeth all understanding, the unnamed and unnamable turning of the soul to God, which is answered by the unnamed and unnamable turning of God to the soul, all that God is to all that the soul is. Then does God utter His divine word of peace, and the soul exclaims: "I will hear what the Lord God will speak in me, for He will speak peace unto His people, and unto His saints, and unto them that are converted unto the heart" (Psalm lxxxiv: 9). St. Dionysius says of these men that they are formed in God. To them did St. Paul speak: "That being rooted and founded in charity, you may be able to comprehend, with all the saints, what is the breadth, and length, and height, and depth" (Eph. iii: 18). Children, the height and the depth revealed to these men neither reason nor sense can understand:—it passes beyond them into the abyss of the deity. But only to those whose external life is wholly purified, whose interior souls are fully enlightened—only to men whose dwelling place is within does God reveal this priceless boon; souls to whom heaven and earth and all things in them are as nothing except for God, for they themselves are to God a heavenly rest and peace.

Our Lord sat in the ship and taught the people. And so does God sit in these men's souls and rests there, and through them does He teach the whole world. But be sure of this: the net of this soul must be broken when it is drawn into this deep place. Though you must not imagine that I myself claim to have arrived at this degree. True, no man should teach that of which he has not had some living experience, or what at least he does not love, and meditate on, and to acquire which he places no hindrance.

As to the breaking of the net, it cannot do otherwise than break, so great is the multitude of the fishes:—that is to say, poor human nature is too weak to abide the strain of so much heavenly joy. Henceforth this man shall never know a day of sound health. St. Hildegarde teaches this very well: "God's dwelling place is not in a strong and healthy body." And St. Paul: "For power is made perfect in infirmity" (II Cor. xii: 9). But this weakness does not come from the Godhead upon and into the soul, which is more than the feeble severe external mortifications can bear, but from the excessive outpourings of bodily forces. God has drawn this soul so deep into Himself that it is, as it were, brightened with the divine brilliancy. It is superessentially new formed in God, who now works this man's work Himself. If one could see that soul thus new formed in God, he would imagine that he behold God himself, though the transformation into God be but the work of grace. God lives in him, and He is the principle of all his acts; God rejoices in him as in Himself. God's glory is bound up in such souls: with them He has launched the ship into the deep, cast forth the net, and taken a great multitude of fishes.

But what is the breaking of the net? When the ship is at the deep place of God and the net is cast for a draught, the number of fishes caught is so great that the ship is about to sink and the net is broken— that is to say all self, and all ownership is broken and torn to pieces. If anything is to become what it is not, then it must first cease to be what it is. Therefore in this case soul and body are, in a certain sense, sunk down into this deep sea and totally immersed. The soul loses its natural activity, and also those devout practices which are seated in the use of the natural faculties. Sunk in this divine depths, a man has no longer any pious exercises, or vocal prayers. Then a man can but do as St. Peter did, when falling at the feet of Jesus he said those foolish words: "Depart from me, for I am a sinful man, O Lord." Pious observances and prayers are gone from him, and perforce he must drop down into his original nothingness, and be a very little thing before God's face. Furthermore, everything that he ever received from God seems stripped away from his soul and restored to the giver; seeming as if it all never had been possessed by him, becoming to him so much nothingness. And it seems to him that by this process, created nothingness is absorbed in a way wholly incomprehensible; it is in reality the abyss of man's being assumed into unity with the abyss of God's being. Thus teaches the Psalmist: "Deep calleth unto deep" (Ps. xli: 8). The divine being takes up this soul, the human spirit is lost in God's spirit—sunk in the fathomless ocean of the Godhead. Then does such a man become wholly virtuous, uniformly kind, and godly; his manners are sweet and cheerful and he is very companionable with everybody; nor shall any fault ever be found in him. To all men he is friendly and trusts all, is very pitiful to all, never stern or exacting—we find it hard to believe that such a man could ever fall away from God's love. God grant that all of us may obtain this grace. *Amen.*

Interior Obedience to God

Synopsis—St. Peter a type of obedient souls—Inspirations—Apparent conflict between inner and outer loyalty—Refinement of soul resulting from inner conformity to God—Sorrows of this state—The folly of resting on anything but a loving interior obedience.

THIRD SERMON FOR THE FIFTH SUNDAY AFTER TRINITY.

(The text is the same as in the preceding sermon.)

The ship in which the Lord sat, from which He preached, which He ordered launched into deep water, into which the great draught of fishes was taken—this ship is Peter's. He stands for a man always and sincerely obedient, in whose soul the Lord loves to sit and to take His rest, a soul that has left all things and followed Him into its own inmost depths. No man can do this easily, and therefore does the Lord often admonish us amid our outward good works to turn inward to Him. Whosoever disregards this warning and clings to his own will and his self-chosen devotional customs, is not obedient to God Not so was Simon; he was obedient to God with a supreme obedience. And supposing a sister in choir singing God's praises, and that He should warn her that this hindered her interior advertence to Him, then (if this could lawfully be done) she should give up the singing and obediently turn inwards to God. If the singing and the interior advertance could go together, that were indeed better still.

Children, do you know how hurtful it is to resist the inspirations of God's grace? If you did, your heart would quake with terror. And yet it is only from God's boundless mercy that it happens that those who, having failed to reach the high perfection God called them to, are yet afterwards permitted to attain it by way of suffering. Again falling short of that, they will feel the pain of it at the hour of death more than less favored ones, and will suffer a great purgatory afterwards. Yet, after all, they will attain a higher place in heaven than those who were called to a lower degree.

Thus in the deep soul of an obedient man does God sit and teach the good doctrine and the wondrous grace of His love. Notice that in one of the miraculous draughts of fishes, our Lord bade Peter "draw out a little from the land." This betokens that in the lowest degree of perfection, a noble-hearted man must draw his affections away from transitory things, and give up all pleasure in creatures. Whosoever shall possess God must have a steadfast endeavor in seeking Him. Never must it happen that a good work undertaken today shall be given up tomorrow. No; if he will reach his best, a man must constantly persevere in his devout exercises—not living for God alone today and for natural ends tomorrow. And this it is that frightens people—they say that it is intolerable and dreadful, and that they cannot hold out so long; and then they turn away to enjoy their natural inclinations as they did before—to take up with all that is not God. The net is broken, the fish all escape. Children, no matter how good our works may be in themselves, if we do not keep God alone in mind while doing them, then there is a certain taint of simony in them. For what is simony? It is buying spiritual things with earthly things; and it is one of the greatest of sins. So, therefore, when one does spiritual things, with the view and purpose of an earthly kind, that is a sort of spiritual simony.

Now we read in the gospel that the apostles mended their nets. And so must we, when we have broken them by sin; and this we do by a sincere return to God. Or another example: when we would make a crooked piece of wood straight, we bend it back and fasten it there. So must an external, animal kind of a man treat his natural tendencies, bending himself back forcibly upright to God. He must be rid totally of all things in mind and body that do not entirely mean God, bowing down his will absolutely in subjection to God. O, after that, give thyself up to the merciful God. In deep humility say to him: Beloved Lord, I have labored all the night and have taken nothing. And is it not true, that the time thou spendest working without God is black night? Dullness and sleepiness of soul is the fate of those who work in that spiritual night, their nature all incapacitated for good. The external minded man shall thus be overworked in hands and feet and back. But from this sad state let him return again to God in his inmost soul.

Children, our Savior said to St. Peter: "Launch out into the deep." That means: Elevate thy soul, and consider the deep things of God.

Pass with thy mental powers over all things of time and earth, for
with these God will not deal in thy case, they are too puny for Him.
The lower powers of man cannot grasp God, they are too coarse for
his infinitely elevated nature. Therefore place thy life in thy highest
powers, far above the things of time, for there sits God and from them
as from Simon's boat He teaches in very truth. His teaching is the
superessential divine Word, in Whom and with Whom are all things
made that are made. Receive this teaching in all gentle meeknss,
for whosoever does so, elevated in spirit above time and into eternity,
to him shall the divine Word be uttered. He shall be enlightened by
Him in a wisdom beyond all that man can comprehend. The kingdom
of God thus established in the soul is ineffable and overwhelming in
its glory.

But now when our Lord is thus born into the soul by the utterance
of the divine Word, and when it is thus faithfully received, it sometimes
happens that God sends a hard trial. That poor, weak human soul
is broken like a net, and the ship seems on the point of sinking:—the
soul thinks that all is lost. But let it not go outward for help of any
kind whatsoever, but rather imitate St. Peter, who beckoned to his
partners, and especially to St. John, to come to his aid—that is to
say use thy own discretion, now enlightened by heavenly wisdom.
Remember that when the uncreated light that is God rises in the soul,
then the created light must give place. The created light must grow
dim in proportion as the uncreated light increases in brightness—
just as the clear light of the sun causes the light of candles to pale
before it. Be but patient; for when a man at last fully enjoys this
divine light, even for a few moments, his peace and joy are far above
aught that this world can ever give. And yet so far this glorious
spiritual sweetness is but in the lowest powers of the soul.

At the other miraculous draught of fishes, our Lord said: "Cast the
net on the right side of the ship, and you shall find. They cast therefor; and now they were not able to draw it, for the multitude of
fishes * * * * Simon Peter went up, and drew the net to land,
full of great fishes, one hundred and fifty-three. And although there
were so many, the net was not broken" (John xxi: 6-11). All this
happened after our Lord's death. And when He had before this asked
them if they had anything to eat, they answered that they had not.
This shows that when a man will be highly favored by God, he must

be entirely destitute. Then it is that he can say as Peter did: Lord, in thy name I will cast the net. It is in the Word of God that a man is granted power high above those lowest faculties of his nature, being changed from human to divine ways and forms, as St. Paul teaches: "But we all beholding the glory of the Lord with open face, are transformed into the same image from glory to glory, as by the Spirit of the Lord" (II Cor. iii: 18). Ere a man shall be granted this, our Lord must be born in him, must die, and rise again. And such a man always says to the Lord what the disciples said, when He asked them if they had anything: he answers, No. Thus are placed all who stand in the truest poverty of soul, and in total self-denial: they have nothing: they desire nothing. Nothing pleases them save God alone. They seek nothing whatever of their own. Often enough do they labor throughout the night and take nothing—in the night of abandonment of all things, destitution and desolation of soul. As far as they can perceive it or feel it, there is neither light nor joy in their souls. But they rest in this darkenss in true resignation, as if (should such a thing be possible) God had required of them to suffer this desolation and inner destitution for all eternity. They freely yield to God's will in this in their interior spirit, and never think of receiving any reward for doing so. Ah, children, that is indeed a poor man, and yet the whole world is his. He has nothing but God's will at heart, he thinks of nothing but how to make God's will effectual in all his undertakings. Nevertheless, he is full of humility, for he answers to our Lord's admonition: "When you shall have done all things that are commanded you, say: We are unprofitable servants; we have done that which we ought to do" (Luke xvii: 10). Now an unprofitable servant does unprofitable work, and that is how God would have us consider our work.

Scarcely anyone wants to be God's unprofitable servant. Each one wants to feel that what he has done is worth something, and on that feeling he builds. No, my child; build on nothing but thy own utter nothingness. And in that spirit sink in deep humility down into the abyss of the divine will, giving thyself up to Him to do with thee whatsoever He may wish. Say with St. Peter: "Depart from me, for I am a sinful man, O Lord." Fall back constantly on thy own littleness, powerlessness, and ignorance, thereby passing over into the high nobility of God's will. Allow no other thought to influence thee; hold thyself poor and miserable in the divine will.

With such men as these, if they but turn their thoughts inward as long a time as it takes to hear one mass, all their affairs are rightly ordered, all their labors are done in great peace, their life with other men is very kindly, and it is full of virtue; and they are entirely resigned to God. They have cast their net on the right side, they have drawn into their hearts the love that is in the bleeding wounds of Jesus. May God help us thus to strive and thus to succeed. *Amen.*

From the Alpha to the Omega of Perfection

Synopsis—Remarks on the worth of the soul—The beginning of perfection is genuine repentance—Plain marks of this—Need of taking God and God alone into account—Next comes confession, which must be very searching, and made in a lively spirit of faith in that Sacrament—Then indifference to all earthly things has place—To this is joined liberty of spirit in the use of devotional exercises— The finishing touch is disinterested love of God.

SERMON FOR THE SIXTH SUNDAY AFTER TRINITY.

And the pasch of the Jews was at hand, and Jesus went up to Jerusalem. And He found in the temple them that sold oxen and sheep and doves, and the changers of money sitting. And when He had made, as it were, a scourge of little cords, He drove them all out of the temple, the sheep also and the oxen, and the money of the changers he poured out, and the tables He overthrew. And to them that sold doves He said: Take these things hence, and make not the house of My Father a house of traffic.—John ii, 13-16.

Ah, children, mark well in these words the dignity of the human soul, which is in all truth the house and dwelling place of God, and God had rather live in it than in any place in earth or heaven. The soul has more that is Godlike in it than the heavens, or than any temple built with hands, or any other of His creations. For in the soul of man is God's heart with all His love and trust and joy. And in the creation of all His other creatures, God has sought nothing else than the honor and dignity and happiness of our soul.

Since God dwells in our soul with all His love, so is He more properly present there than in the heavens or in any material temple. For God does all His work in the soul and for the soul—He gives it to the soul. And there it is that God the Father generates His only begotten Son, precisely as He does in the bosom of eternity. One might ask what we mean by this saying: God is born in the soul. Does it mean the likeness of God, or something divine? No, it is neither the image of God nor anything merely like Him: it is the very same Father generating and the very same divine Son born of the Father before all ages. It is the blessed divine Word, the second person of the Holy Trinity. Him does the Father beget in the soul, and for the soul is He begotten and to the soul given by the Father; and herein consists the soul's dignity.

Thus spoke our Lord: "Take these things hence"—not this or that thing, but all these things—"and make not the house of My Father a house of traffic." Mark well, that whatsoever is born in thy soul which has not God for its cause, or which is not an image of God, existing entirely for His praise and honor, is for thee an object of traffic in God's house. By this means thou dost bargain with God about the blessed birth of His Son within thee. This applies to everything whatsoever to which thou givest thy heart or about which thou engagest thy mind. This is the reason why God cannot be born within thy soul. It may be this world's goods, it may be relatives and friends or other created things that intrude their images into thy soul: they are born within thee if thou acceptest them with pleasure. Be sure that this means barter and traffic of the eternal Son of God, whom the heavenly Father will never manifest in thee as His eternal Word until all these things of barter and traffic are taken out.

I have three things to say, about how a man shall cleanse the inmost depths of his soul, tearing out all hindrances by the roots: or otherwise expressed, how to banish the traffickers from the temple of the soul, leaving it in peace, never to return again. For as God lives thou must make sure of that.

The first is a safe and free conscience. What does that mean? It means a conscience untroubled and cleansed. If one's soul be disturbed, or if it be misdirected by attachment to creatures, if it be evil on account of sinful practices, then it must be cleansed by true repentance. And what is true repentance? Is it that one feels bad and moans and weeps? No, O no. For many a time it happens that convivial and dissipated and sinful men moan and weep, and yet have no true repentance, while others on the contrary weep not at all, and yet these are genuinely penitent. Every creature, if but true to its nature, loves God more than self—but not the sinner; he loves himself more than God. This he proves by seeking his pleasure in creatures, no matter how much pain this may be to God. When a man loves himself above all things, then is he ever looking for what seems pleasant to him, ever avoiding what seems hurtful to him. Hence when it happens that a sinful man realizes that he has lost eternal life and is in danger of being caught and imprisoned in the eternal pains of hell, then he has indeed sorrow, but it is a sorrow as different from true repentance as earth from heaven. It is to self that this sorrow ministers and not to God. Therefore it helps not the sinner, and it may even remove him farther yet from grace, for he is seeking for grace where it is not.

He that will find grace must look for it where it is, namely in God, in God alone, not in creatures nor any imagination of them. Sorrow and pain for thy sins on account of the harm they do thyself obtains no grace, for herein thou restest in self and created things. However good thy work may be, if thy intention is drawn from created things and not from God alone in all loyalty of spirit, no grace can result to thee. Grace is in God and not in creatures. But when in any work the praise and honor of God is had in mind, God takes that work up as His own. Thus it is said: "Amen I say to you, as long as you did it to one of these My least brethren, you did it to me" (Matt. xxv: 40).

Dear children, think how sweet a life is that in which a man practices in time and towards creatures a virtue that God will assume in eternity as if it had been actually done to Himself. Of this meaning are the words: "He that toucheth you, toucheth the apple of My eye" (Zach. ii: 8). Therefore think not only on the poor man who stands before thee but on the person of God, who takes to Himself all that thou dost to him, whether good or evil. Hence when a man has God in mind, so shall his heart be drawn into God and made one with Him, being drawn away from all creatures—and this is where grace is and not with creatures; with whom if thy heart is joined in false love and imaginations, thou shalt find no grace.

And now, dear child, note another good thought. Wouldst thou know whom thou servest, and who is going to reward thee? Mark well for whom thy work is done, and what thou hast in mind as the reason of thy work. That will show thee whom thou servest. As to this all the teachers in the world can tell thee nothing, for thyself alone knowest it. Others know the outside of thy works and they may think them good; but on whose account they are done, thou alone

canst tell for thou alone dost know. Therefore I have elsewhere
written: "The man who gets with his works anywhere else than in God
alone, gets where no grace is, for grace is in God." Not alone with
God is the decision as to whether or not thou shalt have grace, but
with thyself also; for just as thou standest true and loving to God
shalt thou have grace, and just as much grace as thou thyself dost
will. If thou lovest God, then thou sufferest, laborest, avoidest sin
in Him and through Him as much as thou willest. Such is the man
who finds grace, and has right sorrow for his sins—it is one who is
sorry for them out of love and fidelity, sorry that he has angered and
dishonored so sweet and good a God. If there were neither hell nor
heaven, still he ought to be none the less grieved that he had ever
rebelled against God. This is true sorrow, even though one may shed
no tears in it.

And after that one must make his confession. And what is a true
confession? When a man tells all that he knows himself to be guilty
of nor wilfully keeps back anything: then he has rightly confessed,
and he should trust with entire security that all his sins are forgiven
him. It is more to God's honor that He should forgive sins than that
He should punish them. One must also believe in the powers of the
father confessor, according to our Lord's words: "Whose sins you
shall forgive, they are forgiven them; and whose sins you shall retain,
they are retained" (John xx:23). And His other words: "Amen I
say to you, whatsoever you shall bind upon earth, shall be bound also
in heaven; and whatsoever you shall loose upon earth, shall be loosed
also in heaven" (Matt. xviii:18). I tell you in all sincerity that if
any man confesses his sins, and afterwards feels remorse about these
same sins, it were far better than he trust God, believe firmly in the
power of his father confessor, and not tell the sins again—far better
that than tell them over again out of nervousness. Understand this
besides: thou beholdest our blessed Lord's body in the church, thou
knowest full well it is He, thou art ready to go to thy death rather
than to doubt it. Now who hath told thee this? The man who hath
seen it with his eyes does not live: God alone has said it, and by the
power of His word has enclosed Himself in the Sacrament under the
appearance of bread. And out of the same mouth of God has come
forth the word of the forgiveness of sins in confession. Therefore do
not simply believe but plainly know it—as clearly as thou knowest

anything; for nothing is so true as the word of God, as our Lord says: "Heaven and earth shall pass away, but My words shall not pass away" (Luke xxi: 33). In this certainty of the plain truth of God does a man after confession obtain deep peace of conscience. Nor does this confidence rest upon any work of his own, as such, but entirely upon the promise of God. And when he thus trusts God, then does God on His part stand true to what was said in the absolution of the priest, namely that he will be saved.

Furthermore, see to it earnestly that thou standest indifferent as to all earthly things; and that will give thee continual peace of soul. But does it mean that I must be literally indifferent about everything? By no means, dear child, for therein thou mightest go astray. For who can doubt but that, considering works in their intrinsic value, it is better to pray than cook, to think of God than spin, to be in church than on the streets? If one does not agree to this he is a heretic. But thou shalt stand indifferent by not taking things out of their rightful relation to other things. And thus: is it right that thou shouldest now be in church at thy prayers? Then gather together all thy thoughts and lift thy soul upwards to God. But does it behoove thee to be now engaged at some other work, such as cooking or spinning—is this God's will? Even as thou wert recollected in church at thy prayers, so be thou now absorbed in thy present work for His sake. We meet with those who are full of God's love—as they think—when they do honorable work in all peace and in a high station of life. But if it happens that they must quit this work and drop down lower, then they seem to dismiss God from their souls, until they can return to their self-chosen occupation.

Be sure that as long as thou couplest God inseparably with thy particular devotions or any other circumstances of life, thou shalt not have true peace, no, nor shalt thou have God himself. Thou mayst think otherwise, but in very truth thou hast not sought nor found God but thyself and thy own ways. Such persons hurry off to church in the early morning, as if God were not to be found in their homes nor upon the streets in the duties of their state of life. Such a hurrying to church to the neglect of home duties, is an injury to thyself, nor wilt thou therein find God. This is why some do not find peace of heart, do not really find God, now in doing a good work, now in saying a prayer to God or to a saint—hurrying and hurrying in a rush of devotions, one of as little profit to them as the other.

One should in all his good works, keep his mind directed so straight to God, that the figure of the work almost slips out of his mind, and the thought of God remains there alone. This is the way to seek and find grace in every work. Though thou be a woman at home engaged in thy humble household duties, thou shalt find God there if thou give thy mind to Him. Day and night God in His holy wisdom steadfastly waits upon thee, to draw thee to Himself when He finds thee ready, no matter what thy situation, regardless of thy ways of devotion. Thou little knowest when and where God will meet thee. Stand in God's sight indifferent to all things; whatsoever happens to thee, look for God in it, and know that this is all the best for thee. Fear not that thou art guilty of any remissness in this; for that cannot be if thou art doing God's will,—in all things and ways and states make sure of belonging to God, at least in thy intention and purpose. Herein alone is peace and content; apart from this, never. And unless a man seeks God in *all* things, he will not find him in any single thing. Make this a test and apply it to thyself.

Nor should one too anxiously inquire just by what means he has arrived at God. If one is journeying to Rome, he should not tarry to study about the smoothness of the road here and its crookedness there, now over plains and again over hills; if he acts thus he will be forever on the journey. So must a man go straight forward to God in all his devotional exercises, little worrying about this method or that as long as they lead him onward. And in this spirit of indifference there is joy upon joy. Thou mayst ask how one may attain to it. I answer: By denying thyself. Seek thyself in nothing. Seek God and His honor, that alone, that in all things. Scrutinize thyself strictly on this point, and then this virtue will be thine—otherwise not. It rests with thyself; for who but thy own self can tell whether thou hast God in view or thyself in thy conduct and thy thoughts? That man has peace of soul who stands indifferent; and he stands indifferent who seeks not his own.

Besides this, a man must, in a certain way, stand indifferent between God's justice and His mercy. Now there are people who greatly long for God's mercy and love it, but have great fear of His justice. But tell me, dear child, what has His justice done to thee? Dost thou not know that what God does out of mercy He also does out of justice?—and what is done from justice is done from mercy?

Justice constrains God to be merciful to us, because He is our Father and we are His children. He needs must love us out of justice and show us favor—and indeed He ever does. And this is how one should love and long for God's mercy, so that He may exercise justice towards us, according to His adorable will, to His honor and glory.

But to be able thus to think and love, one must be stripped and emptied of all self-will. We must seek the all lovely will of God and that alone, accepting lovingly whatever it pleases Him to do with us and with all creatures. When the will of God thus tastes good to us, then whatsoever His justice does is, we might almost say, as pleasing to our souls as whatsoever His mercy does, whether it be to ourselves or to others. To a man who rightly loves God, everything is welcome, be it pain or pleasure, be it to himself or others, for it all comes from God's will. Ask thyself always: Is this God's will? Then do I set aside my own will in its favor. For thus do we daily pray to God: "Thy will be done!" Which means that it is our will that God's will may be done in all things. Let us be glad of His will working in our will and in all the works He does in us, whether they are the fruit of His mercy or of His justice. If this feeling were deep-seated in us and made truly our own, happy should we be. That this may be granted us, we pray God's merciful justice and His just mercy. *Amen.*

𝔚𝔥𝔬 𝔐𝔞𝔶 𝔊𝔬 𝔒𝔣𝔱𝔢𝔫 𝔱𝔬 𝔠𝔬𝔪𝔪𝔲𝔫𝔦𝔬𝔫

Synopsis—Some should communicate often who dread to do so because they feel no longing—Only bad living men should remain away— Bitter sorrow for sin is God's call to communion—Meditation on Christ's passion is a stimulant to frequent communion—All must be on their guard against the admixture of natural motives.

SERMON FOR THE SEVENTH SUNDAY AFTER TRINITY.

But let a man prove himself: and so let him eat of that bread, and drink of the chalice. For he that eateth and drinketh unworthily, eateth and drinketh judgment to himself, not discerning the body of the Lord.—I Cor. xi, 28-29.

The meaning of this teaching of St. Paul is that one should study himself well, with a view to choosing the right devotional practice to prepare his heart for partaking of this adorable food. For it is good for some, who have no great interior longing for the Sacrament, nevertheless often to receive it, so that they may thereby keep their daily lives well ordered and have grace to maintain their good resolutions against sinning. Even more than this: one should not omit Communion even if sometimes he feels unprepared, and is wholly without conscious longing for it.

Only those should abstain who live according to their own will and do not stop sinning, being overbearing and self-willed, full of backbiting and rash judgments, restless and impatient and abusive, addicted to fleshy pleasures, and fettered with other such defects. As to whether or not such persons should never receive Communion at all, I leave to their own decision, though I would advise them against it, being of opinion that they do themselves more harm than good thereby. The oftener they communicate the worse they grow interiorly and the farther they stray from virtue; for they have no notion of true detachment of spirit; they have never so much as begun to live after the life and example of Christ, though they have doubtless sometimes thought

of doing so, especially when the passion of our Lord is offered for
their meditation. If it happens that the passion moves their hearts
to devotional feelings, they consider that they have gained something
great. Ah, no. This is only the lowest step; and, in fact, the feeling
soon passes away. This feeling about the blessed life and sufferings
of Christ must settle into real imitation, before any actual good shall
come to them,—into real self-denial, dying to all wickedness, whether
of soul or body. Until that happens all resolutions and all outward
devotional practices are vain; they will all be swept away by the first
temptations.

Mark well how you may receive this Sacrament with fruit. Thou
shouldst eat this heavenly bread with eagerness; that is to say, with
great desire and savor in thy inmost soul. What if outwardly thou
dost feel dull and all unfit to receive: that amounts to nothing, as
long as thy will is upright to avoid all that is sinful, as far as thou
knowest, against God's honor and virtuous living, whether thy feelings
respond to this resolve or not. When one avoids all occasions of sin,
and meanwhile practices the ordinary virtues of a Christian life, let
him approach the Sacrament with all joy. His inner soul is not
devoid of great sincerity, though the outward man is heavy and
undevotional—for this inconvenience lies only in our poor human
nature. Any amount of sensible devotion is of little worth, if the
interior will is not upright.

Draw a lesson from the paschal supper of the Israelites, who ate
the lamb with bitter lettuce. This means that thy soul should taste
the bitterness of sorrow for thy sins when approaching the holy table.
Thou shalt obtain this by arousing thy sympathy for Christ in His
passion by means of meditation; also by making atonement to God's
injured honor by leading a life of strenuous penance. This begins by
abstemiousness in eating and drinking, wearing coarse clothes, sleeping
on a hard bed, keeping holy vigils, and the like. When thou hast thus
followed Christ in His outward life, thou shalt be ready to imitate
Him in His interior suffering. He said: "My soul is sorrowful even
unto death" (Matt. xxvi: 38). So shalt thou feel the interior woe of
God's Son, in cutting off entirely all tendency to sensual pleasure, in
total suppression of concupiscence, in treading self-will absolutely
under foot, in entirely giving up self-conceit. Child, this is what it
means rightly to meditate on Christ's passion and to bewail His death.
Without this, other devotional exercises are worthless.

Many seemingly good men have fine appearing and ostentatious virtues, which, however, rest not in essential excellence, but in their own feelings. As a matter of fact, they never get down into their interior life—their whole trust is in outward virtuous acts. Some have a very strong sensible devotion; they are much moved by our Lord's passion, which they meditate from beginning to end day by day with a great feeling of sweetness, the like of which other people do not have. But this is by no means the inner mortification, the humble self-renouncement or the universal love that they should have. They are not at all given up to meekness, or to purity of heart. When the test of self-abnegation is applied to them, their shortcomings are discovered, however honestly they may have imagined themselves humble and single-hearted during their meditations. Ah, no. The purity of virtue comes from other kinds of devotional exercises, namely, the examination and cleansing of all one's thoughts, and the steadfast resistance to whatever is not conducive to spiritual progress.

Along with this let a man meditate on Christ's passion, and study His words and works with the Holy Scriptures before him; then let him follow a good order of devout living; and finally let him free himself from useless and disturbing cares. This is the method of acquiring purity of heart and of thought. Towards that should one earnestly strive—against every evil intention, every sinful desire. Let him be grieved intensely at the danger or the very thought of sin, and steadfastly set himself against it.

When one has attained this cleanness of spirit, whatever bad thing he sees or hears he takes no evil out of it, he forms no judgment about it, for to the pure all things are pure. It is not easy to provoke such a man to anger, and he spreads an air of peacefulness around him, even in the company of the quarrelsome. He is of use to all, of hurt to none, whether in things great or things little. In such a purified soul the Blessed Sacrament works wonders, for in such an interior condition the foundations of virtues are solidly laid; not in showy pious observances, or susceptibility to pious feelings when receiving Communion — in which and in other such things many people put their trust.

These go often to Confession and Communion, thinking themselves entirely worthy to do so, saying they cannot do without it. Yet they rest upon merely natural motives. They are even deluded with the notion that they cannot lose God's friendship; and this arises from their feelings of devotion. But meanwhile they are greatly enraged against those who would admonish them to go to Communion less often, or who find fault with their peculiar devotions. They despise others, they sit in judgment on their neighbors and make little of them, and they slander them. As to those to whom they lawfully owe obedience, they will scarcely look at them or listen to a word from them if they interfere with the practices which they deem so holy. Let it be quite different with us. May God grant us to receive Communion in a holy and happy state of true penance, inner and outer, and with great purity of heart and mind. *Amen.*

Ｔhe Ｊnspirations of Ｇrace

Synopsis—This discourse treats of souls who have gone beyond ordinary Christian virtue—God's guidance is always both inward and outward—Different kinds of imperfect souls—Self-will the principal hindrance to divine inspiration—Next comes the hurt done by spiritual vanity—How good works react on the interior favorably—Disinterestedness, obedience, humility and holy fear are safeguards against delusion.

SERMON FOR THE EIGHTH SUNDAY AFTER TRINITY.

For whosover are led by the Spirit of God, they are the sons of God.—Rom. viii, 14.

All works of all men, done now and until the end of the world, if done without the grace of God, are simply nothing, even though they be the greatest deeds of history—all of them put together are nothing, in comparison with the least work that God does in man by His grace. As much as God is better than man, so much better are His works than man's works.

The Holy Ghost often admonishes us in our inmost souls, or by the voice of His authorized teachers, saying: Wilt thou give thyself up to Me? Wilt thou follow Me alone? If thou wilt, I will lead thee by the right road. I will work within thee, and thou thyself shalt work. ̣O children, it is sad that there is scarcely anyone who knows this. Everyone rests in his own guidance, chooses his own methods, blindly follows external ways, content with self-approval, thereby hindering the gracious influence of the Holy Ghost, neither understanding nor even hearing His voice, giving no place to His guidance. Hence the need of my telling you, that there is no better way to catch the tones of God's whisper in you than to rest still and attentively listen. ̣When God speaks all things must keep silence. If God shall rightly work in us, needs must we give Him room to work, and rest passive under His action. Two cannot do the same work in us at the same time; one must stop while the other acts.

But do not mistake me. I do not mean that young, ardent, inexperienced souls should refrain from good works, waiting for interior guidance. By no means; for these greatly need to follow many good pious customs and do many good works, both in the inner life and the outer. But I refer to souls further advanced, who long sincerely to become God's most perfect children; the methods of these must be far different from those of beginners.

Take the world all around, we find that men are for the most part enemies of God. There are some who are friends of God under compulsion; you must drive them to serve Him; what they do is not inspired by love, but by fear—graceless, loveless men, who pray or attend Mass because you force them. Then there are some commonplace and mercenary creatures who serve God because they have an office and a stipend; were they not sure of their pay they would quit His service and drop back among God's open enemies. For all of these God has no regard; as far as their service of Him goes, it does not make them His beloved children. They may do many outwardly good deeds, but He takes no account of this, for He is not chosen as the motive of their works, but rather they are themselves.

Take another class, that are really God's children, though not the most loved by Him. I mean those who in their outer and inner life act according to their own spiritual methods, and do their own chosen works, and aspire to nothing higher. These souls are content with the bark of the tree of life—they will not climb into its branches after its fruit. Their own ways please them well; they love God indeed, but in their own chosen ways of piety. And God loves them, too, for they are His children, though not the best loved, for they rest in self-chosen ways of religion. Meantime they have no real peace, and they will yet be made perfect.

The best loved children, who are they? St. Paul tells us in our text: "Whosoever are led by the Spirit of God, they are the sons of God." How God leads them, St. Augustine tells: "God's action in man is twofold. The one is that God's spirit always admonishes him, drives him forward, allures him on, so that he may lead a well-ordered life. This He does in the souls of all who wait upon Him, who give Him place, and who will follow Him. The others are those whom He leads suddenly beyond and above all methods and ways, placing them in a much higher degree, pointing them to an end far beyond their own power to reach: and these are God's best loved children." But many will not trust themselves to this divine action; they constantly insist on following ways of their own choosing. They act like a shipmaster carrying a costly cargo across a stormy sea, and steering a wrong course through many dangers and with painful toil, the salt water now and then breaking over the ship and injuring the cargo. Supposing him to meet a skilful mariner, who says to him: Let me guide thee and I will lead thee to a calm and sunny sea, with smooth sailing and a safe harbor for thy ship and cargo; who would not gladly welcome such a pilot? Well, and what sea can be more perilous to cross than that of this world of ours? But the ship in which we are sailing is the life of our senses, which is carried far out of its right course by our following our own lights and ways, causing us infinite labor as we wander amid banks of fog—namely, our ignorance and self-conceit. The enemy of souls casts foul and corrupting thoughts into our minds, like the salt water of the ocean soaking into a precious cargo—these are temptations to be vain of our own ways of devotion, feelings of pride, self-will, self-complacency, self-indulgence, and, again, of despondency. If one feels he has yielded to these suggestions, he cleanses his soul by going to Confession— too often only to fall back again into dissipation of mind. O turn inward and sincerely study thy soul's sickness, bemoaning thy misery to God and avowing to Him thy guilt. And if thou art conscious of grave sin, seek thy father confessor again. Then will the Holy Ghost come and say: Beloved child, if thou wilt but trust Me and follow Me, I will lead thee by a beautiful and a safe way. O who would not entrust himself to the guidance of such a counselor? Happy the man who gives up self-guidance and resigns himself wholly to that of God's Spirit. But, alas, many a poor man will not, but prefers his own devices and rests in his own outward methods of sanctification.

But I must not be misunderstood: it is necessary to practice approved devotional methods having an interior influence, but not with a feeling of proprietorship. Rather should one do these good things with a disengaged spirit, awaiting the manifestation of God's will about them, guarding against self-approval, avoiding rationalizing on such matters. One's soul may be compared to an orchard full of fruit, but the apples fall from the trees unripe, for they are worm eaten, and thus the worms crawl out of them and injure the good vegetables growing on the ground. Meanwhile the worm-eaten apples seem just as good as sound ones, until you pick them up; then they are found to be all rotten. So do our souls look with their fair seeming vain-glorious devotions—till we examine them closely, and among many we shall hardly find one or two that are worthy of God— good observances in themselves, but the heart of them is fatally injured by defective motives. And this applies to both the active and the contemplative life—all one does may be no better than worm-eaten fruit, fatally injured by self choosing and by vain observance. For as to contemplation, do we not read the following in St. Paul? "And lest the greatness of the revelations should exalt me, there was given me a sting of my flesh, an angel of Satan, to buffet me" (II Cor. xii: 7). So might it be needful to thee, even if thou hadst the gift of prophecy, and did great signs and wonders, healed the sick, possessed the key of the future—all may be worm-eaten and rotten, if thou dost not stand watchfully on thy guard.

And now let us explain the lowest and grossest case of empty-hearted religious custom. Suppose a man giving alms, and that he begins by being careful that God alone shall know of this good act of charity; but after awhile he cherishes a sort of longing for human praise, for he is not quite content to be without it:—now this is a worm-eaten apple. Thus it is that one may have selfish motives in wishing that people should praise their good deeds. They put windows and altars in churches with their names marked on them—"they have received their reward." They defend themselves by saying they wish men to pray for them. Alms pure and simple, known to God alone, in whose bosom it is all hidden, were of more benefit to their souls than if they built great churches before men's eyes and all the people prayed for them. God would easily make up to them what men might have petitioned for them, did they entrust their good work to Him alone in all confidence.

Alms out of a heart wholly disengaged from men and from created things, are themselves a better prayer to God than the petitions of admiring multitudes. Many a man for lack of this perfectly pure intention destroys the merit of his good works, sometimes all through his life; whether they serve God or men, in vigils, and fasts, and alms deeds, they calculate what return they shall get, either from God (in a mercenary spirit) or their fellowmen—that is all they think of. If these works filled the whole world, they are no better than worm-eaten apples. Accept this doctrine, not from me, but from truth itself:

"Take heed that you do not your justice before men, to be seen by them: otherwise you shall not have a reward of your Father who is in Heaven. Therefore when thou dost an almsdeed, sound not a trumpet before thee, as the hypocrites do in the synagogues and in the streets. Amen I say to you, they have received their reward. But when thou dost alms, let not thy left hand know what thy right hand doth; that thy alms may be in secret, and thy Father, who seeth in secret, will repay thee." And he continues: "When thou shalt pray, enter into thy chamber, and having shut the door, pray to thy Father in secret: and thy Father who seeth in secret will repay thee" (Matt. vi: 1-6). Children, take heed to these words, which are not mine, but those of everlasting truth; let each one look to God and to Him alone in all the good that he undertakes to do.

Now, there are four preservatives against the worm that destroys the fruit of good works. The first is that a man. should do all his works of the interior and exterior life, not for himself, but for God alone, thinking of God and loving God while he is doing them. | Does he find them sweet to do? Well and good. 'Does he find them bitter? He yet perseveres to do them, for he never chose them for his own joy, but for God's.

The second preservative is an immeasureable depth of obedience under God, yea and under all mankind from the lowest to the highest. An example of this is in the life of the great doctor of the Church, St. Thomas, who made not the least difficulty of humbly accompanying an overbearing brother with a lantern along the streets of the city. Be subject to every human being for God's sake. Thou shouldst in all sincerity esteem. any man better than thyself; thou shouldst never withstand anyone, but yield gently and humbly to all. |

The third is humility, so that a man shall in all sincerity rest upon his nothingness, realizing that it is the only thing he can claim properly as his own, everything besides being not his own. Let him consider as an evil thing whatsoever he has or does on his own account, including his own self. Once as I was in choir alongside of a holy brother of ours, who was a man to whom God had granted many signs of sanctity, and whose holy life was full of marvels of grace—this brother whispered to me from the bottom of his heart: "Brother, believe what I tell thee—I am the greatest and foulest sinner in the whole world." Let every one of us say the same in all sincerity. For I say to you, that if God has bestowed upon the worst sinner the graces

He has granted me, he would have become a great saint. And a man who is thus grounded in humility is wholly incapable of sitting in judgment upon his neighbor, about no matter what affair. If he sees what is plainly bad, he forthwith turns his attention to the consideration of his own defects.

The fourth preservative is that one shall stand in constant dread of the secret judgment of God, not indeed as one who yields to despair, but rather as one deeply anxious lest he shall arouse a friend's anger. Now as to these preservatives, St. Bernard says: "Whosoever does not rest securely upon these, let him do all the good deeds in the world, and they are all worm-eaten fruit."

In the garden of holy Church there grow many and wonderful trees, all full of good fruit; that is to say, many humble-hearted men: on them alone hangs God's true fruit of virtue. Others are there bearing worm-eaten fruit, fair and red to look at, fairer sometimes than the sound fruit: but wait till a stormy wind blows, wait till the time of trial comes: down they fall, and soon they are rotten and spreading rottenness around them.

These are self-indulgent and unmortified men. They vainly trust to their own showy good works, often seeming to do more of them than the truly good souls. They are absorbed in the practice of devotions that have not been prescribed by holy Church, and upon these, with all their grand show of piety, they rest as upon their life's foundation. Meanwhile the weather is calm, their souls are in peace, they bask in the sunshine of their pious observances, they seem to excel God's true servants in virtue. But presently the storm arises, they are assailed by those temptations against the faith common in our time, and presently they are overthrown—and then the worms of doubt and error creep out of their hearts into the hearts of other men, uninstructed and simple-minded, whom they ruin with their false maxims of liberty and their other false teaching. They have been all along treading a broad yet hidden road of destruction, because they give up to their own inborn unsanctified tendencies. They never entered upon the narrow but true path of sincere self-denial; they would not give up self; they were determined to yield to corrupt nature.

But let us not go too far from our subject in pursuit of these worm-eaten souls. "Whosoever are led by the Spirit of God, they are the sons of God," namely, those who perseveringly watch for the will of

God to follow it, who are docile to His inspirations, who obey His interior admonitions. In this way of God they must now and then cross a desert place all full of woe. If they bravely venture into it, trusting loyally to God's Spirit, what a happy lot theirs shall be. Let them but turn inward to their soul's life and keep careful account of it. What wonders of God's working are there, surpassing all sense and all understanding. Let such a man give but one year to this holy interior life and to nothing else, and never was a year better spent. Nay, if God but grant him in that whole year only a single momentary glimpse of the action of His Spirit in the soul's depths, that momentary revelation will give more worth to the year than all the good works he could have crowded into it by immense self-activity. He that works with God can lose nothing, and in this holy matter one indeed works with God.

What! Shall we doubt that God is nobler than His creature? So is His work nobler than His creature's work. With such a man all outward activity not strictly of God's appointment falls away, for he ever has activity enough within his soul. Herein is found perfect security, herein is perfect joy. Alas, that men will not credit this. They cannot comprehend it. In truth it pertains only to perfect souls who are deep rooted in God in all simplicity of heart. As to lower grades of good men, let them be rightly engaged, as indeed they ought to be, in every kind of good works of the active life, lest they lapse into guilty slothfulness.

Believe me, children, "Every plant which My heavenly Father hath not planted shall be rooted up" (Matt. xv: 13). Now can you under- stand how deeply God loves a man who gives Him full room in his soul for His divine work, by which work God is blessed in His own life? It is a love above all love that God bestows on him, and passes all understanding. For such a man is loved with the love wherewith the heavenly Father loves His only begotten Son. No wonder, I say, then, that this spiritual way leads the soul into the abyss of the deity.

The disciples of Dionysius once asked him how it happened that Timothy surpassed them all so greatly in holiness, although they did all the good works that he did. Their master answered: "Timothy is a man who permits God to work within him." This takes place in a living faith in God, which is unspeakably above all the works that by outward act a man can do. But to follow this method what i before all else needed, is to sink down into a deep self-renunciation, by which a man never sees himself in God's work, but sees God alone, leaves himself wholly to God to work His way in him, reserving only what is really his own, namely, his nothingness. If such a man should at last make any account of himself, that were indeed a lamentable fall and a dangerous one. May He who alone can give holiness and perfect it, grant us the grace to yield ever to His will. *Amen.*

Fidelity in Little Things

Synopsis—The littlest work of a member of Christ's body partakes of the dignity of the Head—Each one should do all his works for the sake of all his brethren—Searching for God among little duties— The farmer in a trance, flail in hand—How to obtain heavenly guidance in small affairs.

FIRST SERMON FOR THE TENTH SUNDAY AFTER TRINITY.*

There are diversities of operations, but the same Lord, who worketh all in all, and the manifestation of the Spirit is given to every man unto profit. To one, indeed, by the Spirit, is given the word of wisdom; and to another, the word of knowledge, according to the same Spirit; to another faith in the same Spirit. . . . But all these things one and the same Spirit worketh, dividing to everyone according as He will.—I Cor. xii, 6-11.

Here the apostle names a variety of gifts, but which are all the work of the same Holy Ghost. In the days of the apostles, the Holy Ghost wrought wonderful things among His friends for the proof of the Christian faith, including prophecies; and His final work was the martyrdom of the apostles and their disciples. Miraculous signs are not needed in our days, although it must be confessed that living Christian faith is as little evident in some among us as in pagans and Jews.

Let us consider this teaching—that there are diversities of work in God's service, and yet that one and the same Spirit is in them all. Children, look at the human body, with all its different members and senses, each part having its separate office. Not any sense or member usurps the office of any other, or acts otherwise than as God has ordained for it. So are we all members of the same body, and of this body Christ is the head. Now, the eye in the body of holy Church, that is her teachers. It is an office that does not concern you, for we ordinary Christians must note carefully what our place is, the office to which our Lord has called us, and in the performance of whose

---

*No sermon of Tauler's for the Ninth Sunday after Trinity is extant.

duties we are firmly joined to the Head, our Lord, by means of His holy grace. For no matter how insignificant the work may seem, if it be that of a member of Christ's body, then it is done by the grace of the Holy Ghost to the profit of men's souls.

Well, then, we live among the lowest members. One can spin, another can make shoes, some being skilful at one trade, others at another. And these are all graces that are made active by the operation of the Spirit of God. If I were not a priest, and were only a brother in a community, I should consider it a great thing to be able to make shoes, and I would be very glad to earn my bread by the labor of my hands. Children, the foot or hand should not wish to be the eye, but each should fulfill the office assigned by God; for however lowly that may seem, it could not be done by the other members. Thus our sisters do their part, as, for example, in piously chanting the psalms. St. Augustine says: "God is a most simple being; and yet He works in a most manifold way, being all things in each single thing, and one in all of them together." Every least little work of ours comes to us as a duty from God and each has its particular grace. Let us do it gladly for the sake of all our brethren, who cannot do it as appropriately as we. Thus do we all mutually exchange grace for grace. Believe me, the man who does not pray nor work for his neighbor's sake shall have much to answer for before God, when, as the Gospel tells us, it will be said to him: "Give an account of thy stewardship" (Luke xvi: 2). And each of us is appointed as a steward to do a certain work for God, and to render account of the same.

How does it happen, then, that so many complain that their occupation in life hinders their serving God? God makes no limitations to His service, and how, then, does it happen that thy conscience is afflicted at having to do what He appoints for thee? Dear children, make up your minds that it is not your occupation, but your own ill-regulated way of performing it that disturbs your interior peace. Do thy duty rightly; have God alone in view; be disengaged from all self-conceit and self-love; look not to what is pleasant or unpleasant as thy end in doing or not doing; fear nothing and desire nothing but God; seek no profit, think of no joy in thy work; regard nothing except what is wholly for God's honor:—act this way, and it is impossible that thou shouldst feel distress of conscience in thy usual occupations. It is a shame for any spiritual man to have it said of him, that he is disorderly in doing his daily round of duty, for one soon perceives this defect—the work is not done in God, nor is it done to the benefit of his neighbor.

By this slovenly carelessness thou makest manifest that it is not for and in God thou art laboring; and herein is shown the cause of thy unrest of soul. Our Lord did not reprove Martha on account of her work, for that was holy; he chided her for her excessive solicitude. A man should practice approved spiritual exercises, attend to his bounden duty, and then cast all his care upon God, attending meanwhile to his obligations diligently and in all calmness of minl. And he should be careful to remain at home in his own spirit, looking often there in search of God, with inward intentness and very devoutly, meanwhile carefully attending to every call of duty in his external life. And, besides, he should carefully watch for the inspirations ol the Holy Ghost, whether to action or to suffering for God's sake. By this means he does or he leaves undone according to the guidance of the Holy Ghost, now resting quiet and again pushing onward: such is the way to fulfil thy part in life in all Godliness and peace.

If there is any poor, old, feeble, helpless creature, do thou run quickly to his help. One should outdo the other in this work of charity, thus bearing one another's burdens. If thou failest in this, be sure that God will bestow the privilege upon another with all the accompanying graces, leaving thee empty. Dost thou feel a special joy in any work? Be on thy guard carefully—do the work for God alone, be not carried away by thy feelings. Here, then, children, is the way to acquire virtue, and a very necessary way, if thou wouldst come to God. Do not dream that by counselling quiet waiting for God, I mean that thou art to sit down idle till God shall come and infuse virtue into thy soul.

Put no trust in immature virtue, unearned virtue. If a man claims that the Father and the Son and the Holy Ghost have taken up their abode within him, there is nothing in what he says, unless he has attained to this state by devout exercises of religion, interior as well as exterior, the same that we have been considering. A farmer stands and threshes his grain with his flail uplifted, and suddenly falls into a trance; now the flail will fall on him and strike him, unless an angel from Heaven shall catch it. So with you. None like to thresh, all would wish to be entranced—all the members of the body would be the eye, all for the contemplative and none for the active life. Now this is a sign of stupidity. I knew a man who was a very dear

friend of God, and who was a ploughman all the days of his life—
more than forty years, and, indeed, he is the same yet. Well, he once
asked our Lord whether or not he should give up his labor and spend
his time in church. The Lord said to him: "No, thou shalt eat thy
bread in the sweat of thy face, and in that service thou shalt do
honor to My precious blood." And yet everyone, each following his
own pious method, should daily and nightly retire apart and sink
down into the depths of his soul, choosing therefor a proper time
and place. Those who are so far advanced as to go to God direct
and without the images of the imagination, should follow their method;
others in turn are helped by a different one; for we cannot all be eyes
in the Lord's body. Each one for himself must thus pray just as God
ordains; and in deep love and quiet peace. Whosoever serves God
as He wills, to him shall God respond according to that man's own
will. But if one serves God according to his own will, him shall God
treat, not as he would wish to be treated, but as God in His justice
deems best.

Children, it is in this self-departure, this going forth from selfwill,
that the essential peace of the soul is born within us, which means
the acquisition of well-seasoned virtue. Believe me that essential
peace never comes otherwise—it is false to assert such a thing. Outwardly practiced and inwardly cherished virtue produces peace of
soul; though it is to be said that the peace that arises from the more
interior exercises of religion is a treasure that no man can rob you of.
Men wise in their own conceit will bid you do this and do that to
become perfect—and it is all a set of observances of their own con-
trivance. Such men have sometimes been forty years in religion, and
to this day they do not appreciate their state of life. They are far
bolder in devotional things than I would dare to be.

My vocation is that of a teacher of the people. And yet when I
hear confessions and ask my penitents how this is and how that,
having in view their spiritual direction, at the last I am often unable
to form a judgment about them. Then I pray to our Lord for light;
and if He does not grant it to me, I can but say: Dear children, you
must yourselves pray for the divine guidance, and it will certainly be
granted you. Not so the rash men of whom I have been speaking;
they praise or they condemn quickly, each of them according to his
own chosen standard, and strive to fasten on others their own
favorite devotional customs. And by this means many a plant in our

Lord's garden is worm-eaten in the bud. They say to you: Your way is a novelty and we do not approve of it, it is full of the spirit of innovation; and meanwhile God's ways are wholly unknown to them. Ah, strange things may be expected from men of that kind.

Now says St. Paul: "But all these things the same Spirit worketh, dividing to everyone according as He will." Children, to what kind of men, think you, does God give the knowledge of the divisions He makes among men? Who are they that have the judgment and discernment of different spirits in men? Be sure that they who have this gift are well exercised in the ways of God. The trials of flesh and blood are familiar to them, for they have suffered them in the severest form. The enemy of souls has gone through them, aye, and they have gone through him. Bone and marrow have been searched through and through, and all their souls have been perfected—such are the men to whom God grants the discernment of spirits. If they will but turn their attention to any souls and consider them, they at once discover whether or not their spirit is of God; and they can decide what is the right step to be taken in the road of perfection, or what it is that stands in the way. Meanwhile let us lament how trifling a thing it is that causes us to turn out of the straight road to everlasting truth, doing ourselves a grievous and eternal harm— for God and His love are eternal, and if we neglect His love on earth it will never be ours in the life to come. May God help us to do His work in all truth, and just as His Holy Spirit shall guide us, each one according to his particular inspirations. *Amen.*

Election and Reprobation

*Synopsis—To abide in self-approval is to court reprobation—Also to
serve God in a spirit of buying and selling—Dreadful fate of a
certain unworthy monk—An elect soul keeps God ever in view—A
plain sign of election is feeling spiritual misery on account of
bodily plenty—Again, readiness to hear God's word in a humble
mood.*

SECOND SERMON FOR THE TENTH SUNDAY AFTER TRINITY.

And when He drew near, seeing the city, He wept over it, saying: If thou
also hadst known and that in this thy day, the things that are to thy peace; but
now they are hidden from thy eyes. For the days shall come upon thee, and thy
enemies shall cast a trench about thee, and compass thee round, and straiten
thee on every side, and beat thee flat to the ground, and thy children who are in
thee; and they shall not leave in thee a stone upon a stone; because thou hast
not known the time of thy visitation. And entering into the temple, He began to
cast out them that sold things, and them that bought. Saying to them: It is
written: My house is the house of prayer. But you have made it a den of
thieves.—Luke xix, 41-46.

The city over which our Lord now weeps is Christendom. This is
the first meaning of this Gospel; the second is that He weeps over
worldly hearts, and well may He weep, for we may all weep and
never weep enough over those who know not and who will not be
warned of the time of their visitation. Jerusalem was in joy and
peace when Christ wept over the city. And so are all these men who
live in the life of the senses. They are full of joy and peace as long
as they have this world's goods, power, friends, relatives, honors,
everything to their hearts' content, living as if these were to be theirs
for all eternity. Meanwhile they keep up a show of religion, confession,
and prayer, and dream they are safe. If you say anything to the
contrary, you are lost to them. They abide in self-righteousness and
in perfect security. But mark what comes after this state of security:
their enemy shall come upon them, and leave not a stone upon a stone.

The time of God's visitation is at hand. As they approach death, the
fiend enwraps them in a mantle of despair, they know not which way
to fly, not a thought of God's goodness can enter their souls. No
wonder. God has never been there, they never built on Him, took
little account of Him—they were ever absorbed in transitory pleasures
and the joys of the senses. When the evil one has knocked away that
foundation, then down falls the peace that was built thereon. Now
follows an unbearable tumult of soul, unbearable and everlasting, over
which all men might weep and wither up with terror; yea, they might
well shed tears of blood over such a calamity. Good reason had Christ
to weep over these souls, saying: "If thou also hadst known, and
that in this thy day, the things that are to thy peace." And St. John
writes: "All that is in the world is the concupiscence of the flesh,
and the concupiscence of the eyes, and the pride of life" (I John
ii: 16). How shall God judge such a soul after death? Would that
He might give you to know the terrors of that future tumult of soul
which shall never be followed by peace; which not my words but those
of St. Gregory describe in this day's homily.

Then our Lord entered into the temple and drove out the buyers
and sellers, saying: You have made My house a den of thieves. He
means the soul of man, which is more properly the temple of God
than all material temples in the world. St. Paul says: "Know you
not that you are the temple of God, and that the Spirit of God
dwelleth within you? If any man violate the temple of God, him
shall God destroy. For the temple of God is holy, which you are"
(I Cor. iii: 16-17). Now when our Lord would enter into this His
temple, He finds it a den of thieves and murderers, and a place of
traffic. For what is buying and selling? It is when, for example, a
man gives the corn which he has for the wine which he has not.
Now, a man has nothing that is really his own, except his free will.
And it is by bartering away his free will in exchange for the perishable
things of this world that he plies his traffic: no matter what he gets
in return, he always gives away his free will—seeking joy in food
and drink, in raiment and jewels, both for his own pleasure and for
the admiration of other men. Alas, the day of reckoning is sure to
come. And then they cry out, O blessed Lord, have pity on me! It
was not a sensual love but a spiritual love I indulged in; we must
have our relaxations. Dear children, make no mistake. This is really
the traffic thou carriest on whilst thou canst barter away thy free
will. And as time goes on, God is removed farther and farther away

from thee, and grows stranger and stranger. St. Bernard says: "Divine consolation is of so sensitive and delicate a nature, that it cannot abide the company of any other consolation." One will perhaps exclaim: O Lord, we are in the religious state, members of a holy order. I answer: If thou hadst upon thee all the holy habits thou couldst choose, unless thou dost act up to what these rightly mean, they will do thee no manner of good.

It happened once that a man committed a crime, and then he entered a monastery, wholly unrepentant and unconfessed. Having received the holy habit, he came to his death—and the devil cut him to pieces and carried him off, body and soul, but leaving the holy habit after him. And they that belong to orders should be for that reason all the more holy than the ordinary traffickers of this world. Alas, how vast a subject is this for our meditation, if we did but search it to the bottom. For everybody seems full of his own will, full, full, full! How few strong characters do we meet with, men who subject themselves wholly to God; indeed, the majority of those who act thus are poor, humble women. All seek their own, all are self-willed. Ah, if they would but traffic with God, and give Him their free wills, that would indeed be a prosperous venture. And what is the net profit of their worldly barter? Nothing but disturbance of mind. Yet these half-hearted Christians are all the better off for their pain upon pain of heart, if they but knew it, for by means of this distress of conscience they will at last be saved; whereas those who are content with their state of infidelity to God are in great peril of final loss. St. Augustine speaks thus of the half-hearted: "Ill-regulated spirits provide a martyrdom for themselves, and lay on their souls an oppressive burden; they feel deep unrest and yet know not what ails them." The trouble is that their temple is a place of traffic; they will not give up self-love.

Sometimes one will give up relatives and friends, his goods and his inheritance; but he will not give up self. And all is then in vain. He must be to himself as utterly stripped of all things as when he came naked from God. This is true, even though one must have many cares for himself, like eating and drinking, seeing and hearing, all of which leave their memories in the soul. What then? A man must in all these things keep God in view: he must seek God in all he does, in all he leaves undone. As long as he acts that way, he may disregard his memories and the images of his imagination. He keeps the temple of his soul clean from traffic. He is not entangled by these intrusions of outward things.

The bride in the Canticles says that their bed is full of flowers, that is to say, the soul in friendship with God is full of heavenly flowers, of thoughts and images of divine love and of Heaven. Ah, if thy temple were only totally empty, cleansed of all trafficking, all imaginations, then would it indeed be the temple of God—never until then, no matter what thou mayst do to it. Peace and joy would then possess thy heart; nothing whatever could lead thee astray; all that now annoys thee and even fills thee with anguish would vanish away. The Lord commanded Ezechiel to dig his way through the wall into the temple, and to behold the many abominations there, and the foul images therein to be found—painted by the keepers of the temple themselves. And thus it is with the recollections and the imaginations of men; they themselves paint them upon their souls.

Herein may one distinguish between the elect and the reprobate. The former cannot enjoy full peace in inordinate use of created things, even if they do for awhile lose themselves and go astray in them. They feel the tooth of remorse constantly gnawing their conscience, sorrow and dread haunt them even in their evil hours; and this is the work of the Holy Ghost, as it is written: "The Spirit Himself asketh for us with unspeakable groanings" (Rom. viii: 26). They come at last to sincere repentance, weeping over their wayward and disorderly life, and thus they are saved. This is true even though years may pass before they return to God. What an inestimable grace is this; and he who is granted it may well thank God for the warnings vouchsafed him, and the interior inspirations that stirred him to repentance. But, alas, with others it turns out differently. There are some to whom it avails not to give private warnings or public discourses—nay, there are whole countries that seem to be averted from God.

Therefore do I warn you to hear God's message, while yet it is addressed to you: profit well by it. Admit the word of God into thy understanding, for it is too little understood. It is a blameworthy thing that God's warning remains in the ear and does not reach the heart, for that is filled already; it is all encumbered and overlaid with things of sense. Make room for God's word; drive out of your hearts the joys you take in created things; expel the imaginations and memories of this world—otherwise you cannot understand what God means.

When one preaches a truth of God today, and preaches the self-same truth again tomorrow, his hearers will receive it attentively and with joy, because it is a property of divine truth, that as fast as we learn one lesson in it God makes our hearts ready for another. It is full of undiscovered beauty and instruction, all of which we never can perfectly comprehend. And this ever-increasing power of understanding God's word, is granted especially to those who come to hear it with souls' detached from earthly things. As to the others, much is lost to them, and much is not rightly understood. The truth of God reaches their ears and forms figures in their fancy—not much more. This is on account of the preoccupation of their souls by worldly thoughts. If these thoughts, these traffickers, were but driven out of that temple of God, it would be transformed into a house of prayer, in which God would love to dwell. And presently we shall discourse upon the prayer that should be offered therein. Meanwhile, may God grant us the grace to drive out all traffickers, and make our souls acceptable to Him. *Amen.*

Hindering and Helping a Worthy Communion

*Synopsis—A notable hindrance is despondency over past sinfulness—
Another is lack of sensible devotion—Yet another is discouragement over venial defects—Frequent communion as a reparation
for the wickedness of the whole race of man—Our helps are all
kinds of interior tendencies towards God—Externally, brotherly
love is second to none—Disregard of men's opinion of us is a de-
cided aid—An exhortation to frequent communion.*

SERMON FOR THE ELEVENTH SUNDAY AFTER TRINITY.

Two men went up into the temple to pray, the one a Pharisee, and the other a
publican.—Luke xviii, 10.

Let us take the temple here spoken of to mean the soul of man in
its very depths. There, indeed, does the Holy Trinity love to dwell.
He loves to inspire the soul's activity, making it the place of His joy,
the treasury of His gifts. For the soul is made in the image and likeness of the Triune God. Here then is the temple into which a man
must enter to pray. And if he prays right he does so as two men; one
the inward man and the other the outward man. What the outward
man prays for is of little or no value. And let me tell you, my dear
sisters, that if you would have help to pray and to make real progress
in prayer, there is nothing better than the blessed body and blood of
our Lord Jesus Christ. Receive this at proper intervals and you will
find yourself renewed, yes, newly born, in your spiritual life. That
privilege is yours. Thank God for it with special fervor, and make
good use of it in preference to any other spiritual help. Human nature
is weak and much inclined to evil. We need great assistance if we
shall be able to withdraw from evil; no help can compare with this
divine nourishment. In the Lord's parable, one of the men praying in
the temple was a Pharisee. The other was a publican; that is to say,
a notorious sinner. He stood afar off, not daring to lift his eyes to
heaven, and he said: "O God, be merciful to me a sinner." All went

well with him in this prayer. I only wish that I could in all reality do as he did, ever gazing down into my nothingness; that is the best way to pray, and the most useful. Prayer made in that spirit leads a man to God, straight and without intermediation, for when God, appealed to on the score of His mercy, comes to the soul, He comes with His divine essence, His own very self.

But some enter on prayer with the spirit of this poor sinner, acknowledging indeed their wickedness, but in their humility they would fly from the face of God and from the Holy Sacrament—they dare not receive Communion. Not so, not so, my dear sisters. All the more eagerly should you go to Communion, so that the strength of your sins may fall away from you, saying to our Lord: O come quick, Lord, ere that my soul shall die in its sins. Let me assure you, that if I should find a man inspired with that publican's spirit, deeply and most humbly conscious of his sinful state, and who would gladly be good but much overcome with this praiseworthy fear, yet anxious still to follow God's blessed will and renounce the love of created things with all his might, I say that to such a one I would give the consolation of receiving our Lord's body and blood the very next day; and the prudence of this I am prepared to prove from holy scripture. When we received holy baptism and were dedicated to God, we received full right to Holy Communion; that right all creatures together cannot strip us of—except our own selves by refusing to be contrite for our sins.

Dear sisters, one need not have great sensible devotion in order to worthily receive Communion, nor need one have done great outward good works. It is enough if one be free from mortal sin, humbly stand in fear of God, and confess his unworthiness; all this is indeed necessary and it is at the same time very beneficial. If one will live free from mortal sin, then there is great need that he be fed by this divine food. It elevates us high towards the summit of the spiritual life. Instead of avoiding Communion because thou hast been sinful, rather shouldst thou hasten to receive it, as long as thou dost sorrowfully confess thy wickedness. For from this grace comes strength, holiness, consolation and sweetness. Of course thou shouldst not condemn those who do not go often to Communion, any more than sit in judgment on poor penitent sinners who do go. St. Augustine says: "Condemn no man on any account whatsoever, unless, indeed, Holy Church

has already condemned him for his proud spirit and his open wickedness, and for being obstinately given up to his sinful practices." As
to whether any one receives unworthily, that is not our affair; they
have their superiors who will certainly attend to that. Condemn not,
dear children, lest you become like the proud Pharisee, who sat in
judgment on the poor sinner who stood below him in the temple—
beware of that as you would of the eternal loss of your soul. Meantime be not over anxious as to whether or not your past sins will be
held against you; rather be anxious to avoid the sin of judging your
neighbor.

Once it happened that I was with some brothers of our order who
observed our rule with special strictness, and I was very desirous of
doing as they did. But our Lord willed otherwise, for my health was
too feeble to allow me to do so. This led me to suppose that God foresaw I should have fallen into Pharisaism if I had been permitted these
austerities; I should have been given over to self complacency. Our
Lord is so faithful to us, that sometimes he allows a man of God to fall
into occasional notable faults of a venial nature his whole life long,
because thereby he is constantly forced to enter into his soul and learn
his own nothingness in all humility. Hence one should not refrain
from Communion on account of such defects. Let him meekly exclaim:
Lord, I am not worthy that thou shouldst enter under my roof or into
my heart; yet I implore thee to enter there out of regard for the overflowing riches of Thy merits and Thy boundless mercies. I am in sore
need of contrition, charity and other graces, and all these are plentiful
in Thee, in whom we find all virtue, all aspiration for good.

Children, the awful state of sin in which God found mankind in the
time of our Father St. Dominic, and which almost provoked Him to
once more destroy the world in His wrath, seems to be returned upon
the race in our day. What will happen to us we know not; but we
must seek anxiously for some means of obtaining God's blessed mercy.
And no means is better than for each of us to renounce and cast away
all created things, turn inwardly to God, and invite ourselves to our
Lord in the Sacrament of His body and blood. Dear sisters, adopt
that holy method, observing due order, cultivating the right spirit.
If you detect yourselves in faults, still cherish within you a hearty
purpose to live according to God, regret your defects sincerely, avoid
all dangerous occasions.

In the holy order of which you and I are members, and in which God calls us away from a perilous world, we ought to wait on Him and Him alone with the utmost fidelity of heart.   Dear children, often ponder your holy vocation, mark carefully what progress you are making, and what example of virtue you are setting to others.   All men should behold in your lives the fruit of your Communions, as well as the diligent observance of the holy rule.   I do not mean to urge any unreasonable austerity, as that any aged and feeble sister should fast and toil and watch beyond her power of endurance; but all things to be done with discretion.   Children, if you are thus fervent, the graces of Holy Communion will be inestimably great in you.

Futhermore, let all your words be sweet, kind and peaceful.   What if hard words are spoken to you; suffer this meekly for the love of God, submissive to all men.   To bitter words answer thou nothing but a few kindly sentences, spoken with a cheerful countenance.

Look closely to your interior.   Have no joy in the possession of any thing whatsoever, or in its use.   Make no effort to please self, or to win the favor of others.   Be attached neither to clothing, ornaments nor books; no, nor to any particular companionship.   Whatsoever is really needful for your wants God will provide for you through your superiors.

You ought to have great love for one another, should be subject one to another in all affection, abhoring overbearing manners, or anything that may in the least degree estrange sisterly affections, or disturb interior peace of mind.   Be zealous for good works in the community, exhorting the sisters most affectionately and emulating one another. Lend a hand and a heart to help the weak and aged sisters, antici- pating and relieving their necessities in all cheerfulness and love. And let this be done not only for members of your own community, but for all other persons whom you can induce to accept your good offices.   "For if you love them that love you, what reward shall you have?   Do not even the publicans this?   And if you salute your brother only, what do you more?   Do not also the heathens this?" (Matt. v: 46, 47).

But suppose that you should be ridiculed for doing good deeds, or for some devout practice?   Answer never a word, make no sort of complaint.   Meanwhile, strictly observe your holy silence in choir and in all other places in which it is prescribed.   In choir, you should assist with deep reverence, for you know that our Savior's blessed body is really present there. Cast down your eyes in holy adoration before the face of your eternal King. If a simple maiden stood in the presence of a great queen the object of her monarch's special attention, would she not observe all proper decorum? Thus shalt thou recollect all thy powers of soul and body as thou standest before thy divine Bridegroom, one of His chosen spouses, for He gazes steadfastly upon thee, looking into the secret recesses of thy soul. O, dear sisters, most devoutly spend your time in choir, singing and reading your holy office there with deep devotion and a recollected soul. Nor need you be disturbed in conscience if sometimes your attention wanders, for the law of the office is kept if you pronounce the words; and meanwhile be sure to bring back your wandering mind to your holy work as soon as possible. One's conscience is clear if one does not wilfully yield to distracting thoughts.

The gospel says: "Wherefore, by their fruits you shall know them" (Matt. vii: 20). And in your case, it must be by the outward appearing fruits of virtue that you shall know yourselves as God's servants, and be known by others. To be equal to this test, no one is too feeble in body or too old, if they will but cherish mutual charity and practice patience and mildness of manner. These virtues one can have if he be bedridden. But, again, you shall be known by your interior fruits of grace—forfeiting no opportunity to love God, and totally disengaged from all that is not God. Be glad to pass your time alone with God, united to Him, passive under His influence. Ascend the tree of Christ's holy cross and passion, and hide in His glorious wounds—nay, go upward still, and be absorbed in the infinite Godhead itself. This is the way of the Good Shepherd, who leadeth His sheep back and forth through rich pastures. Thus in your Communions shall the adorable Sacrament give you the fruits of a holy life, and you shall make steady progress in grace.

It may be that some good souls will, out of reverence, receive Communion less often than thou dost, and this is also good; again there may be others who do not at all approve thy going to Communion often, and these will chide thee for thy boldness, or even visit thee with penances. But what then? I say to thee, bear this infliction with all meekness. Hardly any good thing can be done in this life without creating some trouble. It is indeed good that thou shouldst now and then give up Communion in a spirit of unfeigned humility; and yet it is much better for thee (if thou canst) rather to receive it in a spirit of holy love. The sick man needs the physician—here is One whose very presence is itself thy cure. Humble fear thou must not be without; which means that thou holdst up thy sins before thy soul's sorrowful gaze. That is a sign that this adorable Sacrament has worked its ends within thee. But when the medicine has driven out the disease, then comes the time to nourish the patient with good food—he is going to be restored to health, and that soul is sound and well before whose eyes its sins stand out plain and clear. Another good sign is the sincere longing to lead a good life and obey God's law; and if one is thus minded—not in fickleness or presumption, but because he has expelled all vice from his soul—then in this case also let him in all confidence approach the holy table. The more fruitful will his Communion be in proportion to the intensity of his sorrow for his sins.

It may occasionally happen that some of our sisters may have little or no time for thanksgiving immediately after Communion, being called away by community duty, or service in the choir. Let them not be anywise disturbed on that account—the Holy Sacrament will none the less do its work of grace in your soul if you be well prepared. Meanwhile our Lord can wait for your thanksgiving; give Him some time after dinner, even after vespers or compline, and that will please Him just as well as if done in the morning.

A word about venial sins and imperfections, faults that we cannot hope ever to be quite free from in this life. In case some of these escape your mind at confession, be not disturbed—confess them sorowfully to God; and even at confession, it is enough that one touch upon such things in a general way, rather than overtax one's father confessor. As far as real obligation goes, it is only mortal sins that one is bound to tell in confession. Venial sins may be remitted by saying an Our Father, or using holy water, or by a genuflexion, supposing always that one's heart is truly penitent for them. But suppose—you may ask— that we have no sorrow for our sins? I answer: Canst thou not desire to have sorrow? If one is sorry that he is not sorry for his sins, then he is truly sorry. He that aspires after holy ambition is really ambitious to serve God. He that loves to be able to love God already loves God.

But incomparably the most precious virtue is practical, active love of God. This comes to our heart from meditating on all the good which

God has done us and all mankind, and rendering sincere thanks for the same. Concentrate all thy powers upon thoughts of the good things God has done thee, whether in joy or in sorrow, throughout thy entire life. Place all this over against thy pettiness, thy meanness, thy total unworthiness—and then invite all men and angels and all other creatures to join with thee in praising and thanking God, for thou shalt find thyself unequal to the task. Embrace in one single view all the members of Holy Church, both living and dead, and bid them all join with thee in this interior thank offering to God. Often repeat this flight of thy mind and heart to God, and fill it with real sentiments of love. Whatsoever a man has received from God, let him retain no part of it for himself, but return it wholly to the divine giver by frequent and most fervent thanksgiving. And put a stop to all questionings and all thy disputes, as to whether or not this or that interior feeling be from God; fall back constantly upon thy poverty of soul and thy essential nothingness. Leave God's part to God, and as to thyself, consider thy origin, and imitate our Lord Jesus Christ in His constant elevation of His soul to His father. The man who follows Christ best is the best man.

What if one's attention be sometimes relaxed; what if one's soul be now and then preoccupied with creatures; bow down humbly and beg God's pardon; then lift thy soul again to the heavenly Father. Do this and do all else in union with and in thoughts about the life and passion of our Lord Jesus Christ. Thus it will be best done in God's sight. Call to mind the feeling of the woman in the gospel: "If I shall touch only His garment I shall be healed" (Matt. ix: 21). And she touched the hem of His garment and was healed. Now we may consider His garment to mean His Holy Communion, and the hem of it any drop of His precious blood. Thou mayst think thyself so vile as to be unworthy to touch Him, but if thou shalt only have the courage to do so, without doubt thou shalt be healed of thy spiritual infirmity—and this touching of Him means approaching Holy Communion. But as to thy preparation, what is before all else most useful is falling back humbly on thy own nothingness.

If one has attained even to the very highest point of perfection, then, even then has he the very greatest need to sink the roots of humility deep down in the depths of his soul. The higher the tree, the deeper must be the roots. All the height of our perfection springs from the depth of our humility. Hence we see that when that notorious sinner, the publican, was so deeply humbled that he dared not so much as raise his eyes to heaven, then it was that he was raised up high in God's favor, and went home to his house justified. May we be humbled in like manner as was this scandalous but penitent sinner—truly humbled, and thereby fully restored to God's favor. May this be mercifully granted us by God the Father, and God the Son, and God the Holy Ghost. *Amen.*

How Patience Begets Hope and Love

*Synopsis—The sanctification of the saints of the old law was wholly
by patience and hope—An insistence on the need of suffering, and,
therefore, of patience, to live and die well—Suffering God's judgment meekly is the highest form of patience—Fatuity of seeking
human comfort amid divine inflictions—Endurance of God's delays is a noble virtue.*

FIRST SERMON FOR THE TWELFTH SUNDAY AFTER TRINITY.

For the letter killeth, but the spirit quickeneth.—II Cor. iii, 6.

Among God's friends there are two kinds of people, who may be
compared respectively to the old and new testaments. You know that
until Christ came men obeyed the old law with its ceremonies and
customs, and by these they were made pleasing to God; after Christ
we are to be saved by the new law and its usages. The old testament
was introductory to the new, and was its image, preparing men's
souls—if they but rightly viewed it— for the new dispensation, as
every such thing must be announced beforehand and men made ready
for its reception. The old testament imposed many heavy burdens,
severe penalties for sin, and gave very stern manifestations of God's
righteousness, together with only a dim and distant view of redemption. The gates of heaven were shut for five thousand years, during
which men, with all their painful good works, could not enter into
eternal life. Their waiting was tedious enough, ere the new testament
was vouchsafed them, with peace and joy in the Holy Ghost. And now
my lesson to you is this: Some such preparation must each one of us
make if he would in all security attain to the privileges of God's new
dispensation; one must first be practiced in the trials of the ancient
covenant. A man must bear a heavy load of sorrow; he must humbly
bow down under the mighty hand of God; he must endure pains from
without and pains within; he must suffer all kinds of hardships,
whether he be innocent or guilty.

Children, the case is quite different from what I fear you suppose—stand fast by God's teaching, if you would act prudently, and if, as I trust, you have received the grace of God. If you would come to the new testament, you must endure the old. Mistrust in all lowliness of heart any consolation that is offered you, inwardly or outwardly, for by the way of pleasure no man can come to the kingdom of heaven. He must enter there by the way of bitter pain and much tribulation—turn him which way he pleases, so it must be. Before thou enjoyest the holy sacraments, divine illuminations, sweet sentiments of devotion, to say nothing of human comfort, bow down the old man that is in thee beneath the toilsome yoke of God's ancient covenant, with its burdens and humiliations and self-renunciation. And rememeber that in very truth His yoke is sweet and His burden is light. Dear children, I exhort you by the servitude of the cross of our Lord Jesus Christ, that you keep that token of His suffering before your eyes, ever carrying it manfully forward, enshrining it in your souls, glad of its heavy weight, embracing it with total abandonment of all things else, according as God wills and has willed for you from all eternity—this I exhort you from the bottom of my heart. May God lend you courage in all your future pains, desolations, disgrace, and calumny. Thus shall you have the old Adam conquered within you under the ancient covenant, till Jesus Christ shall be born in your souls in His new dispensation of peace and joy. The patriarchs must wait thousands of years, sighing and yearning; but in very truth, children, if you will but have their spirit of patient self-renunciation, your time of waiting shall not be a single year long. If you had a quartan fever for a year or for two years, you must perforce endure it to the end; and so must you endure your suffering in preparation for Christ's coming.

Another trial under the old dispensation were the judgments God visited upon His people; and this represents our interior pains, our suffering from the gnawing of remorse. Some men strive to escape this by multiplying their confessions, little realizing that a thousand confessions of mortal sins are of no avail for solacing the pain of remorse, unless they be accompanied by proper works of penance. Confession being thus made, we can in all humility accept the feeling of remorse that still lingers, full sure of God's pardon.

Others, again, would still their reproaches of conscience by asking many questions of learned men, hoping thereby for some new comfort

to their souls. Spare yourselves the trouble; run here and run there
your whole life long, it is all in vain. Your solace must come from
within or not at all. Await it patiently in thy interior soul. I could
tell you, dear children, of the holiest man in all inward and outward
virtue that I ever saw; and he was a man who never heard more than
four or five sermons all his life. But the sermon that was preached
to him by the voice of conscience, that he marked well, and it was
enough to guide him how to live and how to die.

As to the common run of people, let them go here and there and
listen to all sorts of preaching, lest they should fall into unbelief; but
as to you who aspire to be perfect in God's service, hear good preaching indeed, but turn yourseves inward to God; for if you would acquire
true spirituality you must give up running about and you must stay
at home in your own souls; many words make no man perfect. Love
God from the depths of your heart and your neighbor as yourself, and
all the rest will take care of itself. What you see of good in others
let it be good in your eyes; what you see bad, judge it not nor question
about it. Long to possess God with your whole heart, as did the
fathers under the old law; seek what in very truth you ought to seek;
as to the rest, leave it all to God's blessed will.

The third characteristic of the old dispensation was a dim hope
towards a distant redemption; for the gates of heaven were fast shut,
and no prophet could exactly tell when redemption would come. And
so must we resign ourselves humbly to await God's time and place in
perfect humility, for such is God's will with each of us; and He will
come and be born in us in a perfect life at last and without fail. But
when? Leave that to Him. Some would arrive at perfection in their
youth; some fix their old age as the time; some even at the point of
death. Leave all that to His adorable will, only be true to Him from
day to day. And to thus submit to Him, thou needest no special kind
of spiritual exercise. Learn the commandments of God and keep them;
learn the articles of the Christian faith and believe them; all that
remains is that thou shouldst place thyself at God's disposal in all
things whatsoever. Do these simple things, and there is no manner of
doubt but that Christ will be born in thee in due time to a perfect new
testament of peace and joy in the Holy Ghost. Thou shalt be granted
the grace of an angel's life of gentleness and wisdom. That is indeed
a splendid gift; and yet a better one is the life more than angelic

which the Spirit will work within thee, quite surpassing human under-standing. But by this way of patient endurance must it come to thee and none other. One may dream that he understands all this plainly, and then starts with self-formed plans of devotion to achieve this result, and such a man surely fails. He can only succeed by treading the plain way of mortification; succeed he surely will by that way.

In the old law the Levites carried the ark of God; but in the new law, as we have described it, the ark of God carries the Levites; that is to say, our souls. Whosoever will not submit humbly in this life to God's judgments, that man without doubt will fall under God's judg-ments in eternity. Try what expedient thou mayst, thou must give thyself up to suffering under God. Do that, and then God carries thee forward through all thy pain and trouble; God it is who, as it were, bends His shoulders under thy burden with thee, and helps thee to bear it. Meanwhile, to those who are submissive to God, no burden is unbearable, no misery intolerable. Alas for us if we would do other-wise, and would go forward alone in our weakness bearing our heavy load. In that case suffer we must, labor we must, but all without God. Now may God grant us the grace to carry our burden manfully and with Him. *Amen.*

Spiritual Deafness

Synopsis—In what degree Satan is responsible for our dullness of spirit—The unresponsiveness to God that afflicts worldlings; and even hurts spiritual persons—St. Gregory's remarkable teaching on this point—Thanksgiving is a sign of attentiveness to divine calls—God's inward word in relation to the Seven Gifts of the Holy Ghost.

SECOND SERMON FOR THE TWELFTH SUNDAY AFTER TRINITY.

And they bring to Him one deaf and dumb; and they besought Him that He would lay His hand upon him. And taking him from the multitude apart, He put His fingers into his ears, and spitting, He touched his tongue. And looking up to heaven, He groaned, and said to him: Ephpheta, which is, Be thou opened. And immediately his ears were opened, and the string of his tongue was loosed, and he spoke right. . . . He hath done all things well; He hath made both the deaf to hear, and the dumb to speak.—Mark vii, 32.

We are to inquire to-day into man's spiritual deafness. Since our first parents lent a willing ear to the voice of Satan, we are all deaf to the voice of the eternal Word of God within our souls. And yet we know full well that this divine Word is indescribably close to our souls, closer than our own thoughts, or our very nature to our conscious existence. Within our inmost souls dwells that divine Word, and He addresses us without ceasing. Man hears Him not, for he is afflicted with great deafness. Nor is this a blameless state of deafness, for we are like one to whom something is spoken, and who stops his ears lest he shall hear what it is. We are worse; we have done this so much that at last we have lost knowledge of ourselves, and are become dumb, that is to say, wholly stupid. Ask a worldly man about his interior life, and he is dumb—he knows not if there be any such a life. And the cause of it is that the enemy has crept into that soul, which has hearkened to him, and thus has become deaf and dumb.

Now how does Satan insinuate himself into the soul? Thou shalt detect him in all blameworthy conduct; his guidance is in all the deceit of this world, all inordinate love of created things, such as honors and riches, relatives and friends, and also self love in all its forms. Under cover of any of these does he insinuate himself into thy soul, for he is ever on the watch to take advantage of thy inclination to evil. Sometimes he urges thee to shun a certain pain that thou shouldst manfully bear; again, to seek forbidden joys, whispering inwardly in thy ear, showing pictures before the eyes of thy soul, all that thou mayst shut eyes and ears and soul to the eternal Word. If we but instantly turn away from the enemy's allurements, his temptations are easily overcome. If, on the contrary, one dallies with the tempter, gazes upon his pictures, listens to his suggestions, then is he nigh to destruction; the temptation is grown very heavy. Resist instantly, turn from him instantly, and thou art close to a victory. Soon thy deafness shall be cured, and thou shalt hear the inner voice of the eternal Word.

This deafness afflicts not only people living in the world but also those called to a spiritual life, but who permit their souls to be occupied by love and enjoyment of created things. This is well known to the devil, who tells them things calculated to gratify their inclinations. Some are made deaf by their infatuation for their self-chosen devotional customs and outward observances, which link them strongly to creatures in a spirit of proprietorship. The clatter of all this hinders the soul from hearing the inner voice of the eternal Word. We know well, of course, that we must have approved spiritual exercises and follow them earnestly; and yet without a feeling of proprietorship. Such are devout prayers to God as well as holy meditation, by means of which our sluggish nature is aroused; we are heartened to our work, and we are drawn inward to the Spirit; but never with an obstinate sense of ownership, and always looking inward to God in the depths of our souls. We should not imitate some men, who persist to their very deaths in certain external pious practices and use them in a wholly externized spirit, never seeking to go beyond this. If God wishes to speak to them, the ears of their souls are always preoccupied by other voices. Children, there are so many cases of this sort of spiritual deafness, that at the end of all things we shall be amazed at the revelation of it.

Now God's word is never spoken in any man's ears of whom it may not be said "If any one love Me, he will keep My word" (John xiv: 23). St. Gregory explains this: "Wouldst thou know if thou lovest God?

Take note of thy conduct when thou art tried. What dost thou do when pain comes on thee, or contradiction, or any other distress from round about thee? And how dost thou bear thyself in time of interior distress, when thy mental anguish is so sharp that thou knowest not whither to turn for relief? What is thy bearing in sudden storms of adversity; when beset with difficulties all unforeseen? If thou shalt rest quiet in these visitations, thy soul resting in peace, without any outburst of impatience, with no fault of word or act or even motion, then without doubt thou lovest God truly." On the heart that truly loves, neither outward pain nor pleasure can make any impression. One may give to thee, one may take from thee, if only thy Beloved abide with thee, it is all one to thee, and thou restest in interior peace. Thy outward man weeps—that thou canst not help; the inner man rests content with God's holy will. But if, alas, thou canst not stand this test, then art thou deaf—the divine Word will not be heard by thee.

Another test: art thou full of thanksgiving to God for the manifold favors He has conferred on thee, and on all mankind, and on all creatures in earth and heaven and never ceases to confer? And art thou especially thankful for the unspeakable gift of His Son's holy humanity? Again, thy universal spiritual exercise should be sincere love of all mankind, not only the members of thy own community, but all priests and monks and nuns and sisters, and all humanity besides, of whatever state or condition; and this love should be active, and by no means confined in practice to thy own community, as far as lies in thy power. This universal love is of inestimable benefit; for whosoever are real enlightened friends of God, their hearts are melted with affection for all men living and dead. Had we no such lovers of mankind among us, our lot would be evil indeed. Futhermore, thou shouldst also show thy love by outward works, by making gifts, by speaking words of comfort and counsel, in so far as thy own real necessities will permit. And if thou art unable to give outward help, at least excite thy heart to say in all truth, that thou wouldst do so if it were within thy power. Here then are thy plain signs for true love, and they will show that thy heart is not deaf.

And now comes our Lord to a man deaf and dumb, and He spiritually putteth His finger in his ears, and anoints his tongue with His holy spittal, and immediately the man's soul can hear and can speak.

O children, wonderful words might be said of this act of our Lord; we content ourselves with naming the seven gifts of the Holy Ghost, which thus enter the soul and are granted when it hearkens to God in very truth.

First is the spirit of fear, which is given us that we may renounce all self-will, all self-conceit. It teaches us to fly from every evil thing. After that is granted the gift of piety, making us tender-hearted, hindering all rash judgment, rendering us yielding and kindly towards all. The third touch of the Lord's finger is the gift of knowledge, giving us an interior lesson of divine experience, and guiding us to know the inner ways of union with God's holy will. The fourth is divine fortitude, by which the soul is so strengthened as to be able easily to suffer all pain for God's sake, and courageously to undertake all heavy tasks in His honor. The fifth is holy counsel, making all who receive it lovable men, and acceptable guides to others. And now come two touches of the divine finger that are deep and strong, namely, understanding and wisdom; but as to these, one can more easily feel the worth of them than he can describe them. May God grant that our ears may thus be opened to His truth, and that we may ever hearken to His eternal Word. *Amen.*

Spiritual Blindness

Synopsis—The double vision of man, outward for created things, inward for divine things—How self-will blinds the soul—Differences between seeing and understanding; especially when considering God in the incarnation of His Son—How one's meditation on even Christ's passion may lack true insight.

FIRST SERMON FOR THE THIRTEENTH SUNDAY AFTER TRINITY.

Blessed are the eyes that see the things that you see.—Luke x, 23-37.

On one occasion our Lord, gazing upon his disciples, said: "I confess to Thee, O Father, Lord of heaven and earth, because Thou hast hid these things from the wise and prudent, and hast revealed them to little ones" (Matt. xi: 25). This is appropriate to our text, which was addressed to those same disciples: "Blessed are the eyes that see the things that you see. For I say to you that many prophets and kings have desired to see the things that you see, and have not seen them; and to hear the things that you hear, and have not heard them." Then the holy narrative proceeds: "And behold a certain lawyer stood up, tempting Him, and saying: Master, what must I do to possess eternal life? But He said to him:. What is written in the law? How readest thou? He, answering, said: Thou shalt love the Lord thy God with thy whole heart, and with thy whole soul, and with all thy strength, and with all thy mind: and thy neighbor as thyself. And He said to him: Thou hast answered right. This do, and thou shalt live."

Now let us consider our text: "Blessed are the eyes that see the things that you see." A man has two sets of eyes, interior and exterior. It were a hard lot if a man had no interior eyes; he would be like a beast had he only exterior eyes. And let me ask, dear children, how does it happen that the blessed interior eyes of a man, namely, his glorious reason, are blinded, are in a state of pitiful darkness, seeing no light? This comes from the thick covering that is drawn over them, namely, the love of created things, whether love of self or of other creatures. In this state men receive our Lord's sacred body and blood, and the oftener they do so the blinder they become. It is as if a thick skin had gone over their eyes. Children, what do you think can be the reason that so many men cannot enter in and examine the inner life of their own souls? It is because a veil is drawn over their interior eyes as thick as an ox's horn. Men shut their souls up so close that they keep both God and themselves entirely outside—they shut their spirits up with thick, coarse, black hides, as heavy as the skin of a bear were it even forty or fifty folds in thickness. And what do I mean by these hides? Everything to which thou devotest thy will; all that thou givest thy love to, whether thou doest it by words or works, by favor or disfavor, arrogance, obstinacy or frivolity; in a word, pleasure in anything whatsoever without God.

These are the dark blinds over the eyes of men's souls. But the moment a man feels pained at this lamentable state, and humbly confesses it to God, determined to do his best to remedy it, presently God guides him to good counsel, and the obstacles to spiritual sight fall off. But with some men no counsel avails, and then their darkness grows yet more dense. They will not forsake their idols, but, like Rachel, they hide them away and sit upon them. Their minds are filled with the forms of the created things they love; these blind their eyes; the voices of the world deafen their ears. And when reason is thus deaf and blind, it cannot be saved.

"Blessed are the eyes that see the things that you see." Any man in his senses can see that the creatures that possess our hearts are in themselves merely nothing, and yet they are capable of giving us joy of a certain kind. But why cannot we understand the joy that God will give us, since it is from God that created things have all come forth? The knowledge and appreciation of this would make our eyes blessed, if we would but see it, for we in our day see more than our Lord's disciples at that moment were able to see. They saw their Master indeed; but He was then a poor, rejected and much suffering man, whereas we know Him now, in the light of holy faith, as a majestic being, God and Lord of earth and heaven. Could we but duly appreciate what our eyes thus behold, eternally blessed would those eyes be.

Dear children, the great masters dispute with one another as to which is greater, knowledge or love. But as to us, we shall rather choose for our discussion matters of eternal life:—when we come to that, we shall behold all things in very truth. Our Lord says: "But one thing is necessary" (Luke x: 42). And what is that one thing necessary? It is that thou shouldst know thy own nothingness; recognize this as thy only real self; fully understand as thou dost depend on thyself who thou art. For that one thing necessary has our Lord suffered such agony of soul that He sweat blood. It was because thou wouldst not learn this one thing, that he cried out on the cross: "My God, My God, why hast Thou forsaken Me?" (Mark xv: 34). Why should the one thing necessary for our salvation be given up by us? Dear child, I bid thee to dismiss from thy mind all that I and all other instructors have taught thee, all work and all contemplation, and study henceforth only this one thing necessary—to know thy own nothingness. For our Lord said: "Mary hath chosen the better part" (Luke x: 42). In very truth, didst thou but gain only this part, thou shouldst have, not a part, but the whole of heavenly wisdom. This sense of our nothingness is not what some men conceit themselves to know and teach. They feign a deep humility as they speak of it, but in their soul's inmost depths they cherish a notion of themselves as high as the steeple of the Cathedral. They would be great before men's eyes, and they deceive men, and most of all themselves, by a pretense of humility. Dear child, if thou findest thyself clinging fast to some devout practice, meanwhile unmindful of thy nothingness, then I say to thee it were better to give over this busy method of thine, and turn inward to the thoughts of thy helpless nothingness.

But let us now consider the outward man. Ask thyself: What art thou, and whence art thou? Thy bodily substance is made up of such foul matter, that it is offensive to thy very self as well as to all others. And what shall thy body become? A sack of uncleanliness, emiting a most intolerable stench, turning the costliest food into the worst filth. Yet this fuel for the everlasting fire of hell, is what many a one devotes his whole life to pampering. A dead corpse? It is an unbearable horror to the very ones who once loved it best — it is more disgusting than a dead dog. It would seem as if God had set everything against the comfort of our bodily life, the air and the sun and all the elements. Now we are freezing with cold, again scorched with heat; now it pours down rain, again we are smothered with snow; there is hunger and thirst, there are pleasures and pains; beasts and insects and worms assail and molest us, and many other such plagues; and it is impossible for thee to escape them.

Look at the wild animals, how happily they are placed compared to thee. Their garments grow upon them naturally, and they are always comfortable whether it be cold or hot. As for thee, it is from them that thou must borrow thy clothing; thus art thou poorer than they. All thy pleasure depends on their gifts to thee, and yet thou art proud! Is not this an unspeakable blindness of heart? The cattle are quite content with what God gives them of clothing, beds, shelter, food and drink. And now consider thy marvellous misery, that thou sinnest not seldom by excessive enjoyment of these things that the cattle furnish thee. In former times the saints wept because they were compelled to eat; and they laughed when they had to die.

Yet further consider thy nothingness in the miseries of thy nature. Dost thou gladly pray, and watch, and fast, and weep? By no means canst thou do it. What thou wouldst wish to do, that thou doest not; and what thou wishest not to do, that thou nevertheless must do. What miseries are thine from thy many amazing temptations; and what sins does not God threaten to allow thee to commit. Dost thou never think of this? O that thou didst but learn the lesson of this thy nothingness, the one thing necessary to know. To be sure, the fact that God thus leaves thee in peril of sin is only for thy best good, so that thou shouldst take counsel of thy nothingness—better for thee, perhaps, than if thou shouldst stand high, and wert lifted up among great things.

Men will come to thee with overbearing manners and hard words, telling thee high-sounding and subtle things of the intellect, as if they thought they were Christ's apostles. Dear child, get away from them and sink into thy inmost soul, into thy nothingness, and let these men talk on like the ringing of the bells in a church steeple. Nay, if all the devils in hell were turned loose upon thee, and all other creatures with them—it will all help thee wonderfully, if thou wilt but turn inward to the study of thy nothingness: that is "the best part."

But thou mightst say to me: Brother, I meditate all day long on Christ's passion, His sufferings in Pilate's hall and before Herod,—

and all the rest. Dear child, let me instruct thee. Thou must see
in thy Savior not only His humanity; thou must look upon Him as
the infinite God, who made heaven and earth and all things by His
word only, and by the same word could annihilate them—God whose
greatness is above all knowledge: and who yet became as nothing
for the sake of His miserable creatures. Then shame thyself, thou
poor mortal man, that thou hast given thyself up to pride and vanity.
Bow down beneath the cross of the God-man. Bend thy proud head
and ask for Christ's crown of thorns, and take up thy journey to
Calvary. Do this in all manner of ways interior and exterior,
cultivating constantly a sense of thy littleness. Since thy great God
has for thy sake annihilated Himself so far as to be judged and
condemned by His own creatures, crucified and put to death, so must
thou most patiently suffer thy little pains in all meekness, ever
.dwelling upon the picture of thy Savior's sufferings and sinking it
into thy mind.

But men do not follow this way; rather they think of our Lord's
passion with a blinded love; and it is a love which does not bear
fruit in good works; it does not result in their renouncing pride and
worldly honors. Nor are they led to foreswear bodily pleasures; they
are the same after their meditations as they were before. Alas, how
little fruit is borne by that sweetest of spiritual exercises—meditation
on the passion of our Lord Jesus Christ—if we are to judge by men's
morals. Let it be far different in thy case, dear child. After so holy
a devotion thou shouldst feel so deeply ashamed as to wonder that
the earth could endure thee and that it did not open to swallow
thee up. Remember that there are thousands now in hell who perhaps
were far less sinful than thou. Had God favored them as He has thee,
they would have served Him far better than thou hast; yet has He
spared thee and eternally condemned them. Often think of such
truths. Never taste a morsel of food or drink a drop of water but
with holy fear and deep humility. Use all the comforts of life wholly
for thy mere necessities, by no means for thy pleasure.

And then come forward some men full of high argumentation about
the spiritual life; they talk as if they had scaled high heaven in their
wisdom, but in reality they have not moved a step beyond their own
poor self, of whose nothingness they are quite ignorant. To argu-
mentative truth they have attained, but to living truth, which rightly

is the only truth, no man comes except by the way of his own nothing-ness. Going apart from this way of truth one can but arrive at misfortune, and then remain stationary among shadows. O children, the day will come when such souls will wish they never had any show of spirituality or heard a word about it, or won a great name among men. They will wish that they had followed the cattle in the fields and eaten their bread in the sweat of their face. For then must they render account of every gift God gave them—a just and terrible God, though now so gentle, now allowing His mercy to be so shamefully abused. Yet if one but realizes now this future reckoning, let him not fall into despair, for these thoughts are sent him that he may subject himself absolutely under God and under all creatures in a spirit of entire self-renunciation. Meanwhile beware of a false and boastful humility. Our Lord says: "Unless you be converted, and become as little children, you shall not enter into the kingdom of Heaven" (Matt. xviii: 3). Let us be as unconscious of our humility as little babes, nor ever make it a subject of our thoughts. The Lord says "Suffer little children to come unto Me" (Matt. xix: 14).

The earth is the least of all the elements, and in its littleness it has fled far away from the heavens; and yet the vast celestial spheres, sun, moon and stars, pursue the earth with their kindly and mighty influence, producing on its lowly bosom most useful fruits. Where the valley is deepest the waters do most plentifully flow down, and the lowly valleys are thus more productive than the proud hills. It is so in the spiritual life: the soul sunken into the deepest depths of humility attracts the best gifts of the divine abyss of love. "Deep calleth on deep" (Ps. xli: 8), exclaims the Psalmist. The created abyss, with its boundless knowledge of its own nothingness, calleth into itself the uncreated abyss that is the infinite God, and thus is it made one with Him; in which union the soul knows God, and yet, as St. Dionysius says, knows Him as like nothing that it ever knew before; for God is nothing like the things that man knows or can ever express. Herein the spirit of a man is truly humbled and self-abandoned. So that if it pleased God to annihilate him (if such a thought were possible or were permitted), he would gladly be annihi-lated—for he knows nothing, loves nothing, enjoys nothing, but the One. Children, blessed, indeed, are the eyes that thus see, as our Lord says in the text. May God grant us thus to contemplate our own nothingness. *Amen.*

The Inner Revelation

Synopsis—First is revealed to the soul its own dignity—This consists in its close kinship with God—Another revelation is the difference between the spiritual man and the animal man—Yet another is the perception of the marvellous mutual action of knowing and loving God here and hereafter—Finally, the revelation of God Himself in the remotest interior of the soul—The teaching of Albertus Magnus on this gift to the soul.

SECOND SERMON FOR THE THIRTEENTH SUNDAY AFTER TRINITY.

Blessed are the eyes that see the things that you see.—Luke x, 23.

Here we have a teaching that is the purest truth, showing us where the highest blessedness of eternal life is to be found. And we read that a scribe came and tempted our Lord with his questioning, and yet our Lord received him and answered him very mildly, referring him to the witness of Holy Scripture. Now every man under the old law who would be right, must have had one of three witnesses to approve him. The first testimony might come from God by special revelation; the second out of the depths of his own living soul in the light of natural reason; and the third was that of Holy Scripture. But this man who questioned our Lord had but one witness; to this our Lord referred him when He said to him: "What is written in the law? How readest thou?" And he answered that the law commanded us to love God above all things, and our neighbor as ourself. He had indeed answered truly; he also believed that he had fulfilled that commandment, and upon this he prided himself.

Dear children, two meanings are to be found in the words, "Blessed are the eyes that see the things that you see." One is the blessedness of the interior contemplation of our soul's dignity in its kinship with God, which brings to a loving heart a most blessed grace and joy. Of this dignity of our soul, which is seated in its essential inner life, many masters, new and old, have treated, as Albertus Magnus, Master Dietrich, and Master Eckhart. Some teachers speak of it as a spark of divine fire, others as the inmost depths of the soul, others again as the crown of the soul, or as its origin and source of life. Albertus, however, calls it an interior image, in which the blessed Trinity is manifested to the soul. This divine spark, say others, flies upward so high in the soul, that the understanding cannot follow it, for it is ever passing again upward into the divine centre which is its uncreated source. But you must know, dear children, that these masters have experienced in their minds and in their lives the things they herein treat of; and, furthermore, they have drawn this doctrine from the greatest saints and doctors of holy Church. Even certain teachers before our Lord's birth, as Plato, Aristotle and Proclus, have also diligently studied this subject. As to our devout Christian masters, this close kinship with God has much inflamed their fervor and that of their disciples, and contributed to their eternal salvation, causing in them a sudden conversion of their souls to God. Whereas the false doctrines on this subject have worked eternal harm to souls.

Dear children, let us now carefully examine this road to eternal bliss. It is the way of unfeigned humility, and entire renunciation of self. It makes nothing of self, nothing of all that one can have or can do. For if a man having this way perceives good in himself, at once he knows it as God's and not man's. To this basis of life must thou come, if thy eyes shall be blessed. This is the rule that Jesus Christ the Son of God gave to His elect, saying: "Learn of Me, because I am meek and humble of heart" (Matt. xi: 29). Gentleness and humility are two sisters who are inseparably associated in life's journey. To the humble our Heavenly Father hath manifested the secrets of His high wisdom, and concealed them from the great ones of this world. This meekness of soul it is that we are to understand as the perfect truth in which is hidden the essence of all felicity.

In this same Gospel our Lord says: "Many prophets and kings have desired to see the things that you see, and have not seen them." Dear children, by the term prophets, we may understand those men who glory in their natural reason, its arguments and its subtleties. The eyes of such as these are not blessed. By the term kings, we may understand men of strong character and seeming holiness, powerful speakers, full of self-chosen good works, abounding in fasts and

prayers and vigils which they make much of, meanwhile making little
of other ways of serving God. This spirit of self-praise is not the eye
that is called blessed. These men desire to see, but they do not see,
because they are fixed fast in their own self-will. Children, it is by
self-will that the harm is done; that is the very foundation of all
hindrance to God's work in us; for the will is the eye of the soul.
Consider that when the outward eye is blindfolded it cannot see at all.
And the eye must be entirely unstained with any color whatsoever if
it shall be able to distinguish all colors. So must our interior eye,
the will, be entirely cleared of all desires to have and not to have,
if it shall be the blessed eye destined to see the eternal things of God.
In worldly men the colors that stain the soul's eye are coarse and
material. But spiritual men also are afflicted with their own peculiar
self-deceptions.

Each man, though he be but one person, is, nevertheless, three men
in one. First he is just the external being, animal, living in his
senses; the second is the interior man, whose life is in his reasoning
faculties; the third is the man, that is, the soul, in its highest part,
that part which we call the spirit: and all these three are one and
the same man. Now in this threefold man God should reign supreme.
Children, the will must entirely abdicate its supremacy to God,
according to our Lord's word: "I came down from Heaven, not to do
My will, but the will of Him that sent Me" (John vi: 38). How plain
it is, that as long as thou standest upon thy own will thou art forfeit
of the divine blessedness of thy eyes, for blessedness is found only in
unfeigned renunciation of one's own will. This is born of that lowliness of spirit in which self-will is lost and gone. Self-will is the pillar
on which rests the whole structure of a deordinated life: knock down
that support, and every roof and wall of imperfection falls to the
ground. And the less value a man puts on himself, the less self-will
has he.

Let us consider the love that is theirs who have blessed eyes—
love with the whole heart, the whole soul, all the powers and all
the mind. There is much controversy among the masters as to
whether one's love or one's understanding be the higher faculty—and
that question we leave on one side, being full sure that of the two
love is, at any rate, the more meritorious and useful: for love joyfully
enters in where knowledge must needs remain without. Love requires
no subtle knowledge of things, but a clear, living, Christian faith.

Let us consider the form of love, its matter, and its end or purpose. As to the form of love, that is just love's own self; its matter is our soul and its powers, or, in other terms, our heart, whose work in love is to love in all; and the end and purpose of love is to love God directly and without any intermediation. Finally, the essence of love is simply to love, for love loves for the sake of love. A further explanation is given by Richard of St. Victor "Love in its lowest degree proceeds from the heart and from its thoughts; also from the soul, in its enjoyments and content; and from the soul's powers, in their resistance to and suppression of all that is opposed to love." But all this is not the love that we are to consider.

Albertus Magnus comments on this Gospel as follows: "To love God with all our heart means to love Him with a free and ready will in such wise that we are practically well exercised in love." It often happens that a man will have a love for something, and against that love his reason in the exercise of its freedom will revolt. And many another time it happens that reason constrains a man to love something, to which he has no manner of attraction. But love, to be at its best, should go forth instinctively from a free and a holy heart, needing as little help from the warnings and the considerings and the ponderings of human reason, as is possible in this changeful life of ours.

The words, "With all thy soul," mean a love full of satisfaction and contentment in loving God, with entire freedom of will, engaging every element of the soul's life, embracing the inward man and the outward: this love comes from the soul's knowledge of truth.

The words, "And with all thy strength," mean that a man subdues to the service of this love of God all his animal powers and all his life of the senses. Such a man controls for God's love all his bodily existence, just as an archer strings the bow to shoot his arrow. This is the fulness of love, and it is the highest degree.

To love God "with all thy mind" is a love which embraces all the others, as a measure contains what is to be measured out, fixing the shape and the weight and the distribution. St. Augustine says: "An act does not become an acquired virtue until it gains a certain form, so that a man is grown used to it, does it as easily and with as much pleasure as if it had become part of his very nature." And that state of virtue arises from a foundation of humble love.

Mark well that one's mind is in itself something much higher than the mental faculties, which draw all their force from the mind, belong to it, and flow out from it -- the mind itself being beyond measure above in its own powers. For its being is simple, essential and uniform. The learned tell us that the mind or the spirit is always in action, whether one be sleeping or waking, conscious of act or unconscious. Now, that spirit of ours has a constant longing for God, ever gazing towards Him, ever longing to love Him and enjoy Him. Exactly how that is, we need not now discuss. / Furthermore, the spirit of man beholds God, if it but will it, in itself; for although it be a created being, it is yet made to resemble the uncreated God. / Proclus, a heathen writer, calls this a sleep, a quiet and divine rest, saying: "It is a secret search of one for one, and is a state too high to be comprehended." When the soul turns towards this supernaturally, then it becomes God-like, leading a divine life. As a man goes forth to outward things, he cannot know, he cannot even believe that this state of the spirit can be; yet it really is. The human spirit is planted in such soil and has such a life in it, that it is drawn powerfully to itself; it is a peculiar property of the spirit to be bent and inclined inwards to its own deepest depths, in search of its own origin. This tendency is never quenched, no, not in hell itself, whose worst pain is that the soul must forever endure the activity of this tendency. If a man will but hearken to reason, that will guide all his lower powers and will subject them to its mastery, rejecting whatever is against reason as something alien to its nature. Reason thus raises a man above the influence of his senses, and there he rests free from all disturbance. When the interference of the lower faculties is thus hindered in the Christian soul, it sees its own essence and its power in an intellectual image of Him to whom it owes its origin. Blessed are the eyes that come to this sight; blessed the soul that clings to this holy state essentially, and sinks into it. St. Dionysius teaches that the forms and images of the imagination can in this state have no influence over us.

Albertus Magnus tells of six excellences of this high state. It is most wonderful: the man to whom this spiritual insight is granted can never again be amazed by wonderful or miraculous happenings. It is the very highest: no spiritual state is superior to it. It is most purely spiritual: there is no manner of admixture of the material world. It is the most secure: its safety is its own and is very

perfect, borrowing security from none other. It is inseparably joined
to the spirit: it cannot be influenced by fleshly lusts or temptations.
It is the least hindered state: for in it the spirit walks in the
brightest light, in which it feels at home and which has grown 'to
be, as it were, a habit of its nature; no task of God's appointment
can now be burdensome. It is also the most enduring state: it
encounters no opposition, because it is not rooted in the soul's
sensitive existence.

This is called a state of eternal beatitude, and for three reasons.
First, it is the image of God divinely imparted to the soul. Second,
the soul is immersed in the deity. Third, the spirit enjoys God as if
in His very substance. Hence it is called the action of God in the
soul. All these wonderful things of the soul's unchangeable bliss,
spoken of by Albertus, are not as it were in any state that may be
called human activity, but rather an essential indwelling of the spirit,
living with God in its own depths, in a way superior to that of this
life; for in this life all things change, and unhappiness is born of
activity. To such a man a mishap may occur in his outward life, but
it cannot affect the essence of his happiness in his union with God.
Now when our Savior said: "Blessed are the eyes that see what you
have seen," he meant this blessedness.

Children, to attain to this sort of ecstacy or rapture, one must
carefully choose his times and his circumstances, namely, quiet hours,
solitude, and recollection. Therefore is the night a favorable time,
for it is long and still. Whereas if one waits till morning, he must
provide various things, and run about here and there, and thus
interior detachment is broken in upon. The devil takes advantage
of this, perhaps, to snatch from thee thy opportunity—it may never
come again to thee, but be given to another who will make better
use of it. Dear child, if God gave thee an earthly kingdom, he
would give thee with it what was necessary for thee in order to
possess and govern it. As to this kingdom of blessedness, He gives
thee all that is needed for thy possessing it; but the misery of it
is that thou wilt not procure solitude and recollection to that end.

No one, not even the Pope or holy Church, would wish to disturb
such men as these, but rather be glad to leave them wholly to God,
and this we could prove from the history of the greatest saints.
David calls this state of soul a spiritual slumber; St. Paul, a peace-

that surpasses all understanding; St. John, a stillness lasting half an hour. St. Dionysius and St. Gregory, as well as many other great saints, have written to the same effect. Let us give to such favored souls all careful attention, and leave them to follow God's guidance. St. Augustine says: "When God would work, let us carefully attend to His work, and observe it." Let us bear in mind that the Lord's yoke is sweet and His burden light. Now, a yoke is something drawn over one's head and fastened to his neck. So has God in all sweetness yoked and assumed control over these favored souls, placing a light burden upon them, and leading them by his sweet yoke whithersoever He will. If thou art thyself thus honored, and if thou feelest a sudden stroke fall upon thee, be still, God is fastening his burden of blessedness upon thee. If anyone says that thou hast lost thy senses, be still, answer not: it is thus that God is making thee ready for His blessedness. And, meanwhile, if thou hast to endure something, yet thou are not going to be beheaded, as were the holy marytrs. May the merciful God prepare us to follow His lead, until our eyes shall behold His blessedness. *Amen.*

In What Way a Perfect Man is Like God

Synopsis—God communicates to man His own invisibility—This should make us prefer the hidden life of prayer—Another resemblance is to God's opposition to worldliness—Study of Christ's passion perfects this resemblance—God would also give us His unchangeableness—This is assimilated by the steadfastness of holy living—Besides these, God would endow us with universal holiness, springing from love.

SERMON FOR THE FOURTEENTH SUNDAY AFTER TRINITY.

And put on the new man, who according to God, is created in justice and holiness of truth.—Eph. iv, 24.
Walk in the spirit, and you shall not fulfill the tests of the flesh. For the flesh lusteth against the spirit, and the spirit against the flesh.—Gal. v, 16, 17.

Dear children, if we would walk in the spirit, we must steadfastly turn away from all sin, and from inordinate love of creatures; and we must lovingly turn to God with all the powers of our soul in persevering prayer. To this we must add detachment of spirit, and well-chosen devout exercises. By these means we shall bring the flesh into subjection to the spirit, "and put on the new man, who according to God is created in justice and holiness of truth."

Children, you should know the dignity of your soul. And although every creature of God belongs to Him, yet none other so particularly as our soul. God made use of no other creature to create us, but freely and directly did He make us, taking counsel alone of His goodness, and forming us after His own image and likeness. We are more His than we are any others of His creatures. His image and likeness is sunk so deep in us that it can never be effaced—not even in souls condemned eternally to hell. And, as inwardly we are in God's likeness, so also outwardly we should show forth God's likeness, being in our life conformed to His holiness.

This likeness should follow four attributes of God. The first is that God is invisible, for we know that no man can see God and live. We

copy God in this when we come to a spiritual life; for then whatever
outward form our life may take, no man need be harmed by what he
sees in us.

Dear children, St. Paul writes that by Christ the world was crucified
to him, and he to the world (Gal. vi: 14); which means that the world
with all its joys and luxuries and lusts was exceedingly painful to the
Apostle; he longed for all this infinitely less than for the gallows of
the cross. And what meant he by saying that he was a cross to the
world? He meant that he was such a man in morals and in manners,
and in the whole man that he showed himself to be, that the world
cared for him as little as it cared for the cross. Now it is in this that
the perfection of spiritual men consists; if thou standest there, thou
art in the way of perfection. But, alas, although there are many among
us to whom indeed the world is a cross, for they do not desire it, do we
on the other hand find one man in a thousand so perfect as not to
desire to please the world? Nor am I now speaking of those who
follow sinful courses. No, dear children, no, by no means. But I say
simply this: The man who can truly affirm with St. Paul: I am a cross
to the world, must have reached that point of perfection as to show
plainly in all he does and in every trait of his character that he cares
not to please anybody except God; never dreams of winning anybody's
favor except God's alone. He indeed it is that can say: I am the
world's cross. I range myself against it in everything whatsoever, in
my interior dislike for it, in my outward opposition to it, and to that
degree that it no more desires me than it covets the gallows of the cross.

The second way in which our soul is shown to be like to God is that
we are conformed to His unchangeableness. Thus must we be wholly
steadfast in a good life. We must give ourselves over to Him permanently. Let the whole world be turned upside down, we cannot be
shaken loose from Him, never thrown off into sin, not separated from
Him in any manner whatsoever. Ah, dear children, to the man who is
thus fast fixed in God, all changes are alike, fortune or misfortune,
poverty or wealth, joy or sorrow. O how like unto God the creator,
is the soul that stands immovable in Him who gives motion to all
created things.

The third resemblance to God is that the perfect soul is the image
and likeness of all virtue. We know that in God there is the image of
all things created, namely in His eternal and only begotten Son our

Lord Jesus Christ—an image not like that in the creature, but the living image as God is in God, without beginning and without end. So must a perfect man assemble in his soul the living image of all virtues that he sees around him as they shine forth in the lives of good men and women of all conditions. From one and from another he learns different virtues and acquires various kinds of holiness; this one teaches him humility, that one patience, a third mortification; good order and discipline, devotion, spiritual motives, truthfulness, affectionateness, cleanness of life, obedience. His soul is a treasure house of virtues, gathered in from all directions. It is a picture gallery full of masterpieces of virtue, which he copies in his daily life. And thus never is anything seen in him but holy living.

The fourth trait of his likeness to God is that he is good; he shows forth the divine goodness. God is the fountain head from which all goodness flows. All the goodness in this world taken together and joined in one is called and is good, because it is a single drop of God's goodness, a drop He has permitted us to enjoy. Hence, dear children, must we cleave close to this infinite source of all good, if we would feel the power of good in our lives—the nearer the source the purer and the sweeter the waters of goodness and grace and holiness.

When we give up the world, that is to say, sin, we draw nigh to the flowing spring of divine grace. The man who totally shuts out whatsoever is the world or cleaves to the world, he it is that may be said to leave the world; self-will, self-love, self-opinionatedness, these must one and all be shut out. This done, a man must then give himself up to God, body and goods and liberty, keeping back nothing of self or for self. This is what it means to be a really good and pious man. He must surrender his will in subjection to another man's will, and keep obedience even to his death. He must hand over his goods to another man's ownership, holding nothing back for his own even secret possession. His soul, he must plainly manifest to another, to be by him directed in all things whatsoever. Children, whosoever honestly does all this, and thus goes forth from self in soul and body, and draws nigh to the fountain head of all good and all grace—O how plentifully shall the living waters flow into him, fructifying his soul unto all virtue. Then does that man arrive at essential blessedness; he is like unto God indeed, and "according to God is created in justice and holiness of truth." God grant that this may be our happy destiny. *Amen.*

𝕴𝖉𝖊𝖆𝖑𝖘 𝕳𝖎𝖌𝖍 𝖆𝖓𝖉 𝕷𝖔𝖜

Synopsis—Gentleness is the ideal virtue for dealings with our neighbor —This is made up of affection towards all men for God's sake and humility in our own regard—A universal ideal is found in Jesus crucified—The mingled sweetness and meekness resulting from the study of Calvary—How rightly guided prayer ministers to an understanding of Christ's passion—Prudent mortification is productive of an ideal wisdom in spiritual matters—Observations on the remoter and rarer ideals revealed in contemplation.

FIRST SERMON FOR THE FIFTEENTH SUNDAY AFTER TRINITY.

If we live in the Spirit, let us also walk in the Spirit. Let us not be made desirous of vainglory, provoking one another, envying one another. Brethren, if a man be overtaken in any fault, you who are spiritual, instruct such a one in the spirit of meekness, considering thyself, lest thou also be tempted. Bear ye one another's burdens; and so you shall fulfill the law of Christ. For if any man think himself to be something, whereas he is nothing, he deceiveth himself. But let everyone prove his own work, and so he shall have glory in himself only, and not in another. For everyone shall bear his own burden —Gal. v, 25, 26; and vi, 1-5.

All these words of St. Paul are full of wisdom, but especially the first ones: "If we live in the Spirit, let us walk in the Spirit," that is, in the Holy Ghost. For as our soul is the life of our body, so is the Holy Ghost the life of our soul. Now there are three ways in which we should walk in the Spirit. The first is in outward conduct as to ourself and our neighbor; the second way is after the likeness of our Lord; and the third is a way without any likeness.

St. Paul tells us how to walk according to the first way: "Let us not be made desirous of vain glory," for worldly-minded men diligently occupy day and night in vainglorious thoughts. One can easily see how the Holy Ghost does not come into them. They are not members of God, but are separated from Him; He has no part in them. Then there are other men who, under an appearance of spirituality, carry worldly hearts within them, and are desirous of vainglory in every-thing—clothing, company, relatives and much besides. The longer they thus continue, the worse is their state. The Holy Ghost comes not into them, and their state is a more perilous one than they imagine. Vain-glory is seeking anything in order to be honored and loved by other men. And this taint insinuates itself into all our good religious customs, into our conversation and manners, and into our good works, and this to such a degree that it behooves us all to be on our guard against it, praying God to save us from it; for of ourselves we are powerless to resist it.

And we should walk circumspectly towards our neighbor. We should not quarrel with him, nor in anywise annoy him, nor circumvert him, nor treat him harshly. On the contrary, we should bear ourselves towards our neighbor in the spirit of meekness. Consider thy own self, and meddle not with thy neighbor. Some there are who assail others with abusive language and scornful bearing, often enough about trifling things. Look to thyself in this, for where such conduct is there the Holy Ghost is not.

"Bear ye one another's burdens," and that will make us all one body in Jesus Christ. Superiors should instruct their subjects in all kindli-ness of spirit, and admonish them lovingly. Our holy Father St. Dominic was of so mild a spirit, joined to so deep an earnestness, that no matter how perverse any subject of his might be, he never failed to convert him. St. Paul teaches us how a gentle spirit can by his patience soften a hard man—"in the spirit of meekness." Let each of us thus deal with our neighbor, guarding ourselves carefully, lest we destroy God's temple, that is to say, our neighbor's soul, and thereby fall under God's curse.

Now let us consider the second way of walking according to the Spirit, namely, after the sweet pattern of our Lord Jesus Christ. Let us set His life before us like a mirror, and conform to it to the utmost of our ability. Look at Him; see how patient He is, how kind, gentle and faithful to us; see how candid He is, how truthful; and O how overflowing with love His whole life long. Take all this to thyself after the manner of prayer and meditation, praying Him with the deepest fervor of thy heart that He would help thee to follow along this way in the footsteps of His virtues, bearing in mind that thou hast no power of thy own to do this, but recommending thyself with every earnestness to His boundless goodness. Set thyself and thy Redeemer together before thy eyes, and see how unlike these two are to each other. Consider how strange to thee is this way of salvation, namely, the imitation of Jesus Christ. Offer to the heavenly Father His divine image, His only begotten Son Jesus Christ, as a substitute for thyself, who art unlike God in all things. Remind the heavenly Father of His Son's innocent thoughts, and words, and works; His bitter passion and death—all for thy guilty soul and those of all mankind living and dead.

Dear children, our Lord is so good! And whosoever would stand with Him in His goodness has but to beg Him for virtues as for favors, and all will be granted him. He is easily moved by our petitions, He hears His friends most gladly. Even our purgatory, He readily remits it all, if we but turn to Him with our heart's deepest fervor. Then all our transgressions are pardoned, and the years that were wasted are quickly atoned for. But this transformation God alone can give, God alone can perfect. A man must pray for it day by day with love and humility. He will know that it is at hand, when he is interiorly admonished that he must now give up all hindrances to God's action within him, and then he has but to wait.

Children, the prayer of the spirit pierces the heavens, for in this the soul follows in the steps of our Lord Jesus Christ; upon that rests all that I can teach, or all other teachers, namely, imitation of Christ. St. Peter writes: "Christ also suffered for us, leaving you an example that thou shouldst follow His steps" (I Peter ii: 21). No man can go so high as to reach beyond our Lord's footsteps. The higher one ascends the plainer are Christ's footsteps, who trod that way in His life and death and in His glory.

Here come virgins from the market place and sit them down content, as if the entering of this religious house was their perfection. No, it is by no means so; the way is not so short as that. They must, so St. Paul says, crucify their flesh with its vices and concupiscences. They complain of difficulties—they fall asleep at their prayers. But what wonder if they do? And they complain again that they have no sweetness of devotion. What! Wilt thou seek for sweet feelings forgetful of the awful bitterness of thy Savior's passion and death? Thy slothfulness sets thee far off from His footsteps, for in all thy doings and devotions thou seekest only thyself. Seek nothing of pleasure, not in any mental state nor in its images. Prostrate thyself humbly before the remembrance of His life and death, and carefully consider thy own nothingness. The lower thou sinkest thyself the higher thou shalt stand, for they that humble themselves shall be exalted. Set thy nothingness in contrast with God's infinite majesty, and then consider how He became, as it were, nothing for thy sake and through thy sinfulness; and do not again imagine that thy corrupt nature has yet been overcome. The war against it thou must bravely begin and carry on to victory, for victory will not fly down from heaven into thy bosom.

There are some men so given over to life's pleasures, that God must deprive them of their means of enjoyment by main force. If they were but detached in spirit, even riches and honors might well be theirs, for they would still advance in perfection. But what costs nothing is worth nothing. Young and hearty and unmortified natures, living a life of flesh and blood, complain of hindrances to their spiritual life in their occupations and in distractions. All that may be true, for the reason that thou hast not as yet wisely chosen thy way. It must be another way from thy present one, if thou art going to arrive at perfection. Such souls are of the race of Simon of Cyrene, who carried the cross of Christ by compulsion and not from love. One should under all circumstances offer to carry the holy cross of Christ out of love; he should constantly place himself at the disposal of Jesus crucified. Art thou retiring to sleep? Lay thee down on the cross of Christ, and pray and yearn that the blessed bosom of the crucified may be thy bed, His sweet heart thy pillow, His holy arms thy covering. Those wide open arms should be thy refuge in all thy necessities of soul and body, and well will they shield thee from harm. Art thou sitting down to eat? Dip every morsel in His holy wounds. When our sisters sing their psalms, they should place each holy canticle in His blessed wounds, considering what those wounds mean to us. So shouldst thou identify Him with thyself and thyself with Him in thy thoughts. What simple talk is this, that men boast that they recite the Lord's prayer, and meanwhile fail to follow His example, fail to enter into the Lord's spirit.

The third way of perfection is imageless—a high, short, darksome and sorrowful way is this, my children. Job speaks of it: "To a man whose way is hidden, and God hath surrounded him with darkness"

(Job iii:21). Here it is that women are strengthened tó be men and
all men who here refuse to follow God are brought to naught. O how
dark is this way. For all that had been granted the soul in the other
ways of perfection is now—so the soul feels—quite stripped of it.
Whither it should turn for relief it knows not, and so it stands in the
way in deep oppression of spirit encompassed by darkness, for light
seems departed from it. St. Gregory says: "Many walk in darkness
in this life, thinking to be saved and ending in eternal death." But
these are in the darkness of sin. The darkness we are considering is
the road to eternal life. And this unknown and darksome way we
must be willing to follow, rather than the broad road that leads to
destruction, against which we are warned in the Gospel. This is God's
little path to paradise, and it lies between knowledge and ignorance;
one must keep it in as plain sight as an archer does his target.

We must stop neither at ignorance nor at knowledge in treading this
road, but keep on steadfastly guided by a simple faith. We must avoid
both over security and despondency, trusting entirely to holy hope.
So too we must avoid both false peace of soul and indolence of body,
pressing onward under the guide of true self-renunciation. Excessive
fear and rash presumption must both be avoided, the soul being led
on by unfeigned humility. But, dear children, remember that this
narrow path can be understood only by knowledge of one's inmost soul.
As to our outer senses and the soul's lesser powers, they are useful
to inform us of the circumstancees of life that surround us, for it is a
shame for a man to know many things and not to know himself.

By sticking to this road one is safeguarded against this terrible
fate spoken of by St. Gregory. But one can go astray by knowledge
when it generates pride, and by ignorance when that degenerates into
silliness. But a humble sinking down into entire detachment of spirit,
is a safeguard against any misfortune that may befall us—sinking
down into thy own nothingness, with absorbtion in thy holy faith
joined to living confidence in God. This saves one from those foul
temptations to discouragement, a vice that has stagnated many spirits,
and made them give up all progress, thinking it impossible to finally
succeed. No, dear children; never allow yourselves to be driven backwards; press onward with love and with yearning of heart; lean confidently on thy good and faithful God. When natural goodness exists
and grace is added, then one strides forward swiftly. I myself am

acquainted with several young people of about twenty-five years of age, of noble birth and living in the married state, who have followed this way and attained to perfection. But it happens that when good young souls of a poor condition in life would advance to God in this way, and therein are awaiting God's guidance, they are often driven out of it by others, and are forced to go to work to earn bread—and thereby it may happen that great spiritual advantages are forfeited. Meanwhile, it is a perilous thing to be associated with those who follow this spirit and to be made responsible for their guidance, because they may very easily go astray.

Children, three things are to be considered about this. The first is that it is God who does all these souls' work, just in so far as they allow Him, and in these things they are of course good and praiseworthy. The second is this: If one is turned to God with all his spiritual life, cooperating with Him in love and in every purpose, just so far is such a soul good. Thirdly, if that man yields to self-content and thus gives up to his natural sense of proprietorship, then everything goes wrong with him, his darkness grows deeper and it lasts longer. This darkness casts the natural man into unrest and anguish of soul, for he is placed helplessly between enjoyment of the images of his imagination and deprivation and absence of them. All the sad things we have already spoken of happen to him, and he has no savor of any spiritual joy left to him. What he would enjoy he cannot have, seek it however eagerly he may; and thus he remains in deep desolation and constraint of spirit.

This state of suffering drives many a one away from home on pilgrimages to Aix-la-Chapelle or to Rome; sends many into monasteries. But the more eagerly they search for relief the less they get of it. Others give up the struggle and go back to the lower spiritual methods of imaginative forms in their prayer; they have not the courage to suffer patiently to the end, but fall out of the narrow and rough way. But O children, how blessed are those noble spirits that persevere to the end in this painful darkness; they are God's best beloved. But their poor nature suffers many a death agony before all their task is done. Once a hermit living in a forest had a novice, who asked him what he should do for his perfection. The holy father said: "Go into thy cell and sit there crying out with the Psalmist: 'My tears have been my bread day and night, whilst it is said to me daily, Where is

thy God?' " Children, never leave the footsteps of Christ. What is
the good of devising ways and means of relief, if one will not keep to
this narrow road? And be sure that thy perseverance in this shall not
be in vain.

For what is the end? The Lord will come to thee at the appointed
hour, and He will instantaneously manifest the hidden treasure of His
love, the bright shining light of His truth heretofore covered from thy
eyes. In thy innermost soul shalt thou know why and how thy God
has led thee through darkness to light; thou shalt be fully repaid for
thy steadfast fidelity to His guidance. Then more fully than ever
before shalt thou be granted the gift of deep humility, the boon of entire
self renunciation. The more profound has been thy sorrow, the richer
shall be the gifts of the interior life now bestowed upon thee, and overflowing into all thy works in a most supernatural way. May we all
have courage to follow God in this darksome way to the end; may He
bring us all forth into everlasting light. *Amen.*

𝔗𝔯𝔲𝔰𝔱𝔦𝔫𝔤 𝔊𝔬𝔡

Synopsis—Greed for this world's goods a universal vice: the blindness and folly of it—Seeking for God's kingdom within us—Relation of outward good works to this inner quest—How improvidence is to be guarded against—The final result is the proper union of outward and inward religion.

SECOND SERMON FOR THE FIFTEENTH SUNDAY AFTER TRINITY.

No man can serve two masters . . . . Consider the lilies of the field, how they grow; they labor not, neither do they spin. But I say to you, that not even Solomon in all his glory was arrayed as one of these. And if the grass of the field, which is today, and tomorrow is cast into the oven, God doth so clothe, how much more you, and ye of little faith? Be not solicitous, therefore, saying what shall we eat, or what shall we drink, or wherewith shall we be clothed. For after all these things do the heathen seek. For your Father knoweth that you have n eed of all these things. Seek ye, therefore, first the kingdom of God, and His justice, and all these things shall be added unto you.—Matt. vi, 24-33.

This is our Lord's teaching that we cannot serve both God and mammon, but must hate the one and love the other. You will find a wonderful doctrine taught here, if you study it attentively. Our Savior teaches us as plain as our Pater Noster, in very simple terms, and with beautiful comparisons. He bids us set aside all anxiety about transitory things. In this same gospel He says: "Which of you by taking thought can add to his stature one cubit?" You know full well, children, men's shortcomings in this respect, many a hidden sin of distrust of providence being committed; and that the capital sin of avarice is also committed. These sins work, perhaps, more secret harm among men than any others. Let each one of us consider whether or not in his thoughts and his works he is overanxious to provide for his temporal wants, sometimes even to the injury of his neighbor. A full consideration of this—where would it end? How strange that we cannot trust everything to God, who rules absolutely over all things in heaven and earth. We act

as if we were to live on earth for all eternity. If one but learned
the lesson of this gospel, he would be shocked to think that
he so selfishly seeks his own advantage against all his fellowmen;
all his words, works and thoughts being devoted to his own honor,
or pleasure, or gain exclusively; and that even in the things which
pertain to God's service. Children, this failing is so deep-rooted in
many men that every corner of their soul is filled with greed for the
perishable goods of this world, their soul being bent and twisted by
it, like the poor crippled woman in the gospel, who was bent down
to the ground by an evil spirit.

Poor blinded souls! Why will you not trust God, not in outward
show but in all sincerity. Has He not delivered you from the infection of the solicitude of this treacherous world? Think of all He
has done for you in the eternal things of heaven: and will He not
provide you with the petty necessities of this life? Is it not lamentable, that a man pretending to be spiritual, should be absorbed in
outward occupations—his petty little work, his little garments, and
his trifling engagements? Until at last he can scarcely ever come
to God or enter into his own heart: and indeed is quite content to
forego all thoughts of eternal things, if only his temporal affairs go
on prosperously. These men, though they have the outward show
of spirituality, are yet as much immersed in their miserable little
doings, as are men in the great world with affairs of high importance.
So our Lord bids us seek His kingdom first and its justice, and after
that all these temporal things will be given us. He does not so much
as call them gifts, for they seem to him too trifling to merit so good
a name. I can but be silent about the widespread evil of this foolish
and most useless anxiety over temporal necessities, straight against
the ordering of Gods' good providence. St. Peter says: "Casting
all your care upon Him, for He hath a care of you" (I Peter v: 7).

Carefulness about worldly things does a threefold harm: it blinds
the judgment; it quenches the fire of love, deadening spiritual earnestness; and it hides the interior way to God. It is like a malarious
vapor which chokes a man's breathing. Such is the influence of
earthly solicitude, which without doubt springs from the vice of
avarice.

Let each one of you, dear children, look carefully to himself as long as he remains in this life, setting himself to seek God's Kingdom deep down in his own soul. There it lies hidden, there it will be found, there it will yield you its riches. I say to you emphatically, that whatever spiritual things you neglect now for the sake of temporal advantage, you shall lack in eternity. This earnest devotɔd-ness involves a hard struggle; one must fight manfully against self-interest, against the evil spirit, and against the world. Many a sinful tendency must be overcome ere you shall find God's Kingdom; and this is not to be achieved in a day. It comes with hard striving and patient labor; it involves the withdrawal of our affections from transitory things, and the suppression of all anxiety about them. That a man shall seek his own interest, is a trait rooted deep in our animal nature. Yea, even in his dealings with God will he insist on having consolation of spirit and sweetness of feeling—he must always crave some compensation. He will, for example, join the pleasures of human companionship with the possession of the King-dom of God. But we must learn to suffer in the spirit of faith in Christ; after that, God will gladly fill us with His gifts.

Therefore do good works; exercise thyself in the practice of virtue; God will in due time reward thee. But meanwhile carefully avoid judging thy neighbor, and never esteem thyself his better. Children, suppress all this natural tendency to self-seeking. Avoid doing spiritual things for petty temporal compensation, because this smacks of simony, which is a sin against God's justice, and therefore con-demned by holy Church. God is by His very nature the end and object of all things that exist. Why, then, shouldst thou make some contemptible created thing the end and object of thy virtuous works?

Children, seek God's kingdom and His justice, and make this the foundation principle of your religious life—seek God alone in His kingdom, the object we long for and pray for in our Pater Noster. O how powerful a prayer that is; but you do not know how much this petition in it means: "Thy kingtom come." It is really a prayer to obtain possession of God's own self, for the kingdom of God is God Himself, reigning in all created things. In that kingdom God is our Father (as we begin the Pater Noster), full of fatherly fidelity and fatherly power. If He finds our souls ready, then (as the Pater Noster proceeds) He makes His name known, hallowed and lovingly adored in our interior life. And then follows the coming of His holy kingdom.

in us, He guiding us, and doing His work of justice within us. So, too, His will is done in us as it is in Heaven, that is to say, as it is done in Himself. Alas, children, how often do we give up our will to God's in this His interior kingdom only to take it back again, and use it against God's will. Rise up and restore God thy will, bind thyself fast and firm to God's will in true self-renunciation, trusting for thy care to His fatherly providence. Can He not do all things? Hast thou not often proved His loving care of thee? Trust Him, therefore, most confidently, seeking His justice and His kingdom every day and hour thou livest.

The righteousness of God consists in seeking Him interiorly and clinging faithfully to Him, having Him ever in mind in what thou dost, and giving Thyself over to His guidance. The soul that does all this is ruled by God, and from it all inordinate anxiety about created things falls away.

I do not mean to say that one should be improvident; we must not tempt God. You must exercise prudent foresight for all proper provision for yourself, as well as for others confided to your care. You should also be in a position to do acts of kindness to your neighbor in a spirit of common charity, all things being ordered discreetly. But whatsoever you do or strive to do, conversing with others, eating and drinking, sleeping and waking — in all things whatsoever, keep God in view and God alone, and not your own interests. In this way a noble spirit will go through this mortal life clean of all sordid avarice, passing amid creatures in real detachment, enslaved to none, looking forward to his heavenly country, ever considering His heavenly Father, from whose bosom He came forth at his creation.

You might object, that if God does not abandon those who put their trust in Him, how does it happen that He often permits good and faithful servants of His to suffer painful want? Albertus Magnus gives three reasons to account for this. The first is, that God may test a man's trust in Him, so that it may become sincere and steadfast. Many a one does God allow to suffer want that He may perfectly teach him the virtue of detachment. And then He in due time comes to his help, that he may love his Heavenly Father more tenderly, and pour out his soul in gratitude to Him. In all this he is drawn nearer to God. The second reason is for the sake of penance; for by suffering in this life with a devout resignation to the divine will, a man lessens his purgatory hereafter. And the third reason is that perhaps these servants of God are called on to suffer as an eternal reproach to evil men, who, though well able to assist them, yet culpably refuse to do so.

Dear child, seek this kingdom, for it is nothing less than God's own self. When attachment to creatures ceases, then the will of God is done on earth as it is in heaven. The will of God in heaven is the same as His will in His divine Son. If thou wilt thyself become God's kingdom and be ruled wholly by Him, then desire nothing, intend nothing but God's will. Then shall God be in thy soul, the eternal King seated on His throne and gloriously reigning.

This kingdom is in the deepest depths of the spirit. A man is first practiced in all good outward exercises of piety, and then he retires into the interior life of his intelligence, and becomes, as it were, the union of two different men, one the man of the religious life of the senses, the other of that of the intelligence. Thus being now made a twofold man, he penetrates yet deeper into his spirit, into the secret recesses; there it is that he finds the divine image enshrined. Now he is engulfed in the abyss of the deity, in which he was foreknown by God in the eternity before his creation. When God finds a man thus turned to Him in all self-renunciation, He responds by embracing him in His infinite, paternal bosom. God takes the soul thus abandoned to Him, and new forms its created life, as if He transformed it into the uncreated life, making it one with Himself. If that soul could but see its own being as it now really is, it would see itself so invested with the divine dignity that it might for a moment think it saw God Himself—it would even seem to behold all the words and works of itself and of all other souls.

And what shall be the sign that thou art coming into this inner Kingdom of God to partake of this divine nobility? When all solicitude about temporal things has fallen away from thy soul; for our Lord tells us that it is in this that we seek the Kingdom of God and His justice—the giving up of all care and anxiety into the hands of the all faithful heavenly Father. We know that we can never love God too much, and, just the same, we can never trust Him too confidently, as long as our trust is rightly guided.

St. Paul bids us be "Careful to keep the unity of the Spirit in the bond of peace (Eph. iv:3). And here indeed is a kind of solicitude each one should anxiously cultivate, for interior peace is to be vigilantly guarded. In that peace of the Spirit everything is included—God and His justice and His kingdom. This peace a man must never forfeit, come what will, adversity or prosperity, honors or shame. And what is this peace? It is the love of an undivided heart for each and all of the members of the human race; just as God loves Himself; a love after the sweet example of our Lord Jesus Christ, considering how that love did its task, suffering Himself alone more than all the saints put together. Our Savior was all His days more desolate than any man ever was, and he ended His life by the bitterest death any man ever died. And yet in all this the higher faculties of our Lord's soul were as happy as they are now in heaven. The men who imitate Him most closely in outer abandonment and in interior desolation, and who stand their ground courageously, wholly deprived of help—these are the ones who find the inner kingdom of God of which we have been discoursing. God's justice is found in following Christ's footsteps in poverty and desolation of spirit. That we may thus seek and find, let us lay aside all anxiety. God's Son has said: "Whosoever will save his life, shall lose it" (Mark viii: 35). Our way lies in self-denial, and that means that a man shall essentially go out from all that he is inwardly and outwardly. May God grant us this grace. *Amen.*

The Dimensions of the Soul

Synopsis—The curious double and even triple self in man—Breadth of soul is the state of recollection—Depth of soul is self-annihilation for the sake of our fellowmen—Height of soul is holy thanksgiving. How the outward man serves the inward in the growth of the soul —Christ's example in His agony in the garden.

THIRD SERMON FOR THE FIFTEENTH SUNDAY AFTER TRINITY

For this cause I bow my knees to the Father of our Lord Jesus Christ, of Whom all paternity in heaven and earth is named, that HHe would grant you according to the riches of His glory, to be strengthened by His Spirit with might unto the inward man. That Christ may dwell by faith in your hearts: that being rooted and founded in charity, you may be able to comprehend. with all the saints, what is the breadth, and length, and height, and depth. To know also the charity of Christ, which surpasseth all knowledge, that you may be filled unto all the fulness of God.—Eph. iii, 14-20.

Children, these words are so rich in meaning that there is no need of our searching through authors to expound them. When St. Paul wrote this epistle he was a prisoner, and he wished that his friends should not be distressed on his account. Let me say that if I were myself a prisoner, surely this would be an affliction to my favorite children, and their sympathy would make them all the more dear to me. And from his prison, St. Paul pointed out to his disciples the road to self-renunciation, and bade them not be distressed about anything whatsoever. Some men suffer more keenly from their friends' misfortunes than from their own, and they would say that there is no fault in that; and yet there is fault in every distress of mind. St. Paul would teach us entire resignation and equality of mind under all burdens, all gifts and all graces that God gives us. Trouble of mind is a great obstacle, stagnating spiritual life, clouding its light, and quenching the fire of love. Hence the apostle elsewhere teaches: "Rejoice in the Lord always; again I say rejoice" (Phil. iv: 4).

When he says "I bow my knees," he means not only the outward

act, but especially the inward prostration. What is inward is a
thousand times wider and broader, deeper and longer than what is
outward.   Our outward support is our knees and feet, and these we
take from under us when we outwardly genuflect.   So should one act
interiorly towards God.   All that he is and all that he can do he should
bend down humbly under the mighty hand of God, thereby owning to
his natural and his guilty nothingness; by nature we are nothing
and by our sins our nothingness is full of guilt.   With this double
nothingness let us lie prostrate at God's feet, in all subjectiocn to Him,
in nudity of spirit and in self-renunciation; for these three are like
three sisters covered with the same garment; and the name of that
garment is humility.   A man should stand in a well-balanced equality
of mind between pleasure and pain, possessing and lacking, hard and
easy; and he should receive everything from God and nothing from
creatures.

In every man there are three men.   The first man is guided to the
subjugation of the outward senses, as far as possible, under the sway
of reason, drawing them inward and restraining their outward activity.   Then appears the second man, standing in all detachment of
spirit, greedy of nothing, resting his thoughts upon his own nothingness, making God his lord and master, and wholly submissive to Him.
The third man is now before us, emancipated from servitude, free to
enter deep into the uncreated source of his life as he was predestined
in God's mind in eternity, his spirit in full detachment joined to God
without forms or images.   In this state God grants him "the riches
of His glory"; and he is richly gifted with graces, which perceptibly
strengthen all his powers, high and low; "strengthened by His Spirit
with might into the inward man."

St. Paul says: "That Christ may dwell by faith in your hearts."
This dwelling, therefore, refers to our holy faith, in which men greatly
differ one from another.   For when one man says: I believe in
God the Father Almighty, he may have an interior faith in God in a
more sensible and appreciable way than some other men.   Yet if a
six-year-old child and a professor from Paris make the same act of
faith, it is indeed the same faith in both of them, yet very differently
understood by each.   So does an interior man have his faith in a
clear light, all plain and distinct.   But in the soul of the third and
highest kind of man, just awhile ago spoken of, this knowledge is

darkness, without distinctness and above the need of it, superior to forms and images, in a certain singleness and simplicity of knowledge—enjoying holy faith in all sweetness.

"That Christ may dwell by faith in your hearts." Compare Christ to a healing salve. ⌊Now, when God finds a man turned submissively to Him, into the innermost soul of that man does God pour this healing ointment that is Christ, and it is in this sense that He dwells within our hearts.⌋ Then that heart is made so sweet and gentle and supple that all hardness and stiffness are quite gone from it. ⌊Abandonment to God, nudity of spirit, and freedom from all desire—when these three virtues are deep in a man's heart, then the unction that is Christ soaks down into all its recesses, making it mild and gentle. He, himself, longs to be turned into a healing salve for the saving of men. His love of God has the "breadth and length" to embrace all mankind. St. Paul became a Jew to the Jews and a pagan to the pagans, that he might gain them all; our Saviour ate and drank and consorted with sinners to gain them. And so would this man gladly be ranked with all classes of men to save them.

The same healing ointment penetrates the soul with a universal brotherly love; none are excluded, because God loves all, whether good or bad. That soul is "rooted and founded in charity"; and the deeper a tree's roots, the higher and broader are its branches. Alas! how many showy trees are fallen low; how many fine-appearing blossoms have been torn off and scattered by the stormy wind of temptation. Our Saviour teaches: "Every plant which my Heavenly Father hath not planted shall be rooted up" (Matt. xv, 13). See to it "that being rooted and founded in charity, you may be able to comprehend, with all the saints, what is the breadth, and length, and height, and depth."

Children, to have breadth in God is to realize His presence at all times and in all our doings, as St. Augustine says: "O man, thou canst not escape His presence. ⌉If thou turnest thy back on His countenance, all friendly and smiling, thou shalt face Him stern and angry." ⌊This breadth as it is in God is infinite, and if we bring it into our souls, it becomes universal love.⌋ If you say that it is half quenched in this life, and can only be at best a lovely participation, I answer no, dear child. It is universal, it is as broad as the earth; for it embraces all mankind, and the soul would give all it has and its own

very self to all men. Such souls easily act up to this love, as did our
holy Father St. Dominic, who once sold himself into slavery at a
cheap price, and gave the money to relieve a poor man's dire necessity.
In that sort of love let us work, and as far as possible embrace all
men in its beneficence.

And the length—that is in God's eternity, having no past nor present
and without any change, as the saints now enjoy God in heaven, and
know and love all that God enjoys. Thus let us co-operate unceasingly
with Him in our daily course of life, as long as we remain here below.

The depth that is in God is an abyss that no created mind can
fathom. But this we can do: we can attain to a fathomless annihilation of self, insomuch as we judge ourselves to be nothing and to
merit nothing. Then the soul goes out to all blinded and malicious
sinners, and suffers for them a most painful grief, melted with pity
for their dreadful blindness. This depth of love is so immeasurable, that
it carries the loving soul down to the depth of hell, and if God would
accept the exchange (which indeed it cannot think) it would feel like
emptying hell of all the damned and taking their place there alone
forever. To be sure no one should so pray, nor ever think, for it is
against God's decree. But love and humility have inebriated this soul,
till it resembles Moses, who prayed to God for the Israelites: "Either
forgive them this trespass, or if Thou do not, strike me out of the book
that Thou hast written" (Exod. xxii, 31, 32). This depth of love is
born of God's unfathomable love, which neither angels nor men can
ever reach or even comprehend, for, children, it is too far above us.

The height that is in God is this: He can do all things, and yet He
cannot make any creature so noble, as to enable it by its nature to
reach His own divine height, even though such a creature were far
above all seraphs and cherubim. The highest possible created nature
is immeasurably below God, for it is created and God is uncreated and
is wholly self existent. But the favored souls we have been speaking of
attain God's height in a kind of way, namely by their spirit soaring high
towards God in great thanksgiving and elevation of soul; and because
God has become so great to them and so high, that all that is not God
seems nothing in comparison, according to the prophet: "Man shall
come to a deep heart, and God shall be exalted" (Ps. lxiii, 7).

I declare to you, that the man who rates any created thing great and
high, even though he rates it less than God, to such a one God cannot

be known in His full height and grandeur. When a man has been granted full union with God, his spirit is so elevated in thanksgiving and love, and God has become to him so adorable that nothing whatever in this life can have any savor of sweetness for him, nothing less than God. All created beings taken together, are seen in His eyes to be less in comparison with God than absolute non-existence is in comparison with the angels of heaven. God's super essential height of being draws the soul so high above itself in love and thanksgiving and praise that all possible honor done to godly angels and saints is not to be at all considered; the soul has a loving ambition to transcend them all and render God praise that shall be worthy of Him. As a great heap of coals make a mighty fire whose flame leaps up on high, so is the soul now wafted up above all its thoughts, imaginations and activities, beyond all its faculties, noblest and lowest, away above all its own possibilities and strength, far above all creatures, into the height of the super essential Godhead. In this elevation of spirit, the soul has its own interior depths manifested in a marvellously clear light, and is placed in union with God's inaccessible height and measureless depth and breadth and length.

Herein is fulfilled St. Paul's word: "That you may be able to comprehend, with all the saints, what is the breadth, and length, and height, and depth," namely in the Godhead. Children, if it happens that any man comes to this state without the three virtues of self abandonment, purity of heart, and freedom from desire, then let him at least be securely habited in deep and true humility and enter into the monastery of love. And any man who enters this state without due preparation in the exercises of a devout life, shall surely fall to the ground. But if thou hast entered in furnished with the above named virtues, then thou shalt hold thy place; for if thou ever shalt lose it, it must be by self-seeking and lack of detachment of spirit.

Children, here precious graces are granted, and the seed of them is sown in this soil, and springs up. It is written: "In Me is all grace of the way and of the truth; in Me is all hope of life and of virtue. Come over to Me, all you that desire Me, and be filled with My fruits" (Eccli. xxiv, 25, 26). To attain to this a man must go beyond all creatures; and hence it happens that this new birth is shown to some, who nevertheless do not experience it. But any man who directs all his spiritual exercises to acquiring genuine self-renunciation, to him this birth will be granted, in case he steadfastly continues onward. Let me tell you, children, that I sometimes meet with this in young people. But in those who undertake it when advanced in years, it is usually a failure, because they stand upon their own will, adhere to their old devotions with self will; they are hard in their judgments of others; in a word, they are lacking in the necessary foundation of gentleness and humility. This beautiful virtue has more interior force than self-denial, which belongs rather to our outward life.

To men absorbed in external works, the interior experiences we have been treating of must remain hidden; their souls are too coarse duly to appreciate such things as God's infinite being dwelling in the soul. Many a one who fancies that he has reached a high point of interior spirituality, has as a matter of fact never reached even its lowest degree. God draws men inward to this sanctification by self-renunciation and purity of intention; and upon learning this, many men drive Him away from them as if He were the evil one, holding obstinately to their self-will and self-indulgence. All the fruits of grace are as if struck by a mildew and are destroyed. For no matter how high thou comest, the three sister virtues of abandonment to God, purity of intention and self-denial, grouped and held together by humility, must be and continue with thee if thou shalt hold thy place. When the evil spirit comes to thee looking for his own, and finds thee attached to created things, that gives him his opportunity.

And now what shall I say of how to gain this blessed spiritual state, which outward living men wish not to have, for they are not willing to withdraw from the clatter of externalized spirituality? Dear child, listen to my counsel: If thou recitest an approved prayer once with thy lips, recite it twice besides with a loving interior spirit, and let no one hinder thee in this method. Whatever may be the noise of thy outward devotions, that may not count for much. Meanwhile do not talk about thy interior experiences; but outwardly submit thyself to everyone in sincere humility. Thy outward man should always wait on the inward man as a servant on his master, doing his bidding to the utmost of his power. Such is not the way with those who are exclusively occupied with the external things of religion, and who would constrain others to follow the same course, making a great noise about it. For thy part, dear child, be silent; and be patient with such persons. Abandonment to God, purity of motive, and self-denial—hast thou these lovely virtues? Then let the whole world be in an uproar round about thee the livelong day, and sit thee down quietly; for nothing can do thee harm. If any disturbance or inter-ference injures thy health, quietly withdraw out of reach.

Children, when I find any one led by God in this way, I counsel him as God gives me light. And if somebody curses and swears at me for doing so, I cannot help it—let him curse and swear. In this respect the sisters of our order have a good custom. For whenever one of them feels called to this state of recollection, the others are glad, and she is granted leave to follow her interior attraction. They all feel that such a case is placed beyond their interference. And this is a lovely condition in a community, and one established by the Holy Ghost Himself.

Dear child, dwell always in the monastery of these three virtues, so often named, and beware of those hateful step-sisters, self-indulgence and self-love—nay, set upon them fiercely and cut off their heads. These evil tendencies would drive you to be continually asking privileges, now to leave the house to hear a sermon, again to go to church to visit the blessed sacrament—anything to enjoy some relaxa-tion from solitude and recollection. He that hath ears to hear, let him hear!

Finally St. Paul bids us: "Know also the charity of Christ, which surpasseth all knowledge." This is that knowledge with which our Lord overcame the devil by His bitter death and thereby redeemed us. And yet in that He became the most utterly forsaken of all men on the face of the earth, and at the same time the most perfectly acceptable to His Father that He possibly could be. Did He not exclaim: "My God! My God! Why hast Thou forsaken me?" (Mark xv, 34), being more utterly abandoned by His Father than any saint has ever been. Before this He had felt this abandonment during His agony and bloody sweat in the garden, although in the highest part of His soul He was joined to the Godhead as truly as He is today in heaven. This is the knowledge and, as it were, the skill Christ would teach us, surpassing all other, namely that one should be stripped of all consolation; and becoming miserable, being wholly without support, should abide in total self-renunciation, in imitation of our Lord Jesus Christ. Whosoever does this becomes most pleasing to the heavenly Father.

God rules and reigns in such a soul. In its innermost depths essential peace is born: if thou hast been granted it, let neither man nor angels nor devils ever take it from thee. And yet thou must continue to hold thy outward man in check, wholly subjecting him to thy inward man, and continually suppressing and grieving him, never trusting him, never crediting him, lest he place any hindrance to the progress of thy spirit by his various devices, most especially by his sinful inclinations. To be sure, as long as we are in this life we cannot be wholly without comfort; but place thy reason in supreme control of thy appetites, that all satisfaction of natural cravings may be taken in God and through God, and to this end constantly pray for God's guidance in such things. Our Lord always strengthens those who frequently beg His aid, enlightens them with His wisdom, and perfects their work by His goodness. May God help us to follow St. Paul's blessed counsels in such wise that we may attain to the possession of essential truth. *Amen.*

Beginners, Proficients and the Perfect

Synopsis—Remarks on the vocation to a devout life—Beginners are absorbed in keeping the commandments—How the love of one's neighbor weighs heavy in the balance of newly formed piety— Proficients are led into the Evangelical counsels—How this vocation is related to religious orders—Penalty for rejecting this vocation—The perfect are totally absorbed in imitation interiorly and exteriorly of the life and passion of Christ—Remarks on the different states of souls in purgatory.

FIRST SERMON FOR THE SIXTEENTH SUNDAY AFTER TRINITY.

As a prisoner in the Lord, I beseech you that you walk worthy of the vocation in which you are called, with all humility and mildness, with patience, supporting one another in charity, careful to keep the unity of the Spirit in the bond of peace. One body and one Spirit, as you are called in one hope of your calling.—Eph. iv, 1-5.

Children, four things are to be considered for walking "worthy of the vocation in which you are called:" First, who has called us; second, to what we are called; third, what is the voice that calls us and how is it uttered; and fourth, how shall we worthily obey it?

First, it is the heavenly Father who calls, and into that call He throws all that He is, has, and ever can do. His love, His goodness, His divine being—all leads and attracts us to Him. In very truth God is always striving after us, as if His happiness, nay His very existence, depended on us. All that the Father ever created in earth and heaven with all His wisdom and goodness, was but to call us back into Himself, the fountain head of our existence. A certain teacher says: "All that God ever did, all that He now does, is only to bring the soul of man to hear the divine call, and to love his maker."

Second, to what has God called us? It is to union with His divine Son, to be His brother and His co-heir. He is the highest among His brethren; He is by nature the Heavenly Father's heir; and God calls us to be His Son's co-heirs by grace. Hence our vocation or calling. We are invited to follow His example and to pattern on His character; for He is the way we must tread, the truth to guide us in our journey, the life that shall be our end. All this according to our ability, yet not in mere good will, but in a victim's life and patient suffering.

Third, what is the voice that calls us, and how is it uttered? God's voice is manifold. In our soul's depths God calls us by His inspirations, warnings and admonitions day and night, and sometimes with severe inner visitations. Outwardly He calls us by every happening of life, now in joy, again in sadness. These are all strong voices of God calling us to Him. O, if a man will but be led by these sweet divine tones, he will not need God's harsher measures.

The fourth is that a worthy following of God's vocation is to go onward in all patience, and humility, and mildness.

God calls three sorts of men, beginners, proficients, and the perfect. Let none of us repine on account of the place he is given, for God is the Lord, and He allots to every one his right degree; and He wills that all of us shall be conformed to His only begotten Son. Some things are commanded, some forbidden. The highest commandment is to love God above all things. Many a one says he does this, and meanwhile will not give up certain things that stand in the way of his love of God, and in which he has more joy than in God; this shows how he loves God.

Another commandment is: Thou shalt love thy neighbor as thyself, namely, desiring him to enjoy the same good fortune that thou desirest for thyself. Thou shalt honor thy father and mother; and this precept includes all who are placed over thee. Thou shalt not take God's name in vain. Thou shalt keep Sundays holy and all feast days. Such are the commandments we must observe if we would be saved.

What is forbidden is this: Thou shalt do thy neighbor no injury, in body, goods, or reputation, neither by words or works; nor shalt thou covet anything that is his; and thou shalt commit no impurity. There are still other commandments, but they are all included in these.

Now be well assured, children, that any man who goes straight along this way, and is obedient in the true faith to the holy Christian church, leading an orderly life, such a one is in the lowest class of those who hear the vocation of God and obey it. He is sure to come finally to God, after the fires of purgatory have cleansed him of all defects in the divine service.

The second degree, that of the proficient, is the practise of the evangelical counsels, and is much higher than the first, being the way of chastity, poverty and obedience. That we may follow this vocation rightly and perfectly, holy Church, guided by the Spirit of God, has formed various orders and communities, well adapted to aid us to this end, and they are provided with appropriate rules. When men and women undertake the obligations of this state of life, and then violate them, holy Church sits in judgment on them. But if one feels called to this life of the counsels outside of an order and without its obligations, and then rejects the call (as when a woman has made a private vow of chastity and yet gets married), such a one holy Church does not call before her public tribunal, but leaves that case to God's secret judgment in the tribunal of confession. But as to those living in community, it is a gross perversity if, having an appearance of high spirituality, they yet have only a worldly heart in their bosoms. It is of these that St. Augustine speaks: "Cursed is the man who goes astray in the way of the Lord." This is God's way; He has called these souls to walk in it according to His evangelical counsels. Let every one having this vocation take heed to himself how he walks in it; let him take heed lest he shall be found at the marriage feast without a wedding garment, and be thrust forth into the outer darkness.

Each one should consider interiorly and settle in his mind what is his vocation from God. Otherwise, thou shalt today try one way of life, and tomorrow want to change it and try another, according as thou seest and hearest things round about thee. Know thy own place well, and pay no attention to any other, for it concerns thee not. What is one man's meat is another man's poison. Look to thyself carefully; let nothing cause thee to neglect thyself. I declare to you that there are many men living in the world with wife and children, sitting in the shop and making shoes, having only God in mind and heart and the decent support of their family; and there are many poor peasants who earn their daily bread with hard toil, thinking only of God: and it may well happen that these souls, following their humble calling in all simplicity of heart, shall fare better at the last day than many members of orders, who are not true to their vocation. These simple laymen stand in fear of God, their souls are poor and humble, and they go steadfastly forward in their divine vocation. And thou, lifted up so much higher, see to it that thou be not self-blinded; diligently meditate on the vocation wherein God hath called thee, follow it straight on, go not astray in it.

The third and highest vocation is the imitation of the blessed example of our Lord Jesus Christ in all respects, actively, passively, and in contemplation, with purest motives, in entire detachment of spirit, thereby attaining the loftiest point of perfection. Search your hearts and discover how near to this divine pattern you have come. Only in our innermost souls is our essential life to be found, and here is where we are to be entirely conformed to Christ. It is about entering this state that Jeremias speaks: "Thou shalt call Me Father and shalt not cease to walk after Me" (Jer. iii, 19). And as Laban said to Abraham's servant: "Come in, thou blessed of the Lord, why standest thou without?" (Gen. xxiv, 31), so can I say to a soul faithful to this call: Thou art a blessed man, true to God's vocation, first by obeying His commandments, then in following the counsels of His gospel, and now in walking after the example of our Lord in all humility and patience, as St. Paul teaches. Such a one must go deep into the interior, sometimes by means of forms and images, at other times in the stillness of his spirit without any forms or any works, "careful to keep the unity of the Spirit in the bond of peace, one body and one spirit" in the new forming of the created spirit by the un-created Spirit. Now the spirit of man is all the more newly formed, in proportion as he has walked the more exactly in the adorable foot-steps of our Lord, in all patience, humility and mildness The careful-ness with which one keeps the unity of the Spirit, that is to be measured by the diligence of one's inward faculties, daily and hourly observing one's thoughts and affections; and meanwhile outwardly practising zealously all the virtues of one's state of life. Sometimes one should exercise himself in works of holy charity as opportunity offers; again he will be drawn backward into very interior prayer with the images of a devout imagination; and sometimes his soul will be engaged with God without any figures of his imagination. St. Anselm says: "Draw thy soul away from the multiplicity of external things, and fall asleep to the stormy thoughts of thy mind: sit down and rest and be lifted up above thyself." When this silent peace is established in the soul, then comes the Lord as He did to Elias, "in the whistling of a gentle air" (III Kings xix, 12). In this the Lord only casts a glance into the soul's depths. But when such a man becomes aware of His presence, then, like Queen Esther in the presence of King Assuerus, his spirit faints away within him. And yet the soul's mantle is still drawn over its face as it follows the divine presence in an ecstacy. It was thus that Esther sank down before the King, who then raised her up again. When the Spirit enters this man's soul, all support is drawn away, all that was his own has gone from him, and he sinks into his own nothingness in all things and in all ways. And were he not upheld in the mighty arms of God, he would—so it seems to him—vanish out of existence. This man now deems himself less than all creatures, more miserable than any—corrupt as a corpse, beastly, void of reason or sense, yea, worse even than Satan himself. The King, perceiving that the soul is thus emptied of self, then takes it and raises it up and gives it His kiss of love. And this is due to the soul's lowliness—the lower its self estimate the higher its elevation. Then God and the spirit exchange ineffable greetings, and both are made as one; for God's sovereignty looks downward with especial favor into the deep valley of humility.

Presently this happens: when the soul has attained to so high a state of blessedness, the evil one comes and assails it with temptation to spiritual pride. Besides, it may be that God will allow the soul to fall into some venial fault, as for example wilful anger; and this is permitted to cause the soul to sink yet deeper into the consciousness of its own nothingness, whereupon God can elevate to a yet higher degree of union. Or perhaps it happens that bitter, reproachful words are spoken against that man in the presence of others, and God allows him to be overwhelmed with anguish and shame on that account. If this has happened to thee, be not shocked: thou hast learned a new and a better lesson of thy own nothingness—all goes well; thou shalt now walk more worthily in the way of "the unity of the Spirit in the bond of peace." Whatever man thus walks, following the example of our Lord Jesus Christ in all mildness and humility according to his lot in life, in him shall God's peace be born, a peace that passes all understanding; and a light has dawned in that soul's life that will shine within it for all eternity. May the eternal God help us all to this holy state. *Amen.*

Peace through Patience and Meekness

Synopsis—Patience a very interior virtue—Meekness closely allied to patience—Peace with God is won by absolute abandonment to Him —This is sometimes an exceedingly hard trial.

SECOND SERMON FOR SIXTEENTH SUNDAY AFTER TRINITY.

As a prisoner in the Lord, I beseech you that you walk worthily of the vocation in which you are called, with all humility and mildness, with patience, supporting one another in charity, careful to keep the unity of the Spirit in the bond of peace. One body and one Spirit, as you are called in one hope of your calling.—Eph. iv, 1-5.

These holy words should be constantly before every man's eyes. We should never forget the apostle's admonition to realize the sanctity of our vocation, and we should be true to it in all humility, mildness, and patience, meanwhile bearing with one another's shortcomings in all brotherly love. I exhort all of you by the love you bear to God, to cultivate these virtues with great earnestness; for all good works depend on them, even those attached to receiving the adorable sacrament; namely, humility, mildness, patience and brotherly love.

But one will never acquire them except by suffering contradictions. If a man meditates on how humble he would be if he were oppressed, and if he imagines how patient he would be if he were persecuted— that amounts to nothing, it easily drops out of the soul, it is artificial virtue. But when one is actually shamed and dishonored by works and deeds, and forthwith in all affection and meekness looks about to do some special favor to the one who has injured him: and when in return for his gentle kindness his enemy spits in his face. and yet he continues to serve him—this is indeed meekness. Meekness and patience must be won by hard fighting; for how am I to be patient if no man reviles me? And as patience mostly concerns our bearing outward injuries, so is meekness rooted mainly in interior self-denial. Suppose that I am proclaimed a lying teacher, and that I am covered with reproach and shame and my teaching condemned as false, and a friend of mine should be deeply pained at this; should not his sympathy seem to me like doing me a wrong? For does he not seek to lessen my good fortune in having the opportunity to practise patience? I ought not to love him the better for his condolence but rather the less. How unworthy a Christian should I not be, if I were not willing to walk in the footsteps of my Lord and God, whose whole life and teaching was so shamefully falsified and brought to nought in the hearts of men. Hence my earnest entreaty to you that you should suffer gently and patiently all shame, and tribulation, and all painful inflictions of what kind soever, bearing with one another's faults in universal love.

Now St. Paul says: Be "careful to keep the unity of the Spirit in the bond of peace." And the virtues we have been praising are a true bond, binding all into oneness of spirit in holy peace. And how shall we attain to oneness with God's spirit? The exercises of religion for that end are best placed in the later hours of the night when the winter season prolongs the time of darkness. Go to thy rest early in the evening, if thou wilt seriously endeavor after this holy state, so that being refreshed with sleep thou mayst be able to rise after midnight, search thy innermost motives in holy prayer, making manifest to thy conscience every love thou dost cherish, revealing to thyself every habit of thy mind; and then directing all thy life into conformity with the life of our Lord. And if thou findest no special grace in this, then in God's name, renounce once more all sense of ownership in thy spiritual practices, and devote thyself earnestly to meditating on the passion and death of our Lord, adoring His precious blood and His sacred wounds. By this shall one endeavor to arouse his love, and herein shall his inner life be made manifest to him; for as a great heap of coals or wood blazes up into a great fire, so shall this pious practice inflame one's heart. But let a man soon dispense with the figures of his imagination, and with fiery love penetrate through the middle ground of his spirit into its hidden interior. Such a man now works not but God works within him, God alone, in whose hands he rests passive. And yet his former good pious practices still profitably linger in his soul, and light shines upon him from our Lord's passion; he feels the bitterness of sorrow for his sins; he prays as before for the living and the dead; but all this must now be cast deep into God in great nudity and singleness of spirit. And when the rays of divine light have broken a way into this soul, thus all noble, almost passive under God, then comes essential Truth, namely, God, and draws the spirit into Himself. And His beams are swift as lightning, yea, swift as angels' flights between earth and heaven, whose speed is above that of the lightning. Nor does even this rightly tell how swift and bright are the rays of God's love and truth in the soul's inner life, winning and absorbing the soul, which must refer all back again to God, and be at one with Him.

Here is indeed the true adorer, that adores God in spirit and in truth (John iv, 23). Here true peace is born, and those virtues that lead to it, of which we have been discoursing, and now a struggle commences. For poor human nature is so wasted and weakened as to seem to have lost itself. Then the soul feels like saying to itself: God have mercy on thee, what has become of thy good pious practices? Why is thy psalm singing silenced? This poor man would have something, know something, love something of created existence; and ere these three somethings have faded from his mind, his natural forces are exhausted. All this does not happen in a day; the long combat must be patiently fought out; the soul must exert continually an eager zeal for its sanctification and gradually grow accustomed to conflict; and so win its new spiritual strength; until at last it becomes like the saints, happy and triumphant in its trials: "Afflicted in few things, in many they shall be well rewarded" (Wis. iii, 5). And, as St. Bernard tells us, when nature is at last put totally to death, the soul shall address our Lord words of tenderest love: O love, only love of my heart! Would that I were worthy of a place among Thy best loved and could embrace Thee fast and firm in my soul's embrace, and Thou me in Thy deepest Spirit, and that I might never lose Thee more!—words uttered from the innermost consciousness of the heart.

Dear children, turn to God with all your heart, and do it in any approved way whatsoever, for the way that is given thee by God's providence, that is the way that leads to Him. Whatever devotion attracts thee, follow it faithfully, noting carefully beforehand whatsoever gives thee the most grace. Be sure that a single sweep of thy mind upon the wings of love, into the wounds of Christ, is worth more to God than all bell ringing and organ playing and fine singing and gorgeous vestments in the world. Dear children, if you will but turn to God earnestly, and with your inmost soul, then will your temptations cease, and with them will cease your scrupulous pestering of your father confessor. All will soon be well ordered by your more interior devotional spirit, which gives a clear knowledge of our imperfections, and a humble avowal of them to God; so that when one goes to confession, one can hardly think of anything to tell. May God help us to all this, so that we may devoutly follow our Lord in the practise of virtue. *Amen.*

Inward Pharisaism

*Synopsis—Spiritual self-interest is the root of Pharisaism—The differ-
ent grades of this vice—Warnings about sensible devotion—St.
Bernard's three qualities of love: sweet, wise and strong—Unselfish
love embodies these qualities—How this is perfect in a very supernatural degree of self-annihilation.*

SERMON FOR THE SEVENTEENTH SUNDAY AFTER TRINITY.

And behold a certain lawyer stood up tempting Him, and saying: Master,
what must I do to possess eternal life? But He said to Him: What is written
in the law? how readeth thou? He answering, said: Thou shalt love the Lord
thy God with thy whole heart, and with thy whole soul, and with all thy
strength, and with all thy mind; and thy neighbor as thyself. And He said
to Him: Thou has answered right; this do and thou shalt live.—Luke x, 25-28.

Children, our Lord's questioner thought not of God or of eternal life
for his purpose in asking was treacherous. O how comes it that such
a pharisaical spirit prevails among men, that in word and work they
regard outward things exclusively; as long as an outward show of
piety is observed, they go on with all liberty in their greed for money
and honors and pleasures of all sorts. Now everything that men do
for the sake of show, all that they would have held for great and
wonderful, such works God makes no account of, no matter how high
they may seem. Who caused this or that work to be done? That
question decides whose the work is.

The inward pharisaism is this: No matter what a Pharisee does he
always has himself in view. Some spiritual men are thus infected,
even though they are not aware of it; for thinking that they do things
for God's honor, yet—if only you could read their hearts—they do
them out of self love; and this includes even their prayers. This
fundamental fault is deeper in some than in others; but once made
habitual, it is seldom entirely overcome. Men ostentatiously do great
things; they endeavor to gain indulgences, they beat their breasts,
they pray before pious pictures, here they kneel and there they run in
their showy devotions; and throughout it all they do not consider

God; for their love and their purpose is not given to God but is bent downward to creatures. Created things minister to them; these are their joy, a joy wilfully and knowingly received. Their own inward and outward comfort and profit is the end they have in view. This is not according to this gospel: "Thou shalt love the Lord thy God with thy whole heart;" and therefore God makes no account of it.

Then we find other men who are a little better; they are cured of this delusion, and they have turned away from earthly things as much as they can. But their pious methods smack too much of the life of the senses, and their souls are absorbed too much in gross mental pictures of Christ's holy humanity, the scenes of His birth, the events of His life, sufferings and death. All this is in their soul in a manner far too material. These feelings journey through the soul as a ship upon the waters of the Rhine. This is called by preachers a fleshly love of God, but I would prefer to call it a sensible love—a love dominantly of the senses, thinking only of our Lord as known by the senses, and viewing Him thus from head to foot. These men draw from their devotions a pleasurable love rather than a divine love, and it must be reckoned as savoring of the pharisaical. Such men's souls dwell more intently on the things they do than on the end for which they should do them. Spiritual contentment—that instead of God, is what they strive after. It is not the essential but the accidental, not the goal but the way to it, not the inner meaning but the outer act, that engages their mind: and God has the least possible to do with their religious existence. Natural love and divine love seem so much alike, that we cannot easily distinguish one from the other. It were better for such a man to have no devotional sweetness, if he could but manage to do all his pious actions without it. In this way he would learn to read his own heart far more truly. And yet, although the way of sensible devotion is thus by no means the most perfect, nevertheless would to God that we had more men willing to follow even that low method.

Children, St. Bernard, speaking of the love that is commanded us, says that it is threefold: a sweet love, a wise love, and a strong love; which I can explain by a comparison. The first is a wooden statue gilded all over, the second a silver statue gilded all over, and the third is a statue of solid gold: the wooden one is sweet love, the silver one is wise love, the gold one is strong love.

Now if the wooden statue is well made and finely gilded, every particle of it being well hidden with gold leaf, we prize it highly; but

when the gold begins to peel off and the poor wood shows out we would
hardly give twelve pennies for it. So it is with out devotional sweetness in good works and prayer; it is the fine appearing gold leaf; peel
it off, and our religious life is of small value to us, however much
it may once have delighted our natural sensibility. But by means of
sensible devotion God leads and entices a man onward to a better love,
which is gradually developed in the soul amid these sweet sentiments,
until at last He extinguishes the natural enjoyments which have mingled with pure love. Let us not cast away sensible devotion; let us
receive it with all reverence and humility. But we should ascribe to
our pettiness and meanness that the Lord must thus allure us onward
from the religion of imagination to that which is so far above it,
through outward to inward things, even unto His own divine self in the
depths of our souls, where He would establish His Kingdom of everlasting truth. We meet with many who have much sensible joy in
their devotion, and whose interior hearts are shut in as tight as a
mountain of iron—nothing can come forth from them. This is due
to want of proper spiritual training. Their souls rest upon the forms
and maps of the mind; they are unconscious of that light of eternal
truth that shines in their inmost souls:—they never penetrate those
holy depths. But no man can serve two masters, namely, his senses
and his spirit.

Then we must consider St. Bernard's second kind of love, which he
calls wise love. This is seated in the reason; and it is wonderfully
elevated above the first kind. We have likened it to the silver gilt
statue, which is intrinsically very precious, and if it were a large
statue might be the chief adornment of a church. So is this wise love,
seated as it is in the understanding, a precious thing and exceedingly
lovely. Now mark how thou mayst attain to it. Thou must turn thy
spirit to eternal things. As thou hast been wont to dwell on sensible
images in the mind, as, for example, mental pictures of our Lord's life,
consider now the eternal meaning of each and all of the events of His
life. Think on the eternal birth of the infinite Word of God in the
bosom of the Father; how He was born to us and yet remained with
the Father; consider how the Holy Ghost proceeded in unspeakable
love from the Father and the Son; and consider the divine life of the
blessed Trinity, one only God in three distinct persons. Draw into
that divine sanctuary thy own nothingness, and thy manifold distracted life; look deep into the hidden recesses of the Eternal God-head;

think that to Him there is no past and no future, but only an ever-lasting present, possessing in an infinite way all things whatsoever, embracing them in the divine unchangeableness. Place all this in contrast with thy own variableness in this life of fleeting time, with thy changeable and fluctuating spirit. Thus it will happen that thy sensible love will be elevated above its forms and images in a state of self-renunciation and will approach to a wise love of the understanding, thereby using these lower forms as helps to pass through and beyond into a higher state of holiness.

Children, this wise love leads a man's spirit so far beyond these alien figures of outward things, that he presently is in a state of forgetfulness of them. In his first state, it was a laborious task to turn away from worldly things, and now they drop out of his mind of their own weight. He despises them and feels a downright aversion for them and for all that is not rightly ordered in his affections. This grace raises the mind above all transitory things far more effectually than strenuous external observances: one is now more entirely regenerated. His soul gazes into the divine obscurity; for God the infinitely incomprehensible, is dark to the created understanding, just as the noon day sun, if looked at directly, dazzles and blinds the human eye by its very brightness.

Dionysius says: "God is above every name, or existence, or figure that man can attribute to Him: He is superessentially above all things." As soon, then, as a man is granted to know something of what God essentially is, the knowledge sinks him downwards: it melts and dissolves him into his own nothingness. And the clearer, the more nakedly, God's infinitude beams upon him, the better he understands his own littleness, his very nothingness. It follows that the reality of this inner divine illumination cannot be known in any mental forms and figures, nor by any action of the mental faculties; it can only be verified in the inmost essence of the spirit, and in the sinking of the spirit downward into the sense of its own utter nothingness.

This is against the error of those overbold spirits, who are led astray by false inner illumination. They imagine that they have found the infinite truth, and they are puffed up with self-complacency. Their heads are turned with their false mortification; they dishonor our Lord by their evil treatment of other men, whom they deny to have reached a state of prayer which is beyond that of the figures of the imagination. You may be sure that a really devout man never thinks himself too good to practice the least act of piety, however simple and even contemptible it may seem to proud spirits. And when he does arrive at a state where he feels he can rightly dispense with certain ordinary devotional practises, he by no means despises them—he loves them as much as ever he did when he followed them: in fact he rates himself below all things, and deems that he has attained to no perfection. It is men of a different spirit, men of a proud spirit, who come to you with their heads in the air, and who, if they hear some wild sermon that has neither dovout method nor living truth in it, proclaim it the highest doctrine ever taught. As to the living truth of God, all plain and simple, for that they have no taste whatever. As a matter of fact these souls are stagnated; they bask in their own natural light, parading idly about. They have never broken through their weakness, being regardless of the lessons of our Lord's adorable life. They have never subdued nature by the practise of virtue: the true way of love is unknown to them. They trust to a false inward recollection which flatters their natural pride, and which blinds them to the deep rooted defects of their spirit, inducing a counterfeit state of repose. This evil is very obstinate, and we may well pray a merciful God to pity it and reform it.

In these, our evil days, I would be loath to make men miserable by my complaints, for it is well nigh a hopeless task to wean them from their almost universal self love. But this I will affirm: If any one will attain to this degree of wise love, he must practise self-denial, he must make little of himself, and he must exactly follow the gospel of our Lord Jesus Christ. Such a man falls into no false state of recollection, nor is he infected with a false spirit of liberty—he cares nothing at all for himself. And that is the reason why he is very dear to God.

We are now to consider the third degree, namely, the strong love, as St. Bernard calls it. We have compared this essential love to a statue of pure and solid gold. Now some of this pure love all must have: if any man feels his soul totally devoid of it, his state is a perilous one, and he may well weep day and night. This gold is so brightly polished that it dazzles the eye:—one can hardly gaze straight at it, for it is the brightness of God shining upon the soul: He is present there. The spirit is too weak to endure this brightness, which threatens to melt it away into its original helplessness. And the spirit has no relief but to be lifted into the divine being, and lose all knowledge of self-existence. This peculiar divine presence is simply overpowering. Then the soul does as Elias the prophet did in God's presence in the mouth of his cave. The soul wraps its mantle of helplessness about its eyes in an ecstacy; all mental activity seems still. God appears to assume every act and thought and affection. In this strong love the spirit is immersed in its Beloved, as a litle drop of water in the deep sea. The spirit is made one with God almost as the air with the sunlight at midday. But how all this is, can be better known by experience than told by words.

And what afterwards remains in the spirit? Only a sense of utter self-annihilation, total giving up of all proprietorship in will and in mind and in life. The soul sinks to the bottom: and if it could sink yet lower into actual nothingness, this it would (if such a thought were lawful or possible) be overjoyed to do out of love and out of humility. This self-annihilation comes into existence as if newly born within the soul. Such a man deems himself unworthy to be a man, to enter a church, to look at a crucifix: he is persuaded that he is worse than the evil one. But never before were our Saviour's sufferings so well loved, never did that man love His Lord's blessed humanity so devotedly. It seems to him that now for the first time in his life he has begun to love. And, indeed, he seems only to be beginning to practise virtue, and rightly to go through spiritual exercises. All such things from least to greatest, he now performs in a spirit essentially sincere. Indeed, as God is present to Him in everything, so the simplest and the highest acts of piety are now all alike. The highest heavens—as the soul now plainly understands—work with the lowest earth in God's undivided unity of purpose; the highest works at its best when it fructifies the lowest. So the soul perceives clearly, that God's mightiest influence is displayed in sanctifying man's deepest lowliness of humility.

As the sun absorbs unto itself the moist vapors of the deep hidden valleys, so God seems to absorb this soul into Himself. It is drawn into God and thinks and feels as if it were now even as God; and presently it sinks down back again into itself, and thinks and feels as if it were even less than man. The soul is like an iron vessel half full of water set over a hot fire: it boils up and down and sometimes boils over the sides: taken off the fire, the water sinks down silently to the bottom. Thus does the fire of this strong love affect the spirit, lifting it up into

God, the overflowing point, as if it were about to be thrown out of itself into divine oblivion; and then it drops back into the consciusness of its own nothingness.

This strong, free love has three qualities. The first is that it forcibly lifts the spirit up and casts it into union with Him who is its beloved, far above the working of its faculties of knowing and remembering, and beyond the reach of understanding and the action of the senses. The second is that it sinks the soul down into a fathomless sense of its own nothingness, in a state of humiliation wholly incomprehensible, so that it seems to have lost its place and name in all existence. The third quality is, that this strong love marvellously changes a man's soul into a most peaceful state of contentment; he is entirely restful no matter what happens; he stirs about only very little. remaining tranquil in his place, awaiting the Lord's will to lead him hither or thither. He has become like a servant standing beside his master sitting at table, looking quietly for a signal, ready to do or not to do, just as he is bidden.

Yet after all this great progress, it is quite possible that the evil one will assail him, and even with the most violent temptations. But in vain: these but offer him occasion for an immeasurable increase of love. He stands as firm as a rock, he yields not a single step. When all this is gone through with, the spirit stands like a newly ordained priest before the altar: all that he is, all that he has, all that he does is holy. In his daily conduct he has, as it were, the blessed body or the Lord in his keeping, to lift it up and to set it down where he will. And yet his humility ever abides with him. He dare not say a Pater Noster, without humbly prefacing it with the words holy Church bids her priests utter in the mass: "Admonished by Thy saving precepts, and following Thy divine institution, we make bold to say: Pater Noster." The soul's littleness is ever before its eyes in contrast with the Father's sovereign holiness, which it contemplates and petitions with fear and trembling. Indeed, children, every one of us should thus acknowledge that it is a marvellous thing that his weakness and misery should dare to address God and call Him Father.

And now what is yet wanting to this man thus transformed in God? This condition is wanting, namely, a soul full of God, a body full of pain. And when that state comes upon him, God looks often into him, casting a lightning flash of love into the inmost depths. Then all pain seems too little to that soul. And another effect of these quick visits of the Holy Ghost, is that in them the soul is taught what it must now do, for what intention it must suffer pain, or what it shall proclaim in its preaching.   May God, who is true and essential love, grant us thus to love in this life, grant too that the divine light may shine thus within us.   *Amen.*

𝕽𝖊𝖓𝖊𝖜𝖆𝖑 𝖔𝖋 𝖘𝖕𝖎𝖗𝖎𝖙

Synopsis—Lying, anger and stealing briefly considered—The higher and lower faculties of the human spirit described—How God unites our spirit to His own for our renewal—Times and other circumstances which favor the process of this union—Outward good works, how related to this inward process—The relation of outward suffering to it.

SERMON FOR THE EIGHTEENTH SUNDAY AFTER TRINITY.

Be renewed in the spirit of your mind; and put on the new man, who, according to God, is created in justice, and holiness of truth. Wherefore, putting away lying, speak ye the truth, every man with his neighbor: for we are members one of another. Be angry, and sin not. Let not the sun go down upon your anger. Give not place to the devil. He that stole, let him now steal no more, but rather let him labor, working with his hands the thing which is good, that he may have something to give to him that suffereth need.—Eph. iv, 23-28.

The epistle of St. Paul, read at mass today, is full of meaning and rich in doctrine. Particularly should we hearken to the apostle's admonition: "Be renewed in the spirit of your mind." And he tells us things to do and things to avoid. Three things especially must we avoid, namely, lying, anger, and stealing: these three must first be gone from us ere we shall be renewed in God.

And what is lying? Saying something or showing some sign contrary to one's mind: the heart and the mouth are thus against each other. And there are some men who make a show of spirituality, and yet their hearts are anything but spiritual, being altogether worldly and possessed by love of created things. I am not speaking so much of men placed in a worldly state of life; I speak of worldly hearted men in a higher spiritual state of life, and yet who enjoy their fill of worldly pleasures, not being loyal to God. Even such things as dress and ornaments engage their affections rather than God. But if you tell them this, they blaze up in anger, they instantly find false excuses: they are (so they say) young and they must enjoy themselves; or they do thus and so that God may be all the better served. And all this is a foul lie. Is God better served by introducing things into thy affections that lead thee away from Him? Shall not the blessed God make thee happier than miserable creatures? It is all a base lie.

Then there are other liars, men who do certain good spiritual works, but who even in their piety ever keep themselves in mind more than God. Some of them will be thirty or forty years in this state, and never find themselves out. Nor is this ignorance guileless, for they should have searched their motives. They should have carefully considered whether it was self-interest or God's glory that actuated them — the reward of heaven alone, or God's honor. Children, it needs an earnest endeavor to clearly unveil one's motives. Day and night must one study himself, imagining himself in various ways, investigating deeply what it is that presses him on in his pious deeds. And in all this he must direct every motive, he must expend every force directly for God and God alone. Then one tells no lie in externally leading a devout life. Every good work that is diverted from God is a lie. Every good thing I do that is not done for God is idol worship.

And St. Paul forbids anger, hereby quoting from the Psalmist: "Be angry, and sin not." This means that we must bridle our irascible faculty, constantly mistrusting it. Meanwhile, when we feel an aversion against what is not for God, we must show it only by our efforts to change it for the better, if that be within our power. But we meet with men who seek to change other men for the better, and in doing so make themselves worse. These are hotheaded men, bitter minded men, full of scornful words, threatening gestures, and black looks, enemies of their own peace as well as that of others. Such a one excuses himself by saying: "I have a bad temper." But why should thy neighbor suffer on that account? If thy temper is bad, take pity on thyself as well as on thy neighbor and bridle thy irritability. If thou canst not restrain thy temper, then be silent. It is a great achievement, to be "angry and sin not." Wilt thou put out the fire in thy neighbor's house and meanwhile let thy own house burn down? Thou triest to heal thy neighbor's trifling wound, and givest him two or three heavy ones in the process.

St. Paul says: "Let not the sun go down upon your anger." This means that if you have quarreled with your neighbor, you should do your best to be reconciled to him before sunset that very day. And he means, too, that the sun of Christian prudence should not be obscured by angry passions. Be sure of one thing, dear children, by disobedience to this precept and by thereby gravely injuring your neighbor, you lose God's love and forfeit all the graces you have received.

And the apostle says: "He that stole, let him steal no more." Stealing is unjustly taking and keeping what does not belong to us, and it may refer both to spiritual and material things. Spiritual men steal by appropriating in many ways to their own use and profit what belongs to God alone, using spiritual offices and emoluments differently from what God wills. They interpose themselves between God and what belongs to Him alone. Let no one presume to do this. Let every one accept the emoluments of a clerical office with real fear of heart, for not only may God be offended by self-interested conduct in office, but such a transgressor is liable to be disgracefully deprived of his office. For myself, I will confess that now for these many years, I have not been able to consider myself worthy to be called a son of our father, St. Dominic or a preacher in his order.

Stealing may also be connected with accepting alms, which is a matter very easily disquieting to an enlightened conscience. One should carefully consider why he accepts them and how he has merited them. It is true, children, that both the old and new testament allow me to accept alms on account of my priesthood, (for he that serves the altar should live by the altar); and yet I dread them. If at the beginning I had known as much as I do now, I had rather have chosen to be supported by my family inheritance than by alms.

St. Paul says: "Be ye renewed in the spirit of your mind." A man's spirit has various names, according to its activities, and according to one's point of view in considering it. Sometimes our spirit is called a soul, inasmuch as it gives life to the body, dwelling in every limb, and imparting all movement. Sometimes it is distinctively named the spirit; and in this sense it has a close kinship with God, who dwells in it by ineffable union. For God is a spirit and the soul is a spirit sprung from the divine Spirit. And our spirit is ever inclined to contemplate God's spirit, and to return again to union with its divine origin: this tendency of return to God is never absent from our soul. Sometimes our spirit is called the mind, a beautiful being indeed, the assemblage of all the faculties of will, memory and understanding. And above and beyond the working of these faculties, it has an interior and essential object; namely, God. For if the mind be but rightly directed to God, all its other activity is rightly ordered; and when it is directed away from God, all goes wrong with it, whether one is aware of this or not. The mind is also said to be the soul's depths, in which the holy Trinity lies hidden in its true form; and in this the mind is noble beyond power of words to describe. Sometimes the spirit is called the center or crown of the soul: and as God can have no name that rightly tells of Him, neither can this inner sanctuary of God be rightly named. Whosoever can behold how God dwells in the soul's deepest depths, is made blessed by the sight. But this kinship of God and the nearness of God to the soul is too wonderful for man to presume to discourse of it.

"Be renewed in the spirit of your mind." Now we have said that the spirit is superior to the mental faculties, for they are to it but a drop of wine compared to a whole cask; and it is in this supreme spirit that the apostle bids us to be renewed. This is accomplished by an energetic penetration into the inner life, associated with a practical and very direct love of God, viewing all things in Him only. It is an attribute of the spirit—considered apart from its faculties—that it is able to adhere to God steadfastly and without intermission; while the faculties can have no uninterrupted union with God. And the renewal of a man must be effected in his spirit. God is a spirit uncreated, and hence it must be man's created spirit that shall be united to Him, man being elevated to Him and absorbed in Him in a wholly purified spirit. Before creation man was in the divine Spirit in Eternity, as God foresaw his existence; and now in his created life it must be by the spirit that he shall be united again to God.

The learned ask this: If a man wilfully gives himself up to things that pass away, does not his spirit pass away with them? And commouly they answer yes, as long as he thus remains. But a great teacher says: "As soon as a man returns again to God with his spirit and with his whole will, and directs his spirit into God's spirit as He dwells in eternity, so shall all his spirit's dignity be restored to him, and that instantaneously—all that was lost is recovered." A thousand perversions of the spirit may thus be remedied over and over again in this work of God's love, ending in a true renewing of the spirit and reunion with God. And to this reunion may be applied the Psalmist's words: "This day have I [newly] begotten thee," (Ps. ii, 7). When the spirit is thus mingled with God's being and melted into Him in its innermost life, it is re-formed and renewed. And that transformation of human spirit is perfected in God's spirit, in proportion to the fidelity and purity of intention with which the soul has persevered in this kind of spiritual life, ever keeping God in view. And as the air is so lighted up with the sun's rays that one cannot distinguish air from light, so it is in the union of the spirit of man with the Spirit of God. Who can ever behold this union, so far transcending all natural union—this union all divine, in which the human spirit is immersed in the abyss of its infinite origin? If a common man could see the human soul thus united to God's spirit, he would without doubt think that he saw God Himself. Never did eagle fly towards the sun in the sky so swift as does the soul of man fly to God, in this renewing of the spirit of his mind. And yet in this flight the soul goes onward into a divine obscurity, as Job says: "To a man whose way is hidden, and God hath surrounded him with darkness" (Job iii, 23). He knows now the deep things of God that are far above all that may be described; nameless and formless is this knowledge of God and super essential.

Children, that turning to God is the essential one; and the stillness of night is the most favorable time for effecting it. When one has had a sound sleep before matins, let him then abstract all his senses and powers as if stealing them, and right after matins let him sink them away from him and place himself beyond all the forms and images of these faculties, and lift himself above their activity. But let him not in his littleness aspire to that supernal obscurity of which a certain saint said: "God is darkness to the sharpest eyes and in the clearest light because in His essence He is unknowable in any human fashion." Abandon thyself in all singleness of mind to God, and ask no further questions, thinking God and living God—that alone. Cast everything upon the unknown God, even thy failings and thy sins; give him charge of all thy affairs in a very practical spirit of love, placing all in the obscure, and divine will. Beyond this, such a man must think of nothing, desire nothing, neither devotional methods, nor tranquility, nor activity, nor anything whatsoever, but only to be given over entirely to the will of God.

And now suppose that while a man be thus engaged in this blessed interior occupation God guides him to give it up, and to do an outward good work, as to visit a sick person. In that case let him do it with much joy. If I were one of those favored men, and God called me out of this deep recollection of spirit to preach, it might well happen that God would be especially present with me in my busy work, in which, perhaps, he would de me more favor than in the highest contemplation. Therefore, after some hours of the night and early morning have been given to this interior absorption in God, then as the day opens and God's will places thee in outward labors, do them gladly and in all peace of soul. If thou meanwhile keepest God's presence in mind, thou mayst perhaps receive more graces than in the still prayer of the night.

St. Paul bids us labor with our hands, for the maintenance of ourselves and our neighbor. Now the truly poor in spirit are the men we have been considering; for they deny themselves the bliss of contemplation, for their neighbors' sake, following God's will in either the quiet of recollection or the active care of others. But young and eager souls need to give God much longer time in the interior life; for otherwise when they go forth to outward cares they will be in danger of remaining outside altogether. And if one has no savor of God's deep interior working, let him stand his ground patiently in faith; in this state of pain and desolation he will advance more in perfection than in outward exercises of religion.

Children, you cannot conceive what great progress such a soul makes, a progress extending into every thought, word and act, even the most trifling. All that he does is meritorious. To these men long life on earth is a great boon; for every day advances them in the renewing of their spirit, if they are faithful in all points as I have explained. To be sure they are not conscious of their blessed state, and live in great simplicity of spirit and suffer much. This is because nature might easily be inflated with pride, and so God hides the work of love He is doing in them. Sometimes, however, God selects a deeply humble spirit to whom He manifests it all. Alas, those who can bear this are few in number; for the more a thoroughly humble soul learns of God's love for him, so much the more does he refer it all to God's honor; the deeper does he sink into his interior depths, and the less he attributes anything to himself.

It is mostly in enduring sufferings that such men make progress, for our Lord tries them in every possible manner. And they are sorely tried by all those who are associated with them. If, for example, there are one or two of these holy souls in a community, all the others turn upon them and by words and deeds afflict them, as if they were beating them with strokes of a hammer. Of old the heathen and the Jews martyred the Christians; but now, poor child, thou shalt be martyred by those who seem very holy, and who do more good works than thou dost. They say to thee that thou hast gone wrong; that they have heard and studied much and know much, and that thou knowest nothing; the like of this they say to thee, till thou canst not tell whither to turn or what to try for thy relief. All this cuts thee to the marrow:

and now is the time to be on thy guard, and to suffer in silence, yielding meekly to all. Say interiorly: Beloved Lord: Thou knowest well, that I mean nothing but Thee in all I am, or do, or suffer. The fault-finders would sit in judgment on these interior souls, and force them to stiff uniformity with the common practices of devotion. But this is not to be done, for it is not possible, and everyone must be allowed liberty to follow his own special calling from God.

And so must we all be renewed in holiness of truth, and in justice. Holiness and justice that is our own, children, is all nothing but lack of justice, spiritual uncleanness, a nameless thing before God's eyes. Children, it must all be according to God's justice that we shall be made holy, not in our self-chosen ways or words or anything else of ours, but all of Him and in Him. May we sink deep into Him and be poured out into Him. And may He grant that we shall all be found renewed in Him in all truth. *Amen.*

Attiring the Bride for the Bridegroom

Synopsis—Our soul is called to nuptial union with God—First comes the soul's cleansing from even the pettiest sin—Then it must renounce favorite devotions, if God calls for this—A very interior sense of abandonment to God's will next must follow—All this is accompanied by the ordinary virtues of its state of life.

FIRST SERMON FOR THE NINETEENTH SUNDAY AFTER TRINITY.

FEAST OF ST. CORDULA, VIRGIN AND MARTYR.

The kingdom of heaven is likened to a king, who made a marriage for his son.—Matt. xxii, 3.

This is the feast of the holy virgin, St. Cordula. Left by God to her own feebleness, she sank below all into the lowest place, and overcome with fear of men, she would have escaped from martyrdom by flight. But God, by her interior suffering, gave her the highest degree of sanctity, surpassing all her companions. All the tortures that St. Ursula and her virgins endured, wounds and scourgings and death, she suffered interiorly, for she was martyred in her heart and spirit: she may be said to have died the death of each and all of those martyrs, dying indeed many deaths for each of their single deaths. And then finally she delivered herself up to the power of her enemies, and fell by their sword.

Children, children, let us wonder at the marvellous fidelity of God to us, let us be amazed at the hidden ways by which He leads us to Himself, manifesting to our souls the deepest secrets by means the most astonishing. God leaves a man to himself amid frightful temptations, oppressed with every dire calamity, abandoned to poor human weakness. But if one will only recognize God's guidance in this visitation and follow Him obediently, he will thereby attain to a degree of holiness a thousand times higher than if he had had no bitter conflict to sustain. Let him but earnestly cleave to God in all trustfulness, never despairing of His help, never indulging in unlawful liberty of action; and then no temptation can be so vile or so strong as to do him harm.

In this Gospel we read of a king setting a supper for his son's marriage, and inviting many guests. Now the king is the heavenly Father, the bridegroom is our Lord Jesus Christ, and the bride is your soul and mine. We are all invited, all things are ready for the union of God with our soul, that bride He loves so tenderly. This union is so sweet, so close, so interior, so confiding, so affectionate, as to surpass all comprehension. The loftiest professor of the university of Paris with all his science, could never understand this:—would he prepare to lecture on this, he must first of all rest dumb and amazed; and the more he would desire to speak of it the less should he find that he understood it. Not only does natural light fail in this, but all the riches of grace are incapable of describing God's union with the soul; for all angels and saints would lack words to tell what they know of it. It is only a simple hearted soul, wholly given up to God in deep humility—only such a one can experience something of this spiritual espousals, and that in the inmost recesses of his soul's life. Even he cannot comprehend it, least of all describe it, for it far transcends all created intelligence.

This bride of God, our soul, we must now get ready. We must wash it clean, we must array it in new garments, adorn it with all splendor: as to the old clothes and ornaments, these must we throw away, even if they happen to be good. What the washing means is purifying the soul from sins and imperfections. The stripping off of the old clothing, that means purging out the corrupt tendencies of our fallen nature, every evil habit and natural weakness. The new garments, these are the new virtues that we shall acquire in a heavenly newness of life, formed on the model of Christ. But one might enquire about his former devout practices,—must these be all cast aside?—as being good clothes indeed, but not good enough for these high espousals? Is it right to say (what I will not say) that one must now be dispensed from practising these ordinary virtues, as not being good enough raiment for the heavenly nuptials? To that I answer yes and no. For no man dare say that he shall be above practising any virtues, or loving them. And yet it is also true, that whilst the soul is rapt into ecstactic union with God, he is not engaged in the practise of any particular moral virtue, for example, that of patience or pity. But the moment he returns to an ordinary state of consciousness, then he has to practise all virtues, according to time, place and opportunity.

Another way we can say that one is unclothed of his virtues, namely, by turning them all over to God in entire self-renunciation. One may long to have the grace to practise acts of much holiness: to be so poor, for instance, as not to know where he shall find the next night's shelter; to be so enlightened as to know all God's truth; to feel the deepest confidence in God; and to enjoy divine consolations; or to be like this or that holy friend. From all this must one be unclothed, and in all nakedness of abandonment to God's good pleasure, stand absolutely subject to His will, absorbed entirely in obedience to the divine choice in all such matters. For however desirable they may be in themselves and however intrinsically good, there is a depravity lurking in our nature which tends to pervert all the good that comes to us. It is like good food spoiled by the filthy dish it is served in, or good wine soured by a foul cask. Our loving, faithful Bridegroom knows this, our weakness, full well; and sometimes He allows us to fail miserably by this self choice of virtues, so that we may learn first of all to correct this evil tendency. Unclothing of virtue (understood in this sense), often results in acquiring higher virtue more quickly than would be the case in assuming the practise of great good things prematurely.

Ah, children, whosoever has any self-knowledge and learns his own incapacity, gives up self-guidance and follows God in whatever method and by whatever way He points out. Such a one comes through prosperously and quickly. Let him accept whatever befalls him as sent him by God's appointment, whether in his outer or his inner life; let him submit to the divine judgment upon him and to all divine happenings with deep thankfulness of heart. This way may seem very strange to thee, and yet thou shalt thus be more splendidly clothed with virtue than by the highest appearing good works, if thou dost them by thy own choice, dreaming that great results shall follow. The soul, has, as it were, said to God: O my Lord, I greatly wish to manage for myself, and I long to enjoy interior peace, and am desirous to be like this one and that one. But He answers: No, child, it must be otherwise with thee; thou must be stripped; thou must be thrown back on thy nothingness, and learn what is hidden in thy own soul: stay at home with thyself.

I once asked a man of very high sanctity, what it was that most commonly absorbed his spiritual endeavors. He answered: "Considering my sins; and by that occupation I come to my God." In that he was entirely right. Let God and all God's creatures sit in judgment upon thee for thy sins; then sit in judgment on thyself; and God will no longer judge thee; as St. Paul teaches. But this must be in thy soul without any explanations and interpretations but in all sincerity. It must not be a feigned humility, for that is a sister of pride. And it must be deep seated in thy soul, not a sudden tempest of zeal for perfection; there must be no head breaking recklessness. It is a quiet, gentle, resigned submission to God, in all humble fear of His sovereign majesty.

Therefore do thou lay open to God's eyes thy deep seated evil inclinations in most hearty prayer in thy inmost spirit. Freedom from these thou must seek wholly from Him. Whatever running about for help thou dost will amount to nothing. Following after this leader or that—that is all foolishness. They may be all very good men; but inasmuch as men differ from one another, so do their ways to God differ. What is life to one is death to another. According to a man's mental characteristics, and according to his other natural traits, so are his graces alotted by God. Therefore do not look about thee at men's methods and observances to pick and choose what suits thee; nor at their peculiar virtues. But everywhere observe such things as their mildness and their humility as something to imitate. However, thou shouldst follow their methods and their observances, if thy vocation makes it incumbent on thee. Always and above all things bear in mind thy vocation and thy state of life, and go forward along that road. If thou wilt but advert carefully to that, thou shalt soon find what thou art looking for in the nature of external guidance, and shalt know it as plain as thy right hand.

But alas, thou dost not remain at home in thy own heart; thou dost not seek God's leadership faithfully and loyally in thy interior. Thou lookest for everything on the outside, and that is why thou remainest unknowing both of self and of God. Twenty or thirty years of life is passed as in one leap, and what is the outcome? Thou mayest have led a life of seeming holiness, but as a mater of fact, thou art no closer to God at the end than at the beginning. What a misery is this! Dig down for the roots of thy vices and strike those roots dead; nor should this be the destruction of thy nature. Whosoever does not follow this course, will lose in one hour the store of virtue that he has gathered by perhaps a year of hard striving by outward words and works—spoiled by being tainted by the growth upwards of the roots of imperfection, unknown and undestroyed, hidden in the depths of the soul. As long as a multiplicity of self-assumed pious practices holds possession of thy will, these are on thy soul, which is the Lord's spouse, like very unacceptable garments. While they enwrap thee He cannot clothe thee with the splendid raiment of His love, as He so ardently desires to do. Make account of no spiritual exercises and no good works except as they are in some plain way His divine will. If I had followed all the approved spiritual methods I should be a dead man long ago. Keep God's will in view; love God's will ardently; have nothing of thy own will in view, nor of thy own spiritual pleasure or gain; pray to God enchained in the prison of the divine darkness and unknowingness, of deep retirement of spirit in the hidden depths; then let Him guide thee by whatsoever methods or spiritual exercises He will. Thus it is that He will array thee in the most lovely bridal robes that eye has ever seen. And thy soul shall chant a bridal canticle more ravishing than ever hath been heard or heart ever enjoyed. May the loving Bridegroom grant that all this shall be our happy lot. *Amen.*

Laying the Axe to the Roots of Imperfection

*Synopsis—The depths of our evil tendencies little understood—True
Christians are never without anxiety concerning hidden weaknesses—These often take the form of excuses—Also shown by self-
will in choosing devotions—Rules for alternating prayer and work.
Why inner joy should always be suspected—Danger of indulging a
critical spirit.*

SECOND SERMON FOR THE NINETEENTH SUNDAY
AFTER TRINITY.

Behold, I have prepared My dinner.—Matt. xxii, 4.

After speaking yesterday of how God prepared His Son's marriage
feast, I am now to further explain how the bride, that is to say our soul,
is to be unclothed of all its old garments so that it may be adorned with
new ones.   We shall consider how God gives and takes all things,
arranges and adjusts all things, for the purpose of this unclothing of
His beloved bride so that he may newly array her with appropriate and
divine nuptial robes.   It is much more necessary to attend to this
unclothing than to the reclothing of our souls, for the unclothing is
as far as our part extends.   We may not doubt but that God will do
His part perfectly in the reclothing, once the soul is fitted for it.

I must further explain my teaching that the root of our imperfections must be dug out.   For when one has weeded his garden, there
may remain unnoticed a root or two deep set in the ground, which
will spring up with the good seed and spoil the crop.   By this I mean
that the deep lying defects of our soul, which too often get little notice,
are not destroyed, and are only touched on the surface by our confessions.   Over these the plow of good spiritual exercises passes leaving the evil tendencies still there, rooted in our nature.   It may be
secret pride, or some subtle form of impurity, or some deep aversion
for others joined with scorn and envy.   These spring up in due time
amid apparently admirable virtues, defiling the fruit of a good life.
Be sure that what ever else God does or intends for us, He insists

peremptorily, that we shall uncover these harmful roots of sin and cast them forth from the soul. For as long as they are there, thou shalt have no rest: they will spring up again when thou least expectest. Such was plainly the case with many even of the fathers of the desert, who having lived in solitude for thirty or forty years in all holy exercises without destroying the roots of vicious inclinations, finally were ruined. Be watchful, children. The enemy may sleep long and sound, but he is liable to attack you suddenly, whether by pride, or self love, or inordinate love of creatures. Search your interior soul diligently: and if you find these root-weaknesses, destroy them relentlessly by humility and self-condemnation, appealing to God very fervently for His assistance. Follow this course; and rely wholly on God, for the cause is entirely His own; persistently persevere. For some, as soon as they find relief in their prayers, give over their efforts at purification of heart. For thy part, never be without anxiety concerning these obstinate evil tendencies; never fall into self-trust. The man who is on his guard about his interior weaknesses, is never caught unprepared; when the storm of temptation breaks upon him, he instantly takes refuge in God, who is to him like a safe harbor within his soul. Those who are careless in this matter, are, when overtaken by death, in an awful state of misery. They have wilfully cherished sinful inclinations, and are now justly condemned to purgatory.

What if this painful search and this hard repression of nature does afflict thee? Does it not reveal thee to thyself plainly and honestly? And the pain that thou sufferest will serve thee for thy purgatory. Dear children, there is no blemish of the soul so trifling (for I speak not now of gross sinfulness), but that it may be a serious obstacle to God's divine work in thee, if thou clingest to it wilfully. And it will cause thee more suffering in purgatory than the martyrs endured taking them all together. Thou mayest easily languish thirty or forty years there for such faults: is it not better to suffer for a brief period here in all patience and humility?—to say nothing of the wonderful increase of eternal joy to be thus obtained.

The king said: "Tell them that were invited: Behold, I have prepared my dinner; my beeves and fatlings are killed, and all things are ready." You know how the invited guests refused to come, offering various excuses. And some even laid hands on the king's servants, beat them, and put them to death. So that at last it happened that though many were called but few were chosen. Dear children, the like of this is all too common among us in different classes of people, both secular and religious; for when God calls to perfection, objections and excuses are everywhere heard on the score of worldly occupations and even of mere slothfulness. It puzzles the brain to calculate the marvellous excess indulged in as to clothing and food and furniture. In many cases not a tenth part of what is provided is really necessary. Yet this miserable age of ours leads straight on to eternity; and it is as true today as ever before, that what keeps soul and body together should content us. A man should be willing to perish with want, rather than to wallow in such gross excesses.

Children, lay it to heart that God has called you away from this wretched world to His faithful service. Let us relentlessly cut off all that is not of real necessity, let us avoid every sort of multiplicity and all idleness whatsoever. Turn inward and harken to the call of God in your various vocations, one to the contemplative state of life, another to that of active charity or religion, and a third to that state which is far above both, namely the quiet stillness of the spirit in union with God in divine obscurity. And even these last God sometimes calls to outward activity but in due time returning them again to their interior repose, just as He wills. For if when God calls me to His outward work and I turn inward, then the inner life avails me nothing; and if He would lead me inward and I yet go outward, then my outward labor for Him comes to naught. Stay at home with thyself, therefore, intently listening for God's call: there can be no doubt but that He will sound it plainly in thy soul's ears. Whithersoever it may direct thee, there shouldst thou go and nowhere else.

When one is called to the inner life of stillness and divine darkness, and then insists on never resuming outward works of charity—an unfaithfulness too common nowadays—much harm ensues. A man must under all circumstances do those works of charity that Providence has assigned to him. He must leave the interior, in a spirit of self-denial, not choosing this or that state or work according to his natural disposition, as many, alas, are accustomed to do. All must be done from motives of unmixed love of God's will, and in real detachment from self. A really detached spirit is keen enough to detect danger of injurious multiplicity of mind in devoting himself to external duties; no one knows so well what multiplicity is. Hence he avoids what is dangerous to his recollection, even though it be the companionship of ordinary good people; for their conversation is only too often light and trivial and concerning an infinity of affairs. Turn thou away from all this, and enter into thyself as soon as possible, lest thy soul shall swarm with a multiplicity of useless forms and images.

Once thy work of external charity be done, then hasten inward again. And if entire recollection be not granted thee immediately, then occupy thy mind with deep thoughts of God's unspeakable goodness, such as His overflowing bounty in giving us His divine Son's blessed humanity, and in our Saviour's life, passion and death; as well as the glorious virtues of God's saints. Thus may one be absorbed very profitably in God, in all love and gratitude. Presently this lights up one's soul, revealing one's faults, and it moves one to deep sorrow. All this is good and spiritually stimulating. But better still is interior quiet—as much better as the interior is better than the exterior life. And one greatly errs if he would disturb this restful calm by introducing forms and figures of the imagination—in the same way as one would cripple necessary works of charity by over-much of the restful spirit.

And now a caution: Sometimes men's heads are turned with the favors of the inward rest, and self-gratulation results; true poverty of spirit is forfeited, and the soul enjoys the sweetness of divine grace with the gluttony of a bear devouring honey. The inner of joy, contemplation should have no place in us except as a way to the love of God and God alone. One should seek naught of self, clinging only to the divine honor, lest one's fate should be that of the wicked servant in the gospel, who having appropriated his master's goods to his own use, was stripped both of them and of his own, and then put to death.

From this right relation of the inward and outward spiritual life, is born interior peace amid the silence and obscurity of God's presence in the spirit. About this, much is said in both the old and new Testaments, as, for example, how Moses was led by God into darkness; and in the Book of Kings, how God was not in the stormy wind but in the whistling of a gentle air; and as we read in the book of Wisdom: "While all things were in quiet silence, and the night was in the midst of her course, Thy almighty Word leaped down from heaven" (Wisdom xviii, 14, 15). All our spiritual exercises, all our good works, should serve this holy silence of the spirit, our attention never wandering from it, every effort bent on deepening it.

But some confuse this supernatural quiet of soul with mere natural interior peace. Be on your guard; stand in sincere fear of God, be humble, making nothing of self, suspecting self love in all things, flying incessantly to God's protection. True, this course means a sharp anguish of soul; it is painful in the extreme to be tormented with unceasing yearnings after self-renunciation and simplicity: but it is the anguish of purgatory, whose cleansing fires are thus endured before their time.

Perhaps one may not be able to withdraw his mind from the multiplicity and distraction caused by external works of charity as quickly as he would like. But that should not distress him. If all is done for God's sake, He will shortly abate the hindrance it would otherwise cause: God needs no long time to work His purpose in our soul. Turn quickly inward as soon as occasion serves. When thou hast established the Unnamable in thy soul's depths, all that may be named will be gathered to it, for all must respond to the divine summons within thee. If entire recollection is slow in coming, then exercise thyself briefly and regularly in the interior ways already treated of, till the greater gift of quiet in God shall be granted thee. If a man will but reject self and place God as the only object of thought and act, without doubt God will guide him in whatsoever way he treads.

Now, when simple hearted men hear all this, they directly resolve to make a beginning, and to do it strictly in this manner: always to begin, over and over again to begin, such is their whole ambition, such their life. But men of a critical spirit act otherwise: they take what is taught them in their own meaning of it, and carry it out after their own natural devices and methods. But when death is approaching they find their souls void of God, and are in much distress. They have not, to be sure, departed from holy faith, they are not in a state of mortal sin, but they are to be cast into purgatory to atone for grave venial sins: either that or the eternal fires of hell, if they have unhappily died in mortal sin.

When our Lord says that His beeves are killed, He may be taken to mean outward works of religion; when He says His fatlings are killed, we can apply the term to interior works, namely holy contemplation; and the wedding supper itself, represents the interior quiet of spirit, which the soul enjoys in God as God does in Himself. Finally God the King "went in to see the guests, and He saw there a man that had not on a wedding garment. And He saith to him: Friend, how camest thou in hither not having on a wedding garment? But he was silent. Then the King said: Bind his hands and feet, and cast him into the exterior darkness." The wedding garment is divine love and a divine intention in all things. This excludes all other love, either for self or for any creature: God alone absorbs it wholly. Now we meet with men who claim to possess this love and this purity of purpose: they have heard it explained, they have read of it in books, they know the meaning of it. But this is true only of their reasoning powers, for they have not worked it out in act. They possess it in knowledge and not in essence. It is not in their soul's depths that this love abides-- all love for God alone, every purpose for God alone; no, what they have is self love in disguise. For as a matter of fact what they have in view and what they love is God's gifts and not God alone. Hence the question: "Friend, how camest thou in hither not having on a wedding garment" of real love? A man should indeed use all of God's gifts, but he must not rest upon them with joy, but only on God alone. Hence the King's words: "Bind him hands and feet," that is to say fetter all the powers of his soul, and cast him for a further trial in God's cleansing processes, amid darkness and weeping and gnashing of teeth. Therefore, dear children, think of God alone amid all His gifts, love Him alone, lest your fate should be the same. May God grant us His true light to this end. *Amen.*

On Temptations

Synopsis—In dealing with temptations the cardinal rule is trust in God—Nobility of God's call to conflict—How God grants us favors through and amid temptations—And principally by bestowing humility—Temptations that are peculiar to the devils—Spiritual pride is the worst of all—How a certain kind of divine faith resists this.

SERMON FOR THE TWENTIETH SUNDAY AFTER TRINITY.

Finally, brethren, be strengthened in the Lord, and in the might of His power. Put ye on the armor of God, that you may be able to stand against the deceits of the devil. For our wrestling is not against the rulers of the world of this darkness, against the spirits of wickedness in high places. Therefore take unto you the armor of God, that you may be able to resist in the evil day, and to stand in all things perfect.—Eph. vi, 10-13

Yesterday we spoke of the stripping of the soul of all things in preparation for the coming of the Bridegroom, who will then reclothe it with the true wedding garment. But this seems an awful task; the soul thinks it can never be done, and naturally falls into grievous doubt. And St. Paul's encouraging words are therefore applicable: "Be strengthened in the Lord, and in the might of His power." As if to say: What thou canst not do by thyself, thou canst do by Him. Rely no more on thyself, but absolutely on Him. Rest all thy activity on Him as on a foundation; and thou canst then do all things. Look for success in His sovereignty, His power, His holy humanity. He will do all things for thee, if thou thus cleavest to Him in deepest sincerity and in all steadfastness. Draw all thy force from His hidden might, for His almighty power is secret and silent. But some take a perverse view of this. They act as if they themselves were God; they make no account of any power but what they personally possess, and this delusion extends to both the interior life and the exterior. They resent the exercise of authority of every sort over them, both of Church and state, and meanwhile they strive by every means to rule over one another. But you may be sure that God will not always be silent nor hide His power.

St. Paul says further: "Put ye on the armor of God," which is a warning that we have a battle to fight. But do you know what that armor is? It is the splendid nuptial robe of the bride, made for her and given to her by her Spouse. And how noble a conflict is this, thus to be fought in the Bridegroom's armor. But just what are these holy robes? Our Lord tells us: "Learn of me, because I am meek and humble of heart" (Matt. xi, 29). Thus armed, now let the soul praetise itself in that most necessary of all the arts, how to fight and to overcome in the Lord's battle. It is in temptation that we have our conflict for God, and the victory is that a man learns who and what he is. All the great ones of the earth who have been vanquished in life's combat, failed only from lack of this art of holy warfare. They sometimes have done great things for as long as thirty or forty years; they seemed to be wonderfully virtuous; but when assailed by violent temptations, they were overcome because they lacked meekness and humility of heart, and they did not know their own weakness.

It is amid temptations that we discover our own miserable weakness. This knowledge taken alone is worth more to us than practising virtue without it. Just in proportion as grace is necessary to us, so are temptations necessary. In temptation virtues are rightly begun in us, and in the same are they perfected. And this is a necessary condition if virtue is to sink deep into our being. No matter what may be one's vocation, whether to the contemplative or the active state, it is all one: he must needs be sorely tempted if he is to become perfect. A great spiritual teacher says: "As little can a man be preserved from degeneracy without temptation, as meat can be saved from rottenness without salt." God communicates Himself to us through the virtues and through the sacraments; and He can do the same through temptations. Little spots are cleansed away by them; and imperfections are dug out by the roots; by them holy humility is generated and the deep fear of God. By these trials God admonishes us to constantly fly to Him for help, and to entrust the battle to His direction.

O beloved children, put on this noble armor of God, and without doubt you will conquer in your battle with temptations. Only be humble and mild, only subject yourselves under God and all creatures, and neither man nor devil can ever vanquish you. Let all of God's enemies conspire together to overthrow you, you will put them all to flight. And any man who lacks this armor of humility, will never be victorious. Wrath and pride, the vices opposed to meekness and humility, are born of self-love and self-opinionatedness, as is also self will. The really humble man has no self will nor obstinate opinions: he is detached from his own will, is poor in spirit, and has God for his master and his support and his aim and purpose in all things.

O children, be humbled under the mighty hand of God and He will exalt you. Yield thyself meekly to be condemned by God to do penance, and let all His creatures condemn thee; nay condemn thy own self. Gladly suffer oppression; practise self-renunciation in all things and turn constantly to God: do all this, and without the least doubt it will turn out well with thee in thy temptations. But O children, where shall we find meekness among men? If any one hears a single sharp word, he answers back hotly with ten; immediately evil passions are aroused, and men are suddenly snarling at one another and biting one another like dogs. Meekness? It has vanished away from their souls. Thou shouldst rather be glad to suffer from men, having found out thy unworthiness to receive any other treatment, remembering besides that virtue is born and is strengthened only by such trials. When one assails thee bitterly, quickly turn inward, and hold thyself for nothing; look on thyself as worse than thy assailant thinks thee. And, besides, thou shalt thereby cure his scorn of thee by thy meekness, curing his wounds and suffering none thyself. To overcome all these weaknesses, children, practice deep, earnest prayer in your inmost spirit, and stand fast in the truth unto the end.

Once Peter the Deacon, a disciple of St. Gregory the Great, said to his master: "This is a hard saying—that a man must be always engaged in conflict." St. Gregory answered him: "It is not hard; nor is the victory doubtful, if a man will but place the combat and the victory entirely in the hands of God, receiving all assaults in that spirit arrayed meanwhile in the armor of humility and meekness." Such a man does not strike back, but he quickly turns inward and grasps the buckler of holy faith, and receives all the strokes of his enemies on that.

Clad in this armor, we are "able to stand against the deceits of the devil. For our wrestling is not against flesh and blood." Let all men who practise severe bodily mortifications, but fail to mortify the kinship to the demon that lurks in the bottom of our souls, lay these words to heart. What evil thing has their poor flesh done? These men would break through a stone wall by casting themselves against it head first. Kill your vices and not your body.

St. Paul says that our wrestling is "against principalities and powers, against the rulers of the world of this darkness." He means the devils; but he also means the human princes of this world. These should be the very best of men, but, alas, they are the very horses that the demons bestride, causing them to spread disturbance everywhere, and to oppress the people. They live in pride, they usurp power, they are in many ways wicked men, as is plain to be seen over the whole earth. "Against the rulers of the world of this darkness," adds the apostle. What awful darkness overspreads the Christian world, enveloping both clergy and laity. We can measure its thickness by the fact that Jews and pagans, with all their blindness of heart, live up to their law and their natural reason far better than we Christians observe the gospel of Christ, the teachings of holy faith, and the example of the saints. Our souls are blinded by vice, we are full of vanity, and we are preoccupied with thoughts of created things. We do not sincerely love God nor regard God in our daily conduct. In the end we shall be judged and condemned along with the benighted and infidel nations.

There are those who have given up this darkness, turning away from all selfseeking and walking into the true light of God. They are immersed in their origin—God; they are melted into Him amid the deep stillness of all their mental faculties. It is the holy darkness of the divine solitude that they have sought and found, transcending all intelligence. They are cast away so far from self, that in their union with God they have lost self and all things else, and are conscious now of nothing at all but only God, in whom they are wholly absorbed. And because they are thus placed, all goes well with them; they do not go astray. Coming out of this state, however, and resuming their ordinary activity of mind, they sometimes do not comprehend how it all happened, for it is beyond and above reason's grasp.

And then demons enter this paradise, the most cunning of them all and the most malignant. Well do they know that these godlike men will enjoy the places in heaven that they forfeited; hence they hate them most bitterly, and they give them no rest from temptation. Among other evil thoughts, they suggest to them that they are actually God Himself: for to yield to this illusion were the deadliest calamity of all. Now let the soul raise the shield of holy faith and hold it firmly, exclaiming: there is but one God; there can be but one God: who is like unto God? Upon these acts of true faith as upon an impenetrable shield, the soul receives the fiery darts of the enemy.

The apostle continues: "And take unto you the helmet of salvation;" " having your loins girt about with truth;" "having on the breastplate of justice," which is made up of all the virtues welded together; and take in your hand "the sword of the Spirit, which is the word of God" (Eph. vi, 12-17). Thus armed and shielded, go forth gladly to the conflict with your enemies, to overthrow them and to confound their treason and rebellion against God, that you may "stand in all things perfect." Thus are we to fight in what St. Paul calls "the evil day." We must all prepare for the evil days of the judgment of God, when the pillars of the world shall be moved from their place, and all things be overthrown and cast away. Then those who have built on this deep and hidden foundation of truth and of God, stand in security, liberated from all slavery to self or to other creatures, victorious over all enemies.

Into the inner sanctuary of their spirit these souls daily enter, drawing in with them all whom God has committed to their care; nor need these latter fancy that they are forgotten by such holy souls. No, O, no! All whom they love enter into God with themselves, yea, and they draw in all Christendom, fast bound to them in interior love. And they bring them out again into their external life, expending on them treasures of love in works of charity—to return with them back again into the abyss of divine love. All that comes to such souls in their outer life, they draw inward and place with God, retaining nothing for self—all is for God alone. Such souls are the strong walls of God's Church; had we them not, all would go ill with us; be well assured of that.

Therefore, dearest children, grasp firmly the shield of holy faith, wield manfully "the sword of the Spirit, which is the word of God." And what if you should be stricken down? let it be but for an instant; rise up quickly and fight on bravely. Renew the battle a thousand times over, and stand your ground to the very end, when eternal salvation shall be your victory. God grant us all that victory. *Amen.*

𝔗𝔥𝔢 𝔚𝔦𝔡𝔢 𝔖𝔴𝔢𝔢𝔭 𝔬𝔣 𝔏𝔬𝔳𝔢

Synopsis—The truest lesson of life is how best to love—Love works upward and downward in our soul—Love's relation to keeping the commandments—It gives favors without hope of return—When directed to God love begins with self-condemnation—It then proceeds to entire abandonment to God's guidance—What hinders love is any form of selfishness—Before this is fully cured painful trials must be endured—The more mystical states of love.

SERMON FOR THE TWENTY-FIRST SUNDAY AFTER TRINITY.

For God is my witness, how I long after you all in the bowels of Jesus Christ. And this I pray, that your charity may more and more abound in knowledge, and in all understanding: that you may approve the better things, that you may be sincere and without offense unto the day of Christ. Filled with the fruit of justice through Jesus Christ, unto the glory and praise of God.—Phil. i, 8-11.

Notice with what earnestness St. Paul calls God to witness, of his deep love for his disciples. Had we a return of such love to the apostle and our benefactors generally, it would greatly stimulate us to show ourselves worthy of our friends' affection for us, if for no higher motive than to satisfy their longing for our perfection. And when St. Paul says: "I pray that your charity may more and more abound," he means that it should greatly increase till it overflows and passes beyond every lower motive, and becomes love in all things perfect.

What is the best lesson we can ever learn? Is it not how to possess the greatest love and the best? God demands not great intelligence, nor profound penetration of mind, nor magnificent methods of spirituality, for all good spiritual practises obtain their merit from love. But what God requires of us is only love, for, as St. Paul tells us, love "is the bond of perfection" (Col. iii, 14). As to greatness of intellect and force of character, these are common to us and pagans and Jews; splendid achievements are common to the just and the unjust. It is only the possession of love that divides the false hearts from the true. "God is charity: and he that abideth in charity, abideth in God, and God in him" (I John iv, 16). Therefore before all arts have the art of loving. Inasmuch as God hath first loved us with an unspeakable love, so shall we love Him in return, as St. Augustine teaches. And let our love never cease, never even lessen, but always grow stronger. By love a man merits love; and the more a man loves the more is he made capable of loving.

Now the working of love is both inner and outer. The outer love is given to our neighbor, and the inner is given to God direct. For this latter love a man needs knowledge, as St. Paul says: "That your charity may more and more abound in knowledge, and in all understanding." We must not be content with good love; the apostle exhorts us to win the very best—he wishes that we may overflow with love. Knowledge is one of the gifts of the Holy Ghost, and goes before love as a handmaiden before her mistress to do her service. Now true divine love thou must have interiorly, and it shall be a mark to thee that thou hast it, if thou hast exteriorly a love for thy neighbor. For thou lovest God not, unless thou findest that thy heart loves thy neighbor; as it is written: "He that loveth not his brother, whom he seeth, how can he love God, whom he seeth not?" (I John iv, 20).

Upon love depend all of God's commandments and both the old and new testaments,—that thou shalt love God, and shalt love thy neighbor as thyself. Thou shalt have common joy with him in his good fortune, common sorrow with him in his ill fortune, "one heart and one soul" (Acts iv, 32) with him, as was the case among the whole multitude of the faithful in the time of the apostles, when all things were in common. And if thou canst not exhibit this community of feeling outwardly from lack of means, thou must yet cherish it in thy deepest soul, very unfeignedly, not half-heartedly, very intelligently—"in all understanding"—and with a ready good will to do what lies within thy power. And when thou canst do no more for thy neighbor, thou canst at least say a kindly or a gentle word to him out of a full heart.

And thy love must extend even to a perverse neighbor. Thou must lovingly and patiently suffer his wickedness. Do not fall upon him with hard words, but mercifully bear his defects. Remember that often enough men are not bad from rooted and habitual malice, but from unwariness, or from dullness of mind; or, as St. Gregory tells us, from God's allowing them to fall into sinfulness so that they may be deeply humiliated and thereby learn their own guilty weakness. As to those who are not habitual but only occasional sinners, these thou mayest easily and quickly lead to consider their sad state, to acknowledge their wickedness, and to do penance. The others obstinately cling to their vices, and even justify themselves. But all of them must thou bear with affectionately, and thereby prove the sincerity of thy love. If thou quickly sittest in judgment on thy sinful neighbor, that is a true sign that the love of God has withered up in thy soul: and some are as hasty in judging others as a man in leaping a stone wall. Be on thy guard against rash judgment; if things look bad, cover thy face with thy mantel, and blind thy eyes to the faults of others. Examine thyself very closely, and hold court over thy own shortcomings. Every thing is going wrong, children, because no one will bear patiently with his neighbors' faults for love's sake, and because no one will pity his neighbor's weakness, little considering how much of evil in men is due to feebleness of character, lack of good sense, or momentary unguardedness.

Thus must our brotherly love "more and more abound," and must be directed to all mankind as practically as lies in our power. And hereby shall we discover the genuineness of the love that is turned inwards towards God, the source and origin of our being. The knowledge and understanding in love mentioned by the apostle, is found in the orderly relation between these two loves, the inward and the outward: for the interior love in pregnant of the exterior love, which is continually being born of it: this is the kinship between the two.

When a man wishes to love God, he looks inward, and then he finds that he has a loveless and a graceless heart towards God. But he knows he must love God with all his heart: therefore he rises up in fierce condemnation of himself and he loudly laments his depravity. He in spirit sinks himself deep into hell, or at least into a terrific purgatory; and every conceivable misfortune seems to him to be due to him; and as a matter of fact, God sometimes sends much adversity upon him. Now in very truth this is all just; a man must indeed launch this condemnation against himself. But what shall we do, we poor little worms, crawling about in the dust of the earth? As soon as we feel this deep humiliation, let us say this: O merciful God, have pity on me; save me and help me; inflict such and such judgments on me, so that in spite of all the fires of purgatory, I may at last attain to the kingdom of heaven. Well, we know that without some purgatory, few saints have entered heaven, and yet if one should pray thus to be favored, I do not condemn him for it. But I say that he who has true love for God, will, while he judges himself harshly and knows full well his own defects, yet lovingly sinks down into the abyss of God's being; he will give himself up entirely to God's good pleasure, and this act he will accompany with a perfect abdication of all will of his own.

Love of God when it is true, causes total self-renunciation and the giving up of all self-will. Thus prepared, let a man fall at God's feet and beg Him to sit in judgment on him in love, so that God's holiness may be given him, and God's will be done in him and in all creatures, according to His eternal decrees, whether it may condemn him to purgatory or not,—how soon, how long, how bitter: Lord, let all be ordered according to Thy will; be I much or little in Thy sight, near to Thee or far away, let all be done to me as Thou willest. Thus must thou be glad that God's holiness shall be vindicated upon thy littleness; and if thou seest a holy man treated differently from thee, and God's majesty is shown by this one's virtue, rejoice in his good fortune as if it were thine own. Children, this is indeed true love.

O, if one has committed all the sins in the world, and now coming to the end of his life is granted such a conversion, and has thus given himself up to God's will absolutely and in perfect love, he will go straight to heaven. But no man can bestow this grace in thee, for it is God's gift alone. And as there can be no better death than one blessed with this love, so there can be no more blessed life than one spent in such a love, always more and more abounding in it, the lover finally absorbed in the Beloved.

But sins and temptations stand opposed to this love. As to temptations, these are, taken in themselves, not sinful, being only incidental to our fallen nature's evil tendencies. We must not desire them, nor induce them. But as to the pain they bring in resisting them, that we should welcome, lovingly placing our shoulders under this heavy burden. Would God have thee fight temptations till the day of judgment? Make up thy mind to do so gladly—do it out of love of suffering, and to the praise and honor of God. Every thing that one is thus called on to suffer, let him accept it as from God. And if the merit of it be given not to thyself but rather to some poor Jew or heathen whom thou hast never seen, given him for his soul's salvation, then shouldst thou thank God for it most sincerely, and be glad of it as if it were all bestowed on thyself.

Another enjoyment of love, is the sensible presence of the Beloved, and the sweetness of devotion overflowing the heart. But suppose a

man had all of that joy in every possible fulness he could desire, and
that it was now revealed to him that God would empty his soul of it
all, and give it to his deadliest enemy, what then? He must be glad of
it, and give it over with his heart's best love. Once I heard a great
friend of God say this: "I cannot do otherwise; I am under constraint
to more heartily wish my neighbor to go to heaven than myself." And
that is what I call love.

And there are many other objects of a loving heart's desire. One
would be glad of the gift of divine peace; he would be glad of a state
of life poorer than any orphan in the whole world. But I say to thee,
leave on one side thy own plans and devices; let love do thy planning,
and do thou simply go out of thyself and all that is thine in loving
abandonment to thy Beloved, resting in humility and detachment of
spirit.

One must have love abounding "more and more in knowledge, and in
all understanding;" and that does not mean simply a good way or
degree of loving but the very best. In knowledge indeed: for the prince
of this world has everywhere planted weeds among the roses, so that
the weeds often choke the roses to death, or at least greatly stunt their
growth. One must get away from dangerous company; separations are
inevitable, whether we speak of persons in communities or those who
remain outside. And this does not mean that God's friends should
become little sects among ordinary people in the world, and separated
from them. No; but they should be only separated from others by their
love of God and their virtuous lives.

The love so far treated of is the lower powers of the soul, and by it
nature is granted the enjoyment of many sweet spiritual morsels and
many drinks of the wine of Cyprus. Such was the privilege of the
disciples, whilst our Lord was personally present with them. But at
last He said: "It is expedient to you that I go" (John xvi, 7). That
is to say: If you would enjoy Me in the noblest manner, then you must
give Me up. For be assured, children, that this love in abandonment is
as much higher than the other as heaven is higher than earth. And
unto this love the apostles were now introduced. O how much happier
is the lot of those who are granted this love. Love like this consists
only in denying, not at all in agreeing; it is not possessing God in the
way the apostles had possessed Him in their Master's presence, but
possessing Him in the want of Him.

This is a kind of not knowing that is a superessential knowledge, lifted far above reasoning—superessential and super-wise. But when this process of elevating love is going forward, the soul that endures it struggles like an infant being weaned; cowardly nature, flying from God's face into the hidden corners of the soul is all forlorn and supremely disturbed. For nature is wholly unequal to this trial. To such desolation is the soul reduced, that it dare not look at itself, it seems to itself to have ceased to think, ceased to desire. Nor is the soul able to offer this agony to God—so at least it feels—and it can but cling to a state of apparently absolute unknowingness. And yet that soul loves; it renounces self for love; it dies to all objects of love that it had in those introductory steps we have already considered, assuming in this obscurity a higher love. In very truth, it is God who is now at work in the soul; it is He who loves Himself there, and is the only object of love. As to the soul, there is now nothing for it but self-renunciation, and enduring that process of new formation which is taking place in the divine obscurity, as we find it described in St. Dionysius. Poor human nature is now led in a very different way from the former one; it is the way of perfect denudation of self.

And this is not only in the interior life, but it extends to outward things also—all support, all consolation is withdrawn. Even the sacraments are often directly refused to such a soul, or they are somehow withheld, and this is done by God's own ordering. Before this visitation I would have given such a one holy communion every day—and at present would by no means do so, for God wills otherwise. The soul must now tread another path, leading upward in deep darkness. That spirit must rest in God's Spirit in a hidden stillness as if absorbed in God.

Light at last shines in that darkness, but it is seen only when the soul finds itself in complete single-minded resignation of self to God. And in that state, all multiplicity is unified. This is the day of Jesus Christ spoken of by St. Paul. Now for the first time is Christ rightly received with all the fruits of His passion and death. It is His day bright and clear, in all purification. Not that there is to Him any increase of the fruits of His passion and death; but in us the gain is wonderfully great, because we have Him in this high and noble state of holiness in a way far above forms and images of the mind; in a hidden way, most interior and most divine.

And our Lord offers an instructive illustration of this state. Before His death He allowed himself to be touched by Mary Magdalene, His feet washed, His head anointed. Not so after His death: "Jesus saith to her: Do not touch Me, for I am not yet ascended to My Father" (John xx, 17). Thus in the lower spiritual state, He allows Himself to be touched, washed, anointed by the soul He loves, to that soul's intense joy. But in the higher spiritual degree it is not so: He is now known to the soul only as He is in the bosom of His Father—He is ascended, He has disappeared with all that He is. This is what the soul finds in Christ; true day.

This was foreshown in the generation of the Son by the Father in the divine life, and the procession of the Holy Ghost from the Father and the Son in ever fruitful love. This is indeed the true day, in which true love is born in its proper way and fitting nobility of birth, all in Jesus Christ; as St. Gregory has described it. On this state a great teacher of our order thus speaks: "The light of Jesus Christ shines in our interior soul clearer than the sun in the heavens, and His light is from the interior outward, and not from the exterior inward." Children, there is herein experienced a wonderful increase of holiness, passing all calculation. It goes on not day by day, but every hour and every instant. But one in this state must watch himself very carefully, and he must labor diligently to stand his ground. That we shall do so, all of us who are true friends of God earnestly hope, namely, that we "may more and more abound" in holy love. May God, who is true love, help us to all this. *Amen.*

Self Deception, Its Cause and Its Cure

Synopsis—Sketch of a true conversion—It carries the heart upward through the gifts of the Holy Ghost—A false conversion is always tainted with self-trust—The downward course of this soul plainly traced from apparently high spirituality to open wickedness—This contrasted with the life of a truly converted man.

FIRST SERMON FOR THE TWENTY-THIRD SUNDAY AFTER TRINITY.*

Who hath delivered us from the power of darkness, and hath translated us into the kingdom of the Son of His love.—Col. i, 13.

Dear children, love of God is the beginning, middle, and end of all virtue. For its sake must all that we do be done, all that we leave undone be left undone, all that we suffer be suffered. What we do for the sake of love, be it ever so little, is great before God; what we do without love, however great it may appear to us, it appears quite otherwise to God. Therefore we should bend all our energies to grow more and more in the love of God and of our neighbor. There is our blessedness placed and nowhere else. We should beg the Holy Ghost, who is essential love, that He would light up His love within us, and make it penetrate our sinful nature with its power; for His "love is strong as death" (Cant. viii, 6). And now pay attention, children, to this: if divine love shall spring up and flourish in any man's soul, he must mark certain steps or degrees upward, and those he must little by little learn to climb. This he must do if he would reach the height of divine love. In all the degrees of love—and the Holy Ghost has many,—"love is strong as death." That means that if love shall rightly stand in a man's soul, then he must suffer much ere he can gain possession of it. And this is true in turn of acquiring each particular grade of love.

The first degree of love that God gives His friends is divine fear. It is the first gift of the Holy Ghost, all whose gifts are love, for He is essential love. This gift brings a man to the point at which he

*We have no sermon of Tauler's for the Twenty-second Sunday after Trinity.

loathes all his sin againt God's commandments and the precepts of holy Church. Now this fear stays with a man to the very end of his life. It is mixed with bitterness, for doing penance is a bitter task to beginners.

But when God sees that a man is willing to be converted to Him no matter how painful it may be, and that he goes on steadfastly, then He takes pity on him. After he has atoned for his sins with some bitterness of suffering, God puts honey in his mouth; he grants him a kindly and merciful disposition, a sweetness of charity towards others. This is a new grade of love, and is called piety, or kindly love. It makes a man's penitential works so sweet, that they no longer are a burden to him. He is now able to observe God's commandments and those of holy Church without any opposition of nature; he lives a life of happiness.

And when God sees this joyous courage, this willing devotion and love, and when He sees that this man is humble and by no means thinks that he has become perfect, He grants him the gift of knowledge in his love. This is the third love; by means of which a man is given to understand that he must turn inward to his intelligence, and that there he must overcome the tendencies and desires that incline him to sin. And now he encounters a hard task, for he is made aware of what is meant by anguish of soul. Be sure that love is sweet, but the ordeal of gaining it is a hard one: "love is strong as death."

It happens that some men, when they discover this pain of heart, coming both from without in the battle with their sins and from within in the mortification of their evil tendencies, they act right. They renounce everything whatsoever that is wrong inward and outward; they die to all that they should give up, cutting it totally off. They can be induced by nobody to give up this fight. They regard not their own pleasure nor anything else, resting not till they have found God in all things. In this conflict they need stronger help from God than in any former one, and also good advice from men as well as God's interior guidance. They fail not to receive this exterior assistance, for God never forsakes any one whose good will is given Him. His providence provides all the outward aids that are needful for their increase in virtue; for the work is His, and it behoves Him to perfect it. If we pray to Him and trust in Him—being now brought to a stand still in our progress as far as we can see,—then it is that in reality we are climbing higher in our movement towards Him.

When God's light beams in the understanding, then does the soul turn to Him in yet greater knowledge, which God grants with divine savor. Nor does the soul attribute this to itself; it gives God the glory in all its service of Him and in all its virtues, and it offers itself to God without any choice. Occasionally, however, God withdraws all His light and all His sweetness: the soul finds itself devoid of understanding, and, as it seems to it, even of grace. There is no taste in anything. It can hardly realize that it ever felt God's love. It now feels altogether forsaken, and can only throw itself in blind faith upon God's mercy, waiting sadly and patiently, till God brings about a change.

And now it is necessary that one should not complain to men of his anguish, unless a little to one's superiors and that only to show confidence in them, and submissiveness to the authorities of holy Church. And a man must continue to follow all his spiritual exercises as if they were as sweet as ever to him. Holy Job says: "If we have received good things at the hand of God, why should we not receive evil?" (Job ii, 10). This visitation the soul accepts as a punishment for its sins. By this hard way does the Holy Ghost lead upwards the soul He loves.

But all ways are good that are approved or permitted by holy Church, when followed with an upright intention. Hence let no man condemn the external works of religion saying that they are not the best; for a loving heart and a right intention make men holy in whatever good work they do. It is not the outward character of the work that measures it holiness, but the will of him that does it. Further: when one cannot do a good work, and yet has a loving desire to do it, God is content with this good will, however late we may be in making a practical beginning.

Be assured that whosoever has no such love as this, will go astray. Soon his conscience will be blinded, his sins will give him no remorse, and he will grow lukewarm and then cold in his devotional practises. He at last disregards lesser sins, is quite content with his perilous state; he is guided by the wisdom of the flesh and by his sensual appetites. If he holds a place over others, he neglects to chide them for minor offences, and tolerates their shortcomings out of false tenderness for their weakness. He yields to them that he may not displease them; he allows them unlawful relaxations and pleasures, in order to win and hold their favor. Thus does the fear of God recede from that heart. Meanwhile he is praised as a man of discretion: for he has sought men's praise, and he has found popularity. He really believes that he is as good as his friends rate him; his conscience is at peace; he even increases certain outward penances bcause they win him men's approval. But knowledge of the true state of his soul he has none. He has quite forgotten that he is obligated to die to his disorderly inclinations. And he finds the thoughts of God and holy things very tiresome. He is zealous for those external works that gain him applause, because all that he does is for men's praise. They call him a good man, and he believes them to be right. He feels quite secure of coming to a happy end. He dreads the hidden life and avoids it, for it distresses him with its sharp interior reprimand, and he will not give up his high name for holiness. Thus he falls into a treacher-ous calm of spirit, neglects thanking God for His favors, and fails to do penance for his sins.

Finally he lapses into a state of self-trust; he relies upon his penance in the past, he meditates on his good works and exaggerates their worth; and this is his comfort if any one finds fault with him for his occasional transgressions, or if his popularity begins to wane. Vanity grows stronger in him every day, outward relaxations are indulged in. Even in God's service he is full of vanity; and he does penitential works to be seen of men. But these become wearisome after a while, pious exercises grow irksome; until at last he gives them all up, and falls back on doing some good works of religion or charity to safe-guard his reputation.

And now arise against him those powerful temptations that used to overthrow him before he undertook a pious life, and conscience is gnawed with remorse. For relief, he can but practise some external penances, which avail him but little. He must enter into the depths of his soul; he must learn to know the evil tendencies there wholly uncorrected; he must completely reverse his ways of living, and devote himself to the transformation of his motives of conduct. If he does not follow that way, he falls back into his early sinfulness and soon is sunk in sensuality. He excuses himself: his temptations are irresist-ible—this is his language to his own conscience; he is sickly; he must spare himself and must have some relaxation. And all this time he manages to keep up his good name, he does pious things out of habit, he performs some works of penance.

You notice how clearly he gives reasons and makes excuses. But in reality, he has lost the clear knowledge of the difference between virtue and vice. And this is why his soul is not anxious nor his sorrow for sin sincere, nor even his confessions really valid. The man who performs good works of penance, seeking thereby to be praised by men, is a man whose conscience is blinded. Let him go on teaching and guiding others, let him be busy with works of zeal and piety, it is all profitless to himself and of no great good to others. But suppose that the reproaches of his conscience grow loud and threatening? Suppose conscience thunders at him that he is in an evil state, and his soul's salvation is in peril? What then? He hushes these voices by quoting scripture, perverting its meaning to his own purposes. Soon he is quieted; and he returns to his former perilous condition.

But what if Scripture passages assail him in turn and disquiet him, or God's light, granted him in prayer with interior thereatenings, shows him his danger? What if his self-sufficiency is thus rudely broken in on, and conscience again begins to clamor that he is not what he ought to be? What if, in addition to these warnings, certain deadly temptations to impurity attack him, or to envy, or to sloth? All in vain. He soothes his soul by saying that these are all sent him by God that he may earn more crowns in heaven. With this poor thought he struggles with his inner foes. But his false wisdom deserts him and he is left helpless. He indulges in bodily relaxations, lives in luxury, sleeps and eats and drinks and recreates himself almost like an ordinary worldling, avoiding, however, any external mortal sin.

Then his temptations grow stronger than ever before, and he is finally vanquished, falling in many ways, even before he is himself fully aware of it. And now he is in anguish lest he shall lose his good name. Interiorly, his conscience is so bad that devout practises can no longer please him; rather they disgust him. To follow divine service is intolerable unless associated with some pecuniary profit or bodily comfort.

This man has now come to that pass, that he must lapse into a life of open sinfulness, or God must grant him a new grace of conversion. God must now teach him to understand the admonitions of conscience better than he did before. It is because he would not harken to God's interior warnings, that his present awful state has come upon him. And he must have a new conversion, or fall into a state of undisguised wickedness. But that very fall is often God's chosen means. Open shame brings such men to their senses and back to God's friendship—

that, or very grievous bodily suffering and the worst kind of interior misery are necessary to restore these souls to God's trust and love.

God reveals to them their sinfulness; He imparts the grace of confidence in His mercy; that of courage to begin their spiritual life over again; to correct all evil conduct and repress evil tendencies. It is not now the contempt of men that they dread—no, they are only full of shame on account of their misdeeds against God, which He now grants them to know in all their naked wickedness; and these holy inspirations they by no means resist.

Those who do resist them, return again to their evil ways; conscience indeed makes them miserable, and yet they yield to their weaknesses and they keep on doing so. These follow after the things of the flesh and after worldly goods, seemingly happy enough, for God gives them up to their own devices. But you know, for I have often taught it to you, that before God finally abandons them, He sends them very many warnings, both interior admonitions and external reminders. If they but willed it, they could easily enough be saved.

And how is it with the sincere soul that harkens to God's warnings? He is first of all shamed and grieved for his wicked ingratitude towards God. He is absorbed in the consciousness of his sinful state He is amazed to discover how far he had gone astray in his interior soul, even in the motives of his good works, and how he actually displeased God while seeming to serve Him, so infected with vanity and human respect had been all his conduct. Full of thankfulness for his present graces, he is yet at a loss to find a penance great enough to atone for his past bad conduct. But he humbly goes back to the beginning; he acts as if he were a child new born to holy Church. He learns how to fast and watch in all prudence; he is submissive in his choice of devotions, and very humble, guided by the Church's rules and the duties of his state of life.

Meanwhile he studies the life and example of Jesus Christ most thoroughly, and with all his might he endeavors to imitate Him, patiently reading of Him in holy Scripture, in all things obedient to conscience and the directions of his spiritual adviser. To the best of his ability he conforms his spirit to that of Christ. He learns to die to every evil inner tendency, and to totally abstain from all outward defects; his daily task is to learn this lesson better and better. One danger he dreads above all others:—tepidity in fulfilling the spiritual duties of his state of life; for he knows that that was the original cause of all his delusions and sins. From these has God saved him as from a deep pit, for to save himself he was wholly powerless. He thanks God that this grace was granted him in preference to so many others.

Nor does this change remain a secret. On the contrary, the penitent soul manifests its new life by many signs:—love cannot remain idle. So does this man's love of God now come into notice; he does not spare himself; he gives himself up to all approved penitential practises, yet striving to hide them from the eyes of others. As time goes on, he is bound steadfast, for he vows to God that to the end of his days he will never again fall into lukewarmness. And his love is a prudent one, not striving to destroy nature but rather the sinfulness that rules nature and corrupts the soul: this he is determined totally to destroy.

And his love has a quality of freedom—freedom from creatures: he will tolerate no creature near God in the love of his soul but insists on having all things adjusted to God and His will. Again, his love is a speaking love; for his soul cannot be silent, but addresses all and exhorts all who are out of God's friendship. Furthermore this love is full of longing or yearning, distressed because with all its zeal for God's honor, it knows not how it can win souls to His allegiance.

Then comes to him a burning love, tending to drive the soul beyond all bounds of moderation in its zeal:—nay, even a foolish love, despising the praise of men, and doing things for God that seem to them silly. Yet again, it may happen that there is granted him a love that is all sweetness of joy in the depths of the heart.

Last of all is given that love which is unitive; it comes from intimate union with God here and hereafter; this may well be the love spoken of by the Bridegroom: "Love is strong as death" (Cant. viii, 6). To attain to this divine love, one must love very painfully, and hence the comparison with that greatest of pains, death. But can a man ever serve this fleeting world or sin without great suffering? Wherefore then shall he not willingly suffer to obtain divine love, which never passes, and never grows less in its sweetness? May God grant us to win this His love, and never to perish in everlasting death. *Amen.*

God Alone

Synopsis—Love true or false shown by inner motives—Also love selfish or disinterested—Love is tested by adversity—Also by seeming abandonment by God—The keenest pain is needed to show the best love—All other virtues flow out of love.

SECOND SERMON FOR THE TWENTY-THIRD SUNDAY AFTER TRINITY.

I sleep, and my heart watcheth.—Cant. v, 2.

The more that a loving soul is loved by God, the more restless does it become. It is a trait of love never to be content to be inactive. Love does a great work in a man; and if it does not work it is not love. The noblest part of a man is his heart, and of this, love takes possession. That heart will know no rest until it loves God and honors and thanks and praises Him perfectly. Such is its joy; for loving the Beloved is dearer to it than its own self.

Now it is necessary to distinguish between true love and false love. This is shown by the three traits of a true living and growing love. These are observed in the will, in the intention, and in the desires of the soul. For a man must will and intend, and desire nothing whatso ever, interiorly or exteriorly, except that he love God purely and exclu sively. He must refer all that he has, all that he does, to God alone; and for the reason that God is good, and that out of His goodness He made us and redeemed us by His blood. And he must thank God for the many other good things He has done us and daily continues to do us, yea, and will forever continue to do us—which spirit of thanksgiv ing is a yet better gift. Behold how love can have no rest or respite, but incessantly goes on, watching every chance to thank God and to praise Him, wishing to respond to His love for us, in however feeble a manner.

But this is not all. Our loving servitor will not only always keep God in view and love Him, but all creatures will be dear to him for God's sake. Besides, for God's sake he suffers all kinds of oppression and oppositiou. He forsakes all irregularities of life and conduct for God's ever-lasting honor; himself alone he never seeks under any pretext, whether in matters temporal or external. And by temporal things, we mean all desires likely to lead to sinful pleasures; for by nature, a man holds beautiful things dear and those that attract the senses, or in any wise minister joy to us. Mark well, that a loving soul is bounden to overcome all this with an eager zeal. The need of doing so is soon learned, if one will but carefully consider his life in the activity of the bodily senses, and in what things his affections are likely to go beyond his control.

The lover of Christ who aspires to be perfect, must differ from begin-ners in this holy love. For beginners many spiritual comforts are lawful, such as sweetnesses of devotion, and a smooth course of spiritual experience. Not so the more perfect soul; for he must seek nothing for self, no, not even what comes to him in spiritual guise. Pure love accepts nothing whatsoever for self alone; it will rest in no interior joy, nor cleave to any spiritual comfort. For this would be to put one's trust more in God's gifts than in God Himself, which is straight against upright and clean and perfect love. And it is because some men fail to practise this rightly ordered love, that God often withdraws these same gifts from them. Their souls are presently left dry, they can no longer think of God or spiritual things, and a miserable dull-ness settles upon them. This happens in order that they shall learn to fly to God in perfect abandonment of all spiritual joy, serve Him alone in faith, hope, and love, putting self to death. They must learn to suffer the loss of all spiritual taste. They must rely upon God's self alone, resting wholly in His goodness, thinking only of His boundless mercy; for out of that comes forth His gift of virtue to us and our power to accept it.

It is also a quality of purified love, that a soul shall have as faithful a love for God in this state of desolation as in the time of sensible grace. If this be not the case, then it is manifest that one sets greater store by the gift of God than by God Himself: this is to commit gluttony with God's grace. It is, to be sure, for our own gain that we are practising self-denial of joy in God's gifts; but nevertheless this must be without consciousness of self-interest. We must seek God's graces, His sweet-ness, His goodness, for an end beyond themselves, namely, to arrive by their means at the possession of the interior, spiritual good that is God's very self. He dwells in our inmost soul; and once we have gained Him there, we can come forth to the outward life of truest virtue, practising it in a spirit of detachment. Thus it is that one first gains possession of God.

Yet we must not forget that a good man may lawfully desire devotional sweetness, according to his needs, or for God's honor, or to fit him the better for the salvation of other men's souls; for these gifts make one more zealous for virtue. That is a motive of reasonable self love; and a reasonable enjoyment of any good thing, spiritual or bodily is not to be blamed.

You must also know that for a beginner in the way of love it is lawful to seek for devotional sweetness, so that he may the sooner die to all the sweetness of sin. He thus learns how good and sweet it is to seek God and Him alone, to cleave to Jesus alone, to renounce all the vanity of this earthly life, and all its sinful desires. Thus does he learn to relish God in his devout practises. But when God has thus gifted these souls with spiritual joy, after a while He lessens it; and then the time has come to enter on the way we have herein previously treated of. For while men still hanker after the devotional sentiments which are withdrawn from them, treating them as they do, as if they were the truest spiritual good, they can never attain to what is in very deed the truest spiritual good. Nor can they in that way advance a single step in true virtue. They are under self-deception; they do not really know themselves nor their sinfulness; they cannot appreciate what is or what is not permitted them; nor can they detect and resist the temptations incident to the spiriual life. Wih some of these souls the end is falling helplessly into grave sins. Now all this concerns those transitory spiritual favors, which pure and watchful love of God must not allow itself to seek after.

Listen to this: pure love must not over eagerly seek after certain eternal good things, such as the glory which shall be the heavenly reward of our good works. It is unbecoming pure love of God, it is unbecoming perfect virtue, to seek anything for itself but God alone. It loves and desires everything, all work, all rest, all suffering, with a single mind for God's glory. God gives heaven, He takes heaven away; He saves, He damns: pure love has nothing to do with all this, only hoping to be saved. Pure love has God's honor at heart and God's will: He knows best what to will and to do. Whatsoever He wills, that He loves, and His love is the best love. Yea, this loving soul, if it stand right in this case, would not cease to love God, to advance His glory, to practise His highest virtues, even if it thought (if such a thing were permitted or possible, which it is not), that He would condemn it to hell, there to punish its vices, never to forgive its sins. This thought (however practically impossible), would but stimulate it to greater virtue, for it seeks itself in nothing, it thinks only of God's eternal glory in all things: such a one thus rightly observes God's first and greatest commandment.

The contrary is the case with beginners, for their love is that of the hireling, and is mixed with anxious thoughts about the future, saying: If I could hope for no reward for my labors and penances, I would not do them. To beginners this is allowed, but not to. genuine lovers. God's first commandment says that we must love God above all things, even above ourself. Whosoever will acquire this love, let him search his inner soul, let him scrutinize his outward conduct. In whatsoever thought, word or deed he finds himself falling short of this pure love, let him heartily set about his improvement. Let him aspire constantly to attain to love true and pure. In due time thou shalt have good fruit, thou shalt practise many virtues. Act otherwise, and thou shalt remain in thy defective love until God brings thee out of it, and leads thee to watchful and living love, lest thou fallest asleep in guilty ignorance. God guide us to true love. *Amen.*

Dwelling with God

Synopsis—Christ's dwelling is His school—Its lessons are hard but yet sweet—Every creature yearns for this teaching—Discontent with created things is the divine beginning of the lesson of life—Kind feelings towards men is another divine teaching—How Elias found God in the whistling of a gentle breeze.

SERMON FOR THE FEAST OF ST. ANDREW, THE APOSTLE.

The next day John stood, and two of his disciples. And beholding Jesus walking, he saith: Behold the Lamb of God. And the two disciples heard him speak, and they followed Jesus. And Jesus turning, and seeing them following Him, saith to them: What seek you? Who said to Him: Rabbi (which is to say, being interpreted, Master), where dwellest Thou? He saith to them: Come and see.—John i. 35-39.

Three things are taught us by these words. First, the overflowing wisdom of Christ as our teacher; second, the infinite dwelling place of God's being, the foundation of all being; third, the confidence we should feel in God's invitation to seek Him in spirit, in the dwelling place of His Godhead—"Come and see,"—that we may learn wisdom at wisdom's fountain head, namely, the school of the most holy Trinity. Therefore does the Lord say, Come, O soul, and dwell with Me and in Me: come and see in order that thou mayst learn; I will enclose thee within the depths of My divine heart as in My dwelling, in which thou shalt contemplate and learn all thy eternal good.

And now consider this Master's school. Ah, my Master, (so speaks the soul) teach me how to escape the fate of the five foolish virgins. He answers: Learn of Me to be meek and humble of heart, as I once taught St. Andrew and My other disciples. Then the soul says: But, Lord, this teaching is too hard; for the cares of life, and also anger and contention, disturb my heart, so that I lose meekness of spirit. And our Master, Christ insists: "What doth it profit a man if he gain the whole world, and suffer the loss of his own soul?" (Matt. xvi, 26). It is from thoughts of thy self-interest that all thy pain of heart springs, thy tedium in spiritual exercises, thy dullness of soul: this is why thou losest meekness of spirit; this is why the Spirit of Christ, though overflowing with sweetness cannot pour comfort or joy into thy soul. His kindness cannot bear with thy bitterness, for He is sweeter than honey. Only a man that will not be beguiled by false consolations of men shall receive the sweetness of the Holy Spirit. Therefore, dear child, begin manfully, follow this Master faithfully, sink down under His eyes to the lowly virtue of humility, saying in thy heart: Lord, I am the puniest little creature that ever Thou didst create. Place thyself thus in meekness of spirit, and thou shalt duly appreciate that God is a short word but a long meaning. Diligently pursue this devout practise; for if thou wilt do so and not give it up, thou shalt soon be made aware of a wisdom hitherto quite hidden from thee.

The second teaching is about the way the soul is drawn towards the dwelling of the divine being, our Master. The longing for this is felt by all creatures. They desire their own existence only that they may find the being of God. All the activity of nature is nothing else than a search and an asking: Where is the dwelling of God? Without this the heavens and the earth would not stand. And now, dear child, why dost thou go outside thyself in this search, seeking God in the strange lands of perishable things? Thou shalt not find Him there. They all deny thee, and beckon thee to go back and away, saying: We are not God. St. Augustine says: "Lift up thy soul above thyself into eternal things, for God is there."

And mark well that God may thus be found in many ways, all variously teaching the soul about Him. First, the soul finds God its creator dwelling in holy fear, in the heights of penance and of sorrow for sin. By penance a man freely breaks his obstinate will into subjection under God's will. Learn herein to give up everything great and little, to do hard penances, to chastise thyself for having yielded to thy unbridled will. The more the soul is practised in this, the more does it find. God in itself and itself in God. Thus speaks the lover—"I will go to the mountain of myrrh, and to the hill of frankincense" (Cant. iv, 6). It is in that place of bitterness that God speaks to His beloved. It is the high place of an elevated spirit, which has changed all self satisfaction and treacherous sweetness into feelings of sharp regret for sin. It now finds only bitterness in whatsoever is not according to God's will. Then God speaks deep in the spouse's spirit: "Thou art all fair, O My love, and there is not a spot in thee" (Cant. iv, 7).

But if anyone lives according to his own will and pleasure, he finds

God indeed, but not as does the faithful soul; for God is ever against him in all his works. All that he does hurts him. He may practise bodily works of piety, but they are of little help, unless the rebellious will has first been subdued. One psalm sung by a man who can conquer his own will is many psalms sung:—that is to say, the least work that such a man does, is more acceptable to God than the greatest work of a self-willed man.

Furthermore, we find God's dwelling in the wilderness, in the burning bush: there did Moses find Him. The burning bush means that kind of a spirit in a man which withdraws him from all creatures, and which lives only in the remoteness of solitude, in the loftiness of the eternal Godhead. As the divine essense embraces the three distinct persons of the holy Trinity, so has this spirit embraced God within its three powers by the fires of divine grace, as if they were like the flames of the burning bush encircling and enwrapping God with three branches all flowering with flames.

The soul now grows in fire and light, it waxes strong in every virtue, never a day passes without steady progress; until at last it beholds God in the heavenly Sion with the vision of an angel. Be sure that as thou findest God, thou shalt find a divine method of prayer and a divine power of virtue within thy own self, ever more today than yesterday. But whosoever would thus find God, must suppress all animal tendencies, and must go forward with Moses guided by right reason and the light of holy prudence: flesh and blood shall not possess the kingdom of God. I believe, dear children, that all your venial sins are the sudden uprisings due to the intrusion of outward things into your heart, causing now acts and again words uttered and done before you can turn on them the light of holy prudence.

And, again, God is found dwelling in the mountain within the cloud, where His finger wrote on stone the glory and the light of His commandments. The mountain is the lofty spirit in a man, and the great-hearted soul in him. He can find no content in his works or rest in his endeavors, except when he can see stamped plain upon them the mark of God's will. Then it is that the human soul does not only a human work after human ways, but a divine work according to the divinely prescribed way of God's will. Thus does the soul sanctify the body's work, whose work again is made the soul's work. And thus the work of God's will is made one with that of the soul's will. Now may the soul say with St. Paul: "I live, now not I, but Christ liveth with me"

(Gal. ii, 20). As if the apostle said: I work, now not I, but the power of the divine essence worketh in me. All this takes place within the cloud, and the everlasting splendor of the divine light: for all created light is as dark night when compared to the divine day.

God is also found in the cave, with the prophet Elias, to whom the Lord came in the desert: "He requested for his soul that he might die * * * And he cast himself down, and slept in the shadow of the Juniper tree. And behold an angel of the Lord touched him, and said to him: Arise and eat. He looked, and behold there was at his head an ash cake, and a vessel of water. And he ate and drank, and he fell asleep again. * * * And he walked in the strength of that food forty days and forty nights, unto the mount of God, Horeb. And when he was come hither, he abode in a cave" (III Kings xix, 4-9) : and there it was that he found God. But not in the "great strong wind, overthrowing mountains, and breaking the rocks in pieces;" nor in the earthquake and the fire that came afterwards, but in "the whistling of a gentle air:" in that gentle air Elias found God.

The prophet Daniel saw in a vision the turbulent hearts of worldly men tormented as the sea in a tempest: tossed about with foolish fears and hopes, joys and sorrows. These fears and hopes are what blind men's eyes, those eyes of the spirit with which they must seek and find God. The stormy wind also means bitterness of heart against our fellow Christians, by which rocks are split asunder, that is to say the noble hearts of good men are broken and their peace of soul destroyed. Dear children, suppress all such stormy feelings against others; watch your unmortified nature closely and hold it down in subjection, lest it break away from you like a team of wild horses. It is an awful sight to see men endowed by God with reason's light, and gifted by him with loving dispositions, act so uncharitably. God has given you the power of taming wild beasts, and will you not look at your own wildness and tame it down to reason's guidance? It is a shame to us before God our creator, that we are often more savage than the lions and bears of the forest. This is to live at war with our own nature; it is as if the light of God's countenance had never shined upon us (Ps. iv, 7). I say to you in all truth, that for whatever harm we work by these stormy passions God will exact heavy reckoning, whether the ruin be worked on ourselves—as often enough happens,— or upon our neighbor, who besides being injured, is frequently deprived of many graces by the sin of anger we have caused in him: for this we shall be held accountable. We have our excuses; as for example: we are now sorry that it happened; we are naturally hot tempered; we were provoked to do it. And this is all false self-justification, for nature will never learn without hard discipline how to die to itself, and must constantly be repressed. Let us act quite otherwise; let us turn to God with deeply earnest prayer, very humble self-renunciation. Then we shall find that this evil tendency can never overcome us.

We read that the prophet Elias did not find God in the fire that followed the earthquake. Fire is a thing that never says:—Enough! This figure of fire may signify a heart that can never get enough of this world's goods or of God's earthly gifts. That heart ever burns to amass more and more of those things that are not Godlike nor pure—it constantly burns with the desire of consolations and other transitory things, in which it places all its love and joy—a plain sign that God's spirit is not within it. And in this class I include those spiritual persons who repine in misfortune, as if God had never done them any good thing. They seem to exclaim: Why *did* God create me, since I am stripped of every enjoyable spiritual thing? They little dream that by this deprivation God has saved them from many a fatal fall, withdrawing them with special favor from a sinful world. Nor do they realize that if they would but live up to the standard of their holy state of life, they might well become the solid pillars of the whole Christian Church. I say to thee, dear child, that it is these ungrateful thoughts of thine that dry up the sweet streams of God's grace in its very fountain head. I implore thee by the everlasting love of God not easily to be moved from the holy path which in my heart's fervor I have shown thee—as God is my witness. If anyone of a different spirit teach thee a contrary way, I affirm before God that is only to thy loss; as St. Paul says to the Galatians: "If any one preach to you a gospel, besides that which you have received, let him be anathema" (Gal i, 9).

There came at last to Elias the "whistling of a gentle air," like the sweet breath of May: God came in that gentle air. This may mean to us that gentle spirit which lives a sweet spiritual life, following God's words with holy thoughts and speech, by which the yearning soul companies with God without loud outcry or noise of any kind. God enters the soul with a gentle whisper of love; He comes with the happiness of a shining light, steadily beaming in the spirit. Of this happiness the souls who are easily allured by the alien forms and images of the mind are not worthy, caused as these are by the intruding words of men—aye or even of fallen angels, as St. Paul said to the Galatians:—allured from the right spiritual way into which God had led them.

The right minded soul is like the bride in the Canticles, who bade the north wind to give peace to the south wind: "Come, O south wind, blow through my garden, and let the aromatical spices thereof flow" (Cant. iv, 16). The north wind is the rush of created things into the soul's garden, sowing seeds of evil in the imagination. Says Jeremias: "From the north shall an evil break forth upon all the inhabitants of the land" (Jer. i, 14); an evil wind, withering all the spiritual fruits of God's graces. The soul becomes an intolerable burden to itself when it has lost all savor of interior sweetness. Hence, from amid the desolation of the north wind of earthly thoughts, the spirit cries out "Come, O south wind, blow through my garden." This life-giving breath of God spreads a sweet perfume through all the fruits of the soul's life, the sweet perfume of God.

Finally, the soul will find God dwelling above the angels. For although these are by nature above us men, yet we must soar above them if we find God. The soul finds God in the Eternal Father, by lifting all its works above self, as the Eternal Word is joined to the Father. Thus did the high gazing soul of St. John the Evangelist see God, as he wrote: "In the beginning was the Word" (John i, 1). Thus, again St. Andrew asks very yearningly—and the loving soul asks with him:—"Master, where dwellest Thou?" St. John answers: "In the beginning was the Word." Therefore the soul does not find God in any words that do not introduce our spirit into the beginning. We must penetrate beyond all that is beneath God, and transcend all that is not God, and earnestly seek that beginning from which we have come forth: there alone is our dwelling place, and our place of refuge in eternal bliss. But this can only take place by a quick turning away from creatures to the contemplation of the divine essence, and to union with Him.

Jesus said to the two disciples: "Come and see." Come: turn away from all things which entangle you with inordinate affection, which hinder your interior peace; for you must be emptied of all activity, all understanding, all life of the senses. Come and see: that is to say turn to Me that you may know the purity of God your Lord, to which entire purity of existence your spirit must be joined; the spirit that shall comprehend the divine hiddenness must indeed be entirely purified. In this way must a man be cut off from everything that he feels to be his. St Dionysius speaks to Timothy: "Ah, dear friend, we must no longer hear the sweet, comforting words of our beloved master Paul, at least with our outward hearing, but we must give up everything, and go naked to God." This we cannot do, however, except with darkened eyes, and with our senses inwardly drawn upward to heaven, and until we come far above all knowledge into hidden unity with God. May He help us all to this. *Amen.*

Dealing Honestly with God

Synopsis—No parleying with the tempter—His suggestions not to be met by arguing but by praying—No peace nor even truce with bodily treachery—Upright treatment of God means a steadfast striving after recollection—Curious illustration from Albertus Magnus.

SERMON FOR THE FEAST OF ST. BARBARA, OR FOR THAT OF ANY VIRGIN.

Behold my beloved speaketh to me: Arise, make haste, My love, My dove, My beautiful one, and come.—Cant. ii, 10.

If any one would know whether or not he is a chosen friend, a beloved spouse of our Lord, let him mark well the signs I will give: if he has them, then without doubt he is the elect of God.

The first is, that he is at peace with our Lord in such a way that no created thing can give him interior contentment. The psalmist says: "His place is in peace" (Ps. lxxv, 3). The chosen bride of Christ must have renounced all things. Things may come and go round that soul: divine peace reigns within it. It feels itself able by Him and through Him to renounce all.

Thou mayst ask: with whom must I have peace? I answer, with the world, with the evil one, and with thy own flesh. And how? With the world, because thou carest not what the world may do to thee, give thee, or take from thee: herewith comes perfect patience. Peace with or rather from the evil one. To that a man can scarcely ever come, for the demon strives against him always; he meddles with all our doing and our not doing, for he would hinder us. Now a man can in no way resist the fiery darts of the evil one so efficaciously, as with interior, fervent prayer. This fights fire with fire, and drives the devil out headlong, with all his deceits. Therefore, as soon as one is aware of the demon's attempts to disturb his peace of soul, let him give himself up instantly to earnest prayer, and pay no heed to the temptations that assail him: nothing worse can happen to Satan. Hereby is the soul freed from his hindrance. It is related that the devil once cried out to St. Bartholomew: "Ah, thou burnest me with thy prayer, and thou hast bound me with fiery bands." The third peace is with thy own self. Alas, how can that be? I answer that thou must subject thy body to thy spirit in all things whatsoever. Thou must have the mastery over thyself, so that thy bodily appetites shall in no wise be a hindrance to thee in anything that God requires of thee. So acted the blessed saints of God. They had such a mastery over their bodies, and had so trained them to obedience, that when the spirit willed to go forward the body sprang out of the way instantly, as if the soul said: Away with thee, and give me place: for so it is related of the humble St. Francis.

But if a man shall obtain this mastery over his body, three things are needed. The first is to mortify thy body in eating, drinking, sleeping and lodging. Watch it carefully, and when thou seest it evilly inclined put a bridle on it, and scourge it with a sharp discipline. The second is this: thou must wean thyself from all thirst for worldly affairs and cares of whatever kind. Let the dead bury their dead, and do thou follow after God. Have thy friends died? Or are they come to thee—or gone from thee? Hast thou gained honors? Hast thou been given riches? If thou rejoicest or if thou mournest over such things, then thou hast not gained the mastery. A certain saint says: "What thou rejoicest over, what thou mournest over, about the same shalt thou be judged." St. Paul says: "If we be dead with Christ, we believe that we shall live also together with Christ" (Rom. vi, 8). A dead man cares not whether thou praisest or revilest him, whether thou givest him or takest away from him. A dead or a dying man will not give thee a penny for all gold and jewels, or all possible glory, joy, or friends. Once there came to an old father of the desert an own brother of his, and said to him: "Dear brother, I am in great straits, for my wagon, containing valuable goods, has fallen into the water; help me to draw it out;" and he wept pitifully and begged earnestly. The old hermit said: "Ask thy brother that still lives in the world to help thee." But he answered: "That brother is dead for a year past." And the hermit replied: "So am I dead this twenty years back." And he let him go, and concerned himself no further about his losses.

The third necessary thing is to cultivate an upright spirit in God, that is to say a continual sense of God's presence, and realization of His sovereign majesty. In very truth, if thou wilt have the creator thou must surrender the creature—it cannot be otherwise. The less of creatures, the more of the creator. Is not that an advantageous exchange? Thus says St. Augustine: "The man who is not content with possessing God, is indeed all too avaricious; what canst thou desire that thou mayst not find in Him? Think of anything that heart can desire, thou shalt find it a thousand fold in Him—love, confidence, truth, consolation, unbroken recollectedness, all this is supremely in Him, surpassing all measure and manner. Desirest thou beauty? He is the all beautiful. Riches? He is a divine treasury. Power? He is almighty. All thou mayst think of having is to be had in Him in simple perfection. The infinite, and Eternal God." Therefore expel every thought of creatures with all the comfort they may give thee. Say this: Away from me! Thou are not what I seek, or love, or think about. Say this to all honors, riches, pleasures, friendships. Away with all of you out of my soul; fly away and be gone, for I care not at all for you.

How does it happen that God is so strange to thee? Why does His blessed presence pass so quickly out of thy thoughts? There can be no other reason than that thy spirit is not free and empty; thou art encumbered with created things, and thy soul is full of their images. Says St. Bernard: "Contemplation is nothing else than the soul's cleaving to God in forgetfulness of transitory things." And St. Augustine: "Whosoever is free from earthly thoughts, cleaves to the things of God." And he says again: "O good Jesus, my soul longs unspeakably for Thy love. I beg that I may be rapt away into contemplation of Thee; that I may be absorbed in Thy cross, and in the holy sweetness of Thy humanity, so that I may withstand the vanity of this world and its allurements. I long to be lifted up into heaven, to comprehend the holy mystery of the God-head; I beg to increase in spiritual gifts, so that I may contemplate Thy divine Trinity; that I may see Thy divine will in all my works; and that I may be bound to Thee in Thy own bands of love. And if it happens that I am now and then dropped down to the first or second degree, grant that I may not have too much labor to rise upward again; and that when I see and hear earthly things, I may not dwell in them but instantly die to them, and live to Thee alone."

Be sure that if thou wert emptied of thoughts and images of creatures, thou couldst have God present to thy mind without intermission: He could not keep Himself away from thee; neither earth nor heaven could hold Him back, if He found thee emptied to receive Him. He has sworn it, He must keep His word, He must fill thy soul with Himself. But so long as creatures linger in thy soul, do what thou wilt, thou must make up thy mind to lack God. That thou deprivest Him of thyself and thy love, is a little thing; but O how great a thing does He hold back from thee, namely His own infinite, divine self. It once happened that a beautiful white woman gave birth to a child that was as black as a Moor, and this great misfortune was told to Master Albertus Magnus. Master Albertus searched about her house, and he found a picture of a Moor that this woman had gazed intently upon while pregnant with her child. "Woman," said he, "I have found the father of thy child." He proved he was right; for he took a hen, and he placed it and kept it before the picture of a hawk; and when the hen had hatched out her chickens, they all were formed like the hawk. Thus from divine pictures in the mind, all our actions are born divine; and from the pictures of creatures, all are formed after this pattern.

The fourth is this: thou shalt keep thy senses strictly under yoke, and hold a stiff restraint upon them. Thou shalt see things as if thou sawest them not. Thou shalt never open eye or ear to any vain sight or sound; thou shalt never open thy mouth except to benefit thy neighbor. Thou shalt keep hand and foot and every member in strict control, and securely guarded, so that nothing whatever may happen except what is according to God. Says St. Augustine: "May I die and may I not die." This means that we shall crush to death the depravity of nature and of the senses, so that we may enjoy the true life of the soul in God. Thus it is that God gains the mastery over us; and, without doubt, that gives us the mastery over ourselves. May God grant us this favor. *Amen.*

Holy Severity with Self

Synopsis—Gross tendencies to be hewn off by heavy strokes—More refined ones to be cut off as if with a razor—Always search for the roots of vice—Recollection is a test of true spirituality—Alternating thoughts between Christ's passion and His father's attributes.

SERMON FOR THE FEAST OF OUR LADY'S CONCEPTION.

Come over to me, all ye that desire me, and be filled with my fruits.—Eccli. xxiv, 26.

These words are applied by holy Church to our blessed Lady. Her dignity can in no wise be expressed in words, for it surpasses all human sense. Now as to our theme today, I have before this spoken of the means and methods of beginners in the way of truth, then about those of proficients, and finally of how a perfect man may reach the goal towards which he strives.

The beginner needs to cut off all gross sinfulness, such as impurity, envy, wrath and pride; also all worldly vanity, all silly amusements, all joy in creatures animate or inanimate. In one word, unless a man shall with a determined spirit and with his whole heart turn to God, so that he shall love Him in the depths of his soul and have Him in mind above all things whatsoever, and unless he shall be found thus minded at the end of his days, he shall never come to God. This must be his way and none other. All is profitless otherwise, even though a man had all knowledge, spoke with angels' tongues, gave all his goods to the poor and his body to be burned; as St. Paul teaches us (I Cor. xiii). Now how can men who wilfully enjoy creatures have their hearts turned to God? for they introduce creatures into the place that God has reserved for His own dwelling. What does God care for what a man does, as long as He is robbed of his heart and his love? What cares He for the chaff if another gets the grain?

These coarse vices are to be cut off as a man shears away his tangled beard with a sharp shears. After that, let him sharpen up his razor very keen and shave his soul clean and pure, so that no evil word or evil joy shall be left. What follows is meditation on the secret judgments of God, for no one knows how it stands with him before God's face, favorably or unfavorably. Being thus shorn of vices and humbled and terrified in God's sight, it behooves him to go on further and search for the secret evil tendencies of his fallen nature; for these linger on from force of habit. They are full of excuses; sometimes they would parade even as virtues; for pride can put on a false show; and often enough a defect we think that we have overcome still lies hidden beneath. Vanity of dress takes the name of neatness; sensual indulgence in eating and drinking is tolerated as a necessity; fierce anger and rash judgment are called zeal and keenness of judgment; utter sloth is named bodily weakness. Children, beware of self-deceit about these things; for if you are herein misled by self-conceit and high theories, your end will be evil. Then the devil will come, and he will carry you away with him, though you may have thought that all has been well with you.

Especially is there danger in hidden pride, masquerading in the guise of humility, but full of the vanity of intellect and learning. In very truth men thus affected are training under Lucifer's standard, and the higher they are in their own conceit, the lower in all reality have they fallen down. Children, bear in mind that this is not a matter of trifling importance. If you were shut up day and night in a hot room you would think it a hardship: what shall be the misery of many years in purgatory, or alas! the eternal woes of hell. Children, turn inward; for the Kingdom of God is within you. Diligently study out your place in God's judgment hall. Examine into the roots of vice, find out the whole truth about your old evil habits. If a man continues in sinful courses one or two years, so deep do the roots of vice sink into his nature even in that brief period, that he can scarcely dig them out with all the zeal he can command. Young people should be especially careful to hinder this deep rooting of sin in them. Let them begin at once to examine and to root out these tendencies, for now the task is not a hard one. Especially should one do four things with all diligence against four kinds of poisonous evil weeds.

The first of these are pleasures of the senses. One can hardly describe how greatly these hinder our progress. Good, well-meaning men, longing to be perfect, begin by absorption in devotional joy of a sensible kind; they do not strive for the simple truth of spirituality. They do not look inward; their interior life is a closed book to them. Their inner soul is to them a foreign country a thousand miles off.

External practises usurp the place of the interior life and are to them all in all. They mistake their own selves, and know not where they are in God's sight.

Then comes the discipline of the irascible faculty, which is too often very disorderly. One's anger should be directed exclusively against what is opposed to God in oneself. This faculty is a very noble one in itself, but is easily led astray by a false self-righteousness. One longs to govern others, to direct the good works and the devotions of others; and in doing so he deceives himself and others by an appearance of zeal. He is full of hard words and angry looks, and he has bullying manners.

The third harm is done by a misuse of the understanding, and this hinders many a one's progress. For some rely too much on natural reason, losing thereby the reasonable, living and essential truth. Unless a man shall confess this essential truth he cannot profit by it. A man fancies he has full knowledge, whereas his soul suffers from delusions,—the truth of things is far off. Such a one loses the precious jewel of deep seated humility, content with a false show of virtue, self-deceived and deceiving others.

The fourth obstacle to progress is pleasure in interior devotional sentiments, and this is an injury that many suffer from. They mistake joy in God's gifts for joy in God's own love. They think sweetness of devotion is God's own self. When this sweetness goes, their zeal for perfection goes. Children, take heed to this; many a thing seems to come from God's love, which in reality is but natural feeling, or caused by external devotional happenings. We are often much more influenced by spiritual self-satisfaction than we fancy. Such feelings are due to natural emotional excitability, natural fear of hell or hopes of heaven. ⋅ Be sure, children, that whosoever does not keep God uppermost in his heart's purposes shall not have Him for his end and his reward. Children, these four hindrances must be removed; we must go to work with an iron resolve to cut them totally away; we must consider to that end the stern judgment of God that awaits us and His immovable justice in inflicting chastisement.

But when these great outward hindrances have been shorn away, there yet remain in our inner-nature the roots of former bad habits, the forms and images of evil; these we must banish from the mind by the sweet form and image of our Lord Jesus Christ. The poisoned arrow must be extracted by sinking deep down beneath it the dart of

Christ's love. This love we must cultivate in our inmost souls with great devotion, so that our unworthiness may be lessened. If God gives healing properties to herbs and minerals for bodily cure, what power, think you, shall not the Son of God have for healing all the soul's ills? And this healing is applied by the thought of His blessed sufferings and death. As a man can do nothing by himself alone, so must he take refuge with the passion of Christ in holy prayer. Let him prostrate himself at the feet of the heavenly Father, and implore His aid through the merits of His well beloved Son. Let him dwell upon each point of the Lord's agony and death, begging at every step the Father's pity: for without Christ we can do nothing. This practise should become habitual: Christ's passion should never be absent from our heart, and no thoughts alien to it should ever enter there.

After that, a man should lift his very spirit on high to the company of the glorious God-head, gazing upon Him with humble fear and unspeakable longings. When one has thus placed his darkened and ignorant soul with God, the words of the book of Job come true in him: "When a spirit passed before me, the hair of my flesh stood up" (Job iv, 15). Then follows a great interior movement of the soul. The clearer the Spirit is seen as it passes over and the truer it is discerned, so much the quicker is the change wrought in the soul, and the deeper and stronger and more perfect; and the more plainly does the soul learn its own shortcomings. Then comes the Lord in a sudden flash shining in the innermost regions of the soul, making himself the master workman in the work of perfection. To Him does the soul turn over the task, hailing His glorious presence, and then sinking passive and silent into His arms, all its powers hushed. It seems to find even its own good thoughts a hindrance, so exclusive is God's control: the soul's part is simply to let God act alone. But when afterwards this close embrace has ceased to be felt so vividly, and the soul is left again to itself, then it must return to its usual exercises of devotion and follow them with all diligence.

Thus it is that one should sometimes work and sometimes rest, according as God guides him; or according as he judges that activity or quiet leads him nearer to God. If a man cannot enjoy the quiet of interior recollection, then let him exercise himself in meditation and other practices. That "being rooted and founded in charity, you may be able to comprehend, with all the saints, what is the breadth. and length, and height, and depth" (Eph. iii, 17, 18).

To attain the perfection of this, children, is impossible. But we must yearn for it with an upright intention and deep love. Our spirit should soar upward towards the height of God in His super-essential being, leaving beneath us all earthly, sensible things; confessing that God who has all might, is nevertheless unable to create any being so noble as to comprehend fully with its natural understanding the essence of the divinity. So too is the depth of the divine abyss inaccessible to our reason, and yet we can sink far down within it by a boundless lowliness of spirit. It was thus that our blessed Lady in her colloquy with the angel was silent about all the gifts God had poured into her soul, and named only her unfathomable depth of humility as having drawn Him to her: "My spirit hath rejoiced in God my Saviour. Because He hath regarded the humility of His handmaid; for behold from henceforth all generations shall call me blessed" (Luke i, 47-48).

By the breadth of God we may understand universal love; for God pours out His love upon men in all places and lands, in all their good ways and works. In every part of the universe nothing is so close at hand as God; nothing is so universal as God; nothing is so nigh to our innermost soul as God. If one will but seek Him, he will find Him day and night in the holy sacrament, in every friend of God, in every one of His creatures. Imitate this divine breadth with great diligence and interior zeal; disencumber thyself of all things else but God. Give thyself up with all thy soul's powers to God's presence within thee. By this shalt thou win great freedom of spirit, and very high graces will be granted thee, lifting thee over all created forms and images and all created things. St. Gregory speaks of this: "If we would understand the invisible things of God, then must we transcend visible things."

The length that is of God is His eternity, having no before and after, for He is a tranquil unchangeableness. In Him all things past and future are eternally present in the divine unvarying self-contemplation. This shall a man imitate by fixing his spirit steadfastly on God, renouncing for His sake all love, all sorrow, all created things whatsoever, so that he may rest trustfully in God alone, confiding to Him all guidance. In this manner shall the invitation, "Come over to Me, all ye that desire Me, to be filled with My fruits," be accepted, and the divine generation take place in our souls. It was divinely done in our beloved and blessed Lady, to whom all men, even the most holy, must pay their homage, seeking proper place and time to serve and honor her. May we all imitate her virtues; may God grant that we shall be filled with the graces of her motherhood of the divine Son. *Amen.*

A Dying Life

Synopsis—Murmurs against the severity of the gospel refuted—Cold-heartedness towards one's fellowmen is a hindrance to perfect love of God—Some condemn their neighbor in proportion to their own fancied perfection in loving God—Another hindrance is interior gluttonous joy in sensible devotion—God's favors divert the soul from God's self—Childish folly of this fault—How a wise soul counts on mingled joy and sorrow—Example of Christ's passion.

SERMON FOR THE FEAST OF ST. STEPHEN.

Amen, amen I say to you, unless the grain of wheat falling into the ground die, itself remaineth alone. But if it die, it bringeth forth much fruit.—John xii, 24, 25.

We understand by the grain of wheat our Lord Jesus Christ Himself, Who by His death brought much fruit to all mankind, if men will but reign with Him, and if above all they are willing to live a dying life after His example. That love may indeed be called a dying love, by which a man for the love of God renouncing all gratification of the senses, all pleasures of nature, finally gives up his own will. As often as he dies to pleasure, so often does he offer his death to God, and receives living fruit in return. In so far as a man dies to himself and goes away from himself, so far does he enter into our Lord God, who is life.

Mark well, children, how this dying life is divided into three degrees. The first degree is made up of those who are moved by fear of hell and hope of heaven, mingled with some love of God: their aim is to avoid mortal sin. The love of God can rarely do its work in their souls except by meditation on hell or heaven. As to dying to natural and worldly joys, they are shocked at the very thought of it, nor do they dream of manfully assaulting their natural defects. They have little faith in the tender sentiments that flow from entire detachment from creatures: they only think of saving their skin from the whip of penance and mortification. They are self-seekers and self-lovers, looking everywhere for fleshly gratification and the vanities of the world, frightened at all bodily discomfort. Their dread even of sin comes from fear of hell fire together with the desire of enjoying heaven. Being young in God's love, they appreciate it only as a joyful love, especially as a gift whereby they shall escape hell and gain heaven. Do they meditate with much sympathy on our Lord's passion? Are they grateful to Him for His bitter death and their redemption? All this is much rather from the emotional thoughts about His bodily sufferings for their sakes, than from real appreciation that by his death he practised the highest perfection of all virtues: they dwell little upon His deep humility, intense love, and agony of sympathy for our sad lot, all in the highest degree of excellence, all to the perfect glory and praise of His Father.

Such people would begin to die to self, were they not so full of self-love: they cannot yet appreciate what is meant by being content with God alone, and to give oneself up totally to Him. Although they believe that God does all things for the best, they yet feel great bitterness in resigning themselves to His Providence; and they deem it hard that Jesus Christ should have suffered so much and should lead His followers along the same sad way of suffering. After a while they may really begin to lead a dying life, but even then they are not inclined to follow it to perfection; they addict themselves zealously to fasting, watching and other things painful to nature, little knowing what perpection means. They believe that God most esteems what is thus outwardly painful. When they find that they can suffer all this willingly, they fancy that they have attained to the highest degree of perfection. Presently they sit in judgment on all other men. They condemn other men who are really far more perfect than they are—because they do not practise external austerities, calling them rude names, saying that they know nothing of the spiritual life. Be sure to agree with them, or they will say you have got a false spirituality—everybody must agree with them or suffer condemnation. Meanwhile all that they do, all that they are, is theirs in a selfish pride of ownership: this it is that hinders their entire submission to our Lord in a universal love.

And they fail in brotherly love. They do not love all men, good and bad. Their hearts are divided, loving some and failing to love others. This causes interior unrest. In fact they are essentially self-seekers: self is their thought and self is their love. Toward their fellow Christians they are spiritually very stingy, appropriating all prayer and all devotions to their personal needs. If they do pray for others, they rate it as something wonderful and worthy of the highest reward. In short, as they enter but little into their own interior life, and have but little light about their own inerior state, their progress in the love of God and of their neighbor is very slight. They are so involved in inordinate love of self and created things, that they ever stop short at self, and are never united to any one in the bonds of wise and Christian affection.

That divine love for God and men which they should cherish fails them. They may seem to obey God's law and to be submissive to holy Church, but the law of love they do not hold to. Necessity and fear, these inspire their actions rather than deep rooted love. And since they are inwardly untrue to God, so can they not confide in Him. Their consciousness of imperfect motives—which God causes in their souls—hinders their love of Him. Hence their life-long distress, for they are full of dread, agitation, and pitiable misery. On the one hand they gaze at eternal happiness, and they dread that they will never have it; on the other hand, hell yawns open, and they tremble lest they shall go there. Nor can all their pious devotions drive out this terror of hell, so long as they have not died to self. The greater their self love, the greater their terror of hell. And yet if God our Lord does not give them their own way, they complain against Him; and they weep and sigh at any little contradiction. They spend hours in silly talk, are fond of fabulous legends, and they make their own sorrows a topic of endless conversation. They act and talk as if they had been unjustly dealt with by heaven. They reckon their works, however trifling in reality, to be of great actual merit, and take for granted God owes them a high regard. But if later on our Lord will enlighten them, they will see that they have been like some silly fool, who prizes his walking stick, as much as a noble Knight does his splendid costly sword.

All these men stand on the lowest step of the dying life. And if they do not further mortify themselves, do not better learn what is meant by a dying life, then it is to be feared that they will slip back from even this lowest place. May God guard them from this greater folly and wickedness. But now to save them God grants them great spiritual joy, and by this they are heartened to endure all the severity of penitential works. But when this comes they again dream that they have reached perfection. Once more they begin to condemn their neighbor, and set about forcing everybody to do as they do themselves— so high a point of self-conceit have they reached. Again God visits them in His mercy, for He would lead them out of their delusion, show them just what they are in very truth. He allows the evil one to picture to them the sweetness of sin. Forthwith they are tormented with sinful inclinations, whose grasp upon their thoughts they cannot shake off. Horror of the pains of hell drives them to yet greater external works of penance, and these in turn are a grievous burden, and involve intolerable toil. They are at war with self; they know not where to turn for relief; and they begin to see, although but from a distance, that they have been following a mistaken course of spiritual conduct. Now must God come once more to their help in His blessed mercy. He inspires them to plead humbly for His aid. Presently they are guided by truer principles, and are granted relief in the rightly-directed practise of good works and in a well-ordered life, but especially by properly made meditation on the passion of our Lord Jesus Christ.

The second degree of the dying life of the grain of wheat, is that of those interior touches and tastes of grace as urge a man onward to die more and more to self. In this state he longs with all his soul's powers to advance in perfection. But what if this sweet interior drawing begins to fail him? He knows that he is yet far from perfection., but, alas, he is not content to sit down and wait in all poverty of spirit. He falls into a kind of mistrust of God; he thinks God has forgotten him; he says that God will no longer help him along the road to perfection. He continually debates with himself about doing this or leaving off that, hoping thereby for some relief. If our Lord shows him a kindly face, then he feels right with God: he instantly feels so rich that he dreams he will never again be poor. If he is only free from trials, he enjoys God as if he were His particular favorite:—God is now going to stand by him in all tribulation and to enrich him with all virtues.

But our loving Lord knows how easily he may fall and how deeply, if he is left to this self-assurance. Our Lord knows that to lead him out of his present state of imperfection—and how gladly would He do it!—is to withdraw His perceptible and sensible favors from him for a time. That soul is too deeply involved in self love, in admiration of his own perfections, in the thought of his wisdom and holiness and virtue. Therefore does our Lord fetch him down again into interior destitution, mistrust of self, and humble confession that he amounts to nothing and is wholly unworthy of God's favors.

Then it is that for the first time he perceives that the blessed God had very rightly deprived him of sensible graces, for he had thought himself to be something: how clearly he now sees that he is nothing. He had always sought honor among his friends, and if his good name were assailed he had always fought for it. He prized his good name as a man does his well-loved wife. If anyone said a word against him, he looked on him as an impugner of the known truth. He longed to be praised for holiness as a plant yearns for the summer showers. He seemed to think that men's praises came from true and virtuous hearts and were messages from God. He had wandered so far away from truth, that to find it he never looked into himself. No matter how plain his defects, he esteemed himself actually to be what men said he was—he knew no other way of rating himself.

Now it is to be noted, that any man who will shake off this gross delusion, who will rise out of this unmortified state, must consider three things. First, has he earnestly labored to accept willingly all punishments inflicted on him, all backbiting, all disgrace—to gladly suffer it all for the sake of advancing in virtue? Has he bowed down humbly under all such crosses? Second, how much has he praised and thanked God for all this shame, tribulation and punishment? How kindly has he borne with his persecutors, how much real friendship has he shown them, how much affection has he had in his inmost soul for those who have done him harm? Third, has he in all sincerity and with a thankful heart, prayed to God for the welfare of his tormentors? If he has failed in these three tests, if he knows his soul to be void of these sentiments, if he feels hard and bitter in his trials, then he may be entirely sure that he lives a false life. He is still dependent on the praises of men for his peace of soul. He still lingers in a state of spiritual pride and immortification—he has not yet attained to the second degree of the dying life.

But see how our good God has the heart of a tender mother, full of pity for her wayward child; or, again, how like a skilful physician, who cures an unwilling patient by the hard medicine of letting him suffer bitter pain, till he gives up and accepts the treatment needed for perfect recovery. So does God often allow such a man to fall, so that he may at last learn and confess his own helplessness. Now there come against him temptations of flesh and of spirit, the like of which he never had before. He had thought himself a good man leading a spiritual life—and now he knows not what he is. It is out of mercy to him that God darkens his understanding: he had overmuch trusted in self-guidance. At every step he treads on sharp thorns of sinful inclinations. Finally he concludes that he is a reprobate from the face of God. Now he cries out to God; now he wails and weeps many tears. O God, he exclaims, "Why hast Thou forgotten me? And why go I mourning, whilst my enemy afflicteth me?" (Ps. xli, 10).

When at last from the sole of his feet to the top of his head, he is tormented; when he is overwhelmed with his vileness in comparison with God's holiness; when he is stricken with awful terror at finding out his rebellousness against God: then he is beside himself with the sense of his unworthiness. Misery rushes upon him and overthrows him. The result is that he finally yields to his divine guide; he gives himself up to suffer whatever God may inflict on him. He laments his sad lot with many tears, borrowing the words of holy scripture, and confesses that his sins outnumber the sands of the seashore; that he is unworthy to raise his eye toward heaven; that the wrath of the Most High is enkindled against him. If it happens that his tears are dried up, it is only to suffer a more interior anguish. On the one hand he longs to be trampled under foot of all men and totally to die to self; and yet he feels a secret uprising of very arrogant pride, and longs to assert himself over all. This inner conflict is exceedingly bitter. And he now so despises himself that he is tempted to think that it would be no dishonor to God if he killed himself. I am really of opinion that this trial sometimes enfeebles a man's mental faculties; and that he had rather suffer death than endure it any longer—if such were not against God's honor. Nevertheless all this time he feels that God's grace is yet within him. And he feels confident that in all his strange sorrows and joys and in all that may happen to him in future, he does not and will not, deliberately sin against God.

Sometimes the grace of tears is again accorded him, and he cries out to God: "Arise, why sleepest thou, O Lord? Arise, and cast us not off to the end" (Ps. xliii, 23). He asks God why He has dried up the fountains of His mercy. He invokes all the blessed angels and saints of heaven and appeals to them for pity. To the heavens he cries out: Why are you turned to brass against me? And to the earth: Why art thou hard as iron against me? He calls on the very stones to be

softened towards him and to pity him. He exclaims: Am I become
the accursed mountain of Gilboa, that neither the dew nor rain of
heavenly comfort shall ever again fall upon me? And has it come to
pass that only my single wickedness shall be able to vanquish the
invincible loving kindness of God? Has He whose property is always
to show mercy and to forgive, closed His heart against me, me alone
of all sinners in the world?

Now thus it is that God's work goes on in this second degree of the
dying life, cleansing the soul thoroughly, leading it round and round
through fire and water. It lasts until all self-importance is driven
out of the remotest corners of the spirit. The soul at last is fully
disgraced in its own eyes. It condemns itself with all sincerity. It
falls so low in its own esteem as never again to be able to return to
self-delusion. It now frankly confesses its own feebleness, past and
present. Whatever good anyone may say of it, or whatever graces
God may grant it, it will never again claim any merit. One thing
alone will it say of itself: I am a man all full of faults. Then has
such a man reached the height of this degree, and stands not far from
the door of a great grace—the bridal chamber of the heavenly Spouse,
who is our Lord Jesus Christ. When the day of his death comes
he will receive a joyous welcome from our Lord. But to reach this
degree of the dying life, as we have seen, is a severe ordeal.

We know that little trees sink short roots into the earth: we mean by
this that souls little in their own eyes, really humble hearts, are not
much attached to this world's life; their thoughts and desires are
rooted deep in heaven. These readily give up to God's decree of a dying
life. Not so the prouder spirits, the tall trees deep rooted in love of
this world. They hold on fast and long to their attachments to transitory things. Such is the case with men who are the great ones of the
earth. Many a battle must they fight against God and always lose,
many a death must they die to self, ere they come to this degree of
the dying life. All usurpation of God's rights, all excess of spirit must
be broken up, and they must languish long in the depths of painful
humiliation. At last the time comes when the Holy Ghost finds the
way cleared along which He shall draw the soul to Himself; as we
have above described.

The third degree of the dying life of the grain of wheat, belongs
only to those chosen souls who with earnest purpose struggle steadfastly forward towards perfection. Their life is one of mingled joy

and trouble. The Holy Ghost pursues them with two sorts of trouble and two sorts of joy, and these are always before their eyes. The first misery is an interior suffering. It is an overwhelming sorrow of heart felt in union with the holy Trinity, at the sight of the unspeakable wickedness of mankind, and especially the malice of bad Christians sunk in mortal sin. The other interior anguish is sympathy with the grief of soul that Jesus Christ endured in his human nature, a share of which is granted to them by our Lord. The first of the joys such a soul experiences in this degree of the dying life, is a clear contempla- tive knowledge of Christ, and an overpowering enjoyment of Him: into this state the Holy Ghost lifts the soul, in order to give it a fore- taste of all the perfect bliss that it hopes to possess with Christ in eternal life. The second joy is a participation in the happiness Christ enjoys as a man, and which the soul hopes to possess perfectly in heaven as a member of Christ and coheir of his bliss. Now although this man cannot comprehend the abyss of God's being, nevertheless he is absorbed in its joys. For he knows full well His unspeakable mercies in all their supremacy; and he feels that it is good for him to be over- whelmed with the mystery of God and not to be able to comprehend His majesty. He is glad in his dying to self to bow down in lowly reverence under God.

To this state a man can never come, except when his will has been made one with God in entire self-denial, in perfect self-abnegation. Self-love in every form and all self-will are vanquished by the inpour- ing of the Holy Ghost. And this conquest is so perfect that the Holy Ghost Himself appears to have become this man's will and to be made his power of loving; he can resemble himself and love himself no longer. Yea, even heaven is now longed for purely for the honor of God, and because Christ has merited it for him: God will give it to him as to one of his children. In this degree of the dying life a man loves all things in right order: God over all, then the blessed humanity of Christ, after that the beloved mother of Christ, and then every one of the saints in his own grade of holiness, all according to the divine gifts. And as this glorious company enters his mind, he sits down in the lowest place at the Bridegroom's marriage feast; but when the King who had invited him enters and sees him there, He says to him: "Friend, go up higher" (Luke xiv, 10).

And now this happens: he is endowed with a new life, he is en- lightened with new brightness. He manifestly beholds the secret of his own miserable weakness; he clearly sees that he himself alone is to blame for his former wickedness; neither nature, nor the world, nor the devil can be rightly accused for his sins. He now freely confesses to God, that all his very painful trials and temptations were given him only out of God's great love for him, in order that in overcoming them he might do honor to God and win more crowns in heaven. He further sees and confesses that God had led him along that sorrowful way only that he might at last have no joy in sinning, and that the causes of his baseness might be totally done away, and that he should not fall again. And, besides, he now recognizes and owns a deeper wickedness: namely, that after his conversion he had often felt in a hidden way pained at the thought that he should never again be allowed the joy of sinning. This fills his very life with anguish and repentance, realizing that he is still tainted with some remains of his former weaknesses. But even so he can and does feel very happy, knowing that God's goodness so perfectly meets his necessities and remedies them; and that on account of this alternating distress and happiness, his life may be called in very truth a dying life; that it is conformed to the life of our Lord Jesus Christ, who from beginning to end of His sojourn on earth experienced an incessant change of sorrow and joy.

It was the Son of God's sorrow, that He came down upon this earth from the heavenly throne; His joy, that He was not separated from the glory of His Father. Sorrow, that He was the Son of Man; joy, that He was and still remained the Son of God. Sorrow, that He took the form of a slave. Joy, that He was and remained the sovereign Lord of all. Sorrow, that in His humanity He was subject to death and did actually die on the cross. Joy, that He was superior to death in His God-head. Sorrow, that He was born of a mortal mother. Joy, in His eternal generation, in the bosom of God. Sorrow, that He was of time. Joy, that He was before all time and eternal. Sorrow, that being the divine Word He was yet made flesh and dwelt amongst us. Joy, that He was in the beginning with God and was God. Sorrow, that like a common sinner He was baptized by John in the Jordan. Joy, that the heavenly Father's voice proclaimed Him His beloved Son in whom He was well pleased. Sorrow, that He was tempted by the devil. Joy, that angels came and ministered to Him. Sorrow, that He often suffered hunger and thirst. Joy, that He is Himself the food of men and angels. Sorrow, that He was often wearied with labor. Joy, that He is the sweet repose of all loving hearts and all happy spirits. Sorrow, that His holy life and death shall be fruitless to so many men. Joy, that He shall be the eternal bliss of His friends. Sorrow, that He must beg a drink of water from the Samaritan woman at the well. Joy, that He gave the same woman living water to drink that she might never thirst again. Sorrow, that He must journey across the water in a ship. Joy, that when He willed it He walked over the waves dryshod. Sorrow, that with Martha and Mary He wept over Lazarus dead. Joy, that He waked Lazarus from the dead and restored him to his sisters. Sorrow, that He was fastened to a cross with nails. Joy, that from the cross he promised paradise to a robber. Sorrow, that He was tortured with thirst on the cross. Joy, that by His dying thirst He saved His elect from eternal thirst. Sorrow, that he cried: "My God, My God, why hast Thou forsaken Me?" (Matt. xxvii, 46). Joy, that with this cry of desolation He should comfort all sorrowful men. Sorrow, that He gave up the ghost and died and than was buried. Joy, that on the third day He rose again from the dead with a body all glorified.

Thus was the whole life of Jesus from the crib to the cross mingled of sorrow and joy. And this very life of His He has left as a legacy to His followers in this world, to all who would choose to lead a dying life; so that thereby they might ever be mindful of Him, and walk from the cradle to the grave as He walked. May God grant us that privilege. *Amen.*

Self Deception and Its Root

Synopsis—Remarks on Mary's dignity as Mother of God—Desire to en-joy God and creatures at the same time is the cause of all self-de-ceit—It is increased by delusions about the privileges of one's order—Comparison between the tree and the graft—Rules for choosing a father confessor.

SERMON FOR THE FEAST OF OUR LADY'S NATIVITY.

Come over to me, all ye that desire me, and be filled with my fruits.—Eccli. xxiv, 26.

This is the blessed day in which our Lady, purified and sanctified in her mother's womb, was born into this world. In her has been restored to us what was defaced and lost in the garden of Eden, namely the human soul in all its perfection, made by the heavenly Father after His own image and likeness. She was destined to cooperate with the eternal Father in the restoration of all the members of His family to their original justice. Out of His boundless mercy would God use her, to aid us to rise again from the everlasting death of sin, into which we, as far as it was possible for us to do it, had fallen.

"Come over to me, all ye that desire me, and be filled with my fruits;" that is to say, the graces that followed my birth; such are the Father's words put by holy Church into Mary's mouth, and she would herself in turn apply them to the birth of the eternal Son in the bosom of His Father, and then to that of the same Son, born of her womb into this world: she would invite us to come over to her and be filled with the fruits of that birth. All (as if to say) who desire me, let them desire the birth of my son with joyous love, and in due time they will be granted the privilege of enjoying it. Thus shall your soul be stimulated to a deeper longing. As St. Augustine says: "Lord, Thou hast made us for Thyself, and our hearts are without peace till they rest finally in Thee." This unrest of soul should every man have without ceasing; but our souls are quieted with alien births, namely joy in earthly things and in the senses. We grow content with the possession of created things, animate and inanimate, such as friendship and companionship, clothing and food—anything that ministers to our pleasures. These joys are born in us, and creatures hold the place of father to us. As long as this is with our knowledge and consent, God will not enter: the divine generation shall not be experienced by a soul preoccupied with human pleasures. It may be a mean and trifling thing that thou lovest: it is none the less enough to rob thee of the unspeakably precious good and perfect consolation of the divine birth within thy soul.

Now men will object and say that they have no love for God and no longing for Him. I answer, look within thee for the cause of this, for there alone shalt thou find it—nobody knows that so well as thyself. Do not ask me but ask thy own self wherefore thou hast neither love nor desire. Thou wouldst possess God and creatures together, and that is impossible. Joy in God and joy in creatures—if thou weepest blood thou canst not obtain these two at one and the same time. The trouble is want of perception of what creature comfort is really necessary in this life, or what use of creatures one can lawfully have in God and for God;—such things as the proper satisfaction of hunger and thirst, rest after toil, and the repose of sleep. When these are sought from inordinate appetite rather than from real necessity of nature, they are a hindrance to the birth of God within the soul. I do not say that all sense of pleasure is inordinate, for in satisfying the needs of nature, one cannot extinguish all feelings of enjoyment, for pleasure and necessary refreshment are inseparable.

But if a man wishes to place no hindrance to the divine birth, if he would cultivate an increase in his longing for God, let him keep a sharp watch on all pleasurable emotions of the senses. The less these are, the greater his progress; the more the coldness of heart goes out, the more the warmth of love comes in. Nor does this mean that a man should sink into slothful and slovenly habits, or have a stupid weakness of character. Some degenerate into this state, blindly following a routine of pious observance with little care and attention. Nor should one pester his father confessor about many of these weaknesses and self-indulgences, to which he wilfully adheres: the father confessor has no power to help him unless he fully co-operates himself. If thou goest to confession ten times a day, it will be all the same—back again shalt thou fall into defects of this kind. The fault lies in thy wilful adherance to these failings. As long as thou obstinately cleavest to creatures so long art thou shut out from beholding the face of God.

This is the teaching of holy scripture, and especially of the Gospel of Christ. Thou shalt love God above all things, says the first and greatest commandment; and our Lord tells us that unless we give up all that we possess for His sake, we are not worthy of Him. And again He warns us that not all who call out Lord! Lord! shall enter the kingdom of heaven, but only they who do His Father's will. Do you think that God will give His kingdom to those miserable creatures who have rejected His Son's most precious blood and shamed His holy life? Never believe it. If you but knew how hard God will judge such men your souls would wither up with terror. God has given His only begotten Son to be their way to Him: He is the end, He alone; and do you think He will allow Himself to be despised? Never dream of such a thing.

And never dream that thy holy order is going to take the place of the holiness thou shouldst thyself personally possess. My habit and cowl, my holy cloister and the holy company of my brethren—all that does not sanctify me: there must be in me a holy, a mortified and a recollected spirit before I can be called a holy man. That I often cry out Lord! Lord!—that I say many prayers, read many pious books, have much sacred knowledge and show outward holiness—no! no! There must be much more in me besides this. And now if thou errest in this matter, the blame is thine and not mine, for I have warned thee against the worldly heart and thy proud spirit, against thy vainglory and thy pretence of spirituality. Thou shalt be proved at last as a graft upon a tree—the fruit is according to the graft and not according to the tree. So it is not thy order but thyself that must stand the final test. Thus all thy good works are false before God if thy inner life be not true. For the divine birth is experienced in all thy powers, both inner and outer. In this sense the book of Job teaches: "In the horror of a vision by night, when deep sleep is wont to hold men, fear seized upon me, and trembling, and all my bones were affrighted: and when a spirit passed before me, the hair of my flesh stood up" (Job iv, 13-15). The horror of the vision by night is the anguish that is sure to follow attachment to created things, shaking one's bones with dread of the divine wrath; the passing of a spirit before the soul is the visitation and the judgment of God.

There are two movements of the spirit taught in the Gospel, one being that of God's Spirit into us, the other that of our spirit into God. This two-fold movement must end in God's dominating the soul.

If wood shall become fire, it must cease to be wood; if the seed becomes a tree, it ceases to be a seed. If God's Spirit shall move into ours in the fulness of His generation, then the creature must languish in us. In this sense St. Gregory speaks: "The words of the book of Job, 'the hair of my flesh stood up,' may be illustrated by the cutting off of the hair of the Levites in the old law. As the hair grows on the head and face of a man, so grows his attachment to created things in the lower and higher faculties of his mind, being rooted in his former customs; and these must be shorn entirely off with the sharp shears of holy zeal for virtue." Sharpen that shears on the hard grind stone of God's judgment, before which not so much as an idle word shall escape condemnation. The littlest distraction that is wilfully entertained, must be burnt away with an unbearable purgatory, ere one can come before God's face. But what happens when these matted and filthy locks are sheared off? They instantly begin to grow out again, and we must be ever ready with the shears of mortification again to cut them back. How wise then are those, who are so earnest that the instant any unworthy thought arises they repress it with iron resolution. This seems hard at first, but as time goes on and one is faithful and true, habit makes it very easy: what once took a heavy stroke to remove can now be blown away with a light breath of recollection.

As to one's love for his neighbor, that must be practical. And it must be universal, directed not to this or that particular person, but to all mankind, including no less the wicked than the virtuous, the poor as well as the rich. It is this that we learn of our blessed Lady's father and mother, Saints Joachim and Anna. For it is related that they divided their goods into three parts, giving one to support God's worship in the temple, another in alms to the poor, and the third they used for their own support. Be sure that the soul of a covetous man is a cesspool of all uncleanness. A true man must easily part with the mean things of this mortal life of ours. Says our Lord: "Give and it shall be given to you. * * * For with the same measure that you shall mete withal, it shall be measured to you again" (Luke vi, 38).

The shears must also be used upon an inward growth. For there are men whose souls are covered with a growth of attachments to certain pious exercises, not alone for God's sake but mainly out of the joy they have in them. The deeper parts of their souls they know nothing of; they do not dream but that they are detached and mortified men, for they do not know themselves. It were great good fortune if such a one had a true friend of God, to whose direction he would gladly subject himself, and who would show him the right way of God's Spirit. But to guide such a one no short acquaintance with him is necessary. Such a guide may well be sought over twenty miles of town and country, in order to obtain one with sufficient piety, wisdom and experience. Of course any father confessor of ordinary sound judgment will serve a good purpose, for often does the Holy Ghost speak through our confessors' mouths, even when they are but simple men and hardly realize the purport of the instruction; for their office is by divine appointment. To them we must be submissive, we must never live according to our own lights and guidance. For when our blessed Lady was a little child, did she not obey implicity her old father and mother? Was she not under the direction of the priests in the temple? And in after times, was she not subject to St. Joseph? And at the end she lived under the protection of St. John, to whose care our Lord had confided her. Let us now pray her to take us in turn under her guardianship, on this the day of her nativity; and let us beg her intercession that we may be born again with the birth of her divine Son. God help us to all these favors. *Amen.*

𝔐𝔶𝔰𝔱𝔦𝔠𝔞𝔩 𝔓𝔯𝔞𝔶𝔢𝔯

Synopsis—Remarks on the qualities of ordinary prayer—Higher states of prayer granted only to mortified souls—And the demon singles them out for his fiercest assaults—How the highest prayer is amid deep mental silence—The vision of Elias illustrates this—Invariable effect is humility and love of suffering.

SERMON FOR THE FEAST OF OUR LADY'S VISITATION, OR FOR THE OCTAVE OF HER NATIVITY.

Come over to me, all ye that desire me, and be filled with my fruits.—Eccli. xxiv, 26.

Of our blessed Lady St. Bernard writes: "We cannot praise her enough, and yet we must be silent on account of the surpassing glory of her virtues." And he elsewhere says, addressing her: "However lofty thy place in thy kinship with the deity, yet forget not thy kinship with our poor humanity: enter not so deep into the abyss of the divine nature as to become unmindful of the weakness of our human nature, which thou in thy day hast so well experienced." And there are many other praises of Mary by St. Bernard and other saints.

Now as relates to our Lady's patronage there are two classes of souls. One class prays not to her because, as they say, they cannot pray at all: or rather all their prayer is a sort of vain abandonment to God that He may deal with them and with all that concerns them according to His good pleasure. The other class earnestly and continually pray to our Lady and to the other saints, seeking their intercession in all their necessities. Now both these classes of souls may easily go astray. The first class are wrong in not fulfilling the commands of holy Church, which require them to pray. Our Lord himself taught us to pray, and left us a beautiful form of prayer: He Himself continually prayed to His Father. Such persons offer as excuse that their prayers have not been heard—and this shows their foolishness; for they would have been heard if they had asked no hurtful gift. Some things the Lord will not grant, no matter how earnestly we beg Him. St. Gregory writes: "God desires us to pray to Him. Hence be sure that He will often allow us to suffer want, so that we may be excited to pray to Him." Then God helps us because our loving trust in Him has been stimulated; and our soul is comforted by receiving help from Him.

The others may also easily go wrong, because they pray with unmortified spirits. They would have every things succeed with them just only because they pray: they do not leave the disposal of their affairs to God. Now they should indeed pray, but with real submission to God's will—let Him do as He pleases in all circumstances and about all things. You will remember how we lately said, that beginners must cut off as if with a sharp shears all foul sins; that those more advanced should exterminate their foul inclinations to sin; and that those who seem to be even more perfect, should shave off the slightest tendencies to evil.

As to these latter, the beautiful souls who have disengaged themselves from all love of created things, and turned to God with all their heart to love and serve Him alone,—these the evil spirit assails with temptations so terrible as to affright any worldling who could appreciate them. Worldlings, to be sure, have their temptations, but in a different way, for they arise from their own unmortified nature, from the humors of their flesh and blood all tainted with sin. And how shall such a one escape? By striking down his corrupt nature, and steadfastly resisting the evil one, and casting him forth: so he is defeated and gives over exciting this man's sensuality. But a perfect man has done all this long ago. He is already a mortified soul. His temptation does not come from within, but from without, except the demon may find some remnants of sinful inclination within him, as for example a tendency to anger. Upon this the evil one fastens, here he concentrates his cunning and his guile. The demon as it were throws a burr upon him, then several more burrs, some front and others back, and so on till he is all covered with burrs, that is to say with temptations. If he is inclined to anger, the evil one suggests wrathful thoughts, irritating recollections, until at last the poor man roars with rage as if he were actually beating somebody. Could he but steady himself for a moment, and prostrate himself in spirit before God in deep humility imploring His assistance, and mentally turn towards his enemies and set his soul to be reconciled and at peace, nor offer any excuses or palliations for his angry outburst, but sink down meekly into his own nothingness--if he could but do this, then, children, his defects should be instantly forgiven, and should disappear from before God's face like snow before the sun; the demon would vanish away empty handed. If he can have access to his father confessor, all this will be much facilitated. Whatsoever man acts thus wisely, will gain ground by his trial and be prepared to go higher up in the divine favor.

Now I will speak of something that does not concern everybody; and from speaking of which we poor, weak men naturally shrink, and indeed from even hearing about it, for it is high doctrine, especially to those who never lived according to it. Yet even those who are familiar with it cannot rightly explain it. The book of Job says: "A spirit passed before me, and the hair of my flesh stood up" (Job iv, 15). St. Gregory understands this to mean the apparition of our Lord's sacred humanity, the word spirit signifying His divinity, which is hidden from all creatures. He understands the same of the vision of Elias: "A great and strong wind before the Lord, overthrowing the mountains, and breaking the rocks in pieces: the Lord is not in the wind; and after the wind an earthquake: the Lord is not in the earthquake; and after the earthquake a fire: the Lord is not in the fire; and after the fire, the whistling of a gentle air. And when Elias heard it, he covered his face with his mantle" (III Kings, 11-13). The Lord was thus in "the whistling of a gentle air;" and children, the overthrowing of the mountains, the earthquake and the fire, these were all but preparations for the Lord. St. Gregory says: "The high mountain means proud, lofty souls; the hard rocks, mean unmortified spirits and self-conceited men, fast fixed in self-chosen spiritual ways, doing great things indeed, but all with a sense of personal proprietorship." When the Lord would come to such men as these, he sends an earthquake beforehand, turning everything within them upside down. But, alas, those who profit by this visitation are not many. The reason is that men cling to transitory things, and this is rooted in their dogged resistance to God: they rest in that, and in gratification of the senses.

In some, however, the Lord works His way, with greater or less success; and as His visitations are repeated, it seems to such a man a hundred times over—I have met many a one of them—as if he were at the point of death. Once such a man, dreading day and night that in his agony his life was about to be wrenched away from him, begged our Lord to tell him what to do and whether it was right for him to accept such a visitation at the peril of his life. Our Lord answered him: Canst thou not inwardly dare and suffer what I outwardly suffered in such inconceivable pain, in hands and feet and in all my body and limbs? Children, some men will not endure this trial: they will not rest at home in patience; they turn outward and run hither and thither in search of rest; and they never find it, for they must enter deep into their own souls and there abide in resignation. Alas, what do they suppose is the meaning of this death, which so fills them with terror? It is very wonderful. Children, if a man were as spotless as a babe fresh from the waters of baptism, and never guilty of any sin whatever, yet if he will attain to the truth of God's holiness by the shortest way, he must undergo this very turmoil of soul, this utter self-renunciation, or he will fall behind and remain there.

After the earthquake came the fire, and the Lord was not in the fire. Children, this means fiery love, devouring one's blood and marrow, and making one as it were beside himself. A certain man was so inwardly consumed with this ardent love, and indeed so strongly affected even outwardly, that he felt he would never amount to anything again— he would soon be entirely burnt up with the heat of his feelings. Another one whom I knew could no longer sleep from the burning sentiments of his soul. Only when he could lie down in the snow of a winter's day could he fall asleep—and presently the heat of his body melted the snow into a wide pool of water around him. Behold, children, how this fiery love in the spirit spreads its heat into the body: and yet in nothing of all this did the Lord come.

After that came a sweet, silent air, a soft breathing of the wind like a whisper: in that came the Lord. Children, what think you was this? —coming after the swift and strong wind, the earthquake, and the fire, and all the upheavals of poor human nature in body and soul. O what a wonderful thing must that be, to have such a preparation, and to introduce the entrance of our Lord. Be sure that unless the Lord had supported that man's natural forces with supernatural strength, then would he have sunk beneath the marvellous joy of the Lord's coming, even had he the might of a hundred men together. And yet this coming of the Lord is only a glimpse of Him. For only a glimpse was granted to Elias, and it was so dazzling that the prophet covered his head with his mantle. The cave of Elias may represent our impatience; but the door of the cave, is the grace of beholding God; and the covering of the eyes with the mantle, is to teach us that however fleeting may be the sight of God granted to the soul in this condition, it yet overwhelms it—nature cannot endure it. Children, the Lord God is there in very truth, and His presence is sweeter than honey and the honeycomb. It bears the soul away beyond the life of the senses, beyond even that of its own powers,—far away into the divine depths. As weak eyes cannot bear the sunlight, a thousand times less able is weak human nature to bear the sweetness of this experience. Dear children, whatever one may say of this, or even think about it, is wholly unlike the truth: it is as if I were to point to a heap of black coals and exclaim: Behold the bright sun that shines through all the universe. Children, it is in this manifestation that essential peace is born in the soul, that peace that surpasses every other peace.

The Spirit spoken of in the book of Job was the person of the Son of God; and the Lord that came to the prophet in the whispering of a gentle air, that was the Holy Ghost. And St. Gregory notices that: "Whereas He came to the prophet in the whisper of a gentle air, He came to the disciples on Pentecost day in the rushing of a mighty wind. And this is the reason: the disciples received Him for the outward life and benefit of the whole christian people, and hence He came to them in a public manner, striking and captivating the senses; but this was not necessary in the prophet's case, for to His spirit alone He was sent." Blessed is the man who was born to enjoy this great favor, if it be only for a single instant before his death. Yet you must understand that however high this privilege may be, it is wholly unequal to the sweetness that the soul will enjoy in eternal life hereafter—yes, it is no more than the littlest drop of water compared to the bottomless ocean.

And now how fares it with these interior souls, thus favored with newly discovered joys? They sink down into their own nothingness in a manner quite indescribable; they would be annihilated a hundred times over, (if they could be allowed so to think) for God's praise and glory, so strong is their sense of His majesty, so great is their love of His goodness. For the more they are interiorly taught of His dignity, the more do they recognize their own littleness, their very nothingness. By this sense of their own unworthiness they are so wholly stripped of self-hood, that if God willed to deprive them of their present sweetness of consolation, they would not repine, nay, they would fly from it instantly. And if they freely and deliberately wished to retain it against God's will, that would be a fault in them, and they might easily merit purgatory for it: all is not quite right with a soul thus selfishly yielding to spiritual joy.

The faculty of love in man thirsts for suffering for the sake of the beloved, however much one's reason may revolt against it. And hence these favored souls have a burning desire to suffer. The greatest joy

that God can give them is the privilege of imitating Christ in His
passion, and that in the worst blasphemies, the direst shame, and the
most dreadful agony that He endured. They thirst for the cross of
Christ: beneath that beloved cross they constantly stand, longing for
its sorrows and pains with most interior love, for it is their lover's
gibbet. In their souls, every day is the feast of the holy cross in very
deed, so sweet to them is a share in Christ's crucifixion. The gracious
form of Jesus crucified is imprinted deep on their inmost soul; in
glorious splendor does it shine within them. St. Paul was rapt into
the third heaven, and yet what was his glory? He tells us: "God
forbid that I should glory, save in the cross of our Lord Jesus Christ"
(Gal. vi, 14). And thus speaks the holy man Job: "My soul rather
chooseth hanging, and my bones death" (Job vii, 15). Of all the
favors God had bestowed on him, this was the one he chose in preference to the others. To the soul that we have been considering, hanging
on the cross is indeed the extremity of pain, but yet it is preferred to
every other lot, because its beloved God has hung on the cross for its
sake. And the soul's longing for suffering is now granted: God casts
upon it the most awful darkness of woe, the most terrible sense of
abandonment.

When this happens, how fares it with the soul's power of loving,
being thus ablaze with dreadful fiery love, and yet wholly deprived of
all perceptable consolation? The power of loving is now chided by the
power of reasoning in this wise: Behold, thou lover, and consider the
heritage of love bestowed on thee by thy Beloved:—thou art a soul
filled with God and a body and all natural faculties filled with pain.
And this is the very truth. And as love burns hotter and more painfully, so does this heritage become more welcome and its banquet taste
sweeter. It is the heritage promised of old by the prophets to the
friends of God. The more lovingly the heritage of suffering is cherished
by the lover, the more blissful and glorious shall be the eternal heritage
hereafter. It is what the holy martyrs longed for with sighs of love.
And the favored souls we are considering seem to themselves only now
to begin to live; and they feel like beginners in the life of perfection.
Alas that this most delightful, exceptional and perfect good gift is so
little known. Alas, that it is so commonly neglected, and that men
prefer to it the miserable enjoyments of this wretched world. May
God pity such folly, and may we ever lament it. May God direct us in
this, His chosen path of perfection, and bring us straight to the end.
Amen.

Christian Purity

Synopsis—Unchaste tendencies considered—Temptations arising from carelessness—Self-denial a safeguard—The secret springs of unchastity—Occasions arising from spiritual relationships—Precautions in dealing with the other sex.

SERMON FOR THE FEAST OF ST. AGNES, VIRGIN AND MARTYR.

The virgin thinketh on the things of the Lord, that she may be holy both in body and in spirit.—I Cor. vii, 34.

Two things are becoming to virgins, to be clean of body and clean of soul. To be unspotted in fleshly things, to be temperate in satisfying all bodily needs, as eating and drinking, sleeping and waking; to be of few words, modest in bearing, avoiding vain company and amusements, humble in outward demeanor, busy with all womanly work, diligent in penitential exercises, zealous for every kind of outward chastity; all this is what is meant by "holy in body." If any virgin dreams of safeguarding her chastity or perfecting it in any other way, she is under a delusion. For outward occasions of sin must be met and overcome by outward as well as inward safeguards; otherwise the excesses of the bodily life will sully the purity of the spirit. Yet it is plain enough, that whosoever would tame the flesh with the flesh, will not have much success: hence we shall leave the consideration of bodily purity for that of the spirit, and study how it is saved or lost, a matter which it behooves every spiritual person to attentively consider .

Purity of spirit consists of a conscience clear and unspotted, accompanied with humility. A humble conscience is a pure mind and a clean heart. A pure mind is gained by using the holy scriptures; for these furnish one with good meditations. Let the heart be busied with holy thoughts and it will soon be delivered from vain ones. You may be sure of this: the man who devotes himself to meditating the holy scriptures, will be saved from falling into gross impurity. Thus it was with St. Jerome, who says: "Love the reading of the holy scriptures, and

thou shalt not love thy fleshly inclinations—thou shalt rather despise
them." A man gains a clean heart when he banishes all desire of inordinate pleasure in creatures, especially in men and women. On the
other hand even a really pious man, may in a single unguarded moment
become so disturbed and so weakened by disorderly human affection,
as to suffer from evil thoughts for a long time. Therefore the occasions of fleshly thoughts must be avoided, under penalty of being
harmed by them. This is human nature's weakest spot; this is the
deep rooted taint of our natural concupiscence. A man must all the
days of his life struggle against this enemy—alas that so many men
seem oblivious to this, rashly and thoughtlessly acting as if they had
gained the victory over the flesh finally and forever.

No, no, dear child: if thou hast won a thousand battles over thy
unclean tendencies, lay no store by that. As long as soul and body
hang together, thou shalt have no freedom guaranteed thee against
unchaste temptations. After a hundred years of victory, of a sudden
thy trial will come upon thee. Many a good, pure heart is at last
misled and ruined, without being able to clearly know how it came
about. Nor did the stain come from some outward evil deed suddenly
done; no, not from open fleshly unchastity—although that is sometimes the case. But usually the fall is brought about by gradually
yielding to sinful desires. They get a footing, because the soul has
previously given entrance to affection for transitory things and indulged in bodily relaxations; these have darkened the understanding
and led to forgetfulness of the rules of prudence. The interior spirit of
piety is weakened, and so the fall happens. Then follows a hellish state
of despondency, with the sharp bite of the tooth of conscience to get rid
of. It is in this mood that a man, broken spirited and desperate, walks
straight into the gate of hell and is buried in eternal darkness:—like
one about to be executed for crime, and who loses all sense and reason
in abject terror of death.

This is the road of the unguarded spirit. But sometimes a fall into
impurity is permitted by God, because that alone will ground a man
in true humility. Such a one is thereby fully taught his own miserable
weakness; and, besides, he thus learns how to have pity on the weakness of other men. This is of special good to those who must subject
their intellectual pride to God's sovereign majesty, and attain to naked
poverty of spirit. To these it is necessary—and to them more than to
all others—to be guarded against the company of persons of the oppo-

site sex. The enemy of souls, who never sleeps, and whose cunning is ever ready, will allow no opportunity to escape him.

When men would cultivate an interior spirit of self-denial, entering into themselves in all singleness of heart, they should earnestly endeavor to subdue totally all evil suggestions. Let them subject all their faculties absolutely to God, resisting His grace in no manner whatsoever, giving up every remnant of self-proprietorship in all their works and thoughts: their aim must be that God's will shall prevail within them without the least opposition. Be assured that a man may arrive at such single hearted devotion to God, at such peace of soul, and even of body, that he shall be almost totally unconscious of the opposition of his lower nature. His peaceful conscience scourges him no more. He has, besides, lost the shamefacedness of our degraded nature, so that he is now returned to the happy ignorance of childhood, which does all things that nature requires, unconscious of evil tendencies. An innocent little child feels no need of caution in such things, for it has no knowledge of evil. But as knowledge increases with growth of years, so does evil inclination and the possibility of sin. And a man who has long led a life of self-denial and recollection may recover the simple modesty of childhood. He has overcome—so it seems, and is, at least for a while—the sensuality of nature to that degree, that he no longer feels a temptation of any kind against chastity, no, not even an unclean feeling in his sleep. Deadly occasions overtake him, and do him not the least injury: from every danger he goes forth free and untainted. It may come to pass that he will consider himself no more subject to sensual emotions than a dead corpse: it is possible that corrupt nature may—so it seems at least—be really dead. But let no man, no woman trust to the continuance of this condition, no matter how lofty may seem their purity. No matter how perfectly holy one may be—holy in very truth,—if he dallies with dangerous occasions, he does it at his peril. No matter how entirely dead his passions may seem, if he does not fly from dangerous association with others, his heart will be wounded with sensual pleasure; he will presently be disturbed with gross inclinations towards one or other favorite companion.

Mark well, dear children, how all this comes about, how the net of temptation gradually enwraps such a soul. First of all a pious man cherishes love for individuals on account of their graces; he is affectionately drawn to them because of their spirituality. Now this comes from a secret pleasure of heart; it seems to be a wholly spiritual feeling; it is something to thank God for; one is grateful to the object of one's affection for a new spiritual influence—as it seems to be. And if this sentiment is not forthwith banished from the soul with horror, the most deplorable results may follow. One slips into the notion that he may show these good persons some outward marks of special affection. Special kindness of manner is cultivated, words of affection are used and tender glances are exchanged with overfamiliar smiles and laughter. Then follows yet more dangerous and still closer familiarity, including the usual signs of mere carnal love; and now the heart is indeed wounded with inordinate love. If this inner hurt be not healed by immediate withdrawal from danger, a yet deeper wound is inflicted. Lust of the spirit is changed into lust of the flesh—the devil's snare will hardly fail of its victim. Sensual inclinations are likely to be followed by yet worse things. That poor soul will not easily escape the deadly penalty of trifling with danger.

One may indeed thus gradually fall into mortal sin without being aware of it; he may soon commit the worst sins of thought, making little resistence to his temptations. Behold, dear children, how even a really good man may commit all sorts of sins, if he does not avoid dangerous occasions—yea, even if he has reached the highest degree of perfect virtue. If he will not fly from danger, he stands in the same peril as he did before he began his life of perfection. He is fully in as much danger now as ever he was; never had he so great need of caution as he has now. No man dare count on being exempt from temptation. However holy he may be, he dare not say that he need not guard most carefully against eternal loss. He must stand watchfully on his guard as long as he breathes the breath of life.

Spiritual writers tell us of three snares laid for the feet of spiritual men. The first is the favor and flattery of men. The second is partiality for one's kindred, as brothers and sisters. The third is self-righteousness, by which one relies confidently on his long practise of virtue: and this causes him to be careless of danger. Furthermore, a kind of inordinate and sensual friendship grows up between persons, and then slips down into what is called particular friendship. It is a natural mutual love; they must have their recreation together, and are full of exchanges of friendliness, enquiries after each other's welfare, and the like. This will end wrong, be sure of that; and commonly enough very wickedly indeed, to the heavy burdening and misery of the conscience, especially when the parties to it are of different sexes. No right conscience can tolerate such a relationship for a moment. From it the greatest evils very often result and the deadliest shame:—dark suspicious, envy, anguish of soul, entire loss of interior peace. Hence the urgent duty of all whose office requires it, to admonish the parties to such particular friendships (especially if of different sexes), to immediately give up each other's company. This discipline is necessary for a superior's peace of conscience, as well as for the good of the persons concerned; and it will put an end to any further heartburn and temptation.

If any man will be saved from such or any other sins, let him follow St. Bonaventure's counsel; let him sit with persons of the other sex and act and talk, always as if everybody were looking on and listening: then he will do and say nothing improper. His demeanor will be the same with one as with another. And he must allow no creature any special love under whatsoever name, lest his evil passions be thereby enkindled. He must show marks of particular friendship to no one whatsoever, above all to persons of the opposite sex. He must not indulge in affectionate interviews with them, no, not even on pretext of spiritual conference. He must hold a grave demeanor, deal with them with few words, and hasten his departure from their company at the earliest possible moment.

And now, dear children, seeing that devout persons may, as I have explained, easily fall into impurity by such dangerous occasions, what must be the case with ordinary imperfect souls? We have seen how good souls become demorilized by over-confidence; words, works and thoughts at last are all unclean, because what led to sinfulness was not resolutely shunned; because they would not die to themselves, nor give up superfluities, pleasures, softness of living; and because they began to indulge their appetites. They finally fell by outward occasions. If this be the fate of an incautious good man, what shall be the ruin of a careless ordinary Christian? —self-willed, regardless of every precaution, dull and unwilling in every devout practise. Of these does the Lord speak by the prophet: "I am the Lord who search the heart, and prove the reins: who give to every one according to his way, and according to the fruit of his devices" (Jer. xvii, 10). May God have mercy on us poor sinners, and may He save us from these snares of impurity. May we appear before His face chaste and clean of soul and body, with a conscience undefiled, free from vain thoughts and cleansed from evil desires, resting in no created thing but in God alone, loving Him alone and above all things. God grant us this boon. *Amen.*

The Virginal State

Synopsis—Total freedom from vain glory is the first requisite—Kindly manners are needed—Love of suffering follows necessarily—Busy industry is demanded—The last and most necessary quality is keeping God alone in her intention.

SERMON FOR THE FEAST OF ST. AGATHA, VIRGIN AND MARTYR.

The kingdom of this world and all its pomp I have despised for love of my Lord Jesus Christ.—From the Roman Ritual.

The Church sings these words in the holy office today in the name of every bride of Christ, who has given herself up to His service to persevere in the same forever. Take notice, dear children, what peculiar qualities she should show who would be pleasing to God, be accepted by Him, and led to His eternal espousals, consummating a perpetual union between Him and her soul.

And be it observed that a virgin is not well pleasing to God, unless she despises the kingdom of this world and all its pomp. That means that she sets a watchful guard against pride, vain glory, and the favor of men. This extends not only to personal adornment, but over everything else whatsoever of this fleeting life of ours. She must give all this up for the honor of God. And the same is to be said of spiritual pride, interior vain glory; and also the outward show of piety, the parade of devout words (given forth by a worldly heart), selfish joy of heart over spiritual gifts or graces, and all sorts of spiritual self-satisfaction. Such difficulties as these do the virgins of Christ encounter, and that in many various ways. One can hardly exaggerate the hurt that is done these guileless hearts, and how by all these means the evil one endeavors to mislead them.

Another good trait is watchful guard against a different kind of pride. This is an overbearing manner towards others, arrogance, and boasting, assuming to be wise, putting on airs of prudence. And if she happens to be reproved for her faults, or anywise despised and illtreated, she defends herself hotly, instead of meekly submitting to correction and showing real humility in word and deed, while giving welcome to all efforts to correct her.

A third good trait is this. It is not enough for her to know and to avoid her faults. She must give herself up to suffer willingly all that distresses her, laboring in God's vineyard in all patience, preparing for her Spouse a deeply humbled heart, in which He alone shall be allowed to rest. God's rest is indeed in the heart of a virgin self-abased, very meek, subjected unto God and all men even unto death, if such were God's will. This self-abnegation from the inmost heart, wins from God all that the soul stands in need of, and very much more. God meets such a soul half way, bringing all His graces. He ennobles it with every dignity granted to His holy ones.

The fourth trait of a true virgin, is that she shall gladly be despised and punished and disgraced in this life, and undergo much ill treat-ment, just as the Canaanitish woman endured what she seemed to suffer from Christ. The like treatment He gives to all His elect spirits even unto our own times. If He has a special love for anyone, and if He would infuse into him special graces, then does He scourge him hard in his inner soul; and even outwardly He permits him to be trampled under the feet of all men. Evil things are uttered against him, false and intolerable charges are made against him. When this happens to Christ's virgin, let her revile her own self with the utmost sincerity, let her bow down in true humility, let her esteem her sad lot a real boon from God, of which she is by no means worthy, thank-ing Him for a gift that shows she is one of His favorites.

The fifth trait is a yet deeper humility. Christ's true virgin should despise herself in truest sincerity, suffer every adversity with absolute patience, submit to every one's caprice, and never under any circum-stance utter the least complaint. We meet with virgins who speak evil of themselves with fine words, saying: O I am only a poor sinner. But let anyone else dare to say that to them. This reveals half a heart of pride. A virgin with half-hearted humility is shown in being instantly provoked by even a single little word of contempt and beginning to defend herself. She cannot endure being made light of —— and yet she insists on being considered a humble virgin. No, my dear child; all the contempt thou dost outwardly show for thyself is mani-festly without any real foundation of humility, if thou are not willing to be shamed by thy equals, or better still, by one who is thy inferior.

That goes through the marrow; that will show whether or not thou
hast genuine humility and patience.

The sixth trait, is that Christ's virgin does not idle away her time—
she is not careless of duty or of pious exercises. With much devotion,
and with all the yearning of her heart, she meditates on the passion of
her Beloved. She loves His holy wounds. Nothing pleases her better
than to pass her time in studying the life of Jesus Christ, for whose
sake she has given up all things: no occupation seems to her more
useful. Again, it is peculiar to the virgins of Christ, that they are
diligent in labor all the days of their life; outward and inward occupations absorb them, all being done for the honor of God. They
incessantly offer prayers for the salvation of all mankind; nay, they
offer themselves up as a sacrifice to God for the sins of the common
mass of the people, good and bad together. And it may happen that
God will have His virgin spouse in a state of interior desolation; all
love for God seems gone, for every sort of joy has vanished away; not
a particle of devotional feeling remains; the soul is void, miserable and
abandoned. If in that state the virgin persist in serving God with
her old fervor, full of faith, entirely resigned to her sorrow of heart,
then indeed will God be honored in her, then is He well pleased
with her.

The seventh trait of a true virgin of Christ is in the quality of her
intention. She should see God and mean God in all she does, in all
she leaves undone. Let her disengage her soul from all outward
things. When she does good works, let her feel as if she had done
nothing; and let her think of all good works, as if she were not concerned in them but only in God. Such a virgin of Christ longs to
suffer all the shame and scandal of all men, that God's glory may be
advanced: for herself she craves neither authority nor honors. She
can in no possible way be puffed up with self-conceit, for the Holy
Ghost reigns in her. Such persons are sometimes compelled to govern
others; in which case they rule with much affection and with true
meekness. They fulfil Christ's words: "He that will be first among
you, shall be your servant" (Matt. xx, 27).

The eighth good quality of a virgin of Christ, is that she constantly
strives against all love and desire of transitory things, and all worldly
honor. But it happens that when such desires grow weak in her
heart, then is she first assailed with spiritual pride. This is a powerful sense of self-approval, often coupled with longing for the praise

of others—so strong indeed that God alone can expel it from the heart. No matter how holy any one may be, he must reckon on hard fighting to the end of life, and especially must he be prepared to resist spiritual pride. Now, although in Christ's true virgin no place is usually found for pride, avarice, hate or envy, yet will she now and then be assailed with temptation to sloth, to the vice of gluttony, and even to impurity. These vices are rooted in our flesh, and are sure to rise up to tempt us, if they are not wholly overcome. But such temptations are of great profit to Christ's virgin; for this ardent lover of God enjoys nothing but suffering, and shame, and all that is painful to her interiorly or exteriorly, and this out of tender affection for Christ. These afflictions she covets above all contemplation, before all interior sweetness. When called on to endure some evil thing for Christ's sake, she is better satisfied than if she received all the pleasure that creatures can minister. On this account the movements of the lower appetites cannot drive her into sin—she can now conceive of no joy in such things, for her will is to suffer, her desire is to be afflicted for Christ's sake, and meanwhile always to make herself acceptable to God, her divine Spouse. May God help us to gain and to hold all these traits of a true virgin of Christ. *Amen.*

Mary's Place in the Incarnation

Synopsis—God's love best shown in the conception of His Son in Mary's womb—The interior virtues of Mary—Her purity of body and soul —Her humility—How her soul experienced a mystical generation of God's Son—Close application of this event to our own interior life.

SERMON FOR THE FEAST OF THE ANNUNCIATION OF OUR BLESSED LADY.

Hail full of grace, the Lord is with thee.—Luke i, 28.

In this feast we celebrate the eternal and overflowing love of God, the Lord of lords and the Master of all, by which He had mercy on us poor men, sinful and condemned, brands of hell fire. As St. Paul says: "Who being in the form of God, thought it not robbery to be equal with God: but emptied Himself, taking the form of a servant, being made in the likeness of men, and in habit found as a man. He humbled Himself, becoming obedient unto death, even to the death of the cross" (Phil. ii, 6-8). Of such a love as this can no man rightly discourse, nor can we praise and thank God enough for it. It surpasses the power of angelic and human reason to comprehend it—that our God and our supreme Judge should become our Father, our Brother, and our Spouse. He has taken our debt and our condemnation on Himself; He has redeemed us by His bitter death; He has made us His children, giving us eternal life; He has restored us to our first high place of honor; yea more than that: He has made us like unto the angels themselves, even granting us a heavenly righteousness and a divine kinship, even nearer to God than that of the highest of the angels.

O God, all perfect Good! Who can hold back his deepest love in return for this great love of Thine—his deepest love and praise with all his powers of soul and body. And this Thy work of our redemption has made Thee lovable to us above all things—a work unimagined and unexampled, a humility without limit, a grace so wonderful and so unmerited, a gift without recall. This work of Thine quickly excites our love, sweetly draws our will, binds us to Thee gladly and firmly in all our desires. But oh! sweetest Jesus, what shall we give Thee in return for this gift, so great, so divine? Thou didst give me in my creation a soul, and that soul I ruined by sin; Thou dost now restore it to me, making me doubly indebted to Thee for its possession. And that Thou hast pledged Thy soul in the place of mine, dearest Lord Jesus, what shall I give Thee in return for that favor? Alas, if I gave my poor soul a thousand times over for Thy sake, how could that compare with Thy giving Thyself up to death for me, my Lord and my God?

Dear children, although we can never fully recompense this great love, yet we should earnestly apply ourselves to make at least some partial return by giving ourselves to Jesus. ourselves with all we are and all that we can do; as did His most beloved mother, the Blessed Virgin, out of a heart most perfectly true to Him. Therefore I will show you some illustrations of how we may rightly serve our Lord, helping you to become as it were spiritually our Saviour's mother, God granting us the grace to generate and to bring forth His divine Son. And although your holiness is too little to enable you to comprehend perfectly the mind of the angel when he said to Mary: "Hail, full of grace," yet you can gain some plain notion of how well prepared the Blessed Virgin was for the conception of the Son of God in her womb.

According to her name, Mary was rapt into God and made one spirit with Him in the three powers of her soul. And she was all moved and guided by Him, being absorbed in His blessed will, intensely devoted to His honor—moved and guided by Him as a tool in the hand of a workman. She was poor in spirit. She was lifted up to God from a fathomless humility. She was self-annihilated, willess, passive, and without any longing except for God. And it was by reason of this state of her soul that God found an entrance to her in soul and body. She was clean of spirit; for she did not cleave to any gifts of God, nor did she use them for her joy. She was clean of soul: she felt no attraction towards any created thing, but her soul was adorned with all virtues. She was clean of heart and pure of body: she was never moved to sin, being like the shining angels of heaven. Although she was the fairest among women, yet never could any man look upon her with bad desires, and this was on account of her angelic purity. She was an interior spirit: her sweet affectionate yearnings were all upward towards God, and the outgushing waves of the divine love poured down from the Holy Trinity into her soul. She was deeply recollected: all the powers of her soul were constantly employed in God's praises. She was a faithful heart: her heart was enflamed with love's fiery longings to be lost in the incomprehensible abyss of the Godhead.

Thus had she found her Beloved. She had penetrated the sovereign majesty with her sweetness; she had wounded the eternal wisdom with her comeliness; she had drawn to herself the eternal goodness with her love. Thus had God been poured into her with all His infinitude of being, and thus had He placed her over all His Kingdom. She did not live her own self, but she lived only to Him who is the life of all the living. All her beginning and ending, all her doing and not doing, was in God, and was full of purely divine intention. For she was ever united to God, turning away from His holy presence never a single instant. Hence no creature left any impression on her soul or ever entered there, for like the angels she saw all things singly in God. God alone did she find in her soul's depths, in its essence, in the inmost recesses of her spirit. Hence she was not turned outward with her soul's powers, looking for high things and multiplicity. She has ever turned inward in all single-mindedness—away from self and towards God, as God was towards her and in her. She was most perfectly and with all her faculties turned to her origin. Poor, clean, interior, Godlike, more a creature of heaven than of earth was Mary. In her spirit she was the paradise of God, God's heaven in her soul, God's palace in her body. God's light shone through and through her. Between her soul and God there was union without a medium.

Now consider that God would be born of this holy virgin in three ways, in her spirit, in her soul, and in her body. And she was not so blessed by the birth in her body as by that in her spirit, as St. Augustine says; and as our Lord in the gospel answered the woman who said: "Blessed is the womb that bore Thee, and the paps that gave Thee suck." But He said: "Yea rather, blessed are they who hear the word of God, and keep it" (Luke xi, 27, 28). Therefore had she first conceived and brought forth God in her spirit. By her purity she pleased God well; by her humility she prepared Him a fit dwelling place; by her love did she constrain God to descend into the depths of her spirit, a place all restful in the quiet silence of perfect detachment from created things. There did God unite her spirit to His, there did He utter to her His hidden Word, begetting His only begotten with unspeakable joy and love. This is the eternal generation in Mary; this is the obscure night of the spirit wherein the darkness of the human intelligence receives the dawning of the uncreated brightness. Because where the divine light shines, no created light can remain, for the night is changed into day. That means that the created light of the soul is changed into the uncreated light of eternity. Thus it happened that Mary gave over her spirit into the uncreated being of the Godhead, and her soul sank away into the depths of humility.

And now she drew down into her soul the all-lovely sweet streams of the light of eternal wisdom; for as the Father brought forth His only begotten Son in her soul, He in turn new-formed her in Himself. The Father willed that she should consent that His only begotten Son should assume human nature, and should be born of her in bodily form by the act of the Holy Ghost. From this she shrunk away out of unfeigned humility, and she answered Him fearfully in her spirit: Heavenly Father, I am not worthy. O I had rather be the handmaid of that mother of God's Son. But God willed that she herself should be that mother, and so insisted. Then did she sink into deep self-abasement; and she was given to understand that she was chosen indeed for that high motherhood—God must have her and no one else for His mother. Instantly she was encircled and enshrined in the light of the holy Trinity, and penetrated through and through with the divine glory; the arrows of divine love pierced her soul to its inmost depths; and thus was she made willing to be the mother of God.

At the same moment as she was thus absorbed in the Holy Ghost, the angel Gabriel stood before her and greeted her: "Hail, full of grace, the Lord is with thee" (Luke i, 28). But she was troubled at these great words, both on account of her true humility, and because she was yet entranced in God. But when she said: "Behold the handmaid of the Lord," then the Holy Ghost took from the virginal heart of Mary her purest blood, all on fire with the flames of divine love, and with it He created the perfect body and members of Jesus; and then He created His pure and perfect soul; and He joined body and soul together in Mary's womb. Then at the same instant the person of the Son of God, the Eternal Word, the splendor of the Father's glory, out of merciful love for us and for our eternal blessedness, joined this body and soul to Himself in unity of person. Thus "the Word was made flesh and dwelt amongst us" (John i, 14).

Now this is the third generation of God in the body of Mary, with-

out any injury to her virginal integrity. Thus she became the daughter
of the Father, the mother of the Son, the spouse of the Holy Ghost,
the queen of heaven, the empress of the world and of all created things,
the mother and intercessor of all mankind who desire her aid. 'Mary's
womb is the temple of God and His sweet place of repose as a Bridegroom in His bride chamber, rejoicing with joy in the virginal body of
His mother as in a sweet garden full of fragrant flowers, namely every
kind of virtues and graces. ;

By means of these virtues, therefore, has God changed the heaven of
the blessed Trinity into streams of honied sweetness and poured them
over all of us poor sinners. She has made the sun of justice to shine
upon us. She has reversed the curse of Eve. She has crushed the
head of the hellish serpent. This second Eve has restored by her
Child all that had been lost and ruined by the sin of the first Eve, and
she has procured us much heavenly riches of grace beside. This
is the beautiful star that was to rise out of Jacob, as foretold by Moses,
which was to shed its beams over the whole world. Therefore says
St. Bernard: "In all thy needs, lift thy eyes to this star; call on Mary,
and thou canst not despair; follow Mary, and thou canst not go astray.
By the strength of her Son she will hold thee fast and firm lest thou
shouldst fall; she will defend thee lest thou be hurt; she will bring
thee to her Son. She has power indeed, for almighty God is her
Child; she has the good will, for she is most merciful. Who can doubt
but that this Child shall honor His mother. Who can doubt that she,
in whose bosom He who is all essential love, who is the God of love
Himself, has found His happy dwelling place, shall be overflowing
with love for us."

Whosoever would go very deep into God, his origin, and would be
made more and more conscious of God's indwelling, fixed in God
in his soul's life as the rays are fixed in the sun,—such a one must
follow the example of our blessed Lady. Let him study her inner and
outer bearing towards God, and soon he will receive great help from
her in his own soul and body. Let him first turn himself away from
all transitory things, and gathering together his soul's powers, let him
transfer them into God who dwells within him, deep in the inmost
depths of his spirit. There it is that his soul's three highest powers
are centred, and there he will be made one spirit with God; there will
he be moved and guided by God. His memory will be made fruitful of
good, his understanding illuminated, his will set on fire with divine

love. To him God shall be Himself a food of the spirit, a life to the soul, a guard and defence to the body. Thus turned inward and united to God in our higher powers, we shall be made poor in spirit, clean in spirit, clean in soul and body, all our faculties working towards God in our interior life. Every work shall begin and end in God, all for God's sake alone, as we have shown was the case with Mary, God's mother.

In order that God may have our soul's powers docile in all things, they must be void of attachment to creatures, and rightly ordered towards Him, all will, all desires directed to Him alone. Thus shall a man be absorbed into the solitude of the Godhead, far above all his soul's powers; his being shall be sunk deep into the divine oneness. Therein can the divine birth be accomplished in us without hindrance; and by means of the overflowing and exceeding great gifts of God in the spirit, even the very body shall be made partaker of its blissful privilege.

That we may be blessed in this life and saved in the next, let us beg the intercession of the beloved mother of God; as St. Bernard prays: "Through thee, O thou first finder of divine grace, must we gain access to thy Son, thou mother of life and blessedness: so that for thy sake He may receive us, who by thy means was given to us. Thy purity must pay the debt of our excesses, thy humility—so pleasing to Him—must win His pardon for our vain glory; thy superabundant love must overflow on our sins and hide them from His eyes; thy marvellous fruitfulness must lend us a plentiful store of merits. O thou art our chosen queen, our mediatrix and intercessor; thou wilt commend us to thy Son, nay thou wilt answer for us before Him. O thou blessed mother, we beseech thee through the grace which thou hast found with God, through the high place of election thou hast merited, through the mercy that was born of thee,—we beseech thee to obtain that He, who by thy means condescended to share our weakness and misery, may grant us the privilege to share His blissful glory—Jesus Christ our Lord, with the Father and the Holy Ghost, praised and blessed forevermore." *Amen.*

Self Revelation

*Synopsis—Temptations are permitted to reveal to us our evil tendencies
—From the inward search we quickly pass to the study of our outward conduct—Need of a recollected spirit for these tasks—And of
frequent meditation—On Christ's passion—Deeper penetration of
soul comes in mystical prayer—Danger of deception.*

FIRST SERMON FOR THE FEAST OF THE NATIVITY OF
ST. JOHN THE BAPTIST.

John is his name.—Luke i, 63.

This is the feast of the Nativity of St. John the Baptist, and scarcely
any saint is more highly honored than he who baptized the Son of
God. The name John means one who is in grace. Children, we have
recently considered how one must prepare his soul for God's grace.

There are two human miseries to be reckoned with. One is our
inclination to sin. This is planted in nature itself ever since the fall of
our first parents. Against this we must always strive, turning away
with all our might from whatever is opposed to God's will. The other
misery arises from the first one: it is all the sorrow and pain of our
earthly existence. Now this misery we must accept willingly and
bear cheerfully. It is placed as a duty upon us by God that we follow
after our Lord Jesus Christ, who for our sins suffered the greatest
misery His whole life long.

God often allows men to be oppressed with the first misery, that of
sinful inclinations, in order that in their dire necessity they may find
themselves out. This trial teaches them joyfully to enter the way of
penance, and patiently to suffer all the misery that may happen to
them. Children, it is a blessed privilege thus to accept suffering, for
thereby one discovers his weakness and helplessness, yea even his nothingness before God. Ah, the man who should learn to walk in this
path, and who should devote himself to no other practise than gazing
down into his own helpless nothingness—in that same man would
God's grace truly be born. Dear children, man has nothing of his
own; everything he claims as his is absolutely God's, whether it be

great or little: all comes from God, nothing from man except the spoiling of God's gifts inwardly and outwardly. If you say there is aught in man, then it must be non-existence. This thought must never be absent from our heart: the wisdom of gazing down into one's own nothingness and understanding one's innate tendency,—as far as we are free to act,—to do all kinds of evil. Self-knowledge should be the aim of our busiest efforts. We should get to the bottom of our nature, study our purposes, our preoccupations, our joys. We should go over the garden of the soul searching diligently for weeds. That done, the most interior meaning of our life must be made God and nothing else.

And then thou must ponder thy outward conduct: words, works, manners and behaviour, clothes, companions, all must be scrutinized. Lament before God every shortcoming of thine each day thou livest, breathing sighs of sincere inward sorrow for thy faults and weaknesses. This secures thy forgiveness; but make sure that thy grief is deep within thy soul—a most profitable thing. Such were the interior sighs of the apostles towards God, not only for their own sins, but indeed for those of all men. When God grants a man the taste of eternity if only for an instant, there bursts forth from his heart's cave a deep groan of sorrow. Nor does this feeling rest wholly within, for it works forth into the outward senses, which are thus made the public altar of the most high God, on which are sacrificed the goats and the·oxen of sin atonement. Thus does one offer his outward, bodily flesh and blood as a recompense to God, for the immolation of His divine Son's flesh and blood on Calvary.

In this deep search for his sinfulness, one must cast himself down at God's feet in all humility. He must implore His mercy, full of hope that God will lift from him the weight of his guilt. Thus John, that is to say grace, is born unto us in the home of humility; for the lower we sink the higher we shall rise. Of this St. Bernard speaks: "All the devotional practises that one may do outwardly, are nothing in comparison with passing through the hidden valley of humiliation. In this valley meekness grows, as well as self-abandonment, quiet of soul and kindness: through it lies the straight and the true road. Whosoever treads it not goes astray, no matter how many external good works he may do. These without real humility avail nothing with God; indeed they rather arouse His wrath than gain His favor."

Children, let us consider the gospel of this feast. Zachary was a high priest whose wife was barren, and this was a grief to them. Once as he entered the holy of holies, the people remaining without,—suddenly the angel Gabriel stood before him at the altar, and announced that his wife should bring forth a son, and that he should call his name John, which means grace is in him. But Zachary hesitated to believe this message, and therefore the angel struck him dumb, so to remain till the promise was fulfilled.

Now the name Zacharias means the remembrance of God. The God thinking man it is that shall be a priest, and shall enter the holy of holies, whereas the rest of the people shall remain outside. Mark the essential thing in this priest, and also his office. The office of Christian priests is to offer up the only begotten Son of God to His heavenly Father for the salvation of the people. Now I fear that not all priests are perfect—and that is indeed manifestly the case. They stand before the people personating the Christian religion, and yet some of them are better fitted to lead men astray than to assist them; they rather enkindle God's wrath than placate it. But they do perform their priestly office as representing the holy Christian church, and it is done sacramentally; nor can any but members of the male sex validly do it. They consecrate and offer up the holy body of our Lord Jesus Christ, which none but men in priests' orders can do; for sacrifice is peculiarly a priestly office. As to the spiritual offering of God's Son to His Father, that can be done in the soul's interior shrine by women as well as by men, by night as well as by day. And it is this that we shall mean when we ask how one should enter into the holy of holies, leaving the common kind of people without.

One must enter in alone; with a deeply recollected spirit must one enter into one's own soul, leaving outside all sensible life. Thus minded shall one offer to the heavenly Father a welcome sacrifice, namely His beloved Son, with all His holy words, works, life and passion. This offering the soul makes for every desire of the heart, and into that offering it draws very affectionately all mankind:—all poor sinners and all good Christians in this life and all who are imprisoned in purgatory. Children, this is a mighty act of religion. Albertus Magnus thus tells of the high priests' function: "He entered the holy of holies bearing fire and the blood of a red calf, and with the blood he sprinkled all the golden vessels there. Then he made a bundle of sweet smelling herbs, and he laid it on the burning coals, and as it burnt it filled the room with a fragrant cloud of smoke. And it was in that cloud that God came and spoke to him."

Children, this high priest may be taken as a figure to show forth the interior man. He enters the sanctuary of his soul, bearing with him the precious and thrice glorious blood of our Lord Jesus Christ; and he bears fire with him, too; namely ardent love. And he sprinkles all the golden vessels there with that sacred blood; namely all souls of men in the state of grace, or who shall ever be in that state. And he also comforts with his offering all the poor souls in purgatory, sadly waiting for their release. Children, you cannot imagine how sweet and lovely a work this is. And meanwhile this man does not forget himself; he offers himself up to God's fatherly heart, and enters into entire agreement with the heavenly Father's will that He may do with him as He pleases, in time and in eternity.

Now some may object: if we turn thus inwards, it will happen that the figure of Jesus crucified will drop out of our mind. Dear children, I answer no. When you turn into the soul's depths, you enter the place where alone grace is born in very truth; and in that grace will appear the life and passion of our Lord, all full of love, all simply seen, and as plainly known as if His passion were taking place right before your eyes. Nor is it there seen in multiplicity, but as if I saw all of you in one simple all embracing form as of a single person—so will the events of Christ's life and death appear. One glimpse of this kind of knowledge of our Lord, is more useful to thee, than if thou shouldst spend five months in thinking about Him other ways. Now during this sort of priestly function, where a man enters alone into his soul's holy of holies and stands with all his faculties lifted up in recollection, speaking no word—in that act of spiritual priesthood the angel of God, Gabriel, is presently seen standing beside the altar gazing upon the perfection of the soul's offering. You may take the angel's name to mean the power of God, for he bears to that sacrificial soul the power to do all things in our Lord.

Then this spiritual priest makes a bundle of sweet smelling herbs, and burns them with fire, and out of the vapor of that fire God speaks to him. These are the collection of his holy virtues, especially such ones as mildness and humility. For if a man has not virtues to gather up and offer to God, virtues of the highest or lowest or middling degree, such a one's whole life is false and worthless. The fire that is enkindled in those virtues is the flame of love. From it rises the vapor and the darkness of rapture of the spirit, lasting perhaps not half an Ave Maria; and during that time God takes away thy senses and the natural use of thy reason. Then it is that God speaks to thee in very truth, as it is written: "While all things were in quiet silence, and the night was in the midst of her course, Thy almighty Word leapt down from heaven from Thy royal throne" (Wisd. xviii, 14, 15). And the book of Job says: "Now there was a word spoken to me in private, and my ears by stealth as it were received the veins of its whisper" (Job iv, 12). To the soul this is the announcement of a birth, in which, as in John's case, many souls shall rejoice. From Elizabeth the barren wife of Zachary shall the child be born: meaning a divine fulfillment of the promise of a miracle of love, a happy birth accomplished by the divine omnipotence.

And yet all this takes place in the lowest powers of the soul. And it happens sometimes, that men of mere natural intellectuality turn inwards to the natural depths of the reasoning powers with only reason's native light. They can be absorbed in an inner state of thought void of all forms and images; but they hold this place of light with all self-proprietorship, and treat it as if it were God Himself: but it is mere human nature after all. Yet in this there is more joy than in all pleasures of the senses. But when such high spirits are herein self-contained, and when they hold it all with obstinate self-will, it makes them the wickedest of mankind, and the most dangerous. How can one discover this? By the following signs: they have not attained to this transcendent interior absorption by the way of practising virtue; they have not followed the pious exercises of a holy Christian life, including the mortification of irregular appetites. They make little or nothing of such things, for they trust wholly to their false disengagement and quiet of spirit. This they have not strived after with inner and outer practical charity. They have arrived at the dismissal of inner forms and images prematurely, and without due actual practise of virtue. And now the devil intervenes; he fills them with false light and deceitful sweetness. He so misleads them that often they are eternally lost. Studying their dominant natural tendencies, such as pride, avarice or lust, the evil one draws them on to ruin by such means.

Yet they will call this interior light and their sweetness of sentiment, God's own self—it is only the work of the devil. Why cannot they perceive this? Because they are passionately attached, in all selfishness of enjoyment, to these interior emotions. This explains the unholy freedom with which they follow their natural inclinations.

Such men should be shunned more than the demon himself. Outwardly they so much resemble good men that they are not easily detected. But really right-spirited men show this difference: they have come to their interior peace by the road of common virtue. Humility, the fear of God, detachment from creatures, and mildness of manner:— all this marks their progress. They ever stand in holy fear; they feel that they dare not trust themselves in anything; a weight of sorrow for sin oppresses them; they incessantly turn to God for help. On the contrary, those who boast that they are free, are audacious spirits and inclined to quarrel. Whosoever associates with them, presently encounters bitterness and contention, and overbearing manners. They are too proud to endure contempt or anywise to be made little of. O what marvels of horror shall be seen in the next life, where men who now seem so good, shall be hemmed in straitly, and shall abide in everlasting burning. Beware, beware of this fate, I implore you.

Ah, children, turn inwardly to God, where truth is born to you, and where many great joys are granted you, and through you to all of God's Christian people. Then you shall not be racked with doubt as to whether or not you stand right with God, for you shall have this plain test, the choice of the straight or the crooked road to God. If you have trod the plain, sure road of virtuous conduct, that will be your guarantee of God's friendship, whether your perfection be in the lowest or the highest or the middle state of spiritual proficiency. And when God's joy is born in your soul, its sweetness will exceed the power of words to tell.

Dear children, no one can lead these souls astray without first entieing them from their interior recollectedness and throwing them into multiplicity: they should be left alone with God. The Lord says in the Canticles: "I adjure you, O ye daughters of Jerusalem, by the roes and the harts of the fields, that you stir not up, nor make the beloved to awake, till she please" (Cant. ii, 7). Nor should they seek counsel from those who do not understand God's ways in such things, for that kind of men may easily misdirect them; it is quite possible that thereby they may lose their state of interior union for many years together. They must keep their souls in strict custody, for they are like new wine in active ferment; so strong are the emotions of joy within them that they overcome nature, and sometimes to such a degree that blood bursts from nose and mouth. But this is in the life of the senses and is in the lower degree of union.

The angel Gabriel said of John: "He shall drink no wine nor strong drink" (Luke i, 15). This may be taken to mean, that in whomsoever this birth of God shall be accomplished, he may be led into higher degrees of holiness, and again into yet higher; for there are good and better and best ways with God. Those in the best way shall not drink aught that may make them drunk—that is to say their heads shall not be turned by the joys granted them; they shall not enjoy them with spiritual gluttony, either in contemplation or in action.

On the contrary, they shall be removed into a way that is narrow, dark and comfortless: a time comes when God seems lost and gone from them. Therein they find themselves in a state of intolerable oppression of spirit: nor can they possibly extricate themselves. Whichever way they turn, they find only deepest misery, their soul is desolate, obscure and disconsolate, for God is veiled from their gaze. To this state they must give themselves up. They must abandon themselves to the Lord, being resigned to remain upon this road as long as it shall please Him. And this they must do with as much willingness as if they felt no manner of anguish, and suffered no pain at all. It is a condition of intolerable anguish of spirit, and immense and fruitless longing for God—and yet of perfect resignation. This is in truth the perfect conversion, for which the most essentially perfect reward is reserved. Lesser degrees merit a less essential reward.

Therefore does St. Thomas teach, that great external works of religion—no matter how wonderful—never merit, taken simply in themselves and as good works, more than an accidental, that is to say a less essential reward. But when a man's spirit turns inward to God's spirit, inward to the inmost depths, stripped in all things of what is accidental, seeking God purely and simply, transcending all works and ways and methods, all reason and thought, (a state called by St. Dionysius love unreasoning and unsensible)—when a man has thus placed himself before God, his state may rightly be termed an essential conversion. It must be granted an essential reward. That reward is God Himself.

There is another conversion that may be called essential, but only in an ordinary and external meaning of the term. That is any conversion that keeps God in view with all sincerity, and only God—God for His own sake, God in Himself. But the other above-mentioned one consists in an interior presence of the soul with God, who is formless as the soul is comfortless. It is a supersubstantial drawing of the created spirit of man into the uncreated spirit of God. Oh if a man could thus be drawn into God but once in his whole life, how fortunate for him it would be. Such a man, so docile to God, so true to God amid all his desolation of spirit, He must reward with nought else than His own very self. He draws him into the divine abyss of His own happiness. That man's spirit is so immersed in God and saturated with the deity, that he loses all multiplicity in the divine unity. These are the chosen spirits whose every work on earth is divinized; and they are vouchsafed a foretaste of their eternal paradise. Upon them as a house upon its foundation stands holy Church; if they were not in Christendom, Christendom could not stand. The fact of their very existence among us, that they simply are, is of more honor and of greater benefit to holy Church than a whole world of action by other Christians. It is of them that the Lord speaks: "He that toucheth you, toucheth the apple of My eye" (Zach. ii, 8). Therefore, children, be careful not to meddle with them. May God grant us to attain to this holy state and even by the shortest way, if this may be to His praise and glory. *Amen.*

God the Light of the Soul

Synopsis—Need of looking inward rather than outward for the light of God—Corrupt nature loves created light—The first effect of divine light is to reveal the difference between the Creator and the creature—The second effect is a clear perception of God's love in Christ—Several different kinds of love generated by the light of God.

SECOND SERMON FOR THE FEAST OF THE NATIVITY OF
ST. JOHN THE BAPTIST.

This man came for a witness, to give testimony of the light, that all men might believe through him.—John i, 7.

Our holy mother the Church devotes this week to honoring St. John the Baptist. But if we praise with words, that amounts to little, for our Lord Jesus Christ has worthily praised him, as we read: "What went you out into the desert to see? A man clothed in soft garments? Behold they that are colthed in soft garments, are in the houses of kings. But what went you out to see? A prophet? Yea, I tell you, and more than a prophet. For this is he of whom it is written: Behold I send My angel before Thy face, who shall prepare Thy way before Thee" (Matt. xi, 7-10). Thus does Jesus praise John. And John also said of himself: "I am the voice of one crying in the wilderness, make straight the way of the Lord" (John i,23). Our Lord said on another occasion that he was a burning and a shining light. And our text says that he came to bear witness of the light.

Upon these last words we shall now discourse; for the light he tells us of is light essential, incomprehensible, and glorious above all other light. It shines in the most interior regions of the soul's life. But it happens that when this light begins to shine upon the soul and to stir it into life, the soul often makes a false step. It should wait patiently in the innermost interior; but instead of doing that, it all too readily turns outward and thereby reverses the right order. It will insist on running into outward religious ways, now this one and now that. Therefore the testimony of the light is given in vain, on account of the absorption of the soul in outward pious works.

"He came into His own, and His own received Him not." The soul is here described as in opposition to the light. This is a yet worse condition, for it means downright antagonism to the light, arising from worldly heartedness. Men guilty of this are like the Pharisees, of whom John said that they were the brood of vipers. They called themselves children of Abraham, and yet they were opposed to all who loved God's true light. Ah, that is a perilous position to be in. Such men hang on to the light of truth and to the holy faith by but a single thread.

Now we must realize that nature is spoiled and diseased, and of itself can do little. Therefore has God given us an aid more than natural, namely the light of grace. This is a supernatural created light, lifting the soul upwards high above itself, bestowing upon our nature all the assistance it stands in need of. There is, besides, an uncreated light which is called the light of glory and which beams in heaven alone—a divine light, yea God himself. For if we ever shall know God, it must be through God and with God—God through God; as the prophet says: "In Thy light we shall see light" (Ps. xxxv, 10).

Now God is the all essential and perfect light. He is the light that lighteneth every man that cometh into this world, shining upon all, good and bad, as the sun shines upon all creation. If men are blind to it, that is their misery. If a man were in a dark room, and could open a window wide enough to let his head be thrust out into the sunlight, he would be in the light. So may men open their souls and be presently in God's light.

Let us take notice of the first thing one should do, rightly to receive the witness of the divine light. As this light begins to beam in the lowest powers of his soul, and when it also beams in its higher faculties, a man should cut himself off from all transitory things. The lowest faculties are the concupiscible and the irascible. By the latter one rejects pain. The concupiscible power is the appetite for pleasure, and is shown in one's enjoyment of the company of his fellow men, or of personal adornment, or any other common relaxation of life. As far as necessity goes, God fully allows this appetite to be gratified. But beyond that, it is the wilderness in which God's voice sounds loud and strong, calling for detachment from all pleasures of soul and body.

In the irascible appetite, a man must be endowed with fortitude and perseverence, standing against all aversions to unpleasant things like a mountain of iron. That fits him to accept the testimony of the light. He must not be a reed shaken by the wind, nor a man clothed in soft garments, ministering to his fleshly comfort. We meet with men who are ashamed of a self-denying course of conduct; they are moved by what people say or do as a reed is tossed about by the wind—a sarcastic word, or some petty inconvenience. Ah, dear man, what harm can a scolding word do thee? Knowest thou not that the evil spirit takes advantage of thy unsteadiness?—that it is he who sways thee to the right or left, and throws thee into deep pain by trifles, or lifts thee into inordinate joy by the same? Ah, but thou art a silly man.

And God gives this testimony of the light in our higher faculties, namely in our reason or understanding, and in our will, or power of loving. Now the light in the understanding is indeed a prophet's gift to us; for a prophet is one who sees deep and far. But if the soul be lighted up with this supernatural ray, it has the farsightedness of a prophet. If one then hears some mysterious thing, the voice from the interior of the understanding witnesses to him of its right meaning.

But our Lord said of John that he was more than a prophet. And that has reference to a part of the soul wherein our natural understanding cannot enter. There it is that (if we are entirely illuminated) we see light in light; that is to say, though the interior brightness of the soul we behold most perfect light; we behold the divine light of grace shining amid the created light of our reason. This is at first in an unknown way, and as it were unconsciously. This divine depth is immeasurably beyond the power of the natural faculties to reach. For the breadth of spiritual insight is now become so divine, that there is neither mental figure nor form, nor any such thing as relation of one place to another, but a fathomless abyss. The soul seems to be so still as to be an empty voiceless void; and again its voices are like those of many waters, and threaten to swallow up all existence. This abyss is God's chosen dwelling place, far more so that in all creatures, yea even more than in heaven.

Whosoever comes into these depths finds God most truly, and he finds himself most simply and in God. From these depths God is never absent. To such a man God is present indeed; to him the sense of eternity is most real, as if he touched and tasted it, and the division between things past and things to come is lost in the divine present. Into these holy depths no natural light can penetrate, for God is the light in His chosen abode. When this divine abyss is revealed to the soul, it experiences and knows that not all the creatures that ever lived can fill its void, can satisfy its yearnings. God alone can fill that void with His divine immensity. This is the abyss of the human soul that belongs to the divine abyss, as is written: "Deep calleth on deep" (Ps. xli, 8). Whosoever shall earnestly consider this inner depth of his spirit, will soon perceive the divine light dawning therein, which will finally flood his soul's powers, both the higher and the lower ones, drawing and leading him to his source and origin. But he must closely adhere to an inner solitariness, and he must listen intently for the tones of God's voice sounding in this wilderness, leading him away into deeper and deeper solitude.

And O how waste and barren of creatures is this wilderness, into which never an ordinary thought can come, no not one. All those many learned disquisitions on the most holy Trinity—not a single one of them can enter into this most spiritual union with God, so intimate and interior, so far removed from human activity, having no ken of place or count of time, simple and indivisible. Whosoever has truly reached this state, to him it feels as if he had been there with God from all eternity, as if he were one with the eternal presence now within Him; and yet as if he had been there but one little instant, which seems to generate an eternity of being.

The shining of the light is a witness to the spirit, of how it had been in God's purpose eternally before creation as God's image in God. As St. John teaches: "In Him was life, and the life was the light of men" (John i, 4); and all that was made by Him was one life. Thus the soul learns of the mystery of how in its created life it is the same as it was in the divine idea and purpose before creation and eternally.

So long as a man has not reached the state of purification which God willed for him while he was yet uncreated and existed only in the divine idea, he cannot return again into God. Every inclination to self, every attachment to creatures, every atom of self-satisfaction everything that may stain the inmost soul with self, must vanish away. Every inordinate pleasure of soul or body, whether felt in the understanding or in the will, must be gone—it must be washed away as being an ugly spot on the spirit's cleanliness: otherwise a man cannot return again into his origin in God.

Nor is purification alone sufficient: the spirit must besides be new formed in the light of grace. Whosoever earnestly strives after this transformation, and is a man rightly converted to the interior life,

to him a great boon may be granted: even in this earthly life he may
be granted a glimpse of a perfect transformation. And this is true,
although it is also true that no one can come to God nor know Him
as He is except in eternity in the uncreated light that is God's own
self; for the prophet says: "In Thy light we shall see light" (Ps.
xxxv, 10). But whosoever often turns to God in the inmost depths of
his soul and can make himself at home there, to him many blessed
rays of light will be granted. More and more clearly will he see what
God is, more manifestly than he beholds the sun in the heavens with
his bodily eyes.

This deepest region of the spirit was in a manner known to some of
the Gentiles of old; and as they searched its depths, the knowledge
caused them to despise all transitory things. Such great philosophers
as Proclus and Plato gave a clear account of it to guide others who
knew it not. Therefore St. Augustine says that Plato has proclaimed
the first part of St. John's gospel, "In the beginning was the Word,"
as far as "There was a man sent from God." But all this the philosopher taught with words of hidden meaning. The same philosopher
gained some knowledge of the most holy Trinity. Children, all such
things came from the deep recesses of the soul, in which such men as
Plato lived, and whose stores of wisdom they had access to. Is it not
a shame and a scandal that we who are Christians, and who have such
heavenly aid, we, who are in God's grace, who enjoy holy faith and
have the blessed sacrament, is it not a shame that we should run about
like blind hens, knowing neither our own selves nor the deep things of
God within our souls?

The cause is that we scatter our hearts' love abroad in multiplicity;
and that in religious matters we are absorbed too greatly in what
appeals to the senses. We go by self-chosen ways, and these engage
us and hinder us from entering inward towards God. But, dear children, in case one happens to be inapt for deep spiritual things, let him
at any rate be faithful to ordinary devotional practices. If one may
not offer the wine of Cyprus, let him at least bring gifts of some sort
to God, even if they are cheap and common. It is the empty and the
idle spirit that the evil one overcomes. And certainly one can always
recite the five decades of the rosary with profit.

The testimony of the light is also in the other higher faculty of the
soul, that of loving. During this week, in the churches, we have sung
of John, that "he was a burning and a shining light." Now a lamp has

both light and heat. Thou mayst feel its heat without seeing the light. And if the light be in a lantern, thou canst see it only through the glass or horn. Ah, children, mark well the meaning of this light and heat. It means the wounded heart of love—that love that would lead thee into that same deep foundation place of thy soul of which we have been speaking, that thou mayst there be ravished with love, and there excite thy ardent desire of God as if thou went bending thy bow and drawing thy arrow to hit the mark in the very centre.

It also means that imprisoned love of the heart which is enchained in this deep and secret chamber of the spirit. There must thou surrender thyself to love, for thou hast no longer control over thyself; neither conscious thought, nor exercise of the faculties, nor ordinary practise of virtue now has place. And if love happens to leave thee free for a moment's thought or act, thou soon longest to be again happily enchained; but then thou must wrestle with love, implore its constraining embrace and compel it back to thee. If thou canst not frame right words, at least utter deep inner longings, as did St. Augustine: "Lord, thou hast commanded me to love Thee with my whole heart, and my whole soul, with all my mind and all my strength. Give me what thou commandest from me. Teach me to love Thee and command me what Thou wilt." If while in that state thou are so stupid as not to be able to think even thus much, at any rate, speak the words mechanically with thy mouth. But, children, this humble way is not theirs who, as before explained, enter on a false inner peace, before being well practised in virtue, acting and feeling as if all now were done and over in the work of perfection. These have not the love we speak of.

After this comes languishing love, and then what is called frantic or foolish love. And now alas, children, it strangely seems to this poor, man as if divine love were all vanished and mere natural reason were placed in control. He seems never to have been so keen in worldly wisdom as now, in such matters as buying and selling and all active affairs: and meantime he is foolish and distraught. One in this period of love, which I have called frantic or raving, may be compared to a blindfolded man with a lantern. He knows he has bright love of God within him, but he feels no manner of joy in it, though it runs riot in all his soul's powers. O how he longs for love's joy, for a feeling of love—but he cannot have it; and so he is foolish in his ways, and almost raves. Love devours the marrow of his bones, and yet gives him no comfort. If thou comest to this test of love, I beg thee to beware)

be not frantic.   Do not seek solace in excessive outward penances, which destroy thy natural forces.   Let love alone to do its terrible work in thee.   Thou darest not shrink from this holy ordeal; follow on submissively, even through storm and tempest, until God's plan is accomplished in thee.

Now some may object and say, that they will make sure of avoiding this stormy trial of love: its shame is more than they can bear, it is incompatible with their state of life.   Children, I answer that when this folly of divine love comes upon you, human ways must give place. Then in due time comes our Lord and speaks His word in thy soul, piercing it through and through—Oh, it is a word worth a hundred thousand spoken by men.   St. Dionysius says: "When the eternal word is uttered in the soul's depths, the soul being ready prepared for it and sensitive to the divine whisper in all its meaning, capable of assimiliating its meaning not in part but in all its fulness: then is the soul's most interior self made one with the same divine Word."   Nor does a man in this union lose his essentially created life.   This union did our Lord speak of: "That they all may be one, as Thou, Father, in Me, and I in Thee; that they also may be one in Us" (John xvii, 21). And so did He speak to St. Augustine: "Thou shalt be changed into Me."   But to this state of union can no man come, except by the way of this foolish degree of love.

St. John the Baptist said: "I am the voice of one crying in the wilderness, make straight the way of the Lord."   This way is in the practise of virtue.   This road is very level.   Again he says, that he is to prepare the Lord's paths.   Now these footpaths are not so level as the open and public road of the Lord, and they are harder to find and to keep.   Whosoever would go to the Lord in his deeper consciosness by the short cut through the fields, must make up his mind to suffer much; and furthermore he may easily go astray; yet this way is indeed much shorter than that of the open and common highway.   If one will but study his deeper soul carefully, his journey will be safer.   Let him be absorbed in his own faults to correct them, in God's guidance to follow it, difficult though it may seem, and dark and strange.   Whosoever behaves thus shall not be overwhelmed when opposition comes, nor altogether oppressed with anguish of soul.   Nor shall he break out into the defects to which men are liable in this journey.   But God will now lead and again drive him forward, until he has reached the depths of the interior life.

In this manner let a man smooth the way of the Lord in his spirit's relation to God and God to him. The difficulties are serious, and they are unexpected and hidden. Many souls for the sake of relief are misled into outward exercises of religion and charitable good works— holy in themselves, but unless imposed by duty, they are not now oppor- tune. To go deeper into the interior spirit is now the task, and for this one should not go outward. That is like a man starting for Rome and taking the road to Holland: the faster he walks the farther he is from his journey's end. So does a man act who travels into external devotions instead of absorbing himself in interior medita- tion:—if he is to attain a deep state of peace and recollection he must devote himself to his interior life. Perhaps after growing old in this misdirected way, these souls at last turn into the right one. But then they are weak and nerveless, and their heads cannot stand the stress of love's storm in the final trial.

And when love's storm does break on a man's spirit, then, children, let him not stop to think fretfully on his past sins or anxiously ques- tion about his humility or about anything else except this: am I rightly responsive to God's love as it does its work in me here and now? For now a man must battle with love while suffering coldness of heart and from a sense of total abandonment. Oh, let him give up to love in all fidelity of heart, stript of everything that is not purely love of God, his soul destitute and miserable for love's sake. Have deep and constant longings for God's love; have firm trust in God; keep thyself true to love and firm in love. In due time thou shalt be granted in one hour as many graces as in another way thou wouldst acquire in a lifetime.

Especially cherish firm trust in God's love: if that weakens, thy longing for God sinks away, and the hidden love is soon quenched within thee. Be sure that if thou dost lack this sign, namely con- fidence in love's final rescue of thy distressed soul, then all other signs together are deceitful—thou must totally fail. This is the testimony of the true light. The demon will leave all else, if only he can unsettle thy confidence. He will even leave thee a treacherous show of love itself, if only thou wilt give up this true witness of genuine love,— confidence in God's love during the time of desolation of spirit.

If one now questions as to whether or not he has true love, let him search deep in his soul and ever deeper, and light will be granted him to know how he stands towards this degree of love. All the harm that can befall thee is in this: thou canst not fathom thy inmost soul, or perhaps thou wilt not. Once thou enterest there, God's grace awaits thee, admonishing thee incessantly to keep up a courageous spirit about thy standing with Him. But many a one resists this inner voice and keeps on doing so until he at last becomes unworthy of it and it ceases to be heard, and that forever. The cause of this misfortune is nothing else than self-trust. But if one be only humbly submissive to the divine guidance, it will finally lead him into such a divine union, that he shall enjoy in this life somewhat of the bliss proper only to life eternal. May God grant that this shall happen to us all. *Amen.*

Fraternal Correction

Synopsis—A kind heart is made better by seeing other people's sins— Praying for a faulty brother is often a better favor than chiding him—Many rules for guidance of superiors in administering correction—The strict rule that fraternal correction should be preceded by self-correction—Need of great gentleness of manner.

SERMON FOR THE FEAST OF ST. TIMOTHY.

Preach the word; be instant in season, out of season: reprove, entreat, rebuke in all patience and doctrine.—II Tim. iv, 2.

Thus does St. Paul instruct his beloved disciple St. Timothy, whom he had set over men to rule them in Christ's name. And the apostle's words apply to all who hold office, including father confessors.

First, they are to discipline open sinners, if they may hope to reform them, especially those who are committed to their pastoral care. Furthermore, many good books tell how pastors should teach their people, and correct and admonish them, each according to his needs; especially St. Gregory's Liber Pastoralis.

But we should more attentively consider the second point, which applies the apostle's injunction, given elsewhere, to all men, and even directs us to admonish ourselves in a very interior spirit. It inculcates that any one who aspires to be an interior man shall keep his eyes off other men's conduct, and especially shall not sit in judgment on their sins, lest he fall into bitterness of spirit and rash judgment. Oh, children, this fault does a lamentable amount of harm in men's souls. For the love of God turn away from rash judgment of your neighbor, and keep your keen eyes fixed wholly on your own life. Now you may have committed sins in your past life, and indeed you may have your faults at the present time. Be sure that one reason why God has permitted these, is that when you see the like things done by your neighbor, you may be stung with remorse for your own bad conduct, led to deeper penance, and be more entirely reformed: meanwhile praying for your poor neighbor that God may change him as He has done you.

In this way is a kindly heart made better by other people's sins. Of course this supposes a close guard against uncharitable thoughts. It is a bad heart that sits in judgment on a sinful neighbor. The sins of others sink him deeper by adding uncharity to his other vices, causing him to make the worst of any bad act he sees. A good man has true love for and faithful trust in his fellow man. His gentle heart makes him think other men blameless in their lives. If he cannot help noticing wicked things in his neighbors' conduct, he manages to believe that they are not as bad as they look; that however ugly they seem his poor neighbor may have meant well; or that bad as these deeds are, God allowed that man to do them to admonish him of his weakness, and thereby to save him from more fatal falls.

The sight of other men's sins, makes a good man anxious to die to himself in holy penance for his own and his neighbors' sake both; makes him realize better God's constant presence, and His great patience with sinners. All this helps one's neighbor, for it is an offering to God; it often serves a better purpose than admonitions and punishment, even though these be lovingly administered. Sometimes a man fancies that he corrects his neighbor out of charity, but it is not really so. And I say to thee, dear child, that if thou wilt but conquer thyself by patience and by peace of soul, establishing thereby purity of heart within thee, thou shalt have overcome all thy enemies. This is a higher victory than to subdue the whole world with the scripture's best wisdom, losing mastery of thyself meanwhile by injurious thoughts against thy neighbor, for the Lord says: "Why seest thou the mote that is in thy brother's eye; and seest not the beam that is in thy own eye?" (Matt. vii, 3).

As to prohibition of judging others, we of course except those whose office in holy Church requires them to judge. And these must prudently examine persons and cases; they must avoid an overbearing manner, hot words, or anything that provokes resistance or unnecessarily troubles hearts. Their discipline is intended by God for the reformation of their subjects. Alas, superiors fail in this often and seriously, and instead of bettering the lives of their wayward subjects, they but fill them with bitterness, and turn their hearts yet further away. If one should but guide his subjects into the fear of God with mildness, how different would be the results. The guilty ones would plainly see that the sole purpose of their superior was their soul's welfare, they would receive correction peacefully and would much sooner be reformed. But they plainly see that the superior's motive is his own honor or profit. They submit as to mere force, and in their hearts they remain more rebellious than ever. Many superiors fancy that they are actuated by zeal for virtue in their administration of discipline; but as a matter of fact they are driven on by their angry moods. They think it is hatred of sin that stirs them, and in reality it is hatred of the man who committed the sin.

I beg thee to closely examine thy heart and find out whether or not true charity dwells there, kindly feelings towards those whom thou hast so bitterly pained by thy correction. I fear that instead of true zeal for right order, it is only violent impatience that controls thee: I am speaking especially of those superiors who have little interior life, and have not yet tasted the sweetness of divine love in their souls these are the ones who storm at their subjects, and agonize them with sour looks and cutting words. The soul that knows nothing of God's interior sweetness of love, cannot command prudent ways and kindly words in correcting others. How to deal with delinquents, is a lesson to be learned only from genuine love of God.

Whosoever feels called on by his office to correct others, should bear in mind how easily God may be dishonored by faulty exercise of this duty, and how easily souls may therein be injured. Let him use kindly words, let him cultivate gentle manners and a patient bearing: so that weak spirits may plainly see that the one only object in view is their happiness. It may happen that God will allow thy subjects to revile thee and heap dishonor on thee. Take no notice of this, and never repay it with any sort of discipline, as far as is consistent with the common good. If thou actest otherwise, it is likely that thou thyself shalt become sorely embittered; and, besides, it is likely that thou canst never make any good out of thy subjects. The worse thou art treated by any one, the more sweetly shouldst thou feel and act towards him, in all patience, and with friendly words. Such trials as these are commonly sent by God as His hardest test of superiors, by which they shall either win or lose the merit of martyrdom. Be ever eager to suffer such things; for meekness, and forgiveness of injuries are the best virtues of superiors.

They should avoid flattery. They should shun all partiality in thought or conduct, holding all their subjects equally dear to their hearts, as a true mother does her children. But if any difference may be allowed, then they should love with the deepest affection and treat with the greatest confidence, those who are weakest in character; and this they should, with prudent safeguards, manage to show. Meanwhile they should lift up their hearts to God, and ever earnestly entreat Him to keep watch and ward over their subjects, and that He may save themselves from all self-love. Again, they should, as far as is at all possible, do first themselves the tasks they impose on their subjects. For all goes well when superiors are manifestly full of love and of virtue:—God then guides the community and helps it. The superior's example constrains subjects to do right, even if these are hostile in spirit and inclined to evil doing.

As to those who hold no office over others and are simply members of the community, it behooves them secretly to sit in judgment over themselves and condemn themselves and nobody else. They should refrain strictly from judging anyone else, or criticising the order and arrangement of the community affairs. As a rule, a man goes astray from truth in such judgments, things being quite otherwise than he supposed: sad experience often proves this. There is a motto that says, that that man has true wisdom who finds good in everything. May God help us to this state of brotherly love. *Amen.*

v. Mean-
...estly en-
... ...at He
... as far as
on their
...ll of love
... it. The
... these are

... members
...ent over
... should
...der and
... ...s astray
... than he
that says,
...g. May

Cutting off Superfluities

Synopsis—This means almost the whole of our part in the work of perfection—How it applies to shunning persons as well as things— Separation and solitude are the sum total of the negative side of perfection—Attachments breed unrest and falsehood—The folly of a half-hearted spirit in spiritual conduct—A good description of perseverance—The penitential aspect of detachment.

SERMON FOR THE FEAST OF ST. MARY MAGDALENE.

Martha, Martha, thou art careful, and art troubled about many things; but one thing is necessary. Mary hath chosen the best part, which shall not be taken away from her.—Luke x, 41, 42.

Dear devout children of God, I greet you in our blessed Lord Jesus Christ and in His coming, which shall be to you fruitful of eternal life. I have this day gathered into one discourse that divine doctrine that is the straightest way to eternal happiness. *Amen.*

Dearly beloved, earnestly observe your own hearts and their failings; and at the same time take careful account of the Divine inspirations sent you. Be not deluded by the attractions of transitory things, nor the evil tendencies of your own nature. Would you become the best loved friends and followers of our dear Lord Jesus Christ? Then you must wholly cut off from you all perishable things whose use does not lead you to God. You must dispense with their use except in cases of real necessity. You must rest upon God alone in all circumstances of life, quite cut off from reliance on created things. As to your fellow-men, you must likewise cut off all unnecessary communication with them, whether in deeds or words; and especially must you be averse to the human and natural pleasure of their company. You are to banish from your soul the images of creatures, and stand free of natural joy in them, or even consciousness—as far as duty allows—of their existence. This was what the Blessed Mary Magdalene did; this is what our Lord praised in her. All this being done on thy part, the Lord can do His part within thee,

His supernatural work after His own holy will. He can inflame thee with His burning love; He can overflow thy soul with Divine grace. He will meanwhile impart to thee heavenly prudence, giving thee all guidance necessary to bring thee to sit at His feet and contemplate Him as Mary did.

Be assured of this, dear children, that if we only knew it, all outward superfluity in things and in works has power to blind our soul's eyes to true perception of God's inspirations and our own transgressions. Even when these external things engage us from motives of divine love and are far from being bad, they are often the less perfect ways to God. For did not our Lord Jesus Christ praise Mary Magdalene for her total detachment when He said that she had chosen the best part? And did He not rebuke Martha for being careful and troubled about even important outward service? And yet she was engaged with ardent love in the very seemly duty of providing for the comfort of Himself and His dear disciples. Wouldst thou, therefire, have God's special consolations, and wouldst thou understand His high spiritual doctrine, so full of fruit, so very needful; and wouldst thou be provided by Him with all things necessary for body and soul? Then must thou cut off all superfluities. Thou must dispense with what is not truly necessary in thy every day life, both inner and outer, guided herein by the voice of God in thy conscience.

Above all must we shun all those persons whose memory dwells with us, whose image interposes between us and God. And it matters not how holy they may be; if dealing with them halts us on the way to God, then they must be given up. In that case they are not truly our friends or helpers in acquiring real loyalty to God, whether they be religious or secular or even father confessors.

One never finds God so perfectly, so fruitfully, as in separation and solitude. So did the Blessed Mother of God find Him, St. John the Baptist. St. Mary Magdalene, the other saints of Christ, and the patriarchs of old. They fled from the world and the company of men. They shook off the cares of human society, and then withdrew into wastes and forests the most remote they could find. Ah, children, amusements and company and conversation and all unnecessary dealing with creatures, lead to a sad old age, even when such intercourse is well intended and all seems innocent enough. The reason is that when our heart is full of the images of these things—all alien to our end as they are, and unnecessary to our real happiness—then God must remain outside. He cannot enter our souls thus preoccupied, any more than one can pour sweet wine into a vessel full of filthy ashes. Alas, turn where you will in this poor life of ours, you will find in all outward things, in all human companionship, nothing but falsehood and unrest. A man dreams he will find comfort and relaxation of mind, and he ends in wholly losing inner comfort; he is robbed of that peace of heart which he had gathered by long-continued self-denial and recollection. We become encumbered with all sorts of superfluities, we become addicted to petty lying, and we waste precious hours of time. Our hearts are cooled towards God, love is quenched, conscience is gnawed with remorse, and we are made impatient and easily provoked to bitter anger.

Oh the misery of not being able to understand this truth: that neither comfort nor peace, neither true joy nor veritable relaxation of mind can be anywhere found except in God alone. If we did but turn to Him in whole-hearted fervor and waited on Him with gentle patience —as did the souls of the ancient fathers in limbo for thousands of years—how happy would be our lot; though our waiting can be at most only for the short space of our natural life. He will grant us His sweet comfort in due time, however unworthy we may be of it. He hides Himself for a little while, but that if for our best advantage so that He may inflame our love the more later on, and lead us to higher perfection. Whatsoever is for our spiritual advantage He neither will nor can withhold from us, whether it be external favors or interior graces; and He best knows what we stand in need of.

Alas, how pitiful it is that we so foolishly allow trifling things to hinder us, even to hurt us. We fancy that our fine discourses, full of eloquent things about God, will be pleasing to Him, forgetting how exceedingly simple was His own address to His well-loved disciples. Or, again, we fancy that with noisy and showy works—eating up our precious time—we may serve God rightly and best help our neighbor. Others are not even as good as that; they idly gad about among pious people, making useless visits, and filling their souls with images that obscure the all-lovely figure of our Lord Jesus Christ. We fail to remember that even our Lord's most holy presence in bodily form had become a hindrance to His disciples, as He said: "If I go not, the Paraclete will not come to you; but if I go, I will send Him to you" (John xvi, 7).

Another delusion is that we can possess and enjoy with all feeling of proprietorship many things in this life without spiritual hurt—temporal goods, favorite company, amusements, friends in the world and those in religion, relatives; not recalling that He Himself chose to be disgraced, a wretched outcast, and destitute of all things. And listen to His doctrine: "Every one that hath left house, or brethren, or sisters, or father, or mother, or wife or children, or lands for My name sake shall receive an hundredfold, and shall possess life everlasting" (Matt. xix, 29). And in another place: "If any man come to Me, and hate not his father and mother, and wife and children, yea, and his own life also, he cannot be My disciple" (Luke xiv, 26). Ah, if we did but look deep into our Lord's blesed doctrine, many a one of us would find that their whole life had gone wrong, and that they have been living amid dreams and delusions.

If we shall ever attain to true Divine peace, if we shall be united wholly to God, then all comfort from transitory things must cease, as well as all recreation from them. Reasonable necessity must be the exclusive rule in their use; all beyond that, whether for solace of mind or pleasure of body, must be given up. Whatsoever thing lodges thougts in our mind diverting us from God, must be renounced. God insists on being our heart's only guest. He will tolerate no rival there. Divine tenderness must have the field entirely to itself.

Ah, children, honor the death of our Lord Jesus Christ, and prize His infinite merits. Consider the shortness of this miserable life; learn the deceitfulness of this poor, evil world. Consider the danger of men's company, no matter what appearance of spirituality it may have. Remember that the last hour of life may sound at any moment; that death is surely creeping onward to snatch us away. Consider all this and turn your hearts earnestly to hearken to God's inspirations. Do this, and in one hour God will take charge of you, teach you more truly and sweetly in one hour than all men together in a thousand years. Dear children, make good use of the precious hours of this life; let no creature lead you astray, give your confidence to none, lest you forfeit your eternal salvation. If we lose our worldly goods we can recover them again, and at any rate they serve us no purpose except this side of death. But it may happen that in one fatal hour we shall lose what, once lost, can never be recovered—the glory of eternal life.

I tell you in all sincerity that I forbode the evil fate of many among us. They trust in creatures, for they cleave to them. Their souls are filled with thoughts of them and affection for them. They race here and there after idle stories to hear or to tell. They are crippled spiritually with a heavy weight of superfluities. Thanks be to God's boundless mercy that He often holds us back from gross, deadly sins. But think how perilous a state is that of tepidity—coldhearted, stupid, stuck fast and motionless on the road to perfection. For this we must at last endure a bitter purgatory.

We are like a miserable jackass; his only song is his loud discordant bray; his only movement is his slow, dragging pace; his only food is coarse hay—all this is the joy and sweetnes of his life, and meanwhile he is bitterly cursed and cruelly beaten. In his favor it must be said that he deserves far better treatment; but not so the reasonable and christian spirit that grovels along in his cowardly imperfections. Now this besides: if we would not cut off our attachment to creatures for God's love and our own eternal happiness, then we might do it wisely for a selfish reason, namely, the sweet peace of heart that it gives us during this life. God's love sets us free from many an inner pang, and soothes away many an oppression of spirit.

This is not our highest motive, and yet a most reasonable one. The man who busies himself with all sorts of earthly things, who would set every wrong thing right, who meddles with other people's affairs, who resists when attacked and attacks when angered—such a man is full of unrest. He goes astray; he reaps trouble on all hands. And if the whole world leaves him in peace he none the less devours himself with irritation and discontent. If we want peace we must commit all our affairs into God's hands with childlike confidence. In all our works of soul and body let Him be the master workman, planning and doing as He wills; that brings full peace, and brings it surely. Is not He a better workman and a wiser one than I am? Does not He know what is best for my outward welfare and for my soul's estate? And He undertakes this care of us the moment He finds us doing and thinking and speaking all things solely for His praise and glory. That is our part, that and nothing more. Neither for our bodily welfare nor our interior happiness need we make any provision, except to give ourselves up to Him with deepest sincerity of heart and real humility. From time to time

He will show us ways and means of acting wisely in all our affairs, both spiritual and temporal. Does He not know what we need? And will He not provide for us perfectly, if we will only place all our trust in Him?

The misery is that we insist on ruling ourselves and all our affairs, and our guide is self-love. We trust usually to mere natural light. We act as if we thought ourselves wiser than the very fountain of all wisdom. What is it that deeply concerns us? It is some trouble to be shaken off; some person to be quit of, because he annoys us; to have this or that office; to enter a certain society—one or other of such things as these we fasten on as the best thing in the world. If we only knew ourselves thoroughly well, we should find traces of the evil spirit in all this. He is misleading us; he is gradually winning control of us by taking advantage of our unsteadiness.

Steady perseverance is that virtue which gathers other virtues into one; hence the evil spirit does his best with all of us to throw us off one good purpose onto another. His aim is to make us unstable. If we knew our own hearts better we should discover that it is self-seeking that inspires our life; or that we unconsciously, perhaps, are striving to at once be rid of some cross that God would have us carry a while longer. But this must not be. Our beloved Lord will have His chosen ones constantly crucified. He brings this about in many strange and secret ways, but always acting out of His merciful love. He will not allow created things to make us happy, for He is determined that the enemy of souls shall never gain mastery over us. Our Lord crucifies one man in this way and another in that. He causes one to suffer more, another less, according as He perceives our necessities, our readiness for certain graces, and our progress in perfection. Hence we must suffer as submissively under one infliction as under another, according as God may bring it about.

Meantime we should not rashly draw conclusions from the occurrences of our life, as if God's will was this or that; let us wait till His designs are maturely developed, or seek and follow the guidance of His devout friends. In all this we tread the road of real peace. It sometimes happens that in running away from a slight suffering we run straight into a very serious one.

Would to God that we were not so silly. Did we but appreciate how closely a little anguish of soul joins us to God and sinks us into God, we should suffer willingly enough. Did we but know how quickly the cross of Christ drives out the evil one, we should run many a mile to meet and embrace it. If we knew the precious worth of suffering, we should sincerely thank those who any way oppress us. Therefore must we anxiously seek out the way of the cross, glad and thankful when we find it; yes, happy to find several crosses at once to carry for Christ's sake. What did the holy Apostle St. Andrew do? When he came in sight of the cross on which he was to die he overflowed with joy. It was an ecstacy to him to feel that in his death he was so much to resemble his divine Master. Christ was crucified for us all. What, then, shall be our best joy but to bear Him company. Ah, what a wonderful and eternal reward of glory may we not earn in this poor, fleeting life of ours in this matter of suffering, if we will but gladly give ourselves up to God's guidance. It is every way a noble thing to suffer; it is fruitful of joy here and eternal joy hereafter; it makes men like God, and that is why He will not dispense His friends from suffering. Rather than allow His elect souls to be without the heavenly benefits of suffering God would create new sufferings out of nothing; He would set over us the whole universe of dead and senseless things, to painfully exercise us in the virtues that lead to eternal joy.

But, alas, we are unworthy of such precious favors; we are unreceptive of such gifts, and unregardful of our opportunities. Nay, we incessantly run away from sufferings. Especially are we unwilling to suffer from one another; we cannot tolerate the least annoyance by words or deeds. If any man attacks us, forthwith we strike back; among our adversaries we are like savage dogs. Interiorly we are full of bitterness; right or wrong we defend ourselves vehemently and with burning words. We will not bear to be put down by anybody whatsoever. O misery, misery, how wild is our nature, how utterly unmortified, and how very foolish. We ought to deem ourselves unworthy of so high a principle as suffering in common with Christ. Besides, do we not know this to be needful for our perfection? We should accept trouble and annoyance as gifts from heaven, receive them in real thankfulness, and humble ourselves silently and meekly beneath the blows that are dealt us, imitating the wise and prudent and constant patriarch Job.

Another sentiment that should inspire us is that of penance. We should gladly suffer all inflictions as a chastisement well merited by our sins. No matter how ill treated we may be we should feel that the pain falls far short of what we have deserved. This brings us into a state of true peace. This fits us to exhort and lead our neighbor to the practice of virtue. And this way is far more profitable to us, far more conducive to God's honor, than all manner of self-chosen devotional or penitential exercises.

Surely, dear children, if all teachers were dead and buried, and if all books were burnt, we should have learning enough and wisdom enough in the life of our Lord Jesus Christ. Whatever virtue we may lack let us but fix our eyes on Him and study Him earnestly, and we shall abound with grace; how He has gone before us in all patience and mildness, enduring every conceivable opposition from men and devils, in abandonment and desolation, in disgrace and shame and destitution, in the bitterest pains and griefs. O let us often look at ourselves in this wonderful mirror, for that will strengthen us cheerfully to endure every infliction without and anguish within. This tells us how to overcome temptations and patiently bear misfortunes, no matter from where or from whom they may come. This study of Jesus crucified makes toil and pain easy to bear.

And this shows us how to take good out of all the events of life. For if we would enter the harbor of peace in God we must diligently learn to turn everything to a good use. This custom gives us, besides, a natural tranquility of mind, and saves us from the world's unrest— bearing ourselves mildly and gently towards all, whether rough men or smooth. Serving God faithfully, we must expect to be often mistreated by our fellows, and so be ready to make all allowances for them. We shall constantly be tempted to say of one that he talks too much, and of another that he is too silent; one displeases us because he goes too slow, and another because he goes too fast. People's manners offer many occasions for our falling into interior defects against charity and justice. All this we must strenuously resist, never allowing such thoughts to get a hold upon us. We may be too weak to quite exclude them from our hearts, but we must at least totally repress every outbreak of impatient words correcting nobody whatsoever. Nor is it right to make people's manners and ways and words topics of conversation, neither with one or many companions, no matter what compulsion may be put upon us. There is certainly much merit in such charitable conduct, besides the advantage of a peaceful soul and the happy facility of bearing adversity.

Our beloved Lord Jesus Christ taught that doctrine well and truly by His example. Consider how gently He treated Judas and all His other tormentors. He showed them every sign of affection, well as He knew their deadly hate. He could easily have punished them; yet He was the most innocent Lamb of God among them. To be sure, no man can reach that degree of perfection, or say that he is without sin. Let any of us but examine his conscience sincerely and he finds many faults to lay to his own charge—too many to allow of his presuming to administer punishment to others. And that is true of my own poor self, whose faults you are well aware of. Learn by my faults to guess at your own, and humbly to acknowledge them.

Lay to heart the words you have heard from me. I assure you, as God sees me, that I have studied you all out of the book of my own transgressions. My purpose has not been to preach doctrine to you, for I am in need of your teaching rather than you of mine. But I have given you a brotherly warning, that if any man will not live a recollected life he will become a failure. Any man who does not cultivate entire purity of motive, namely, God alone, and who is not rooted in real humility, shall not be able to offer stout resistance to temptations, nor can he hope to attain to perfection in truth. Better is voluntary and spontaneous poverty than all worldly gods; better is union with God than the empire of the earth and the heavens, even if God filled them with riches for you to give to the poor. And now may God's everlasting peace be with you in time and in eternity. *Amen.*

Guidance: Human and Divine

*Synopsis—Corrupt nature demands self-guidance—God claims our alle-
giance, painful but necessary—Is God my only motive? this is the
supreme question—Trust God blindly and exclusively—This can
only be learned in the interior life—The secret insinuations of self-
love are to be detected and rejected.*

SERMON FOR THE FEAST OF ST. LAWRENCE, MARTYR.

If any man minister to Me, let him follow Me; and where I am, there also
shall My minister be.—John xii, 26.

There is rich meaning in these words. One could write a whole
book on each of them. Here we shall only explain what kind of a
man Christ's true minister is, serving God in truth and following
Him wherever He leads. God does not lead His minister in one way,
one work, one manner of devout living; He leads him where He is
Himself, namely, into all ways, works and manners of devout life.
God is in all things; He is the only and supreme Good. And hence
a man does not minister to God rightly, who cannot serve Him except
in his own self-chosen way, whether it be in choir or in certain ways
of praying—all according to his own choice. If such a man cannot
serve God as he chooses, or if God would lead him to some other
way, he turns his back on Him, and then he pours himself out on this
thing and that which interests him. Such a man is not God's minister, for he has turned away from God. One can be God's minister
only if he follows God in all places, and in all works and ways of
piety. For in all these God is; His minister must simply and solely
follow Him in his choice of them; Him alone must he keep in mind
and serve in all his conduct. God is not in any man who herein fails.
Such a one becomes involved in multiplicity, his spirit is externized;
and besides the self-injury he does, he is a disturbing element to the
people about him in whatever place he may be, and in whatever way
he may be occupied.

What is the cause of this state? It is this: God is not within thy soul. Thou hast, indeed, a fictitious God within thee, but essentially it is not God. Hence as soon as thou hast interrupted thy devotions the Divine presence is gone from thee; this shows that thou art not truly God's minister. The other reason is that a man empties his soul out on the external things of the senses and cleaves to them. If any man would be freed from multiplicity, he ought to let things of the senses flow on past him. If he must be concerned with them out of duty, it should be as one who stops for a little while to attend to something in which he is by no means deeply interested, and then hurries away; nor should he touch such matters except out of necessity. He has no inner converse with them; he is empty and free of creatures, giving them no time nor place to engage him, except when God's interests are plainly involved. It is exactly as if he said: I seek nothing, I mean nothing, I pursue nothing but God alone. Whatsoever crosses my path I say God bless you to it, and go on my way to God.

What worse harm can hell and devils do to me than hinder my loving Him for whom all creatures continually yearn? Let a man press onward with all his might to God through everyone of his life's happenings; let him make no great matter of what occurs to him, whether sweet or bitter. Let it all flow away behind you; meddle with it no more, for it has ceased to concern you; follow God with all your best reason. Thus may one attend to every external duty without externizing himself; thus does God remain present to his mind amid a multiplicity of affairs, while he remains safe from the effects of that multiplicity. That happy state comes only from refusing to fasten one's spirit upon anything whatsoever except God alone. Go not forward or backward or sideways; take no account of pleasure or profit, men's favor or their disfavor, but simply and solely consider God.

If thou shouldst unwittingly fail in this, and some motive that is not God should for a moment control thee, rise up again very quickly with an act of thy reason; turn the good ship into the right course by the rudder of holy discretion. If God's servitor begins his work with an upright intention, and so continues it, then no matter what feeling of multiplicity he may experience, it will not essentially hurt him; it will not be enough to mislead him. God may not be present to his understanding, but without doubt He dwells at home with him in his more inward spirit. If he makes sure to commit no deliberate faults, nor to cleave wilfully to creatures, let not his outward occupations or any occurrences whatsoever disturb his peace of soul. In case his devotional exercises or his external duties do disturb his peace, that plainly shows that he has failed in interior recollection, and has not done his task rightly; he has not based his doing and his not doing exclusively upon God.

When a man becomes aware that God is not his only motive, then he must strive with all his might to make Him so. He must cast out all else but God, of whatever name or nature it may be. Otherwise he is like a man shot with an arrow, and which he will not allow to be extracted because of the pain that it will cause—meantime his flesh swells and putrifies. So in very truth is it with thy soul. If anything that is not God, or not on account of God, holds place there, be sure that God will not abide in thee. If thou wilt not suffer the first sharp pain of detachment from creatures, then the later pain will be much worse, misery upon misery increasing beyond all comprehension. The spirit of a man must go to God clean and empty of creatures. It must stand ready for the word and beck of God, as if to say: Dear Lord, if I could but give Thee joy in all my good works and in all my dealings with men, to that task I would humbly devote myself. Another thing is this: Whenever opportunity serves, one must fly from multiplicity and gladly choose to turn inwardly to solitude with all his faculties.

A man must serve God not as he himself wills, but according to the blessed will of God, and this rule extends to everything, both of the outer and the inner life. When one has not God as his interior guest he goes onward with uncertain step, as the Scripture says: "Woe to him that is alone, for when he falleth he hath none to lift him up" (Eccles. iv, 10). But if a man be on his guard, and if his soul is like a well-garrisoned fortress, then the enemy assaults him in vain. God is our soul's garrison; keep Him with you securely, always realize His holy presence. When one thus possesses God he stands in need of little else; any little provision of this world's comfort suffices him; nor is he disturbed by contradictions in his labors, or opposition from the men around him. If God be felt within the soul, it makes more progress in virtue under external difficulties than when all is favorable. But, of course, nature feels this unpleasantly, and one stands his ground only with an effort; especially does he need constant recollection of the spirit in God.

The best state of things for us is not prosperity; then everything goes on of itself, and very smoothly. How can one tell if he be in reality a true minister of Christ if he suffers no adversity for Him? But thou mayest ask: Suppose a man fails in fidelity under stress of adversity? Let him rise up again quickly, acknowledge his misery and nothingness before God, and renew his spirit of recollection— all this the sooner the better. But do not dwell too long on thy faults, discussing sadly how this happened or how that; such a practice is indiscreet. Hast thou been unequal to duty? Then how shalt thou be made equal to it but by secretly entering deep into God? How shalt thou better run away from death than by running into Life? Life eternal and essential. Is there any better way to be warmed than to come near the fire? Lay all thy cares upon God, and He will arrange everything for the best. For thy part, trust Him implicitly and in everything that concerns thee; that done, accept all the happenings of thy life in peace of mind, and make the best of them.

But if a man will not trust God nor abandon himself to Him, if he insists on striving and straining and worrying, God often permits him to fall into deep misery and want. This is to show him how far he can go under self-guidance. But if a man sincerely turns all care over to God, then does God better manage his affairs than could all creatures together. Oh, God is full of grace; He is the fountain head of wisdom; and whoever seeks his guidance with sincere trustfulness will undoubtedly obtain it. We cannot love God too much; we cannot confide in Him too blindly—supposing our intention to be entirely upright and our fidelity unfeigned.

Now how shall this way of life be learned? How shall we acquire trust in God, all peaceful and joyful, extending over all our devotions, all our good works, felt in every place and under all conditions? This can only be learned in the interior life; it comes to us from constantly turning into the inmost depths of our spirit. For this end one needs holy leisure, some freedom from external duties, fit places and times for retirement. It is in interior recollection that this peculiar virtue of trust in God is planted and grows, puts forth

branches and bears fruit. In this inner detachment a man is given
to know God's ways and means; and the more he dwells thus alone
with Him the clearer and truer does his knowledge grow. And when
this guidance fails then it is plain that the spirit of recollection has
not been fostered; proper hours and sufficient time and fit places have
not been set apart for God's intimate communion; His guidance has
not been honestly sought.

You should know, children, that some men, while outwardly spiritual, are in reality devoted to their own self-chosen spiritual ways, and
on that account their lives pass along and away without their knowing how they stand with God. And they finally grow to be content
with this state, calling it resignation. But, as a matter of fact, it
is nothing but gross spiritual negligence. Into this slothful emptiness of soul other defects insinuate themselves; God's holy rights in
the soul are usurped by self-love or other love of creatures. For it
is as impossible not to have some love or other in one's soul as to
exist without any soul at all. Whether one is or is not quite aware
of this sad state, it often enough exists; and one goes along blindly,
trusting to a certain sort of spirituality, certain devout practices and
good works, but with no real spiritual fruit. Such a man thinks he
stands on solid ground, bcause he never investigates the foundation
of things in his inner spirit. At last he comes to the end and passes
into eternity. He has not trodden the way that is Christ, who says:
"I am the way, and the truth and the life" (John xiv, 6). Whosoever
walks not in that way goes astray. It is a deadly shame that a man
will study and learn many things, and himself he will neither know
nor want to know.

Dear children, no man should remain in doubt about his interior
life; he should know it positively—not merely by surmise, but actually
—how deep God dwells in his heart, and how strong is his own yearning for God. If he is void of this holy wisdom, then let him seek it
from devout and instructed men. Not fancies and surmises, but something like certainty should possess his mind about his standing with
God. Let him realize that what he neglects now he shall never make
up for hereafter, where the Blessed Virgin and all the Saints could
not win him a hair's weight of merit; no, not with tears of blood.
They themselves, in their lifetime, were ever ready; they responded
instantly to the heavenly Bridegroom and entered into the wedding

feast with all joy. The others waited too long, and when the cry was heard, "Lo, the Bridegroom cometh!" their lamps were not trimmed, and they came too late; and He answered their call and their knocking with an oath: "Amen, I say to you, I know you not" (Matt. xxv, 12). They were not His own; they were not in the ranks of His familiar friends gathered now close around him.

St. Augustine says: "Nothing is so certain as death, nothing is so uncertain as the hour of death, or the place or circumstances of death. Who knows the time, who knows the manner of his departure?" Hence, nothing is so necessary as that we shall be well prepared; that we shall be sure we are well prepared, not trusting to fancies or surmises. It is to that end that we are here in our time of probation; it is not for the sake of good works alone, but for the sake of that truly instructed mind from which the good works spring as the fruit is generated by the tree.

Let all our pious exercises have that aim—more knowledge of God's interior ways, and a nearer approach to union with Him. Whatsoever man has broken away from his life's externalism, and is elevated in spirit above the things of time, and has ordered his ways according to God's intimate guidance, the same cannot be involved in multiplicity. Whatsoever touches him cannot lay hold on him, nor distract his thoughts and affections from his inner life. The more a man's spirit is joined to God the more quiet-minded he is the better ordered is his life, the less likely to be worried by his responsibilities. Here is a sign of a right-minded man: that all his work and rest shall be motived and done in such a manner as shall win his approval afterwards when he is in his better spiritual condition. So that when his dead body shall be buried in the earth his soul may instantly be united to the infinite Godhead. It is for this end alone that God has placed us in this life; and if we fail to attain it now we fail forever.

Whose image and superscription is stamped on the coin? To him, whether God or a creature, the tribute must be paid without fail. Look often, therefore, into thy deeper thoughts, and read the superscription on them: that is to say, who or what is thy best beloved? Whom dost thou have mostly in view in thy purposes? What, for the most part, solaces thee and rejoices thee and stirs thy affections? Thou art, perhaps, really inclined towards God and heavenly things, lovest the company of God's friends, art pleased with public divine service, thy mind, will, words and behavior given to God. But ask thyself if thy motive be not thy own advantage, thy honor among religious persons, thy comfort and convenience, thy friendships, alas, perhaps, even thy pecuniary advantage. Is it not all this, or part of it, that draws thee and holds thee, rather than divine things considered in themselves? If any man will discreetly question his soul about these matters, he will obtain true knowledge of himself. That will give him humble confidence that he really knows himself; surmises and guesses and uncertainties are done. If there is anything in thy deeper spirit that is not simply and purely God or has not God for its origin, whether it be thy own self or anything else, great or little, then thou hast not God within thee—supposing, of course, that this be wilful and deliberate. Thou mayst weep an ocean of tears, that helps nothing; thou must give thy spirit up wholly to God, or do without Him in time and eternity.

O, children, what ails these poor men, that, having open eyes, they yet will not see? They are not alarmed at the cunning self-deceptions of our fallen nature, its secret tendencies to selfhood, its constant return to self, its steadfast regard to self alone in all communication with creatures, and even in the service of God. A man must hasten forward without stopping. Time is short, and whatsoever has to do with God, even the smallest of His affairs, is of greater weight than all this earth's treasures put together. Therefore, set to work earnestly, both inwardly and outwardly, to make everything point to God, and to God alone. Pray for a heart quite disengaged, so that God may work His blessed will within thee. May He help us to that freedom and detachment of spirit. *Amen.*

𝔚𝔞𝔱𝔠𝔥𝔦𝔫𝔤 𝔣𝔬𝔯 𝔉𝔯𝔦𝔢𝔫𝔡𝔰 𝔞𝔫𝔡 𝔈𝔫𝔢𝔪𝔦𝔢𝔰

Synopsis—Watching is a universal religious obligation—For souls aspiring to perfection, it is needed especially in regard to interior defects—These range from hidden lusts to foolish delusions of spirit—God sharpens the gaze of faithful souls—A watchful spirit is constantly rewarded with precious graces.

SERMON FOR THE FEAST OF ST. AUGUSTINE.

Watch ye, therefore, because you know not what hour your Lord will come.—Matt. xxiv, 42.

The evil spirit strives with all his might and all his cunning to lead us astray into eternal loss. He watches for an unguarded hour, yea, even a thoughtless moment, to destroy us. As a robber watches for a window left open through forgetfulness, so does the prowling demon take note of our omitting our daily devotions, or performing them sluggishly; then he slips into our soul's house and steals our treasure. Therefore, carefully close your windows; that is to say, be wide awake and on your guard against temptations. Hold all your soul's powers well together in recollection; watch incessantly. As soon as thou art conscious of a proud thought or stubborn self-will or self-conceit, be sure that the enemy of souls is at hand hoping to carry off a rich booty of thy spiritual goods.

Children, there are those in this world who practice fine devotions, hold high names and bear great fame as religious men, but who are full of self-approval; and this has so far cut down their merit that in the life to come they will be very thankful to have a place among rude Christians of no name and wholly ignorant, poor peasants, but humble servants of God. And there are poor, simple creatures whom nobody notices, without learning and without showy good works, but yet sunk down before God in real humility, who will be placed so high that many a pretentious and self-satisfied Christian will hardly be able to see them. Watch, therefore, with a wakeful spirit. Keep your soul's eyes wide open. Look to divine truth only in all your thoughts, words and deeds; yea, even in your virtuous actions; abound in patient suffering; ever glance warily around, both in your outward and your inward progress towards perfection.

Children, you little dream how perilous is your state of natural weakness, and how deep a stain your miserable sins leave on your soul. You little appreciate the inestimable favors God ever stands ready to grant you, and which you fail to get by reason of your supineness. Let me ask: Do you appreciate what it means to pass incessantly under the eye of God, searching your inmost soul? Do you realize that all your evil comes from your not living and acting in God's truth? How we sinners should wither away with fear and shame as we read: "The just man shall scarcely be saved" (I Peter iv, 18). St. Augustine explains this as follows: "Woe, and again woe, to all our righteousness if God will not judge us according to His mercy." Hence, if you but understood the deadly danger of all who, in practicing religion, think of anything but God alone, your human weakness could not stand it. Thus does the holy man Job speak: "I have sinned: what shall I do to Thee, O keeper of men? Why hast Thou set me opposite to Thee, and I am become burdensome to myself?" (Job vii, 20).

The Lord bids us watch for Him, our loins girded, burning lamps in our hands, awaiting His coming to the marriage feast. Of this watching I have just now discoursed to you. But you must observe three points. The girding of the loins may be like binding a man with a rope, so that he can be drawn about against his will, as you would lead a well-broken horse, keeping him on the safe road, pulling him back from the edge of a pit. The loins may mean the lusts of our sensual nature, which we break under the discipline of reason, hold together in bondage, never allowing them free play. The second point is to have lighted lamps in your hands. And this means the sweet zeal of burning charity, both felt within and active without. That lamp must never leave your hand; you must do works of affection on every possible occasion, and with all eagerness, but especially among your nearest brethren. The third point is waiting for your Lord's coming to His marriage feast: "Blessed are those servants whom the Lord, when He cometh, shall find watching. Amen, I say to you, that He will gird Himself and make them sit down to meat, and, passing, will minister to them" (Luke xii, 37).

This marriage feast is in the inmost soul of a man, the place in which God's blessed image is set up. The nearness of the soul to God and God to the soul there, the wonders He works in that inner sanctuary, the sweetness of the joy He dispenses there—all this passes sense or reason to understand. Men usually know nothing of this celestial banquet, except those who have diverted their hearts' desires from all created things, and have resolved with eternal steadfastness to be content with God alone. The rest of men, whose satisfaction is found in themselves and in what they own, who rest on creatures whether alive or dead, who do this wilfully and deliberately—with them has God nothing to do in this spiritual union.

Upon these tardy and slothful souls the enemy fixes his eye. Seeing their Lord is long in coming, he insinuates some treacherous joy into their hearts, hoping that they will be absorbed in it. Dear child, be not deceived by this. Be resigned to wait for thy Lord: "And if He shall come in the second watch, or come in the third watch, and find them so watching, blessed are those servants" (Luke xii, 38). Then will He sit them down to serve them; that is to say, He will give them a foretaste of the everlasting marriage feast. And while they patiently wait He will secretly visit their souls with comfort, lest the tedium of delay should overcome them—He imparts some drops of the sweetness of His own love to strengthen theirs.

St. Gregory comments on these words of the Psalmist: "Lo, I have gone far off flying away; and I abode in the wilderness" (Ps. liv, 8). "When," says he, "an interior man has waited on God, and when he has yet again waited, then let him still further wait and withdraw himself from all things and enter into the wilderness." This wilderness consists in giving up all the multiplicity of one's outward powers; but more than that, it includes the renouncing as much as possible the multiplicity in the interior powers of the soul, namely, the images of the mind, the forms and figures of the imagination, the multiplicity of the thoughts. Thus removed from forms and figures, a man's interior life is lived in solitude. Now this is painful to human nature. But when one has endured the pain patiently and lived through the strain and stress upon his mind, at last the Lord comes to him—that Master whom he has so lovingly waited for. In an hour he dreamed not of the Lord is with him. Sudden as the winking of an eye is His coming to reward his beloved's faithful waiting.

But when this has happened, and has endured I know not how long, what follows? Then the Lord would elevate him yet higher in His love. And with that purpose He strikes him down again, and oppresses him with a tedium of waiting more dreary than before. He thus withdraws His conscious presence lest the soul should cleave with proud self-complacency to the interior sweetness [already granted.

It is for him that Jeremias speaks: "I sat alone, because Thou hast filled me with threats" (Jer. xv, 17). What does that mean, but that after a man has entered into his quiet rest of soul the Lord comes and threatens him terrifically, as if with both hands.. One hand casts over him a thick inner darkness in his sad, solitary journey; he knows nothing now; he has nothing; and he feels that all calamity has come upon him. Especially, sins and temptations seem to overwhelm him—pride and impurity and denial of the faith and all else that he dreamed he had got rid of forever. As this awful hand of God is raised in threat against him, these direful temptations are upon him. The other hand is the portent of eternal loss. God seems to be ready to arraign him for his sins, and to condemn him to the deepest hell. O how these two awful hands crush this poor man's soul. And yet all this cruel trial is intended by God to purge that soul of the venom of pride. Children, in those who bow down humbly beneath these two threatening hands all evil love is quenched; in a single instant it is cured more perfectly than by many years of external religious exercises.

Now, when one has thus journeyed into the prophet's solitude and patiently dwelt there, at least a partial relief comes at last. The storms of passion are stilled, the forms and figures of distracting thoughts are wiped away. Then God, accompanied by His holy angels, enters the wilderness and finds the soul, and in an instant of time endows him with a gift of active love. Some noble mission of love is committed to him, perhaps an affair of deep moment for all Christendom, for the living or the dead—in one quick flash is this given to him. Then it is as if our Lord said to him: Thou needst say no word to Me; I well know what thou dost desire—and then He grants that man what he wishes. This is the one who fulfils the words: "The true adorers shall adore the Father in spirit and in truth" (John iv, 23). But yet the demon is allowed to tempt him;

and he now once more casts into his mind thoughts of woe and suffering. Let him pay no heed to these. If he is not regardful of them, then the evil one must go his way shamefaced and empty-handed; and that soul remains much benefited by Satan's onslaught.

In some countries men are met with who have a false detachment of spirit. These quit doing all good works whatsoever. They even avoid good thoughts; and they boast that they have attained to freedom of spirit. They refuse to join in devout exercises, and they will not practice virtue; they have got beyond all that. But in reality there is an imp of Satan seated in such a soul, who hinders all interior or exterior means of disturbing these misguided spirits and getting them out of their delusion. He keeps them restful in thought and act, so that he may finally lead them into eternal unrest; this is the secret of their spurious quiet of soul. Just men have no such deceitful calm. They practice religious exercises as God, by interior inspirations or by His lawful representatives, leads them, both interior and exterior devotions. They suffer God to guide them in all their trials and darkness of spirit; nor do they for a moment presume to think that they have arrived at a state of spiritual quiet. And yet they are not really in unrest. They journey along a narrow path between rest and unrest, between hope and unreasonable fear, between the sense of security and that of distrust. When they are vouchsafed a momentary glimpse of true peace, of real confidence, of spiritual freedom, instantly do they cast this gift into the abyss of God's being; nor do they cleave to it with affection.

Children, the men who are in this narrow road should, before all things, tread in the footsteps of our Lord Jesus Christ. The stricter they observe this the more perfectly detached will they become. Then in due time God's hands shall cease to threaten; these are now become open hands, beckoning with all love; and presently our Lord's hands and arms and heart will embrace them most tenderly, and lift them upwards high above all created things. Now falls away every thought of natural existence, and it wearies them to so much as think of anything that is not purely and simply God.

Then the Lord turns their eyes back on the narrow, dark and toilsome road they have travelled, and instructs them fully in its meaning. After that no man can hurt them, and they are well repaid for all their misery.

To those who glory in a false freedom all this is not right. They presume upon a counterfeit detachment of spirit. They will sometimes continue in this delusion for forty years or more, doing great works meanwhile, and following in all things their self-chosen spiritual methods. They will not walk in the narrow path; for in a great multitude there will, perhaps, be scarcely one or two willing to do it. And all the others will look on these with disapproval, trying them sorely, and thereby unwittingly helping them in their hard task. If one of these favored souls does the least thing amiss, the others chide him very severely. Dear child, if that be thy misfortune, bear it patiently. If a bitter answer escapes thee, do not be disheartened. Enter into thyself, confess thy fault, and bear the reproach of conscience manfully. Keep still and thank God that thou hast the grace to own thy defect. And it is consoling to know that if thou hadst been very patient under reproof it might have been the occasion of a greater sin, namely, that of spiritual pride. Humble thyself and go on thy way. Everything, be it straight or crooked, will prepare thee for God's coming. All things will work together for thy good, if thou wilt but be watchful over thyself. Whosoever thus waits for the Lord with watchful eyes, as did St. Augustine, him will the Lord sit down at His heavenly banquet, and He will serve him with all joy. May God grant this to happen to all of us. *Amen.*

The Supremacy of the Cross of Christ

Synopsis—Jesus crucified rules mankind from His cross—This means the law of sacrifice in our lives—Some reflections on Holy Communion—How the love of Christ leads us to crucify our flesh.

FIRST SERMON FOR THE FEAST OF THE EXALTATION OF THE HOLY CROSS.

And I, if I be lifted up from the earth, will draw all things unto Myself.—John xii, 32.

Today we celebrate the Exaltation of the Holy Cross, on which our Lord Jesus Christ, the salvation of the whole world, suffered and died out of love for us. By the Cross of Christ we are born again into that high nobility in which God first created us. Let us love it well in this new birth of love, for its dignity cannot be expressed in words. Said our Lord: "And I, if I be lifted up from the earth, will draw all things unto Myself." He means our hearts' love; He would draw our hearts away from all joy in creatures, draw them to Himself. He would draw us away from proud self-complacency, and from attachment to things of the senses. He would be lifted up in our hearts and be made great and powerful there. Wheresoever God is great there all creatures are little. In Him all transitory things are as nothing at all.

This blessed cross is nothing else but Christ crucified, who is exalted high above all saints and angels, all bliss and happiness of all creatures taken together. And as His rightful place is the highest, so will He dwell within us elevated to the highest place, the most interior, the most receptive place in our spirit. By that means He will draw the lowest powers of our nature into submission to the highest, and both highest and lowest He will draw into union with Himself. If we will but yield to Him in this, then will He draw us out of ourselves and into Himself, into His highest and most interior life. And that must needs be. For if I shall be drawn into His life, I must of necessity receive Him into mine; as much of mine, so much of His. Such is the even trade between Him and me.

But, alas, how much is this holy cross forgotten. How very generally is the interior ground of our hearts shut against it; it is barred
out by love of created things.   Love for created things rule souls in
our day, souls of men in the world, and those even in more spiritual
states of life.   Many hearts are lost to God by loving creatures, the
blindest love and the direst misfortune in the world.   If we could
but appreciate God's anger over this when men's souls are arraigned
in His court, we should wither away with fear.   But men go so far
as to make jokes about this, doing it sometimes habitually.   Disregard of eternal penalties is deemed a mark of honor—a misery over
which God's saints in heaven, were such a thing possible, would weep
tears of blood.   The wounds of Christ would bleed afresh over so
awful a deed as shutting out Christ's cross from our souls, for whose
welfare He lived His Divine life on earth and suffered His cruel death.
May God pity us all.

Children, this is no invention of mine, for you know that all holy
Scripture holds up the supremacy of Christ's cross.   Says the Gospel:
"No man can serve two masters.   For either he will hate the one and
love the other, or he will sustain the one and despise the other.   You
cannot serve God and mammon" (Matt. vi, 24).   And again does
Christ teach: "If thy right eye scandalize thee, pluck it out and cast
it from thee" (Matt. v, 29).   And about fixing our heart on worldly
goods, He says: "Where thy treasure is, there is thy heart also" (Matt.
vi, 21).   St. Augustine comments on this: "Dost thou love the earth?
Then thou art of the earth earthly; for thy soul is more truly present
with what it loves than it is present with the body to which it gives
life."   And St. Paul teaches: "If I speak with the tongues of men and
of angels * * * and if I should distribute all my goods to feed
the poor, and if I should deliver my body to be burned, and have not
charity, it profiteth me nothing" (I Cor. xiii, 1-3).

Now, my dear children, be very thankful to God for the wonderful
privilege of receiving the body and blood of the Lord in Holy Communion, a favor often granted you as members of your order.   For this
brings you very close to the cross of Jesus crucified.   Often receive
our Lord.   I trust with all my heart and soul that this devout practice of frequent communion shall not be discontinued in these dangerous times.   Nature cannot stand alone; either it must fall lamentably,
or with all its powers cling to God for support.   And do not suppose
that this is a question of perfection; no, but rather of preservation from

our innate weakness, and salvation from eternal loss. Our Lord teaches that the well need not a physician, but the sick. And this need of vital help is seen in our times far and wide, and even among persons consecrated to God.

But let no one sit in judgment on those who are not perfect in their good works. If these observe the rules of their holy order as far as they are able, that is enough, so long as they have a good will to do all the rest, and are lawfully dispensed from stricter observance. It takes no great learning for this much. Let them cheerfully comply with their rule as far as they can, meanwhile keeping their eyes wide open against all deadly dangers. To this end let even our younger members often and gladly approach Holy Communion. I will answer for the older ones. They have communicated often and fervently in former years, when times were not so wicked. They have been devotedly attached to our order and lovingly obeyed its rules. They will, therefore, keep up their pious custom of fortnightly communion. It sufficed for their perfection in better days than these. But the degeneracy of our younger people calls for a yet more frequent use of Holy Communion on their part, in order to overcome their evil inclinations. We need more help of divine grace and more frequent Communion nowadays, if we would keep our footing in the higher ways of perfection. Alas, everything seems sinking down into the pit of beastly lust and sensual enjoyment.

I ask no greater perfection of you than that you love your holy order, and that you resolve to keep its sacred rules to the best of your ability. Observe strict silence in every place and time prescribed, but especially at table and in choir. Be on your guard against the least familiarity with any who may lead you away from God—the older members for the sake of edification and recollection, the younger ones on account of natural frailty. Do this with deep sincerity, and God will grant you His own familiar company, and then it will be easy enough to fly from all that may sully the purity of your heart. I assure you that the intolerable evils that have fallen on certain monasteries have come from neglect of this rule about dangerous association; and if this shall continue it will bring them to utter destruction.

Dear children, if in your spiritual life you do not feel sweetness of devotion, let that not distress you. What is worth more than all taste of sweetness is to do what good lies in your power, and to be interiorly detached from earthly things. Bitterness of soul suffered for

God's sake will bring you nearer to Him in living truth than all manner of sensible devotion. Our Lord cried out on the cross: "My God! My God! why hast Thou forsaken Me?" (Matt. xxvii, 46). And in the agony in the garden He exclaimed to His Father: "Not what I will, but what Thou wilt." (Mark, xiv, 36). Will you, dear children, be afraid to follow Him? Listen to Him again: "If any man will come after Me, let him deny himself and take up his cross daily and follow Me." (Luke ix, 23).

Children, the cross means Christ crucified. He must be born in us, and in all our soul's powers, will, memory and understanding; yes, and even in our outward life of the five senses must Christ crucified be given full mastery. St. Paul teaches: "They that are Christ's, have crucified their flesh with the vices and concupiscences" (Gal. v, 24). That means the taming of our unruly sensual tendencies under the dominion of Christ crucified. And our irascible tendencies must also be subjugated. We must easily give up to others, and that in all lawful things whatsoever. We must easily believe others are right and ourselves wrong. We must abhor strife, and become kindly-mannered and good-natured, silent under insult, and as easily led by our neighbor as a feather is wafted by the wind.

If thou art in a gathering of men, and seest the others chattering and noisy, dear child, learn a lesson of silence from that, turn into thy own thoughts and sit still. If a man would learn a trade how is he going to do it if he will not let himself be taught?. If thou undertakest a fencing bout, thou shalt be worsted and suffer hurt unless thou dost practice beforehand under a master. Thus, also, in the Lord's warfare we learn how to win the victory over ourselves by suffering contradictions. As to the two interior faculties, the understanding and the will, the powers of knowing and of loving, the cross of Jesus crucified must be taken up and carried in them most manfully, that the all-loving Redeemer may be borne in our inmost spirit.

Thus it is that we are to be born again in God, to be made the fruit of His spirit. St. Peter says: "As new-born babes, desire the rational milk without guile" (I. Peter ii, 2). If thus you live to God, every day of yours is a day of the dedication of God's living temple; all your sins will be forgiven by this new birth in Christ crucified. May God help us to His Son's blessed cross, that we may be nailed to it and hang upon it, and that by it we may be constantly born into newness of life. *Amen.*

Interior Crucifixion

Synopsis—Christ crucified draws all our being inward to Himself—The interior life is a sweet and bitter crucifixion, followed by resurrection—The hard truth that not in joy but in pain we are joined to God—Warning against despondency.

SECOND SERMON FOR THE FEAST OF THE EXALTATION OF THE HOLY CROSS.

And I, if I be lifted up from the earth, will draw all things to Myself.— John xii, 32.

This is the Feast of the Exaltation of the Holy Cross, whose dignity passes the power of words to tell, by which all glory of time and eternity is given us; for when we think of the cross we call to mind Him who died upon it. On this day religious communities with all solemnity pay high honor to the Cross, and, when their rule requires it, they begin today a season of fasting—a practice profitable, not only to them, but to all others who may be able to observe it.

We recall today how a Christian Emperor recovered the true cross from a heathen King, and how he began to bear it with royal pomp into Jerusalem. But his pomp was not suitable to that symbol of pain and sorrow, and, therefore, God miraculously closed the gate of the city against him, and stationed an angel there to bar him out, who said to him: "Thou comest here carrying the cross with majestic splendor, whereas He who died upon it was driven out of this city in shame and ruin, bearing it on His bruised shoulders and walking painfully along barefoot." Upon hearing these words the Emperor quickly got down from his horse, stripped off his precious robes, even to his shirt, laid aside his glittering crown and took off his shoes; then in that poor plight, shouldering the holy cross, he started forward. The gates flew open before him, and he entered the city and set the cross up in its place, and many miracles were wrought by it on the blind and lame and sick.

Our Lord said: "And I, if I be lifted up from the earth, will draw all things to Myself." Man is what is meant by all things, for, as St. Gregory says, man has in him all forms of matter and of life. Now we meet with men who have found the cross, for God has drawn them to it and to Himself with many sorts of pains, and with various pious exercises. But these sufferings must not only be found by us—as was the material cross of Christ by that Emperor—but they must be exalted in the soul and made supreme there. If a man will but enter into himself he will find the cross twenty times a day. Painful things are always happening, and these crucify him, if he will but have it so. But it is quite possible that he does not exalt these crosses to their proper height; he does not make right use of them. We should lift up the full weight of the cross of life in God; that is to say, we should accept all our own pains and troubles, inner and outer, both those of the soul and those of the body, with hearty and cheerful willingness. It is thus that a man is drawn into God; for, as Christ says, it is when He is lifted up that He will draw all things to Himself.

Again do we find men who bear the cross, indeed, but it is in the way of outward piety, following too mechanically the routine of their order, in choir, at holy reading, in the refectory. A little honor is, indeed, done our Lord in this way of the outward life. But, dear children, do you think that God has created you to be his little singing birds? No, but He would have you to be His special friends, and the spouses of His Holy Spirit. Yes, you carry Christ's cross outwardly, but you are careful to keep it out of your interior life, and you lay it aside and take a rest from it whenever you can. Such as these carry the cross, not with our Lord, but with Simon the Cyrenian, who was forced to carry it. But after all, even this is good. They do carry Christ's cross; it guards them from many defects, it helps them against gross frivolity of mind, and it saves them many a pang in purgatory, perhaps even from the eternal pains of hell.

"I will draw all things to Myself," says our dear Lord. Now, if one will draw things, he first gathers them together. And so our Lord, when He is going to draw us, gathers our senses, our words and works, our thoughts and intentions, our imaginations and our longings, our understanding, our will and our love—all these he attracts towards Him. And when they are well assembled together He absorbs them into Himself, and away from all alien attractions. For be sure of this:

if thou shalt be drawn to Christ, then all that thou cleavest to must be cut off, all and every satisfaction whatsoever, interior and exterior. This detachment is, indeed, a heavy task, all the heavier in proportion to how strong the attachment was. For all joy and love thou hast in created things, call it by what name thou pleasest, however holy and godly it may seem to thee—all must be stripped off thee, as the royal robes were stripped from that Emperor, if thou art to be drawn to God and exalted on His holy cross.

This is the first degree, and it concerns a man's outward life. Should he, however, wish to raise the cross in his interior life, then he must needs give up all interior joy. He must renounce all attachment to the joys of his spirit, even such as flow from the practice of virtue. Learned men dispute as to whether or not a man may lawfully enjoy the pleasure of virtue as such, maintaining that we can only have the profit of a virtuous act, and must reserve all our joy for God Himself, and for Him alone. Yet it must be said that one cannot practice virtue without feeling some joy in it; but this must be without any sense of ownership.

Children, what do you think joy or satisfaction really is? Is it that a man can fast, watch, pray, keep the rule of his order? But I tell you that our Lord, when He would have me keep my order's rule in the right spirit, will deprive me of joy in doing all this. What do you suppose God means by sending dry times into your observance of the rule? Seldom is one day like another. Now I am full of devotion; yesterday I was empty and barren. At one time I am attentive to prayer; at another my mind is overrun with all sorts of distractions. Dear children, this is the cross of Christ. Accept these dreary changes from His hand in all patience, and they will become a lovely cross to your souls. If thou wilt but offer them all up to God in total resignation of spirit, and thank Him sincerely for them, thou shalt by their means be drawn close to Christ crucified and exalted with Him, magnifying God in all the happenings of thy life.

The Son of Man must be lifted up on the cross. Many among us, dear children, are clean of heart, but they fail in this: they are too hungry for the sweet feelings of religion. They would have their minds full of emotional happiness. Dear child, give over all that. Attend diligently to real disengagement of spirit. Be afraid of interior sweetness; look on thyself as unworthy of such favors. Love

the cross that is found in trial and-temptation; love it better than
the sweet flowers of pious emotion. Make up thy mind that thou,
like everyone else, must bear the cross. Our Lord said to the two disciples on the road to Emmäus: "Ought not Christ to have suffered
these things, and so to enter into His glory?" (Luke xxiv, 26). Can
it be otherwise with thee, His disciple? Now, therefore, if any bright
light illumines thy inner soul, or any great sweetness refreshes its
taste, let not the enjoyment of that gain control over thee. Stop
not with it so long as to ask: What is this gift of God? But quickly
fall back on thy own nothingness and do no otherwise.

Our Lord said: "If any man will come after Me, let him deny
himself and take up his cross daily and follow Me" (Luke ix, 23).
It is not with prosperity, but with the cross that a man follows God.
When St. Andrew saw his cross he cried out: "All hail to thee, thou
most lovely cross. Long have I craved with all my heart to have
thee. Lift me up from among men and place me with my Master."
To be made like-minded with that apostle is not the work of a day
or two. Thou must set thyself to constantly search thy soul and
overcome thyself in all things. Thou must also keep strict account
of thy sins and imperfections. What if thou art weak and fallest
seventy times a day. Never give up; rise again each time and go
forward courageously. Return to God so quickly and so sincerely
that thy sins are pardoned thee even before thou hast time to tell
them in confession. Let not thy sinful tendencies affright three.
Many a fault of thine is permitted by God, not so much to hurt
thee as to help thee. For does it not cause thee to own to thyself
that thou art but nothingness? Does not the shame of it lead thee
to mortification and detachment? Carefully avoid all despondency.
When a man knows that he has a good will, that he is glad to obey
God, then no matter how weak he may be let him be full of courage.
No one in this life is free from sin as our Blessed Lady was. Therefore, be content to strive manfully, to suffer patiently, to bear thy
cross in union with Christ. St. Paul says: "We know that to them
that love God all things work together unto God." (Rom. viii, 28);
and the gloss says that this includes even our sins. Be silent; fly
to God; consider thy nothingness; stay at home in thy own interior
life, nor need thou run to thy father confessor after every little defect. St. Matthew, all unprepared and all uninstructed as he was,

yet rose up the moment he was called and followed the Lord. And if thou catchest thyself in some fault, do not make too much ado about it. Let Divine truth itself guide thee about it, and be thou faithful in all peace of soul. Nothing can condemn thee eternally if thou dost not mortally turn away from God and wilfully give thy affection to creatures. All thy faults may be turned to good account by humbling thee, if thou wilt but keep God in thy mind and in thy heart.

But let me warn you frankly. If you allow creatures to absorb you, and that wilfully, and if you seek dangerous occasions of sin, therein is your damnation. And if God does afterwards give you the grace of true repentance (but upon this you dare not reckon), you shall, at all events, suffer an awful purgatory—if you but knew how bitter, you would wither away with fright. And if in that state of mortal sin you receive Holy Communion, it is as if you took a sweet, delicate little child and cast him into a filthy cesspool. Thus do you treat the Son of the living God, who gave Himself for your salvation. And, furthermore, your confessions will be sacrilegious if you are not resolved to avoid the proximate occasions of mortal sin—a calamity from which the Pope and all his cardinals could not save you; for your sorrow is vain, and you become guilty of the body and blood of the Lord.

I have already quoted our Lord's words: "If any man will come after Me, let him deny himself, and take up his cross daily and follow Me." Many a devout Christian takes this doctrine of self-abnegation so seriously that words cannot express how hard they are driven onward to every sort of self-denial, and how deeply they long for the cross. And very rightly, too. What costs little is worth little. "And this I say: He that soweth sparingly shall reap sparingly" (II. Cor. ix, 6). So says St. Paul. And our Lord: "With what measure you mete it shall be measured to you again" (Matt. vii, 2).

But, dear children, what is the good of my exhorting you to take up the cross if you will still obstinately cling to your old ways of external devotions? Thou must give thyself up; thou must die to thyself in thy interior. The Lord has said: Follow me. And, indeed, the servant always follows his master; he does not go before him. Nor are things arranged to suit the servant's will, but the Lord's. This applies to the inner no less than to the outer life. We need no higher learning than duly to understand what it means to be a servant of God interiorily—to give all our mental energies to do our Master's will in all things.

Child, the grain of wheat must die before it can bring forth fruit; so must thou in all sincerity die to thy own will: A man must go out and away from his own will. If he then gives himself up interiorly to God it is with him as if he had not possessed any will of his own. Once a devout nun stood singing in choir, and in her heart she sang as follows: "Lord, this time is now thine and mine, but if I turn inwards to thee, then this time is thine and not mine."

If one is going to give himself to God, he must do so by unlimited renunciation of his own will. Every man is, as it were, three men: the animal man, living according to his senses; the reasonable man guided by his understanding; and finally the Godlike man, or the man formed on God's pattern. This is the highest man, and it is the interior man. Into this interior manhood must we turn our thoughts, with it must we lie prostrated at God's feet in the abyss of His diety, delivered over to Him bound hand and foot, quite gone out of ourselves. The two lower natures we must trample under foot. In view of this it is that St. Bernard speaks: "We must withdraw the animal man from the things that he possesses with love. How hard a cross that is you know full well." And he continues: "It is not a whit less hard to draw the outward man back into the inward man; to change from a life of visible things to one of things invisible, deep in the recesses of the soul." And St. Bernard is in this justified by St. Augustine. All the afflictions of the two lower orders of life, which seem to hinder our turning inward to the highest order, if we did but accept them as crosses and offer them lovingly to God, instead of hindering us will help us to our inner perfection: and this includes all trials of the mind as well as pains of the body. We should readily leave them behind us, and diverting our souls from them, turn quickly to God in our highest spirit.

Thus did Abraham. When he went up the mount of vision to sacrifice his son, he left his servant and the ass at the foot. Our animal nature is but a beast, our natural understanding is but a servant; these serve us to bring us to the mount of vision and of sacrifice. Let them both remain below, while we go up alone with our son, namely our interior spirit. Ascending to the summit we shall there offer our best and highest gift, our very spirit itself, to God. Give thyself up instantly to God. Enter into His hidden depths, and there give Him the hidden life of thy soul. As the Psalmist says to God: "Thou shalt hide them in the secret of Thy face (Ps, xxx, 21). In this secret union with God, the created spirit has returned again into conformity with its uncreated type, as it existed in the Divine plan in eternity, though yet remaining in its own created existence: and nevertheless it is in God, because in the Divine abyss all things are as it were in God. When a man reaches this state, says Proclus, all that may affect his outer nature, as poverty and pain, he no longer adverts to. As the Psalmist again says: "Thou shalt hide them in the secret of Thy face," and then adds: "From the disturbance of men" (Ps. xxx, 21). These souls now follow our Lord in His union with the Father, as He said: "In that day you shall know that I am in the Father, and you in Me, and I in you" (John xiv, 20).

That we may all thus be drawn to our Lord, God grant us in His mercy. As Christ crucified would draw all things to Himself, may He draw us; and may He exalt us with the exaltation of His cross, placing us in the holy heights of His true love. May all this be granted us by Him who has gone before us bearing His cross and ours, and on it has died for us. *Amen.*

Jesus Crucified

Synopsis—Perfection summarized is union with Jesus crucified—Need of adjusting our motives to those of Calvary—Lessons drawn from the four parts of the cross are humility, purity of heart, love of God and of neighbor—How the cross attracts even hard sinners.

THIRD SERMON FOR THE FEAST OF THE EXALTATION OF THE HOLY CROSS.

I was exalted like a cedar in Libanus, and as a cypress tree on Mount Sion.—
Eccles. xxiv, 17.

This is the feast of that glorious cross, whose praises no words can rightly express. Let us apply our text to the cross's lessons.

On Mount Libanus grows the incense, whose fragrant vapor typifies a spiritual offering of great excellence made by man to God. They say that the smoke of burning cedar wood cures the poison of snake bite, as the cross of Christ cleanses our souls of the devil's venom. Cypress wood, they tell us, is that medicine which stops vomiting, and helps a sick man to retain good food in his stomach. Even so, if a man will but take and keep within his soul the cross of Christ, the sweet and nourishing food of God's word will abide in him. All the teachings of God's holy servants and prophets will feed his soul, not a morsel of the Divine food being lost; and it will strengthen him unto eternal life: this is the effect of one's loving Christ's cross. And the cross has a sweet fragrance of its own besides, very attractive and very strengthening, a sweetness surpassing all other, a power to win above all other. As the Lord said of His exaltation "And I, if I be lifted up from earth, will draw all things to Myself" (John xii, 32). As He was Himself attracted to the cross, so fondly drawn to it that He must be hung high upon its arms, so would He draw all men to it with the same power, namely the power of humility, and of patience, and of love. Just as He suffered, so must we in like manner suffer, each one imitating Him to the best of his ability; so that we shall in spirit be apprehended and bound with Him, condemned and put to death with Jesus crucified.

Our Lord Jesus Christ was stripped naked when He was crucified. Not a stitch of clothing was left on His body, and right before His dying eyes his garments were gambled for. Now I know as sure as there is a God, that if thou shalt come to thy best spiritual state, thou must be stripped naked of every single thing that is not God—not a thing must remain to thee. And then all that thou hadst must be made a joke and a game of before thy eyes and counted as nothing worth, and thy fellow men must reckon thee to be a fool. The Lord said: "If any man will come after Me, let him deny himself, and take up his cross daily, and follow Me" (Luke ix, 23).

And again He said: "If thou wilt be perfect, go sell what thou hast, and give to the poor, and thou shalt have treasure in heaven: and come follow Me" (Matt. xix, 21); that is to say, follow Him in the way of the cross. And this is the practical lesson of the feast of the exaltation of the holy cross. We read in the Apocalypse, of the dreadful plagues that God shall send before the day of judgment, but the exact time is not written, and we are still expecting them. But an ancient prophet tells us how men may be saved from these horrors. God said to His destroying angel: "Go through the midst of the city, through the midst of Jerusalem, and mark Thou upon the foreheads of the men that sigh, and mourn for all the abominations that are committed in the midst thereof" (Ezech. ix, 4). And these men were to be spared. Now this, mark Thou, was the last letter of the Hebrew alphabet, and was made thus—T, like a cross: the men saved were thus marked with a cross, and the rest were destroyed. The word cross means to us pain. God spared the men who had suffered pain and sighed and mourned for His sake. He did not command the angel to spare the learned, nor contemplatives, nor actively zealous men; no, it was only patiently suffering men who were to be spared. Our Lord did not say to mankind: Whosoever will follow Me, let Him become a contemplative; by no means; but let him take up his cross of daily suffering and follow Me.

A word more about the cross. The man who takes up the cross of Christ perfectly is the best man on earth. No plague can ever strike him. He shall suffer no purgatory. Nor, all things considered, is there any great pain in the cross. But alas, we have come to this: nobody nowadays thinks that he can endure any pain at all. People are grown weak-spirited and delicate-natured. The diligence and earnestness of former times has almost disappeared, the fire of love is quenched. Men will not tolerate the least discomfort. If we could find some new way of perfection involving no manner of suffering, we might preach and propegate it with success. In our day men love only themselves.

Yet the cross may not be what people think it is. It is not necessarily fasting, or watching, or going on pilgrimages, or great alms giving, or total poverty. All these serve a good purpose, indeed. Do thy share of them faithfully according as thy state of life and thy opportunities suggest. But remember that no man is too weak of body, or too old, or too stupid, but that he may yet take up Christ's glorious cross and journey with Him to eternal life.

The cross is framed of four pieces, one upward, another downward, and two sidewise. The upward piece is true Divine love. The left arm is deep humility: to this a man is nailed by genuine self abasement and renunciation of all things belonging to him. This is a better virtue than pretentious belittling of self, which may easily be mixed with secret pride. The right arm of the cross, is true, interior purity of heart. By this one is nailed fast in entire voluntary absence of whatever can stain the soul with the least fleck of creature love inner or outer. The lower part is what holds the feet fast nailed in holy obedience, true and perfect: it means quick and entire abandonment of every sense of proprietorship in thy own will. These four beams are fastened together in the midst into one cross, and it is done by this strong bolt: *Fiat voluntas tua*—Thy will be done. This makes four pieces one cross. That bolt is a true and perfect surrender of one's freedom to God.

Now notice first about the left hand—humility. With St. Augustine, we consider a man humble who gladly accepts suffering for God's sake, and willingly continues in it. Again, a humble man must be reduced to nothing in his own eyes, likewise in those of his fellowmen. He must go forth naked out of all his belongings, out of all that he is. Let men throw dice, if they please, over his very clothing; and let them despise him and make sport of him—it is all welcome to him, because he is nailed to the cross with Christ crucified. Thy whole life must be despised; thou must be regarded as an imbecile; thy opinions must be turned on thee. And when thou sufferest all this and are direfully railed at, thou must not answer back a single word; thou must feel ashamed to say a syllable in thy own defence. Thou must never say:

The man who accuses me is a liar; or this: Thou dost me an injustice. But rather shalt thou love to keep silence, and to think within thee: Ah this is a favor; I am unworthy to suffer all this; my accusers are good and noble men: God does me unmerited honor in this visitation: And thou shalt bend thy back and patiently bear thy burden.

The right hand, (to apply our figures of speech in a variety of ways), is disengagement and purity of heart. By this a man is nailed to the cross by willing destitution of all things that are not God, all that may put a spot on the soul's brightness, all joys of the senses. The lower piece is holy obedience, to which we are nailed securely by entire submission to all our superiors in holy Church. This obedience is driven home by the nail of detachment from self-will in everything whatsoever. The cross's centre, is our going forth out of selfhood; it is resignation under no matter what affliction God or man may lay upon us; suffering willingly for Christ's sake; and cheerfully ready for the cross at all times.

Perhaps thou mayst protest: Alas, sir, I cannot do this, I am too weak. But I answer thee: In thy soul there are two wills, a higher and a lower, as Christ had His Divine and human wills. Now thy lower will wants always to be free from suffering; but the higher one says with Christ to His Father: "Not what I will but what Thou wilt" (Mark xiv, 36).

The head of the cross is the love of God. Thus the soul rises upward without any interruption from God or man, looking to God in a state of entire abandonment, and saying: "My God, why hast thou forsaken Me?" (Matt. xxvii, 46). Mayst thou also utter those words with Christ crucified. Our Saviour's head as He hung dying was without any support, and in His desolate abandonment, His love gave forth those words. Once a good man asked our Lord, why it was that He allowed His friends to suffer so dreadfully. Our Lord answered: "Man is always inclined to harmful satisfaction of the senses; and therefore I restrain him and hinder him in this, so that I alone may become his satisfaction." The head of Christ, which here may mean love, hung down helplessly, having no support; and that is the universal lot of good men.

Children, turn which way you will, you must carry your cross and hang upon it. To be a good man desirous of coming to God, always means suffering. Some cross or other he must have. If he runs away from one, he will run into another. The man was never born who could preach well enough to disprove that proposition; you cannot escape suffering. Fly this way or that, try this thing or that, suffer

you must, there is no escape. It may indeed happen that God will
now and then place His own shoulders under thy burden, and lift
its heavier end off of thine; thou wilt sigh with relief, and think thyself at last totally free. But presently God withdraws His aid, and
then the weight again crushes bitterly down upon thee with intolerable oppression. Now Christ suffered all this before us in the
severest possible pain; and He has drawn after Him in this trial all
those whom He most dearly loves. His cross is Elias's fiery chariot,
bearing our prophet upwards to heaven, and from it He casts forth
His prophet's mantel on Eliseus, His disciple. Our Lord does this for
us from His cross.

Take an example. A certain sister of our order had often longed
to behold our Lord as a little child, and once during her devotions
He appeared to her in that form. But the Divine Child was wrapped
in a thorny robe. That she might embrace Him, she had to brave
the sharp points of many thorns and to suffer bitter pain from them.
Thus was she taught, that if any one would enjoy our Lord in close
embrace, he must be willing to suffer sharp, piercing pain.

But someone might object: If I am only pure and innocent, all
this teaching might profit me better; but my sins are too great that
I should merit any such favors on account of suffering. But I answer:
A man who has repented of very grievous sins, may gain extraordinary
merit from suffering, and that in several different ways:—nay, his
merit may possibly be greater than that of one who had always been
innocent. He may be compared to one who would make a great leap:
the farther he would leap the farther backwards he goes to get space
for a long run before springing into the air. So any man who goes
far back from God's face, that is to say retires into deep humiliation
of spirit on account of his sins, will on that account spring forward
into God with all the greater force. The more relentlessly one de-
grades himself in his own eyes—not simply with words, but most
truthfully in his deepest soul and because he has been a vile sinner,—
the more powerful will be his impulse of love; the more perfectly will
he become absorbed in God.

That we may permit ourselves thus to be drawn to Jesus crucified,
may He mercifully grant us. And may He enable us to give up willingly all created things for His sake. May He who suffered and died
on the cross, exalted high in the air for our sakes so that He might
draw all things to Himself—may Jesus crucified exalt us into His
company by giving us the grace of holy suffering. *Amen.*

Giving Up All

Synopsis—How striking is St. Matthew's example—Sense of ownership must be excluded from all dealings with God—We are not to be discouraged by occasional or involuntary faults against this difficult obligation—On the more hidden and painful detachments of perfect souls—Christ's passion the school of all self-renunciation.

SERMON FOR THE FEAST OF ST. MATTHEW, APOSTLE AND EVANGELIST.

And He saith to him: Follow Me. And he arose up and followed Him.—Matt. ix, 9.

This blessed apostle St. Matthew is a moving example to all men. He was at first a great sinner, as scripture tells us, and afterwards he became one of the greatest friends of God. Our Lord spoke to him; and as he heard the words they sank deep down into his soul; he instantly rose up, left all things, and followed Him. Everything depends on our doing like St. Matthew, following God in all truth.

But that means forsaking everything whatsoever that is not God and that has gained a foothold in one's soul. For God is a lover of hearts; He is not content with anything else; no gift of outward things will satisfy Him. He is concerned with the interior life of a man; He would have a man cultivate an inner inclination to all that is virtuous, all that is Divine. God is in the interior life; He is more truly there in one minute of recollection than in hours of wordy prayers, or in singing loud enough to echo through the whole earth, or in any amount of fasting and vigils, if these are done with little interior spirit.

Our Lord said: "Follow me," and to obey Him means six things, three in the lower and three in the higher faculties. In the lower, there must be humility, gentleness, and patience. The other three virtues left are high above all our powers, being supernatural: faith, hope and charity. He says: Follow. We do this, in one way, after His own example, namely, by thanksgiving and praise to His Father.

In another way we come closer to Him, transcending all methods, and yielding to a certain interior quiet. In this state our spirit is turned inward, and simply waits for God, letting Him do His will just as it may please Him. We meet men with whom all seems to go well in outward religious exercises, as prayer, fasting and vigils. But they have so absorbing a joy in these practices that God is not much reckoned with—at least directly—sometimes is quite forgotten; and then He withdraws Himself. The reason is because these men make themselves the object of their devotion, cherishing a sense of ownership of spiritual things in great self contentment. They forget that every good thing is God's and not anything is their own.

One may inquire how he shall be able to separate a good thing from the joy there is in it. I answer by a comparison. In the old law the priest was forbidden to eat the fat of the sacrifice; that was commanded to be burnt as an offering to God. But yet the fat that was in the intestines of the victim he was allowed to eat. Now we may compare the sweetness of all external devotions and good work to the outside fat of the victim. These sensible joys we must cast into the fire of love, and burn them in God's honor: He has appropriated them to Himself. But yet a certain sense of satisfaction inherent to these good works by the necessity of the case and by their very nature, these emotions one may enjoy in a single-hearted way, though without any self complacency.

Now let us apply to ourselves the spirit in which St. Matthew left all things and followed Jesus. The man who gives up everything, and includes himself in this renunciation, must follow the Lord in His outward life in all virtuous practices, and in universal love. As to the interior life, he must follow Jesus with sincere self abandonment, embracing a real freedom of spirit about all devotional practices, whether inner or outer. And listen to what I have to say about myself. From God I have received the gift of Divine grace; from holy Church I have received my holy order of St. Dominic, my habit and cowl; and from her also comes my holy priesthood; and so I am appointed to preach and to hear confessions. Now if it should happen that the pope and holy Church, from whom I have received all these privileges, should as far as possible deprive me of them, then if I were a truly detached man, I would humbly accept the deprivation nor so much as ask why it had been done. I would put on a rough gray coat—if I could get one,—and go my way. And if I could no longer live with my brothers in the monastery, than I should submit to go out of it. If I were stripped even of my priestly functions and of my power to hear confessions, and also to preach, I should say this: In God's name I give it all up; they gave me these privileges, they have taken them away from me, as they had the power to do: I will not presume to ask them why they have done so. I do not wish, indeed, to be called a heretic, nor would I like to be excommunicated. Well, then, if I had the grace to bear my trial in that spirit, I should in truth be a detached man, resigned to God's will. But take a different case, suppose someone not invested with lawful authority should try to rob me of these gifts, I should rather suffer death than submit to it; and yet in resisting with due moderation I should remain a man really detached and resigned to God's will. And should holy Church deprive me of the sacrament outwardly, I must yield with all submissiveness; but to hinder me from spiritual communion, that can no one do. Whatsoever the Church has given us, she can take away, and to her rule we must bow without the least murmuring or contradiction.

So much for disengagement of spirit in outward things. But we should go yet farther in resignation of proprietorship in inward things. What have we that God has not given us? Hence all that He gave us must be yielded up to Him again in sincere detachment just as if we never had received it. Dear people, you whose souls are occupied with devout forms and figures and thoughts, whose time is employed in the ordinary methods and good works of religion—I am not now addressing you, do not apply my words to yourselves. No; I am now speaking to those led by God in special ways of interior darkness, who have been guided into that narrow path trodden by only a few. Their way is very different from that of others, both in doing and refraining from doing certain things.

One must hold his spiritual gifts in his soul's powers without any feeling of ownership. Indeed, God's work in such a soul is in a region above the soul's powers. Let it rate all things as nothing except for God's sake alone. But meanwhile all men are naturally formed to possess, to know, and to will; and this is operative in the acitvity of the powers of nature. In this you must recall the six things I already named. In the lower faculties are humility, gentleness and patience; in the higher, faith, hope or confidence in God, and charity. And when God leads thy soul to close union with Him, He sends faith to despoil thee of thy reason, and of all knowing, and to make thee mentally blind. And when this happens to thee, thou must deny thyself thy use of reason, and of knowing, and of mental vision. And after this comes hope and robs thee of all natural confidence. Finally charity spoils thy soul, thy will, of all sense of ownership.

And these three high virtues pass from the superior faculties of the soul into the inferior ones, and they are projected into the virtues dwelling there, humility, mildness and patience. Humility vanishes away into a blank feeling of one's very nothingness, losing even its name. This meek grace had already robbed the will of the pride of selfish ownership; but now all things are become alike to the soul because all are reduced to nothingness in the soul's esteem. One no longer seems conscious of being virtuous; virtue loses its name, and its very being is lost in the one supreme virtue, love. All things are had in even minded peace. As to patience, love so rules the soul that its thirst for suffering seems but love, and patience is known no more by its own name.

Dear children, amid all this state of detachment one may commit faults. A fit of anger may seize one, and an ugly word may escape one; but this should not discourage thee. God allows this in order to sink thee yet deeper in thy own nothingness, causing thee to know how unworthy thou art of receiving even a good thought from God. Upon one thing everything depends, namely, a bottomless sense of thy own perfect nothingness. As to the spiritual exercises of persons thus placed, they are not the ordinary outward devotions, nor ordinary methods of prayer with forms and figures in the imagination. Let those who have not reached so far diligently cultivate all these, and God will forgive them their sins, and lead them through purgatory to the kingdom of heaven. You must know that it is not by self-chosen pious practices that one arrives at the more perfect state we have been considering, no, nor even to be made servants of the servants of these favored souls. If such chosen ones are only well advised, they are above measure fortunate; and yet it is as perilous a state as that of the wildest men in the world, for it places souls on a darksome road; as Job says: "A man whose way is hidden, and God hath surrounded Him with darkness" (Job iii, 23). In that desert road all depends on a man walking in a state of entire self-abasement, detached from every thing that may possibly arise before him. To such a soul our Lord would say: Follow me—come onward through and past all things: whatsoever thou seest is not Myself—forward! follow Me, never stop.

Then the soul may ask: Lord, who art Thou, that I must follow after Thee in this dark, wild and gloomy road? And Jesus may answer: I am Man and God, and far more God than thou canst understand. And O how happy for that soul, if it can but respond to the Lord: Thou art God, and I am nothing and less than nothing. For in truth the infinite and unnamed God can have no other place or state to work His will in, than in the depths of a soul that confesses itself to be nothing.

Philosophers tell us that when a new form of existence enters a substance the old form must needs be destroyed; as when in the mother's womb mere matter gives place to the animal form, and then in God's due time the animal form receives the rational soul, forming the human nature—quality, quantity, shape, color, and the like, all being assimilated to the new form. So I affirm of the transformation of the soul by this superessential process: all its forms must needs, in a sense, yield place to God, such as the powers of knowing, willing, acting, feeling, self proprietorship. When St. Paul at the gate of Damascus was struck blind, he saw God. When Elias covered his head with his mantle, the Lord appeared to him.

And now all rocks shall be rent asunder: all that the spirit rested on, is shattered and torn away. And when all natural forms and conditions are gone, the very same instant the soul is transformed. Therefore must thou ever keep on and go forward. The heavenly Father says: "Thou shalt call Me Father and shalt not cease to walk after Me" (Jer. iii, 19). As if to say: On and on must thou go, deeper and deeper into the unnamed and unknown abyss, nearer and nearer to Me: far above all methods, and all figures of the mind, thy soul stripped naked, thy mental faculties lost in Me. Into this lost state of soul no ray of light ever flashes but only one; and this lights up and reveals the all sufficient being of God—one in essense, one in life, above all. A man may say of this rapture that he is so absorbed in God, that in himself he is devoid of consciousness, of love, and of spirit. But this is not to be understood to mean the effacement of one's natural individuality, but tells of the transformation which the Spirit of God works in the created spirit out of His own free goodness; and it tells of the created spirit's bottomless feeling of being lost in God, and its immeasurable disengagement from all that is not God. Of this state we may also say that in it the soul learns to know God, to love Him and enjoy Him in a transcendent manner, for now there remains to it nothing at all but one life, one being, one act—God. But if it should happen that a soul thus favored, should bear itself with undue freedom and should follow after any false guidance, it would be in the most perilous condition possible in this life.

The way and method to reach this happy state, is the study and imitation of the life and passion and death of our blessed Lord. For He is the way that we must walk, He is the truth that lights up the way, He is the life that we must attain to live. He is also the door; and He tells us that whosoever enters unto God through any other door is a thief and a robber. Through this blessed door, then, all must enter, breaking down nature's resistence in the steadfast practise of·virtue, especially humility, mildness and patience. Be sure that anyone who fancies that he has come to perfection without treading this road, is under a delusion. From such persons God is far removed, and they are blind and self-blinded.

As to those who have sincerely trodden in our Lord's footsteps and obtained this state of perfection, the authorities of holy Church from the pope down, feel no uneasiness about them, nor need they. For they obey all laws out of love. As St. Paul says: "If you are led by the Spirit, you are not under the law" (Gal. v,18). Life is never weary to such souls, for tedium never oppresses them. The same cannot be said of any world-lovers, for their love palls on them. Whereas in these heavenly lovers, their very existence has in the superior powers of the soul, been lifted above time and its weary changes. And even in their inferior faculties their life is full of freedom, for they are detached from affection for all things: they have come into a land of essential peace. From God they accept instinctively all that happens to them, and in the same spirit they offer up all to Him again, and so they abide in sweet tranquility of mind. And this is true of them even while their outward man is much disturbed and sorely pained. O what happy men are these. Wherever they are found, they should be honored by all. But I fear that such Divine seed is but thinly sowed among us. Let us beseech our Lord to grant us the grace to follow Him in this manner, and that we may acquire these high privileges. *Amen.*

The Holy Angels

Synopsis—The angels are actively engaged in our behalf—How dear to us should be our guardian angels—How the different choirs of angels are engaged with different states and classes of men.

SERMON FOR THE FEAST OF ST. MICHAEL AND ALL HOLY ANGELS.

Their angels in heaven always see the face of My Father who is in heaven.—Matt. xviii, 10.

This is the blessed feast of the holy angels, and we have seen how it arose from the apparition of St. Michael on Mount Gargano. With what words one may rightly tell of these holy spirits, I do not know, for they have no bodily form, no hands or feet or outward appearance. How can we so much as imagine them?—least of all describe them. Nor is it any wonder we know so little of them, for what do we know of our own souls, by which we are constituted human beings? Why wonder, then, that we cannot understand these transcendent angelic beings, whose nobility so far excells all human excellence. Hence it is not of their essential being that we can speak, but only of their work with us. Now their activity among and with us, is conditioned on this: they ever behold us in the mirror of the Godhead, each one of us in his own distinct form and essence. As God acts universally upon us and without distinction of this one or that one, because He is the infinite God, so do the angels act upon each of us separately. God's activity in us is infinitely more noble, and is exclusively His own; their's is in cooperation with His, as the rays of the sun in the sky distribute its light throughout the earth. Or, again, as the stars give us the reflexion of the sun's light, so do the angels bear the Divine brightness to our souls.

The angels are divided into three hierarchies, and each of these into three choirs. Each hierarchy has its own peculiar office in God's work with us, and its special relation to the three lives we lead: first, the outward bodily life of the senses; second, the interior life of intelligence, our reason; third, the high, Godlike, most hidden and interior man. All of these together are one and the same man, over whom the angels have custody. Each of us has his own special angel, given him in baptism, the angel guardian. He is always with us, sleeping or waking, working or resting, whether we are bad or good. O, if we had nothing else to thank God for, how deeply should we love Him for binding each one of us so fast and firm to such glorious being as an angel of heaven. But, be it remembered, every man has also his particular devil, ever actively scheming against his welfare, just as the angel strives for his salvation. And let me say this: if a man were only wise and diligent, the devil's warfare would serve him better than the angel's care, for without a battle there is no victory.

As to the hierarchies, the lowest is called that of the Angels, pure and simple, who serve us in our outward life, warning, guiding, and helping in the way of virtue and peace with sleepless zeal. Without this guardianship, what calamity, think you, would not fall upon mankind. We should be exposed helplessly to the plots of the malignant demons. Against these the good Angels ever assist us.

Above the Angels are the Archangels, and these are like angelic priests, for their office is to help us to profit by the sacraments of holy Church, especially by the worthy reception of Holy Communion. Above these again stand the order of blessed spirits called the Virtues, ever urging us onward in the practice of various kinds of natural and moral virtues; and in addition to that, they win us by their secret influence to the practice of the holier virtues of faith, hope and love. Happy are the men who obey their sweet whispers, and who live in familiar friendship with them. To such men the practise of virtue grows so easy and its fruit so delicious as to become, as it were, a part of their very nature. Children, against these good men, the fiends who have fallen from this order of the Virtues, level their fiercest strokes. All their cunning devices are set to work to hinder their salvation; for they, if they but persevere to the end, will be given the places in that rank of heavenly spirits from which those demons themselves have fallen. The maliginty of these evil spirits is inevitably great, and it works incessantly. We must stand our watch against them with sleepless vigilence; for often times their deadliest scheming takes the form of something good. Especially do they strive to divide and scatter our affections away from God, and to waste them upon a multiplicity of created things. Often enough, when one has reached a state of moderate virtue, the demons will do their utmost to hinder him from advancing to that further state of perfection which God would have him reach. This is a very dangerous condition to him, and the devil is well aware of it: in our times there are more souls thus halted, while God calls them to go forward, than at any previous time. St. Bernard says: "In the way of God, to stand still is to go backward."

In this state of stagnation are all those worldly hearts, who say: We do as many good works as others do, and that amply suffices for us; indeed, we are better than those who pretend to greater perfection; and we will continue in the good ways of those who have gone before us. But when some great trial comes upon these men, then shall we hear their lamentations: it will be shown that they were not as good as they thought they were. The evil spirits will work their fiendish will upon them, and at last lead them away without resistance. The contrary will be the case with fervent spirits, who have hearkened to the counsel of these good Angels. When their trials are passed and gone, they will be found all purified and made holy by them; they will be, as it were, on terms of familiar friendship with those bright spirits, who will continue to conduct them towards a happy end.

Of the other and superior orders in the hierarchy of blessed spirits, we are told that they are given custody over men's intelligence, by which we are raised above all other bodily creatures, and are made like the Angels themselves. They are called the Powers, the Principalities, and the Dominations. These principally assist those men who have made some progress in virtue, aiding them to self mastery, as well over the senses and the outward life as over interior faculties of the soul. By their aid a man can rightly guide his thoughts, and words and deeds, attaining a noble freedom from our naturally vicious inclinations. Thus it is related of St. Francis, that he was given such a mastery over his external nature that when he made up his mind to do any good work, his body seemed instantly to respond and to say: Behold Me before thee, ready to obey. These men are as it were the princes of this world, for they are free from nature's corrupt constraint and subject to no weakness, ruling all movements of their inner and their outer nature according to God.

And when the evil spirits see these souls thus full of power for good, they are devoured with incredible hate; they cannot bear the thought that these shall take the places in heaven they themselves have forfeited.

One can hardly imagine the violence of the temptations they launch against them, the like of which commonplace worldlings have never known. But when these souls are almost driven mad with their trials, then come the angelic Princes, members of the choir of the Principalities, and rescue them from their enemies: thus the victory is won. After that the fiend molests them no more. The demon's pride is now fatally hurt, and he dreads another conflict with so powerful a foe. And then a mighty angel of that choir called the Powers, becomes active in such a soul. By his means a man's reason becomes so strong, that he is able to detect the treacherous purposes of the demons, as St. Paul says that neither the mighty ones of this world nor those of hell itself could ever overcome him. After this comes the third hierarchy to do their holy work in the innermost soul, where man is transformed and new made in God.

Of these the first choir is called the Thrones, the second the Cherubim, the third the Seraphim. The first makes a man's inner spirit a royal throne for God. There He rests and dwells and rules with Divine joy; there He judges and rewards this soul, and guides all its activity, both interior and exterior. Now does such a man become so immovably fixed in his freedom from evil, that scarcely anything is so hard or so enticing, so sweet or so bitter, as to be able to disturb him. As St. Paul says: "I am sure that neither death nor life—nor any other creature, shall be able to separate us from the love of God, which is in Christ Jesus our Lord" (Rom. viii, 38, 39). A hundred deaths could not move such a soul from God. He is like a man on the point of death, to whom all honor and shame are alike indifferent, for he is now turned to the other life. So is this interior man always turned with a life and death determination, towards God enthroned in the remotest chamber of his spirit. Peace of soul possesses him under all happenings, for he has the Prince of peace within him; as David said of God: "His place is in peace" (Ps. lxxv, 2). Dear child, may God grant thee this place of peace in thy soul, and may His holy angel help thee to guard it securely from all disturbance. Be silent, avoid men, suffer patiently, and sit down in peace. In all confidence remain at home with thyself, seldom go abroad, keep careful watch over thy thoughts, shrink away from contentions and disturbances; watch Him who is enthroned within thee all powerful, all glorious. Never let there be the least interruption to His peaceful sway over thee.

And after this the Cherubim take up their part, which is to pour a brilliant light into the soul, casting as it were with quick flashes the tints of the Divine beauty upon that soul. By these Divine gleams of heavenly splendor, the soul is so penetrated with the light of wisdom, that were it necessary it could instruct the whole race of mankind with the brightest teaching. And this enlightenment is given in flashes, ever growing quicker, truer, more splendid, and more certain.

Finally come the burning Seraphim with their blazing fire of love. In an instant these set the soul's depths on fire. Then does a man's love blaze out so wide and so hot, that it enwraps and includes in itself all things whatsoever. He feels as if he would set fire to all men and to all things and consume them with his love—and this feeling comes to him instantaneously. And it is so vehement a fire that he would himself love to be burnt up with love.

All this happens in the inmost depths of the enlightened soul. But yet it is exhibited in both the interior and exterior faculties. These are now Divinely ordered. Such a man is so far detached from affection for earthly things, so virtuous, peaceful and quiet, that not the least imperfection can be noticed in any of his words or acts. And meanwhile he reckons himself as nothing at all. All these marvels of grace, of angelic inter-position in his spirit, seem to him no more his own than if they had been operated in another man a thousand miles distant. He cherishes no attachment whatsoever for all that God does in him or can do—only to God is he given over, and to Him wholly and entirely. He places himself last of all in the entire race of mankind. These souls are the very heaven in which the Divine Spirit dwells, as our text says: "Their angels in heaven always see the face of My Father who is in heaven." May God grant us all the grace to reach this holy state. *Amen.*

The Beatitudes

*Synopsis—The multitude who heard the Sermon on the Mount is typi-
cal of heaven—Poverty leads the holy throng—Involuntary poverty, a state dear to our Lord—Voluntary poverty includes a deep
love for the poor—The other beatitudes considered in detail.*

FIRST SERMON FOR THE FEAST OF ALL SAINTS.

And seeing the multitudes, He went up into a mountain, and when He was set
down, His disciples came unto Him. And opening His mouth, He taught them
saying: Blessed are the poor in spirit: for theirs is the kingdom of heaven.—
Matt. v, 1-3.

Thus it was that our Lord taught us the eight Beatitudes. The mountain into which Jesus went up, may be considered as His own Divine
beatitude, by which He is one with His Father. There followed Him
a great multitude of all His beloved saints, whose solemnity we this day
celebrate. And how variously did all these follow Him, each one according to his different calling from God. It behooves us to do likewise,
everyone of us observing closely what his vocation from God may be,
and therein to abide in peace.

Let us honor these great servants of God with all earnestness. And
now what is the best honor we can do them? It is to cultivate entire
detachment of spirit from all created things; and then to sink deep
into the heart of God as they did, and to be lost there. That is their
beatitude; no other can be ours. This sentiment is the best celebration
of their holy feast.

Let us closely study this holy multitude, assembled on God's mountain, each one placed and ranked as God has differently drawn and
appointed him. First came the ancient Fathers of the old law, who
spent their lives in ardent sighings for the coming of the Redeemer.
They were filled with God's hope and love; and not only outwardly but
inwardly they were disengaged from all things that were not God.
With great charity did they share all their possessions with God's
chosen people. They were deeply concerned lest any fault should stain
that race, out of which was to spring forth the Saviour of the world.

They lived without any proprietorship of their own flesh, which was dedicated to the birth of the Messiah. Of this race it is read today in the Apocalypse, that out of each of its twelve tribes, twelve thousand were signed with God's special favor; and after these followed on a multitude so great that no man could number them.

After them came the glorious company of the holy apostles, called by our Lord to a far higher perfection. Not only by secret longings, but in actual possession did these have the Redeemer. They were with Him in true poverty of spirit and of body; indeed they attained the highest degree of holy poverty that a man can ever reach.

Then came Christ's martyrs, a vast multitude of heroic souls. They not only gave up all things for His sake, but they gave up their very lives, just when and where and how God willed.

Then came the great army of holy confessors of Christ's faith, who had variously followed Him in many a sacred calling. Some of them were hermits, and spent their lives in solitude, far removed from all men. There they sat still and hearkened to what God, the eternal Word, spoke within them, dwelling in deserts, in caves and in forests. Others again passed their lives in the state of holy orders, as God provided for them. These labored in holy church in preaching God's word to her children, in writing about Divine things, hearing confessions, teaching, governing congregations; all done with ready good will as God guided them, in true submission to Him, and detachment of spirit from both themselves and all things else that are not God.

Then there followed the Lord the great choir of the pure and spotless virgins, chaste in soul as well as body. O how lovely a thing is that—to be found at death as clean as an angel of God, to be clothed in that robe of virgin whiteness that our Lord and His holy mother prized above all other adornment. Whosoever is granted this privilege, may laugh to scorn all the troubles of life. As long as he holds fast to this priceless pearl, no pain that is known to man can reach his heart. But thus to retain holy chastity, one must make ready to fight a hard battle. He must suffer many a pang from the rebellion of his senses and the foolishness of this world, besides the plots of the devils. But be well assured that such striving every way brightens the purity of a chaste soul with renewed splendor. Dear child, keep a close guard over thyself, and often call to mind the wondrous reward of chastity in the company of Christ's holy virgins.

After these the great multitude of the Christian people follow our

Lord, men and women who have lived in the world and been occupied in the common walks of life. These were upheld and saved by the prayers and ministration of the closer friends of God; and ere they come into the Father's kingdom, they must for the most part be purified in purgatory. As we celebrate the perfectly sanctified souls in this festival of All Saints, so tomorrow we shall commemorate the souls not yet perfectly sanctified, namely those in purgatory. And we should realize that for one earthly self satisfaction, one venial sin, we shall suffer sharper pains than were endured by all the martyrs whom today we honor. This needs must be, as we can see if we consider what it is to stand against the infinite God even in the smallest matter.

Now all these beautiful groupings of holy men and women, form the great multitude that have followed Christ to the mount of His Beatitudes. And having them gathered about Him, He opened His Divine mouth and He proclaimed His eight Beatitudes. Let us say a few words about each of them. First: "Blessed are the poor in spirit, for theirs is the kingdom of heaven." This virtue is given the first place, because it is a capital or head virtue, and a beginning of all perfection. Children, whatever way you look at Christian perfection, the inmost soul of a man must, to begin with, be free, and unencumbered, and therefore destitute. If God is to do His work in thy soul, it must be stript of all ownership. That is a foregone conclusion, if God is to make thy soul His own.

One kind of poverty is to be poor against one's will. Persons who are thus poor may have their faults, but let no man judge them harshly, for our Lord overlooks their defects all the more graciously on account of their poverty.

The second kind is spoken of by St. Thomas. Herein man loves poverty and practises it according to his lights, because he knows that it ministers to his freedom of spirit and detachment; but yet he retains his own necessary goods. Many a one is only the more elevated in spirit if he is placed so as not always to feel want, rather than if he must daily struggle for life's comforts. When one lawfully possesses the goods of this world, offering thanks to God for the same, he is sometimes more pleasing to God, than if he must look out constantly for his bare support. But in case one finds his ownership of goods absorbing his mind and becoming inordinate, hindering the practice of such virtues as meekness, temperance, humility, disengagement of spirit, then he should give up his goods and should join those men who practise outward poverty.

The third kind of poverty is that in which God is so dear to a man, that none of this world's goods can hinder his love for Him. More: everything in the world helps him to love God. St. Paul says: "We know that to them that love God, all things work together unto good" (Rom. viii, 28). Such a soul is untouched by anything that is not simply God, his whole spirit being immune from the love of earthly goods, remaining under all circumstances poor and detached. The apostle tells of this kind of spirit: "As having nothing, and possessing all things" (II Cor. vi, 10). Such a man may own the treasures of a kingdom without harm to his inward spirit.

The fourth kind is a deep love to be poor, with the motive of being in the company of our blessed Lord Jesus Christ in His state of destitution. This poverty is embraced out of unfeigned desire to have a soul unencumbered of all that is not God, interiorly and exteriorly. It helps the return of our spirit into God its origin by detaching it from all creatures. It makes it harder for any sudden danger to fetch us down, for it clears the spiritual perceptions, and smooths the way to our turning inwards to God. Children, this is the purest poverty. For the highest dignity of poverty is this: it facilitates our soul's flight to the heart of God; or will increase the beatitude of the soul in eternity.

And now let us consider the second Beatitude: "Blessed are the meek, for they shall posses the land." This lifts us a grade higher in beatitude. True poverty, indeed, frees us from certain hindrances: but this blessed meekness goes deeper, and banishes from our hearts all bitterness, wrath, and untruthfulness. For it is written: "All things are clean to the clean" (Titus i, 15). To the gentle minded, bitterness is unknown, and this comes from the solid foundation of goodness in him, which makes all things good.

Dear child, in former times the pagans tortured God's friends, but nowadays good appearing Christians persecute those who would closely follow Christ. Ah yes, these thy neighbors inflict deep wounds upon thee. If thou wouldst serve God perfectly men say to thee: Thou art raving to do such things, thou are guilty of singularity, thou art a deceiver. Then comes meekness to thee and leads thee back into thyself; and now thou acceptest all this as from God and not from man. And then thou restest peaceful, and sayest to thyself: What harm can men do thee, if thou remainest a faithful friend of God? Thus does the soul that is meek possess the land, namely interior peace; that heritage remains his no matter what befalls him. If thou shalt act otherwise, then thou failest in virtue and losest thy peace, and art no better than a snarling dog in thy quarrelsome resistence to God's visitations.

The third Beatitude is, "Blessed are they that mourn, for they shall be comforted." And who are the mourners? In one sense they are those who have any suffering whatever to endure. In another sense, they are those who mourn and weep in sorrow for their sins. Yet again it is those faithful friends of God who have done true penance, and have already bewailed their sins and been entirely pardoned. They need not weep any more for their own sins, but they do weep bitterly for the sins and imperfections of their fellowmen. We read that once our holy Father St. Dominic asked one of his companions why he was weeping so bitterly. "Dear Father," said he, "it is on account of my sins." Then the saint answered: "No, dear son, weep not for them, I pray thee, for they are pardoned and all penance done for them. But I beg thee to weep now for the sins of those who will not weep themselves for their wickedness." God's true friends weep over men's blindness of heart, and over the miserable sinfulness of the whole world. When we see the threat of God's wrath upon us, in fire and flood and storms and darkness and famine, then do we weep and mourn before God's face, day and night imploring Him to spare us. And so he holds back His hand and gives us space for repentence. But if we do not use this respite well, He visits us with yet greater plagues. The dark cloud of God's judgment hangs over us, but God's servants keep it back with their tears. But be sure that if we do not repent, the Divine wrath will break forth against us with such fury as will make us dread that the day of judgment is at hand. Those who now rest in the false peace of sin, will then feel the heavy hand of justice. They easily omit hearing mass; they readily neglect hearing God's word—these Divine things are growing very strange to them, as one of them goes here and another there in his guilty ways. But others there are, whom the faithful God will find true to Him. These weep and mourn for their sinful brethren.

The fourth Beatitude is, "Blessed are they that hunger and thirst after justice." Children, this is a virtue that few men have possessed in such measure, as that all their hunger and thirst and desire was after God's justice and nothing whatsoever besides. That would mean longing for neither the favor nor disfavor of men, neither for my profit nor that of my friends, caring neither for praise nor blame—only for God. Such a man as that is well worthy our admiration, for whosoever has reached so high a degree as to care only for God's righteousness, nor can enjoy the thought of anything else except God alone, may indeed be called blessed.

The fifth Beatitude is "Blessed are the merciful, for they shall obtain mercy." Of mercy it is written: "The Lord is sweet to all, and His tender mercies are over all His works" (Ps. cxliv, 9). Therefore is a truly merciful man a Godlike man, for mercy is born of Divine love and kindness. Hence it happens that real friends of God are more merciful than other men, and are more trustful and patient with sinners than those who love God less than they do. Mercy springs from that mutual love that men should have one for another. At the last day our ·Lord will demand an account of this brotherly love, and if we cannot show that we have had it He will withhold His mercy from us. He will say nothing about all other perfections, and will found His sentence on this question alone: Were you merciful to your fellowmen? Nor does this virtue consist alone in giving gifts. No, it extends to a merciful regard of all the faults our neighbor commits, and patient endurance of all the injuries He may inflict on us. Whosoever does not feel a loving sympathy for his neighbor's misery, whosoever does not overlook his faults with kindly feelings—such a man may well forbode that the Lord will not show him mercy, for with the measure with which thou metest it shall be measured again to thyself withal. See to it, that thou dost not condemn thy neighbor, lest thou thyself shalt be condemned eternally.

The sixth Beatitude is: "Blessed are the peacemakers, for they shall be called the children of God." Men of truly peaceful hearts are indeed blessed men. No man can take their peace away, either in time or eternity. For all their will has gone out from them into God's will, in joy or sadness, in weal and woe, for time and eternity. All their doings are according to God's ways and not men's, for they are guided supernaturally, Divinely. They are baptized in the power of the Father, in the wisdom of the Son, and in the sweet love of the Holy Ghost, and this Divine influence has penetrated so deep, that their peace is beyond man's reach to disturb. The tranquility of the blessed Trinity has so entirely sanctified them, that they could order and rule the whole land with their peaceful wisdom; for the eternal wisdom has filled them with its light. And they are just as full of love. Gladly would they overflow upon their fellow men in great floods of love and of peace, expending their inner and outer life entirely for their welfare. Touch them how you please, peace and love come forth upon you. These hearts are indeed the peacemakers of mankind, having that peace which passeth all understanding. Well may they be called the children of God. For the fountain of peace that is Christ's because He is by nature the Son of God, that same is theirs by the participation of grace, for they are truly begotten in the heart of God. Nor can any such peace as theirs be otherwise obtained, than by a most interior union with God. This Beatitude can not be gained by self chosen methods of piety of an outward description.

The seventh Beatitude is: "Blessed are the clean of heart, for they shall see God." What is a clean heart? It is a heart free from the entanglement of creatures; a heart whose depths God finds empty of all love, naked of all attachments to creatures. These clean souls will truly see God. Purity of heart is stained, when a man willfully seeks satisfaction in created things and rests in them. In whatever degree a man finds content in creatures, in the same does he cut himself off from God. And the effect is such darkening of his soul's vision as to hinder his seeing and finding God in the interior life. Outward conditions of chastity aid the soul's interior cleanliness, as St .Paul says: "He that is without a wife, is solicitous for the things that belong to the Lord, how he may please God" (I Cor. vii, 32). As with bodily chastity, so with purity of heart. As the former is sullied by unguarded mingling with outward company, so is the Godlike integrity of the spirit, soiled and even destroyed by wilful contact with what bears not the stamp of God. The soul's eyes become darkened, so that it cannot recognize the Divine source of all purity within its depths. It requires a soul all cleansed from worldly and fleshly satisfaction to enable one to flow back without ceasing into God, our creator and our beginning. Cleanness of heart is a most admirable virtue, inasmuch as it prepares the human spirit to be the spouse of God, and fixes all its desires upon Him alone.

The eighth Beatitude is: "Blessed are they that suffer persecution for justice's sake, for their's is the kingdom of heaven." No man can fully explain, or indeed understand, what an amount of good lies hidden in suffering. Our faithful God, who has set apart His chosen ones for close union with Himself, when He sees that their life is not conducive to that, visits them with quick and terrible suffering. By that means, whether they will or not, they must partake of his beatitude And that is a trait of fidelity in God that we should be exceedingly thankful for. That I must suffer is a favor from God that I am unworthy of. And it causes a great hope to rise in my heart that God has a special love for me, for it makes me like His Divine Son, and compels me to imitate Him. St. Bernard says: "It is a far greater honor to suffer slight pain with holy patience, than to perform many good works for God." And St. Thomas says: "There is no pain so slight, whether in our interior or exterior life, but that in suffering it patiently we may image forth the adorable passion of our Lord Jesus Christ; and in every suffering we endure, we can, if we will, obtain a share of the merits of Jesus crucified."

But I must speak of a nobler kind of suffering, and a sort that brings us yet closer to God, than even these wonderfully beneficial pains and deprivations. I mean suffering from the direct act of God in our inner life. As high as God is above creatures, so is this pain greater than any that man can inflict on us. It is the pain of being compared with God's greatness and holiness now fully revealed. We should love Him dearly for securing our eternal beatitude by suffering direct from His own self. Our beatitude thus becomes God's work and not ours; we have but to accept Him and yield to Him.

By nature a man is better fitted to suffer than to act, to accept than to give. Every gift of God makes our longing for all His gifts a thousandfold greater, if we will but passively sit still and wait for God's action in us, giving Him all room in our souls to continue and complete His blessed work. For God's is most pure act, and the soul, on the contrary, in this supernatural relation to Him, is purely passive. If a man will but rest tranquil under God's action, only accepting and longing and nothing more, God will perfect His plans upon him, and impart to him His marvelous beatitude. May God grant us to be still, patient, and passive under His hand, and to experience the fulness of His loving influence. *Amen.*

Interior Cleanliness

*Synopsis—The pain of holy purification—Unbridled passion described
—How virtue succeeds vice in the purifying process—Vigilance,
courage and patience the virtues principally needed for gaining
purity of heart.*

SECOND SERMON FOR THE FEAST OF ALL SAINTS.

Blessed are the clean of heart, for they shall see God.—Matt. v, 8.

Dear children, be assured of this: all who would be well pleasing to
God, must be free from every spot and blemish, or God will not accept
them, rather does He leave them to their devious wanderings. A man
should aspire not only to be quit of his sins, but to lead a life of detachment from creatures, and this with the purpose of giving Himself
wholly to God's service. This cleanness of heart is indispensable if one
would hearken to God's loving inspirations in his soul. Now, if this
be needful for the present life, so is it for a high place of glory in the
next life.

To have us clean of heart in this sense is the end God has in view
in giving us His graces. The first effect of these is to set one to examining his conscience diligently, and then to the banishing from his life
every sinful thing by means of earnest mortification of the outer senses
and the inner weaknesses. And what is meant by a good conscience?
It is a very peaceful spirit, making little of self, humbly devoted to
God's will, eager for His honor. It causes one to stand indifferent
as to all giving and getting, quite without choice, except that the soul
craves to enjoy that beatific state in which God's will shall be done
in it without resistance.

But ere the soul arrives at this state of freedom and of peaceful
detachment, it must be heavily oppressed with sorrow, and hence God
scourges it with inward pain. First comes a burning knowledge of
the malice of its mortal sins. It bewails them with deep sincerity and
great pain, and hates and avoids all wickedness with steadfast courage, including all dangerous occasions of sin. During all this the soul
eagerly yearns to be clean of heart, and never again wilfully to trans-

gress God's law. After that the soul begins to practice works of penance, setting itself relentlessly to mortify sensuality in every way, refraining itself even from lawful pleasures, as in eating and drinking, visiting and conversing, rest and work. All this it does to advance in perfection, following the gospel counsels of poverty, chastity and obedience. In due time a great change is seen. Whereas once the soul found its joy in self indulgence, the very thought of such things now causes it pain. Thus it is that the heart is made clean of the least stains of venial sin, while formerly it thought it sufficient to guard against gross mortal sins.

And now the spirit would conquer the body, and the lower nature resents that, for it means a heavy bodily discipline and the retrenchment of its accustomed pleasures. The brutish nature of a man repines at this, and may not easily and patiently yield to reason's sway: the perverted lower spirit revolts. Naturally one does not brook restraint in his indulgence of the life of the senses. He craves to idly gossip and chatter with his friends and hates holy silence; he would have liberty to complain; he must have leave to boast. Whatsoever he does not like, he resents accepting. If he has aversion for anyone he insults him; the instant he is pained he flies into a passion; he follows his prejudices blindly; what is sweet to him is good, what is bitter is bad; if he praises anyone, all must echo him; and if he condemns anyone, none dare praise him.

Now against all this one strives manfully, if he would become clean of heart. First he studies it all over very carefully, playing well the part of self-observation. He would know above all else what sort of a man he is, and what power he has over his natural forces. But the cleansing of his heart he finds to be a heavy task. Oppression of spirit he will not endure, nor inward shame: he must force these upon himself violently. But one thing he has: much contrition and real humility before God; and even to his fellows he owns his miserable weakness. Yet, thus far he has hardly learned the real meaning of Christian mortification; and he may easily make a misstep, for in his nature's depths his evil propensities still lie hidden. They drive him towards outward sins, which he can hardly keep away from. And now his greatest need is the practice of the outward virtues, following the pattern of our Lord Jesus Christ; and ever and everywhere to shun the dangerous occasions of sin.

After some progress has been made in this heavy fight against the

grosser vices, a man gradually acquires a spiritual tone of life in his
practise of virtue. His part is now to practise most fervent prayer,
springing out of a heart weary with the struggle against sin. A sure
result is far deeper contrition than before. He is overwhelmed with
shame, as God gives him a clearer knowledge of his former depravity.
He begins more easily to accept pains and miseries and contradictions
and disgrace, as being a fit offering to God in atonement for his wickedness. Love soon begins to take the ruling place, and with it comes
the virtue of detachment from created things, together with firmer
faith and more lively hope in Christ Jesus. He will now have nothing
of his own, lest the sense of ownership should stain the purity of his
motives in the least degree. Self hatred often quite posesses him, and
by that humble condition of soul he is hindered from judging others.
The instant he is conscious of temptation, he shuts and locks all his
senses; he avoids every danger lest he should give the enemy the least
advantage.

Soon he begins to cleave to God with all his heart, and would think
of nothing else. Come what may against him, he is ready with holy
patience, and waits meekly till God comes to his relief, for he will by
no means loosen himself from the cross by seeking either mental or bodily solace. Along with this there comes to him much docility of spirit.
He seeks and easily follows good counsel; and he obeys his superiors
because he is submissive to God. He looks straight at the duty of the
moment; is it to do some good work? He straightway does it. Is it
to patiently resist temptation? He resolutely does so. And he thanks
God for all that comes and goes. If he suffers want, he learns to utter
no complaint except, perhaps, very humbly to God. He boasts of nothing, is self complacent over nothing—God and God alone is his joy, and
that above all things To Him he offers thanks for sweet and bitter
gifts with equal fervor. As to his imperfect brethren, he has no pride
over them, but much kind heartednes for their weakness. He shuns
outward silliness, and puts a rein on his tendency to excessive mer-
riment.

He dreads a spirit of routine in performing spiritual exercises,
and hates lukewarmness of spirit. Nor will he gluttonize in the sweetness of sensible devotion. With him, that alone is good which is close
to God. Watch and ward is his motto in dealing with himself. It
comes at last to this: he cannot help belittling himself in his own
mind. If he advises against any defect, he leads the way in shunning

it, and especially every form of self-will. He busily labors to raise the house of perfection on the solid foundation of self abasement, in which he offers himself to God, bearing in his soul and body the life, passion and death of Jesus Christ. On no creature will he place the least reliance, but only on God. O how he longs to love God more ardently; how ambitious he is to be a true lover of God, clean hearted, clearly guided by Divine truth towards his eternal beatitude. God grant us all to come to that blessed state. *Amen.*

Perfection the Pearl of Great Price

*Synopsis—The first practical rule for acquiring perfection is loving
imitation of Christ's life and passion—This involves daily meditation on His words and deeds—The need of an interior spirit in this
exercise—The second rule is rigid fidelity to the routine of a pious
life—This must be based on principle—Peace and joy resulting
therefrom.*

SERMON FOR THE FEAST OF ST. CATHERINE, VIRGIN AND MARTYR.

Who, when he had found one pearl of great price, went his way, and sold all
that he had, and bought it.—Matt. xiii, 46.

We may understand this parable as referring to a Christian virgin,
who, for the sake of safely keeping holy chastity, has given up all
things. Or, again, the virgin of Christ has found the pearl of great
price in His sacred passion, and in that passion she has followed
Him, renouncing for His sake all natural and worldly pleasure.

The shortest way to serve God perfectly is found in two things:
the first is faithful observance of the common religious practises of
holy Church, including a life of obedience, poverty, chastity, and the
other pious practices handed down by the fathers. This course disciplines our outward conduct and trains us to the acquisition of
virtue.

The other is imitation of Christ in His passion. Once a day we
should meditate diligently on His life, sufferings and death, conforming ourselves as strictly as possible to them as to our model. Especially
should we note the various happenings of our life, receiving them as
from God's hand, and studying His meaning in sending them, so that
we may thus the better give ourselves up to Him and follow His guidance. A careful consideration of what daily occurs reveals God's
great mercy in dealing with us. Not a day passes but He would lead
us higher up towards Himself, conforming us more and more nearly
to the image of His Divine Son in all He gives us to do and to suffer.
Meanwhile a man should direct his intention strictly to God's honor

in every act of the day or night. He should, besides, suppress the inordinate activity of his senses, having in near view the quenching of all love of worldly things. May not all this truly be called a pearl of great price—doing all these holy things after pious meditation on Christ's passion?

The sufferings of Christ are the brightest jewels that can adorn a virgin's soul. The thought of Jesus crucified, of God's Son dead, buried and gloriously risen again, is a treasure worth all this world's goods; and when it has become habitual in the soul, it is worthy of the most heartfelt thanksgiving. By pondering the sufferings of Christ, evil inclinations are restrained, foul imaginations are banished, our own mortal weakness is shown to us, and deep rooted humility acquired. Soon the soul gains the grace of heartfelt compassion for our Lord in His crucifixion, and of deep sympathy for all men in their woes and miseries. On the other hand, if one fails thus to study our Redeemer's life and death, he will not learn to know himself; and such a one usually sticks fast in external exercises of religion, which his cowardice hinders of interior sweetness.

One of the fruits of meditation on Christ's passion, is the grace of readily offering our own sufferings to God in all singlemindedness, and without self deception. God Himself takes charge of such souls, and especially does He teach them the virtue of true mortification, helping them to recover from their petty defects. He draws them from loving creatures to loving Him; and He gives them the grace of discernment to know in advance what to do and what to avoid to make progress in His love. How faithfully do they confide in Him. How well do they understand the folly of trusting themselves. Thus minded they make bold to believe that they are not under deception, for well they know, that whosoever trusts self is surely deceived.

A yet further grace is the discernment of the various movements of grace and of nature, as they form our motives of conduct—a very needful wisdom. For many an apparently faithful Christian, good in outward religious practices, yet harbors self-complacency in his inmost soul.

Good virgins cherish the sound and commonly received principles of the spiritual life as held in holy Church and taught in the scriptures; to these they adhere with all their might, full of inner faith and outer profession. And their spirit is ever an interior one. They cleave directly to God. To Him and not to men do they look for relief from their difficulties. But it happens that if one would turn away from men to God, he is likely to suffer persecution and be visited with shame. In such a case our good virgin bears her burden silently and cheerfully, ever and again returning to meditation on Christ's life and passion, never failing to receive strength from on high to stay at home in her own heart, even though she be despised for her choice of this devout custom. But she does not yield to pride. She does all with a holy fear, ever blushing with shame as she stands before God, as being unworthy of so rare a mortification as suffering the charge of hypocricy, and of being called a fool for Christ's sake. But in her conscience God witnesses to her guilelessness. And she is very thankful that God's love makes her so happy interiorly.

The enemy can hardly disturb the peace of such a soul, because her glance is always turned upon her own self. And she is not guided by the light of natural reason, or by men's talk, and lays no hope upon good outward appearances, or upon sweet feelings, as if these things could mark her union with God, whereas they too often are snares of the evil one. On the contrary, she always falls back on honest self knowledge, approved spiritual practises, and seeking union with God with all her might. And when her external exercises are over, and her bodily senses are relieved from strain, her soul does not cease quietly and spontaneously adverting to God's presence, offering Him thanks for his favors, beseeching His aid against all that may divert her from His love. Such souls humbly beg God to pardon them their past sins, simply because they are displeasing to Him—not alone to escape hell and obtain heaven,—begging Him to do with them whatsoever will best advance His glory here and hereafter. They by no means pray God that their sins may not displease Him, but that He will forgive them, so that they may not be hindered of His graces, by which they shall be taught to advance in virtue—not even to be relieved of punishment, for that they leave to God, as far as they may rightly do so. To this happy state do men arrive, who persevere in meditation upon the passion of Christ.

But alas, how few spiritual men reach thus far; for most of them rest in the external things of religion, not turning earnestly inward to God. Therefore is there such a difference between man and man. The problem is to reconcile a life of active religious work with the cultivation of the interior spirit. There are souls who will not rest satisfied with external works of religion unless they can at the same time diligently labor interiorly for advancement in virtue. To these it is a hard trial to be associated with men who exclusively give themselves up to outward religious cares. Misunderstandings naturally arise; and the externized souls often cause the more interior spirits a great deal of suffering. But when the latter understand that this arises from ignorance and not malice, they can bear it with better patience. They will be the means of leading many others into the better ways of the spiritual life, if they will but go deeper and deeper into self knowledge and Divine love.

Whosoever does not go out of self love before he enters the depths of the spiritual life, will go astray before he knows it. One easily slips back into self indulgence, and presently he stops short in his spiritual progress. If God still endures his service of the senses, He is nevertheless not satisfied with it, for all the fruit of holiness above spoken of is lacking in them, and in those whom they might have led onwards, if they had themselves been turned inwardly to God. Few ever recover from this externalism. How much better it is to give up entirely to God's all lovely will—better for God's honor, better for the good of souls, many of whom for lack of wise guidance constantly provoke God's anger and mislead their fellowmen.

Thus is the pearl of great price fruitful of interior sweetness, in self knowledge, in love, and in all holy practises. And yet one must go deeper down for the best fruits, namely below sweetness into a certain bitterness of self abandonment, choosing sufferings from motives of love, and manfully dying to one's own selfish sense of proprietorship. The freer a soul is from love of self and love of joy, the safer it is from the snares of the enemy, the more exempted from the anxieties of this world, nay, the more secure from danger of hell, even of purgatory.

By constant self-renunciation, practised for God's love, one may be so safeguarded by grace as to be scarcely able to fall into sin. At first the soul enters a way of sweetness, practising many virtues. But there remains a higher and holier degree requiring, however, heavier labor, deadlier grief of conscience, and more painful inflictions from God . Let all this be borne patiently, with sincere faith in God's love and confident trust in His purposes, and He will not be found wanting to the soul. A man will be tempted to think God has forsaken him, so keen shall be his anguish of soul thinking of God's majesty, remembering his own sinfulness. But he must stand fast in holy hope, giving himself to God to do with him what He wills, in time and eternity. Behold, then, what comes from devout meditation on our Savior's passion. In the end a yet greater perfection is granted, when a man is made one spirit with God. May we all find this pearl of great price, and with it may God grant us every good gift. *Amen.*

How Holy Love Joins us to the Three Divine Persons

Synopsis—Love begins by keeping God's commandments—As love be-comes purer it instinctively adores the will of the Eternal Father as its inspiration—Then the wisdom of God's only begotten Son is felt—The peaceful submission of the soul to Christ as its Master and reward—How union with the Father is perfected by that with the Son—Union with God the Holy Ghost is a clearer perception of divine truth and love—This is joined with the loftier graces of contemplation.

SERMON FOR THE FEAST OF ALL THE HOLY APOSTLES.

If you love Me, keep My commandments.—John xiv, 15.

St. John tells us that Jesus "Having loved His own who were in the world, He loved them unto the end" (John xiii, 1). And many a proof had He given of this His tender love; but He especially showed His love for His disciples at the last supper. Then it was that He reminded them of the great debt of love they owed Him, which they could only rightly pay by observing His commandments. And He promised them to pray His heavenly Father to send them another Comforter, "That He may abide with you forever, the Spirit of truth, whom the world cannot receive, because it seeth Him not, nor knoweth Him" (John xiv, 16, 17).

Therefore, dear children, I will once again speak to you of holy love, to discourse about which is always a sweet task and very com-forting; and far sweeter yet is it to taste its savor. Our God bids His lovers hold Him dear to them by keeping His commandments, and He tells us that whosoever keeps them not, does not love Him. It is mani-fest, therefore, that God hates the man who lives in sin. On this sad theme I will not discourse; but I will speak according to my lights about the man who serves God with the highest kind of love.

Whosoever would love God must keep His commandments. That means that they must be subject to God's will. They dare no longer have any will of their own, but only God's. They must say in all truth: "Not My will, but Thine be done" (Luke xxii, 42). God's will is good love, and good love knows nothing of self-love, and loves only the will of the beloved. Three points are here to be considered: First, a watchful guard of the outward senses, shutting up close and fast those five doors of the soul, lest inordinate desires should arise, enter in, and gain force. In this way must one be vigilant, lest interior hurt is done by means of the outward senses.

The second is mortification of interior self complacency. By this one readily gives up his own chosen practises of piety and manner of life when God's will so indicates. He guards against self will in such matters. He stands firmly opposed to hell's five gates, namely: perverse self will, self complacency, spiritual pride, self flattery, and self conceit.

The third is placed in the motives of one's daily life. A man in all his deeds and words and thoughts, in all that concerns himself, his neighbor and God, should be actuated purely and simply by love. In this he makes a living sacrifice of himself to God, standing in perfect awe of the Almighty before all mankind. And this can be done in a grade of love so marvelously high as to pass the power of words to express; to be understood it must be experienced, transcending as it does all nature's powers. The soul goes beyond itself into the freedom of the Spirit that is given it, and therein it is united to the heavenly Father. This is accomplished with a sense of self abandonment for God's greater praise. The soul is entirely subjected to God, immersed in the Divine abyss, praying Him meanwhile to make it fruitful in His service, according to His eternal good pleasure. And the soul also prays Him to perfect it and every creature He has made, so that His all lovely will may be done in everything without exception. Again, the soul, as it is become an example of God's mercy, now offers itself to be made an example of the Divine Justice. But it does not wish that its works shall deserve damnation. And in this way it prays God for the perfecting of his holy will.

From the Father the soul goes onward to the Son, the eternal Wisdom, subjecting itself to Him in all simplicity, as being nothing, knowing nothing, feeling nothing—as far as its powers go—as to what it shall do or not do for God's praise and to carry out His blessed will. Only does the soul pray Him to perfect His will in itself and all creatures with His Divine wisdom, just as is best for His praise and glory and most fruitful of good for mankind. In all this the soul pays no regard to itself, but all to God.

And now, peacefully content in all things, the soul is established in unfeigned simplicity, waiting God's action, trusting without doubt that He will assume control of it and do His will in it. Then whatsoever happens to it, that the soul accepts as from His hand and to His praise. This is the soul's firm foundation. If it stands in doubt about God's will in particular cases, it follows whatever course it believes nearest to it. And if it is forced by circumstances to follow its own judgment, that often seems to be unwise and to contradict sound reason. Not willing to act thus, it can only give up again to God, trusting confidently that He will finally guide it. And now God is exalted in the soul in His sovereign wisdom, and the soul itself is proportionately sunk down before Him in the littleness of its understanding. And this state abides in the soul even while engaged in the most petty duties of daily life. Thus is it united to God's wisdom in much simplicity, and attains to the immensity of the deity, amid the darkness of His unknown being, in which He dwells elevated incomprehensibly high above all created life. He is a simple being, to whom the created human faculties cannot attain, but to whom they may be united through the work of grace, namely, supernatural faith, hope and charity.

And when this has all been completed, the loving soul goes onward to the Holy Ghost, who proceeds from the Father and the Son. To Him the soul subjects itself so perfectly that it is raised above all created things, and almost transcending faith and hope, it enters into God by love. This degree of love is more precious than all gifts; by it the soul is absorbed so deep into the uncreated life as to surpass comprehension, for the closeness of union and the Divine freedom there attained is unspeakable. And, if one may be allowed to say so, the soul in its union with God is now a faint resemblance even of the humanity of Christ. No longer does it hesitate from timidity, but takes up its company with Christ more lovingly and freely than ever before.

When such a soul would obtain a favor from the Father, it takes Christ with it, especially in holy communion; and it thus offers itself to the eternal Father in union with the Son. Particularly does it then pray for the fruitful life of holy Church, saying with Christ on the cross: "Father, into Thy hands I commend My spirit" (Luke xxiii. 46). Again and again does the soul thus pray. It is as if it said: O Lord, rule freely over me, as Thy Father ruled over Thee; help me to pray, that the will of the most holy Trinity may be done in me; and may it be perfected in my miserable imperfection, as once it was in Thy glorious perfection; and permit me to be one with Thee for the welfare of holy Church. O Lord, once Thou didst suffer, and thus didst Thou redeem the world; and now Thou canst no longer suffer. But I can suffer in Thy stead. Therefore, spare me not, as Thy Father spared Thee not. My heart is ready for all that pleasest Thee in time and in eternity. Lord, Thou knowest in what manner I can most rightfully thank Thee, and how I can be most helpful to mankind: order my life to that end, I beseech Thee. Thus it is that this soul gives itself over to God, that the Divine honor may in it and by it be advanced. But ere the soul attains to the degree of perfection in which such an oblation of self can be made, it must journey over many a desert road, and die many an unheard-of painful death.

To this third way does God elevate those who have trodden the two first ways. God comes to these loving ones and leads them Himself, teaching them the higher path, and uniting them to Himself in the manner we have described. But alas and alas, that so few men nowadays are really spiritual-minded. It is due to the fact that they are not willing to go this way of God and be made fruitful for other men's salvation. But any man who will turn to God's commandment of love thus to keep it, such a one will do more good than any ten other men, who would indeed serve God but yet turn unguardedly towards the world; who do not rest in patient waiting and are not single-minded towards God. They are absorbed in the active and external service of religion, rather than in the interior work of love, as we have explained it. For we have shown how a man awakes from the sleep of darkness into the true light of God.

But what if this new grace were held out to us, and we should wilfully fail to grasp it? It will escape us in a way that we shall not be able to understand. Therefore, let us one and all implore God in simplicity of heart and deep humility, for help to abase ourselves and despise ourselves, reckoning ourselves the lowest, basest, most contemptible and worthless creatures that ever lived. Let us beg Him to inspire all who meet us with contempt for us, that they may revile us, wag their heads at us and despise us. Let us beg Him to so manifest our misery to His mute, inanimate creatures, that even they will rise up and condemn us—anything, everything to teach us how to die to our own will. By this prayer we may obtain grace to shake off all sense of proprietorship inner and outer, and learn how to immolate ourselves totally to the Divine honor, to do God's good pleasure in all things, giving over to Him mastery of all we possess, not excepting our own personal selves, not excepting anything at all of time and eternity. May God help us to do this, and to do it not out of self-approval, but only from an ardent desire to please Him. *Amen.*

𝔗𝔥𝔢 𝔖𝔲𝔣𝔣𝔢𝔯𝔦𝔫𝔤 𝔬𝔣 𝔞 𝔅𝔩𝔬𝔬𝔡𝔩𝔢𝔰𝔰 𝔐𝔞𝔯𝔱𝔶𝔯𝔡𝔬𝔪 𝔞𝔫𝔡 𝔦𝔱𝔰 ℭ𝔯𝔬𝔴𝔫

Synopsis—True spirituality craves the martyr's crown—All of God's drawings to virtue point to heroism—Need of a resolute purpose to suffer in union with the King of martyrs—Heaven forecast and described—Curious explanation of the marvels of the apostolic era.

SERMON FOR THE FEAST OF MANY HOLY MARTYRS.

God, our heavenly Father, honored these holy martyrs with special glory; they were transformed into the close likeness of His only begotten Son. He pressed to their lips that bitter but precious chalice which His Son drained to the dregs. For these martyrs suffered death for the name of Jesus Christ. Therefore it is that this day we sing the praises of these dauntless warriors of Christ and favorite friends of God.

Now take notice that there are two kinds of martyrdom . One is outward martyrdom by the sword; the other is inward martyrdom by the stroke of dying love. And we read of St. Martin, that although untouched by the outward sword, he was yet not deprived of the glory of martyrdom. Here let us realize that a Christian man should experience the sufferings of Christ our God, seeking after them in due and proper penance for his sins in a dying life; thus does he become a friend of God. But these sufferings come to us in two ways.

The first suffering of a dying life is outward, by withstanding all concupiscence and sinfulness. St. Paul says: "They that are Christ's have crucified their flesh with the vices and concupiscences" (Gal. v, 24). The other suffering is interior. It consists in an oppression of spirit; God deprives the soul of all sensible or perceptible joy in His service, and dries it up totally. In this trial men are usually found wanting; and yet by this means are they most effectually forced to turn to God. Some think that all is lost if they cannot enjoy high illumination in their thoughts, and are lacking sweet feelings of devotion. But this is a trait of beginners, and is set aside by those who aspire to the best form of love; for these make little of sensible devotion. It is a good preparation, to be sure, to something nobler, but taken in itself, our sensible feeling of religion is not of much worth.

Alas, true lovers of God are not many. Men will follow Christ only in sweetness. This sort of love may be called wounded love, and God, seeing that men's hearts will not be otherwise drawn to Him, imparts to them the sensible sweetness of devotion they feel in His service. Gradually, however, He leads them to that love which is called the imprisoned or the captive love; and then they cannot escape Him. After that there is the degree of love called the raving, or frantic, or foolish love. In this state of love souls are granted great strength. Well are they compensated by their graces for the loss of all things; easily do they endure men's contempt and derision. Whatsoever suffering God permits, they instantly offer it to God in the deep abyss of the Godhead. With perfect trustfulness they say: O God, whether Thou wilt save me or damn me, may Thy will be done (if one could possibly or lawfully say this of his future state) : all power and all love is in Thee. Now when a man has reached this love, he has won the prize to gain which God started him forth. But as to how and by what processes this is brought about, that is God's secret.

It is to attract each soul to Himself that God bestows His gifts so affectionately, serves us with His graces so tenderly. For He would have us offer back these gifts and graces to Him in all detachment of pirit, and without reluctance or parleying. When He grants great piritual sweetness, it is to induce us to self-renunciation. And when Ie leads us from sweetness to aridity, it is to place us in a higher rade of the spiritual life. He takes away, seemingly, everything He as given us. Our soul seems to stand miserably poor, and all outside f God. The purpose of this is to force us to make a beginning of the oblest self-denial, to force us to rest upon no created thing whatsoever, ut only upon God. Now there are two ways of arriving at God's true ove.

The first is the way of joy in Divine grace. O how happy one is in he holy exercises of religion. And God causes that in order that we ay contrast spiritual joys with fleshly ones. These last are now uenched in the former. A man sells himself to God for these spiritual weetnesses. He despises bodily pleasures, and he shows this so plainly hat his friends wonder at the sight of it. For we read of many saints, hat when they were first drawn hard to God, they fled from the comorts of life so suddenly and so violently that men were amazed. This is doubtless the work of the Holy Ghost, whose love is strong as death.

The second way is that of spiritual sorrow and suffering. And now all these joys we have been speaking of are snatched away. And it is precisely in this trial that the spiritual strength of our martyr is generated—in utter aridity, barrenness of devotional feeling. Meanwhile you must know that amid all this sorrow of heart and in this spiritual vacuum, souls continue to hold God very dear, and to purpose and practice virtue no less than before this visitation. But they are sorely embarrassed, and know not which way to turn for relief, for God seems to them to have quite given them up. They can but stand fast in faith, hope, and charity, in a very thick darkness of soul. As to sinning, oh! no matter what might come upon them, they are firmly resolved never to sin, for they ever bear in their bosom a deeply humbled heart, overflowing with contrition. When they see the signs of God's grace in other men, they are cut deep with pain; but they blame only themselves for not being equally favored, accusing themselves of wanting in fidelity. And when they strive to obtain grace by diligence and zeal in good works, they only grow dryer within. A stone is not dryer or harder than their heart feels.

Sometimes all patience seems to vanish away from them. Forebodings of the future haunt them; their sadness steadily increases in bitterness. And presently they accuse themselves of envying others the graces they enjoy; and that brings sorrow upon sorrow. By all these tribulations they are utterly worn out, and know not what they shall do. They would not willingly fail in fidelity to God and in the practice of virtue, and yet they feel unequal to any good work. They dread lest they have aroused God's anger by their impatience; they fear that they have been guilty of the awful sin of despair—and that pains them intensely; for they really hate sin because it is rebellion against God. This feeling of intense aversion to sin heartens them somewhat, for they know that they would not wilfully provoke the Divine wrath. But at last they fall back upon mere patience and arrive at peace, even though continuing under heavy depression of spirit. They resign themselves to suffer on until it pleases God to give them a change; for they now perceive that they cannot do otherwise than blindly trust God. And this is the way God teaches detachment from all things and submission to Him. And presently a change comes over them; these souls now appear more like others who have great sweetness of devotion; but in various respects they are far nobler spirits. For their way is more like that of Christ, whose life was full of suffering.

Such a man thinks himself the poorest of the poor in spiritual gifts. But in God's sight he is very rich. Such souls are the farthest away from God, to their own seeming, but as He sees them they are the nearest. To themselves they are God's outcasts, and to Him they are the chosen ones. They rate themselves the most untrue to Him, and He knows them to be His most steadfast friends, most reliable to resist His dishonor, most eager to advance His glory; for they suffer only for His sake.

On account of this interior poverty they are open to severe temptations, but to these they will in no manner give place. Yet they cause them much mental torture—worse indeed than the agony of death. This is especially the case when they scruple that they have yielded to the tempter. They would gladly overcome their petty imperfections; they long to practice good works; and they find themselves powerless to do either. The pains of hell itself seem less to them than the torture this causes, this and their other interior tribulations. But it all arises from their great fidelity to God, for meanwhile their heart's trust is ever His, but they are not able to realize this. They reckon themselves as the basest sinners in the world; in God's eyes they are the most spotless.

One thing in them displeases God, namely, that they make so much of this their sad condition. To punish them, He now and then allows them to show impatience with others, or to commit some petty imperfection against pure love. If they were entirely faithful, God would not thus visit them; they would then simply make their sorrows their only peace. In that case their progress would outstrip that of all other men. This advantage they lose by yielding to excessive despondency.

This fault of theirs comes from their inadvertence to the wonderful fruit that must result from God's discipline. Or perhaps from some hidden lack of self-abandonment, some weakness of resolve to suffer on and on to the end—they forebode that the term of their sorrows will be longer than they can endure. They should understand that this lack of patience only prolongs the agony, and lessens the benefit to be gained. What alone can shorten their trials is patient and gentle endurance, simply giving themselves over to sorrow for God's love. The more simply they do this, the nobler shall be their triumph, the brighter their final illumination.

For if a man will but tread this darksome way faithfully, a bright light at last will burst upon him, flooding his inmost soul with the splendor of eternal truth. Thus before God—however different he may seem to men—he will have reached the purest state of love. He will have given up self and all things else for God's sake alone. He is now made, as it were, one love with God. That love no man or any other being but himself can deprive him of or anywise disturb. To will or not to will is now, as it seems to him, all one in his soul's life, for God and all God's elect have taken up their abode in him.

Yet more is to be said of this blissful state, for it leads to a happy death. O, my soul, consider over and over again, the unspeakable bliss of heaven; of a soul that looks directly upon the face of God, the infinitely lovely God; think of the joy of possessing the sovereign good that God is. In Him is found all joy, power, beauty, all that is holy, all that our heart can desire. Think of possessing God with everlasting security—being very closely united to God; joined to Him, never to be again separated. O, how supremely blissful will be the sight and presence of the most holy Trinity; how sweet the company of Mary, our beloved Lord's holy mother, with all the heavenly choirs of the angels, with all the ancient patriarchs and prophets, the apostles and the martyrs, the confessors and the virgins, and all the saints. How glorious to dwell forever in that company, so mutually affectionate, and ever rapt in the divine love. The greatest of the saints in that loving family, would, if it were possible, gladly share his joy with the least, as the least would gladly add his share of glory to that enjoyed by the greatest. So shall the souls whose proving we have been considering, having been tried and found faithful, receive in this life a foretaste of these overwhelming joys.

O how foolish are the men who turn their backs on eternal happiness, for the sake of fleshly joys on the passing good things and honors of this world. Study this matter, O my soul, whilst thou art in the way of grace and probation. Do good works. See to it, lest thou dost forfeit everlasting happiness. Hasten on to a life of virtue. Let no toil dishearten thee, but labor steadily during the short span of thy earthly existence, and with real fidelity to God, that thou mayst gain an eternal good, an eternal joy. Let there be nothing so dear to thee that thou shalt allow it to hinder thy gaining the eternal friendship of God. Canst thou not plainly see, that all possible pain, adversity and misery of this life is as nothing, if we but keep in mind the joys of eternal life? Think of all the glorious saints of God, and how they all obtained their paradise by an upright Christian life, Set them before thy eyes; imitate their virtues, so that thou mayst be made a sharer of their glory. O my soul, consider the joys and the honors of the heavenly Jerusalem, and its gracious loving citizens. All of them have journeyed thither along this road of Christian virtue and self denial, passing out of this valley of tears into its open gates of everlasting joy.

There are five signs of God's favor attached to the lives of mortified men, as our Lord teaches. The first is that they cast out devils in the name of Christ. All men who have confessed their mortal sins with true contrition, can enjoy that prerogative, for they have expelled the demon from their own souls. The second is that they shall speak with new tongues. Such is the privilege in a certain sense of all who renounce sinful and idle words, and speak good and useful ones; and of all those who preach the word of God, who read the holy gospels, who recite devout prayers, who admonish and correct sinners, and who instruct the ignorant. The third sign is that they can take up serpents and not be hurt by them. This is enjoyed by all who banish bad thoughts from their souls, and withstand them manfully. The fourth sign is that they can drink any deadly thing, and it shall not hurt them. This is fulfilled in those who patiently suffer persecution and contempt of men for justice sake. The fifth and last sign is that faithful souls can lay their hands upon the sick, and they shall recover. The like of that do all good men, who forgive their enemies out of whole hearted kindness, no matter what harm has been done them; and also those who give alms to the poor. Of all those who show these signs, as given in the holy gospel, one can safely say that they truly belong to God's faithful friends, and that if they but persevere, they will be taken up to Christ in eternal life. God grant all of us that happy lot. *Amen.*

How to Meet Temptations

*Synopsis—Temptations are allowed for our advancement in virtue—
The various kinds of temptations and how to deal with each of
them—How they cure a tendency to misuse sensible devotion—A
sorely tempted man is well taught the supreme virtue of humility
—Explanation of the more subtle interior trials—The dread of
sinning—how it may be utilized.*

SERMON FOR THE FEAST OF A HOLY MARTYR.

Blessed is the man that endureth temptation.—James i, 12.

The holy man Job tells us that our life on this earth is a state of
warfare. Indeed the saints often speak of life as a long series of temptations; when one goes another comes. The reason of this is our
Lord's purpose that we should go onward, and should bring forth the
fruit of victory, moving ever forward on God's road and conquering in
His name. From temptation we can extract the hidden joy of the spirit,
as the bees do honey from thorn bushes and weeds. Solomon says: "What
doth he know that hath not been tried?" (Eccli. xxxiv, 9). And the
holy doctor, St. Bernard, enlarges upon that teaching. There are more
than a thousand passages of Holy Scripture showing the good uses of
temptations. It is a special sign of God's favor over a man, if he has
fought a good fight and come forth victorious. To such a one the
crown is given, as it was to our martyr, of whom Holy Church sings
today, that he was blessed because he had endured temptation, had
won the victory and had received the crown of life reserved for those
whom God loves.

One kind of temptation is that of the external senses. By this a
man is tempted to place his joy in men, whether friends, relatives or
others. It leads to anxious care in personal adornment, as clothing
and jewelry; or in fine books, elegant and luxurious dwellings, delicate food and drink. These cleave to him as a burr to a dog. Some
times a man will be far from these temptations, but assailed by yet
more unusual ones, being tormented with impure thoughts. But,

however foul the temptations may be, they can do us no harm, except as St. Gregory teaches, we are careless of resisting them. We should turn quickly away from them.

The other kind of temptation is interior, and would set up an alien rule in the kingdom of the mind. The activity of soul and that of body are mingled together. Our inward turning to God in this life is closely joined to our outward tendencies, and this gives rise to temptations. Scripture says that Satan can transform himself into an angel of light; and that takes place in his temptations while our soul is absorbed in contemplating God.

Now notice further, dear children, how St. John divides all sin into three classes: "For all that is in the world, is the concupiscence of the flesh, and the concupiscence of the eyes, and the pride of life" (I John ii, 16). And as these rule in the world, so do they seek to rule in our flesh; and then to reign in our interior life by assuming a spiritual appearance. Outward sins are plain enough, if one will but see them. But sins of the interior life are more hidden. They take on a disguise of spirituality so cunning that a man is on the point of falling before he is aware of any danger.

And I ask you to observe that there is a certain kind of spiritual unchastity, which name we give to spiritual self indulgence. I mean the excessive pleasure one takes in interior sweet feelings of devotion. The one who yields to that temptation, insists on having unbroken interior peace of soul; he resents being corrected or admonished for his faults; he neglects his ordinary duties in order to attend to his own particular devotions. All this is due to the sensible sweetness he enjoys in his spiritual exercises. When that fails, he is utterly unhappy, irritable, impatient of the most trifling annoyance. He loudly complains of the terrible temptations he suffers from. And this is all nothing else but absence of sensible devotion. St. Bernard says: "Our Lord, in His mercy, often grants interior sweetness to souls quite unworthy of it, in order that He may the better draw them to His love. On the contrary, He often withholds it from nobler souls, who are truly deserving of it, being long practised in solid virtue." Yes, sometimes He deprives such souls of devotional joys their whole life long, so that in the life to come they may receive all the greater reward. And, indeed, our spiritual fruit is not in such things, nor our highest gratitude; but, rather in interior trust in God, firm loyalty to Him, entire absence of self-seeking, whether in pain or pleasure. Our true felicity lies in a constant offer of ourselves to God as His poor, humble servitors, glad to minister to His will at our own cost, and so to do, if it were lawful to say such a thing, for all eternity.

And yet, one may be allowed to pray to God for sensible sweetness of devotion, in case he happens to be a young and weak beginner in the spiritual life; for our kind heavenly Father may by that means induce him to a stronger service and gradually strengthen him in His love. But mark the danger. It is quite possible that we may value this sweet tranquillity of soul over much, even loving the gift—however unconsciously—more than the Giver. Anyway, we should never forget that these tender feelings are not of our earning—they are God's mere gifts to us. We may, besides, fall into spiritual gluttony in their enjoyment. This is plain and gross disloyalty to God our Savior, Who won all these favors for us by His own life-long self-denial, and who has merited better treatment at our hands.

Spiritual gluttony is a temptation to ever crave more favor from God than is necessary in our earthly pilgrimage. Now what more should a pilgrim take with him on his journey than what he would bring back home again. Believe me, it is an open stain on our outward state of poverty as religious men, to seek to have more bodily comfort than is necessary for us. And the same kind of a stain is fixed on our inward poverty of spirit, yes, a much uglier spot, if we long for more spiritual comfort than is necessary. Ah, which of us men has ever been so poor as Jesus Christ? He gave up all heavenly riches and took a life of the greatest earthly distitution, and was finally abandoned by all creatures, and even cast helplessly back on Himself by His divine Father—as He complained from His cross: "My God, My God, why hast Thou forsaken Me?" (Matt. xxvii, 46). Now all this was for our instruction; He would teach us to cherish spiritual destitution of all things.

But thou mayst answer: Alas, I could bear it better if it was not all my own fault; I could bear it more patiently but for my former neglect. I am myself the cause of all my trouble. But I answer: Do not let that thought distress thee. Knowest thou not what the wise man says? "A just man shall fall seven times" (Prov. xxiv, 16). And dost thou dream that thou shalt always stand? Yes, I agree that it is all thy own fault, and that thou dost richly deserve this desolation of spirit. But yet it is all for the best that thou shouldst trust our good God for pardon. He knows thy weakness full well, and will forgive thee thy imperfections seventy times seven times a day: better wait on His loving kindness than reproach thyself in so mean-spirited a way. Oh child, hast thou fallen? Then rise up again. Go to thy Father with childlike confidence, and say humbly with the prodigal son, "Father, I have sinned against heaven and before thee; I am not worthy to be called Thy son; make me as one of Thy hired servants" (Luke xv, 18, 19). Thinkest thou that God would treat thee otherwise than the father in the parable treated his son? Mercy is God's most precious treasure, and it will be a small thing for Him to forgive thee, if thou wilt but put thy trust in Him. His hand is not shortened that He should not save thee. Therefore, be on thy guard against spiritual avarice, for the poorer in spirit thou standest in God's presence the more acceptable shalt thou be, and the more richly will He endow thee with His gifts.

Spiritual pride is that vice by which a man is not ashamed of his sins, excusing himself and sparing himself in everything, never being willing to submit. It often happens that such a man uses abusive and injurious language to exculpate himself, and even falsehood. Those men forget that if plain truth will not help a man, lies are of little use. A simple man, humbly submissive under God's will, is infinitely better than one with some pretence to virtue, but full of interior pride, and swaggering about with arrogant manners. Tell me, dear child, what is all our righteousness? Let the prophet Isaias answer: "We are all become as one unclean, and all our justices as the rag of a menstruous woman" (Isaias lxiv, 6).

And when were we really just in God's sight? If God our Lord would but show us our deservings, we must needs confess our guilt in His sight, and own that all our virtue is due to His grace. Many a time does our Lord favor a weak and wayward soul because it casts itself humbly at His feet and craves his mercy. God demands that every knee shall bend before Him, and strictly exacts thanksgiving for all the virtues we possess. And be it remembered that spiritual pride is often a very secretly-hidden vice; and this accounts for much of the harm it does. Whosoever, on the other hand, carefully guards against spiritual gluttony, avarice and pride, will be held fast in God's true way, and his interior life will not go astray.

To this end three rules will help. First, that he should remember that any interior difficulties and contradictions which discipline our spirits into the likeness of our Savior's humility, which tend to form us after the manner of Christ's saints,—that we should be sure that such trials are not due to depraved nature, nor are they the suggestions of the evil spirit. All such trials undoubtedly come from God. As He is the supreme God, nothing but good can come from Him, and whatsoever results from His interposition can only be good. All life flows back to its fountain head, and all existence rejoices in its return to its Divine origin. But mark well that whatsoever distorts our likeness to God in Christ is due to an evil cause, either our perverted nature or the wicked demons. These are ever bent on drawing us away from God. The same is to be said of every influence that makes for separation from Christ, as He says: "He that is not with Me is against Me, and he that gathereth not with Me scattereth." (Luke xi, 23). Now this rule is useful against the first spiritual evil I spoke of, namely, spiritual excess or gluttony in enjoying devout feelings.

The second rule is this: Whatever inner tendency or happening forces a man nearer to his own heart to observe it; whatever concentrates and unifies the spirit of a man into greater simplicity; whatever tends to increase his loving trustfulness in God's fatherly care, diverting him from thoughts of his own works and feelings; this is all, without doubt, from God. So that when a man stands before God confessedly a sinner and a beggar, thinking nothing of how good he may seem in men's eyes; when a man finds himself out, and plainly avows to God and to himself that he is devoid of virtue; when he rates himself as a poor, lost, good-for-nothing, empty-hearted creature, who can be cleansed by God alone and by Him alone filled with virtue; when he cleaves to God in utter self-abandonment, avowing his total powerlessness to help himself:—when a man is conscious of this interior state, let him be quite sure that it is entirely the work of God. None but God can drive a soul inward to learn and acknowledge its own utter destitution. Depraved nature and the evil one would rob a man of all his spiritual goods, all his graces or virtues; and their opportunity is when a man does not know himself, and when he thinks he has virtues that he really has not. Then he is open to the condemnation found in the Apocalypse: "Because thou sayest: I am rich and made wealthy, and have need of nothing; and knowest not that thou are wretched and miserable, and poor and blind, and naked" (Apoc. iii, 17). And this has a mixture of spiritual avarice, mingled with the leaven of spiritual gluttony.

The third rule is this: Whatever makes a man little in his own eyes; whatever humiliates him under the mighty hand of God and under all creatures in sincere lowliness of spirit; whatever makes him long to be downtrodden and made nothing of: all that without doubt is from God. For, inasmuch as Lucifer and his rebel angels were swollen with pride and presumption, and were for that cause banished from heaven, so, on the contrary, shall we be led into heaven, because of our sincere humility; as of the three holy kings it is written: "They went back another way into their own country" (Matt. ii, 12).

According to each one's essential being does he act, and after the pattern of his own nature would he form all others whom he can influence. Now the evil spirit is besotted with self-love; pride and effrontery are permanently hardened into his intelligence and will. Not to obtain heaven itself would he humble himself to God; no, not for a single instant. And all proud spirits tend to become like the demon. From him they have learned to prize their own opinion above the sense and reason of all mankind. Hence their constant quarrelsomeness, hence their fierce insistence on their own views and their own will. And hence their incessant unrest, evil thoughts about others, and violations of brotherly love. They will suffer correction from no man, they are so stiff-necked. They even disregard the warnings that Divine Providence sends them, and they despise the admonitions of their best friends. God characterized them plainly, when condemning hypocrites in the words of Isaias the Prophet: "I have spread my hands all the day to an unbelieving people, who walk in a way that is not good, after their own thoughts" (Isaias lxv, 2).

Furthermore, our dear Lord is Himself all meekness and humility, and toward these virtues he is constantly drawing all willing souls. Yet think of his greatness. His being is the cause of all things and their beginning and essence. He is the life of the living, the resurrection of the dead, the restorer of souls ruined by their own sinfulness. He recalls the wandering, He upholds the falling. Of those that stand He is the strong support, of those that journey onward to heaven He is the safe guide. He is the dawn of day to every enlightened spirit, the manifestation of all heavenly secrets, the first beginning of all our beginnings of eternal life. And He is the infinite and incomprehensible and unnameable God. And, nevertheless, He is the meek and lowly Jesus.

Let us praise His mysterious divinity with silent awe, and never more praise aught but what honors Him. Let us reverently salute the first rays of His Divine light in our souls, turning our spirits to Him to reflect His brightness as burnished mirrors. Always, amidst all our love, should we cultivate a fearful awe of Him, according to the words of God to Moses sanctifying Mt. Sinai: "Everyone that toucheth the mount, dying he shall die. * * * Whether it be beast or man, he shall not live" (Exod. xix, 12, 13). That is to say, let not our beastly nature presume to come nigh to God's holy mountain in our souls; let all that is animal within us sit down outside the bounds in the lowest place. And when we are thus properly humble-minded, the Lord will call us up higher, saying: "Friend, go up higher" (Luke xiv, 10).

And then, not by his own power, but drawn and elevated by God's grace, a man ascends to divine union, his life of the senses entirely cleansed, his soul lighted up with heaven's splendor. By this means of holy humility, silence, patient waiting, does a man attain to God; and by this means more effectually than by a more active spirit in outward exercises of religion. The divine nature of Christ is the power that would draw to God all spirits, all hearts that follow His example and daily unite themselves to Him in holy love. Richard of St. Victor says: "I am to receive Christ, not only as He is cruci-fied on Calvary, but also as He is transfigured in glory on Mount Tabor. But to receive Him thus glorified I must have His duly ap-pointed witnesses, Peter and James and John, Moses and Elias." That is to say, when Christ comes to us in deep anguish of heart we may instantly trust that it is truly our Redeemer. But if He is man-ifested to us in interior contemplation, amid the light of glory within our soul's Mount Tabor, then must we pause. We must have wit-nesses and external approval; we must take precautions, lest we should indulge to excess in this feast of light, and thereby commit spiritual gluttony. As a man can eat more sweet things than he can digest, so may we abuse the gifts that God generously bestows in our interior life. We must incessantly humiliate ourselves in His sight; we must never forget the danger of spiritual pride. The vir-tues of humility, meekness, obedience are the witnesses approving our free enjoyment of the transfigured Christ in our inmost souls. Against these guardians of truth and peace no false angel can ever prevail. God grant us this happy lot. *Amen.*

On Human Respect

Synopsis—Love of a great name the ruin of many, and why—Serving men at God's expense—How bitter disappointments attend the love of men's praise—Vainglory as a substitute for recollectedness of spirit.

SERMON FOR THE FEAST OF A HOLY BISHOP, CONFESSOR.

And in My name shall his horn be exalted.—Ps. lxxxviii, 25.

Self-glory and proud boasting is, as you know, my dear children, the sin most offensive to God. It is giving to a man's own self the glory that belongs to God alone. God cannot endure that His creature shall usurp to his own honor the good repute that is granted him only for the divine honor, and for the spiritual benefit of other men. And how plainly do God's servants show their appreciation of this, as did the holy prelate whose feast we celebrate today. He sought his own glory in nothing, God's glory in everything. Hence holy Church chants his praises in today's office: "In My name shall his horn be exalted"—that is to say, his glory in heaven and on earth. As if God should say of him: His name shall not be his glory, for he never cared for that, as he cared but for me alone; therefore he shall be exalted even in My name and with My glory.

And in another place the Psalmist says: "For His name alone is exalted" (Ps. cxlviii, 13). Now, nothing is more hateful to God, nothing goes straighter against Him than ambition to acquire a great name. In many men this sin is hidden deep in their souls, and they little realize their perilous plight. Men in high places demand, as of personal right, that all should bow down to them; and woe to anyone who says or does anything at all likely to lessen their public honor. Of the secret pride from which this springs David speaks: "Who can understand sins? From my secret ones cleanse me, O Lord" (Ps. xviii, 13). Which means in some cases: Cleanse me from the secret desire of a great name. Again we read: "Let not the foot of pride come to me" (Ps. xxxv, 12). Which means the first steps or inclinations towards pride; for in the earliest movements of the heart are the causes of all iniquity. I say to thee, that if thou wilt not renounce thy love of an honorable name, thou canst not find God in whatsoever thou doest, no matter how good it all may be in itself. St. Chrysostom says: "Forsake thy great name, and thou shalt easily be superior to all the sorrows and sufferings of life." If God could but obtain from penitent sinners self-abasement in the same degree as they formerly had pride and self-complacency, He would obtain from them all that He desires. Every chastisement that God visits on a man is for the purpose of lowering him in his own self-esteem. And when ordinary correction fails, then will God often allow His friends to suffer public shame, even to a most pitiful degree of degradation, in order that they may be disenchanted with self.

Mark this well: When a man is overpraised by others, when more virtue is ascribed to him than is really his in God's sight (for He alone knows all man's shortcomings), then if God would advance him in perfection, He wrecks and ruins this fair fame and turns it into evil repute. For this stolen spiritual treasure must be given up in shame and ridicule in this life, if one shall come safely through to eternal life. But if a man's great name does not puff him up, then it will help his spiritual state; let him but keep a clean heart, guard well the grace of God, and stand humbly and fearfully before Him, avowing his innate sinfulness. Let him hold himself merely as God's steward of all the gifts and graces he possesses, nor rate himself in the least degree a more deserving man that he was before his elevation to his office. This he should administer with a single-hearted purpose to honor God and holy Church, and advance his neighbors' salvation. Herein is much merit in God's eyes, much profit for men. When such a man hears the praises of the worldly-minded, it affects Him no more than if he were in any common state of life. And if he were suddenly turned out of office it would be all one to him, for he holds his spirit indifferent to all things whatsoever in this life.

Dear children, another kind of great name, and one that is a deadly danger, is the reputation for holiness. Make sure that you dread and avoid this most sincerely. The man that does not live up to the reputation he holds among his fellows, who rejoices in a fair fame of virtue that he does not actually possess, must pay the penalty of bitter shame and disgrace here or hereafter, and all the more painfully in proportion to the esteem he shall have enjoyed.

But sometimes a good man may be distressed lest his motives in doing good are tainted by love of human praise. He may dread lest men's applause, rather than holy obedience, inspires him. But if he has an upright intention, let him not be troubled, only keep himself upright in conscience while doing all his good works, repressing vainglorious thoughts as best he may; for we must never cease doing good on account of scruples.

But all depends on the intention, for if that is not upright, virtuous acts are not meritorious. If one's name is highly lauded, and his intention is meanwhile to please men, he is easily made proud; soon he is overbearing in his manners; he will not do anything good unless it attracts attention; his main object is always to be noticed and praised by men. He parades pious ways of talking and of acting; nor will he be content with anything less than the first place in the opinion of his fellows.

The sign of this vice is principally that such men do not win their fame with the people because they advance them in the virtues of divine faith and hope and love. It is soon noticed that their reliance is not upon the love of God. Men begin to mistrust that they are true servants of God, and soon their high repute is lost. Then they begin to be anxious about themselves. They lose confidence in God's love and fall into a very dangerous frame of mind. Ask them to do some good act which they fear they are not equal to, and they will refuse you: they dread that God will unveil their feebleness and they will be exposed to contempt. All that holy Scripture teaches of trusting God cannot induce them to risk the danger of exposure of their lack of virtue—a dozen preachers could not persuade them to it. And so they rest in their obstinacy and pride, and become quarrelsome. They find it impossible to live peaceably even with kindly-natured people. Only a new, strong, very attractive light of grace can change them, can teach them self-denial, instruct them in love for all those with whom they must live. So they continue in bitterness of spirit toward their neighbor. Brotherly love—the very thought of it is painful to them, and all the gentle and affectionate virtues are hateful to them. Now they dream of obtaining relief by entering an order, separating themselves from men by solemn vows, thinking they will never again see and hear what may annoy them. But no, dear children. That is not the road to peace. In the monastery such men are only the more unsettled; they are a prey to envious thoughts, rash judgment, community gossip, and other such evils—they are all the worse for being greatly withdrawn from men's company. For the evil one sits on his throne in their bad hearts, and until he is driven out by true repentance, peace cannot enter in.

If they will have peace, let them turn inward and study their souls. Let them cleanse their thoughts of pride and self-complacency. Let them, as far as is seemly, communicate their false interior state to others, that they may be rated for what they really are, shameful sinners, worthless creatures. And let them persevere in this painful exercise till they have purged their whole being of their passion for human praise. Then and not before will they gain the sweet gift of peace, then and not before will they be fit for the good works to which their calling obliges them.

They sometimes fancy that a mechanical use of confession will serve them for peace of soul. But if I allowed them hours and hours of confession daily, it would not relieve them; they would still be tossed about with trouble of mind, and would be hateful to their neighbor. The more they go to confession without true sorrow and deep humility, the more occasions of sin will the evil spirit throw in their way— anger, envy, hate, trouble-mindedness, despondency, mistrust of self and of all others. Often they live in thoughts of the past. They beguile their minds with vain memories of what happened twenty or thirty years before, rather than with the will of God at the present moment. And all this misery must they continue to suffer, until they learn their own weakness and humbly confess it, giving up wholly and finally their love of men's praise, and their absorption in outward appearances of virtue.

But they may say: We must set the people a good example and not scandalize anybody. But I answer that if you would set the people a good example, then acquire virtue and give the people edification; give them to know what in very truth you are; show out real Christian good qualities, and let these be at least the commonplace virtues of kindliness, patience, promptness to serve them, receiving ill-treatment good-naturedly: better this than a pretense of virtues you do not possess.

Ah, children, these men were neglected in their training. They were not subjected to ridicule by their superiors, they were not thwarted by them. They were allowed to see how pleasing they were to the people, being praised no matter what they did. That hardened them into habitual love of praise, and soon without that motive they would do scarcely anything. The result is that now one must pray and weep to get them to do their ordinary tasks—a most pitiable spectacle. Of these the Lord says: "Amen 1 say to you, they have received their reward" (Matt. vi, 2). Alas that men are found who will praise them and thereby gratify their vanity, a sin like murder in God's sight, misleading these soft-natured creatures. Naturally inclined to serve God, they are perverted by ill-considered compliments, and finally degenerate into obstinate self-love. This state may lead to the eternal death of the soul and exclusion from God and His saints in heaven. Such indiscreet praise is often given from selfish motives, to win their favor, to profit by the service of these defective charac-ters in worldly affairs.

Ah, children, longing for worldly advantages means turning away from heavenly things; and this continues until it too often happens that both one and the other are forfeited. Seek first whatever is needful for eternal life, and God will provide for your temporal needs, and that in sufficient abundance. Yet for some small temporal gain we mislead soft-natured souls with our fulsome praises. We thereby instill vain glory into them, a vice ever leading one to resist God, ever hurtful to grace, laying men open to the demon's fierce assaults. A man fully possessed of this form of pride may become capable of any sin, even the most inhuman. The foulest depravity springs from this devilish root of evil. And if this root be planted in early youth, it strikes so deep into our nature that in later life infinite pains are necessary to pluck it out.

Hence we should admonish our young brothers and sisters against the influence of men's praise. Bid them act wholly for God's glory, Who for love of us and to save us humbled Himself even unto the death of the cross. He has granted us strength, knowledge and many graces wherewith to win eternal happiness. Children, these begin-ners in the spiritual life had best be made little of, corrected with kindness, and exercised in the ways of holy humility: they may thus be made holy men. By lavish praise they are ruined; later on they are too much hardened in habits of self-complacency to suffer cor-rection.

At last it happens that if one does not flatter such men they are bitterly discontented; they think that they are hated; they are dis-satisfied with their superiors and father confessors and are evil-minded about them: they are sunk in despondency; and they are full of suspicions. They say that nobody cares for them or wants them to do anything of importance. They boast of the great things they have done, and of how great use they have been to others; and all this they whisper around to those who will listen to them. Dear children, see the effects of flattery upon a certain class of simple characters. It finally imperils their eternal salvation. It prevents genuine brotherly love, and plain, honest obedience to superiors. If these are lacking, of what account are fasts, vigils, disciplines, reading and singing prayers, genuflexions, and all other bodily exercises of religion? These are all good; but with them we must have true humility; we must acquire real self-abasement and mortification; we must establish a fixed intention to do all and everything for God's honor and our neighbor's good, and for that alone.

Furthermore, consider that once a man sincerely disregards a great name, longs ever to be hidden, covets humiliations, is quite willing to be despised and to be ranked the lowest of all, then will God begin to do great things with him and through him. When a man never seeks honor, name or position, when he is well content that nobody praises him, and really feels better when he is last and least, then I say that before God he is just as he ought to be. If such a man happens to be given a high place, the flattery that is offered him does him no harm; and the honors that are done him only help him the better to serve the people. But yet the praises of men afflict his humble spirit very keenly, and his pain thereat is one degree of that interior death that he must experience in becoming united with God. It will clarify his soul more and more brightly, until God's light shall shine more perfectly in him—a state of soul not easily understood except by one who has gone along this path of self-abnegation.

How happy a lot is this; and how lamentable the state of those who have failed to secure it, having given up their lives to men's praises. Everyone of us should be on his guard against vain glory. And we should be ready and quick to enter the dark road of humility, to which God would draw us. The true man lives only upon faith and hope in God. He says in all sincerity : Lord, I will serve Thee in this darksome way; and I confidently trust that what lies before me in this marvelous experience on which I am entering is no delusion; and I give myself up to be guided passively by Thee forever. Sometimes faith, hope and love all fall away from him—as far as he can feel: but his good will, his upright intention remains firm and fast within him, and that suffices him. Sometimes his lower natural faculties, and even his understanding, are, according to his perception, wholly emptied of love. But meanwhile love of God is hidden safe and secure in the higher part of the spirit. And as long as he retains some feeling of loyalty to God in real self-abandonment— even in spite of the emptiness of nature and of his understanding— and as long as he is content to be thus forsaken by God, and as long as he harbors no thought of despair, nor seeks to relieve his interior pains by any sort of bodily self-indulgence:—then he may be sure that all is well with him. But if he seeks relief in the solace of the enjoyment of the senses, or if he plunges for solace into active labors— even those of a good and spiritual kind—for the stated purpose of escaping the interior oppression that God has imposed on him (the feeling that he has no faith, nor hope, nor love), then he has made a false step. He has snapped the tie of painful love that bound him to God, and all unconsciously he is likely to fall into a lower degree of the spiritual life. But if he will only stand his ground, true to God though God seems to have abandoned him, then is he intimately bound to God in the highest degree of love, however little he may be aware of it.

And when the darksome time is past and gone, then the soul is found cleansed in its very depths of all sense of proprietorship. Now he brings forth abundant fruit to God in the practice of virtue, and he finds a sweet rest in God, and knows God in all things. Then, too, is his zeal for souls very fruitful of his neighbor's salvation. This is easier felt than described, for without having experienced it one can never fully understand what it is to love God in truth. May we have grace to exalt the name of God above all things and not exalt our own. May God grant us the grace of true self-renunciation, and teach us how to make little of ourselves. *Amen.*

𝕿𝖍𝖊 𝕸𝖎𝖘𝖙𝖆𝖐𝖊 𝖔𝖋 𝕿𝖚𝖗𝖓𝖎𝖓𝖌 𝕺𝖚𝖙𝖜𝖆𝖗𝖉 𝕴𝖓𝖘𝖙𝖊𝖆𝖉 𝖔𝖋 𝕴𝖓𝖜𝖆𝖗𝖉

Synopsis—How some practice devotion without keeping the command-ments—The strange desire to be holy by external practices alone—Doing pious things without taking God into account—That many really good souls are partially addicted to formalism.

SERMON FOR A FEAST OF MANY HOLY CONFESSORS.

The light of thy body is thy eye.—Luke xi, 34.

Dear children, today we celebrate the memory of holy confessors of the faith of Christ. By their heroic Christian virtues they have spread abroad the glory of Jesus Christ. And this they did not only by splendid examples of all virtues, but by interior self-abandonment in mind and spirit and heart, being dead to the life of the senses. They were ever eager and diligent in serving God, and their eye was single to do His will.

Now, you have noticed in these times that there are many who keep up a show of spirituality, and who busy themselves with inordinate zeal in spiritual exercises of many kinds, and yet they do not work that change in their lives that they had hoped for. They fast and they watch over night, they say many prayers, they often go to confession and holy communion, they practice meditation on the blessed passion of Jesus Christ, they do many charitable works, they go in search of indulgences—these and many other such holy things they do, and yet their lives are not changed. They do not keep God's commandments; they do not practice Christian virtue. They have wasted their strength out of God; they have not received His approval; little profit has come from it all to their souls; and they still stand in danger of eternal loss. And what is the reason? Their intention has been fatally defective, and in this: they have turned outward in their religious life, and not inward.

They do not know themselves. How, therefore, can they tell how to manage themselves and increase in virtue? Hence, instead of increasing in virtue, they are just as apt to decrease. They are under the delusion that they amount to something, and, as a matter of fact, they amount to nothing at all in God's sight; and, therefore, they are trying to serve God without knowing what they are about. They imagine that they are seeking God, but such is not at all the case. And now as they go on in this wise, following their own fancies and given over to self-contented indulgence of the senses, it is no wonder that they grow no better for the good practices of religion they have followed. The older they grow the more irritable and impatient they are; the more oblivious to their evil words and their defective works. And yet these all dream that they are high up in the spiritual world.

It all comes from serving God because of the natural joy that there is in it, and out of an excessive desire to be something holy. They give themselves to good works for the feeling of devotion they find, and often exceed their ability. Then they change from one pious practice to another, thinking that one helps and another hinders, all done without foresight or prudence, with a vague notion of some inward gain of virtue. While it tastes sweet it is good; when the taste is gone they declare it does not help them. Therefore are they unstable and hold to nothing long. While thus they run about, be sure they cannot lay a solid foundation of spirituality. Ask them if they mean only to please God. They answer, Yes, and they mean to tell the truth, but they are deceived.

Of course, nobody wants to serve the devil; who is so base as deliberately to choose the evil one for his master? And yet not a few of these persons do his will without knowing it. As long as a man undertakes to serve God by external works alone he has not yet begun to serve Him in truth, and in the right devotional spirit. The foundation of a perfect Christian life is not in external devotions and good works alone, however much these may help; but it is far rather in interior good works, by means of which sins are avoided and virtues are brought to life.

And I say this in addition: We find people in monasteries who lay the whole stress of their life in the order on external and bodily exercises. And there are men living in the world who afflict their body with fasting and other mortifications, and who are doubtless good men, giving alms with the hand, but this is all done without reference to the foundation of almsgiving in their heart. They do not advert to the strict duty of cleansing their life from sin. With all those noble, good and religious works of theirs, they are still hot-tempered, envious, arrogant, given to backbiting) and ever seeking praise for their virtues. And persons with these blemishes are in some places all too common in the various conditions of life. I affirm that these souls are entangled in the meshes of the evil one, and are subject to gross self-deception.

They think that they can be made righteous by external works alone, and be by them alone eternally saved. But that can never be; God must have the heart besides. They may be compared to gilded statues; outside they look like solid gold, and in reality they are stone or wood. In the gospel Christ compares men to sepulchres, beautiful on the outside, and within filled with dead men's bones. Therefore do I insist that there is no merit in fasting, saying prayers and doing other such outward works of religion, unless the spirit of a man is chastened and cleansed of wickedness.

It is seldom enough, alas, that men live as they ought, and yet there is nothing impossible in it, if one will only exert himself a little. Whatever rule is required will not be accepted and followed; what is not required, that is embraced, and great spiritual bliss is expected from it. So it happens that men take up heavy burdens, and labor long and hard to find God, and seldom come to Him in the degree of union they ought to have gained. Herein lies the failure; herein do men try to do the impossible. What they could do easily enough, what, in fact, no one could hinder their doing, that they will not do—they find no manner of joy in the right and simple way to God. But they rejoice in attempting the impossible. In whatever direction overdeveloped spiritual emotion points — especially when it affects the bodily senses—by that way they press onward, little knowing what they are about, though they may talk wisely concerning spiritual things. If they would stay close in the true road to Christian perfection, they would soon know how to speak and to act intelligently. Nor is their going astray due to lack of knowledge. No, for their conscience reproaches them for their remissness. If they did all that they understood was right, whether it were litle or great, God would acquit them of blame; for He would then ask no more from them, otherwise He would give them more light.

Finally, dear children, be well assured, if any man will be made different by grace from what he is by nature, he must bestir himself to seek God in his inmost heart, to mean God in everything, and to love God and not self. That is the righteousness required of every Christian; that is genuine devotion. For what do I mean by genuine devotion? Some think it is sweet emotionalism. So it sometimes is, but not always; for often enough one has such sweetness from natural causes. This leads many astray. True devotion is a willing submission to God's service; and it belongs to true spirituality that every man should at least once during each day or night enter into himself and diligently take account of his thoughts, words and actions, going over the whole day's life; and thus will he fully become informed of his sins and weaknesses.

It can hardly happen but that he has done something amiss. If he has not, then let him call to mind and sincerely repent of his previous transgressions. Furthermore, a man should earnestly set to work to cleanse out the folly and sinfulness of the past still lurking within him. He must then hold fast to God's commandments and keep them faithfully. And men in religious life should know that they are more strictly held to observe the commandments than ordinary laymen.

Yet, again, every man should associate himself, and that gladly, with the active religious life of the holy Christian Church, and if he be a religious, he should do so according to the rule of his order or congregation. These solid Christian ways are of more worth than all self-chosen practices of fasting, vigils, labors and the like—all very good in themselves, all of much help to beginners in the spiritual career, but taken alone they are not true and fundamental spirituality. For we meet with many well practiced in such things, and who none the less stick fast in plain faults—they are self-willed, disobedient, proud and bad tempered. May God grant us grace to acquire true devotion. *Amen.*

The Triple Crown of Holy Love: Self-abnegation, Patience and Earnestness

Synopsis—Five introductory external virtues: Temperance, modesty of demeanor, love of retirement, industry, openness of character—Self-abnegation as opposed to pride of vocation—That many lay people lead saintly lives—A humble soul is ever amazed at God's goodness to it—Patience waits on God with confidence in spite of many signs of His disfavor—Earnestness is best shown by uniform regularity in the ordinary practices of devotion.

SERMON FOR A FEAST OF MANY HOLY VIRGINS.

And five of them were foolish, and five wise.—Matt. xxv, 2.

Thus does our dear Lord compare the kingdom of heaven to two very different kinds of souls, the foolish ones, who live according to the flesh, yielding to its temptations; and the wise, who shun all such dangers, and who live according to the spirit. The wise virgins refrain themselves from all those things against which the foolish ones take no precautions whatsoever.

As to governing our outward life, five things are to be practiced, if we would be like the wise virgins. The first is temperance. We must practice moderation in eating and drinking, and in providing for all other necessities of nature, so that while provision is made for what is needed, we shall not pamper our dangerous appetites.

The second is simplicity and modesty; let our clothing be plain and ordinary, our bearing manly and open, our conduct every way modest and retiring.

The third is avoiding vain company, especially those whose talk is light. And we must be attentive to all our duties.

The fourth is to live by the labor of our hands, never to be idle; for idleness is the open door of all impurity.

The fifth point is diligently to restrain every sense and member, so as to escape the temptations incident to our daily life; to resist them strenuously, and never to yield to them. To this end nothing is better than the candid manifestation of our temptations to some holy man, done fully and humbly, so that we may get and keep his counsel for the prudent chastisement of our flesh and for interior offerings of prayer to God.

All who do not thus govern their outward life are to be reckoned as foolish virgins before God. But it behooves the wise virgins to furthermore adorn their interior souls for their Bridegroom; and the foundation of all this is humility of heart. They should consider themselves God's sisters because they do His will; and they should not sit in judgment on those who serve God in the married state. They should not strive to please anybody with their virtuous practices except God alone; for that would make them like the Pharisees. Virginity is not a commandment of God, but humility is. A proud virgin is a thousand times worse in God's sight than a meek housewife. A virgin dare not hate anyone, and must love everybody; she dare not think highly of herself, but ever must stand before God in fear and trembling. As sins begin secretly to germinate in the soul and to be pleasing to it, in the same degree does love cool and virtue wane. Virgins follow the Lamb whithersoever He goeth only if they maintain chastity and humility; but if they yield to pride, or if they are stained with grosser sins, then will pious married people be alotted places far higher than they.

Virginity has its origin in God Himself, and from Him have the angels learned it, for in heaven is it found, and there it remains till the resurrection at the last day. In heaven there is no marrying nor giving in marriage, but human souls there are like the angels of God, with Whom they have celebrated everlasting espousals. Virgins in this life are exempt from all fleshly bands, and bound only to God in order that they may bring forth eternal fruit. They are endued with great power against the devil. They sing the new canticle before the throne, which none else can sing. In these His chosen daughters has God set His throne, and it is His delight to dwell with them; but that is conditioned on their living an interior life of humility, meekness, self-renunciation, their hearts born again to God in holy love.

To God's love can no man ever come except through humility, which is a gift of God more precious than all earthly treasures. Humility establishes the heart in true peace, for no man is restless or quarrelsome except first he breaks away from humility. If a man be but truly humble, and so remains, he never will sin again. The reason why

Mary could not sin was because she was truly humble; and where God finds a humble soul, He does great things to it. St. Augustine says: "Whosoever is the humblest man on earth, the same is the greatest saint."

The signs of a humble man are these: He always begins by considering himself; and he at once acknowledges himself unworthy of every good gift. He accounts it an amazing thing and an injustice that God should think of him at all; that God should have made him a man; that He should continue to feed him and care for him. And yet he unceasingly thanks God for all those gifts with very deep humility. He exalts himself in nothing whatsoever, nor praises nor plumes himself. On the contrary, if he is conscious of virtue, he considers this wholly as God's gift, and holds himself only the more deeply involved in indebtedness to God on that account. God, in fact, is his last and only intention in everything, and the meaning of every act he does.

A wise virgin shall by no means set two purposes for any of her acts, meaning God for one purpose and some transitory end for the other. If we prize anything, it must be ever in subordination to the love we have for God; it must help us to love God and to come to God: thus acts the wise virgin and not differently. One must hold the Lord more dear than any of the messengers He sends forth—we mean the gifts He bestows.

A wise virgin esteems herself no more for her virtues than if she never had been born. Whatever favors God bestows on her with them He bestows Himself, and the gifts are for the purpose of His own unhindered action within her soul. For that end only God would make her perfect; nor can He ever cease to do so as long as she yields Him place, and her heart is loyal to Him, and suffers His guidance without any mixture of self-love. A humble man deems himself unworthy of whatever place he has, and of whatever company he is in.

He ever seeks the lowest place; he wants the meanest and least share of everything; and this feeling of his embraces everything, extends to all the affairs of life. He complains of his sufferings to nobody. He dares not complain against God in the sorest distress, not even when it grows so bad as to be intolerable; he accepts everything from the hand of God. Nor does he fret against any creature that troubles him, no matter how base may be his enemy. If he is unjustly accused, he cannot lay the blame on others, for he is persuaded that all such things are done by God's ordering, and that all is arranged for his best perfection. Thus it is that the wise virgins live, and thus in all contentment do they die.

Behold the shortest road to God, and to the bright company of the wise virgins who follow the Lamb whithersoever He goeth. How different with the foolish virgins, though they are quite unconscious of it. Whosoever would live truly in God must be made a fool in his own eyes and in those of everybody else. Whosoever would make sure of saving his soul, must give up and lose all the vain honors of this life. Whosoever would acquire humble charity of heart, must learn three lessons—self-renunciation, patience and love.

By self-renunciation we not only give up great sins, whether of the outer or inner kind, but in the interior life we renounce all joy of ownership in spiritual gifts. In our fasts, vigils, prayers and holy readings; in our devout feelings and pious thoughts; in our flashes of interior illumination; in our hunger and thirst for the rewards of eternal life; in our holy communions, jubilees, visions and contemplations:—in all these things of the spirit we must practice self-renunciation. One must come to be persuaded, that of all the contemptible men in the world he is the most contemptible, the coldest, the least pleasing to God, the most shiftless and negligent in religious duty. And yet meanwhile he must diligently perform all his spiritual tasks, nor ever pretend that he is exempt from any duty. Thus does a man come to account himself as nothing. Self-will and self-conceit are lost and gone, as well as all self-praise for good works.

The deeper a man's sincerity in all this the more truly is he humble, and the straighter is his path to God's own self. For God is in the abyss of our humility; there it is that the soul obtains possession of Him, there God unites the soul to Him. And now such a man is changed in God till he becomes, as it were, another man altogether. This is the work of the Holy Spirit, who now lives in him and rules him.

The second lesson is patience, for humility has need of patience. A man must suffer with as peaceful a mind as possible all kinds of ridicule. Pleasant things or unpleasant, good fortune or ill-fortune, contempt, belittling, losing or gaining—all must be received with equal balance of mind. And this must be so, even when one is persuaded that things are all wrong, that these troubles hinder his virtue, that they destroy his happiness. Give yourselves up to all suffering with the best grace of patience you can command, single-minded for God's will, trusting Him implicitly, no matter how little you can understand God's ways. Great fruit of humility comes from all this. Self-complacency and self-conceit will in this manner be wholly rooted out. You will learn to make the best of everything— if you can only learn patiently to suffer. If you sometimes think that harm is being done you in things temporal or spiritual, be sure of a compensation a hundred fold in God, and a great increase in solid virtue, if you will only humbly and patiently endure.

The third lesson is love, which serves greatly to increase humility. For never is love so nobly active as in giving up our own and in suffering. It is indeed true that love greatly increases when one receives God in unity of will with Him; but it is also true that God comes down into the self-abased soul, bringing with Him all that He is. Then and there does the loving soul embrace Him, then and there is it absorbed into Him, lost in Him, returned again to its Divine source of life. In that union is the soul assured, as far as may be in this life, that it will enjoy God forever hereafter. True humility is essential for this happy lot—the contemplation of God to the greatest degree permitted here below.

Three things are needed for this. The first is that a man shall have a pure intention, set and determined to desire nothing but God, to hold nothing dear but God, and Him alone to please and to love. Behold, these are they who contemplate Him rightly in this life.

The second is that we view God's action upon us with the eyes of self-denying love, sunk down deep in our lowly opinion of ourselves and full of love; carefully repressing all feelings of elation should God manifest hidden mysteries to us.

The third is great earnestness in performing our spiritual exercises, elevating our thoughts to God in whatever way we are led: sometimes in meditating on the Lord's humanity, again on His divinity, or on the blessed Trinity; or pondering the life and passion of Jesus Christ, the virtues of our dear mother Mary, or those of other saints. Every sentence of holy Scripture contains a divine meaning, did we but strive to find it. Thus will a man obtain from God what God wills him to have, if he cultivates those three virtues, namely, purity of intention, readiness to suffer while waiting on God in all meekness, and diligence in spiritual exercises. To this end a sound bodily constitution helps, a strong brain and a well-balanced mind, together with a penetrating judgment; and thus with God's grace one may advance rapidly in the spiritual life.

All virtues and all religious good works depend on these six points: First, true humility; second, patience in suffering; third, self-renunciation in all things; fourth, unfeigned love; fifth, to keep God in view in everything we do; sixth, earnestness in our spiritual exercises. And may God help us to be wise virgins. *Amen.*

Human Nature Depraved and Sanctified

Synopsis—Fallen nature seeks perishable joys, sanctified nature the possession of God Himself—The one craves outward life, the other hidden life—Nature prefers mercenary motives in religious activity, grace demands disinterested ones.

FIRST SERMON FOR THE ANNIVERSARY OF THE DEDICATION OF A CHURCH.

This day I must abide in thy house.—Luke xix, 5.

Dear children, we are celebrating the anniversary of the dedication of the mother church of the diocese, the great cathedral, and this solemnity was observed yesterday in many places in this city of Cologne. As I said yesterday, so say I today: all the devotions and outward observances of holy Church point inward to men's souls. There it is that in the best reality a temple is dedicated to God, and there should constantly take place a Divine renewal of our life. All external rites call us away to perfect interior festivities with God, call us, admonish us, and prepare us. Church dedication means giving to God a new temple, and so must we do in our souls, our nature denying itself, and curing itself of all attachments, as, for example, those we cherish for friends and relatives. All must be given up that comes from our outward natural life, and all that ministers natural joy to our senses and faculties in every way and work. To this end bodily mortifications serve, such as the various fasts and vigils we are able to endure. But, children, you are not aware of how cunningly nature seeks her own good, and how often she causes one to enjoy pleasures where he had only thought of serving some necessity.

The reasonable man must earnestly set to work to master the animal man that is in him. But at the outset of this, one feels deep pain, he begins to discipline his disorderly appetites, as in eating and drinking, seeing and hearing, talking and acting. Children, if this hostile attitude of our nature were but fully set right by the death of animal pleasure, it would be a sweet odor of sacrifice before God. As the

Apostle says: "For we are the good odor of Christ unto God" (II. Cor. ii, 15). When these hindrances of thy corrupt nature are removed, then may it be said of thee: "Who maketh the clouds thy chariot, who walketh upon the wings of the winds" (Ps. ciii, 3). The meaning is, that when one is set free from earthly ends and purposes by real mortification, then does God come into close company with him and give three wings, as it were, on which he may be said to fly—the wings of the dove, the wings of the eagle, and the wings of the wind.

The wings of the dove mean the holiness of those purified men who live in simplicity of heart, devoid of suspiciousness, free from rash judgment, kind, quiet natured, keeping the meekness of Christ ever before their eyes. Our Lord guides their dove-like flight ever upward, sanctifying their desires and filling them with His gentle spirit. The wings of the eagle carry souls so high that ordinary mortals can scarcely follow them with their eyes. They are interior spirits, soaring aloft in wisdom and in love, bearing with them all their outward and inward faculties, passing beyond the harmful reach of the life of the senses. And the souls that have Christ's wings of the wind are yet more spiritual. The wind is very swift, and blows thou knowest not whence or whither. And so there are souls who are the most perfect in all spiritual things, transformed in God in the mysterious ways of the hidden life, exceeding sense and reason to understand. Such a soul wings its way back to the fountain head of its existence, God, its created life merged in the uncreated, its light joined to and, as it were, extinguished in the infinite light that is God: for all created light compared to Him is but darkness. When the sun rises in the morning the stars that shone so brightly are now obscured into darkness: so does God's light extinguish all natural light when He shines in the deeper depths of the human soul—an overwhelming flood of divine brightness, wholly impossible to comprehend. Compared to God's brightness, all created intelligence is like the eyes of a little bird compared to the great fiery globe of the sun in the heavens. Look, if thou darest, straight at the sun at noonday, and presently its blazing disc is a dark spot in thy troubled eye. Thus it is with our soul's eyes and the brightness of God's spirit. A heathen king said: "God is darkness in the soul after all light has shone; a man knows Him in the unknowingness of his spirit." It is a shame to us that a heathen, and a heathen king besides, should understand this. What are we Christians about?

We read in the Gospel of this feast of the dedication of a church, that Zachaeus, the publican, was anxious to behold our Lord, but could not on account of the crowd, for he was short of stature. What, then, did he do? He climbed up a sycamore tree. So must we do. We long to behold the Being who has created such a disturbance in our souls, but we are too short of stature; that is to say, too petty, mean, and cowardly. What then? We shall climb up above our pettiness, and rise high over our imperfections by mortification of the life of the senses, repression of our depraved natural inclinations. Let us become interior men, for among such does God walk in familiar companionship.

But thus to repress nature is utter folly to the wise ones of this world—a man is a mere idiot in their eyes if he leads a hard life in order to come closer to God and to see Him: and these are men who own and read a hundred marks' worth of learned books. They think pious men are utter fools. But, children, I say to you in all truth, that is the foolishness that God honors, as our Savior taught: "I confess to Thee, O Father, Lord of Heaven and earth, because Thou hast hidden these things from the wise and prudent, and hast revealed them to little ones. Yea, Father, for so it hath seemed good in Thy sight" (Luke x, 21).

Many grateful revelations were granted St. Hildegarde illustrating this high spiritual flight; they are shown in some pictures in her book, copies of two of which are in our Sisters' refectory. One shows what the fear of God is—a blue-mantled figure all covered with eyes, and yet without head or face. But this is not fear in its common meaning, it being rather a careful self-searching in the light of God's justice, our soul scrutinizing with a thousand eyes, as it were, all our words and works and thoughts. The figure has no face and head, to show self-forgetfulness, total indifference to human love or hate, praise or blame. Nor has it any hands; and this shows detachment from all selfishness whatsoever.

The other picture is a form clothed in a white garment, with blue fringes, standing barefoot, hands uplifted, but without any head. Above it God is represented in pure gold, His being streaming down upon the figure so as to take the place of its head. This picture represents entire poverty of spirit. God is that soul's only head; the whiteness of the garment is single-heartedness towards God, together with total self-renunciation. The bareness of the feet means following Christ in strict imitation of His detachment. The blue fringes mean steadfastness in well doing unto the end. The uplifted hands mean perfect readiness to accept and to do God's will in all things, whether in acting or in suffering.

One may compare this to the sycamore tree, or that elevation of spirit above worldly things so necessary if one would see God in time and eternity.

The Lord hurried Zachaeus down from the tree, saying: "This day I must abide in thy house." That is, go down very low and learn thy own nothingnes in being and in doing; it is thus I must have · thy soul prepared for My coming. And in truth, whilst one is still up in the tree, although he sees God's everlasting truth, yet it is not with perfect clearness; his nature, with its inclinations, is still struggling against grace; he is not arrived at entire self-abasement. Be well assured that whatsoever nature does is always stained with some faults—it cannot be entirely perfect. Hence men whose spirituality is of mingled nature and grace, God calls down from their sycamore tree into a state of more thorough self-renunciation. And our Savior said: "This day I must abide in thy house." This day means the day of eternity, and tells the promise of salvation—which may God grant to all of us. *Amen.*

Faith as a Practical Means of Sanctification

Synopsis—Preliminary observations on Christ expelling the traffickers from the temple—True faith not always the sign of a truly faithful soul—Sign of a living faith: when one's inner knowledge is brighter than one's outward profession possibly can be—A perfect Christian's heart is a chronicle of God's truth in words of love—The prayer of faith.

SECOND SERMON FOR THE ANNIVERSARY OF THE DEDICATION OF A CHURCH.

My house shall be called the house of prayer.—Matt. xxi, 13.

Our Lord would show us how it may be brought about that our interior soul shall be made a house of prayer, for man is essentially God's holy temple. But first of all the traffickers must be driven out; this means the alien forms and pictures of our imagination, as well as enjoyment of created things, and self-will. To this is added the cleansing of the soul, which must be washed with the tears of penance in God's love. Then is the temple clean. Now, temples are not holy because they are houses made of fine material and beautiful design, here, there or in Rome or elsewhere, for they are made holy by God. And of all temples, that of our soul is God's favorite temple, for there God dwells in all truth, if room only be given Him, and if whatsoever is incompatible with His presence is removed.

But what sort of dwelling for God shall that soul be, which, ere it gives one thought to God often gives forty thoughts to other things? And this indicates who are the traffickers in God's house, and how they happen to be there. Whosoever wilfully lives in the enjoyment of creatures, the same is a trafficker in the house of God. There can be no manner of doubt, therefore, that any man who would have God dwell in Him and work His divine work in him, must put away all that stands between him and God; he must drive out of his soul all pleasure in created things that God is not the cause of. If any one would say that ten hurtful human friendships are not worse than a single one, he would talk foolishly; any child would know better. Therefore, the fewer hindrances to God we have to expel the easier our task will be. But yet mark this: Ten imperfections that a man knows and acknowledges to be such, are less dangerous than a single one that he will not own to be a fault, and that he obstinately cleaves to. Therefore, cultivate humble fear about your hidden faults. For when thou liest prostrate before the merciful God in all lowliness of spirit, owning frankly to thy imperfections, then art thou well advised. A man who is full of excuses can never be rightly guided. Avoid that spirit as you would eternal death. Thou mayst come across the holiest man in the world, and likely enough thou wilt find him weeping bitterly for his sins; and if thou askest him if he has not wept enough during so many years of penance, he will answer thee that it is not a thousandth part of the tears that are due to God for his wickedness, and that he is now only beginning to weep. If this be the mind of wise and holy men, shouldst not thou look carefully to thyself? You may ask me if I mean to teach that one should weep all the time. I answer yes and no, according to God's guidance of different souls. Only this I maintain—no man should imagine at any time that he has completely done all the penance that is due to God for his sins.

But when thou hast driven the traffickers out, when thou art come so far as not to permit joy in creatures to abide in thy soul, what then? Why this: Thou must keep a strict guard on thyself. For these vile traffickers soon will try to creep back again, once more to begin their huckstering; and then they must be driven out a second time. But observe that if they linger within thee—these earthly tendencies—and if that be straight against thy will, they cannot harm thee. But whether their intrusion be long or short, out at last must they go through the same door they came in. Yet more: All the foul and evil things that they may have left behind them—thoughts, feelings, weaknesses—if they be the accumulation of even twenty years, all must be cast out along with what caused them.

"My house shall be called the house of prayer." Now, to prayer belongs devotion, a word which means devoted to God or vowed to God, an interior binding to God joined to a great longing for eternity. When thou art thus bound, thus vowed to God, thou hast devotion wheresoever thou art, whatsoever may be thy good work. It needs not always to be celebrating jubilees to have devotion; or to feel great spiritual sweetness. All this is but incidental; for the essence of devotion is in totally giving oneself to God interiorly, or being united to Him, or bound to Him. That brings one very close to Him. Devotion thus understood is like a battering ram; it hammers down the walls of God's kingdom and opens a wide passage for the soul to enter in.

St. Hilary names three means of gaining entrance into God's interior kingdom. The first is true faith; the second an intelligent knowledge of God; the third, interior, devout prayer. And now what is faith? I make bold to say that not all the Christian people are faithful Christians. You know that the churchyard is full of the dead and the church building full of the living; so in holy Church there are many that seem to be alive, but are really dead, for their faith is not a living faith. And what is a living faith? Nothing else but a living taste for God and for all that savors of God. A man may hear and read things that belong to our holy faith, as about our Lord's divinity or humanity, or the blessed Trinity. But he has a living faith within him, if interiorly he knows that God is, and when that is interiorly more plain to him than all his teachers can say; and this because he lives and dwells in the interior kingdom. There does this life of faith pour forth its living waters from its own fountain head.

Another kind of Christians—and, alas, they are not few—hang on indeed to the life of faith; but its light is easily obscured in their souls. If sunlight were a living creature and a cloud were another, then the latter could destroy the life of the former. So may the life of faith, already weak enough, be devoured by the cloud of sinfulness in a Christian's soul. But when one is strong in the faith with the living strength of knowledge and love of God, then if clouds of sin happen to overhang that soul—for all men are liable to sin—soon the sunshine of Divine life breaks through those sin-threatening clouds and disperses them: the soul quickly recovers its former sense of living faith. The life within such men has struck deep roots, its fruit soon reappears: in plain words the soul quickly flies from sin. Meanwhile the others, those of weaker faith, lie where they fall. If they enter into themselves they find themselves a dead dog, dead and reeking with corruption. Drag that dead carcass of a soul away out of our sight—we might say: it is lifeless and cold, it is empty of God and of all that belongs to God. Whatever means God is heavy and dull to that soul. Or there may be a faint spark of life left; the sinner may feebly cling to Christian faith. In that case the soul shall be finally saved if it will but enter into real and living faith by true repentance. But it may easily happen that such a man shall fall away totally and finally. By and of himself he has no ways or means of returning to God, for he lives in outward things alone; spiritual things are vain and tasteless to him and his own interior condition strange and unknown.

Those souls who abide in the life that is within, know well of the interior movements of God and of His truth. As to what befalls them in the outer life, that also makes for God, ever newly awakening their inner life, now with holy purposes, now with deeper love, again with praise and thanksgiving to God. This life is within them and none other. They live in a divine interior kingdom. They savor God in everything—a state of soul that must remain hidden from all who have not been granted its privileges.

St. Hilary's second road into the interior kingdom of God is an intelligent knowledge of God. That is found in a man of living faith— he has not far to seek for it, for it manifests itself to him. Entering, as he does, by the right door, the light of this knowledge beams full upon him—he does not intrude himself by any forbidden passage, and therefore it must be said to him: "Lo, the kingdom of God is within you" (Luke xvii, 21). He finds the truth in a degree of brightness unknown to all who are not familiarly at home in this interior dwelling. He finds a knowledge here above all thought and reason and understanding, as St. Dionysius writes: "It is light in light, the soul's light in uncreated light." The great teachers of the University of Paris read great books, and turn over the leaves with much joy. That is very good; but those devout men we have been speaking of read in a true living book in which every word is a living force. They turn over earth and heaven as a man turns over the leaves of a book, and therein they read the wonderful works of God. They advance to the knowledge of the different orders of the blessed angels of heaven. They penetrate into the eternal life of the blessed Trinity, how the Father eternally begets the Son our Lord Jesus Christ, how the Son everlastingly rejoices in the bosom of the Father, how the Holy Ghost proceeds from both the Father and the Son, how the holy Trinity pours itself forth into all blessed spirits, and how these all return into their origin and fountain head. This is the beatitude of which our Lord spoke: "Now this is eternal life: That they may know Thee, the only true God, and Jesus Christ, whom Thou hast sent" (John xvii. 3). Such is the life in God's living temple, the noble and glorious entertainment of all God's chosen friends. Here dwells the Divine High Priest in His own palace, for here is the true presence of God, in which all good is centred and where all pain vanishes away. Whosoever has experienced this, knows it well and knows nothing else. It is a knowledge unknown to all the masters of worldly science. Whatsoever man best acquires it in this life and goes deepest into its secrets is found closest to God, and shall be made the happiest.

St. Hilary's third road to the kingdom of living faith is prayer. It is the elevation of the soul to God. In a stricter sense, it is the turning inward of the created spirit to union with the uncreated Spirit of God. By this means the spirit of a man shall be moved and guided by the essence of the Godhead. Such men are the true adorers, who "adore the Father in spirit and in truth" (John iv, 23). And our Savior adds: "For the Father also seeketh such to adore Him" (ibid.). What they seek in their prayers they find—they receive what they ask. And in this prayer there is finding and there is losing. How losing, and what is lost? Even the temple now is lost—the man's spirit and all the life of it that we have been describing are lost. What has become of it all? It has all flowed back into God and is now embraced by His being and absorbed in Him. The human soul is made one spirit with God, as our beloved St. Paul tells us: "He who is joined to the Lord is one spirit" (I. Cor. vi, 17). What all that is, and how all that is done, is more easily felt than told: all discourse about it is as unequal to its reality as a needle point is to the great heavens above us. May God grant us the grace one day to experience it—God the Father, and God the Son, and God the Holy Ghost. *Amen.*

TWO USEFUL INSTRUCTIONS ABOUT CONFESSION.

Children, I counsel you, and I admonish and implore you, to learn how to confess all your sins interiorly to God, and to acknowledge yourselves guilty before Him with the utmost sincerity. Ponder over your sins very deliberately before His eyes and with much love; but do not make your outward confession to the priest too long, nor dwell too particularly upon the fine distinctions between different venial sins. There is little profit in such a practice, and it robs your father confessor of his valuable time, annoying and perhaps distressing him. Children, by such minuteness of confession your sins will not stop, and, as I have elsewhere taught you, your father confessor has no power over sins which you have not made up your mind to quit.

Turn into yourself; arouse your memory; work inside your soul. For the outward telling of your sins brings little fruit if not joined to interior repentance, especially when there is (as in this case) no question of mortal sins, but of venial sins. Such superfluous telling of sins is often the sign of a man all too careless in the work of interior confession. If the interior confession of venial faults be done rightly, these defects are so obliterated from one's conscience that he can scarcely recall or describe them with any particularity; but that presupposes that he has dealt with God about them with deep sincerity. And now you understand that all this has reference only to venial sins.

As to mortal sins, O may God preserve you from them. Children, it is every way necessary that a man should keep a strict watch over his interior life. He may be said to have many skins drawn over his soul, hiding its true state from him. We meet with men who, though they know many things, do not know themselves—there are thirty or forty interior disguises hiding some men's souls from their own knowledge, one disguise beneath the other, each of them as hard as the hide of an ox. And these self-deceptions hinder one's getting away from and keeping out of mortal sin: for they cannot be stripped off by confession alone, as you might suppose they could, but only by interior sorrow. And just what are they? Everything that thou hast in thee, or meanest, or enjoyest, whose true end and object is not God. These are all a man's false gods—evil images harbored in the mind, self-will, self-indulgence in the life of the senses. A man hides these from himself—these as Rachel hid and sat upon her father's ·idols in her tent. To these are joined presumption, boastfulness, and spiritual sloth in Divine things. These are all interior disguises. I do not say that they are all matter for confession to a priest, but I do say that they must be seriously taken account of and humbly confessed to God. If a man will but prostrate himself at God's feet and acknowledge himself guilty of these things, all will be well; he will then begin to turn away from them to the best of his ability, and our Lord's help will not be wanting. *Amen.*

II.

One may confess his venial sins to his father confessor with words such as these, according to each one's particular failings: I have been guilty of proud and useless thoughts in reciting my office and in my prayers instead of giving careful attention. I have been negligent; I have broken silence without necessity at times and in places not permitted; I have spoken scoffingly, hastily and imprudently; I have been silly in my language, restless and uneasy in my conduct, unguarded in my manners; thoughtless of God's will; forgetful of the holy rule in and out of choir; I have been disobedient and ungrateful; I have not loved God and praised Him as I ought; I have not attended to His interior admonitions; I have not given my brethren a good example; and I accuse myself in general of having not duly observed poverty, chastity, obedience, and the holy rule according to my vows, as well as of all other of my sins and imperfections.

And thou mayst beg of God the granting of an indulgence as follows: Dear Lord, if it were possible for me to do so, I would seek to gain this indulgence by journeying through frost and snow, through rain and cold. But that is not in my power to do; nor can I do more than humbly implore Thee to grant me this indulgence as Thy generous alms. I beg Thee to make me a sharer in all the holy devotions in Thy Church everywhere, giving me a plenary indulgence from all my sins, by the most precious blood flowing from Thy Divine wounds, the source and fountain head of all Thy graces. Dear children, say that prayer with sincere faith and deep confidence in God, and thou shalt be raised above all the miseries of this world.

ON THE ATTRIBUTES OF GOD.

Moses said to his people: "Hear, O Israel, the Lord our God is one Lord" (Deut. vi, 4). So can we make much progress by meditating on the different attributes of God and His various names, as we apply them to His Divine being; but meanwhile we ought to sink down into our own nothingness. I have already explained, that after one has duly meditated on our dear Lord's birth, life, passion and death, he should then elevate his spirit above time and fix it upon the eternal ways and being of God.

In considering the Divine attributes, one may, as it were, mirror

God in his soul, and consider Him as a pure being and the essence of all beings, and yet He is nothing of all things as we understand them. But all that is, and all that is being and has being and is good, in all that God is. St. Augustine says: "Seest thou a good man, a good angel, the good heaven? Abstract man, angel, heaven; and that which remains, that is to say, the essence of good, that is God; for He is all in all things, and yet far above all things. All creatures have indeed good in them, have indeed love; but they are not the good, they are not the love, but God alone is the essence of good, of love, and of all that one can name." Then let a man compare himself with this essential good, and exerting all the powers of his soul let him contemplate it and become absorbed in it, so that his own nothingness may be merged in God and renewed in His Divine essence, which is alone the being and the action and the life that is in all things.

Let a man contemplate the attribute of the simplicity, the absolute oneness of being, and he will see God as the final end of simplicity, in whom all multiplicity is made unity and simplified in unity of essence. Again, God's essence is His action. God's knowledge, love, justice, mercy, righteousness are all one. Enter therein, drawing with thee thy own incomprehensible multiplicity, which He will make simple in His own most simple essence.

Let a man contemplate God's unspeakable hiddenness. He is hidden in all things; as Isaias says: "Verily, Thou are a hidden God" (Isaias xlv, 15). To everything he is nearer than it is to itself. He is in the depths of the soul, hidden there from all sense and unknown. Penetrate there and enter into union with Him with all thy powers, transcending over all the thoughts of thy external existence; for thy external existence is as far from thy real self and from thy interior existence as is any beast, which lives only in its bodily senses, and knows and understands and feels nothing besides. Hide thyself away in this hiddenness of God, away from all creatures and all that is alien to essential being. But this does not take place by the way of images and forms in the mind; no, nor by the use of the understanding, but in an essential way, all the soul's powers and aspirations being lifted above the life of sense into the way of perception.

Then let a man contemplate the solitude of God, in which never a word in the essence or in the essential way is spoken. All in God is silent, secret and solitary—nothing but simply God, and never has entered there anything alien to God, whether it be creature, or form, or image. God meant this solitariness when He spoke by the prophet: "I will lead her into the wilderness; and I will speak to her heart" (Osee ii, 14). This wilderness is His silent, solitary Godhead, into which in time and eternity He leads all who will be attentive to His interior inspirations. Into this still Godhead introduce thy own vain and waste soul, which is a wilderness full of a rank growth of weeds and empty of useful fruit, a wilderness given up to the wild beasts that are thy senses and faculties.

Then contemplate the Divine darkness; for by reason of His unspeakable brilliancy, God is darkness to all created understanding, whether of men or angels, as the noonday sun is darkness to the unprotected eye that gazes straight upon it. The created light of the mind of man or angel compared to God's mind is as the eyes of a little bird compared to the sun in the sky. When any created spirit looks full upon God, it must instantly close its eyes and rest in blindness and, as it were, unknowingness. Into this brightness of Divine light introduce thy fathomless darkness, devoid as it is of all true light. Give over thy darkness to the abyss of the Divine darkness, which alone knows Itself, and in the degree it knows Itself is unknown to all else. But this abyss, this unknown and unnamed, is divinely blissful, and it ravishes the soul's love more than all that it can know else in the eternal beatitude of the Divine essence.

INDEX

NOTE—The reader should bear in mind, that nearly all of Tauler's Sermons deal with Christian and religious perfection, and with the various degrees of mental prayer. Therefore, the following and kindred subjects will be found treated of nearly everywhere: Poverty, chastity, obedience, purity of heart, mortification, humility, the passion of Christ, the divine attributes, meditation and contemplative prayer in every degree and aspect, sensible devotion, aridity, spiritual direction, guidance of the Holy Spirit, and all the rules for the interior life.

INDEX—Continued

INDEX—Continued

INDEX—Continued

INDEX—Continued

INDEX—Continued

WS - #0016 - 160420 - C0 - 229/152/44 - PB - 9781332948192